TOWN CLASS CRUISERS

TOWN CLASS CRUISERS

by

Neil McCart

Previous Page: HMS Belfast *in Plymouth Sound in 1942 (Syd Goodman Collection)*

First published in the United Kingdom in 2012 by Maritime Books, Lodge Hill, Liskeard, Cornwall, PL14 4EL

CONTENTS

ACKNOWLEDGEMENTS

Mr T. K. Anderson, Ulster Folk & Transport Museum, Holywood, Co Down: Mike Critchley and Steve Bush, Maritime Books, Liskeard: All the excellent and helpful staff at Cheltenham Public Library: Mr Michael Cassar, Valletta, Malta: The late Mr C. H. G. Heath BEM MBE, Cowplain, Hampshire: Sarah Hogben, Imperial War Museum, HMS Belfast, London: All the staff at the Repository and Readings Rooms of the National Archives, Kew, London: Dr Richard H. Osborne, World Ship Society, Bristol: The late Mr Anthony J. Perrett: The late Lt-Cdr R. G. Robertson RNVR, Edinburgh: Mr Frederick W. Stephen, Newry Co Down: Mr A. K. Vicary, Maritime Photo Library, Cromer, Norfolk. Finally to my wife Freda, for her unstinting help.

INTRODUCTION

For a quarter of a century, through some of the most turbulent years in Britain's history, the Town-class cruisers served the Royal Navy and the country well. During the six years of the Second World War, from the Arctic Ocean to the Atlantic, Mediterranean and the South China Sea, they were in the thick of the action, as evidenced by the fact that four of them were lost to enemy action. Three were sunk in the Mediterranean, and the fourth in Arctic waters while escorting convoys to and from northern Russia. That a fifth ship was not lost is due in large part to the skill and tenacity of *Belfast*'s officers and men when, only 15 weeks after leaving the shipbuilder's yard, she fell victim to the newly developed magnetic mine which broke her back and left her out of commission for longer than it had taken to build her.

The origins of the Town-class cruisers go back to the early 1930s, just over ten years after the Great War during which Japan had been a valuable ally, but was now an Imperial rival in the Far East. The London Naval Treaty of 1930 limited by tonnage the numbers of light cruisers which each major maritime power could build, and the news that the Imperial Japanese Navy had begun work constructing its Mogami-class light cruisers, which it was said would be armed with 15, 6.1-inch (155mm) guns and achieve a speed of just over 30 knots, set alarm bells ringing in London. These Japanese ships were more powerful than many heavy cruisers, and at the Admiralty there were calls for similar ships to be built for the Royal Navy; these would be the Town-class cruisers.

Originally the plan had been that eight ships of the class would be built, sufficient for two squadrons, but in the event, between March 1937 and August 1939 ten cruisers of the class were commissioned. Initially, to match the Japanese vessels, the Admiralty had wanted ships of 8,500 tons, able to steam at over 30 knots and armed with 15, 6-inch guns, but the Director of Naval Construction ruled this out and in the autumn of 1933 a revised design was accepted. The first two ships of the class had a standard displacement tonnage of just over 9,000, whereas by the summer of 1939, when the final two cruisers were commissioned, their displacement tonnage had risen to 10,550. The cruisers had an overall length of 623ft 6in, a beam of 63ft 4in and a maximum draught of 18ft 3in. They were powerful ships with a main armament of 12, 6-inch guns in four triple turrets, and their armour plating ranged from 4½ inches on the ships' sides, 4 inches to the front and sides of the main gun turrets to 1¼ inches on the decks. In addition to the main armament the design provided for a secondary armament of 12, 4-inch, high-angle guns in twin mountings; two, four-barrelled pom-poms; eight 0.5-inch machine-guns and two sets of triple, 21-inch, torpedo tubes. Originally it was envisaged that the cruisers would carry and operate five seaplanes, but the practicalities of stowing and operating that number in the very limited space available proved too difficult to resolve and the number of aircraft was reduced to three. One would be stowed on the catapult and the others in two large hangars built into the superstructure on each side of the forward funnel uptakes. Capable of a maximum speed of 32 knots, they were quadruple-screw ships powered by four sets of Parsons geared steam turbines, with the superheated steam being provided by four Admiralty three-drum boilers. The main propulsion machinery developed some 82,500 SHP, while their four propellers gave a high degree of manoeuvrability. As designed they carried a complement of 748, but during the Second World War those numbers increased dramatically.

Today the last ship of the Town-class cruisers that was commissioned lies permanently in the Pool of London. She is the only major pre-Second World War warship to have been preserved and she remains a fitting tribute to one of the most successful classes of cruiser built for the Royal Navy.

Neil McCart
Cheltenham
2012

Chapter One

HMS SOUTHAMPTON
1937-1941

HMS Southampton *at Chatham in April 1937 soon after her arrival from the builders. She is seen wearing the flag of Rear-Admiral T. P. Calvert CB CVO DSO.* *(Author's Collection)*

In May 1934 the Clydebank shipbuilders of John Brown & Company Ltd received an order from the Admiralty for what was described as, '...a large M-class, or Minotaur-class, cruiser to be named *Polyphemus*. The *Polyphemus* is to be a vessel of 9,000-tons and will provide welcome work for both shipyard and engine works.' With shipbuilding still at a low ebb following the lean years of the great depression it was indeed a good order for the workers of Clydebank, and preparation of drawings began at once. Six months later, on 21 November 1934, at No 1 berth in John Brown's East Yard, the first keel plates for *Polyphemus* were laid. Five days after the keel-laying ceremony, however, the First Lord of the Admiralty announced to the House of Commons that the *Minotaur* which was building on the Clyde was to be renamed *Newcastle* and the *Polyphemus* under construction at John Brown & Co, was to be renamed *Southampton*. He then went on to say that both ships would be built to a different design and that the name of *Southampton* had been substituted for *Minotaur* as the class name. It was thought, correctly as it turned out, that the city names would prove to be popular in the localities concerned.

It was the spring of 1936 before Yard Number 542 was ready for launching, and on 5 March, just five days before she took to the water, the uncrowned King Edward VIII inspected the cruiser during a visit to the shipyard. The launch, which took place at 1300 on 10 March, was one of the most important on the Clyde that year, and after a short religious service, Lady Sarah Haddington, the wife of a notable Scottish peer, sent *Southampton* down the slipway into the waters of the River Clyde. Ten minutes later the cruiser was safely secured in the same fitting-out basin as the passenger liner *Queen Mary*, which was being completed for the Cunard White Star Line. At a luncheon in the shipyard offices afterwards Lord Aberconway, the chairman of John Brown & Co, presented *Southampton*'s sponsor with a small casket containing a jewel as a memento of the occasion. Two weeks later *Southampton* had to be towed from the fitting-out basin and upriver so that *Queen Mary*, with seven tugs in attendance, could be manoeuvred out of the basin and into service, but it was not long before work recommenced on *Southampton*.

In November 1936 *Southampton*'s first commanding officer, Captain A. M. Peters DSC RN, was appointed. The selection of Captain Peters was fitting, in view of his service in the previous ship of the name, the fourth *Southampton*, which had been in commission between 1912 and 1926, and which had also been built by John Brown & Co on the Clyde. During the Great War he had taken part in all the great North Sea actions, and had been awarded the DSC at Jutland. In February 1937 it was announced that *Southampton* was to become the flagship of Rear-Admiral T. P. F. Calvert, in command of the 2nd Cruiser Squadron, Home Fleet (CS2), in succession to *Orion*. She was dispatched to the America and West Indies Station to relieve the elderly cruiser *Dragon*, which returned home to pay off into reserve. Just over three weeks later, on 6 March, at John Brown's shipyard, *Southampton* was commissioned for service and shortly afterwards she sailed to undergo her acceptance trials. Following these, sailing via the Pentland Firth, she set course for Sheerness and Chatham, arriving alongside the latter's No 3 basin during the forenoon of 10 March. Next day her ship's company was brought up to full strength and on 7 April Admiral Calvert hoisted his flag on board.

HMS *Southampton*'s operational career began in earnest on 12 April 1937, when she left Chatham for Portland to begin her work-up which continued through to the end of the month. On 6 May she left Portland for the River Thames and Gravesend where, with her sister *Newcastle*, she anchored in

HMS Southampton *at Spithead for the 1937 Coronation Fleet Review.* *(David John Weller)*

mid-river. The two cruisers were in the Thames as part of the Coronation celebrations for King George VI, and during the six days she spent off Gravesend her gangways were opened to the public each afternoon. On 13 May, after leaving the Thames Estuary, *Southampton* and *Newcastle* steamed round to Spithead to take their places in the Coronation Review. The Review itself took place during the afternoon of 20 May when, at 1505, the Royal Yacht *Victoria & Albert*, carrying King George VI, left Portsmouth Harbour to steam down the rows of assembled warships, which included the German heavy cruiser *Admiral Graf Spee*. That evening there was a searchlight review and firework display and at 1135 the next day the King paid a short visit to *Southampton*. Four days later, on 25 May, *Southampton* resumed her work-up exercises with a series of day-running trials from Spithead, and later from Portland, which took her through to the second week of June. On 14 June *Southampton* left Rosyth to take part in her first major fleet trade defence exercise, which also involved the RAF. It was designed to exercise both Services in the tasks which would fall to them in any war as well as investigating any problems that the rapid advances in aircraft technology might impose on sea warfare.

The situation on which the exercise was based involved an enemy force, most of whose ships were neutralised in their own distant home waters by the British fleet, but which had succeeded in getting a heavy cruiser and an auxiliary cruiser into the Western Approaches to disrupt the essential seaborne supplies to British ports. As it turned out it was a scenario which would be encountered during the early months of the Second World War. Admiral Calvert was in command of the 'Blue' force, with his flagship *Southampton* representing the enemy heavy cruiser, while RFA *Prestol* took the part of the auxiliary raider. The defending force came under the command of Rear-Admiral T. H. Binney, flying his flag in the aircraft carrier *Glorious*. Along with her squadrons of fighters and torpedo bombers, *Newcastle* also came under his orders. The scene of the exercise was a rectangular area stretching some 240 miles south and 400 miles west from a point close to Lundy Island in the Bristol Channel. During the manoeuvres the co-operation of the Merchant Service was secured, and British merchant ships passing through the area were liable to 'attack' or 'capture' by *Southampton* or *Prestol*. However, if they did fall victim to such an 'attack' they would not be delayed but just send out radio calls for help. One of the aspects which was of interest was the effect of using an aircraft carrier to protect trade routes, a tactic which in the first weeks after the outbreak of war in 1939 was to have tragic consequences for *Courageous*.

In the event *Southampton*'s career as a commerce raider was brief, for within 24 hours of leaving Portland a call for help was received from SS *Cordillera* and aircraft from *Glorious* had soon found and 'sunk' the cruiser. The *Prestol* had a slightly longer career, but three days into the exercise she was located and 'destroyed' by *Newcastle*. The exercise was repeated during the days which followed, and this time the giant Cunarder *Queen Mary*, which had once shared a fitting-out berth with the cruiser, was 'captured' by *Southampton*, but once again both she and *Prestol* were located and 'sunk' by aircraft from *Glorious*. The series of exercises concluded with an 'attack' on the defences of Plymouth and Portsmouth by a force which included *Rodney, Courageous, Southampton* and *Newcastle*, with the defending force including *Ramillies, Revenge, Cairo* and *Exmouth*, after which the whole fleet anchored at Portland.On 19 July, with the exercises over, *Southampton* left Portland to steam up Channel, through the Solent and up Southampton Water to make her only visit to the city after which she was named. During the five days she spent alongside berth 107 in the new Western Docks, her officers and men attended a number of official functions organised by the Civic Authorities for Merchant Navy Week, which was being held in aid of the Missions to Seamen charity, while civic dignitaries were entertained on board the ship. On four of the five days the cruiser herself was opened to the public and the people of

HMS Southampton *in 1938, as completed, with a square-fronted bridge, tripod masts and four triple 6-inch turrets.* *(Syd Goodman Collection)*

Southampton, who were more used to seeing the great liners in their port, flocked over the brow to see the warship named after their city.

After leaving Southampton Water *Southampton* rendezvoused with her sister *Newcastle* and the two cruisers steamed north to Stranraer from where, on 28 July, they escorted the Royal Yacht to Belfast and back for a day-long visit to the city by King George VI. Both ships then returned to their base ports, with *Southampton* arriving alongside at Chatham on 30 July. Next day the Lord Mayor of London opened Chatham Navy Week, at which *Southampton* was the star attraction. It was 9 September when, with seasonal leave having been taken, *Southampton* left Chatham to steam north to Invergordon for the Home Fleet's autumn exercises in the North Sea. These continued through into early October, after which the ship returned to Sheerness for storing and refuelling before leaving the Thames Estuary to set course for the Northern coast of Spain. For seven months the Royal Navy had been patrolling the Basque and Asturian coasts, which were being blockaded by General Franco's Nationalist forces, a blockade not recognised as legitimate by the British Government, and the patrols had been maintained in order to protect British shipping and, if necessary, to evacuate British nationals from the civil war which was raging in Spain.

HMS *Southampton* arrived off the French Biscay port of St Jean de Luz, close to the Spanish border, from where the Royal Navy's patrols operated, on 12 October and six days later she sailed for the patrol area. Two days into her patrol, during the forenoon of 20 October, the cruiser received a call for assistance from the small, 516-ton British registered steamer, *Stangrove*, which had just left the Spanish port of Gijon carrying refugees, but had been detained by a Spanish Nationalist armed trawler. *Southampton* was quickly on the scene and, on the grounds that the detention was outside territorial waters, she took the *Stangrove* under her protection until she was well on her way to Bordeaux. With the town of Gijon under siege by Nationalist forces there were hundreds of Republican refugees attempting to escape from the area and on 24 October, some 20 miles north of Santander, she sighted a drifting launch with 49 refugees aboard who had been drifting for three days. After embarking the occupants she sank the launch by gunfire, and next day she came across another launch with a further 31 refugees aboard. They too had been drift-

Looking forward from HMS Southampton*'s hangar deck. The door to the starboard hangar can be seen immediately to the right of the forward funnel.*
(Maritime Photo Library)

ing for some days and had every reason to be grateful to the Royal Navy, for their boat was slowly heading out of the Bay of Biscay and into the Atlantic Ocean. That evening all the refugees were disembarked at Biarritz and *Southampton* resumed her patrol. Next day, at 0800 on 26 October, the cruiser sighted a Spanish trawler, *Mario Tero*, adrift off Cape de Penas with 291 refugees aboard. After the trawler's engines had failed, sheets were being used as sails and initially the refugees mistook *Southampton* for a Nationalist warship. However, they were soon reassured by the sight of the White Ensign, and they hoisted the Spanish Republican flag. *Southampton* manoeuvred alongside the vessel and took on board 283 men and eight women, before sinking the trawler with a depth charge. That

Looking aft from HMS Southampton*'s hangar deck at the second funnel, the aircraft cranes, and, on the starboard side, one of the twin 4-inch gun turrets.*
(Maritime Photo Library)

HMS Southampton *departing Portsmouth in June 1938.* *(National Museum of the Royal Navy)*

evening she anchored off La Pallice and all the passengers landed. Five days later, with Franco's Nationalist forces having captured the last Republican enclaves on the Asturian and Basque Biscayan coast, the British naval force was withdrawn and on 2 November *Southampton* arrived at Portland. Later that month she steamed round to Chatham for maintenance and to give seasonal leave.

On 18 January 1938 *Southampton* left Chatham to steam round to Portland from where, in company with *Glasgow, Newcastle* and *Sheffield*, she sailed south for Gibraltar and the annual combined Home and Mediterranean Fleet exercises. Also taking part were *Hood, Nelson, Warspite, Galatea* and *Cornwall*, with the first phase of the manoeuvres taking place in the Eastern Atlantic and the second phase in the Western Mediterranean. For *Southampton* there were short visits to Majorca and Valencia before she returned to home waters on 25 March, together with her squadron and *Nelson*, arriving at Chatham on the last day of the month to undergo a six-week docking and refit period.

It was Wednesday 11 May when *Southampton* put to sea again to steam round to Portsmouth to join *Nelson*. Both ships then rendezvoused with the Home Fleet at Portland, from where *Southampton* carried out day-running exercises with her sisters *Glasgow, Newcastle* and *Sheffield*, which included firing at the target ship *Centurion*. In late June she was at Portland for the visit of King George VI to the Home Fleet. She spent a day carrying out evolutions with the Fleet, which ended with the Royal Yacht *Victoria & Albert* steaming through the lines of assembled warships. She spent the last week of June at Portsmouth, secured alongside *Sheffield* at Middle Slip Jetty, and in the first week of July she operated from Portsmouth. One exercise involved the embarkation of an Army Infantry Brigade in *Southampton* and in the transports *Clan Macalister* and *Lancashire* to carry out a landing exercise. The commander of the brigade, who was embarked in *Southampton*, was one Brigadier Bernard Montgomery who, with his staff, occupied the

Admiral's quarters. Also involved in the landing exercise were the battleship *Revenge* and two destroyer flotillas. Leaving Portsmouth on 5 July the convoy steamed down Channel, round Alderney and back to Start Bay where they anchored, at midnight on 6 July. The landings took place at Torcross, Slapton and Strete with *Southampton*, *Sheffield* and *Revenge* providing naval gunfire support, which must have been somewhat disconcerting for the residents of Kingsbridge and the local villages. As far as the Army was concerned the landings went as planned and the exercise ended with counter attacks and a withdrawal back to the ships. By the afternoon of 7 July the whole convoy and the escorts had returned to Portsmouth. For *Southampton* there followed a passage into the North Sea and a four-day visit to the seaside resort of Whitby, before manoeuvres with *Revenge, Sheffield* and *Cornwall*, after which, on 26 July, she returned to Chatham to give seasonal leave and undergo maintenance.

On 7 September 1938 *Southampton* left Chatham to steam north to Invergordon where she joined other ships of the Home Fleet for the annual autumn manoeuvres. The exercises continued through September and into October, with air defences playing an important part and aircraft from nearby RAF Everton attacking the ships at sea. With the exercises over *Southampton* remained in northern waters and, together with *Sheffield*, hunted down the submarine *Swordfish*. In mid-November *Southampton* returned to Chatham where she remained until the middle of January in the fateful year of 1939.

On 2 January there was a change of command when Captain F. W. H. Jeans RN took over from Captain Peters. A specialist gunnery officer, Jeans had served in *Duke of Edinburgh*, the monitor *Havelock, Resolution, Revenge* and *Centaur*, with *Southampton* being his first command. By this time the cruiser was the flagship of Rear-Admiral Edward-Collins who, in May 1938, had taken over from Calvert.

On 17 January 1939 *Southampton* left Chatham for Portland where she joined other ships of the Home Fleet, including *Nelson, Rodney, Royal Sovereign, Glasgow, Newcastle, Sheffield* and two destroyer flotillas, for the passage to Gibraltar for combined Home-Mediterranean Fleet exercises. During these intensive manoeuvres there was still time for a short visit to Lisbon, but by now, with dark clouds of war gathering once again over Europe, the fleet exercises were taking on a new urgency, and it was 10 March before they were concluded and the fleets returned to Gibraltar. By mid-March *Southampton* was back at Portland and four days later, on 20 March, together with *Rodney, Glasgow, Sheffield* and the 5th Destroyer Flotilla, she steamed up Channel to anchor in the Dover Roads. Just six days earlier, in defiance of promises given at Munich, German and Hungarian troops had occupied Bohemia and Ruthenia respectively. These were the rump provinces left to Czechoslovakia after Munich, and as Neville Chamberlain told the House of Commons: '*For the first time, the Fűhrer has occupied territory not inhabited by people of Germanic race.*' *Southampton* and the other ships were at Dover to welcome the President of the French Republic, Monsieur Lebrun, who was paying a two-day, highly-publicised, official State Visit to London. He arrived at Dover in the steamer *Côte d'Azur*, escorted by French destroyers. Two days later the French President returned to France after top secret meetings, during which, for the first time, there was a hasty Anglo-French military agreement to go to the aid of Poland if it were attacked by Germany. As large parts of Germany had been ceded to Poland in 1919-20, it was apparent that this would be next on Hitler's agenda. Britain and France would soon pay a heavy price for the grievous political errors they had made at the Palace of Versailles some 20 years earlier.

After the French President's return to Calais *Southampton* made the short passage to Chatham for dry docking and maintenance and at the same time large numbers of the ship's company were changed. On 28 April she left Chatham for Portsmouth from where, eight days later in company with *Glasgow*, she was to escort the Canadian

Pacific liner *Empress of Australia*[1] She had been chartered to carry King George VI and Queen Elizabeth to Quebec for an important visit to Canada and the USA as part of the British Government's forlorn attempt to cement a military alliance with the USA. They arrived in the St Lawrence Approaches on 16 May, and next day steamed upriver to Quebec. The tour itself lasted for four weeks and during this period *Southampton* spent the first two days at Quebec, before steaming south to New York where she secured alongside the prestigious Pier 90. For eight days the ship's company enjoyed the legendary hospitality of New York, before sailing to Boston for a week, and then north to Halifax, Nova Scotia, where the royal visitors were scheduled to join the liner *Empress of Britain* for the passage home. Leaving Halifax on 15 June, both *Southampton* and *Glasgow* took up their escort positions on either side of the liner. There was a brief overnight stop at Conception Bay, Newfoundland, after which the five-day transatlantic passage began. During the forenoon of 22 June, with *Empress of Britain* taking her royal passengers into Southampton, the two escorting cruisers anchored at Portland, and five days later *Southampton* sailed for her home base at Chatham.

HMS *Southampton* was scheduled for service on the Africa Station, based at Simonstown, and was due to arrive there in October 1939 to become the flagship of the C-in-C Africa Station, Vice-Admiral G. H. D. O'Lyon. However, as the political situation in Europe continued to deteriorate, this time over the Baltic port of Danzig, the city at the mouth of the Vistula River, her move to Simonstown was cancelled and she was ordered to remain with the Home Fleet. Under the Treaty of Versailles Danzig had been declared a 'Free City'; the problem was that the population of Danzig was overwhelmingly German, and ever since the Treaty in 1919 German militias had been smuggling arms into the city. Now it seemed Hitler was trying to overturn the Versailles agreement and get Danzig returned to Germany. For Britain and France it brought the prospect of a second European War closer, for their Governments had given Poland hasty promises that if the Poles felt obliged to use force to maintain the status quo in Danzig, then they would go to her aid; promises which neither country could easily fulfil.

On 30 July 1939, with her maintenance completed, *Southampton* left the Thames Estuary to join the Home Fleet, including *Rodney, Royal Oak, Glasgow* and *Sheffield*, for exercises in the North Sea, based at Invergordon. For *Southampton* there was time to relax for the weekend when she visited Grimsby on 11 August. On 23 August, when Germany signed a non-aggression pact with the Soviet Union, thereby denying Britain and France the one ally whose influence might just have deterred the German invasion of Poland, *Southampton*, *Glasgow* and *Sheffield* were steaming north to their war stations at Scapa Flow. En route they passed through a large German fishing fleet which, no doubt, reported the course and speed of the three cruisers. On 29 August, some five days before war was declared, with her ship's company at Defence Stations, *Southampton* left Scapa Flow to begin her first patrol of the North Sea. On the last day of August she anchored off Grimsby, but this time no shore leave was granted and when war was declared on 3 September she was still patrolling the North Sea.

During the first weeks of September, operating from Rosyth, *Southampton* patrolled the North Sea, between the Firth of Forth and Sheerness. On 9 October she was at sea, in company with *Edinburgh* and *Glasgow*, off the coast of Norway, south-west of Stavanger, when all three cruisers were attacked by German Heinkel He-IIIK bombers. Although one bomb exploded astern of *Southampton* there were no casualties and the ship was unscathed. The attacks continued for most of the day, and on board all three cruisers the 4-inch high-angle and pom-

[1] Ironically, *Empress of Australia* had begun life as the German Liner *Admiral von Tirpitz*, and had been ceded to Britain under the treaty of Versailles in 1920 and renamed *Empress of China*. In 1922 she was renamed *Empress of Australia*.

pom crews were closed up and kept busy firing barrages of shells at waves of high-level and dive-bombing attacks. At 1700 the onslaught ceased and next day the cruisers anchored at Scapa Flow. *Southampton* resumed her patrol, and on 16 October she and *Edinburgh* returned from the North Sea to anchor at Rosyth. At 1430 the next day a force of 14 He-IIIKs carried out an air raid on the Firth of Forth, their prime target being the Forth Rail Bridge. A second wave of bombers turned their attention to the two cruisers and at 1435 a 500lb bomb hit *Southampton*, passing through the flag deck on the port side and right through the ship, exiting through the ship's side at No 84 station, five feet above the waterline. Fortunately it did not explode, but one rating was killed and three were seriously wounded. The ship, however, remained seaworthy and six days later she left for her next patrol, which took her south to Immingham and north to Scapa Flow. The North Sea patrols were interspersed with convoy escort duties and continued through to 23 December, when she was ordered to the River Tyne to undergo a five-week docking and maintenance period.

While *Southampton* lay high and dry in the Middle Dock at South Shields, for most of the ship's company there was an opportunity for at least one week's leave. On 1 February 1940 she left the River Tyne and set course for Scapa Flow from where, often in company with *Glasgow, Manchester, Newcastle* or *Sheffield*, she began patrolling the Norwegian Sea between Shetland and Iceland. In April 1940, however, the European war was about to begin in earnest and, like most ships of the Home Fleet, *Southampton* would be heavily involved in the Norwegian campaign. Both Britain and Germany harboured designs on occupying strategic parts of Norway. In Germany many strategists formed the view that their country's failure to take Norway during the Great War had enabled the

HMS Southampton *in Topsunhet Fjord, Norway in April 1940* *(Syd Goodman Collection)*

British blockade to be devastatingly effective and in Britain, although it is difficult to believe today, the Government was laying plans to invade both Norway and Sweden through the northern port of Narvik. Such an invasion would, according to British planners, enable Britain to control iron ore exports from Sweden and also to go to the aid of Finland which was struggling to fight off a Russian invasion. Such a campaign, when Britain was already at war with Germany, would have seen the country commit unprovoked aggression against both Norway and Sweden while waging war with the Soviet Union at the same time. Perhaps it illustrates just how out of touch with the realities of the country's military limitations British politicians were. These plans were formulated shortly before Chamberlain's, '*Hitler has missed the bus*' speech, and it was *Cossack*'s audacious rescue of almost 300 merchant navy prisoners from the German supply ship *Altmark* in a fjord near Bergen in February 1940 which galvanised the British, French and German governments into action. In the event the German invasion convoy sailed on 7 April, exactly the same day that a joint British and French invasion fleet left Scapa Flow and other Scottish ports bound for Narvik. *Southampton*, together with *Glasgow, Manchester* and *Sheffield* left Scapa to act as escort and to support the landings. For *Southampton*'s ship's company it was the start of a very busy two months.

On 10 April, having escorted the first troop convoy as far as the Norwegian coast, *Southampton* returned to Scapa Flow where she embarked 500 troops, including the Army's GOC, General Carton de Wiart, and his staff. Two days later, escorted by *Electra* and *Escapade*, she sailed for Harstadt, north-west of Narvik where, on 14 April, the troops were landed. The ship then lay at anchor for three days, coming under regular air attack, but despite near misses she remained undamaged. On 17 April

A camouflaged HMS Southampton *seen in the North Atlantic on 22 May 1940.* *(Syd Goodman Collection)*

she escorted two troop transports out of Norwegian waters, but by the following morning she had returned to her anchorage at Harstadt where, for the next ten days, she and other warships were subjected to fierce air attacks. On 1 May, while escorting a convoy from Harstadt to Sullum Voe she came under another heavy air attack, but once again she emerged unscathed. After leaving Norwegian waters *Southampton* returned to Scapa Flow and then sailed to Rosyth where she remained alongside for 14 days.

On 10 May 1940, 136 German Army Divisions slammed into Belgium and the Netherlands, and within 24 hours they had swept aside the vital Belgian defences at Fort Eban-Emael, outside Liège. They were now poised to deliver the Schlieffen Plan and overrun France in a way which, earlier in the century, the less mechanised armies of the Kaiser had never been able to accomplish. Meanwhile, in Norway, despite some spectacular naval successes, the German invasion forces moved swiftly and efficiently and very soon the combined British, French and Polish force at Narvik was under severe pressure. On 22 May *Southampton* left Rosyth for Harstadt where she anchored two days later. At 1230 next day she came under heavy air attack, during which a 500lb bomb landed very close to her starboard side where it exploded, ripping three underwater holes in the ship's side and causing casualties in two messdecks. Later that evening the most severely wounded were landed for medical treatment ashore, and three days later, with the holes in the ship's side having been shorn up by a cofferdam, *Southampton* moved up to Vestfjord in order to provide naval gunfire support ashore. However, it was not long before she was ordered back to Harstadt where she remained on patrol until Sunday 8 June when, with the allied evacuation under way, she sailed in company with HMS *Campbell* to escort a convoy back to Scapa Flow. Being in need of urgent repairs, however, she left the convoy in the Pentland Firth and continued her passage round the north of Scotland to Greenock: by 0600 on 13 June she was high and dry in Glasgow's King George V graving dock for her hull repairs.

During the nine days spent in dry dock there was a change of command when, during the evening of Tuesday 18 June, Captain B. C. B. Brooke RN took over from Jeans. Four days later the ship left the dry dock to head north to Scapa Flow. During the last week of June and the first week of July *Southampton* carried out a nine-day work-up programme before, on 6 June, she sailed south to Rosyth. During the passage she was attacked by enemy bombers, but she emerged unscathed and anchored in the Firth of Forth the next day. On 19 July she was ordered to sail south down the North Sea, and once again she attracted a number of bombers en route to the River Medway. For just over four weeks, during the period when the country was on a high state of alert, *Southampton* remained in the Thames Estuary. Both she and her sister *Birmingham* were there to boost the naval defences of south-east England, where an invasion, if it came, was most likely. In early August *Southampton* shifted from her buoy at Sheerness, where no shore leave at all had been granted, and both she and *Birmingham* anchored off Southend Pier. Some limited shore leave was given here, although it was a period of high alert, with both cruisers at an hour's notice for steam on the main engines. On 17 August the monotonous routine was broken when she left the Thames Estuary to escort convoys first to Rosyth, and from the Firth of Forth to Immingham, where she remained for two weeks. Finally on 16 October, she left the east coast to make the passage north to Scapa Flow, where she joined the Northern Patrol in the waters between the Shetland Islands and Iceland. By early November most patrols were being carried out in atrocious weather conditions, with heavy seas, blinding snowstorms and only five hours of daylight.Along with other ships on the Northern Patrol, many of which were armed merchant cruisers, *Southampton* was ordered to keep a close watch on German auxiliary cruisers attempting to break the blockade and escape into the Atlantic. In June and July 1940 two

raiders had successfully evaded the patrols, and in November it was thought that the commerce raider *Kormoran*[2] would attempt a breakout. On 8 November *Southampton* was ordered to intercept the Swedish merchant ship *Hera*, which had been chartered by the Finnish Government for a voyage from Petsamo to Portland, Maine. When she encountered the ship at 2052 that evening the weather was rough and stormy and totally unsuitable for boarding, and the merchantman's master refused to put into Reykjavik to be searched. However, before any further action could be taken *Southampton* was ordered to break off and proceed directly to Belfast for dry docking in order to be '*ready to leave the Clyde on 15 November on a most important operation, the duration of which cannot be foreseen'*. She was, in fact, being deployed for service on the East Indies Station, sailing via the Mediterranean where she would carry out convoy escort duties en route to Alexandria.

After leaving the Northern patrol and refuelling at Reykjavik, *Southampton* steamed south to Belfast where, on 13 November, she was briefly dry docked in order to clean what was described by her commanding officer as '*a very foul bottom and to repair the Asdic dome*'. During the forenoon of 15 November she was towed out of dry dock to anchor in Belfast Lough and await a southbound convoy, of which she would form part of the escort.

HMS *Southampton* had, in fact, been ordered to join 'Operation Collar', under the command of Vice-Admiral Sir James Somerville, Flag Officer Commanding Force H at Gibraltar. The object of the operation was, '*...to secure the safe and timely passage through the Mediterranean of two Southampton-class cruisers, three merchant ships and four corvettes.*' The two cruisers were in fact *Southampton* herself and *Manchester*, and between them they would be carrying some 1,370 RAF personnel bound for Alexandria to reinforce the hard-pressed Western Desert Air Force. With both cruisers carrying almost as many embarked personnel as their own ship's company it was accepted that their fighting efficiency would be seriously impaired. In fact, Vice-Admiral L. E. Holland (Vice-Admiral Commanding 18th Cruiser Squadron who, in May 1941, was lost in HMS *Hood*) expressed serious concerns about including them in the convoy at all and would have preferred to sail them independently. In the event his doubts were overridden and when the C-in-C Mediterranean asked the Admiralty for clarification as to whether the safe passage of the cruisers carrying the RAF personnel, or the merchant ships carrying supplies should receive priority, he received the contradictory reply that the personnel should receive priority, but this was subject to the overriding consideration that if Italian forces were in sight, '*...action taken by the cruisers must be the same as if personnel were not embarked.*' Not only would *Southampton* and *Manchester* be included in the convoy, they would be fought as if there were no military passengers aboard.

Escorting the convoy was the battlecruiser *Renown* (flag Vice-Admiral Somerville), the aircraft carrier *Ark Royal*, the cruisers *Despatch* and *Sheffield* and nine destroyers. Somerville also had permission to include the battleship *Royal Sovereign*, but as she was undergoing repairs which could not be completed in time, she did not sail. At 2330 on 17 November *Southampton* weighed anchor to sail south and join the five merchantmen, *Clan Fraser, Clan McNab, Clan Forbes, New Zealand Star* and *Franconia*, a fast Cunard liner which had been converted for use as a troopship. She was carrying the 1,370 RAF personnel who, on arrival at Gibraltar, were to transfer to the two cruisers (760 in *Southampton* and 660 in *Manchester*). Routed well out into the Atlantic it took four days to reach Gibraltar, and as they sailed along the Spanish coast past Tarifa the RAF personnel were ordered to remain well out of sight below deck. During the afternoon of 22 November they arrived in Gibraltar, and that night under cover of darkness

[2] *Kormoran* was a powerful ship which, in November 1941, was engaged by *HMAS Sydney*. During the ensuing battle both ships were lost.

they were transferred to the two cruisers. Finally, at 0730 on Monday 25 November, the convoy left Gibraltar bound for Malta and Alexandria. It now consisted of the two cruisers and three merchantmen, *Clan Forbes, Clan Fraser* and *New Zealand Star,* all of which were carrying tanks and mechanised transport for the Army; four corvettes whose speed was limited to 16 knots; the destroyer *Hotspur*, whose speed was also limited, and the main escort force consisting of *Renown, Ark Royal, Sheffield, Despatch* and nine destroyers. At around the same time Force D, which consisted of *Ramillies, Newcastle, Coventry, Berwick* and four destroyers, left Malta to steam west for Gibraltar. The forces were due to rendezvous at around noon on 27 November, south of Sardinia, which was the most dangerous section of the passage.

The first day of *Southampton*'s eastbound voyage passed quietly, with *Ark Royal*'s aircraft carrying out regular reconnaissance missions. At sunrise on 27 November *Renown, Sheffield, Ark Royal* and four destroyers were some 20 miles to the north-east of the convoy, which was off the coast of Algeria, south-west of Sardinia. The four corvettes, having been unable to keep up, were some ten miles west of the convoy. At about this time *Ark Royal*'s fighters shot down an Italian Z506 reconnaissance aircraft which had been shadowing the convoy. By 1016 it had been established that an enemy battlefleet, consisting of two battleships, six cruisers and seven destroyers, was situated some 40 to 50 miles to the north. *Renown* and *Sheffield* both increased speed to 28 knots and turned to engage the enemy force, and by 1130 they had been joined by *Ramillies, Newcastle* and, despite the fact that they were loaded with military personnel, by *Southampton* and *Manchester*. The Italian force, which included *Vittorio Veneto, Giulio Cesare*, six heavy cruisers and 11 destroyers, had been ordered to remain within range of the Regio Aeronautica air bases on Sardinia, and to that end the Italian force retired north-eastward, chased by the British ships. At 1215 the Italian cruisers were sighted by *Southampton* and within a minute both sides had opened fire, but by 1300 the Italian ships were out of range and *Southampton* ceased fire. Soon after this Somerville realised that not only was there no hope of overhauling the enemy force, but that they were drawing his ships ever closer to the Sardinian coast where they would be vulnerable to air attack, and he ordered his force to retire. Soon afterwards he received a report of a damaged enemy cruiser some 30 miles north of his force, but only ten miles from the Sardinian coast. He considered it most unwise to place *Southampton* and *Manchester* in danger of being sunk or badly damaged by bombs, and any other ships of his force which searched for the cruiser would be singled out for air attack; if any were disabled his whole force would be placed in great danger trying to extricate a damaged ship, thus putting the whole convoy at risk of destruction. Under these circumstances he decided against searching for the damaged enemy ship. At 1407 his decision was vindicated when the first enemy air attack came close to seriously damaging some of the escorting destroyers, and this was followed by two more air raids before the force was out of range. Somerville's impression of the Italian air raids was that: '*Apart from a few bombs which were jettisoned as a result of interception by our fighters, most accurate bombing was carried out.*' By 1700 the escorting force was back with the convoy, and during the forenoon on 28 November the Malta section was detached. Finally, by 1015 on 30 November, *Southampton* and the other ships had arrived at Alexandria and three hours later all the RAF personnel had been safely disembarked, which had been the primary objective of 'Operation Collar'.

Having arrived safely at Alexandria *Southampton* joined the 7th Cruiser Squadron, but there was barely a 48-hour break before she resumed her voyage, south through the Suez Canal, to set course for Durban. Eight days into her passage, however, she was ordered to close the port of Kismayu (Kismaaya) in what was then Italian Somaliland, just north of the Kenyan border, to bombard shipping in the harbour. It was only days before the

British Army invaded Eritrea, Somaliland and Ethiopia and it was vital that as much disruption as possible was caused to both shipping and the harbour installations. *Southampton* finally arrived in the Mozambique Channel during the forenoon of 18 December where she rendezvoused with *Devonshire* and *Shropshire*, who were escorting a troop convoy between Durban and Aden. After transferring mail *Southampton* took over the escort of this important convoy, WSB4, which included the troop transports *Andes* and *Duchess of Athol*. For seven days the convoy steamed north, but on Christmas Day, just south of Aden, *Southampton* was ordered to return to Alexandria from where she was to take part in a special operation.

During the first week of January 1941 the Royal Navy mounted 'Operation Excess', another joint operation by Force H at Gibraltar and the Mediterranean Fleet at Alexandria, to reinforce and resupply the now besieged island of Malta, and the newly created British Army garrison in Greece. The operation involved the entire naval strength from both sides of the Mediterranean, and with naval intelligence sources indicating that Axis forces had over 300 long-range bombers and dive-bombers available, it was clear that the threat of air attack was very real. This massive operation was mounted to escort just four merchant ships and it was the first of several such convoys over the next 18 months. The plan was that they would be escorted from Gibraltar by Force H as far as the Skerki Channel, and the timing was such that they would arrive at the Sicilian Narrows at nightfall, where the ships of the Mediterranean Fleet would take over the escort and by dawn the next day the convoy would be within range of fighter protection from Malta.

At 0900 on 7 January 1941 four merchant ships, *SS Essex, Clan MacDonald, Clan Cumming* and *Empire Song*, escorted by *Renown* (Flag), *Malaya, Ark Royal, Sheffield, Bonaventure* and 11 destroyers, left Gibraltar to sail east. At 0500 the same day Force A, which consisted of *Valiant, Warspite, Illustrious* and eight destroyers, left Alexandria bound for the Skerki Channel where they were to take over the escort duties from the ships of Force H. Both *Southampton* and *Gloucester* would eventually join the escort, but they had left Alexandria at 1300 on 6 January to sail for Suda Bay and Malta with troops for both garrisons. They arrived in Malta at 1000 on 8 January, and after disembarking the troops and refuelling they sailed at 1445 to join Force A as part of the convoy escort. The remainder of the day passed quietly, and on 9 January they joined the convoy. That afternoon there were air attacks, but *Southampton* came through unscathed. At 0430 on Friday 10 January, when in a position 36°29'N 012°10'E, south of the island of Pantelleria, two enemy torpedo boats operating from the island were engaged by *Bonaventure* and *Hereward*, with *Southampton* and *Jaguar* standing by. Between them they fired seven torpedoes before one boat was destroyed and the other escaped. Four hours later *Southampton, Gloucester, Bonaventure, Griffin, Hereward* and *Jaguar* were ordered to stand by the destroyer *Gallant* which had hit a mine and had her bows blown off. She was eventually towed at 6½ knots to Malta, with *Southampton* and *Gloucester* providing an escort, before finally leaving her off Grand Harbour at 0500 on Saturday 11 January, and returning to join the convoy.

At 1500 the same day, *Gloucester* (from 0500 flag of 3rd Cruiser Squadron (CS3)), *Southampton* and *Diamond* were in a position 35°03'N 018°10'E, roughly 180 miles south-south-west of Malta, and some 195 miles from the North African coast. The sea was calm and the weather was fine, with only a gentle southerly breeze. The ships' companies were in third degree of readiness with guns' crews and fire and repair parties closed up. All three ships were steaming at 24 knots on a zigzag course. Suddenly, at 1520, without any warning, *Southampton* was attacked by 12 Junkers Ju-88, twin-engine bombers, one of the most versatile aircraft of the early war years. The first five aircraft dived low on *Southampton* from the sun which was on the starboard quarter. A second group simultaneously attacked from astern, and a third from the port quarter. Although they were quickly engaged by the

ship's four-barrelled pom-poms none of the aircraft was brought down. The first 500lb bomb pierced the port hangar and exploded on the protective deck above A boiler room, and almost immediately a second bomb pierced X gun deck, passed through the wardroom flat and exploded on the protective deck above the wireless transmitting office. The second bomb was almost certainly an incendiary device and fierce fires broke out. A third bomb was a very near miss, with fragments of shrapnel piercing the ship's side and causing casualties forward.

The first bomb started some small fires, but in A boiler room the front of the superheater was blown off and oil and water pipes were fractured. The escaping superheated steam, mixed with smoke, quickly made the compartment untenable and the boilers were shut down and all personnel evacuated. This bomb killed or incapacitated 18 ERAs, Mechanicians and Chief Stokers, and wounded some 150 other ratings. The after bomb killed or seriously wounded 27 officers, including the ship's Executive Officer, Commander C. B. Tinley OBE, who later died in hospital, and three senior engineer officers. Although the ship was steaming on the after machinery units and was still able to manoeuvre, the second bomb had caused raging fires which were described thus by Captain Brooke, who had gone aft to see the devastation for himself: '*The after bomb, which had incendiaries attached, started serious fires around the magazines and caused great structural damage to watertight doors and decks, and wrecked the flood shafting to all explosive chambers except Y turret. Nothing was known of the hit aft, due to the fact that the Damage Control Officer, the Executive Officer, and almost everyone else in the vicinity was killed or rendered unconscious. Above the upper deck the whole Wardroom flat was enveloped in flame and burned fiercely with oil fuel from the galleys on fire. The port screen was blasted away from the deck by two feet (60cm), and the upper deck was bulged upwards on either side of the quarterdeck screen. The wood planking was split with smoke and steam rising through it. Above the main deck a fire blazed from 155 to 227 Stations, which included the Engineer Officers' flat, the Gunroom flat and all the cabin flats. The after engine room was very hot and could not be entered, and on the Platform Deck the main wireless transmission office had been put out of action and no communication with it had been established, nor had anyone escaped from it.*'

Although the ship was steaming at 20 knots the heat in the after machinery spaces was intense, and with flames raging around it personnel had great difficulty gaining entry and exit. By 1600 the fire which had spread through four compartments was blazing furiously, and an hour later, owing to lack of feed water, all power in the ship was lost. In the attempt to evacuate the boiler and engine room personnel it was found that those in the after engine room, with the flat above and abaft the engine room burning fiercely, could not escape and they were in danger of suffocating through inhalation of smoke. Fortunately, a very determined effort by a firefighting party from forward managed, with great difficulty, to extricate them. At 1800 a fire was observed in the forward funnel, and although firefighting efforts continued in the after part of the ship, cordite had started burning, and fierce fires were raging out of control above and around X warhead magazine. By 1830 the moment of decision for Captain Brooke had arrived, for if he delayed abandoning the ship any chance of saving most of his ship's company would be gone and any destroyer coming alongside risked being blown up by the rapidly overheating magazines. By this time *Diamond* had come alongside the cruiser's forecastle to evacuate the wounded and so at 1859, some three hours and 39 minutes after the attack, Captain Brooke ordered that all sea cocks and doors which could safely be approached be opened, and the ship was abandoned. By that time, with the whole ship aft of B turret burning out of control, only *Southampton*'s forecastle was tenable and Captain Brooke had to climb down the fore side of the bridge by way of an emergency rope ladder, which with the intense heat was already starting to smoulder. He was the last person to board *Diamond*.

At 2020, with *Southampton* still burning fiercely, and listing heavily to starboard, CS3 ordered *Gloucester* to fire one torpedo at the burning hulk. This hit the ship forward, but even after the resulting explosion the ship showed no signs of sinking , with the list increasing only slowly. An hour later *Orion* fired four torpedoes, one of which caused a massive explosion, and within minutes the still blazing hulk which had once been HMS *Southampton* rolled over and sank.

Altogether 80 officers and men lost their lives and CS3, Rear-Admiral E. De F. Renouf CVO, confirmed Captain Brooke's decision to abandon the ship had been the right one. Of his ship's company Brooke wrote: '*The behaviour of officers and men while fighting such fierce fires over unflooded magazines was exemplary. Many acts of individual heroism in saving life came to my notice. I was deeply impressed with the patience and cheerfulness of the badly wounded from whom I have yet to hear evidence of cry or complaint. I much regret that there were many fatal and other casualties.*'

Chapter Two

HMS NEWCASTLE
1937-1959

HMS Newcastle, *at speed, shortly after completion.* *(Syd Goodman Collection)*

On Thursday 4 October 1934, at a small ceremony in the Walker-on-Tyne shipyard of Vickers Armstrong Ltd, the keel plates were laid for a new class of cruiser. Originally it had been intended that the new cruisers would be the Minotaur class, with the first ship being named *Minotaur*. However, before the keel was laid the First Lord of the Admiralty had announced that owing to the trend in foreign cruiser design it was necessary to increase the tonnage in order that the new ships would not '*be inferior to those being developed by other powers*'. As he made this announcement he had his eyes firmly fixed upon Germany and Japan. He also revealed that the eight new cruisers would be named after cities in the United Kingdom. The fact that the first order had gone to the Walker shipyard was a welcome boost for Tyneside for in 1931, following the completion of the passenger liner *Monarch of Bermuda*, and the onset of the Great Depression, the company's order books had dried up. In September 1934 the very welcome order for the first of the Town-class cruisers had enabled the management to reopen the yard and prepare the slipway.

For 15 months after the laying of the first keel plates work proceeded apace, and by the new year of 1936 the ship was ready for launching. The ceremony took place on 23 January, but as it was only five days after the death of King George V, the Government instructed that the launch was to be carried out '*with as little ceremony as possible*'. The very subdued affair, with just nine representatives of the Admiralty and the builder present, took place after a short religious service with music from the Band of the Northumberland Fusiliers, when the Duchess of Northumberland named her *Newcastle*

as she sent her down the slipway into the waters of the River Tyne.

In September 1936 *Newcastle*'s first commanding officer, Captain J. G. P. Vivian RN, was appointed to stand by the ship. He had just completed a period as Naval Attaché to the British Embassy in Tokyo and before that he had commanded the cruiser *Dauntless* in the Caribbean. During the Great War he had been Navigator of the cruiser *Venus* and the battleship *Iron Duke* and in 1920, after promotion to Commander, he had seen service in the battleships *Conqueror* and *Thunderer*. In 1923 and 1924 he had been the Squadron Navigator of the Special Service Squadron which had travelled round the world with Admiral Field.

On Friday 5 March 1937, with *Newcastle* having completed her builder's trials, she was secured to buoys in the River Tyne abreast the Albert-Edward Dock at North Shields and at 1930 that day she was officially accepted into Royal Naval Service. Half an hour later she slipped her moorings and put to sea for the 48-hour passage south, through the Strait of Dover to Devonport, anchoring in Plymouth Sound during the evening of 7 March. Next morning, as dawn was breaking, she weighed anchor and slipped quietly up harbour to secure alongside Devonport Dockyard's No 7 Wharf, where she joined the 2nd Cruiser Squadron.

During the cruiser's first week alongside at Devonport her ship's company was brought up to full strength, and she embarked stores and ammunition. On 10 March one of Vickers Armstrong's workmen, who was still completing some fitting-out work on board, was killed in a fall. Five weeks later, on 13 April, the ship began her initial trials off Portland. It was during this period that she was joined by her sister *Southampton*, which had been built on the Clyde and was also undergoing trials. On 7 May the two cruisers steamed into the River Thames where they anchored in midriver at Gravesend to take part in celebrations to mark the Coronation of King George VI. Both ships provided ceremonial platoons to march in the Coronation Procession in Central London, and during the six days they spent on the Thames they opened their gangways to visitors. On 13 May they left Gravesend for Spithead and the Coronation Fleet Review. *Newcastle* arrived off the Nab Tower shortly before the German Navy's heavy cruiser *Admiral Graf Spee*. On 24 May, with the Review over, *Newcastle* returned to Portland where she continued her trials and work-up. On 29 May, while at anchor in Portland Harbour, she suffered an electrical fire in one of her forward gun turrets, but fortunately it was quickly extinguished and later that day she got under way to anchor at Spithead. Three days later she steamed up harbour where she secured alongside the battlecruiser *Repulse* at Pitch House Jetty.

On 10 June *Newcastle* steamed north to Rosyth from where, in company with *Southampton*, she carried out ten days of gunnery exercises, and the ship's Walrus aircraft was put through its paces. The exercises ended in Largo Bay, after which *Newcastle* sailed south and both she and *Southampton* took part in a major trade defence exercise in the Western Approaches and the Bristol Channel. The exercise, which involved both the Navy and RAF, was designed to investigate the problems of maritime warfare, by the development of the faster, bigger and longer-range aircraft which were being developed in the mid-late-1930s. The Navy was still coming to terms with air power, while many in the RAF believed that powerful bombers would, on their own, decide the result of any future war, despite the fact that many senior officers were still thinking in terms of static trench warfare across the flat fields of northern France and Belgium. One aspect of future warfare which was fully understood, however, was the need to protect Britain's trade routes. The scenario of the exercise was based on an enemy 'Blue Force', whose naval forces had been neutralised in their own distant waters by the main British fleet, but who had succeeded in detaching a cruiser and an armed and disguised merchant raider to the Western Approaches to disrupt British seaborne trade. Rear-Admiral T. P. F. Calvert was in command of 'Blue Force' and his flagship, *Southampton*, was designated as the

'enemy' cruiser. The defending 'Red Force', under the command of Rear-Admiral T. H. Binney, flying his flag in the aircraft carrier *Glorious*, also had *Newcastle* and the destroyer *Brazen* under his command. On board *Glorious* was 802 Fighter Squadron, with Hawker Nimrod biplanes, and 823 and 825 Torpedo-Spotter-Reconnaissance Squadrons, equipped with Fairey Swordfish aircraft; in addition Binney had the use of the RAF's 201 Flying Boat Squadron. The exercise took place in a rectangular area stretching 240 miles south and 400 miles west of Lundy Island. The co-operation of the Merchant Navy was secured, with any British merchant vessels in the area being liable to 'attack' or 'capture' by the 'Blue' ships. Such a 'capture' was signalled by the warship remaining in the vicinity of her 'prize' for 45 minutes, which represented the time required to remove the occupants of the ship and to 'sink' her.

HMS *Southampton*'s career as a hostile raider was brief, for almost immediately after the defending force left its base at Falmouth on 28 June, a call for help was received from the merchantman *Cordillera*, in a position some 130 miles to the south-west. *Newcastle*, together with *Glorious* and *Brazen,* made for the spot with aircraft from *Glorious* searching ahead. Two other merchant ships were 'attacked' before aircraft from *Glorious* located and 'sank' *Southampton*. The official records show that 18 Swordfish attacked with bombs and torpedoes, and that *Southampton* was adjudged to be 'sunk'. It is an interesting rebuttal of the allegation that the Royal Navy was unprepared for the advent of air warfare and the exercise bore an uncanny resemblance to some early Second World War engagements against enemy commerce raiders. It shows that the Navy was well aware of the devastating effects of air power which could be projected well beyond the range of a battleship's guns, but they were hampered by second-rate aircraft, a legacy of almost 20 years of RAF control.

The exercises continued until 5 July when all the ships involved anchored in Tor Bay. After further exercises in the Channel, which also involved the

A port quarter view of HMS Newcastle *during the 1937 Coronation Review at Spithead.* *(David John Weller)*

aircraft carrier *Courageous*, and attacks on the sea defences at Portland and Portsmouth, *Newcastle* steamed north to Loch Ryan, from where she escorted the Royal Yacht *Victoria and Albert*, carrying George VI on an official visit to Belfast. Two days later, on 30 July, *Newcastle* returned to Devonport where, over a period of eight days, she took part in the annual Navy Week and played host to some 57,000 visitors.

On 8 September *Newcastle* left Plymouth Sound to sail via Spithead to Invergordon, from where the Home Fleet's autumn manoeuvres took place. In 1937 the ships taking part included *Rodney, Royal Oak, Resolution, Revenge, Ramillies, Courageous* and *Furious*. During the exercises which continued into October, *Newcastle*'s gunners had the opportunity to fire the main armament at the radio-controlled target ship *Centurion*. On 7 October *Newcastle* sailed south to pay a five-day visit to her birthplace on the River Tyne, where a silver bell was presented to the ship by the city of Newcastle on Tyne. She then spent 12 days at anchor off Shoeburyness before steaming round to the south coast and Portland where the Home Fleet reassembled for a further three weeks of exercises before leaving for their base ports and the Christmas leave period. On 15 November *Newcastle* and *Royal Oak* left Portland, arriving alongside in Devonport later that day.

The year 1938, the last full year of peace for over seven years, began for *Newcastle* on 18 January when she left Devonport bound for Portland, where she rendezvoused with her sisters *Sheffield* and *Southampton*, and set course for Gibraltar. With civil war still raging in Spain, which affected shipping in the surrounding waters of the Atlantic Ocean and Mediterranean Sea, all three cruisers had red, white and blue recognition markings painted on 'B' turret. It was not long before this savage civil war, which preceded Europe's second destructive war of the twentieth century, directly affected *Newcastle*'s operational commitments.

On 31 January 1938 the three cruisers had begun a series of visits to the Spanish coastal cities of

HMS Newcastle *prepares to recover her Walrus while at anchor. Note the port side aircraft handling crane has been swung outboard ready to receive the aircraft.* *(Ken Kelly Collection)*

Valencia and Palma, Majorca; they arrived in the latter port during the forenoon of 4 February. That same evening *Newcastle* was ordered to proceed immediately to Barcelona, where she anchored off the breakwater next morning. She was under orders to embark the master and 16 crew members of the British merchantman, SS *Alcira*, which had been bombed and sunk by Spanish Nationalist seaplanes some 22 miles off Barcelona. As the vessel had been well outside Spanish territorial waters, and clearly displaying neutrality markings, the attack had caused a diplomatic incident. *Newcastle*, fortunately, did not become embroiled in that, but, nevertheless, after embarking her passengers for an overnight transfer to Marseilles, she kept full anti-aircraft and surface lookouts posted. After disembarking *Alcira*'s crewmen for them to continue their journey home overland by rail to Calais then Dover, she returned to Palma from where she took part in joint Home and Mediterranean Fleet exercises, which also included *Hood, Nelson, Glasgow, Sheffield, Southampton, Cornwall, London, Aurora* and two destroyer flotillas. The exercises ended on 19 March and six days later the ships left Gibraltar, with the Mediterranean Fleet returning to Malta and the Home Fleet ships to their base ports. *Newcastle* accompanied *Nelson, Glasgow* and *Sheffield* north, arriving alongside at Devonport on 29 March.On 10 May 1938, having given seasonal leave and undergone essential maintenance, which included dry docking, *Newcastle* left Devonport for Spithead where she embarked her Walrus aircraft and flight personnel before steaming to Portland to join other ships of the 2nd Cruiser Squadron. For the next six weeks *Newcastle* was involved in exercises with the Home Fleet, and these culminated on 21 and 22 June with a visit by King George VI; he had travelled by train to Weymouth where he had embarked in the Royal Yacht *Victoria and Albert* which was lying in Weymouth Bay surrounded by ships of the Home Fleet, including *Nelson, Rodney, Ramillies, Resolution, Royal Oak* and *Revenge*. The Town-class cruisers were represented by *Newcastle, Glasgow, Sheffield* and *Southampton*. Also present were the 4th and 6th Destroyer Flotillas and, most importantly, the aircraft carrier *Courageous*. The latter, as far as the press were concerned, appeared almost to have been added to the list as an afterthought.

During the forenoon of 21 June, *Nelson*, flying the Royal Standard, led the fleet to sea for two days of intensive exercises. Once clear of Weymouth Bay the cruisers each launched their aircraft, and the destroyer flotillas delivered a mass torpedo attack on the battlefleet. Aircraft from *Courageous* were adjudged to have caused most damage to the battleships, after most of the torpedoes launched by 18 Swordfish hit one or more of the leviathans. This spectacular success was somewhat overshadowed when, during the next serial, the cruisers let loose their anti-aircraft guns and shot down the 'Queen Bee' target drone with a direct hit, but only after the drone had made three clear runs over the battlefleet and emerged unscathed. The final serial of the day, before a thick fog closed in around the fleet, was a rapid-fire gunnery shoot at the radio-controlled target ship *Centurion*. The second day of manoeuvres was largely spent carrying out harbour evolutions, with *Newcastle* and the other cruisers engaged in fire-fighting and damage control exercises. That evening the King returned to London and on 23 June the battlefleet carried out a final day of manoeuvres, which concluded off Land's End. Eighteen ships of the fleet, led by *Nelson* (flag C-in-C, Admiral Sir Charles Forbes), then steamed north to the Clyde where, in conjunction with the Empire Exhibition in Glasgow, Scotland was holding its own Navy Week. Other ships present were *Rodney, Royal Sovereign, Courageous, Glasgow, Newcastle*, the 6th Destroyer Flotilla and the submarines *Narwhal* and *Seahorse*. During the nine days at Glasgow *Newcastle*, her sister *Glasgow* and four destroyers, berthed in the city's King George V Dock, and when they opened their gangways to the public thousands of visitors from the city and surrounding areas formed long, patient queues along Shieldhall Wharf as they waited for their opportunity to look round the ships. Meanwhile, at anchor

off the Tail of the Bank, the battleships *Nelson, Rodney* and *Royal Sovereign*, and the aircraft carrier *Courageous*, kept the Clyde pleasure steamers busy ferrying day trippers round the fleet.

The visit to the Clyde ended on 4 July, and after leaving the river *Newcastle* steamed north to the island of Lewis, where she paid a three-day visit to Stornaway, after which she steamed across to Denmark and the port of Aarhus. During the visit King Christian of Denmark visited the ship and, being an honorary Admiral of the Royal Navy, the Danish Royal Standard and his Admiral's flag were hoisted. During the short, hour-long visit, the King inspected the ship's company at ceremonial divisions. When *Newcastle* left Aarhus on 18 July she rendezvoused with *Nelson, Rodney, Revenge, Royal Sovereign, Glasgow* and *Aurora*, which formed 'Blue Force', in North Sea exercises which were designed to test the defences of the main east coast ports, including Harwich, the Forth, the Tyne and the Thames, against air and sea attacks. The defending 'Red Force' consisted of *Sheffield, Cornwall* and four destroyers. During these manoeuvres *Newcastle* carried out dummy bombardments of Harwich and, on 22 July, she 'attacked' and 'bombarded' the Medway defences before returning to Devonport for Navy Week.

On 6 September *Newcastle* sailed from Devonport for annual naval manoeuvres. This was at a time when Czechoslovakia was dominating the headlines, and German threats to invade the mainly German-speaking region of the Sudetenland, and with France and Britain bound by a Treaty of January 1924 to go to that country's aid, the dark clouds of war were hanging over Europe. Just 20 years after the end of the Great War it seemed that Europe was about to tear itself to pieces once again. As diplomatic tensions mounted, military preparations began, first with the French Army cancelling all leave and reinforcing their garrisons on the Maginot Line, and with martial law being declared throughout Czechoslovakia. For the Royal Navy, the manoeuvres in the North Sea now took on a more serious significance. On 24 September, when war appeared imminent, the Home Fleet was ordered to its war station at Scapa Flow, where it was designated as the North Sea Force – a pale shadow of Jellicoe's Grand Fleet of August 1914.

During the two weeks spent at Scapa in the autumn of 1938 *Newcastle* exercised with other ships of the 2nd Cruiser Squadron, including *Southampton, Sheffield, Glasgow* and *Aurora*, but for most of the time she remained at anchor. On 29 September Neville Chamberlain flew to Munich for his third and final meeting with Adolf Hitler, during which he and the French premier Daldier gave Hitler the Sudetenland. Next day Chamberlain flew back into Heston aerodrome, which was near to where Heathrow is situated today, to be met by cheering crowds. That evening, in a stage-managed event from a first-floor window at 10 Downing Street, he uttered the fateful words borrowed from Disraeli: '*I believe*', he said, '*it is peace for our time.*' Although Munich is popularly perceived to be a watershed in the discredited diplomacy of Appeasement, it was, in fact, another step in the unravelling of the Treaty of Versailles which had been going on since the 1920s. British politicians had often supported revisions to the Treaty, but in the case of the Sudetenland Germany's diplomacy had been backed by the threat of force, which had made any further revisions to the Treaty unacceptable to the British and French. However, as far as Germany was concerned the most despised part of the Treaty was the loss of East Prussia and the cities of Königsberg[1] and Danzig to the newly formed Poland. Hitler was unlikely to take much heed of British and French objections to further revisions of the Treaty, particularly since Poland had taken advantage of the Munich Agreement and had invaded and annexed parts of Moravia. In the meantime, however, the apparent success at Munich meant that there would be no European War in 1938, and on 6 October the Home Fleet returned to Invergordon to

[1] Königsberg is now called Kaliningrad and is in a small enclave which has been Russian since the end of the Second World War.

continue the autumn manoeuvres, following which *Newcastle* returned to Devonport in mid-November.

On 17 January 1939 *Newcastle* left Devonport to join *Southampton, Echo* and *Eclipse* for the passage to Gibraltar and en route they subjected any passing merchant ships to dummy attacks. On arrival in Gibraltar the Governor of the Colony, General Sir Edmund Ironside, accompanied by his personal staff, embarked in *Newcastle* for the short passage to Casablanca where he disembarked for an official visit to what was in those days the French Protectorate of Morocco. He was the guest of General Nogués, the Resident-General, to discuss mutual defence arrangements in the event of a European war which was now looking inevitable. On the same day that Ironside disembarked from *Newcastle* at Casablanca, Adolf Hitler travelled from Berlin to Hamburg to launch the battleship *Bismarck*. The General's visit to Morocco took him to Rabat, Meknès, Marrakesh, Fez and Tangier from where, on 19 February, he re-embarked in *Newcastle* for the passage back to Gibraltar.

At the end of February and during the first two weeks of March *Newcastle* exercised from Gibraltar with other ships of the Home Fleet, during which she acted as escort to the aircraft carriers *Ark Royal* and *Glorious*. On 13 March she left Gibraltar and set course for Portland, where the personnel and Walrus aircraft of 712(C) Flight were disembarked. *Newcastle* herself then continued up-Channel and anchored off Dover. On 21 March, together with *Rodney, Southampton, Sheffield, Glasgow* and nine destroyers of the 5th Flotilla, she formed part of two lines of warships which would undertake the ceremonial welcome for the French President, Albert Lebrun, who was making a State visit to London. The visit came as the spectre of German troops marching into what remained of Czechoslovakia was hanging over Europe and as Chamberlain told the House of Commons: '*For the first time the Führer has occupied a territory not inhabited by people of the German race.*' Within days of Lebrun's visit to London the British and French Governments had made a hasty but 'whole-hearted pledge' to defend Poland against attack, a pledge which neither country could ever fulfil, and which ensured that both countries would be hostages to Polish foreign policy decisions. While these momentous events unfolded, *Newcastle* was at Dover to salute the French President as he left for Calais, and on 24 March she returned to Devonport to undergo a five-week maintenance period.

On 23 April 1939, when *Newcastle* put to sea again she joined *Rodney* and three destroyers for the passage to Portland and eight days later, after embarking journalists from the *Sunday Graphic* newspaper, she sailed with *Ark Royal, Rodney, Sheffield, Aurora* and 11 destroyers for a position off the Isle of Wight. Here, at just after 1700, the fleet met and saluted a royal squadron including the passenger liner *Empress of Australia*, which was carrying George VI and Queen Elizabeth to Quebec. They were on what was considered to be an important State visit to the USA in an effort to draw the USA closer to the British and French alliance; this proved unsuccessful. With salutes and steam past over, the Home Fleet returned to Portland from where, during May and into June, *Newcastle* carried out a series of day-running exercises. During the remaining weeks of peace she continued to operate from Portland, with the only break being a weekend visit to Teignmouth. On 6 July she returned to Devonport where, over a period of six weeks, an early seasonal leave was given. On 26 July there was a change of command when Captain F. Figgins RN took over from Vivian. Figgins had joined the Navy at 15 years of age in 1902, and by 1911 he had attained the rank of Chief Warrant Officer (Gunnery). He had a distinguished record during the Great War, and in 1933 he became the first officer to be promoted to the rank of Captain via the grade of Mate. On 3 September, when war was declared, *Newcastle* was completing her maintenance at Devonport, and it was during the forenoon of 12 September that she left Plymouth Sound and sailed north to join the Home Fleet's North Sea Force at Scapa Flow.Two days

after her arrival at the wartime base, during the afternoon of 16 September, 80 officers and men from the cruiser were ferried over to *Royal Oak* for a pep talk by the visiting First Lord of the Admiralty, Winston Churchill. During the remainder of the month she exercised in and around the Flow, but on 1 October she began her first patrol in northern waters enforcing the Northern Blockade. During the seven-day patrol she intercepted three Norwegian merchantmen and dispatched them to Kirkwall for a full inspection. At 1915 on 12 October, just over 24 hours before the first of *U-47*'s first torpedoes slammed into the side of *Royal Oak*, *Newcastle* left Scapa on her second patrol, and also to carry out convoy escort duties which took her south to the Western Approaches and the Bay of Biscay where, for a brief period she joined company with the French battleship *Dunkerque* and the submarine *Surcouf*, which was armed with two 8-inch guns. On 26 October, with Scapa Flow having been temporarily vacated by the fleet, *Newcastle*'s ship's company enjoyed a rare wartime treat when they put into Devonport for five days.

On the last day of October *Newcastle* left Plymouth Sound and after pausing briefly at Spithead, which enabled her to pass through the Strait of Dover at midnight, she continued north to Sullum Voe, from where, on 4 November, she began her third patrol of the inhospitable waters between the Shetland Islands and Greenland. At 1315 on Sunday 12 November, in a position 66°54'N 022°57'W, north of Iceland, lookouts sighted smoke on the horizon. After three hours' steaming a merchant ship was sighted displaying the Russian name *Iama*. After an hour of carrying out checks the ship was positively identified as the German steamship *Parana* and she was ordered to stop. Before *Newcastle*'s whaler with an armed guard could be lowered, the *Parana* turned out her boats and fires were seen to be burning. The armed guard did manage to get on board, but quickly reported that the merchantman was making water fast, and the fires were burning fiercely. By 1900 it was clear that the ship could not be saved and the armed guard was recalled to *Newcastle*, which had been busy picking up members of *Parana*'s crew from their lifeboats. At 1936 *Newcastle* opened fire with her main armament, but at 2311, when she had finally rescued all the crew, she resumed her patrol. During the night *Newcastle* remained in the vicinity of the blazing wreck, and at 0958 next morning, with no sign of the vessel sinking, the cruiser's Marines, who were manning X turret, were given some target practice. Finally, at 1039 the still blazing wreck rolled over and sank. Two days later, in extremely rough seas south-west of the Faeroes, sadly one of *Newcastle*'s Boy Seamen was lost overboard and despite a thorough search of the area he could not be found. Finally, on 16 November, the German PoWs were landed at Kirkwall, after which the cruiser completed her patrol and anchored in the temporary base at Loch Ewe.

During the afternoon of 21 November, after a four-day break, *Newcastle* left Loch Ewe to begin another patrol, and only a few hours into her passage north, lookouts spotted the conning tower of an enemy U-boat some 400 yards off the port beam, which was already awash as the boat was diving. As it was in an ideal position to fire torpedoes the cruiser took evasive action and turned away to starboard before continuing her passage north. Two days later, at 1553 on Thursday 23 November, urgent signals were received from the armed merchant cruiser *Rawalpindi*[2], reporting that she was being pursued by what she thought was an enemy heavy cruiser. In fact she had been intercepted by the battlecruisers *Scharnhorst* and *Gneisenau*, which obviously heavily outgunned the former liner. The *Rawalpindi* gave her position as 63° 32'N 011°40'W, which was just off the south-east corner of Iceland and some two to three hours' steaming. *Newcastle* immediately increased to full speed and headed towards *Rawalpindi*'s position; at 1735 the ominous glow of a ship on fire and gun flashes were sighted. *Newcastle* immediately went to Night Action Stations and at 1815 she sighted the dark-

[2] *Rawalpindi* was a former P&O Liner.

ened silhouettes of two heavy warships some 13,000 yards away, but as the two battlecruisers appeared to turn towards her *Newcastle* altered course away, intending to shadow them until further assistance arrived. Two minutes later, however, a heavy mist descended over the area and visibility was reduced to 400 yards, so contact was lost. Although visibility did improve, in the inky black darkness of the northern waters *Newcastle* was unable to regain contact and at 1918 she broke off the search to return to the blazing hulk of *Rawalpindi*. With survivors being picked up by the armed merchant cruiser *Chitral*, another former P&O liner, *Newcastle* resumed her search for *Scharnhorst* and *Gneisenau* and it was not long before she was joined by *Edinburgh, Glasgow* and *Sheffield*. For *Newcastle* the search and the patrol ended on 28 November when, for the first time since 12 October, she anchored at Scapa Flow to fuel and to embark stores. Nine hours later she was back at sea and heading to a patrol area off Iceland. Four days into the patrol, she was in a position close to where *Rawalpindi* had been lost. The only sign of enemy activity, however, was a German flying boat which shadowed the cruiser and almost got within range of her guns, giving *Newcastle*'s anti-aircraft gunners some practice. Otherwise the patrol was uneventful and on 6 December she returned to Scapa Flow.Two days after her return from patrol *Newcastle* sailed once again, this time to a patrol area west of Iceland, where she rendezvoused with *Repulse* and the aircraft carrier *Furious* to escort an inbound troop convoy from Canada, which included the transports *Duchess of Bedford* and *Empress of Australia*, on the final leg of their passage to the Clyde. On 17 December she returned to Scapa Flow, and for the next 11 days she spent only a few hours at sea. She spent Christmas at Scapa Flow, but on 1 January 1940 she left in company with *Devonshire* for another patrol of the grey, icy-cold waters of the Norwegian Sea, with further patrols following throughout the remainder of the month and into February and March. On 26 March, with machinery defects mounting and the ship urgently in need of a refit, *Newcastle* left Scapa Flow to steam south to the River Tyne, where she was taken in to Palmer's shipyard for a two-month refit.It was on 30 May that *Newcastle* left Palmer's shipyard to secure to a buoy in Jarrow Slake in order to refuel and ammunition ship, and three days later she left the Tyne to carry out machinery trials en route to Rosyth, where she paused before continuing north to Scapa Flow. By now, however, the military situation in Europe had changed out of all recognition, for while *Newcastle* had been refitting, the German Army had conquered virtually the whole of Europe and within hours of her return to Scapa Flow, the British Expeditionary Force, minus all their heavy equipment, had completed its evacuation from the port of Dunkirk and the beaches as far north as the Belgian towns of De Panne and Nieuwport. Hitler's mechanised army, closely supported by a powerful Luftwaffe, had spectacularly succeeded in its execution of the 'Schlieffen Plan' in a way which, in the Great War, the Kaiser's less mobile forces could only have dreamed of .*Newcastle*'s post-refit work-up consisted of just three hours of exercises within the confines of Scapa Flow before she left on 5 June in company with *Ark Royal, Renown, Repulse, Sussex* and a destroyer screen to search the Iceland-Faeroes gap for *Scharnhorst* and *Gneisenau*, which were known to have sailed from Kiel the day before. Although the Allied armies had been ejected from Belgium and France, they still had a toehold at Narvik in northern Norway and on 7 June, as the withdrawal started from there, large vulnerable convoys began sailing to and from the port. During the evening of 7 June *Newcastle* and the battlecruisers were off Iceland and they were still in the same vicinity the next day when the two German warships sank *Glorious, Acasta* and *Ardent* north-west of Trondheim. During the next six days of her patrol *Newcastle* escorted convoys returning from Narvik before she returned to Scapa Flow on 14 June. Two days later she was again on patrol, this time in the North Sea in company with *Sussex*. On 21 June the two cruisers rendezvoused with the submarine *Severn* off Scotland's east coast where they were attacked by two Heinkel He-111 bombers. Fortunately, with daylight fading fast, *Severn* was able to crash dive and the bombs missed her, exploding astern of *Newcastle*. Next day the cruiser returned to Scapa Flow. On 25 June *Newcastle* steamed south to Rosyth where she remained for six days before she accompanied *Manchester* and *Sheffield* south through the very dangerous waters of the North Sea, headed for her base port of Plymouth as a reinforcement for the south coast defences. Leaving Rosyth at 0515 on 1 July the three cruisers steamed south, passing Aldeburgh at 2230. On arrival at the Thames Estuary *Sheffield* was detached to Chatham. By 0830 on 2 July *Newcastle* and *Manchester* had passed through the Strait of Dover, and later that forenoon *Manchester* detached to her base port of Portsmouth. At 1512 *Newcastle* passed Portland and just over an hour later she came upon a westbound convoy of merchantmen sailing from London to the safer waters of the River Clyde. The largest and most important ship in the convoy was the 10,000-gross ton Blue Funnel Line passenger/cargo ship SS *Aeneas* which had arrived in London from Shanghai on 22 June. Having disembarked her passengers she was in the process of unloading her cargo when it was decided to move her north to the Clyde; at this point she was the second of the merchant ships in a line-ahead formation. As *Newcastle* was approaching the convoy to overhaul it, a German Ju-88A fighter-bomber attacked the ships and *Aeneas* was hit by at least one bomb which severed her main steam lines, blasted a huge hole in her starboard side and started fierce fires. The ship took on a severe list and began to sink rapidly; *Newcastle*, together with the destroyer *Witherington*, was able to rescue her crew. By 1850 all the survivors had been transferred to *Newcastle* and three hours later the cruiser secured to a buoy at Devonport. During the weeks which followed *Newcastle*'s move south to Devonport she made regular patrols of the Western Approaches and on 15 August, while at anchor in Plymouth Sound, there was a change of command when Captain E. A. Aylmer DSC RN took over from Figgins, who went on to take up an appointment as Rear-Admiral at Lowestoft.

During the rest of August and into September *Newcastle*'s sea time was limited to one day each week, when she made a foray into local waters to carry out various exercises. The remainder of this period was spent secured to a buoy in Plymouth Sound, which for the ship's company was a great improvement on the beer canteen at Scapa Flow. At 1900 on 10 October *Newcastle* accompanied *Revenge* and a screen of seven destroyers to sea, bound for the German-occupied port of Cherbourg. At 0240 next day, after almost eight hours' steaming, they arrived in Cherbourg Roads and while *Newcastle* fired starshell to illuminate the port installations, *Revenge* and the destroyers carried out an hour-long bombardment. At 0335, when they set course for home, fierce fires could be seen burning in both the docks and the city, and by 0830 the force had returned safely to Devonport.

Following her return *Newcastle* underwent three days of maintenance and on 15 October moved back out to Plymouth Sound. Two days later, in company with destroyers of the 5th Flotilla, she left to patrol an area between the Isles of Scilly and Ushant. At 1600 on 17 October she was off Land's End, in a position 49°53'N 004°22'W, when she sighted a German destroyer. Speed was immediately increased and at 1607 'A' and 'B' turrets opened fire at extreme range. By 1621, with the chase well and truly under way, three more enemy destroyers were sighted but they quickly put up a thick smokescreen into which they disappeared. *Newcastle* launched her Walrus aircraft, which almost immediately came under fire from a Dornier 17 light bomber. The bomber then attacked *Newcastle* and she retaliated with her high-angle guns. In avoiding the bombs the force had widened the gap between their ships and the enemy destroyers, and at 1810 the chase was abandoned. All that remained was for *Newcastle* to recover the wounded pilot from her aircraft which had been shot down, and next forenoon she returned to Plymouth Sound.

HMS Newcastle *at full speed engaging German destroyers off Ushant, 17 October 1940.*
(T. Ferrers-Walker Collection)

For the next three and a half weeks *Newcastle* remained at her buoy in Plymouth Sound, or alongside Devonport Dockyard, but on 13 November, having embarked some 200 RAF personnel, she left Plymouth Sound escorted by six Spitfires, bound for Gibraltar and Malta. She was taking the main part in an operation code-named 'White' which was to provide air reinforcements for the besieged garrison at Malta. The three-day passage to Gibraltar was uneventful, and at just after midday on 17 November, she left the port to make a fast 45-hour passage to Malta's Grand Harbour, arriving alongside Hamilton Wharf during the forenoon of 19 November. At the same time that *Newcastle* was making her solo passage, Somerville's Force H carried out a separate operation to fly 12 Hurricane aircraft from *Argus* to Malta. On her arrival in Grand Harbour the RAF personnel, their stores and equipment were quickly disembarked, but *Newcastle* remained at Malta for another seven days while urgent repairs were carried out to her boilers. When she sailed on 26 November, her return passage to Gibraltar had been timed to link up with 'Operation Collar' by the ships of Force H, which involved *Manchester* and *Southampton* carrying troop reinforcements into the Mediterranean. *Newcastle* was part of what was designated as Force D, which also included *Ramillies, Berwick, Coventry* and a screen of five destroyers. The passage west was timed to coincide with the eastbound passage of the important troop convoy carrying an armoured brigade to Egypt. *Manchester* and *Southampton* had on board some 1,400 Army and RAF personnel, and would be escorted from Gibraltar by Force H.

Admirals Somerville (Force H) and Cunningham (C-in-C Med) had concluded that the Italian Navy would attempt to intercept and destroy the military convoy as it approached Malta, which was why Forces H and D were to rendezvous on 27 November. In the event the two forces met at 1127 that forenoon in a position 37°57'N 008°24'W, close to La Galite Island off the coast of Tunisia. Just over an hour earlier, however, *Ark Royal*'s aircraft had spotted a formation of enemy cruisers and

HMS Newcastle *entering Devonport in late 1940. UP mountings can be seen on both 'B' turret and the quarterdeck. (Ken Kelly Collection)*

destroyers to the north and they appeared to be on a converging course. She had immediately flown off a strike force, and *Renown* from Force H, *Berwick, Sheffield, Manchester* and *Southampton*, despite the fact that the latter two were loaded down with troops, set course to chase and if possible intercept the Italian naval force. At 1206 the three Italian cruisers and three destroyers were sighted. As well as the cruisers, however, the Italian force was being led by the battleships *Giulio Cesare* and *Vittorio Veneto*, and by retiring at speed towards Sardinia they were not only drawing the escorts away from the convoy, but also to within an easy flying range of the airfields on Sardinia and Sicily. At 1220 three more enemy cruisers were sighted and a minute later the first enemy salvo straddled *Manchester*. Almost immediately *Berwick* and *Manchester* opened fire, as did *Newcastle*, but with a range of 25,000 yards and the Italian ships making thick smoke, accurate fire was impossible. By 1234 *Renown* had opened fire on the two Italian battleships, but again at extreme range and with thick smoke hanging over the targets there were no hits. At 1235 *Newcastle* was forced to cease fire when A turret jammed and there was a fire on X gun deck caused by a blast which had ignited inflammable material. Six minutes later, when she opened fire once again she managed six broadsides before thick black smoke again obscured her target. At just after 1300, with the Italian ships having disappeared, the order was given to cease fire. Soon afterwards, however, as *Newcastle* stopped to hoist in her Walrus, the first formation of ten enemy bombers appeared right ahead of the ship. As *Newcastle* quickly got under way again the Walrus aircraft's crew were rescued, but the plane itself was swamped and it capsized as *Newcastle* surged forward. During the afternoon several waves of enemy bombers attacked the fleet and although there were a number of near misses there were no hits or damage. At 1930 that evening *Newcastle* and Force H were ordered to leave the convoy and make their way west, and some 45 hours later *Newcastle* secured to a buoy in Gibraltar Bay.

Although the action off Cape Spartivento was indecisive, the primary purpose of the operation,

the safe passage of the convoy and troop-carrying cruisers, was a complete success. Nevertheless, at Churchill's instigation, a Board of Inquiry was ordered to investigate Somerville's failure to force a decisive action against the enemy fleet. Fortunately common sense prevailed when it became known that not only would a prolonged chase have failed to intercept the enemy warships, but the absence of the main escorts would have left the convoy vulnerable to attack. In addition it had been apparent that the Italian Fleet was keen to get an action on its own terms, and by luring Somerville's force close to Sardinia the ships would have been open to aerial attack. Having heard the facts, the Inquiry quite rightly upheld Somerville's decisions.

On 1 December 1940 there was a complete change of scene for *Newcastle* when she left Gibraltar to head south into the Atlantic Ocean for Freetown. On 10 December, five days after arriving at the West African port, *Newcastle* sailed for her first mid-Atlantic patrol which would take her close to the coast of South America as she scoured a vast area of the ocean for the German armed raider *Thor* which, just five days earlier, had been in action with the armed merchant cruiser *Carnarvon Castle*, during which both ships had suffered severe damage. On 21 December, after a fruitless search, she anchored off the island of São Sebastião, just south of Rio de Janeiro, where she replenished fuel and stores from *RFA Arndale*. Next day, after resuming her patrol, she rendezvoused with *Cumberland* and on 23 December the two ships met *Enterprise*, after which they jointly patrolled the sea lanes off the River Plate estuary. Both Christmas and New Year's Day were spent at sea, with the three cruisers taking it in turns to anchor in Samborombón Bay in Argentinean waters on the south side of the estuary, from where *RFA Arndale* kept them supplied with fuel and stores.

During the first three months of 1941 *Newcastle* continued to patrol the sea lanes off the River Plate, and there were only limited distractions such as a 24-hour visit to Buenos Aires and two similar visits to Montevideo, during which she passed close to the wreck of *Admiral Graf Spee*, a vivid reminder of the purpose of the seemingly endless patrols. In mid-March the three cruisers held a joint exercise off the mouth of the River Plate, during which *RFA Browndale* represented *Admiral Scheer*. During the second week of April, however, *Newcastle* left the River Plate area and set course for the other side of the Atlantic Ocean where, on 15 April, she took over from *Nelson* as escort to the southbound convoy WS7, bound for Durban. *Newcastle* escorted the convoy round the Cape of Good Hope to a point off Cape Natal Light, where she handed over to an escort from Durban and retraced her course south to the naval base at Simonstown where, two days later, she began a three-week refit and docking period.

On 14 May, after hoisting the flag of Rear-Admiral South Atlantic, *Newcastle* sailed for Freetown. Four days into her passage, when she was some 250 miles off the coast of South-West Africa (Namibia) she sighted a large merchant ship ahead, steaming on an opposite course. The vessel was quickly identified as the Vichy French *Saint Lombort Bie*, and after intercepting and stopping the ship it was found that she was sailing from Marseilles to Madagascar and then on to Saigon, in what was then French Indo-China. She was carrying demobilized Annamite (Vietnamese) troops who had been fighting for France on the Western Front in Europe, and after putting an armed guard aboard, *Newcastle* escorted the ship towards Cape Town. Next day the armed merchant cruiser *Pretoria Castle* took over the escort and *Newcastle* resumed her passage to Freetown. However, she had not gone far when she received orders to set course for the River Plate area once again and on 27 May she rendezvoused with *Cumberland* and the armed merchant cruiser *Alcantara*. Once again the cruiser's patrol area covered the area between the River Plate and the island of São Sebastião, with anchorages at either end of the patrol line where the *RFAs Abbeydale* and *Broomdale* kept her fuelled and supplied. On 8 July the ship's company had a welcome break from the vital, but monotonous

patrol, with a 48-hour visit to Montevideo. In mid-July the armed merchant cruiser *Carnarvon Castle* relieved *Alcantara*, and she took part in a series of exercises with *Newcastle*.

At 0945 on Friday 25 July 1941, in position 41°25'N 050°44'W, some 600 miles south-east of the River Plate estuary, *Newcastle* sighted and intercepted the elderly 6,000-ton, coal-burning, Norddeutscher Lloyd freighter, *Erlangen*. This slow merchant ship had been plying its trade in the Pacific Ocean for months and on 26 August 1939 she had left Dunedin bound for Port Kembla, New South Wales, but on 31 August when she failed to arrive she was reported as 'overdue', and Royal Navy Intelligence was informed. She had, in fact, diverted to Chile, but not having sufficient fuel to complete the voyage her enterprising master took the ship to the uninhabited and heavily-wooded Auckland Island, some 300 miles south of New Zealand and anchored in one of the many sheltered coves. Her crew quickly learned to become very competent lumberjacks, cramming the ship's stokeholds with wood for the boiler furnaces. Good fortune was with them when *Leander*, which had *Erlangen* on her list of German merchantmen known to be at sea, but unaccounted for, searched the island's bays and inlets, but failed to find her. Eventually, on 12 November 1939, with her stores almost completely depleted, she reached the temporary safety of Puerto Monti in southern Chile. There she lay low for 18 months before, painted dark grey and carrying a cargo of honey and wool, she sailed round Cape Horn to the Argentine port of Mar del Plata, where she arrived on 3 June 1941. By now, however, her movements were being tracked by British Intelligence sources and diplomats were pressing the Argentine Government to get *Erlangen* to sea again and into international waters. Finally, on 21 July she sailed and four days later her luck ran out.

At 0955, as *Erlangen* turned away in a vain attempt to escape, *Newcastle* fired a 6-inch broadside from A turret ahead of the merchantman, which had the desired effect of bringing her to a stop. As *Newcastle*'s boarding party were preparing to lower their boat, however, smoke was seen billowing from *Erlangen*'s bridge and the ship was clearly beginning to settle by the stern. Within minutes of this one of the ship's lifeboats was being launched and, in order to prevent this and to deter others from launching boats, a burst from the cruiser's anti-aircraft guns was aimed and fired above the lifeboat. Unfortunately, the gunner's aim was poor and a number of the German crew members who were manning the boat were hit and badly wounded. This unintended incident had the desired effect and no other boats were launched. Soon afterwards *Newcastle*'s boarding party began attempts to prevent *Erlangen* from sinking, for not only had the crew set fire to the ship, but they had also opened the sea cocks. Around midday, as the boarding party struggled to put out the fires, they allowed another boat to leave the ship and soon afterwards *Newcastle* had embarked 16 officers and 73 seamen, a number of whom were seriously wounded. At 1730 the cruiser's gunnery officer, who was leading the boarding party, reported that the fires were almost out but in the engine room the condenser doors had been removed and all the pumps damaged beyond repair, so little could be done to stem the flooding. Shortly after dark the boarding party was recalled and the cruiser began to steam in circles round her prize. Suddenly, however, at 2315, *Erlangen* disappeared from sight. She had been swamped by floodwater and had sunk. During the next 24 hours three of the German PoWs died of their wounds, and at 1630 on 26 July, with full naval honours and in the presence of their shipmates, they were buried at sea. Next day the surviving prisoners were transferred to *Carnarvon Castle*, which was better able to accommodate large numbers of men.

HMS *Newcastle* resumed her patrol, but on 5 August there came a welcome break when the cruiser put into Buenos Aires for 48 hours, during which time some shore leave was granted to both watches. After leaving the Argentine capital and the River Plate *Newcastle* patrolled for another week

before, on 13 August, she anchored in Samborombón Bay where, next day, she was relieved by her sister *Birmingham*. At 2345, after transferring the Admiral and his staff, together with large quantities of stores, *Newcastle* weighed anchor and set course for Freetown, where she arrived on 26 August. Three days later, in company with *Dorsetshire* and *Eagle*, the cruiser left Sierra Leone as part of the escort for a transatlantic Caribbean-bound convoy. Once in mid-Atlantic *Eagle* and *Dorsetshire* were detached and on 9 September *Newcastle* and her convoy arrived safely in Trinidad. Next day she left to escort another convoy as far north as Bermuda, from where she was detached to the US Navy's shipyard at South Boston, Massachusetts where, on 19 September, she began a three-month refit.

During the refit both watches of the hands were given some well-earned station leave at a US Navy rest camp at Fort Townsend, north-west of the city. When the refit began the USA had been officially neutral, but just days before the work was completed Japanese aircraft bombed the US Pacific Fleet at Pearl Harbor, and Germany declared war on America, so when she sailed on 16 December the USA was an ally. After four days of post-refit sea trials *Newcastle* left US waters and set course for the naval base at Ireland Island, Bermuda, where she remained just long enough to refuel and embark stores before sailing for Devonport, reaching her base port on 29 December. For three weeks *Newcastle* was taken over by the dockyard for the fitting of new Type 273 and 291 radar equipment, together with Type 285 fire-control radar. With just a care and maintenance party looking after the ship, the ship's company enjoyed was the luxury of 21 days' leave.

On 27 January 1942, having been re-allocated to the 4th Cruiser Squadron, *Newcastle* left Plymouth Sound to steam north to Scapa Flow where she arrived two days later. For the first three weeks in northern waters she carried out work-up exercises in and around Scapa Flow. On 15 February Captain P. B. R. W. William-Powlett took over command from Aylmer, and soon afterwards the ship sailed to escort a vital troop convoy, via Freetown and the Cape of Good Hope, to Durban. Once in the Indian Ocean *Newcastle* continued to carry out convoy escort duties along the east coast of Africa. In March she operated with *Glasgow* and in April with *Birmingham*, *Emerald* and *Enterprise*. In late May, together with *Birmingham*, *Fortune* and *Griffin*, she left Kilindini Harbour (Mombasa) for the Mediterranean via Aden, to replace the appalling losses suffered by the Mediterranean Fleet during 1941. During the passage to Aden she intercepted an Italian hospital ship which was allowed to proceed unmolested, and after refuelling in Aden she set course for Suez, making her northbound transit of the Suez Canal on 6 June and arriving at Alexandria the next day.

At 1700 on Saturday 13 June *Newcastle* sailed from Alexandria in company with *Arethusa, Birmingham, Cleopatra, Euryalus, Hermione* and a destroyer screen, as escort to a convoy of 11 merchant ships bound for Malta. The operation was code-named 'Vigorous' and the first day at sea passed quietly. On 15 June, some 90 miles north-west of Derna, *Newcastle* was sailing in company with *Arethusa* astern and the destroyers *Sikh, Zulu, Hasty* and *Hotspur* in close company. At 0350, just as a new zigzag had begun and the four destroyers were passing ahead from their starboard side position, a wake was sighted on *Newcastle*'s starboard bow; at first it was thought that it had been left by the fourth destroyer, but as it could also have been an enemy E-boat, orders were given to investigate. Meanwhile, as part of her zigzag *Newcastle* was turning towards the wake which, when illuminated by searchlight, turned out to have been created by the German E-boat *S-56*, which was some 500 yards away. On board *Newcastle* full starboard wheel and full speed ahead were ordered so as to swing the ship into the E-boat's wake, but two torpedoes had already been fired before the enemy craft lurched across *Newcastle*'s bow and disappeared into the inky darkness on the port side. Both torpedoes ran on the surface and were clearly visi-

HMS Newcastle *is seen here at Brooklyn Navy Yard, New York, on 21 November 1942 on completion of repairs. The ship had been torpedoed, while on operations in the Mediterranean, by German E-boat S56.*

(Courtesy of James Flynn)

ble in the cruiser's searchlight beam. One passed ahead of the ship, but the second slammed into *Newcastle*'s starboard bow abreast of frame 14 and six feet below the waterline, where it exploded. The explosion ripped a 20-foot by 15-foot hole in the shell plating which, although it did not affect the ship's fighting capacity, allowed large waves to enter which tore away at the shell plating. Next day bombers attacked the convoy, damaging *Birmingham*, and on 16 June, while returning to Alexandria, *Hermione* was torpedoed and sunk. In the event the convoy did not reach Malta, and the surviving ships returned to Alexandria during the evening of 16 June. Four days later *Newcastle* left Alexandria to steam south through the Suez Canal to Aden and on to Kilindini Harbour, Mombasa, where temporary repairs could be carried out. Soon after leaving Aden, however, *Newcastle* and her escorts ran into severe gales and heavy seas, and very soon serious leaks developed when the pitching of the ship forced water up a vent trunking from the empty Fleet Air Arm messdeck. Although the vent was eventually blanked off, other leaks continued to cause problems and two days into the passage splits were noticed in the port bulkhead at frame 22, the Asdic Cabinet Flat. Closer inspection found that the ship's plating was being torn away, flooding the compartment, which had to be sealed off. Later that day, with a heavy sea still running, the ship was hit by a very heavy roller which forced open a hatch at the after end of the Fleet Air Arm messdeck, and water flooded into the ship and engulfed the forward seamen's messdeck. This meant that all compartments forward of bulkhead 30 had to be evacuated, closed down and hatches shored up. Further inspections revealed that the ship's side plating on the port side had been torn out by the heavy seas, leaving a hole to port roughly the same size as that caused by the torpedo. It was not known how long the port side plating had been damaged, but with Kilindini Harbour still over 1,000 miles away, the ship would not be able to complete the passage by steaming ahead. An attempt was made to steam stern first by turning the

starboard shafts at maximum speed, while the port shaft speeds were modified for manoeuvring. However, with little improvement in the weather the ship could only make three knots at best. Finally, at 0730 on 28 June, it was decided to turn back and some 72 hours later *Newcastle* arrived back in Aden Harbour. The attempt to sail between Aden and Mombasa had been made at the height of the monsoon season, and the heavy seas had caused more damage to the cruiser's hull than had the original torpedo.

Following temporary repairs at Aden, which included a 20-foot thick concrete cofferdam being constructed aft of 22 bulkhead, extending from the lower deck to the baseline, *Newcastle* sailed for Bombay where she arrived on 30 July and was taken into dry dock for more substantial repairs. These included replacing missing shell strakes and temporary decks being added. Finally, on 7 September, the ship was seaworthy enough to begin the long voyage to New York where, under the Lend-Lease Scheme, permanent repairs were to be carried out. Five days into her passage the cruiser went to the aid of the Polish merchantman *Narvik*, whose master was seriously ill, and after transferring him to the cruiser's sickbay the passage continued. On 13 September she paused at Mauritius for fuel and six days later she arrived at Cape Town, where there was a break of 48 hours and *Narvik*'s master was transferred to hospital. There then followed an eight-day transatlantic voyage north-west to the Brazilian port of Pernambuco (Recife) and from there *Newcastle* steamed north to Bermuda, before finally arriving in New York on 10 November, where she was taken into the US Navy yard at Brooklyn. During her seven-week stay in the US Navy yard the garboard and A strakes in the vicinity of the damage were replaced, as were the transverse frames and longitudinal. As well as replacing *Newcastle*'s forward hull plating on both port and starboard sides, all forward messdecks, bulkheads, flats, compartments and their contents were replaced to the original designs. On 2 December *Newcastle* was once again fully seaworthy, and she left New York to carry out five days of trials in and around Chesapeake Bay, after which she left US waters to return via Bermuda to Devonport. During the afternoon of 18 December 1942, in plenty of time for Christmas, she arrived in Plymouth Sound.

For 12 weeks after her return to Devonport *Newcastle* lay alongside No 5 Wharf or in dry dock, during which time new radar outfits and additional 20mm Oerlikon guns were fitted in order to improve the ship's close-range anti-aircraft defences. For the ship's company there was 14 days' leave for both watches. Finally on 12 March 1943 *Newcastle* left Devonport to undergo four days of trials, before setting course for Scapa Flow. After an absence from the fleet of nine months she was fully operational again.

HMS *Newcastle* arrived in Scapa Flow on 19 March where she joined the Home Fleet for just over two weeks. During this period she carried out a series of work-up exercises before steaming south to Greenock and upriver to Dalmuir Basin for a seven-day maintenance period. On 16 April, having returned to Greenock, she left to take up station as ocean escort to convoys WS29 and KMF13, bound for Freetown and Gibraltar respectively. By 26 April she was off Dakar, where more merchant ships joined the convoy, and two days later she delivered them all safely to Freetown where there was a seven-day break before the passage south continued. On 8 May there was time for a little relaxation as the equator was crossed with full ceremony. Nine days later *Newcastle* and her convoy arrived at Cape Town, from where she sailed north for Kilindini Harbour to join the 4th Cruiser Squadron of the Eastern Fleet during the forenoon of 27 May.

Her operations with the Eastern Fleet began in the second week of June when she joined *Kenya* (flag Rear-Admiral Tennant), *Frobisher, Suffolk* and the armed merchant cruisers *Alaunia, Canton* and *Carthage* for work-up exercises off the East African coast. In the last week of July she began her first patrol of the Indian Ocean, which took a triangular

route from Kilindini, via the Seychelles, Colombo, Addu Atoll and back to Kilindini. At the end of August she sailed south to Simonstown for a three-week refit and docking period, but by the end of September she had returned to Kilindini where she hoisted the flag of Rear-Admiral Tennant. During the last weeks of 1943 *Newcastle* spent most of her time on patrol in the Indian Ocean, and exercising with the other cruisers of the squadron, including *Danae, Hawkins, Kenya, Emerald* and *Frobisher*. During the second week of December, together with other ships, she arrived at Trincomalee, which, for the first time since the dark days of April 1942, marked the reopening of the naval base. It was here that the 4th Cruiser Squadron spent Christmas 1943, and saw in the new year of 1944.

Early 1944 saw a very different strategic situation in South-East Asia from that of two years earlier, with the US offensive in the Pacific rapidly gathering momentum - drawing Japanese forces away from South-East Asia to the much more important Pacific theatre of war. This in turn meant that the British forces which had been pushed back through Burma and over the border into India would, in mid-1944, be able to contemplate offensive operations of their own.

For *Newcastle* the first weeks of 1944 saw her exercising off Trincomalee with the cruisers *Ceylon, Kenya* and *Suffolk*. On 10 January, after a 17-hour passage along the Coromandel Coast from Trincomalee, *Newcastle*, *Kenya* and *Suffolk* secured alongside the North Quay in Madras (Chennai) Harbour for a short 48-hour visit, after which they returned to Colombo. No sooner had they left the area, however, than the Japanese *I-165* torpedoed and sank the 10,000-ton merchantman SS *Perseus*, just south of Madras. There were three Japanese submarines in the Bay of Bengal at this time, and four German U-boats in the Indian Ocean, and between them they would sink 55,994 tons of Allied shipping. In mid-January *Newcastle* left Colombo for Mauritius from where, on 8 February she and *Relentless* were ordered to search an area up to 900 miles south-east of the island in an attempt to locate the German oil tanker *Charlotte Schliemann* which was in the Indian Ocean supplying the enemy submarines. On 12 February it was *Relentless* which found and sank the supply ship. The sinking of the tanker meant that *Newcastle* could return to Mauritius, and a few days later she steamed north to

HMS Newcastle *at Colombo during her service with the Eastern Fleet.* *(Maritime Photo Library)*

Colombo to undergo a week's maintenance. By the end of February, however, she had returned to Mauritius.

In early March Intelligence sources learned that another German oil tanker, the *Brake*, had sailed from Japanese-occupied Batavia to take the place of *Charlotte Schliemann*, and that on 11 March she was due to rendezvous with three German submarines. On 5 March, in order to try to intercept this new supply ship, *Newcastle* and *Battler* left Mauritius to rendezvous with *Roebuck*. The operation was code-named 'Covered' and the three warships were designated as Force 67, with *Suffolk* and *Quadrant* forming Force 68. In order to make the search easier for the warships all Allied merchantmen were ordered to keep clear of the area of operations, and at 1620 on 12 March an aircraft from *Battler* reported sighting the tanker in company with two U-boats some 250 miles south-west of Mauritius, some 40 miles north of Force 67. *Newcastle* immediately detached *Roebuck* to intercept and destroy the tanker which, by 1800, she had done. In the meantime *Battler* flew off aircraft to locate the U-boats and although one was attacked, both boats managed to dive deep and escape. That evening and through the night into the next day *Battler*'s aircraft continued to patrol over the area in case either of them surfaced to rescue *Brake*'s survivors who were adrift in boats. On 15 March, however, the force returned to Mauritius, and two days later *Newcastle* and *Suffolk* sailed for Colombo where the former underwent a nine-day maintenance period.

On 1 April 1944 *Newcastle* returned to Trincomalee, and over the next couple of weeks she exercised with *Valiant, Nigeria, Gambia* and *Illustrious*. On 16 April, she joined *Queen Elizabeth* (Flag C-in-C Eastern Fleet, Admiral Somerville), *Valiant, Nigeria, Ceylon, Gambia*, *Tromp*, FS *Richelieu* and eight destroyers to form Force 69. Together with Force 70, consisting of *Renown* (flag FO2 Eastern Fleet), *Illustrious*, USS *Saratoga*, *London* and six destroyers, they were deployed on 'Operation Cockpit'. It was the first major joint operation for the Royal and US Navies, and the force was to provide a diversionary attack on the port facilities and airfield at Sabang, an island situated some 12 miles from the northern tip of Sumatra, while in the Pacific area Allied forces prepared an attack on Hollandia, in occupied New Guinea. It was hoped that Somerville's raid would prevent the Japanese from transferring a large proportion of their 500 aircraft south during the invasion of New Guinea. The two forces arrived off Sabang in the early hours of 19 April, and strike aircraft were flown off the two carriers at 0530. Although the raid was a success, with little enemy opposition, it did not deflect the Japanese from their main defensive strategy of maintaining the bulk of their forces in the Pacific area. By 21 April the two forces had returned to Trincomalee, and two days later *Newcastle* sailed via Mauritius to Simonstown where, on 3 May, she began a 20-week refit.

Five days into her refit there was a change of command when William-Powlett relinquished command of *Newcastle*, but it was not until 11 June that his successor, Captain J. G. Roper OBE RN, joined the ship and assumed command. The refit ended on 25 September, and after nine days of trials she steamed north to Kilindini Harbour from where she carried out a short work-up before sailing for Trincomalee, where she arrived on 25 October to rejoin the Eastern Fleet's 5th Cruiser Squadron. A week after her arrival *Newcastle* began training exercises with other ships of the squadron, which included *Cumberland, London, Nigeria* and *Suffolk*. On 17 December, together with *Indomitable* (flag Admiral Sir Philip Vian), *Illustrious*, *Argonaut, Black Prince* and five destroyers, she sailed from Trincomalee. Designated as Force 67 the ships were headed for a point off northern Sumatra from where aircraft from the carriers were to have attacked oil refineries at Pangkalan Brandan, but thick cloud over the target meant that the bombing raids were switched to the port facilities at Belawan Deli. The force arrived off Sumatra in the early hours of 20 December, and the first strike was flown off at 0640, with the second following later in the day at

1620. Both raids were successful in that complete surprise was achieved, with no fighter opposition and little in the way of anti-aircraft fire. By 22 December the force had returned to Trincomalee.

On 30 December 1944 *Newcastle*, together with *Nigeria, Phoebe* and three destroyers, sailed from Trincomalee bound for Chittagong, where they landed stores and ammunition for the Army. During the weeks which followed, *Newcastle*'s operational commitments continued in support of the Army's advance into Burma, and on 23 January 1945, flying the flag of Rear-Admiral Read (CS5), she sailed in company with *Kenya, Nigeria, Phoebe* and five destroyers across the Bay of Bengal to take part in the capture of the island of Cheduba, off the Arakan region of Burma. The assault was entirely a naval operation with the cruisers carrying a force of 500 Royal Marines who were to land and capture the island in order to provide a bridgehead for the Army in the Arakan. Air cover was provided by the escort carrier *Ameer*, and the force (TF 65) arrived off Cheduba Island at 0500 on 26 January. Just over an hour later, under cover of a bombardment from *Kenya, Nigeria* and *Newcastle*, the marines were landed. Once ashore they were opposed by some 200 Japanese troops, and during the days which followed the cruisers provided gunfire support and kept them supplied. On 30 January *Kenya* brought 400 Indian troops to replace the Marines, who were able to return to their ships. Although only a small operation, it has gone down in the Marines' history as almost a textbook working of their motto, "*Per Mare Per Terram*" and back again. On the last day of January the cruisers carried out their final bombardment, before *Newcastle* set course for Trincomalee where she arrived on 2 February. *Newcastle*'s arrival at the Ceylonese naval base effectively marked the end of her operational commitment in the Eastern/East Indies Fleet, for she was badly in need of a major refit and dry docking. Prior to this, however, there was time for a five-day visit to Calcutta, after which she sailed to Colombo where, on 24 February, she began a three-week docking and maintenance period.

On 18 March *Newcastle* did make a brief return to Trincomalee, but she did not stay long and on 25 March, after striking the flag of CS5, she sailed for a fast 11-day passage to Sydney where, after only a seven-hour refuelling stop at Fremantle, she arrived on 5 April. Originally it had been intended that after maintenance she would join the British Pacific Fleet, but after two weeks it was decided that instead she would return home to the UK, and after a slower return passage she arrived in Colombo on 6 May. Next day, as escort to the fast troop transport *Empress of Scotland*, she left Colombo bound for Suez and on 15 May she made her northbound transit of the Suez Canal. Eight days later, after only the briefest of pauses off Gibraltar, she arrived back at Devonport.

For eight weeks *Newcastle* remained swinging at a buoy in the Hamoaze, and she became a familiar sight to those using the Torpoint Ferry, but in mid-July she was sent north to the River Tyne to undergo a major overhaul which began at Hebburn on 19 July. The original intention at the end of the refit had been to return the ship to the British Pacific Fleet, but the surrender of Japan on 15 August changed the whole situation. Not only was the ship not required for service in the Pacific, but Britain's shattered economy needed to be returned urgently to a peacetime role, with the export of manufactured goods being the top priority. *Newcastle*'s berth at Hebburn was required for the reconditioning of passenger-cargo liners, two of which were ex-German ships, therefore, on 26 September, she left the Tyne and steamed north to the naval dockyard at Rosyth where the refit was completed. On 28 October, when she left Rosyth to return to Devonport, her profile had been altered by the removal of X gun turret, a change which put the ship a foot down by the head.

When *Newcastle* arrived alongside Devonport Dockyard's No 8 Wharf on 30 October 1945, she found that she had been given a completely new and unexpected role, that of a makeshift troop transport. The sudden end to the war in the Far East and Pacific had left many long-serving 'Hostilities

HMS Newcastle *leaving Grand Harbour in 1948.* *(Syd Goodman Collection)*

Only' conscripts in different parts of the world, and with the Government's policy of discharging the longest-serving men first, there came the task of getting them home and, where necessary, replacing them with regular servicemen or those who had been conscripted much later in the war. On 3 November, *Newcastle* left Devonport on her first trooping voyage bound for Freetown and South Africa. She had on board as passengers a dozen naval officers and 270 ratings. In order to provide sufficient accommodation her ship's company had been drastically reduced and, wherever possible, all the passengers were given a job to do and responsibility of some sort. On arrival on board the drafts were employed striking down their heavy baggage, hammocks and steaming kit, and the space of X turret's empty barbette was filled to capacity as a makeshift baggage room. Once stowed, however, there was no way any individual bag could be retrieved until the end of the voyage when the space was cleared. The passengers invariably provided additional watchkeepers in the engine and boiler rooms which enabled a four-watch system to be kept instead of the usual three.

Twenty-four hours after leaving Plymouth Sound *Newcastle* rendezvoused with the troop transport *Carisbrooke Castle* for a sea boat transfer of stores, and then the cruiser settled down to her passage south at a steady 19 knots, with few variations of course or speed. On 10 November she made a brief refuelling stop at Freetown, and eight days later she arrived at Simonstown where her detail of officers and ratings disembarked. For her homeward voyage, however, she embarked 677 officers and ratings, together with six truckloads of gold bullion, the latter being stowed in an empty ammunition magazine, as were many tons of food for austerity Britain; one empty 6-inch magazine on board was loaded up with 40 tons of strawberry jam – a luxury indeed for the people at home. On 24 November *Newcastle* left Simonstown, and after embarking a further 22 passengers at Freetown she reached Spithead during the forenoon of 8 December. Next day, after she had disembarked all the drafts and their baggage, she steamed back down-Channel to Devonport where her cargo was unloaded. On 3 January 1946 *Newcastle* left Devonport for her second and last trooping voyage, this time bound for Colombo, via Gibraltar, Malta, Port Said and Aden. She made her return passage by the same route and

arrived on 11 February at Spithead where the passengers were disembarked into landing craft. Next day *Newcastle* secured alongside Devonport's No 8 Wharf. It would be almost two years before she put to sea again.

For 18 months *Newcastle* was laid up in reserve in Devonport's No 4 basin, and at one stage it was thought that she might be destined for an early demise at a shipbreaker's yard. However, that particular fate was deferred, and in the late summer of 1947 she was taken in hand by the dockyard for a refit. On 7 November that year Captain S. H. Paton CBE RN took command and she was recommissioned. Three weeks later, on 4 December, she left dry dock to begin six days of trials which ended with an inspection by C-in-C Plymouth and on 13 December, having embarked two civilians, six naval officers and 88 rating passengers, together with seven motor cars, two motorcycles and surface mail, she left Plymouth Sound to join the Mediterranean Fleet. She arrived in Malta's Grand Harbour in time for the Christmas and New Year festivities and on 23 December, Admiral Sir Algernon Willis, the C-in-C Mediterranean, hoisted his flag in *Newcastle*.

During the whole of January 1948 *Newcastle* underwent work-up exercises in the waters off Malta, and at various times she exercised with *Ocean, Chieftain, Chevron, Volage* and *Whitesand Bay*. In mid-February, in company with *Chevron*, she made official visits to Port Said, Alexandria and Beirut. At the latter port the C-in-C hosted an official reception for the President of Lebanon, after which the ship sailed south through the Suez Canal to the Saudi Arabian port of Jeddah, where the C-in-C entertained the Emir Feisal. The British Government was trying to persuade him to support an Anglo-American plan for the partition of Palestine, which would have awarded most of the country to the mostly immigrant, and East European, Jewish population. After leaving Jeddah *Newcastle* steamed north once again, spending 48 hours at anchor in the Great Bitter Lake off Fayid, which in those days was within a British base area, and shore leave was granted to the ship's company. On 12 March the cruiser arrived back in Grand Harbour where the C-in-C transferred his flag ashore and the ship prepared for a more difficult operational commitment. On 30 January she sailed with *Mauritius* to Haifa in Palestine where, four days later, they anchored in the harbour.

In 1948, as now, the Levant was in a state of unrest and the problem then, as now, was the future of Palestine, where the consequences of British colonial decisions made during the Great War and before Britain even controlled the country were coming home to roost. In late 1947 the Foreign Secretary, A. J. Balfour, in what has become known as the infamous 'Balfour Declaration', promised Lord Rothschild, who was one of a number of wealthy and influential Zionists, that the British Government viewed with favour: '*...the establishment of a national home for the Jewish people.*' In short, as one more far-sighted Westminster MP described it, it was: '*... a false promissory note which was morally wicked because it amounted to one nation (Britain) promising to a group of people (Zionists) the country of a third people (Palestinians) who have never been consulted as to whether they wish to hand over their country.*' Replying to this damning criticism Balfour said: '*Are we never to have adventures? Are we never to try new experiments?*' This casual dismissal set the scene for a catastrophe and a running sore in the Middle East which continues to this day. Over the years which followed, fuelled by the Nazi excesses and atrocities in Germany, huge numbers of European Jews emigrated to Palestine and many of the hard liners among them made no secret of the fact that they were determined to take over and forcibly deport the indigenous Palestinian population. In 1936 the Palestinian outrage and indignation at having an alien race thrust upon them exploded into a violent uprising, referred to clumsily in British history books as 'The Arab Revolt'. There is no doubt, however, that it shook the British colonial authorities and thereafter strict quotas were imposed on the numbers of Jews being allowed to

settle in the country. Following the end of the Second World War, however, and the appalling crimes perpetrated on Jewish people in Germany and many Eastern European countries, hundreds of thousands of European Jews were attempting to enter Palestine illegally and the only viable way to do this was by sea. The Royal Navy had the thankless task of trying to prevent them from landing and deporting those who were caught.

This then was *Newcastle*'s role in Palestine, and for the ship's company there was only very limited canteen leave at Haifa where tensions between Palestinians and Jews were running high. There was also an extremely vicious insurgency going on mainly by three Jewish terrorist groups, which made any shore leave highly dangerous for British servicemen. In order to provide a more relaxed atmosphere for libertymen the naval ships would steam a short distance up the coast to the northern Lebanese port of Tripoli[3] (now Tarābulus) where shore leave could be safely granted. *Newcastle* visited the port for five days in early April then on the 11th of the month she was ordered back to Haifa, where she arrived at just after midday. That evening *Virago* entered harbour towing the illegal immigrant ship *Vivara*, an auxiliary schooner with the name *Rina* painted on her bow, which was carrying 822 people. By 2300 she had been secured alongside *Newcastle*, which in turn was secured alongside the troop transport *Empire Rival*. The illegal immigrants were transhipped under armed guards from *Vivara* on *Newcastle*'s port side to *Empire Rival* on her starboard side. The transfer began at 2325, and as each person passed over *Newcastle*'s quarterdeck they and their baggage were searched and sprayed with DDT insecticide. Fortunately, in this case the immigrants were not uncooperative and by 0130 on 13 April *Empire Rival* had sailed for Cyprus where the refugees were detained in camps. During the forenoon of 13 April *Newcastle* and *Virago* both sailed for Cyprus and for ten days they remained in the Kyrenia area.

During the morning watch of 24 April *Newcastle* returned to Haifa where, once again, she was required for the transhipment of illegal immigrants; this time it was 785 passengers from MV *San Michele*, which had been arrested by HMS *Chevron*, to the *Empire Rival*. As before, the operation was conducted quickly and efficiently, and at just after midnight *Empire Rival* was on her way to Cyprus. Two days later *Newcastle* was back at Haifa and once again preparing to transfer illegal immigrants to the transport *Empire Comfort*. This time the immigrant ship was the dilapidated *Tadorne* which, at 0645 on 27 April, carrying some 558 immigrants, was towed into port by *Pelican* and secured alongside *Newcastle*'s port side. By 0935 the transfer was complete and the cruiser left Haifa to steam south to Port Said, arriving on 28 April.

With the British Mandate over Palestine due to end at midnight on 14 May 1948, the heavily armed Jewish insurgents in the country began the long-awaited and well-planned all-out attack on the densely populated Palestinian areas of Haifa, driving people out of their homes and towards the borders of Lebanon and other surrounding areas. By this time the British Army was concentrating its forces and equipment for the final withdrawal through Haifa, and although some reinforcements were sent in an attempt to impose order, there was little hope of any effective intervention, although the Navy did do its best to assist Palestinians fleeing by boat to get clear safely. By 1 May the bloodshed and the flood of Palestinian refugees was causing questions to be asked of the British Government, which resulted in some attempts to mediate with Jewish organisations which, until the Mandate expired, were still classed as terrorist organisations. *Newcastle* was recalled from Port Said and ordered back to Haifa where she remained until 9 May, just five days before Britain's Palestine Mandate expired. She then left for Malta, where she arrived three days later. The appalling problems

[3] Tripoli was a port familiar to men of the nineteenth-century Royal Navy. It was off here in 1893 that HM Ships *Victoria* and *Camperdown* collided with tragic results.

facing the Palestinian people had, however, only just begun.

HMS *Newcastle*'s arrival in Malta coincided with the departure of the outgoing C-in-C Mediterranean Fleet, Admiral Sir Algernon U. Willis, who had been succeeded by Admiral Sir Arthur Power. Willis's departure took place with full ceremony and a 17-gun salute from Fort St Angelo as he was rowed out to *Newcastle*. Once the cruiser was clear of the harbour, however, Willis disembarked into a tug and was taken ashore for a flight home to the UK. During June 1948 *Newcastle* underwent three weeks of maintenance, before carrying out exercises with the aircraft carrier *Triumph*. She then joined the rest of the fleet, including *Liverpool* (flag C-in-C), *Euryalus, Venus, Troubridge, Volage, Widemouth Bay* and the submarine *Templar*, for exercises in Greek waters, which meant for *Newcastle* visits to Poros, Salonika and Argostoli. It was 29 July before she returned to Grand Harbour, where the whole of August and the first week of September was spent undergoing maintenance. *Newcastle* sailed again on 7 September, to carry out manoeuvres with *Triumph* and *Venus*, and to make a series of visits to Italian ports, including Palermo and Venice, and what in those days was known as the free port of Trieste[4]. In late September she returned to Malta in time to sail with the rest of the fleet to Aranci Bay for the annual Mediterranean Fleet regatta and general drills. On 7 October, following the presentation of prizes by the C-in-C, the fleet sailed for combined exercises between Malta and the Libyan coast, from where guests were embarked for a Sea Day. By mid-October, however, *Newcastle* had returned to Grand Harbour. During November and December she undertook a series of day-running exercises from Malta, and in mid-December she underwent an 11-week refit and docking period.

On 1 March 1949, *Newcastle*, in company with *Euryalus* and *Liverpool*, sailed for Gibraltar from where they carried out joint manoeuvres with ships of the Home Fleet, before visiting French and Italian ports. By the end of March *Newcastle* was back in Malta and in April she took part in exercises off Cyprus, which ended with a three-day call at Kyrenia. This was followed by further training exercises combined with a visit to Beirut and a day at anchor off Tobruk. By mid-May *Newcastle* had returned to Grand Harbour, and on 23 May there was a change of command when Captain A. F. Campbell RN took over from Paton. Over the next three months *Newcastle* took part in local manoeuvres with *Phoebe* and in July with the battleship *Vanguard*. At the end of August, and flying the flag of the C-in-C Mediterranean, *Newcastle* made an official visit to Istanbul. The C-in-C's visit to the city was considered in political circles to be extremely important, and he was received by the Turkish President and top military leaders. *Newcastle* followed this with visits to Izmir, Venice and Trieste, and at the end of September to Cannes and Rapallo, before returning to Malta to undergo maintenance. It was mid-November before *Newcastle* put to sea again, and her final weeks on the Mediterranean Station were spent day running from Malta. *Newcastle*'s commission in the Mediterranean ended on 5 December 1949 when she left harbour at 0815. She had on board a passenger in the form of retired Admiral Arthur Bedford, who had been in Malta to visit the grave of his son who had been killed during the Second World War. However, shortly after clearing the breakwater, sadly the Admiral was found dead in his cabin and the cruiser had to return to harbour. In the event it was later in the afternoon before she could leave and on 13 December she secured alongside the battleship *Anson* in Devonport Dockyard. With the ship about to be taken over by the dockyard to be placed in reserve, de-ammunitioning began immediately and on 20 January 1950 Captain Campbell relinquished command. On 10 February

[4] In 1945 the Allied Powers had been releuctant to allow Trieste to go to Italy, which had been a belligerent nation. However, for ideological reasons they were also reluctant to award the city to Yugoslavia, so the idea of a neutral "free city" was invented.

all officers and men remaining aboard moved into *Anson*, the accommodation ship, and 17 days later, on 27 February, the cruiser was paid off into dockyard control.

For two years *Newcastle* remained static in Devonport Dockyard, but in late 1951 work began to refit her for further service. By this time Britain, at the USA's behest, had become involved in the Korean War and suddenly at a time when the country's economy could ill afford it, defence expenditure rocketed. As far as the Navy was concerned the conflict involved the recommissioning of ships which would have otherwise languished in reserve before being scrapped. One of these ships was *Newcastle* and on 3 March 1952, after a new ship's company had marched down to the ship from the Royal Naval Barracks, *Newcastle* was recommissioned for trials under the command of Captain W. F. H. C. Rutherford RN. In the event it was mid-April before the ship put to sea, and she then undertook four weeks of intensive trials and work-up exercises in the Channel and off Portland. On 14 May *Newcastle* secured alongside in Portsmouth Dockyard and four days later a more formal recommissioning ceremony was held on board. Next day she sailed for Gibraltar and Malta and on 19 June she left Grand Harbour for Suez, Aden and the Far East.

She arrived in the naval base at Singapore on 5 July, where the ship's company enjoyed a brief respite before she sailed for Hong Kong and the Japanese port of Sasebo on the western tip of Kyushu, north of Nagasaki, which was now a US naval base and the operating base for the warships deployed off Korea some 160 miles away across the Korea Strait. Less than 24 hours after her arrival at Sasebo, having relieved *Ceylon*, which left for Singapore and Trincomalee, *Newcastle* sailed for her first patrol off Korea's west coast. Her duties were to enforce the United Nations blockade of North Korea, to carry out planeguard duties for the aircraft carriers operating off the coast and to provide naval gunfire support to the troops ashore.

Just three days into the patrol, during the evening of 22 July, *Newcastle* carried out a 6-inch bombardment of the North Korean Amgak Battery on Chodo Island, which had opened fire on a US landing craft earlier in the day. Despite several direct hits, however, only a few days later *Newcastle* herself was hit by a 76mm shell fired by the battery. The remainder of the patrol passed quietly and on 29 July, having been relieved by *Belfast*, she steamed to Kure for a short break. The cruiser's second patrol began on 2 August and lasted for five weeks, during which time she operated with *Charity, Crusader*, and *St Brides Bay*, as well as acting as planeguard escort to *Ocean*. On the last day of August, in support of a commando raid on enemy gun positions at Choppeki Point on the island of Paengyong-Do she carried out a sustained bombardment over one and a quarter hours. During September and October *Newcastle* continued to patrol the west coast of Korea, often in company with HMAS *Anzac, Cossack, Morecambe Bay* and *Ocean*. In mid-November she underwent a three-week docking and maintenance period at Kure, and it was 3 December before she was operational and on patrol once again. Flying the flag of Rear-Admiral E. G. A. Clifford, FO2, FES, the cruiser made a tour of the operational area, but was interrupted on 10 December when she was ordered to patrol the area off Sok-To Island[5] which was under threat of invasion by North Korean troops. Eight days later there was a portent of future advances in naval aviation when a US casualty evacuation helicopter landed on *Newcastle*'s quarterdeck with a wounded Korean soldier, who was treated in the sickbay. Next day *Newcastle* concluded her patrol and sailed for Hong Kong, where she spent Christmas and the New Year.

On 2 January 1953, after embarking 50 Army personnel as passengers, *Newcastle* left Hong Kong for Sasebo, and four days later she was back on patrol off Korea's west coast. During the winter months of January and February weather conditions off North Korea were similar to those experienced in Arctic

[5] The island was north of the 38th Parallel but was held by Republic of Korea troops.

waters and the ships on patrol were frequently surrounded by pack ice, while the watches on deck were continually clearing ice accumulations from the superstructure and masts. By this time *Glory* had relieved *Ocean* as the Royal Navy's operational aircraft carrier in Korean waters, and the flying operations were carried out in bitterly cold weather conditions, with frequent snow showers and blizzards. On 13 January, and again six days later, *Newcastle* bombarded North Korean military buildings and command posts south of Chinnampo, but on 22 January the patrol ended at Sasebo. Three days later she sailed for Kure and it was 3 February before she left on her next patrol.

During March 1953, as long drawn-out peace negotiations between the United States and the North Koreans dragged on, *Newcastle* continued her patrol duties in the Yellow Sea, and over three days in late March she carried out a 6-inch bombardment of enemy positions. During the weeks which followed, the patrols took on a routine as the cruiser operated first with *Glory*, and then in late May with *Ocean*. More and more days were spent at anchor, and regular storing and refuelling was carried out from RFAs. There were periods of busy activity, such as the bombarding of enemy positions which, on 24 and 25 May, were carried out in conjunction with the battleship USS *New Jersey*. Above all else was the constant need to be on the alert for unexpected air attacks and the ever-present threat of mines. In June there was a major offensive when some 30,000 Chinese and North Korean troops attacked on a 30-mile front, which gained some ground for the north, but peace negotiations continued and on 27 July 1953, after three years of heavy fighting, the guns fell silent, an Armistice was agreed and the fighting stopped. *Newcastle* remained on patrol right up to the end of June, but on 2 July she left Sasebo bound for Hong Kong and Singapore, arriving at the naval base in the Strait of Johore on 13 July to begin an 11-week refit. For the ship's company relief came in the form of a move to the comfortable shore accommodation at HMS *Terror*, and the ship herself spent nine weeks high and dry in the base's King George VI dry dock.

During the refit there was a change of command when, on 23 September, Captain Sir St John Tyrrwhit DSO, DSC, RN took over command of the ship. Three days later the ship's company moved back on board and on 30 September *Newcastle* sailed for three days of post-refit trials. No sooner had the cruiser slipped her moorings at the naval base than the new captain gave an example of how he intended to handle the ship, as Fred Stephen who was an Able Seaman at that time recalls: '*The new captain showed he was a destroyer man when, after trials, he wasted no time in steaming down the Johore Strait to rendezvous with* Comus *and* Consort. *We then took part in an air defence exercise in which we represented a Sverdlov-class cruiser making a foray into the South China Sea as a commerce raider and on occasions we outmanoeuvred and ran rings round the two destroyers.*' Once the trials and work-up exercises were completed the cruiser returned via Hong Kong to Sasebo for further patrol duties off Korea. Although the fighting had ceased only an armistice had been agreed, so it had been decided that the UN ships would continue their patrols and during the weeks which followed *Newcastle* continued to patrol the waters of the Yellow Sea, in the vicinity of the 38th Parallel. On board, however, there was a far more relaxed atmosphere and there were more frequent calls at Sasebo, Kure and the port of Pusan.

Christmas and the New Year were spent in Hong Kong and in mid-January *Newcastle* sailed for her final weeks off the Korean peninsula. An indication of the high morale on board came when a detachment of the King's Regiment was embarked as part of a series of exchange visits. Among the soldiers was a lance corporal who quickly earned himself a reputation for having an insatiable appetite. Every meal time he would quickly devour his own food, before looking around for leftovers, which he dispatched just as rapidly. His reputation for eating soon became the talk of the whole ship, and on 8 February 1954, shortly before the detachment was disembarked at Hong Kong to return to their garri-

HMS Newcastle *after her 1952 modernisation. She has a new outfit of 40mm Bofors, a completely new bridge structure and a lattice foremast.* *(Steve Bush Collection)*

son duties, the ship's company organised an elaborate presentation ceremony, at which the Gunnery Officer, Lieutenant-Commander Henry Leach[6] presided. The Army detachment was mustered on X gun deck in front of the assembled ship's company, all of whom were smartly fallen in and ordered to attention, at the same time as trying desperately to keep straight faces. Leach then solemnly read out an award citation which accompanied a larger than life purple-ribboned medal, complete with three bars, which was engraved 'Breakfast, Dinner and Supper'. The lance corporal himself obviously had a good sense of humour and he too had a good laugh at the citation which was headed '*Mentioned in Victualling Dispatches*', and read: '*While attached to* HMS Newcastle *in Korean waters, continuously for three weeks Lance Corporal Harry M was exposed to the rigours of General Messing. Although several times grievously wounded by the ship's cooks so that his stomach flapped against his backbone, Lance Corporal M never for an instant allowed duty to stand in the way of more food. To the end he ate more than the rest of the mess put together, stuffed day and night long after all others had succumbed. By his capacity, his steadfast devotion to eating, and his firm denial that he had ever had enough, Lance Corporal M excited the admiration and inspiration of all.*'

On 27 February 1954, after undergoing FO2's inspection in Hong Kong, *Newcastle* and *Birmingham* left for Korean waters and joint exercises with the US 7th Fleet, including USS *Missouri*. Fred Stephen remembers the exercises: '*The "enemy" comprised one battleship, two carriers, one cruiser and a handful of destroyers. The "battle" was at its height when I took over seaguard radar duty for the middle watch, which gave me a special view of all that was going on.* Newcastle *steamed constantly at high speed, often making tight 360-degree turns to avoid giving the destroyers a target. The captain impressed us all with his ship handling and tactically it was first class, especially when he used a spur of rock to thwart possible torpedo attacks. We did not know the word then, but that night the adrenalin flowed.*'

With the exercises over *Newcastle* returned briefly

[6] Later the First Sea Lord, Admiral of the Fleet Sir Henry Leach.

to Sasebo and then to Hong Kong for docking and maintenance, but finally, on 21 April, the cruiser left Hong Kong bound for Yokosuka, Pearl Harbor and Panama. At 0830 on 6 May *Newcastle* anchored off Kauai Island, part of the Hawaiian group, where the ship was smartened up. Fred Stephen remembers: '*The ship was painted from masthead to waterline in the old traditional manner by the whole ship's company, with only Captain Tyrwhitt being excused. Everyone wore any type of rig and everyone was given a paintbrush. I remember the padre, wearing just a pair of shorts and sporting a Panama hat, thoroughly enjoying himself as he splashed Pusser's grey on the wardroom screen. After about eight hours at anchor, with the ship looking as smart as a new pin, we weighed anchor and made a slow overnight passage to Pearl Harbor, where we arrived alongside at 0900 the next day. The Americans were their usual hospitable selves, but we didn't know whether to be pleased or indignant when the local press reported the arrival of, "The little light blue British cruiser".*'

On 24 May *Newcastle* made her eastbound transit of the Panama Canal and during the homeward passage, with the ship due to be paid off and then recommissioned within the space of 24 hours, the ship's company made every effort to ensure their departments were cleaned up ready for the new complement. There was time for relaxation at Kingston, Jamaica, but after leaving the island on 29 May there was a non-stop, 11-day passage home. Fred Stephen remembers the final days: '*I picked up the UK on my radar set at 0600 on 9 June, and I remember being amazed at how this tenuous link was so heart-warming; even a gale warning for south-west England and the Channel didn't dampen our spirits.*' Later that day *Newcastle* anchored in Falmouth Bay where, as Fred Stephen remembers: '*The Side Party, with plenty of voluntary help from those off watch, slapped another coat of Pusser's grey on a hastily washed hull.*' Next day at 0700 *Newcastle* arrived at Spithead where, for five hours, everyone waited patiently for Customs clearance. Finally, at 1353, with her paying-off pennant flying, *Newcastle* weighed anchor and steamed slowly up harbour, passing the cheering holidaymakers on Southsea beach, to secure alongside South Railway Jetty, where relatives and friends were waiting to go aboard.

Five days after her arrival in Portsmouth *Newcastle* paid off, and Fred Stephen remembers the day thus: '*At 0730 we landed our kit on the jetty for transport to RNB, then at 0915 we marched the short distance to the barracks. In Lion Terrace we passed the "new boys" marching down to "our" ship, and I have to say I felt rather sad to be leaving her.*' By 0940 on 15 June 1954 the new ship's company had joined the ship and at 1130 *Newcastle* was recommissioned under the command of Captain R. B. Honnywill RN. Captain Tyrwhitt, meanwhile, took command of the battleship *Vanguard*.

HMS *Newcastle* was to be the first Royal Navy warship to try out a new system of 18-month Foreign Service commissions, and on 29 June she sailed from Portsmouth bound for Malta, where she arrived six days later. During the remainder of that month she carried out an intensive series of work-up training exercises, and it was not until 3 August that she left Grand Harbour, bound for Suez, Trincomalee and Singapore. On 24 August she arrived alongside the naval base at Singapore to begin a 13-week refit and docking period, which for the ship's company meant moving ashore to the spacious accommodation at HMS *Terror*.

During the refit the ship's Royal Marines detachment joined up with the Sikorsky S55 helicopters of 848 Naval Air Squadron for operations in the thick jungle of the Malay State of Perak, but by mid-November they and the ship's company were back on board. On 27 November *Newcastle* carried out a short trials period before leaving for Hong Kong, where she joined her sister *Birmingham*. During the first two weeks of 1955 the two cruisers exercised together around Hong Kong, but by 22 January *Newcastle* had returned to Singapore where she anchored in the Singapore Roads, south of the city. On Sunday 23 January the ship was opened to visi-

tors, and next day she steamed north to anchor off the coastal town of Port Dickson. She was taking part in an Army operation code-named 'Nassau' to clear Communist insurgents from the area between Port Dickson and Port Swettenham. The cruiser's task was to provide naval gunfire support, but she was also there on a flag showing mission. This was only ten years after the end of the Second World War and the debacle at Singapore in February 1942 had dealt a severe blow to British prestige in the area. *Newcastle*'s other function in the area, in the words of the official order to Captain Honnywill, was: '*To heighten British prestige with His Highness, the Sultan of Selangor*'.

At 0645 on 25 January, with an Army Auster aircraft acting as spotter, Y-turret opened fire, with targets being engaged continuously until 1120. That afternoon, between 1430 and 1830, and during the night between 2300 and 0300 next day, further bombardments were carried out. At 0900 on 26 January the bombardments were resumed, but that afternoon with the Sultan of Selangor due to be entertained on board, the vacant Admiral's cabin which had been set aside for him was in darkness and covered by mounds of glass from a shattered skylight and broken electric light bulbs. Inside the cabin there was a similar scene and it was apparent that whatever damage had been caused to insurgent camps ashore, the sustained firing of Y turret had also taken a heavy toll on fixtures and fittings in its own vicinity. Fortunately, the ship's company set to with a will to clean up the mess and to replace all the glass and shattered bulbs, and they were assisted by the fact that the VIP guest was two hours late in arriving. After Captain Honnywill had entertained his guest to lunch, the Sultan and his entourage were taken to the Operations Room to watch the final bombardment, while a small working party stood by to replace any broken light bulbs. After a short lull, during which the Sultan departed, *Newcastle*'s bombardments continued until 2140 that day, after which she weighed anchor and returned to Singapore Naval Base. In all she had fired 349 rounds of full-charge, 6-inch shells, and it was thought she had destroyed two insurgent camps.

Once back at the naval base the Admiral's quarters were again cleared of broken glass, and after embarking the C-in-C FES and his staff, together with a Royal Marines Band, *Newcastle* left Singapore in the middle of a tropical deluge, bound for Rangoon. The cruiser made a four-day goodwill visit to the Burmese capital which, since Independence in 1948, had not enjoyed particularly good diplomatic relations with the British Government. The visit involved a busy programme of official calls and functions, leaving very little spare time for the ship's officers, but the efforts at goodwill appeared to have been effective, for when the ship left during the afternoon of 5 February, she was given an enthusiastic send-off, with the Burmese Navy at the Ratnabon Naval Base manning and cheering ship. During the passage back to Singapore the ship's Principal Medical Officer (PMO) and his staff were kept busy performing two appendectomy operations in the space of 24 hours, which the sickbay staff claimed as a naval record. On 14 February *Newcastle* arrived back at Singapore.

On her return to Singapore the C-in-C struck his flag and FO2 hoisted his. Later in the month the cruiser made the passage to Hong Kong for a short maintenance period, before steaming on to revisit many of the old haunts which had been familiar ports of call during the Korean War, with Inchon, Chinhae, Sasebo and Yokosuka featuring in the list. At the end of April she was back in Malayan waters and taking part in fleet exercises in the South China Sea. On 18 May she anchored in the Johore River to carry out another bombardment of Communist insurgent positions in the south-west tip of Johore State, following which she joined more exercises in the South China Sea along with the cruiser HMNZS *Black Prince*. On completion she paid another visit to Hong Kong. She then returned to Singapore to undergo a five-week maintenance period.

On 26 August, having hoisted the flag of Vice-Admiral R. F. Elkins, FO2, FES, *Newcastle* left

Singapore to begin an extended cruise in Australian and New Zealand waters. During the cruise the C-in-C flew down from Singapore to attend meetings with senior naval officers in Australia and New Zealand; his schedule ensured that he was in Melbourne, Wellington and Auckland at the same time as *Newcastle*, which called for a great deal of formal ceremony in those ports. The cruiser's first call was Fremantle, after which she moved round to Melbourne and then across to Dunedin in New Zealand. On 24 September she arrived in Wellington where there was a formal cocktail party on board, attended by the Prime Minister of New Zealand, senior government officials and senior diplomats. After leaving Wellington *Newcastle* crossed the Tasman Sea once again to visit Sydney and Newcastle, NSW, before steaming north to Hong Kong, and arriving back in Singapore on 15 November. It had been a successful cruise and it marked a fitting end to the ship's commission.

It had been decided to recommission *Newcastle* at Singapore, and on 1 November 1955 the RAF began what was at that time the largest single trooping commitment by air ever undertaken. It was also the first time that a major warship of the Royal Navy had recommissioned this way. During the first two weeks of November, in a fleet of Hermes aircraft, some 750 officers and ratings were flown from Britain to Singapore, with a similar number of the old ship's company returning to the UK in the same way. On 15 November the cruiser's new commanding officer, Captain A. R. Kennedy OBE RN joined the ship and at 1100 he was followed by the main body of the ship's company. Four hours later, at 1500, *Newcastle* was recommissioned.

On 6 December, after completing a short maintenance period, *Newcastle* sailed for a short work-up with *Cockade*, before both ships set course for Hong Kong where they would spend Christmas and the New Year. On 2 January 1956 *Newcastle* left Hong Kong to return to Singapore, and after a few days anchored off the city, where she was opened to the

HMS Newcastle *steams past the Royal Yacht* Britannia *in November 1956. Together with the destroyers* Consort *and* Cockade, *she provided escort to the Royal Yacht on passage to Australia for the opening of the 1956 Olympic Games. (Steve Bush Collection)*

public, she moved round to the naval base to begin a 19-week refit and dry docking period. The ship's company moved into HMS *Terror*, where they spent the next three months, during which time the ship became virtually uninhabitable. By 13 May, however, they were back on board and five days later the ship was carrying out post-refit trials and work-up training exercises. On 25 May FO2 hoisted his flag and in early June the cruiser, in company with *Cockade* and *Consort*, left for a cruise of Korean and Japanese ports whose names would have been very familiar to those who had taken part in Korean War operations. By August 1956 she had returned to Singapore and suddenly the Egyptian nationalisation of the Suez Canal Company was dominating the newspaper headlines. In the Far East, however, this all seemed rather remote and during the months which followed *Newcastle* took part in two major fleet exercises in the South China Sea.

On 2 November, as the joint British and French invasion forces were sailing between Malta and Suez, *Newcastle* left Singapore to rendezvous with the Royal Yacht *Britannia*, which she, *Cockade* and *Consort* escorted via Port Moresby to Sydney and Fremantle. *Britannia* was carrying the Duke of Edinburgh, who was officially opening the sixteenth Olympic Games at Melbourne - an event which was overshadowed by events in the Middle East and in Hungary. *Newcastle* arrived in Melbourne on 21 November where she remained for two weeks, but mechanical problems with her steering gear meant that she was unable to lead *Cockade* and *Consort* on planned visits to New Zealand ports; instead she steamed north to Hong Kong for Christmas and the new year, and a nine-day period in dry dock.

After leaving Hong Kong on 16 January 1957, and disembarking FO2 off Singapore's Changi Point, *Newcastle* continued west, refuelling at Trincomalee and arriving at Bahrain on 12 February. After the humiliation of Suez the British Government was keen to bolster its political and military position in the Persian Gulf, and during the remainder of February and the first two weeks of March the ship made a series of high-profile visits to Muscat, Dubai, Basra and the Iranian oil refinery port of Abadan. During these visits she received VIP visitors in the form of local rulers, but on 18 March, to the relief of most of the ship's company, she left Bahrain to return to Singapore, calling en route at Karachi, Bombay and Trincomalee, and arriving in the Johore Strait during the forenoon of 18 April.

On 24 April, after a short six-day break at the naval base, *Newcastle* sailed for 'Exercise Tradewind', a series of international naval manoeuvres which also involved HMAS *Melbourne, Queenborough, Quickmatch, Tobruk* and *Warramunga*, as well as the US Navy ships *George* and *Spangler*. The exercises took *Newcastle* as far north as the Gulf of Thailand and south to Subic Bay, with short recreational breaks at the island of Pulau Tioman. When she arrived at Singapore Naval Base again it was to pay off, and over the two weeks which followed her arrival the ship's company, who had flown out some 18 months earlier, were flown home again. On 23 May, with a new commanding officer, Captain A. H. C. Gordon-Lennox, and a new ship's company, *Newcastle* was again recommissioned at Singapore. Next day the cruiser began her work-up training exercises in the South China Sea and in the Strait of Malacca, which included visits to Penang and the town of Malacca itself. During the last week of June, having been joined by *Anzac* and *Cockade*, she steamed to Hong Kong from where, in company with *Newfoundland*, they operated for the whole of July.

On 1 August, in company with HMNZS *Royalist* and RFA *Wave King*, the cruiser left Hong Kong to return to Singapore by way of the Gulf of Thailand, which included a short visit to Cam Rhan Bay, Cambodia, and Brunei's Seria, before she began a 15-week refit at Singapore Naval Base. In was late November before she put to sea again to undergo post-refit trials and as soon as these were completed she was pitched straight into a major fleet exercise in the South China Sea. On 10 December, when this was concluded, she joined *Cavalier* for Christmas

The end of the road - Demolition is under way as the former HMS Newcastle *sits alongside at Faslane in 1959.*
(T. Ferrers-Walker)

and New Year at Hong Kong. She had in fact completed her last full year of operational service.

On 6 January 1958 *Newcastle* left Hong Kong to join *Cavalier* and *Cheviot* for training exercises in local waters, but by the end of that month she had returned to Singapore. In early February she visited Rangoon, and later in the month she took part in the 'Fotex' exercise in the South China Sea, off Malaya's east coast. During March, wearing the flag of FO2, FES, she visited the Malayan west coast ports of Port Swettenham (Kelang) and Port Dickson, and in April FO2 transferred his flag to *Newfoundland*. On 21 April *Newcastle* left Singapore for the last time for Hong Kong from where, in company with *Newfoundland*, she sailed for visits to Sasebo, Kobe and Yokohama. It was the first stage of *Newcastle*'s homeward passage, and although the Suez Canal had reopened, it had been decided to send her via the Pacific. On 21 June she left Yokohama and arrived at Pearl Harbor nine days later. This time there was only a short 48-hour stopover before she continued her passage to the Canadian West Coast and the naval base at Esquimalt. During the ship's 13 days in Canada she took part in a mini-naval review, which had been arranged for an official visit by Princess Margaret, and as well as *Newcastle*, other ships present were HMCS *Ontario* and *Crescent* and five US Navy warships, including USS *Bennington*. On 22 July *Newcastle* continued her homeward passage, calling at San Francisco and passing through the Panama Canal on 8 August.

Three days after leaving Cristobal the cruiser arrived at Kingston, Jamaica, where it had been arranged she would embark the island's Governor for an official visit to the Turks & Caicos Islands. However, on 13 August, with the ship skirting the edge of a particularly severe hurricane and mountainous seas, the Governor was landed in the Dominican Republic and the cruiser continued her voyage. At 2150 on Sunday 24 August 1958, having been away from Britain for over four years, *Newcastle* anchored at Spithead. Next day, at 0955, she weighed anchor to steam up harbour where, having secured alongside North Corner Jetty at 1045, 'Finished with Main Engines' was rung for the last time and families of ship's company members streamed over the gangway.

By the end of August *Newcastle* had been reduced to reserve. With the big post-Suez Defence Cuts the size of the fleet was being drastically reduced and it was apparent that the cruiser's days were numbered. In October 1958 it was announced that she was to be scrapped, and on 14 August 1959 she followed *Bellona, Dido, Cleopatra, Glasgow* and *Liverpool* to the scrapyard, when she was towed from Portsmouth Harbour bound for the breaker's yard at Faslane.

Chapter Three

HMS SHEFFIELD
1937-1967

On 24 July 1936, HMS Sheffield *is launched into the River Tyne.* *(Steve Bush Collection)*

After weeks of back-door intrigues, 31 January 1934 saw the first anniversary of Adolf Hitler's appointment as the Chancellor of Germany and already seriously disturbing accounts of organised excesses against political opponents and Jews were beginning to filter out of that country. However, despite the rhetoric, he had not at that stage turned his attention to the wholesale revision and repudiation of the Treaty of Versailles. In Britain, supported by some roughneck 'stewards', Sir Oswald Moseley harangued a crowd of supporters in Birmingham, but Parliament was already considering measures to ban uniformed private militias. As this time, in Europe generally there were no serious thoughts of a second European War. Also on that day, at a little publicised ceremony at Vickers Armstrong's Walker-on-Tyne shipyard, the first keel plates were laid for another of the Royal Navy's cruisers provided for under the 1934 building programme. It was the third keel for what was then called the Southampton-class, and the hull was to take shape on a slipway adjoining that of *Newcastle*, whose keel plates had been laid some three months earlier. The two ships provided very welcome work for the shipyard which, just 12 months earlier, had been empty with only a handful of lucky men employed carrying out essential maintenance work.

Eighteen months later, at 1820 on Thursday 24 July 1936, a dull, wet day in the north-east of England, the Duchess of Kent named the new cruiser *Sheffield* and sent her down the slipway into the River Tyne. That same month the first key naval personnel were appointed to stand by the ship. These included Captain W. P. Mark-Wardlaw DSO RN, who until this appointment had been Commodore in charge of the new naval base under construction at Singapore. Just over a year later their numbers had been augmented by a navigating party, made up mainly of seamen and engine room personnel, and during the forenoon of Friday 20 August 1937 *Sheffield*, which was still wearing the Red Ensign at her masthead, slipped her moorings and steamed out of the River Tyne to undergo five days of builder's acceptance trials. These manoeuvres included a full-power trial at the conclusion of which steam to the ahead turbines would be abruptly shut off and the astern turbines opened to full speed. Unfortunately, the subsequent vibrations damaged one of the ship's A brackets, but otherwise the trials were successful and at 1700 on Wednesday 25 August the ship hove to off the entrance to the River Tyne where, at a small ceremony, she was formally accepted into the Royal Navy. At the masthead the Red Ensign was lowered and the White Ensign was hoisted for the first time. At 1850, after disembarking officials from Vickers Armstrong, *Sheffield* steamed clear of the river entrance and set course for the Thames Estuary. Twenty-four hours later she passed the Nore lightship and soon afterwards she had secured to a buoy at Sheerness. Next day *Sheffield* steamed into the Medway where she was manoeuvred through the north lock and into Chatham Dockyard's No 1 basin, and from there to No 9 dry dock.

During the days which followed, while repairs were carried out to the A bracket, *Sheffield* loaded stores and ammunition and by the end of the month she was back alongside the wall in No 1 basin. At 0900 on 31 August, with her ship's company having been brought up to full strength, *Sheffield* was commissioned, but she remained alongside at Chatham for another three weeks. On 23 September she left Sheerness to make an overnight passage to Spithead where she embarked her Walrus aircraft L2185, together with Fleet Air Arm stores and personnel. She then left for Portland from where, over a period of two weeks, she carried out her first phase of trials and work-up. On 12 October there came a break in the arduous routine when she steamed north to Immingham on the River Humber, which was the nearest port to her namesake city of Sheffield, and where she secured alongside the port's Timber Pool. During her six days alongside at Immingham a number of official functions were organised for the officers and men, and over the weekend of 16 and 17 October the ship was opened to the public, for which the London & North Eastern Railway Company put on special trains from Sheffield to Immingham Docks. In all over 22,000 people visited the ship, with long queues winding round the dockside sheds. On one day two officers and 200 ratings took a special train in the other direction to watch a local Sheffield football match, before being entertained at a civic reception, a cinema show and the Lord Mayor's Dance at Sheffield Town Hall, where 200 young women, who had been 'specially chosen' by a committee of Sheffield 'ladies', had been invited to be dancing partners for the sailors. No record now exists of what qualifications or vetting process the Sheffield 'ladies' used when selecting the 200 suitable candidates.

The visit to Immingham ended on 19 October and *Sheffield* steamed north to Rosyth where, next day, she joined the 2nd Cruiser Squadron of the Home Fleet, which also included her sister *Newcastle*. For three weeks, until the second week of November,

A pre-war photograph of HMS Sheffield *at anchor as completed.* *(National Museum of the Royal Navy)*

Sheffield continued her work-up in the North Sea before returning to Chatham to give seasonal leave and to undergo a nine-week maintenance period. When she left the Thames Estuary on 18 January 1938, the last full year of peace, *Sheffield* was bound for Gibraltar where she joined her sisters *Southampton* and *Glasgow*, together with other ships of the Home Fleet including *Courageous* and *Rodney*, for two full months of intensive exercises, broken in late February when *Sheffield* spent a weekend at Tangier. With the Spanish Civil War still raging when the ships put into Gibraltar, leave was confined to the Colony itself. On 31 March there was an alarm when a small merchantman, SS *Olarus*, sent out an urgent call for assistance after being approached by a hostile Spanish Nationalist armed trawler. At the same time *Sheffield* and *Southampton* were exercising nearby and as *Sheffield* went to the coaster's aid the ship's company went to Action Stations. Fortunately, the sight of the cruiser warned off the armed trawler and the manoeuvres could be resumed. It was the end of March before *Sheffield* returned to Chatham, this time for a six-week maintenance period which included two weeks' dry docking.

When *Sheffield* left Chatham on 10 May 1938 the shadow of Hitler's rearmed Germany hung over Europe, and although Britain had signed the Anglo-Italian Agreement which was intended to ensure that Italy did not become a belligerent power in Europe, the last vestiges of Versailles were falling apart and, as the historian A. J. P. Taylor has suggested, war in Europe would resume as a continuation of the Great War of 1914-18. *Sheffield* spent the summer of 1938 exercising off Portland, operating with other ships of the 2nd Cruiser Squadron, including *Aurora*, *Newcastle* and *Southampton*. On 21 and 22 July, with the rest of the Home Fleet, *Sheffield* took part in exercises staged for the visit of King George VI to Portland, during which she put on an impressive display of gunnery, firing at the target ship *Centurion*. On conclusion of the exercises she spent a long weekend at Portsmouth before taking part in what was a combined landing

HMS Sheffield, *followed by her sistership* Newcastle *and the County class cruiser* Cornwall *exercise with the Home Fleet during the visit of King George VI to Portland in 1938.* *(Ken Kelly Collection)*

exercise involving close co-operation between Army, Navy and Air Force. With *Southampton* she escorted two troop transports down Channel, round the Channel Islands and back to Start Bay where five companies of infantry, together with equipment, including guns, tanks, transport and artillery were landed on three beaches in the neighbourhood of Torcross. Following the landings, battle exercises took place which involved the re-embarkation of the troops under the cover of a naval bombardment from *Sheffield* and *Southampton*, before the troopships were escorted back to Spithead. Two days later *Sheffield* anchored off Scarborough, where once again she was able to renew her links with the city after which she was named. Leaving the seaside town on 19 July she joined *Southampton* for joint exercises in the North Sea, in which the German fishery protection vessel *Elbe* took a close interest. Six days later she returned to Chatham where she was the star attraction during Navy Week. The main event here was a re-enactment of the Zeebrugge Raid of 1918, and *Sheffield* herself put on a popular display which mimicked a bombardment of an enemy fort. Both displays looked back to the Great War and were an indication of how the horrors of that conflict still haunted the country. On 9 August, three days after the end of Navy Week, there was a change of command when Captain E. De F. Renouf CVO RN took over from Captain Mark-Wardlaw.

On 16 September 1938 *Sheffield* sailed from Sheerness north to Invergordon for Home Fleet exercises. Eight days later came the Munich Crisis over the future of the German-speaking Sudetenland, which since 1919 had been part of the newly formed Czechoslovakia, but prior to the Great War had been part of the Austro-Hungarian Empire. As Neville Chamberlain and Edouard

Daladier, the prime ministers of Britain and France, struggled to agree terms with Hitler, which meant reneging on an agreement of April that year to defend Czechoslovakia against German aggression, it appeared that war in Europe was imminent. On 24 September the Home Fleet at Invergordon was ordered to curtail its manoeuvres and proceed to its war station at Scapa Flow, which in late 1938 was far from ready to receive the fleet. Mobilising the Home Fleet Chamberlain announced: '*I am a man of peace to the depths of my soul. Armed conflict between nations is a nightmare to me, but if I were convinced that any nation had made up its mind to dominate the world by force I should feel it should be resisted*'. Six days later he and Daladier chose not to defend Czechoslovakia and the crisis ended with Chamberlain's '*I believe it is peace for our time*', a phrase borrowed from a speech by Lord Beaconsfield (Disraeli) in 1878 after the Congress of Berlin. The Munich Agreement, however, would bring only a brief respite, delaying the outbreak of war by some 11 months. In Scapa Flow, meanwhile, on 6 October the Home Fleet was stood down and the ships, including *Sheffield*, steamed south back to Invergordon where they resumed their autumn manoeuvres.

Following her return to Invergordon *Sheffield* resumed her exercises with other cruisers of the squadron, including *Cornwall*, *Coventry* and *Newcastle*, with an emphasis on anti-aircraft defences. On 18 November she returned to Chatham to give leave and to undergo maintenance, and in mid-January 1939, when she put to sea again, she steamed via Portland to Gibraltar, from where she took part in combined Home and Mediterranean Fleet exercises. Also taking part were *Ark Royal*, *Nelson*, *Rodney*, *Warspite*, *Glorious*, *Newcastle*, *Southampton* and two destroyer flotillas; after the scare of Munich the manoeuvres took on a new intensity. On her way south *Sheffield* called at Lisbon, but this was the only respite from seven weeks of intensive day and night exercises. On 13 March, however, with other ships of the Home Fleet, she sailed north again for Dover and seven days later, led by *Rodney*, and in company with *Glasgow*, *Newcastle*, *Southampton* and the 5th Destroyer Flotilla, she anchored off the port to welcome the French President, Monsieur Lebrun, on a high-profile State Visit to London. Tuesday 21 March dawned clear and sunny with a strong northerly wind and at 1100 the assembled fleet, which was anchored in two lines, dressed ship. Shortly afterwards the destroyer flotilla steamed into mid-Channel to meet *Côte d'Azur*, with the President and his party on board. Overhead a flight of RAF aircraft flew by in salute, while at sea in the sunshine the warships formed an impressive sight with their upper decks manned and flags, including the White Ensign and Tricolour, flying at the mastheads. As *Côte d'Azur* approached the lane between the warships a 21-gun salute was fired and the Presidential vessel passed between the lines. On board *Rodney* the Royal Marines Band played the Marseillaise and cheers rang out from the assembled ships' companies. The ceremonial arrival was a public signal to Hitler that the Anglo-French alliance was unshakeable, but the two countries had overestimated both their influence and power, and such diplomatic subtleties cut little ice with the politicians in Berlin.

With the French President ashore and on his way to London by train, *Sheffield* and the rest of the fleet anchored in The Downs, but on 24 March they returned to Dover to salute the French President when he re-embarked in *Côte d'Azur* for the return to Calais and onward journey by train to Paris' Gare du Nord Station. Later that day *Sheffield* steamed north to Sheerness and at the end of the month she was taken into the dockyard at Chatham. For the ship's company there was the relief of seasonal leave, but for Europe the dark clouds of war were once again gathering. In mid-March Hitler had presented the Government of what was left of Czechoslovakia with a demand for independence for the provinces of Slovakia and Ruthenia, and a new pro-German government in Prague. Two days after the demand German troops invaded Czechoslovakia. In London Chamberlain, who had expected this move ever since the Munich Agreement, emphasised that for the first time Hitler had occupied territory not inhabited by German people. Two weeks later he announced a hastily drawn-up Anglo-French-Polish military alliance. Neither Britain nor France could do anything which would assist Poland in the event of that country being invaded, but the two Allied Governments were counting on the alliance to act as a deterrent to Hitler. There is a great deal of evidence to suggest that Chamberlain soon regretted giving the guarantee to Poland, for he quickly found that the Polish Prime Minister, Joseph Beck, when the tensions were building over the future of the 'International' city of Danzig (Gdansk), another hangover from the Treaty of Versailles, would not be willing to contemplate any compromises whatsoever in his dealings with Germany. Although five more months were to elapse before hostilities began, few people in Europe doubted that the second major European war in the space of 25 years was very far away.

On 3 May 1939, when *Sheffield* left Sheerness to make the passage down Channel to Portland, her ship's company were making preparations for the ceremonial departure of King George VI, who was travelling to Canada and the USA in the chartered passenger liner, *Empress of Australia*. The main purpose of the visit was an attempt to cement a military alliance with the USA. In that respect the visit would fail, but in Germany Hitler was far more successfully negotiating a vital neutrality pact with the Soviet Union. Back in the Channel, meanwhile, *Sheffield* took up her position in Weymouth Bay, and at 1750, when *Empress of Australia* steamed through the two lines of warships, her ship's company manned and cheered ship. Five days later *Sheffield* and other ships of the Home Fleet, including *Royal Oak, Royal Sovereign*, *Rodney*, *Nelson*, *Aurora* and *Newcastle*, began a series of joint battle exercises with the new French battlecruisers *Dunkerque* and *Strasbourg*, and the cruisers *Leygues*, *Gloire* and *Montcalm*, which took them all through the North Sea to Rosyth, where the French ships paid a highly publicised goodwill visit. The French squadron was under the command of Vice-Admiral Gensoul, C-in-C l'Escadre de l'Atlantique, and after a weekend of entertainments, which included a fleet dance at Rosyth, guided tours of Edinburgh and finally an official civic reception in the city's Assembly Rooms, the combined British and French Fleet put to sea for more joint exercises and manoeuvres. However, for two major navies which in time of war would have to work closely together the co-operation was too little and far too late. During the exercises, however, *Sheffield* did get a chance to fire 6-inch reduced-charge shells at *Centurion*. During the last week of June *Sheffield* spent a weekend anchored off St Helier, but on 27 June, with German demands for Danzig and the Polish Corridor to be returned becoming ever more strident and insistent, the political situation was such that the Admiralty ordered the ships of the Home Fleet to their base ports and for summer leave to be advanced by a month. This decision also allowed essential docking and maintenance to be carried out and, with the heavy workloads in all the Royal Dockyards, Navy Weeks at Portsmouth, Devonport and Chatham were cancelled. For *Sheffield* the order meant an immediate return to Chatham for four-weeks' maintenance, which included two weeks in dry dock where the ship's bottom was completely scraped and repainted.

On 28 July 1939 *Sheffield* manoeuvred out of Chatham Dockyard's No 3 basin to a buoy off Sheerness, and next day sailed to meet *Resolution* and *Royal Sovereign* for exercises in the North Sea, before anchoring off the Kentish Knock lightship where, on a warm summer's evening, 'hands to bathe' was piped. On 30 July, having been joined by *Southampton*, the four ships weighed anchor and set course for Invergordon where the Home Fleet's autumn manoeuvres were starting a month earlier than usual. The first three weeks of exercises took place in the North Sea, with the ships operating as far south as the River Humber. At one stage *Sheffield* was given the role of a German auxiliary cruiser with orders to break out from the North Sea into the Atlantic Ocean. On 24 August, the day

before Hitler's original date for the invasion of Poland, the Home Fleet was ordered to its War Station at Scapa Flow, and next day *Sheffield* anchored in the massive natural harbour in the Orkney Islands. For the next two nights the cruiser put to sea to take part in night encounter exercises, but at 2200 on 27 August she was ordered to sail for the Norwegian port of Bergen to embark some 'special' diplomatic passengers. During the passage, at 2016 on 28 August, as darkness began to fall over the Norwegian Sea, a large merchant ship was sighted, which on closer investigation turned out to be the crack, 55,000-ton North German Lloyd passenger liner, *Europa*, Germany's largest merchant vessel. At that stage, although it was known that the German Army had massed on the Polish frontier, no invasions or declarations of war had been made and the liner, which was on passage from New York to Bremerhaven, had to be allowed to continue. The encounter was not unexpected for *Europa* had been scheduled to call at Cherbourg and at Southampton earlier that day and, indeed, some 40 German citizens desperate to get home had been ferried out to the Solent where, at noon, they had been due to embark. The failure of *Europa* to make either the Cherbourg or Southampton calls had led to speculation that she was sailing direct to Bremerhaven by way of the Iceland Faroes gap, so *Sheffield*'s sighting confirmed that when the war did start the German liner would be safely in her home port.

When Chamberlain had announced the Anglo-French military alliance with Poland, the veteran politician David Lloyd George had taken him to task with the words: '*If we are going in without the help of Russia we are walking into a trap. It is the only country whose arms can get there... If Russia has not been brought into this matter because of certain feelings the Poles have that they do not want Russians there, it is for us to declare the conditions, and unless the Poles are prepared to accept the only conditions with which we can successfully help them, the responsibility must be theirs.*' Lloyd George was right in that the Soviet Union was the only European power with the arms and position to defend Poland, but not only were Chamberlain and his ministers accepting without any serious argument Poland's absolute refusal to allow Soviet troops onto its territory, they themselves had an ideological disdain and aloofness towards the Soviet Union and its leaders. We now know that the Soviet Union would have welcomed an alliance with Britain and France and, indeed, immediately after the German occupation of Prague in April 1939 Stalin had proposed a conference of 'peaceful powers', but the British Government had rejected this idea out of hand. By August 1939, however, Chamberlain and his Government were becoming desperate and to a certain extent they were prepared to abandon their ideological distaste of the Soviet Union. As a result, on 6 August, they dispatched a joint diplomatic and military mission led by Foreign Office official William Strang and Admiral Sir Reginald Plunkett-Ernle-Erle-Drax[1], both of whom were unknown to the Soviet leaders. They left Britain by a slow merchant ship bound for Leningrad (St Petersburg) and Moscow, where they arrived five days later to '*string out negotiations until the October snows in Poland*'. This lack of seriousness on the part of the British Government was not lost on Stalin and negotiations stuck on the fact that Britain wanted to cloak an agreement under the League of Nations, which the Soviets considered a recipe for no action at all, and on the fact that there was no agreement on the exact circumstances which would trigger joint Soviet, French and British action. The final, and perhaps the most basic sticking point, was the fact that Poland refused to allow Soviet troops onto its territory. In the event the utterly unscrupulous, but more realistic, German Foreign Minister, Joachim von

[1] Born Reginald Aylmer Ranrurnly Plunkett, second son of Baron Dunsany, he assumed by Royal Licence the additional surnames of Ernle-Erle-Drax. His long series of titles, surnames and postnominals are said to have inspired P.G. Wodehouse when lampooning the British airistocracy, but, in fact, Drax had a brilliant mind and was an early pioneer of solar heating.

Ribbentrop, met Stalin and his Foreign Minister Molotov in Moscow and, on 23 August, in a move which surprised and completely stunned the British and French Governments, Germany and the Soviet Union signed a non-aggression pact, which made the outbreak of a second European war virtually inevitable. The British and French had been completely outmanoeuvred and, in the words of A. J. P. Taylor: '*It is pointless to speculate whether an Anglo-Soviet alliance would have prevented war in 1939. But failure to achieve the alliance did much to cause it*'. For the ill-fated British mission to the Soviet Union there remained only the question of how to return home safely, for by late August British shipping had been warned to avoid the Baltic. In the event they travelled by train from Leningrad to Norway, but at noon on 29 August when *Sheffield* anchored off Bergen the 14-man mission was still on its way from Oslo. For the ship's company this allowed seven hours shore leave for the non-duty watch, and in the event it was 2200 before the passengers were embarked. Twenty minutes later *Sheffield* weighed anchor and set course for Thurso where they were to be landed, but soon after leaving Norwegian waters, the cruiser was ordered to make for Scapa Flow where she arrived during the evening of 30 August. Thirty-three hours later the German Army swept over the frontier to begin their invasion of Poland.

Meanwhile, on the last day of August, *Sheffield* and *Aurora* left Scapa Flow to begin their first patrol of the Iceland-Faroes gap. This time the ships' companies were at Defence Stations and additional lookouts were posted. At 1100 on 3 September 1939, when war was declared against Germany, *Sheffield* was on patrol in the North Sea, some 130 miles west of Duncansby Head, and that evening for 24 hours before returning to Scapa Flow, she took station on the battlefleet. During the weeks which followed *Sheffield* and *Aurora* continued to patrol, with the only break in a monotonous routine being 24 hours spent at Sullum Voe.

On Monday 25 September, *Sheffield* and *Aurora* were on patrol together when they came under heavy air attack. The two ships were in the North Sea, just north of the Great Fisher Bank when, at 1300, they were shadowed by Dornier flying boats which were flying as low as 100 feet, and well outside the range of the cruisers' guns. On a fine clear day, with little cloud and no wind, conditions were ideal for a bombing raid, the first of which came at 1500. Nine Dornier aircraft were sighted flying in three flights in line abreast, some 11 to 12 miles on the port beam, and 15 minutes later they attacked from the direction of the sun, which meant that the gunners on board the two cruisers were unable to get them in their sights for more than a few seconds at a time. At this point *Sheffield* was some four cables abaft of *Aurora*'s port quarter, steaming on a parallel course, when the first formation of bombers flew high over the two ships. When Captain Renouf considered the formation was just about to release its bombs he ordered full speed and put the ship hard-a-port. Almost immediately the first bomb was seen to fall off *Aurora*'s port beam with a second off her starboard beam, while a third fell between the two ships. The last two bombs from the first wave of bombers, flying at 14,000 feet, fell some 20 to 30 yards off *Sheffield*'s starboard bow, abreast B turret, and close on her port beam, with the 60-foot plume of spray falling right over the ship. Although at 1518 the aircraft were reported as directly overhead, it was impossible to open fire as the angle of sight was too great. The second wave of bombers came in at the same height and eight bombs were seen to explode within 20 feet of *Sheffield*'s stern, as did the bombs dropped by the third wave. No sooner had the bombers departed than an enemy fighter was seen attacking an escorting destroyer, its bombs exploding close to the ship's stern. Less than an hour later five more Dornier bombers were sighted some ten miles away, but with low cloud, poor visibility and rain showers, an attack failed to materialise. Fortunately, *Sheffield*'s damage was confined to broken lights in a number of compartments, and leaking steam pipes in the engine rooms, where joints had been loosened. In his report Renouf describes the attacks as, '*...of a very high*

HMS Sheffield, *at anchor in 1938. Note the awnings on the quarterdeck and the booms rigged forward and aft for small boat operations. The cranes are also in operation for handling the boats.* *(Steve Bush Collection)*

standard in the first attack. Subsequent bombs were avoided by continual alterations of course.' That same night, at 0230, *Sheffield* returned to Scapa Flow, where there was a six-day break and the ship's company were able to sample the delights of the 'wet canteen'.

For some years after the Great War Scapa Flow had lain littered with sunken and derelict warships, and soon after the end of that war it had ceased to exist as a naval base. In September 1938, at the time of the Munich Crisis, the C-in-C Home Fleet, Admiral Sir Charles Forbes, had taken the fleet to what he knew would be its war station in the Flow. It is said that on arrival the sailors had found two oddly contradictory activities going on there, with working parties dismantling the Great War gun emplacements, while boom defence vessels were preparing anti-submarine nets. Of one thing which Forbes was certain, Scapa's defences were wholly inadequate, but in the 12 months between September 1938 and the outbreak of war, despite his urgent recommendations, very little was done to improve them. As to amenities for the sailors, in September 1939 these consisted of wooden huts in a quagmire of mud. The wet canteen was described by one sailor as '*...a large wooden hut, trestle tables and two or three large beer barrels, with the beer strictly rationed. The noise, the stench of stale beer and the beer-sodden floor, had to be seen to be believed. A large corrugated iron shed housed the billiards room and this building, its roof riddled with rust holes, also doubled as the cinema. The two ancient billiard tables, which also dated from the First War, were moth-eaten, but they were still well-used.*' This then, was what *Sheffield*'s ship's company could look forward to when taking canteen leave.

For two days in early October *Sheffield* carried out full-calibre gunnery exercises within the confines of Scapa Flow, but during the afternoon of 5 October she sailed south to Invergordon where she joined other ships of the Home Fleet for a two-day visit and inspection by King George VI, who had travelled north to Scotland by train. During the forenoon of 6 October the King spent an hour and a half on board *Sheffield*, and no sooner had he disembarked than the cruiser weighed anchor and returned to Scapa Flow. *Sheffield*'s next patrol began during the forenoon of 8 October and she was still at sea six days later when *Royal Oak* was torpedoed and sunk in the anchorage at Scapa Flow. Admiral Forbes' concerns of September 1938, which had been largely ignored by government, had become an appalling reality and the Home Fleet

was forced to abandon Scapa Flow until its anti-submarine defences had been improved. On 14 October, when *Sheffield* completed her patrol, she anchored in Loch Ewe, which was providing a temporary haven for the fleet, but 48 hours later she was at sea again on her next patrol.

In the early months of the war the ships of the Northern Patrol had been very successful in intercepting German merchant ships which were attempting to use the Iceland-Faeroes gap and the Denmark Strait to return to home ports in Germany. By the end of 1939 some 17 ships had been sunk or captured by ships on the patrol. During the evening of 18 October, west of Iceland, *Sheffield* had intercepted a neutral ship and sent it into Kirkwall for a contraband inspection, and two days later, at 2215 on 20 October, when she was just south of Iceland, lookouts sighted the silhouette of a darkened merchant ship, which was quickly identified as the 5,896-ton German SS *Gloria*. As she was unable to safely put a prize crew aboard that night, *Sheffield* took station on *Gloria*'s starboard side. Next forenoon at 1100, an armed boarding party was put aboard the merchantman and she was steamed to Kirkwall, where it was found she was carrying a valuable cargo of wheat. Four days later, at 1035 on 25 October, *Sheffield* went to the assistance of the armed merchant cruiser *Transylvania*, which had captured the 5,800-ton German steamer *Poseidon*, but which was having some difficulty in escorting the vessel to Kirkwall. When *Sheffield* arrived on the scene her Commander (E) was sent across by whaler to the German ship, where he found the coaster's crew had destroyed the main engines. By 1345 *Transylvania* had managed to secure towing lines and she began towing the vessel towards Kirkwall. For *Poseidon*'s crew the vigilance of the Northern Patrol had been their downfall, for they had managed to avoid detection by the cruiser *Ajax* off the River Plate area, and they were almost within sight of safety when the armed merchant cruiser had spotted them. On 27 October, however, a severe storm blew up and the tow wires parted, so after her crew had been taken off, *Poseidon* was sunk by gunfire. *Sheffield*, meanwhile, made a refuelling stop at Sullum Voe before steaming south to Rosyth.

During the first three weeks of November 1939 *Sheffield* continued to patrol the stormy Norwegian Sea, between the Shetland Islands and Iceland. She was frequently pounded by seas so heavy that the ship's boats were smashed to matchwood on their davits, and the blinding blizzards reduced visibility to just a few yards. On 21 November, at the end of one such patrol, she anchored in Loch Ewe for what was to have been a five-day break. Two days later, at 1615 on 23 November, a signal reporting an engagement between the vulnerable armed merchant cruiser *Rawalpindi* and what was at first thought to be the German heavy cruiser *Deutschland* (1940 renamed *Lützow*), but was, in fact, two battlecruisers - *Scharnhorst* and *Gneisenau*. In the one-sided engagement which followed, *Rawalpindi* was quickly sunk, but in the meantime all available ships of the Home Fleet were ordered to the area to search for the enemy warships which were thought to be in the Iceland – Faeroes gap. By 1800 *Sheffield* had raised steam and was leaving Loch Ewe. For the next nine days, in conjunction with *Devonshire*, *Glasgow* and *Newcastle*, she scoured the Norwegian Sea, but to no avail for, by hugging the Norwegian coast, the two enemy ships had returned to their base at Wilhelmshaven. By 2 December the search had been called off and at 0820 that day *Sheffield* anchored in Scapa Flow, which was again back in use as the Home Fleet's northern base.

HMS *Sheffield*'s stay in Scapa Flow lasted just long enough for her to refuel before she was once again at sea and on patrol. The weather conditions in the Norwegian Sea were much as they had been during November, and in the early hours of a very stormy night of 3 December *Sheffield*'s encounter with the small British coaster *Arlesford* illustrates the difficulties faced by ships of the Northern Patrol. At 0402 the cruiser's lookouts sighted the darkened merchant vessel, but her master chose to ignore three challenges ordering the ship to identify

herself. After numerous attempts to communicate with the ship *Sheffield* ordered her to stop, but her obstinate master ignored these signals as well. *Sheffield* then fired a warning shot across her bow, but even this had no effect and the merchant ship continued on her way. Finally, at 0615, over two hours after first intercepting the ship, *Sheffield* identified her as British and wasted no more time over her. The cruiser's patrol ended on 10 December, when she secured alongside Wallsend Slipway Quay on the River Tyne where, without any delay, the starboard watch left the ship for long leave. At 1800 on 13 December, Captain Renouf relinquished command and left the ship; at noon next day Captain C. A. A. Larcom RN assumed command.

HMS *Sheffield*'s refit was to be carried out in two stages. The first phase lasted for just eight days, and on 18 December *Sheffield* sailed again for the patrol line in the Iceland – Faeroes gap. The winter of 1939/40 was bitterly cold in those northern waters and once again the cruiser was operating in temperatures well below freezing, with heavy seas and blinding snowstorms. Christmas Day on board *Sheffield* was no different from any other day at sea as she steamed through more snowstorms and mountainous waves. She returned to Scapa Flow in time to welcome in the new year. It was 7 January 1940 when, in company with the armed merchant cruiser *Derbyshire*, she returned to the patrol line. Three days later, at 1030 on 30 January, when the ship was steaming through a heavy sea east of the Faroe Islands, a young Stoker, John W. Penn, was lost overboard. Although *Sheffield* searched the area for well over an hour, with blinding snow, subzero temperatures and a heavy sea, there was clearly no chance whatever of finding the missing man and the ship resumed her patrol. On 4 February she returned to Scapa Flow and next day she steamed south to Rosyth before, on 8 February, securing at buoys in the River Tyne to complete the refit which had been left unfinished before the new year, and to give leave to both watches.

It was Sunday 17 March when *Sheffield* left the River Tyne again to return to Scapa Flow prior to North Sea Patrols off Scotland's north-east coast, protecting the continuous supply convoys sailing north to replenish the base at Scapa Flow. In early April, with *Cairo* and *Penelope*, she escorted a convoy from Scapa to Greenock, after which she joined the Home Fleet, including *Nelson*, *Rodney*, *Glasgow*, *Manchester* and *Southampton*, in order to investigate large numbers of German ships which had been seen off the Norwegian coast. On 9 April the four cruisers were steaming ahead of the battlefleet when they came under heavy air attack and although *Sheffield* emerged unscathed, there were several near misses. The fleet returned to Scapa Flow on 10 April, at the time that the British Government was laying plans to occupy various Norwegian ports which had been occupied by German forces. Unfortunately, the plans had been drawn up hastily, and the resulting operations were to prove both costly and embarrassing for both Britain and France.

Following the German invasion of Norway the British and French Governments decided to land two expeditionary forces in that country; the first in northern Norway and the second in central Norway, in order to provide encouragement for the Norwegian Government and to form rallying points for their hard-pressed armed forces and, most importantly, to secure bases for any subsequent operations in Scandinavia. It was with the latter that *Sheffield* would be involved from the very start of operations. Together with *Glasgow* she was ordered to land a joint, 300-strong, Royal Navy and Royal Marines Battalion at Namsos, in order to forestall a German landing and to ensure an unopposed landing for a larger force which was due to arrive in mid-April. Both cruisers embarked additional Royal Marines and equipment, and at 2240 on 11 April they left Scapa Flow bound for central Norway. Three days later they arrived in Namsenfjord where, at 1930, they anchored and the destroyer *Matabele* came alongside *Sheffield* to disembark her 150-man landing party of marines and sailors, who were under strict orders not to attempt an opposed landing. By the evening of the next day the landing parties had secured the main quay at Namsos, the quay at Bangsund and an important road bridge over the River Nagsun. During the night of 15 April *Sheffield* and *Glasgow* left their exposed anchorage at Namsos and two days later the cruisers returned to Namsos to re-embark their landing parties who had been relieved by stronger Army battalions. By now, however, the ships in the fjord and the Army units ashore were coming under heavy air attacks, but fortunately *Sheffield* and *Glasgow* were able to complete the embarkation and clear the fjord unscathed. By 21 April the two ships had landed their additional Royal Marines at Scapa Flow and steamed south to Rosyth where they each embarked some 700 Army reinforcements, together with military stores and ammunition.

Meanwhile, back at Namsos, the scale of enemy air attacks was increasing, and with few Allied aircraft available it was clear to the Army Commander, General Carton de Wiart, that unless his force was withdrawn it would be overwhelmed. For *Sheffield*, however, there was one more trooping passage to Norway to undertake and at 2035 on 23 April, some 38 hours after leaving Rosyth, she disembarked her 700 reinforcements and their equipment at Molde Pier. She left the port in the early hours of 24 April to join *Ark Royal*, *Glorious* and *Berwick* off the Norwegian coast and two days later she returned to Scapa Flow for fuel and stores. During the 28 hours spent at the fleet anchorage the military situation for the Anglo-French force in Norway had rapidly worsened and by the end of April a full-scale evacuation of the Allied forces in central Norway was in full swing. For *Sheffield* there was just one more passage to Norway, this time to Andalsnes where, at midnight on 30 April, she began embarking some 800 troops who had been ferried out in the destroyer *Walker*. At 0100 on 1 May, *Sheffield* left Norwegian waters for the last time, and ten hours later she passed *Birmingham* and *Manchester* who were on their way into Andalsnes to evacuate the rearguard units. *Sheffield* arrived at Scapa Flow at 0630 on 2 May, her part in the ill-fated Norwegian campaign over.

During May and June 1940, *Sheffield*, *Birmingham* and *Manchester* operated from Rosyth, patrolling the east coast from Immingham northwards, as they provided anti-invasion defences. During the evening of 21 June, while in close company with *Birmingham*, *Manchester* and *York*, in the North Sea just south of Rosyth, having been shadowed for most of the day by enemy aircraft, the four ships came under heavy air attack, with four bombs exploding close alongside *York*.

On 1 July, together with *Newcastle*, *Sheffield* steamed south to Sheerness to reinforce the Nore defences, and she remained in the area of the Thames Estuary for three weeks, after which she returned to Scapa Flow. For the next ten days in the waters of the Pentland Firth *Sheffield* carried out a mini work-up, before steaming south to Glasgow to undergo a 14-day refit and docking period at Govan. On 13 August she left the Clyde to return once again to Scapa Flow, but only temporarily for on 22 August, in company with *Valiant*, *Illustrious*, *Coventry*, *Calcutta*, *Ajax*, *York* and a destroyer screen, she left Scapa bound for Gibraltar as part of a convoy escort. Once at Gibraltar she was to join the newly formed naval force which would be based at Gibraltar and would be responsible for the defence of the Western Mediterranean, as well as for convoys approaching and departing from Gibraltar and the Atlantic Ocean as far north as the Bay of Biscay and south as far as Freetown. It was the legendary Force H.

At 0700 on Tuesday 27 August, after a passage of five days which had seen the convoy routed well out into the Atlantic, *Sheffield* was some 300 miles west of Gibraltar when the battlecruiser *Renown*, the flagship of Vice-Admiral Sir James Somerville, Flag Officer Force H, together with *Ark Royal* and ships of the 8th Destroyer Flotilla were sighted. They had come out to welcome the addition to Force H, and some 24 hours later *Sheffield* secured alongside Gibraltar's Coaling Wharf. For the cruiser's ship's company, however, there was little time for relaxation and the day after her arrival she sailed

HMS Sheffield *at Gibraltar. Although this image is undated it is believed to have been taken early in the war as she still has her aircraft embarked and there is a distinct lack of radar aerials.* *(T. Ferrers-Walker Collection)*

in company with *Valiant*, *Illustrious*, *Coventry*, *Calcutta*, the old aircraft carrier *Argus* and a destroyer screen for what appeared to be a foray into the Atlantic. That evening, however, under cover of darkness, they reversed course and steamed east into the Mediterranean. The cruiser was part of 'Operation Hats', the aim of which was to fly off reinforcement aircraft from *Argus* to Malta, a role which the elderly aircraft carrier would perform well. At the same time in the Eastern Mediterranean, Admiral Cunningham's Mediterranean Fleet, based at Alexandria, steamed west to meet Force H south of Sardinia. The first objective, the dispatch of *Argus*' Hurricane fighters to Malta, was carried out while *Ark Royal*'s aircraft attacked Cagliari. Once the two fleets met, *Illustrious* would continue her passage east to Alexandria, while the elderly and slow *Royal Sovereign* would leave the Mediterranean Fleet and continue her passage west to Gibraltar. During the evening of 1 September the two fleets finally came together in the dangerous waters south of Sardinia, and that evening they were subjected to high-level bombing attacks, but there were no casualties, and during the forenoon of 3 September Force H and *Royal Sovereign* returned safely to Gibraltar. Once again, however, there was to be no respite for *Sheffield*'s company, for in Britain it was thought that a German invasion was imminent and on 5 September she was ordered to make a fast passage to the Clyde; three days later she anchored off Greenock where she would remain until early October. Initially she had been due to escort a convoy to Sierra Leone and, indeed, in the early hours of 11 September she actually sailed with the convoy which included six large and important troop transports, but when only a few hours out of the Clyde she was recalled and ordered to return to Greenock. Finally, on 3 October, she was ordered to sail and to rendezvous with a southbound convoy which she would escort as far as Gibraltar. At 2000 that evening, in heavy seas and howling winds, the convoy was sighted, but instead of the six ships there should have been, there were only five. The MV

Highland Brigade was missing. For over 48 hours *Sheffield* searched for the missing troopship, and at 1013 on 8 October she launched her Walrus aircraft P5670 to assist with the hunt. Although the severe weather had eased somewhat there was still a long Atlantic swell and at 1225, after the aircraft had landed and was being hoisted inboard it was caught by a particularly large wave and became waterlogged. Fortunately, the crew were rescued uninjured, but as the aircraft was beyond salvage it was put to use providing target practice for the pom-pom crews. Six days later, after a fruitless diversion to the vicinity of the Azores to search for two German blockade-runners, *Sheffield* returned to Gibraltar. On 27 October she was once again at sea and bound for the area of the Azores where two German merchantmen were thought to be about to sail in an attempt to break through the Northern Patrol's blockade. She spent ten fruitless days patrolling the area, and shortly before she returned to Gibraltar she encountered the Vichy French troopship *Messilia*. The vessel had been given clearance to proceed to Liverpool to embark troops who had been evacuated from Dunkirk and other French ports, but had chosen to be repatriated. In the event *Messilia* would eventually take her passengers to Senegal. On 6 November *Sheffield* returned to Gibraltar, but next day in company with *Ark Royal*, *Barham*, *Berwick* and *Glasgow*, she sailed east once again. This time her mission was to escort *Barham* and *Berwick*, which between them were carrying over 2,000 Free French troops to Malta. During the evening of 8 November a shadowing aircraft was shot down, and next day *Ark Royal*'s aircraft bombed the airfield at Cagliari. Two days later, without any further incidents, the cruiser reached Gibraltar.

At this period of the war there was little respite for the ships of Force H, and in the early hours of 15 November *Sheffield*, *Ark Royal*, *Argus* and *Renown* left Gibraltar to steam east to a point south of Sardinia where, two days later, *Argus* flew off 12 Hurricanes and two Skuas as reinforcements for the air defences of Malta. The whole operation took three days and during the early evening of 18 November the force arrived back at Gibraltar. Less than 24 hours later, however, *Sheffield* was at sea again, this time heading to the area around the Cape Verde Islands where there had been reports that the heavy cruiser *Admiral Scheer* was operating. For four days in atrocious weather conditions *Sheffield* patrolled the seas around the Portuguese islands, and although there was no trace of the German raider, during the afternoon of 20 November she intercepted the Brazilian freighter *Sequeira Campos*, which was carrying a German contraband cargo. Despite difficulties with one of her whalers in the heavy seas, a boarding party was put aboard the freighter, which was then steamed back to Gibraltar for inspection. *Sheffield* herself continued her patrol, and during the afternoon of 21 November she rendezvoused with *Manchester* and *Southampton* which were escorting three important merchantmen, *Clan Forbes, Clan Fraser* and *New Zealand Star*, all of which were carrying vital supplies for the besieged island of Malta. Three days later the cruisers put into Gibraltar where they were able to refuel, load stores and, in the case of *Manchester* and *Southampton*, to embark 1,370 RAF personnel who were bound for Egypt to relieve men on front-line squadrons, many of whom had been in Egypt since before the outbreak of war.

At 0812 on 25 November, some nine hours after her arrival, *Sheffield* left Gibraltar to rendezvous with *Manchester* and *Southampton*, both of which were now loaded with troops, *Ark Royal*, *Renown* and a screen of nine destroyers, to set course eastwards towards Malta. The primary and overriding objective of the operation was to ensure the safe arrival at Alexandria and Malta of the convoy and the two troop-carrying cruisers, *Manchester* and *Southampton*. Should either of these two be sunk or seriously damaged the consequences would be catastrophic, and if one or both of them were disabled within range of enemy airfields their recovery by other ships of the force would put the whole convoy operation at risk. The merchantmen *Clan Forbes, Clan Fraser* and *New Zealand Star* were laden with

much-needed tanks and equipment for an armoured brigade, and at the time it was the most important Mediterranean convoy of personnel and equipment to sail through the Mediterranean since Italy's declaration of war.

Flying his flag in *Renown* Somerville considered it likely that the Italian fleet would attempt to intercept and engage the convoy with a substantial force, and initially he had wanted *Royal Sovereign* to reinforce Force H for the operation, but this had not been possible. The plan was for Somerville and his force to escort the convoy to a point between Sicily and Tunisia where they would rendezvous with *Ramillies*, three cruisers and five destroyers from Cunningham's Mediterranean Fleet. Here the convoy would be handed over and the ships of Force H would return to Gibraltar. The Italians knew from their Intelligence reports roughly what was happening and the battleships *Vittorio Veneto* and *Giulio Cesare*, six cruisers and 11 destroyers were available to attack the convoy. They were, however, ordered to remain within range of air cover from Sardinia and, if possible, lure the warships of Force H to within easy striking distance of the Sardinian airfields.

At 0956 on 27 November, with Force H some 100 miles west of La Galite Island, *Ark Royal*'s Swordfish reported the presence of five enemy cruisers and five destroyers to the north-east. *Renown*, *Sheffield*, *Manchester* and *Southampton* increased speed towards the enemy force. At 1200 smoke from the enemy cruisers was sighted and five minutes later *Sheffield*'s lookouts sighted three of the enemy ships, which altered course eastward towards Sardinia. At 1218 the two Italian battleships were sighted and within a matter of minutes they had opened fire on Force H; at the same time they too steamed east to bring themselves within range of air cover. At 1224 *Sheffield* opened fire on the left hand cruiser and increased speed to 31 knots to give chase. At this point Force D, consisting of *Ramillies*, *Berwick* and *Newcastle*, had joined from the east and the five cruisers, *Sheffield*, *Manchester*, *Southampton*, *Newcastle* and *Berwick*, were charging in line abreast at 30 knots towards the enemy at a range of 22,000 yards. At 1230 *Sheffield* launched her Walrus in order to carry out spotting duties for *Renown*, and although it took off safely it suffered damage from the blast of the cruiser's own guns. In the event *Southampton*, despite the fact that she was laden with RAF personnel, hit and badly damaged the destroyer *Lanciere*, but *Berwick* suffered a direct hit to 'Y' turret, which caused casualties and knocked out both guns. At 1302 two French passenger ships crossed through the battle area, but by 1320 the enemy force had withdrawn out of range and Somerville, realising that not only was his force being drawn into a dangerous position where they would be vulnerable to attack from the air, but the three merchant ships, which were covered only by *Coventry* and the destroyers, were also dangerously exposed to air attack, ordered his force to return to the convoy. Without doubt this was the correct decision, for less than an hour later large formations of Italian high-level bombers began to attack the convoy. Fortunately, no damage was caused to either the convoy or escorts, and at 1930, with darkness having fallen, the force split as planned, with the convoy, including *Manchester* and *Southampton*, continuing eastwards and Force H, with *Ramillies* and *Newcastle*, steaming westward. During the afternoon of 29 November Force H, including *Sheffield*, arrived back in Gibraltar to an enthusiastic welcome. The action, which became known as the Battle of Cape Spartivento, had succeeded in delivering the convoy unscathed and in repulsing enemy air attacks. However, for Somerville there came the unwelcome news that, before he had even submitted his report on the operation, Churchill, who wished to replace him with Rear-Admiral Henry Harwood, the hero of the River Plate action, had ordered a Board of Inquiry into why he had called off the pursuit of the enemy battlefleet. In the event the Inquiry found in Somerville's favour and he was not replaced.

Meanwhile, *Sheffield*'s ship's company enjoyed a six-day break in Gibraltar before, on 5 December, she sailed into the Atlantic Ocean to make another patrol in the area around the Azores. Two days into the patrol, 200 miles west of Cape St Vincent, she came across a drifting lifeboat from the recently scuttled 5,848-ton German steamer *Klaus Schoke*. She also carried out a search for the 8,777-ton German merchantman, SS *Madrid*, which had been reported as attempting to run the blockade in an effort to get back to her home port of Bremen. There was also the ever-present threat posed by the heavy cruiser *Admiral Scheer* which, just a few weeks previously, had sunk the armed merchant cruiser *Jervis Bay* and wreaked havoc on the transatlantic convoy HX84. In the event the search for *Madrid* was unsuccessful and on 15 December the cruiser returned to Gibraltar. Once again, however, there was only a short respite for *Sheffield* and on 20 December, with *Renown* (flag), *Ark Royal* and 11 destroyers, she sailed east into the Mediterranean in order to rendezvous with and escort the battleship *Malaya*, five destroyers and the returning merchantmen *Clan Forbes* and *Clan Fraser*, on their westward passage from Malta. Leaving Gibraltar at nightfall the force initially steamed west, but after dark they reversed their course and steamed east and into the Mediterranean. On 22 December the westbound force was met, and two days later they all arrived back in Gibraltar, with the only casualty being the destroyer *Hyperion* which was torpedoed off Cape Bon.

With less than 24 hours between operations, at 1310 on Christmas Day *Sheffield*, accompanied by *Renown*, *Ark Royal* and eight destroyers, was ordered to sea at short notice following a report that in the Atlantic a convoy of 20 ships, WS5A, was being attacked by a German heavy cruiser. In fact, during December *Admiral Hipper* had left Germany, broken through the Northern Blockade and entered the Atlantic, where she had made contact with WS5A some 700 miles off the Spanish coast. Fortunately, the convoy was being escorted by three cruisers, including *Berwick*, which had driven her off and raised the alarm. On board *Sheffield* Somerville had just addressed the ship's company, and was doing his light-hearted Christmas Day rounds of the messdecks when the alarm signal was received and the force sailed into a cold, wet and windy Atlantic storm. For five days, as the cruisers and *Renown* rounded up the scattered convoy, *Ark Royal*'s aircraft flew reconnaissance missions over a radius of some 150 miles, but there was no sign of the raider. Finally, in the early hours of 30 December the force returned to Gibraltar.

For *Sheffield* the new year of 1940-41 was spent alongside in Gibraltar, and it was the forenoon of 7 January before she put to sea again, this time as part of 'Operation Excess', which also included *Renown*, *Malaya*, *Ark Royal*, *Bonaventure* and ten destroyers. They were to escort a convoy of four merchant ships, one bound for Malta while the other three were heading for Piraeus as part of the ill-fated attempt to reinforce the Greek Army. Two days into the passage east *Sheffield* escorted *Ark Royal* ahead of the convoy in order to fly off five Swordfish aircraft bound for Malta. At noon that day, as they approached the narrows between Sicily and North Africa, the escort was reinforced by *Gloucester* and *Southampton* who had come out from Malta. That afternoon ten Italian Savoia SM 79 bombers attacked the force, concentrating on *Malaya*, but not causing any damage. During the evening of 9 January, having handed over the convoy to ships of the Mediterranean Fleet, Force H turned round and set course for the return to Gibraltar, where they arrived during the evening of 11 January. However, following the departure of Force H, the convoy had not fared so well and had come under heavy air attack during which both *Gloucester* and *Southampton* were damaged, the latter so badly she had to be sunk.

HMS *Sheffield*'s return to Gibraltar was followed by a very welcome and much-needed maintenance period, and it was during this time that some thought was given by the powers that be to sending *Sheffield* into the Eastern Mediterranean as a replacement for the lost *Southampton*. In the event, however, a combination of Somerville's determination to hang on to the cruiser as part of Force H and

Cunningham's preference for *Bonaventure* with her better anti-aircraft armament, meant that *Sheffield* remained with Force H, where she worked easily and efficiently with Somerville's flagship *Renown* and *Ark Royal*. By the end of the month *Sheffield*'s maintenance period was over and her next foray to sea began during the evening of 27 January when, in company with *Neptune*, she left Gibraltar to head out into the Atlantic to rendezvous with, and safely escort, a slow northbound convoy past Casablanca. Part of the convoy consisted of Vichy merchantmen which had been taken as prizes and it was thought that French warships from Casablanca might attempt to recover them, but after an uneventful three days, on 30 January, *Sheffield* returned to Gibraltar. No sooner had she secured alongside, however, than she was under sailing orders for 1330 the next day.

On 31 January, *Sheffield* accompanied *Renown*, *Malaya*, *Ark Royal* and a screen of ten destroyers to sea for the first British offensive action of the war against the Italian mainland. Code-named Operations 'Picket' and 'Result', the objectives were an air attack by aircraft from *Ark Royal* on the Tirso Dam in Sardinia, and the bombardment of the naval base at Genoa by *Renown* and *Malaya*, where it was thought there were two battleships and at least one heavy cruiser. Despite some atrocious weather, during the morning of 2 February eight Swordfish from *Ark Royal* attacked the dam, but with little success and the ferocious anti-aircraft fire led to the loss of one aircraft. With the weather worsening the proposed bombardment of Genoa was cancelled and on 4 February the ships of Force H returned to Gibraltar. The ferocity and preparedness of the Italian defences on Sardinia led to suspicions that there had been a security leak, and two days later when the same ships sailed for Genoa on 'Operation Grog', the postponed bombardment of the port, an elaborate subterfuge was used to make it appear that the force would be carrying out a sweep against Vichy French ships in the Western

HMS Sheffield *at sea in 1941. By then she was wearing a disruptive camouflage scheme and her AA armament and electronics outfit had been updated.* *(Syd Goodman Collection)*

Mediterranean. Passing between Ibiza and Majorca during the night of 7 February, the following night Force H passed within 50 miles of an Italian fleet, but both groups were unaware of the other's presence. Fortunately, the Italian air reconnaissance patrols failed to detect Force H, and in the early hours of 9 February 14 Swordfish aircraft from *Ark Royal* took off to attack the oil refinery at Leghorn (Livorno) while four more were to lay mines outside the harbour. At 0715 *Renown*, *Malaya* and *Sheffield* began an intensive bombardment of targets in and around Genoa, including an aircraft works, railway yards, factories and the city's docks, causing large explosions and fires. Where *Sheffield*'s 6-inch guns targeted factories and industrial installations, at least two huge explosions were seen. At 0745 the ships ceased fire and set course to rejoin *Ark Royal* for the return passage to Gibraltar, where they arrived during the afternoon of 11 February. The raid received a great deal of publicity in the British press, out of all proportion to the limited strategic value, but for a hard-pressed country which was suffering nightly air raids it was a morale booster.

Following her return from this action there was to be no respite for *Sheffield*, and just over 24 hours later she sailed on her next operation, this time into the Atlantic Ocean to assist with the search for the German battlecruisers *Gneisenau* and *Scharnhorst* which, earlier that month, had evaded the British blockade and broken out into the Atlantic, as well as to escort vulnerable convoys. First of all, with *Renown* and *Ark Royal*, she was ordered to protect two important convoys, the first of which, HG53 was made up of 21 ships, the largest of which was the ex-Cunarder White Star liner *Britannic*. She had left Gibraltar on 6 February and was due to arrive in the UK on 19 February. Reports of the German raiders at large in the Atlantic meant additional escorts were necessary. During this period at sea *Sheffield* also escorted convoy SLS64, a slow convoy of 19 ships which had left Sierra Leone on 29 January and was also due to arrive in the UK on 19 February. On 4 March she returned to Gibraltar to undergo a seven-day maintenance and dry docking period.

During the afternoon of 8 March, while *Malaya* was south-west of the Canary Islands, escorting a homeward-bound convoy, she sighted *Gneisenau*. The old battleship was far too slow to stand a chance of catching the German battlecruiser, which, in fact, was in company with *Scharnhorst*. The two enemy vessels were not taking any chances and they retired westwards, but *Malaya* sent an urgent signal requesting assistance. At the time *Sheffield* was high and dry in Gibraltar's No 1 dry dock, but the old battleship was quickly joined by *Renown*, *Ark Royal*, *Arethusa* and two destroyers. As for *Sheffield* it was 10 March before the dry dock was flooded and she was able to move alongside the sea wall. Next day she put to sea to join *Arethusa* and three destroyers to escort the P&O liner turned troopship SS *Strathmore* to the Clyde. The passage north passed without incident and at 1335 on Monday 17 March *Sheffield* anchored off Greenock. For a lucky few off-watch members of the ship's company there was just over four hours' shore leave granted that evening, but over the next three days most of the ship's company were able to get ashore for a short time. On 21 March *Sheffield* weighed anchor to join a fast troop convoy, which included the Union Castle liner *Dunotter Castle* and HM ships *Argus* and *Maidstone*, for the passage back to Gibraltar. In the event it was a slow, roundabout voyage south, with the convoy routed into mid-Atlantic, and it was the afternoon of 29 March before *Sheffield* secured alongside Gibraltar Dockyard's coaling wharf. Once again there was no respite, for no sooner had she berthed than she was once again under sailing orders and all shore leave was cancelled. Initially she had been ordered to put to sea at 2015, but severe weather conditions delayed her sailing and it was 2230 before she steamed through the breakwater. *Sheffield* and four accompanying destroyers had been ordered to intercept a convoy of four Vichy French merchant ships, which were being escorted by the destroyer *Simoun* en route from Casablanca to Oran. They had origi-

nally come from Saigon in what was then French Indo-China, and it was recognised that the interception of the French convoy would be a 'difficult and delicate' operation. However, it was considered important that one of them at least, the *Bangkok* which was believed to be carrying a cargo of rubber, should be prevented from docking and be escorted to Gibraltar. The operation was code-named 'Ration', but the operational order proved somewhat contradictory for it had been stated that French 'territorial waters should not be respected', but that there should be a desire to 'avoid creating an incident.' There was also an instruction that Spanish territorial waters were 'under no circumstances to be violated', which meant that the convoy could not be intercepted in or near to the Strait of Gibraltar. In the event *Sheffield* and the destroyers *Faulknor, Fearless, Forester* and *Fury* were ordered to intercept the convoy and escort *Bangkok* to Gibraltar or, if necessary, sink her. However, owing to severe gales *Sheffield* and the destroyers were delayed and it was not until 0840 on 30 March that they sighted the French convoy in a position 35°18'N 001°57'W, five to six miles from the port and anchorage at Nemours, Algeria (now Ghazaeuet), within 30 miles of the border with Spanish Morocco.

Weather conditions at the time of the first sightings were far too rough to contemplate the dispatch of boarding parties, and as the British ships approached the convoy *Simoun* employed delaying tactics by making a series of signals to *Sheffield*, while the French ships turned in towards the shore. Larcom was confident that once into calmer inshore waters he would be able to send a boarding party over to *Bangkok* and get her back to Gibraltar, but at 0945 the situation changed completely when a French 6-inch shore battery, situated close to the lighthouse at Nemours, opened fire on *Sheffield*. Its first salvo straddled the cruiser but *Sheffield* immediately replied with six main armament broadsides, which appeared to silence the battery. However, a few minutes later it opened fire once again, this time on the four destroyers, and *Sheffield* once again replied with her main armament. This time there was a heavy explosion and a fierce cordite fire, almost certainly the result of at least one direct hit on the battery's magazine. As Larcom stated in his report: '*The existence of shore defences was quite unknown to me and prevented any further delay. The alternatives were to withdraw, or sink* Simoun *and the convoy without more ado. I regarded the sinking of the convoy such a drastic step and likely to have such serious political consequences that I refrained, and at 0956 ordered all ships to withdraw.*'

During the passage back to Gibraltar the force was attacked three times by French Air Force bombers escorted by fighters and flying in waves of five. In the event *Forester* sustained hull damage and five casualties during the attacks, but at 2315 the force reached Gibraltar. Even before they returned, however, the Foreign Office in London had sent placatory telegrams to both the Spanish and US Governments telling them that an 'incident' had occurred between British and French forces but: '*In view of the action taken by the French batteries our warships would have been fully justified in firing on the French merchant ships and their escorts, but in the interests of humanity did not do so and the merchant ships succeeded in entering the port of Nemours.*' Although the government in London were critical of Larcom's decision to withdraw, the Foreign Office was quick to reassure Spain and the USA by playing down the incident, and as for Somerville at Gibraltar, he was well aware of the folly of adding the Vichy French to the enemies he was already fighting in the Mediterranean.

On 2 April, just three days after arriving back at Gibraltar, *Sheffield* was at sea once again, this time with *Renown*, *Ark Royal* and five destroyers, to steam east to a point where the carrier could fly off 12 Hurricane fighters to Malta. This operation was completed satisfactorily and during the afternoon of 4 April *Sheffield* and the rest of the force returned to Gibraltar. No sooner had the cruiser secured alongside, however, than she was once again preparing

HMS Sheffield *in a scheme comprising white, blue and shades of grey. She appeared as such during most of 1941/42. (Steve Bush Collection)*

for sea and at 1940 the same evening, in company with *Renown*, *Ark Royal*, *Furious* and four destroyers, she put to sea again. Somerville's judgement regarding the wisdom of not sinking the Vichy French ships was proved correct, for Intelligence reports were received that a heavy air raid against Force H ships at Gibraltar was imminent and so to avoid unnecessary damage he put to sea. At the same time the opportunity was taken to exchange ten Fulmars from the newly arrived *Furious* with ten of *Ark Royal*'s Skuas. The exchange of aircraft took place during the forenoon of 5 May, and at just after midnight the next day Force H returned to Gibraltar. In the event the French air raid did not take place, but Somerville could take no chances with his fleet. Once again, however, *Sheffield*'s time alongside in Gibraltar was limited and at 0405, less than three hours after her return, she had refuelled and put to sea once again. A signal had been received that *Gneisenau* and *Scharnhorst* were at sea and so *Sheffield* joined *Renown*, *Ark Royal*, *Fiji* and three destroyers to patrol the Bay of Biscay. *Sheffield*'s patrol lasted until the forenoon of 14 April, when she returned to Gibraltar.

For *Sheffield* and the rest of Force H mid-April brought some short but welcome relief from the constant operations at sea, and the cruiser had a full six days to carry out essential maintenance. On 20 April she left Gibraltar as escort to *Argus*, which had brought out Hurricane aircraft from the UK for transfer to *Ark Royal* and onward dispatch to Malta. *Sheffield* returned to Gibraltar during the morning of 24 April, and just 16 hours later, in company with *Renown*, *Ark Royal* and 13 destroyers, she sailed on 'Operation Dunlop' which took the force east into the Mediterranean. During the morning of 27 April *Ark Royal* flew off 24 Hurricanes and three Fulmars bound for Malta, after which the force returned to Gibraltar. Next morning, when they were some ten hours' steaming from their base, one of the carrier's Fulmars crashed into the sea. *Sheffield* was ordered to search the crash area, and after an hour she spotted a raft with two survivors. Later that afternoon, after returning to Gibraltar, the cruiser was taken

into No 2 dry dock for a very overdue docking period to repair the hull damage which had been caused by French bombers at the end of March.

For the Royal Navy's ships during the Second World War, refits which in peacetime would have lasted for weeks, were usually completed in a matter of days, and so it was for *Sheffield* in early 1941. By 2000 on 2 May she was back alongside Gibraltar's Coaling Wharf and three days later she was once again putting to sea. Initially she sailed west into the Atlantic Ocean to rendezvous with the battleship *Queen Elizabeth*, which had steamed north from Freetown, and a convoy from the Clyde which was carrying tanks and vital heavy equipment for Wavell's Army of the Nile. Passing through the Strait of Gibraltar that night the convoy was joined by the rest of Force H, including *Renown*, *Ark Royal*, *Gloucester* and six destroyers, as well as *Sheffield*, *Queen Elizabeth, Naiad* and *Fiji*, the latter three being reinforcements for the Mediterranean Fleet. The first enemy bombing raid came at 1345 on 8 May when eight Italian torpedo-bombers attacked the fleet. One torpedo came within yards of hitting *Renown* before its motors failed, and two of the aircraft were shot down. This raid was quickly followed by more bombing attacks, the last of which took place at 2030, but, fortunately, there were no hits. It was during the final attack that an explosion in P2 gun on board *Renown* killed six ratings and badly wounded an officer and a further 25 ratings. At the same time *Queen Elizabeth, Fiji, Gloucester* and *Naiad*, together with a destroyer screen and the five merchant ships of the convoy, parted company for Malta, and during the evening of 12 May Force H arrived back at Gibraltar.

After a break of four days *Sheffield* carried out exercises and manoeuvres in the Gibraltar area, during which she provided a target for Swordfish pilots practising torpedo attacks. During the evening of 17 May she returned to Gibraltar's Coaling Wharf to enjoy a 31-hour break after which she was due to begin operations again. Meanwhile, in northern waters the powerful German battleship *Bismarck*, together with the cruiser *Prinz Eugen,* had left the Baltic port of Gdynia in the Gulf of Danzig heading for the Norwegian port of Bergen. Grand-Admiral Raeder had planned to have four major surface warships capable of launching raids on British convoys in the Atlantic and, indeed, their very presence there would tie up most major units of the Royal Navy's Home Fleet and prevent any meaningful reinforcements in the Mediterranean and Far East. The sailing of the two German ships had not gone unnoticed as the Swedish cruiser *Gotland* had sighted the pair and passed on a report to London, thereby alerting the C-in-C Home Fleet at Scapa Flow. Back at Gibraltar, however, there did not appear to be any immediate cause for alarm and early on 19 May *Sheffield* accompanied *Renown*, *Ark Royal*, *Furious* and six destroyers on 'Operation Splice', the delivery of 47 Hurricanes and four Fulmars to Malta. The aircraft were flown off at 0600 on 21 May, after which Force H returned to Gibraltar where *Sheffield* arrived alongside at 0100 on 23 May.

Back in northern waters, at noon that day *Bismarck* and *Prinz Eugen* were sailing north of Iceland and had entered the Denmark Strait. That evening the cruiser *Suffolk* sighted the two German ships and, together with *Norfolk*, shadowed them. At just after midnight on 22 May *Hood, Prince of Wales* and six destroyers left Scapa Flow to make for Hvalfjord, from where they would be in a good position to cover whichever route the enemy ships took. *Hood* and *Prince of Wales* were within hours of arriving at the Icelandic fjord when they were ordered to cover the area south-west of Iceland, and by the evening of 23 May they were racing for the Denmark Strait in their doomed attempt to intercept the German warships. Next morning, at 0305 on Saturday 24 May, *Renown*, *Ark Royal*, *Sheffield* and six destroyers left Gibraltar to escort a southbound convoy, and were ordered at the same time to remain on the alert in the event that *Bismarck* and *Prinz Eugen* somehow managed to evade the British blockade. At a few minutes past 0600, however, *Hood* and *Prince of Wales* made contact with the German ships. *Hood*, the 22-year-old outdated and virtually obsolete pride of the Royal Navy, was

hit and blown up and the new, but unworked-up *Prince of Wales*, was damaged. The loss of *Hood* was a severe shock to the British public, but in reality she was an elderly and vulnerable battlecruiser. The myth and public sentiment which, between 1919 and 1941, had surrounded the 'Mighty *Hood*' had somehow been defrauded.The loss of *Hood* and the breakout of the two German ships into the Atlantic galvanised the Royal Navy into action, with all air and naval resources diverted in a search for the enemy vessels. Swordfish aircraft from *Victorious* were able to launch an attack on *Bismarck* and the pilots reported that she appeared to be leaking oil. This was the result of a hit by *Prince of Wales* during the Denmark Strait action and although the damage was not serious it was to have a decisive effect. Soon afterwards however, contact was lost.

The C-in-C Home Fleet, Admiral Sir John Tovey, had rightly guessed that whatever damage *Bismarck* had sustained she would require dockyard facilities to carry out repairs, and that the two most likely destinations for these to be undertaken were either Brest or St Nazaire. Although the 14-inch shell fired by *Prince of Wales* had not exploded, it had penetrated two oil fuel tanks and isolated other fuel tanks resulting in a loss of speed. *Bismarck* was also down slightly by the head, she had a list of some 9 degrees to port and she was leaving a tell-tale trail of oil in her wake. She was in need of urgent repairs and it was not long before decoded signals from the German battleship showed that she was indeed making for north-western France. At 1100 on 25 May Somerville received an urgent signal telling him to assume that *Bismarck* was heading for France, and by 2000 that day Force H was at sea and approaching the southern end of the Bay of Biscay. Although the ships were suffering fuel shortages they were in the best position to intercept *Bismarck*. Somerville was also aware that *Gneisenau* and *Scharnhorst* might also take the opportunity to leave Brest and attempt to join the powerful German battleship. At this stage Somerville was steaming through some very stormy weather which not only slowed his force down, but also made air reconnaissance difficult. By 0700 on 26 May, Force H was south-west of Ireland and half an hour later, despite heavy seas which in peacetime would have 'grounded' the aircraft, *Ark Royal* launched her first air reconnaissance patrols. At 1110, to quote *Sheffield*'s official log: '*Aircraft reported one battleship 120 miles to westward*', which made it clear that Force H was within striking distance of *Bismarck*. At 1145 *Sheffield* took station astern of *Ark Royal* and there she remained until 1325 when she was detached to '*close and shadow* Bismarck.' For some reason the signal was missed by *Ark Royal*, with what might easily have been very serious consequences.

After leaving *Renown* and *Ark Royal*, *Sheffield* increased speed to 31 knots and by 1600 she was some 15 to 20 miles from the German battleship. The aircrew of the 15 Swordfish which had been launched to attack *Bismarck* were, however, unaware that there were any other ships in the vicinity and at 1645 the understated entry in *Sheffield*'s log reads: '*Attacked in error with torpedoes by nine Swordfish aircraft. Courses and speeds as required to take avoiding action. No damage.*' In bad weather and not being aware of *Sheffield*'s presence so close to *Bismarck*, all but a handful of the pilots had mistaken the cruiser for the battleship. Captain Larcom had ordered his anti-aircraft gunners to hold fire while he manoeuvred the cruiser at high speed to comb the torpedo tracks, which he accomplished successfully. This unfortunate case of mistaken identity did highlight the fact that the duplex magnetic pistols with which the torpedoes were armed were exploding prematurely, and after refuelling and rearming the 15 Swordfish were launched again, this time with their torpedoes set to run at a depth of 22 feet, and armed with contact pistols. This time they had orders to locate and make contact with *Sheffield* before launching their attack on *Bismarck*.

Meanwhile, having survived the attack by *Ark Royal*'s aircraft, *Sheffield* steamed closer to *Bismarck*'s position until, at 1740 at a distance of

some ten miles, she sighted the German battleship and began to shadow her. Meanwhile, despite the appalling weather conditions, the second Swordfish strike on *Bismarck* found the target and flew in to attack. The battleship put up a formidable anti-aircraft barrage, including firing its 15-inch guns on a flat trajectory in order to put up what was literally a solid wall of water through which the attacking aircraft had to fly. As is now well known this attack, which lasted for over an hour, was pressed home with great courage and determination and two of the torpedoes found their mark. The first hit the battleship at the stern, seriously damaging the tiller flat and jamming her rudders at hard-a-starboard. The great battleship was no longer manoeuvrable, for although her engines were intact she could not be steered and she was unable to hold a course. She was, in fact, steaming in large circles. At 2107 three of the attacking Swordfish passed over *Sheffield* on their way back to the aircraft carrier; just over 20 minutes later the cruiser once again sighted *Bismarck*, apparently making smoke. At 2137, however, the German battleship suddenly emerged from her own smokescreen, having closed the range to about nine miles. Almost immediately, in the darkening sky pinprick flashes could be seen coming from *Bismarck* and seconds later came the scream of six salvoes of 15-inch shells, all of them accurately ranged, which straddled the cruiser with near misses. The splinters from the exploding missiles wounded 14 members of *Sheffield*'s company, three of them critically. At this stage Larcom had to quickly retire under cover of his own smokescreen as the cruiser moved out of range, and *Sheffield*'s contact with *Bismarck* was lost. During the night *Bismarck* was harried by destroyers, who at intervals fired starshell in order to indicate the battleship's position. At 0100 on 27 May, on board *Sheffield*, Ordinary Seaman D. T. George, having been critically wounded by one of *Bismarck*'s salvoes, died of his injuries.

At 0655 on 27 May, as soon as dawn broke, *Ark Royal* flew off a reconnaissance patrol and at 0844, with *King George V* and *Rodney* having arrived and manoeuvred into a position where they could open fire to finish off the crippled German battleship, *Sheffield* and *Renown* were ordered to close the enemy. *Renown*, which suffered similar hull weaknesses to those which had proved fatal to *Hood*, was ordered not to engage *Bismarck* before the arrival of *King George V* and *Rodney*. At 0955, when both British battleships were engaging and battering *Bismarck* with 14- and 16-inch salvoes, *Renown* was able to join the action. Finally, at 1036 the crippled and helpless German battleship was sunk by torpedoes from *Dorsetshire*. Fortunately, *Bismarck*'s steering gear had been disabled before she got within easy range of shore-based aircraft, but enemy planes did appear and at 0956, as *Sheffield*'s log states: '*Opened fire on enemy aircraft.*' By 1010, however, Force H had set course for Gibraltar. That evening a second member of *Sheffield*'s ship's company, Able Seaman A Ling, died of his wounds and finally, at 1340 on 28 May, Able Seaman A. C. Taylor succumbed to wounds that he received when splinters from *Bismarck*'s near misses had hit the ship. At 1050 on 29 May, in a position 36°12'N 008°16'W, as she approached the Strait of Gibraltar, *Sheffield* slowed down for a funeral service before she once again took station on *Ark Royal*. At 1334 *Sheffield*'s Walrus aircraft L2228 was launched to take correspondence to the flagship *Renown*, then to carry on to North Front at Gibraltar. She carried a crew of three, plus a passenger who was bound for Gibraltar in order to pick up the ship's mail. Five minutes after launching, as the aircraft passed over *Renown* to drop the correspondence, it is thought it passed through the hot gases from the battlecruiser's funnel uptakes which caused the pilot, Lieutenant (P) B. A. H. Brooks RN, to lose control of the machine, strike *Renown*'s stern awning tripod and crash into the sea. The pilot, his observer, Lieutenant (A) A. Nedwill and the RAF crewman, Ldg Aircraftsman J. A. Seville, were all killed instantly. The only survivor was the passenger, RPO J. W. B. Marjoram, who was picked up by the destroyer *Wishart*, but he died later of his injuries. At 1900 *Sheffield* secured alongside

38 berth at Gibraltar; for her the mission to hunt and sink *Bismarck* had proved costly.

HMS *Sheffield*'s return to Gibraltar brought five days of relaxation for the ship's company before, on 3 June, she put to sea for the day to carry out gunnery exercises. Two days later, at 1020 on 5 June, in company with *Renown*, *Ark Royal*, *Furious* and a destroyer screen, she left Gibraltar to steam east as part of 'Operation Rocket', a mission to fly off 43 Hurricanes and three Fulmars to reinforce the air defences of Malta. Next forenoon the aircraft took off from the carriers and by 0900 on 7 June the force had returned safely to Gibraltar. However, that evening, with Intelligence reports indicating that Vichy French aircraft were about to launch an attack on Gibraltar, Force H sailed west into the Atlantic. Two days later *Sheffield* detached from the main force to search an area in mid-Atlantic, west of Biscay, for a German oil tanker which was known to have left St Nazaire some two weeks earlier, and was thought to be biding her time before attempting to break through the Northern Patrol. *Sheffield*'s search bore fruit when, at 1722 on 12 June, in a position 44°10'N 019°55'W, she sighted what appeared at first to be a Panamanian oil tanker with the name *Leda* painted on her bow. By 1820 *Sheffield* had positively identified the tanker as her quarry, the German *Friedrich Breme*, and she steamed to overhaul her. At 1915 the cruiser went to Action Stations and she signalled the tanker to stop, adding, '*If you scuttle will open fire.*' Within minutes, however, it was apparent that the oil tanker was settling in the water and her crew were swinging the boats out to abandon ship. At 1943 *Sheffield* opened fire with 17 salvoes from her main armament and at 2000 the tanker sank. It was almost two hours later before the cruiser had rescued and taken on board some 88 survivors, including 12 who had been wounded by the gunfire. She then set course for Scapa Flow and Rosyth, arriving at the latter on 20 June where the prisoners were disembarked and the wounded were transferred to a hospital ship. Next day *Sheffield* was taken into dockyard hands to undergo a seven-week refit.

On 22 June 1941, the day after *Sheffield*'s refit began, the course of the European war was changed drastically and, although it was far from obvious at the time, the scene was set for Germany's eventual defeat. Three German Army Groups, consisting of over 3,000,000 men, 3,350 tanks and 3,000 aircraft, the largest military force ever assembled for military operations, in what was code-named 'Operation Barbarossa', invaded the Soviet Union. In 1939 British politicians had desperately wanted the Soviet Union as an ally, but ideological differences had inhibited them and Stalin had not taken seriously the low-key British and French attempts to form some sort of alliance. Now Britain, with its back firmly against the wall, and the Soviet Union, which for at least another 18 months would be in the same position, were fighting a common enemy. Eventually the epic battle for Stalingrad (Volgograd) would see the Red Army decisively break the military power of Germany, but all Britain could contribute in mid-1941 was to ship weapons (mainly American) and supplies to hard-pressed Russia.

Meanwhile, back at Rosyth, on 2 August 1941, Captain A. W. Clarke RN superseded Larcom in command of *Sheffield* and eight days later the cruiser left the dockyard to anchor in midstream. On 12 August she sailed for Scapa Flow to carry out an eight-day work-up period and on 29 August, after completing her exercises for the day, *Sheffield* steamed south to Greenock from where, at 0035 on the last day of the month, she sailed with *Repulse*, *Furious, Cairo, Derbyshire* and a destroyer screen, bound for Gibraltar and Cape Town. No sooner had they left Greenock, however, than the elderly *Furious* began to suffer engine problems and *Sheffield* escorted her back to Belfast Lough. Two days later, with repairs completed, she saw the elderly carrier back to the convoy to continue the passage south to Gibraltar. *Sheffield*, meanwhile, was ordered back to Scapa Flow where she arrived two days later. By 11 September the cruiser was once again back at Greenock and preparing to act as escort to another convoy, this time into the

HMS Sheffield *in a revised camouflage scheme following her 1942 refit.* *(Steve Bush Collection)*

Mediterranean for an operation code-named 'Halberd', the purpose of which was to attempt the safe passage of eight merchant ships, together with HMS *Breconshire*, the fleet supply ship which would be carrying ammunition and stores, to Malta. First of all *Sheffield* made a fast, independent passage to Gibraltar which passed without incident, although off Cape St Vincent she encountered a number of drifting lifeboats and life-rafts which, on closer inspection, turned out to be empty.

After arriving alongside at Gibraltar during the afternoon of 17 September *Sheffield* spent four days alongside, during which time the convoy escorts formed up for, as would repeatedly be the case, a formidable naval force was required to escort just a handful of merchant ships to ensure that Malta was kept supplied and reinforced. During 'Halberd' the nine merchantmen[2] would be escorted by two groups of warships. Group 1, the ships of Force H, would consist of *Nelson* (FOH), *Ark Royal*, *Hermione* and six destroyers. Group 2 was made up of *Prince of Wales* (FO2, HF), *Rodney*, *Kenya* (CS10) *Edinburgh* (CS18), *Sheffield*, *Euryalus* and 12 destroyers. The convoy was to keep close company with Group 2, which left Gibraltar during the forenoon of 20 September and steamed westward until 2130, when its course was reversed and it passed through the Strait under cover of darkness and rendezvoused with the convoy during the morning of 22 September. It was five days later, during the afternoon of 27 September, that the first air attacks began, and by that time the convoy was in a position 37°48'N 008°40'E, off the Tunisian coast. At 1255 radar indications showed two formations of torpedo-bombers approaching, one from the east and the other from the north. Although one aircraft was shot down by *Ark Royal*'s fighters the remainder got through and although there were

[2] The merchant ships were: *Imperial Star, Rowallan Castle, Clan MacDonald, Clan Ferguson, Ajax, Leinster, City of Lincoln, Dunedin Star* and *City of Calcutta*.

some near misses, none of their torpedoes hit their targets. A second attack at 1327 was more deadly, for although the aircraft was shot down by either *Prince of Wales*'s or *Sheffield*'s anti-aircraft gunners, one of its torpedoes hit *Nelson*'s port bow and reduced her speed to 18 knots. Within minutes a third attack developed, but this time there was no damage to the convoys or escorts. That evening, between 2000 and 2040, there were four more torpedo-bomber attacks and the sharp manoeuvring of the ships caused two merchantmen, *Rowallan Castle* and *City of Calcutta*, to collide, but neither ship was seriously damaged. At 2027 came the fourth and final air attack of the day and during this raid *Imperial Star* was hit on her port side aft, with the explosion blowing away both her propeller and her rudder. Another torpedo that dropped on *Sheffield*'s port bow forced the cruiser to make a successful emergency turn to port in order to avoid it. Attempts were made to take *Imperial Star* in tow, but in the absence of large tugs this proved impossible and the destroyer *Oribi* was ordered to sink her with depth charges and gunfire. At 1212 next day *Sheffield* arrived in Malta's Grand Harbour and that evening, after embarking 83 Army and RAF officers, she left Malta to make a fast passage to Greenock. The voyage was broken for an hour on 3 October when the cruiser stopped and sent a boarding party to inspect the Portuguese merchantman, SS *Alforarede*. Three days later she anchored off Greenock and from there she steamed north to Scapa Flow.

During the last two weeks of October *Sheffield* completed her much delayed work-up, and on the last day of the month, in company with *Edinburgh*, she sailed north to Iceland's Hvalfjord. During November, in atrocious weather conditions, both cruisers patrolled the waters between Iceland and the Shetland Islands, and on 30 November *Sheffield* left Seydisfjord to escort her first Arctic convoy to Russia's Kola Inlet. The passage east through icy-cold waters, in almost permanent darkness and through blinding snowstorms, passed without incident and after eight days at anchor in the desolate Kola Inlet she made a fast, independent passage back to Scapa Flow whose own bleak shores then seemed a very welcome sight. *Sheffield* did not stray too far from Scapa Flow until early in 1942 when, on 17 January, in company with the battleship *King George V*, which was flying the flag of Rear-Admiral Sir Stuart Bonham Carter, she steamed north to Hvalfjord. Four days later, the C-in-C Home Fleet, Admiral Sir John Tovey, paid a brief visit to the ship. During the weeks which followed the cruiser resumed her patrols of the waters between Iceland and the Shetland Islands, escorted a supply convoy to Iceland and escorted minelayers in their operations off the north coast of Norway. At 1100 on 2 March *Sheffield* left Hvalfjord to patrol the waters around Iceland. She steamed into strong winds and heavy seas and two days later, as she approached Seydisfjord to refuel, a mine passed very close down the starboard side of the ship. Fortunately, the device did not explode and two hours later she was alongside an RFA and pumping started. By 1800 she had taken on 259 tons of FFO and at 1815 she cast off from the RFA and left harbour to resume her patrol. At 2119 she was off the south-east corner of Iceland when, suddenly, there was a huge explosion on the port side aft, which tore a large hole some 35 feet long in the side of the ship, flooding the Commander's Cabin Flat. Miraculously there was only one serious casualty, Marine F. W. Wint, who was the keyboard sentry in the Captain's Cabin Flat. Sadly he died of his injuries early the next morning. For a time the cruiser was not under control, and the two destroyers *Eskimo* and *Faulknor* circled her to provide an anti-submarine screen. At 2156 *Sheffield* managed to get under way and she began the slow return to Seydisfjord, where she anchored just before midday the next day. It was clear that without temporary repairs *Sheffield* would not be able to steam home, but facilities at the Icelandic anchorage were very limited. However, despite the lack of equipment, over the next three weeks the ship's company worked hard to clear and cut away wreckage, and used cement to shore up and strengthen bulkheads

as well as building cofferdams. Wooden planking was provided by the Army, much of which was used to cover the gaping hole in the ship's hull. Finally, on 27 March, having carried out six hours of sea trials over two days, with the destroyer *Ledbury* acting as ocean escort and an RAF Catalina flying boat providing air cover, *Sheffield* left Seydisfjord to make a 48-hour passage to Scapa Flow. Once she was safely at anchor CS18 hauled down his flag and after another survey, further strengthening work was carried out to the ship's hull. On 1 April *Sheffield* left Scapa Flow to make a 30-hour passage to the River Tyne where, at 1845 on 2 April, she secured alongside Tynemouth Wharf.

During the three and a half months that *Sheffield* spent in dockyard hands at Hebburn-on-Tyne there were major changes to the ship's company, with many old and experienced hands leaving the ship. On 3 July a draft of 291 ratings arrived on board, mainly seamen and engine room ratings, all of whom were newly recruited 'Hostilities Only' conscripts. On 11 July *Sheffield* was shifted from dry dock to the Tyne Commission Quay and five days later, at 2108 on 16 July, the collier *Shearwater*, which was being manoeuvred in the river, collided with the cruiser's port waist, tearing away the refuse chute and denting the ship's side armour. Fortunately, the damage was superficial and it did not hold up the progress of repairs. On 19 July the main engines were turned as the ship underwent a basin trial, and next day *Sheffield* left the River Tyne to make an eight-hour passage to Rosyth where the refit was completed. Finally, on 24 July she arrived back at Scapa Flow where she rejoined the 18th Cruiser Squadron.

For the first five weeks of her return to operational service *Sheffield* carried out an intensive period of work-up exercises, often in company with *Aurora*, *Scylla*, *Jamaica* and *Suffolk*, and in the first week of August there was some relaxation when a travelling ENSA party entertained the ship's company. Otherwise there was little respite from the seemingly endless days of training exercises in and around the waters of Scapa Flow. On 1 September the training took on a new aspect when *Sheffield* joined the battleships *Anson* and *King George V* to practise naval gunfire support, by bombarding targets on Cape Wrath. Five days later there was a change of scenery when *Sheffield* was ordered south to Greenock, where she embarked 14 Norwegian Army and Naval personnel. She then steamed via Hvalfjord to Isfjord on the island of Spitsbergen, where the Norwegians were disembarked for the nearby radio station at Barentsburg. By 22 September the cruiser had returned to Hvalfjord where, next day, she once again became the flagship of the 18th Cruiser Squadron when Vice-Admiral Bonham Carter hoisted his flag. For the next three weeks the cruiser continued to exercise close to Scapa Flow, but on 5 October there was a reorganisation of the cruiser squadrons, which coincided with the departure of Bonham Carter to his next appointment as FO2 at Malta, and the arrival of Rear-Admiral Harcourt, of River Plate fame; he hoisted his flag in *Sheffield*, which then became the flagship of the 10th Cruiser Squadron, which included all the Home Fleet's cruisers. On 10 October there was a visit and pep talk by a government minister, the austere Sir Stafford Cripps, and ten days later *Sheffield* sailed south to Greenock.

At Greenock there was no leave for the ship's company as *Sheffield* began preparing for her role in 'Operation Torch', the American-led invasion of north-west Africa, with troop landings at Morocco and Algeria. After 24 hours on the Clyde the cruiser sailed for Belfast Lough where she arrived during the afternoon of 24 October. During her three days at anchor *Sheffield* took on board huge quantities of US military stores and equipment; during the afternoon of 26 October the reason for this became clear when she embarked 49 US Navy personnel and 614 men of the US Army's 135th Regiment for the purposes of the 'Torch' landings code-named 'Terminal Force'. *Sheffield* left Belfast Lough during the middle watch of 27 October, and by the forenoon she was on station with the 'Torch' invasion force. The huge convoy had come together off the north-west coast of Ireland and as well as small

HMS Sheffield *in 1942. She is fitted with Type 281 air search radar at the top of the masts and Type 273 surface search radar behind the main DCT.* *(Syd Goodman Collection)*

escort vessels and supply transports, it contained 12 former crack passenger liners including P&O's *Viceroy of India, Strathnaver* and *Mooltan*, each of which was carrying thousands of troops. In order to minimise the risk of a successful submarine or air attack, the ships steamed out almost into mid-Atlantic before turning south, and on 3 November *Sheffield* was detached to make a fast, 36-hour passage to Gibraltar to refuel. She arrived during the morning of 5 November and once alongside the south mole severe restrictions were placed on the movement of the US Army personnel, forbidding them access to the upper decks. That evening, at 1935, *Sheffield* steamed out of Gibraltar, this time with the elderly aircraft carrier *Argus* for company. After steaming back into the Atlantic to join the other ships *Sheffield* then continued the passage in company with the main convoy, which took her back through the Strait of Gibraltar, and during the afternoon of 7 November, when she was off the coast of Morocco, rendezvoused with the destroyers *Broke* and *Malcolm*. Then, at between 1615 and 1718, she carried out a remarkably efficient and well-executed transfer by landing craft and tenders of the 614 US Army personnel to the two destroyers. *Sheffield* then rejoined the convoy which was bound for Algiers where, with *Bermuda*, she was to have bombarded and silenced the defensive guns of the fort at Cape Matifu. However, when she arrived off the Cape the fort, and, in fact, the entire Algiers garrison, had surrendered and *Sheffield* joined *Scylla, Argus* and *Avenger* to escort a convoy of three troopships from Algiers Bay to the port of Bougie (now Bejiäi). Arriving in Bougie Bay well before daylight on 11 October, they found the area swarming with invasion traffic and at 0346 the Algerine-class minesweeper *Cadmus*, steaming at speed, collided with the cruiser's port side, scraping alongside the side of the ship. Although damage to *Sheffield* was confined to superficial scrapes, one of the ship's boiler room personnel, Stoker A. Spong, who was on the hangar deck getting a breath of

fresh air, was killed. That forenoon *Sheffield* stopped in Bougie Bay, and during the afternoon she was ordered to join Force O and return to Gibraltar. At 1530 that afternoon the body of Stoker Spong was committed to the deep and three days later the cruiser secured alongside at Gibraltar. This was only a brief stopover, however, for 12 hours later she was ordered to return home, and on 20 November she anchored in Scapa Flow.

Having been at sea on operations for some four weeks with hardly a break, some respite was now to be had while essential maintenance was carried out, but for the ship's company shore leave meant only the 'delights' of Scapa Flow with its beer canteen and rather makeshift cinema. During the first two weeks of December there were occasional days at sea, sometimes in company with the battleship *Anson*, and when Rear-Admiral R. Burnett (CS10) hoisted his flag on 13 December, it soon became clear that another major operation was planned. At 0515 the next day the cruiser weighed anchor and steamed south down Scotland's west coast to Loch Ewe, where she joined *Jamaica*, two destroyers and a convoy of merchant ships which had left Liverpool on 15 December. The convoy, designated JW51A, and escorts left Loch Ewe during 16 December and over the next eight days they made their way slowly, but safely, through rough and icy-cold weather into the Barents Sea to the Kola Inlet, where they arrived with their upper decks, superstructure and masts encrusted in thick ice. *Sheffield*'s passage home, again in company with *Jamaica* and this time escorting the empty westbound convoy, RA52, began during the afternoon of 27 December when they left the Kola Inlet, once again sailing into stormy and icy seas, with blinding snowstorms.

During the night of 30/31 December the stormy weather conditions eased somewhat, and at 0800 on the last day of December *Sheffield* was in a position 74°01'N 028°33'E. She was steaming some ten miles north of the convoy route in order that during short daylight hours, when there was some visibility, she would have the advantage of light over any enemy ships which might appear, and also so that she might avoid air reconnaissance which would lead enemy aircraft to the ships in the convoy. *Sheffield* was intending to sweep eastwards, covering the convoy from astern. The sky was overcast with cloud, there was a seven-to ten-knot northwesterly wind, the temperature was -9° Centigrade and, except for the armament, the ships masts and superstructure were covered in a thick coat of ice.

At the same time, steaming east towards the Kola Inlet was convoy JW51B, which had left Liverpool on 22 December and was being escorted by destroyers of the 17th Flotilla, including *Onslow* (Captain D17), *Obedient, Obdurate, Orwell, Achates* and two corvettes. By New Year's Eve the two convoys and their escorts were approaching to pass each other, with the Russian-bound convoy some 30 to 40 miles south-east of *Sheffield* and *Jamaica* and their empty homeward convoy. Meanwhile, at Altenfjord in northern Norway, the German Navy was putting together 'Operation Regenbogen', a detailed plan for an attack on convoy JW51B by the heavy cruisers *Admiral Hipper* and *Lützow*. Together with six destroyers, these two were to be dispatched to wreak havoc among the Arctic convoys. At 1240 on 30 December the submarine *U-354* sighted and reported the position of JW51B and at 1745, after darkness had fallen, the eight German ships put to sea. Although they were under orders to locate and destroy JW51B, they were also ordered to '*avoid a superior force*', an order which is generally thought to have led to overcaution. By the morning of 31 December the German force had located JW51B, but it was past 0900 before the German destroyers opened fire on the British destroyers escorting the eastbound merchant ships.

At 0858 on board *Sheffield* a radar contact was obtained bearing 320°, at a range of some eight and a half miles, and at 0904 a ship was dimly sighted. As the contact was 'suspicious' Burnett decided to track it. At 0932 gun flashes were sighted over the horizon to the south which at first were thought to be anti-aircraft fire. *Sheffield* continued to track the

original radar contact, but at 0946 further heavy gunfire was seen to the south, and shortly after this a report of three enemy destroyers was received by Captain (D) in *Onslow*. Burnett ordered *Sheffield* and *Jamaica* to haul round to 170° and increase speed to 25 knots towards the gunfire. By this time it was realised that the original radar contact had been stragglers from JW51B, and as *Sheffield* and *Jamaica* worked up to 31 knots Burnett signalled to Captain (D) that the two cruisers were approaching his position. At 1020, as they steered toward the action, Burnett saw two separate engagements taking place, one ahead and the other on the port bow. However, because of the smoke and poor light it was not possible to identify the ships taking part, but one large vessel was observed in the easternmost engagement. This ship was firing salvoes containing tracer and not using flashless cordite, so was almost certainly an enemy.

At 1030 *Sheffield*'s radar picked up another large ship bearing 180°, about ten miles away and steering east, then at 1032 another radar contact was made, this time some 16 miles away on the port bow, steering north-east and closing. Shortly afterwards the vessel was sighted and identified as larger than a destroyer, therefore it had to be the enemy. In his report Burnett referred to this ship as Target A, which was, in fact, *Hipper*. The second radar contact, which he refers to as Target B, was *Lützow* with two destroyers in company. At 1054 Target B made a large alteration of course to starboard, with which both *Sheffield* and *Jamaica* conformed, but the enemy ships were soon out of sight. At 1112 Burnett's two cruisers altered course to 190°, directly towards Target A, *Hipper*, which was seen to be firing to the eastward. At this time *Hipper*'s speed was thought to be 30 knots and at 1125, at a range of some 16,000 yards, *Sheffield* and *Jamaica* opened fire and almost immediately several hits were seen. In his report Burnett states: '*The enemy appeared to be taken unawares and did not open fire until after* Sheffield*'s fourth salvo. She appeared to be firing at* Jamaica, *her fire was very accurate but, unlike ours, was ineffective.*' At 1135 the enemy cruisers altered course into the cover of a smokescreen laid by the attendant destroyers. In fact, a 6-inch shell had hit *Hipper* and had penetrated her armoured belt on the starboard side, damaging a boiler, and reducing her speed to 23 knots. She had also been hit on the port side, starting a fire in the aircraft hangar. *Sheffield* and *Jamaica* both turned to follow the damaged *Hipper*, when an enemy destroyer was sighted approaching on *Sheffield*'s port bow. Burnett immediately ordered *Sheffield* to switch target to the destroyer, which was *Friedrich Eckoldt*; at a range of just 3,500 yards the destroyer was hit by the first salvo, and with the third salvo was heavily damaged. As *Sheffield* approached to within 1,000 yards, *Friedrich Eckoldt* could be seen to be down by the stern and blazing and, when fire was checked after the sixteenth salvo, a complete shambles. Passing within five cables, *Sheffield* engaged her with 4-inch armament and pom-poms, and when last seen the destroyer was still on fire, listing heavily and emitting red and white pyrotechnics. Before losing sight of her those on board *Sheffield* saw two large explosions, which almost certainly marked her end.

Throughout *Sheffield*'s action with *Friedrich Eckoldt*, *Jamaica* was engaging another of the enemy destroyers, *Richard Beitzen*, which quickly turned away and was lost to sight, thus avoiding her sister's fate and escaping intact. At 1154 *Sheffield* altered course back to the westward, and radar contact with *Lützow* was again made, but she also was retiring quickly. At 1223 *Sheffield* sighted two more German destroyers, which were in fact *Lützow*'s escorts, and as Burnett stated in his report: '*One of these destroyers challenged with a bright light, making LLL and later GGG; Sheffield replied with the same letter.*' While *Sheffield* targeted these destroyers, the cruiser's lookouts sighted another large ship, which was in fact *Lützow* herself, some nine to ten miles away. At 1229, with the range down to eight miles, *Sheffield* and *Jamaica* opened fire on her, but spotting conditions were difficult and four minutes later both cruisers came under fire from *Hipper* and *Lützow*; they were forced to alter

course away to avoid being engaged from both sides, and to avoid a torpedo attack from the German ships. Burnett continued to shadow the enemy force until 1400, but by then he was confident that the German ships were retiring. *Sheffield* and *Jamaica* continued to sweep the area around both convoys until well after dark, which in those latitudes was before 1600, and nothing more was seen of the enemy. The British cruisers had suffered some splinter damage, ten of *Sheffield*'s aerials had been shot away and *Jamaica*'s Type 273 radar aerial was damaged. However there had been no casualties in either of the ships. The powerful German attack on convoy JW51B had resulted in the sinking of the destroyer *Achates* and the minesweeper *Bramble*, with over 100 casualties. The destroyer *Onslow* had also been damaged and 17 men killed, but only one merchant ship had suffered damage and the convoy arrived safely at the Kola Inlet. The Battle of the Barents Sea was described by Admiral Tovey as '*...one of the finest examples in either of the two world wars of how to handle cruisers and destroyers in action with heavier forces*'. As for *Sheffield*, she and *Jamaica* arrived in Seydisfjord on 4 January 1943, and next day they made a fast eight-hour passage to Scapa Flow.

On 9 January *Sheffield* arrived in the River Clyde at Greenock, where she was de-ammunitioned before steaming upriver to Dalmuir Basin for repairs to the damage sustained in the Barents Sea. For the ship's company it was a welcome break, but on 18 January she arrived back at Scapa Flow. Later in the month, in icy-cold weather, she was once again in Arctic waters and this time operating out of the Icelandic port of Akureyri. With a destroyer flotilla and the battleship *Anson*, the force exercised a scenario whereby the powerful battleship *Tirpitz* was attempting to break through the blockade of the Denmark Strait as *Bismarck* had done almost two years earlier. On 11 February, however, *Sheffield* was back at Scapa Flow, and that evening a new commanding officer, Captain C. T. Addis RN, joined the ship. Three days later, having been prevented from landing by gale force winds which were sweeping northern Scotland, Captain Clarke left the ship and on 16 February *Sheffield* sailed from Scapa Flow to patrol the Norwegian Sea. During the forenoon of 19 February she ran into a severe storm, with wind speeds of up to 63 knots and huge waves, which caused serious structural damage to the ship, with half of A turret's top being torn away by the heavy seas. Next forenoon the cruiser anchored in Seydisfjord where, over a period of four days, temporary repairs were carried out. During the afternoon of 26 February *Sheffield* arrived in Greenock where de-storing and de-ammunitioning took place, and 11 days later, while in *Glasgow*'s Dalmuir Basin, she was handed over to John Brown & Co Ltd for emergency repairs and a 15-week refit.

During the refit the aircraft catapult was removed, although the cranes were retained, and additional 20mm Oerlikon anti-aircraft guns were fitted. The main hangar doors were blanked off, but the hangar structure itself which, since the loss of *Gloucester* off Crete, had been considered an attractive target for attacking aircraft, could not be removed altogether. On Sunday 6 June 1943, *Sheffield* slipped her moorings, was towed from Dalmuir Dock into the River Clyde and then steamed down to the Firth of Clyde to undergo machinery and degaussing trials, after which she returned to Glasgow's Princes Dock for final adjustments to her machinery. On 11 June she left the Clyde and next day arrived in Scapa Flow, where she joined the 10th Cruiser Squadron and her sisters *Belfast* (flag) and *Glasgow*. For six weeks after her return to operational duties *Sheffield* carried out work-up exercises in and around Scapa Flow. On 22 July Admiral Burnett (CS10) transferred his flag from *Belfast*, and two days later the cruiser steamed south to Plymouth Sound. After pausing just long enough to refuel she was at sea again, this time in the warmer waters of the Bay of Biscay and the Western Approaches, as she covered the arrivals and departures of convoys. During the forenoon of 29 July, when *Sheffield* was escorting convoy SL133 west of Ushant, several German Focke-Wulf 200

Condors attacked and bombed the convoy. Despite a heavy anti-aircraft barrage from *Sheffield* the bombers managed to get through, but fortunately none of their bombs hit their targets. Two days later the cruiser returned to Plymouth Sound, and in the first week of August she steamed up-harbour to the dockyard for a three-week maintenance and docking period. For the ship's company the spell in Plymouth was a welcome break from long periods at sea, and it was the end of August before the ship resumed her convoy escort duties in the Western Approaches.

Her resumption of patrol duties off south-west England did not last for long and on 21 September, after two nine-day patrols, she left Plymouth Sound for Malta. Pausing only for a refuelling stop at Gibraltar, on 25 September the cruiser arrived in Grand Harbour where she secured alongside the battleship *Rodney*. Following the surrender of Axis forces in North Africa, the summer of 1943 would see Allied invasions of Italy, the first being the invasion of Sicily in July. Overall, however, it was on the Russian front that the Second World War in Europe was being decided, and in January 1943 the German 6th Army which, almost three years earlier, had gained easy victories over the French and British Armies, was forced into a crushing and humiliating defeat by the Red Army at Stalingrad. It was the first major defeat for the Wehrmacht. In early September came the Allied invasion of the Italian mainland at Salerno, which led to the surrender of Italy and the German occupation of the whole of that country. In the third week of September, however, after a strong German counter-attack on the Allied bridgehead, it was the Salerno landings which were causing American and British generals most concern and at one stage it appeared that the whole landing force might have to be evacuated. In the early hours of 27 September *Sheffield* left Grand Harbour to make a 14-hour passage to Salerno Bay from where, next afternoon, she provided naval gunfire support when she bombarded enemy mechanised and infantry units ashore. During the days which followed the cruiser continued her support of the Army ashore, and provided anti-aircraft cover for the mass of shipping in Salerno Bay. These duties continued through to 5 October when, with the Allied bridgehead finally secured, she was ordered to Augusta, where limited shore leave was granted to the ship's company. Four days later she returned to Grand Harbour where there was a break as she was fuelled and stored, and on 13 October she sailed for Naples, which was now in Allied hands and safe enough for shore leave to be granted. With the military situation at Salerno having stabilised, *Sheffield* was able to steam south to the Gulf of Taranto where, on 8 November, she embarked Vice-Admiral Power and his staff for the overnight passage to Malta. Here the ship's company enjoyed some welcome respite from operations.

On 18 November *Sheffield* left Malta to sail west to Mers-el-Kebir where, over a period of 48 hours, she provided accommodation for the new C-in-C Mediterranean, Admiral J. H. C. Cunningham (who was no relation to the previous C-in-C), while he was in conference with other Allied military leaders. With that duty having been completed *Sheffield* was ordered home, and during the afternoon of 24 November she secured to a buoy in Plymouth Sound. For her ship's company *Sheffield*'s return to Plymouth marked a welcome break of 11 days before she sailed north again to Scapa Flow and on to Arctic waters and the Icelandic base at Seydisfjord. During the summer of 1943 the Arctic convoys to Russia had been suspended, mainly due to the menacing presence of *Tirpitz* and other heavy ships, including *Scharnhorst* and *Lützow*, at Altenfjord. Although *Tirpitz* had been damaged in a midget submarine attack a few weeks earlier, her very presence had the desired effect of causing the cancellation of convoys during the summer months, when there was virtually no darkness to hide the ships, and the tying down of the Royal Navy's battlefleet in northern waters. In November 1943, with *Lützow* in refit, *Tirpitz* damaged and only five destroyers to escort *Scharnhorst*, the British Government was under pressure from Russia to

restart the convoys to Murmansk, and during November three outward bound and two inward bound convoys were run without any serious incidents. By mid-December, aided by the 'Ultra' code-breaking ability, the new C-in-C Home Fleet, Admiral Sir Bruce Fraser, had a strong feeling that *Scharnhorst* would come out and endeavour to attack convoy JW55B[3]. In fact, between 12 and 20 December, Fraser in *Duke of York* accompanied by *Sheffield*, *Belfast* and *Norfolk* had escorted convoy JW55A from Iceland to the Kola Inlet, after which *Duke of York* had returned to the northern Icelandic port of Akureyri to refuel and prepare to escort the next convoy of 19 merchant ships, JW55B, which would leave Loch Ewe during the forenoon of 21 December.

Meanwhile, *Belfast* (flag CS10), *Sheffield* and *Norfolk* remained at anchor in the Kola Inlet in order to provide escort cover for convoy RA55A, an empty, homeward-bound convoy. Fraser's plan was for the two convoys to pass each other in the vicinity of Bear Island and, to all intents and purposes and as a temptation to the German Navy, both would appear to be lightly defended by a force of destroyers. Unknown to the Germans would be the presence of Force 1, consisting of *Belfast*, *Sheffield* and *Norfolk*, which would sail west from the Kola Inlet, and Force 2, consisting of *Duke of York* (C-in-C Home Fleet), *Jamaica* and three destroyers. At 0312 on Thursday 23 December the three cruisers left the Kola Inlet with convoy RA55A, and three days later, at 0400 on Sunday 26 December, they were in a position 73°52'N 027°12'E, south-east of Bear Island, steering 235° at 18 knots. Meanwhile, Force 2, which had sailed from Akureyri in Iceland at 2300 on 23 December, was in a position 71°52'N 010°48'E, south-west of Bear Island and steering 080° at 24 knots. The two convoys and their destroyer escorts were in between the two forces and, as Fraser had hoped, they were under surveillance by both German aircraft and submarines. The final piece in the jigsaw came about at 1900 on Christmas Day, when *Scharnhorst* and the destroyers *Z29, Z30, Z33, Z34* and *Z38* sailed from Altenfjord in an operation code-named 'Eastern Front', the purpose of which was to destroy convoy JW55B, thus providing much needed relief for the hard-pressed German Army on the Eastern Front, which for the first time during the Second World War was being decisively beaten by the Red Army. Although Rear-Admiral Erich Bey, flying his flag in *Scharnhorst*, was aware that Force 2 was at sea, he did not know its position and the fact that it was a very real threat to his force. He personally would have preferred to let his five destroyers attack the convoy, with *Scharnhorst* lying back in support, but he had been overruled by Grand-Admiral Doenitz, who it is said wanted a spectacular victory to mark his first year as the C-in-C of the fleet. In the event Bey kept his destroyers some ten miles ahead of *Scharnhorst*, well beyond visual signalling range, and with the battlecruiser keeping radio silence this left them unaware of *Scharnhorst*'s movements. At 0820 Bey turned the battlecruiser to the north, thus increasing the distance between himself and his destroyers and, more importantly, leaving them with no knowledge of his change of course which meant they were heading away from him.

At 0840 *Belfast*'s radar picked up *Scharnhorst* at 35,000 yards, bearing 295°, only 35 miles from the convoy, and by 0915 the range had dropped to 13,000 yards. At 0921 *Sheffield* reported 'Enemy in Sight' bearing 222°. At 0924 *Belfast* opened fire with starshell and five minutes later Force 1 was ordered to engage *Scharnhorst* with main armament. At 0930 *Norfolk* opened fire at a range of 9,800 yards, but had to drop back to clear *Belfast*'s range. *Scharnhorst* altered course to turn away, but *Norfolk*'s fire was fast and accurate and within minutes she had fired six full broadsides and a shell from the third salvo hit *Scharnhorst*'s foremast, completely carrying away her radar aerial, putting a high-angle director out of action and wounding an officer and several ratings. Another shell penetrated

[3] Convoy numbers prefixed JW indicated that they were bound for Russia, while those prefixed RA were returning from there.

her upper deck and ended up in a messdeck without exploding, but the vital hit was the one which destroyed the battlecruiser's radar. The appearance of the three cruisers took *Scharnhorst* by surprise, which had been Fraser's intention, and although the battlecruiser turned away from them she was still intent on finding and attacking JW55B. As far as this first action went, however, with *Scharnhorst* steaming southward at 30 knots she was soon out of range of the cruisers, but Burnett realised she was trying to work round to the northward of the convoy and, in order to get Force 1 between the enemy and the convoy, at 1000 he altered course to 305°. Six minutes later, at a range of 36,000 yards, all contact with *Scharnhorst*, which was steaming to the north-east at 28 to 30 knots, was lost.

During this first brief engagement the convoy had been ordered to turn northwards, but when contact with *Scharnhorst* was lost it was ordered to resume its original course. By 1045 Force 1 was in radar contact with convoy JW55B, and had been joined by the escorting destroyers, *Matchless, Musketeer, Opportune* and *Virago* (36th Division). The cruisers then took up a position some ten miles ahead of the convoy, with the destroyers acting as a screen ahead of them. At this stage, with contact having been lost, Fraser in *Duke of York* was not at all confident that he would be able to bring *Scharnhorst* to action, but Burnett was convinced that the battlecruiser would return to the convoy from the north or north-east. At 1205, when the convoy was about nine miles on the port quarter of Force 1, *Belfast* made radar contact with *Scharnhorst* at 30,500 yards, bearing 075°. Immediately, Fraser knew that there was every chance that he could catch her.

At 1209 *Sheffield*'s own radar picked up the German battlecruiser, and 12 minutes later, at 1221, *Scharnhorst* was sighted at a range of 11,000 yards and Force 1 was ordered to open fire. At the same time the destroyers of the 36th Division were ordered to attack the battlecruiser with torpedoes, but the weather conditions and poor visibility prevented this. Shortly after this, however, at a range of some 7,000 yards, *Musketeer* opened fire on *Scharnhorst* and continued rapid firing for 14 minutes, but with the battlecruiser retiring at high speed there were no hits and no possibility of a torpedo attack. This very determined second action by Force 1 at ranges from four and a half to eight miles lasted for only 20 minutes, but it was effective in driving *Scharnhorst* away from the convoy. She had quickly altered course from west to south-east and once again, as she increased speed from 18 to 28 knots, the range began to open. During this action *Sheffield*'s main armament had been in action from start to finish and *Scharnhorst*'s 11-inch salvoes had straddled her and hit *Norfolk*. During the opening salvoes several of the cruisers' shells had hit their target and prisoners later confirmed that their fire had been unpleasantly accurate. On board *Norfolk* one of *Scharnhorst*'s shells hit the barbette of X turret, which put the guns out of action, and a second shell hit the ship amidships rendering most of her radar unserviceable and killing one officer and six ratings, while seriously wounding five more ratings. By 1242, with *Scharnhorst* on a course of 110° at 28 knots and the range having opened to 12,400 yards, Burnett decided to check fire and, with the whole of Force 1, shadow her until she could be engaged by Force 2. For the next three hours the ships of Force 1 followed and reported the enemy battlecruiser by radar from just outside visibility range; as she was on a course which was so advantageous for interception by Force 2 Burnett decided not to engage her.

Following this second exchange Bey decided to return to Norway with *Scharnhorst*, but he broke radio silence to order his destroyers to attack the convoy at a position which had been reported by a U-boat. However, the information was not up to date and the destroyers missed the convoy. For several hours, with Burnett's cruisers shadowing him, *Scharnhorst* steamed south at 28 knots. At 1406, however, the gearing on *Sheffield*'s port inner shaft stripped, and two minutes later her speed was reduced to eight knots as engineers worked to lock the shaft. It was not until 1821 that she was able to increase speed to just short of 23 knots, but the

delay meant that for the rest of the action she remained some ten miles astern and could only conform to the general movement of the battle, following at a distance.

At 1632 *Duke of York*'s radar had picked up *Scharnhorst* at 29,700 yards, and some 15 minutes later *Belfast* opened fire with starshell, followed at 1658 by *Duke of York*. By 1650 the now brilliantly lit *Scharnhorst* was found by *Duke of York*'s fire control radar and the battleship opened fire and achieved early hits. *Scharnhorst*'s return fire was erratic and during the engagement she would fire a broadside at either *Jamaica* or *Duke of York*, and then turn end on until she was ready to fire the next one, making gunnery difficult for the British battleship. Meanwhile Fraser ordered the destroyers to carry out a torpedo attack, and this was delivered by *Savage, Saumarez, Scorpion* and the Norwegian destroyer *Stord*. Although four of the torpedoes hit *Scharnhorst* she was still able to maintain a speed of 22 knots, but this was not enough to outdistance *Duke of York* and with starshell '*hanging over her like a chandelier*' she was virtually a sitting target. By 1915 the British ships were subjecting *Scharnhorst* to a deluge of shells and the end came at 1945, after *Matchless, Musketeer, Opportune* and *Virago* fired a total of 19 torpedoes at her. Of *Scharnhorst*'s complement of 1,968 only 36 survived.

By 2100 *Sheffield* had rejoined Force 1, and soon after this Fraser ordered the vessels to proceed independently back to the Kola Inlet. At 1730 the next day *Sheffield* anchored in the approaches to Murmansk, and an hour later Fraser ordered 'Splice the Main Brace!'

At just before midnight on 29 December *Sheffield*, in company with *Belfast* and *Norfolk*, left the Kola Inlet and some 97 hours later she anchored in Scapa Flow. Three weeks later she weighed anchor and set course for the River Mersey where, during the afternoon of 23 January 1944, she secured alongside Liverpool's Princes Pier. Three days later she was moved into dry dock to begin a two-week maintenance and docking period. During the afternoon of 9 February, with her refit completed, *Sheffield* left the River Mersey to return to Scapa Flow where she rejoined Burnett's 10th Cruiser Squadron and spent seven weeks carrying out intensive exercises, including naval gunfire support bombardment practice. Unknown to all but a few government ministers and Chiefs of Staff, D-Day and the invasion of France was only a few months away. However, *Sheffield*'s next operational duties were not concerned with those momentous events, for in Norwegian waters the powerful German battleship *Tirpitz* was operational and *Sheffield* was one of a number of ships led by *Duke of York* (flag C-in-C), and including *Anson*, *Belfast*, *Jamaica* and six destroyers, which were to escort the aircraft carriers *Victorious* and *Furious* to Norwegian waters, just south of Hammerfest, from where they would launch air attacks on *Tirpitz*. Leaving Scapa Flow on 30 March, by the morning of 3 April the force was off northern Norway, with the first air strikes being launched at 0415. As far as the escorts were concerned the operation passed off quietly, with some damage being inflicted on the enemy battleship. On 6 April the force returned to Scapa Flow, and seven days later *Sheffield* took part in 'Operation Pitchbowl', a 48-hour air defence exercise west of the Shetland Islands. On conclusion she returned to Scapa Flow for 48 hours before leaving for Greenock, where she arrived on 18 April. Three days later she shifted her berth and was secured in Scott's Cartsdyke East shipyard at Greenock for a two-week docking and maintenance period. By 9 May, with the work completed, *Sheffield* was ready to steam north to Scapa Flow where, on 12 May, detachments of the ship's company were sent over to *Furious* for the King's visit to the fleet. That afternoon, however, all leave was cancelled as *Sheffield* sailed on 'Operation Potluck', which involved escorting *Furious* and *Victorious* to Norwegian waters to search for and sink enemy shipping, and to divert German attention away from preparations for the forthcoming landings in Normandy, which had been set for the first week of June. By 16 May *Sheffield* was back at

HMS Sheffield *as she appeared in May 1945, towards the end of the Second World War.* *(Syd Goodman Collection)*

Scapa Flow from where, during the next six weeks, she carried out training exercises in local waters. On 20 June, however, she made her last wartime foray into the Norwegian Sea before returning to Scapa. By 29 June she had moved down to Greenock, from where she sailed on up the Clyde to Gareloch where she remained at anchor for almost three weeks. Finally, on 18 July, having embarked drafts of ratings bound for Canada, she left the Clyde bound for the USA and a long overdue major refit. She would take no further part in wartime operations, and it would be almost two years before she returned to operational service.

On 25 July 1944, after a seven-day transatlantic passage, *Sheffield* arrived at the US Navy's Yard at Boston, Massachusetts, where she secured alongside the North Jetty. Six days later Captain Addis addressed the ship's company for the last time before handing over command to his Executive Officer. *Sheffield* remained in Boston until May 1945, and on 14 February that year Captain J. W. M. Easton RN took command of the ship. During the refit the ship was prepared for service with the Pacific Fleet, for at that stage of the war it was still generally thought that the war against Japan would last for another 18 months at least. In addition, as well as completely overhauling the machinery, additional AA armament in the form of four quadruple 40mm Bofors and 27 Oerlikon guns was fitted, but with the removal of X turret three of her 6-inch guns were lost. In May 1945, however, the sudden cancellation of the Lend-Lease arrangement with the USA, whereby US military equipment and services were supplied in return for long-term leases on military bases in Commonwealth countries, brought *Sheffield*'s Boston refit to an abrupt end. On 15 and 16 May a series of basin trials were carried out and five days later *Sheffield* joined two US destroyers for a short trials and work-up period. On 29 May, after full-power trials on the measured mile off

Cape Cod, *Sheffield* left US waters for the transatlantic passage to Portsmouth. Six days later she passed Eddystone Light and on 5 June she anchored at Spithead, before steaming up harbour to secure alongside Portsmouth's North Corner Jetty. Soon after her arrival *Sheffield* was taken in hand by the Dockyard and shifted to No 14 dry dock and this is where she was on 14 August 1945, when the Second World War ended.

HMS *Sheffield*'s refit, which had been intended to prepare her for service east of Suez and in the Pacific, included the installation of a great deal of new equipment, such as target acquisition radar, improved air warning system, barrage directors for main and secondary armament and updated gunnery equipment. The preparations also included the issue of white tropical uniforms to the ship's company, and all the vaccinations necessary for service in the eastern theatre of war. However, with the complete cessation of hostilities *Sheffield*'s refit ground to a halt. She was not required in the British Pacific Fleet which, during the 18 months after the end of the war, would be run down; ships sent east of Suez would once again be based at Singapore, Hong Kong and Trincomalee. *Sheffield*, however, remained in Portsmouth Dockyard and on 14 November 1945, Captain K. L. Harkness DSC RN took command of the ship. In mid-February 1946 she received a short visit from her sponsor, the Duchess of Kent. It was on 3 May that the ship underwent basin trials, and six weeks later she shifted to a buoy in Portsmouth Harbour. Finally, on Monday 24 June she left harbour to carry out a series of trials, first from Spithead and then from Portland. On 6 July, immediately after completing a full-power trial and embarking a few passengers, she left Portland to steam south via Gibraltar to Malta, where she arrived on 17 July.

For almost four weeks after her arrival at Grand Harbour *Sheffield* carried out work-up training exercises from Malta, and on 10 August she received a visit from Vice-Admiral Sir William Tennant, C-in-C designate North America and West Indies Station, who would fly his flag in *Sheffield* during her service in the Caribbean area. At 0900 on 12 August, with her work-up satisfactorily completed, *Sheffield* left Malta to steam west to Gibraltar, after which she took part in impressive naval exercises off Portugal, which was a reminder of how, after the Second World War, the balance of power in Europe had changed. With the exercises led by the new US Navy aircraft carrier *Franklin D. Roosevelt*, with her 125 aircraft and a host of escorting destroyers, it was evidence as the historian A. J. P. Taylor wrote that, '*Europe ceased to be the centre of the world*'.

After leaving the exercises *Sheffield* refuelled at Ponta Delgada, where there was a four-day break, and after leaving the Azores she continued her passage south-west until, on 30 August, she secured alongside the South Basin of the naval dockyard at Bermuda's Ireland Island. Two days later Admiral Tennant hoisted his flag onboard and in mid-September the cruiser left for her first flag-showing cruise in the Caribbean which, as far as the Royal Navy was concerned, had become something of a backwater during the war years. During this tour Captain Harkness had been ordered to provide generous hospitality for local dignitaries, and his recollections of the cruise were of '*strenuous and almost unceasing hospitality, both ashore and afloat*', with the intermediate sea passages providing an opportunity to rest and relax. In the event the various cocktail parties exposed petty jealousies and rivalries between government departments in these small outposts of what was soon to be a rapidly diminishing Empire. The most obvious of these arose at Antigua where, on *Sheffield*'s arrival on 9 October, it was found that apart from the Colonel in command, no British Army officers based on the island had been invited to *Sheffield*'s 'At Home'. The omission, it transpired, had been deliberate for relations between government and the Army had long been strained.

The first stop on *Sheffield*'s itinerary was Nassau where she anchored on 18 September. Two days later, however, came orders to weigh and proceed to Jamaica at best speed, for in what were the first stirrings of civil unrest, which would eventually lead to self-government and independence, the island's Police had gone on strike. No sooner was she under way than the strike was over, and during the forenoon of 23 September the cruiser was able to arrive alongside Kingston's No 1 Pier as scheduled. In the event, instead of being called upon as an aid to the civil government, the ship's company were able to enjoy a warm welcome ashore. The popularity of the Royal Navy was illustrated when the ship was opened to the public, and during the course of one afternoon some 10,000 visitors flocked to the pier. Although the numbers were more than the ship's sentries could control, there was plenty of goodwill, which made the day a success and was the object of the visit. After leaving Kingston *Sheffield* called at Trinidad, Grenada, Barbados and Antigua, after which she returned to Bermuda where, on 15 October, she secured alongside at Hamilton. Four days later she was at sea again, this time bound for New York for a flying visit to pick up the C-in-C. At 0915 on 21 October the Ambrose Light was abeam, and two hours later she was steaming past the famous skyline, of which the ship's company had only the briefest of glimpses, to secure alongside Pier 90. The visit lasted just four hours and at 1652, having embarked Vice-Admiral and Lady Tennant, the cruiser was sailing out of New York Harbour and setting course for Bermuda, where she arrived on 23 October.

During November and December *Sheffield* underwent a maintenance and docking period at Bermuda, and during the forenoon of 22 December there was a change of command when Captain G. B. H. Fawkes CBE RN took over from Captain Harkness. The end of 1946 and the new year of 1947 was an unsettling time for the ship's company, a good proportion of whom were Hostilities Only

HMS Sheffield *returns to harbour in June 1946 following post refit trials.* *(National Museum of the Royal Navy)*

ratings. They had been called up before the end of the war and were due for release during early 1947, so there were big changes as time-expired men left the ship, their places often being taken by young new recruits.

On 31 December 1946, with her maintenance completed and with the C-in-C having arrived on board, *Sheffield* left Bermuda to carry out a series of exercises and manoeuvres with *Kenya*. At that time the America and West Indies Station employed two cruisers and at least four destroyers, but in post-war austerity Britain such a large squadron in an area which was inevitably dominated by the US Navy was difficult to justify and it would not be long before it was cut drastically. On the first day of January 1947, after 24 hours of exercises, *Sheffield* left Bermudan waters for what was to be the Royal Navy's first showing-the-flag cruise for over seven years to South American ports. After a short refuelling stop at Jamaica, on 8 January *Sheffield* passed through the Panama Canal, to spend 48 hours alongside at the US Navy's base at Balboa. On 12 January, while steaming south through the Pacific Ocean, there was a full Crossing the Line ceremony, and two days later the cruiser made a full ceremonial entry into Peru's Callao Harbour, the port for the capital city of Lima. After a five-day stopover she steamed south again, to Antofagasta, Valparaiso and Talcahuano, following which she continued her passage south to Puerto Montt and Punta Arenas, before heading out into the South Atlantic to Port William in the Falkland Islands, where the ship's divers were kept extremely busy clearing kelp from the engine room cooling water inlets. From the Falkland Islands *Sheffield* steamed north to Montevideo where she arrived on 28 February to represent the Royal Navy at ceremonies to mark the inauguration of the President of Uruguay. On 7 March *Sheffield* left Montevideo Harbour to make her way up the River Plate to the Argentine capital - Buenos Aires. That afternoon, however, just as she was approaching the harbour, she grounded by the bows. Fortunately, prompt manoeuvring with the main engines got her clear and she was able to make a ceremonial entrance into the city. Three days later, during the evening of 10 March, *Sheffield* was visited by the President of the Argentine Republic, General Juan Peron. After leaving the River Plate *Sheffield* steamed north to the Brazilian ports of Santos, Rio de Janeiro and Recife, before returning to Bermuda by way of Trinidad in mid-April.

For ten weeks after her arrival at Bermuda *Sheffield* remained in local waters carrying out various exercises and manoeuvres, often in company with *Kenya, Snipe, Sparrow, Padstow Bay* and the Canadian aircraft carrier *Warrior* and destroyer *Haida*. On 27 June, having embarked the C-in-C, *Sheffield* rendezvoused with *Padstow Bay, Porlock Bay* and *Haida*, to sail north for Halifax, Nova Scotia. The cruiser was to remain in Canadian waters for over two months, and during the first few weeks she sailed round Newfoundland calling at some of the more remote settlements, including St John, Port Saunders, Cornerbrook and Arriege Bay. On more than one occasion she negotiated the narrows of the Strait of Belle Isle and in the process passed what remained of the forlorn and rusting hulk of *HMS Raleigh*, the former flagship on the North America Station, but which had been lost some 25 years earlier after foundering on the Labrador coast. Later in August *Sheffield* steamed up the St Lawrence River to the cities of Quebec and Montreal. On 4 September, after leaving the latter, she rendezvoused with *Padstow Bay* in the St Lawrence River to transfer stores and then steamed south to make important visits to Boston, where she had last berthed some three years earlier in the closing stages of the Second World War, and New York. Both visits lasted for a week, after which the cruiser called at Philadelphia and Annapolis, from where the C-in-C travelled to Washington for discussions on the proposed NATO organisation, which would take another 18 months to come into being. After leaving Annapolis she steamed back down Chesapeake Bay to Norfolk, Virginia, where she secured alongside Pier 7 in the US Navy Shipyard. From Norfolk, where the C-in-C rejoined the ship,

HMS Sheffield *alongside, probably at Hamilton, Bermuda, during her 1948 commission on the America & West Indies Station.* *(Maritime Photo Library)*

Sheffield returned to Bermuda to undergo an eight-week maintenance period.

In late October, whilst she was high and dry in the floating dry dock at Bermuda, *Kenya*, which had been on station since December 1946, *Padstow Bay* and *Porlock Bay* were withdrawn from the America and West Indies Squadron, leaving *Sheffield* and the two sloops *Snipe* and *Sparrow* as the only permanent ships on the station. They would, however, be reinforced on occasions by visiting ships on temporary deployment to the Caribbean region. When *Kenya* left Bermuda for Chatham in early November she took with her *Sheffield*'s last Hostilities Only ratings, who had been exchanged for the same number of the Colony-class cruiser's ratings. On 4 December, three weeks after *Sheffield*'s move out of dry dock to the dockyard basin, *RFA Gold Ranger* collided with her port side, punching a hole in the plating and demolishing a scuttle. Fortunately, the damage was quickly repaired, and on 15 December she left the dockyard to carry out two days of trials, before returning for the seasonal Christmas and New Year break.

For *Sheffield* the new year of 1948 began on 2 January when, in company with *Sparrow*, she left Bermuda for a cruise to the Caribbean, which began with a visit to Nassau and New Providence Island in the Bahamas. From there the two ships steamed to Havana for a six-day stopover, followed by eight days alongside Toulouse Street Wharf on the Mississippi River at New Orleans. On 30 December, after leaving New Orleans, *Sheffield* steamed south through the Gulf of Mexico and the Yucatan Channel to anchor off Belize City, which in those days was the major town and port in the Crown Colony of British Honduras[4]. This small area of Central America which shares borders with Mexico to the north and with Guatemala in the west had been acquired by Britain in the 1860s, when it had been seen as a possible pivot for naval and

[4] Now independent and renamed Belize, British Honduras was the last British colony on the continent of America.

commercial power on the Central American isthmus, but right from the start Guatemala had disputed Britain's possession of the territory. The original intention to use it as a base in Central America had been scuppered by the Monroe Doctrine, which had been aimed primarily at Britain, in which the USA warned that any attempt to extend Empire over, for example the Isthmus of Panama, might mean war with the United States. The Monroe doctrine had ensured that the America and West Indies Station remained a backwater and as a result British Honduras had remained an isolated outpost of Empire. In 1919, however, there had been serious civil unrest in the colony, and again in 1934 when there were strikes and riots in Belize City. At the same time Guatemala had never dropped its claim to the territory and from time to time, as threats of invasion were rumoured, the small resident garrison was often reinforced by Royal Marines. However, when *Sheffield* anchored during the forenoon of 2 February all was quiet, and the visit passed without incident.

From British Honduras *Sheffield* visited Kingston, Jamaica, La Guira, the port for Venezuela's capital Caracas, and the Colombian port of Cartagena, where she arrived on 21 February, and from where the C-in-C flew to Bogotá for talks with Colombian defence chiefs. The first indications of a possible Guatemalan invasion of British Honduras came during the evening of 23 February, but as the source was thought to be unreliable they were not taken seriously. By the following morning however these early indications had been confirmed and *Sheffield* was ordered to sail immediately. In the event it was 1250 on 25 February when, after re-embarking the C-in-C, she managed to put to sea and arrived off Belize City during the forenoon of 27 February. Immediately the Royal Marines Detachment went ashore to guard the airport, and armed platoons of the ship's company were landed to guard and patrol the town itself. On 1 March *Sheffield* was joined by the training cruiser *Devonshire*, with troops and additional Marines who had embarked at Jamaica. By 3 March, with only 200 or so poorly armed Guatemalan troops known to be on the border with British Honduras, normal leave routines were restored in *Sheffield* and *Devonshire* sailed for Jamaica to repair damage to a propeller shaft. Although *Sheffield* remained in the area until 16 March, the emergency was effectively over and the 2nd Battalion Gloucestershire Regiment had taken responsibility for the defence of the colony. During the second half of March *Sheffield* visited Jamaica and Antigua. In early April she took part in exercises with *Sparrow*, the Canadian cruiser *Ontario* (ex-HMS *Minotaur*), the destroyers HMCS *Crescent* and *Nootka*, the US Navy's aircraft carrier *Coral Sea* and the destroyer *Rodman*. On 5 April, with the exercises over, she returned to the naval base at Bermuda.

On 6 May 1948, as *Sheffield* lay in the south basin at Bermuda's dockyard, there was a change of command when Captain C. P Yorke RN took over the ship from Captain Fawkes. During the second week of June she spent three days alongside at Hamilton, and on 28 June left Bermuda for her second foray into the Pacific Ocean. On 6 July, after three days at Balboa, she sailed for Acapulco; Long Beach, California: Portland, Oregon; the Canadian naval base at Esquimalt, British Columbia, where she took part in Navy Week; Vancouver, then back down the West Coast of the USA to Seattle and San Francisco. On 5 October she returned via Panama to Bermuda, but two days later, with *Sparrow* and *Gold Ranger*, she had to put to sea in order to ride out a hurricane. Although she was only at sea for 24 hours, when she returned to Bermuda two of her whalers had been smashed beyond repair, the forecastle breakwater had been badly distorted by the heavy seas and numerous wooden gratings had been lost overboard. It was, however, almost the end of the commission, and on 26 October she left Bermuda bound for Chatham, where she arrived on 5 November 1948. It would be over two years before she was operational once again.

During 1949 and 1950 *Sheffield* remained either in reserve or under refit. In April 1950, while she

HMS Sheffield *arrives at Esquimalt naval base, Vancouver in 1952.* *(Steve Bush Collection)*

was being refitted at Chatham, it was announced that in November that year *Superb*, the flagship of the 2nd Cruiser Squadron, was transferring to the America and West Indies Station for some 12 months, and during her absence *Sheffield* would recommission in April 1951 and take *Superb*'s place in the Home Fleet. It was also announced that in November 1951 *Sheffield* would return to the America and West Indies Station, taking the place of *Superb*. On 15 December 1950 Captain M. Everard RN took command, and in early March 1951 *Sheffield* steamed round to Portsmouth, which was to remain her home base port for some five years. During Navy Days at Portsmouth over the three-day bank holiday Easter weekend *Sheffield* was opened to the public and she proved to be a popular attraction, with over 10,000 people streaming over her gangway. On 15 April she was recommissioned and 11 days later she sailed to Invergordon to join *Swiftsure* (flag CS2), *Agincourt, Corunna* and the submarine *Sea Scout,* for anti-submarine exercises in northern waters which continued almost to the end of May. She then steamed round to the River Mersey where, two days later, she secured alongside Liverpool's Princes Landing Stage. Next day, 31 October, amid tight security on the dockside and very little ceremonial, the Queen and Princess Margaret embarked and at 2100 the ship sailed for an overnight crossing of the Irish Sea, arriving alongside at Belfast at 0915 next morning. The Queen's visit to Belfast lasted four days, during which time *Sheffield* remained in the city, and when the royal visitors flew back to London on 4 June the cruiser returned to Invergordon to take part in a major anti-submarine exercise which included 18 submarines and 30 surface ships. The object of the exercise was for the submarines, in the face of opposition from anti-sub-

marine ships and naval and RAF aircraft, to make an 'attack' on an escorted convoy in the North and Norwegian Seas. For *Sheffield* the exercises ended on 25 June when she arrived at Rosyth, after which she visited Hull, Swansea and Cardiff, before returning to Portsmouth on 25 July, in time for the summer Navy Days.

Sheffield remained alongside at Portsmouth undergoing a docking and maintenance period until 1 October when, in company with *Superb*, she left for the America and West Indies Station. On 25 October, just 12 days after arriving at Bermuda, *Sheffield* and *Sparrow* left for Puerto Rico and a major training exercise with the US Navy, which included USS *Midway, Newport News* and *Tarawa*. On 5 November a new dimension was added to naval warfare when *Sheffield* was ordered to make black smoke and to simulate being 'hit' by an atomic bomb. The official record makes no mention of what anyone thought would be left of either the cruiser or her company if she had actually been 'hit' by such a weapon. On 14 November, with the exercises over she returned to Bermuda and seven days later the C-in-C of the America and West Indies Station, Vice-Admiral Sir William Andrews, who had just arrived on the island from London, hoisted his flag in *Sheffield*. No sooner was he aboard than *Sheffield* left Bermuda for an 11-day visit to Baltimore. On 7 December, having steamed through severe gales and mountainous seas, she arrived back at Bermuda where she remained until early January 1952, spending Christmas alongside in Hamilton.

Sheffield's first Caribbean cruise of the commission began on 4 January 1952, when she left Bermuda for the islands of Antigua, St Lucia, Barbados, Grenada and Trinidad. After leaving Port of Spain on 22 January she steamed to the Venezuelan port of La Guira, and from there to Willemstad on Curaçao Island, part of the Netherlands Antilles. The cruise continued to Jamaica and then to the US naval base at Guantanamo Bay on the south-east corner of Cuba. There she joined ships of the US Navy, including the battleship *Missouri* and the destroyers *Murray, Beale* and *Sherwood*, for four days of joint manoeuvres in the Caribbean. On 21 March she returned via Jamaica to Bermuda where she underwent a five-week maintenance period. On 5 May, with the dockyard having completed their work, *Sheffield* left Bermuda for the cooler waters of Canada's east coast where she called at Halifax and Montreal, returning to Bermuda on the last day of May. On 17 June Captain Everard handed over command of *Sheffield* to Captain J. G. T. Inglis OBE RN who, 14 days later when Vice-Admiral Andrews struck his flag as C-in-C, was temporarily promoted to Commodore. Just two hours after hoisting his pennant Inglis took *Sheffield* to sea for the first time on a cruise into the Pacific Ocean via Jamaica and the Panama Canal. After leaving Balboa on 11 July the cruiser steamed north along the West Coast of the USA to San Francisco. Here she hosted one of the biggest children's parties seen on board when 340 disadvantaged children swarmed over the ship, enjoying rides on a home-made carousel on the forecastle and consuming enormous quantities of ice cream and jelly. From San Francisco *Sheffield* steamed north again to Seattle, Esquimalt, Vancouver and Portland, Oregon, before returning south to call at Long Beach, San Diego and Acapulco. On 2 October she returned to Balboa, from where it was intended she would steam east back into the Caribbean, but she was ordered to remain at the US naval base in the Panama Canal Zone, before being sent south to the Peruvian port of Callao and, on 29 October, to Valparaiso, Chile, to represent Britain at ceremonies and celebrations to mark the inauguration of the country's new president, General Carlos Ibañez, who had been elected earlier in the year. On 1 November, when the ship was opened to the public, she received almost 5,000 visitors and two days later, with other foreign warships, the cruiser took part in a review by the new president. Finally, on 7 November she sailed north to Panama. Seven days later, in a torrential thunderstorm, she made her westbound transit of the canal and returned to Bermuda by way of Trinidad, where she paused to refuel, and Guantanamo Bay, where she stopped to land an acute appendicitis case, arriving back in Bermuda on 20 November. Four days later, having been relieved by *Superb*, she sailed for home and at just before midnight on 3 December she anchored at Spithead. Next afternoon, having cleared Customs, she steamed up harbour to secure in the tidal basin alongside the South-West Wall. Ahead lay a 16-week refit which would take the ship into the new year and spring of 1953.

By mid-March 1953 *Sheffield* was lying alongside *Kenya* at Portsmouth's South Railway Jetty, and on 27 March she put to sea for a day of machinery trials. During the first week of April she took part in Navy Days at Portsmouth, and on 20 April her post-refit trials and work-up began. In late May there was a five-day break at Liverpool, and midway through the visit severe storms which swept across north-west Britain prevented the cruiser from leaving the Gladstone Dock in order to anchor in midriver from where she had been scheduled to fire a 21-gun salute as part of the Coronation celebrations. This, however, was only a minor inconvenience, for in Llandudno Bay the destroyer *Verulam* was forced to cancel a fireworks display and hastily put to sea, leaving behind some 70 officers and men. *Sheffield*, in the more sheltered waters of the River Mersey, was able to complete her visit before sailing south again to Spithead, where she took her place in the lines of warships attending the Coronation Naval Review on 15 June. Two days later, with the review over, she returned to Portsmouth Dockyard for another 13 weeks of maintenance, this time to replace the superheater tubes on all her boilers.

During the two full months that *Sheffield* languished in C-lock the deafening noise of dockyard hammers resounded through the ship and, to escape the shambles of tubing, pipes and often loss of shore-supplied electrical power, the ship's company were able to catch up on all leave owed, including some foreign service leave, for it had been confirmed that before the end of the year the ship was bound once again for Bermuda and the America and West Indies Station. On 15 September she carried out a day of boiler trials before returning to Portsmouth Dockyard, and two days later there was a change of command when Captain K. McNeill Campbell-Walter (known as Campbell-Walter) took over from Captain Inglis. Next forenoon *Sheffield* sailed north to Invergordon to join *Eagle, Apollo, Crossbow*, *USS Wasp* and other ships to take part in the major NATO naval exercise 'Mariner'. *Sheffield*'s part in the manoeuvres was to patrol the area between Iceland and Greenland, and for those members of the ship's company who had served in the war, the severe gales and mountainous seas brought back memories of the Northern Patrol blockade duties. During one spell of severe weather one of the ship's whalers was carried away, and the radio mast on top of Y turret also disappeared. Down below almost all of the ship's crockery was broken, and among the many young ratings there were some very 'green' faces. However, for the Scotsmen on board it was good news on 3 November when the cruiser put into Greenock for minor repairs and to store ship; during the unscheduled stop of four days many of them were able to get ashore to their homes. Shortly before the ship left Greenock during the forenoon of 7 October the Governor of Bermuda and his aide were embarked.

After an eight-day transatlantic passage *Sheffield* arrived at Bermuda on 15 October, where everyone was expecting a three-week stay in the dockyard, but after just 48 hours she put to sea for Port of Spain, Trinidad, where she relieved *Superb* and hoisted the flag of the C-in-C, before returning to Bermuda. On 16 November 1953 *Sheffield*'s deployment began in earnest, when she sailed from Bermuda bound for Kingston, Jamaica, where she was to take on the duty of escort to the Shaw Savill liner *Gothic*, which had been chartered by the Government to act as a royal yacht and carry the Queen and Duke of Edinburgh on their 1953-54 Commonwealth Tour. The cruiser arrived in Kingston Harbour on 20 November, and next day *Gothic*, which had completed an 11-day passage

HMS Sheffield *arrives at Boston, Massachussetts, in September 1954. She was greeted alongside by the RCAF Pipe Band, from Ottawa, in Boston for the Highland Games.* *(Ken Kelly Collection)*

from London, joined her. On 26 November the royal passengers flew in to Jamaica from Bermuda, to be welcomed by a Guard of Honour from *Sheffield*'s Royal Marines Detachment. That evening the Governor of Jamaica, Sir Hugh Foot, gave a reception at Government House, during which the Royal Marines and platoons of *Sheffield*'s seamen gave displays of marching and countermarching. During the afternoon of 27 November *Gothic* and *Sheffield* left Kingston bound for Panama. Two days later both ships completed their transits of the Panama Canal, and on the last day of November they left Balboa bound for a rendezvous point some 200 miles south-west of Fatu Hiva, one of the group of French Marquesas Islands, where HMNZS *Black Prince* would take over the escort. On the last day of November, just 24 hours out from Balboa, *Gothic* and *Sheffield* stopped to allow the Queen and Duke of Edinburgh to be transferred by royal barge to the cruiser. In the event the visit lasted for just half an hour during which time the ship's company mustered by Divisions on the quarter deck and marched past. On 4 December the two ships crossed the equator with full ceremony and five days later *Sheffield*'s surgeon was transferred by jackstay to perform an emergency appendectomy on one of the liner's crewmen. On 11 December *Black Prince* took over the escort and, after refuelling at the Marquesas Islands, *Sheffield* returned to Balboa, where she arrived on 23 December to spend Christmas and New Year.

On 8 January 1954 *Sheffield* made her eastbound transit of the Panama Canal, after which she cruised in the Caribbean, calling at Curaçao, Trinidad, Grenada, Barbados, Antigua, Jamaica, Havana and Vera Cruz, arriving at the latter on 15 February. During the visit over 100 officers and men visited Mexico City, where the Royal Marines Band Beat Retreat in front of the Presidential Palace. After

HMS Sheffield *midway through her final refit at Chatham.* *(B. Newton)*

leaving Mexico *Sheffield* negotiated the Mississippi River to secure alongside at New Orleans, where once again there was a full programme of official functions, the visit being enlivened by the Mardi Gras festivities and parades. *Sheffield*'s next ports of call were Houston, Texas, and Pensacola. In mid-March she made a three-day visit to British Honduras (Belize), followed by Jamaica and Trinidad, before arriving back at Bermuda to undergo some much needed maintenance on 10 April.

On 14 May *Sheffield* left Bermuda to join ships of the 7th Frigate Squadron, including *Bigbury Bay*, *Burghead Bay* and *Cygnet*, to carry out anti-submarine exercises, with *Tally Ho* acting as their quarry. The manoeuvres included night encounter, replenishment, towing and gunnery exercises, which ended on 16 May when *Bigbury Bay* set course for the Falkland Islands, *Cygnet* to Charleston and *Tally Ho* to New London. *Sheffield* and *Burghead Bay*, meanwhile, made the passage to Norfolk, Virginia, arriving off Fort Monroe the next day. Although the two ships were rather overshadowed by the battleship *USS Missouri*, the aircraft carrier *Bennington* and the heavy cruiser *Macon*, the White Ensign flew proudly and the ceremony of Beating Retreat, which was performed on the jetty by the Guard and Band of the Royal Marines, drew a spontaneous round of applause from American sailors in all three ships. After leaving Norfolk *Sheffield* and *Burghead Bay* visited Annapolis and Baltimore, from where the C-in-C travelled to Washington for an audience with President Eisenhower. After leaving US waters on the last day of May, four days later the two ships arrived back in Bermuda.

HMS *Sheffield*'s last deployment of the commission began on 6 July, when she sailed to Newport, Rhode Island, Portland, Maine and on to the Canadian cities of Montreal, Quebec, St John's, Newfoundland, Halifax, Nova Scotia, and south again to Boston, Massachusetts, and New York, where she remained for seven days, returning by way of Philadelphia to Bermuda on 1 October. Just over two weeks later, having been relieved by *Superb*, she left Bermuda for the last time, and arrived in Portsmouth on 26 October, where she paid off.

Soon after arriving back in Portsmouth *Sheffield* was in dockyard hands and undergoing a refit and dry docking period. On 22 December a new commanding officer, Captain T. E. Podger RN, took over command of the cruiser, and by the end of January 1955 *Sheffield* had been shifted from No 14 dry dock to South Railway Jetty. On 15 February she put to sea to run three days of trials, and seven days later she left Portsmouth bound for Gibraltar, Malta and the Mediterranean Fleet. After a short 48-hour stopover at Gibraltar she arrived in Grand Harbour on 5 March to begin a seven-week work-up, during which time she operated with *Glasgow*, *Jamaica*, *Albion*, *Centaur* and the Malta-based destroyers. In early May she visited Cannes, in time for the world-renowned Film Festival, but by mid-May she was back in Malta where she was visited by the flamboyant Maltese Prime Minister, Dom Mintoff, who had just won a General Election on a platform of 'integration' with the UK, which would have worked rather along the lines of the Channel Islands model[5]. At the end of May, following exercises with the fleet, she visited Istanbul, followed by Alexandria then Turkey and the port of Marmaris. During August she exercised with the fleet carrier *Eagle* and visited Leghorn (Livorno) and Venice, but by 11 September she had returned to Grand Harbour. On 18 September, after a farewell address by FO2 Mediterranean Fleet, *Sheffield* left Malta bound for Portsmouth and a refit which would include essential work on her now troublesome main boilers, her future now being uncertain.

During her return passage there was a 48-hour stop at Gibraltar, and on 27 September she arrived at Spithead. Next day she steamed up harbour to secure alongside Pitch House Jetty. By late October she had been shifted, via moorings off Whale Island, to No 3 basin where she was de-stored and placed in reserve. Here she remained for the rest of 1955, and persistent rumours of her imminent demise circulated constantly. During the forenoon of 5 January 1956, however, she was taken in tow by four dockyard tugs to make a slow 24-hour passage to Sheerness. Five days later she was towed into Chatham Dockyard's No 3 basin to be prepared for a major refit.

The cruiser's final major refit had been planned prior to the Suez Crisis of 1956, and before the post Suez Defence Review, which saw most of the Royal Navy's pre-war warships reduced to reserve and scrapped. Had her refit not already been under way it is likely that the elderly cruiser would have not seen any more operational service, and it is unlikely that so much money would have been lavished on her. As it was, however, renewal and refurbishment work was carried out on the ship's boilers and her forward tripod mast was replaced with a more up-to-date looking lattice-work affair. Much of the accommodation for both officers and ratings was completely refurbished and on 27 February 1957, with the end of the refit in sight, a new commanding officer, Captain L. D. Bourke CBE DSO RN, was appointed. The ship, however, was still a shambles of dockyard equipment, with a myriad of pipes and hoses cluttering her passageways, and it was not until 1 May that Captain Bourke temporarily commissioned the ship for machinery trials. These took place between the 7th and 16th of the month in the North Sea and two days later the cruiser steamed up harbour from Sheerness to secure in Chatham's No 3 basin once more.

During June 1957 *Sheffield* was dry docked and after that a semblance of order was slowly restored to the ship. On 11 June she received a visit from the Lord Mayor of London, and soon afterwards came her end of refit inspection by the C-in-C Nore. On 19 June *Sheffield* left the dockyard for Sheerness and next day she began two more days of machinery trials before returning to Chatham Dockyard. Finally, at 1500 on Monday 1 July 1957, *Sheffield* recommissioned for the last time; four days later she steamed round to Portland to begin her work-up. On 4 August there was a short break from the daily grind of training exercises to visit Immingham Docks on the River Humber. Despite damaging one

[5] The 'integration' proposal for Malta foundered on the thorny subject of financial aid.

HMS Sheffield, *with new enclosed bridge and lattice foremast, is seen departing Malta.* *(Crown Copyright/MoD)*

of her propellers while entering the locks there, the visit was a success and during September she steamed north for NATO exercises, which also included *Eagle* and *Gambia*. Most of October was spent in the Channel, working out of Portland, but also calling at Devonport and St Peter Port on the island of Guernsey. At the end of that month, however, she steamed north for another major exercise, this time code-named 'Sharp Squall II', which also involved *Apollo, Cavendish* and *Contest*, as well as Canadian and Norwegian ships. The exercise ended at Rosyth on 14 November and after a weekend break she took part in 'Exercise Phoenix II' with *Ark Royal*, *Eagle* and *Bulwark*. These manoeuvres took place in atrocious winter weather conditions and there were sighs of relief all round when they ended at Rosyth on 23 November. Five days later *Sheffield* secured alongside the brand new Europa Hafen terminal at Bremen for a four-day visit, and when the ship was opened to the public some 8,900 visitors swarmed over her. On 6 December, having been delayed by fog off the Great Nore, *Sheffield* returned to Chatham to give leave and to carry out maintenance work. She was about to begin her last full year of operational service.

It was some three weeks after the new year of 1958 had been seen in that, on 22 January, she left Chatham bound for the warmer waters of the Mediterranean. Five days later, at Gibraltar, she hoisted the flag of the C-in-C Mediterranean, Admiral Sir Charles Lamb, and on 3 February, in company with *Ark Royal*, sailed for Malta. For the next few weeks *Sheffield* operated from Grand Harbour with the aircraft carrier and the cruiser *Kenya* in the waters around Malta. In early March, however, *Sheffield* joined 39 other ships of the Mediterranean and US 6th Fleets to begin a three-day programme of combined exercises. Also taking part were *Ark Royal* and *Eagle*, *Birmingham* and *Kenya*, as well as the US aircraft carriers *Essex* and *Saratoga*, and the cruisers *Des Moines* and *Salem*. The exercise was designed to familiarise the two fleets in combined operating; in overall command was Vice-Admiral C. R. Brown of the US 6th Fleet, with the carrier groups being commanded by Flag Officer, Aircraft Carriers, Rear-Admiral A. N. C. Bingley, flying his flag in *Eagle*. The gunnery phases of the exercises were under the command of Vice-Admiral L. Durnford-Slater, who flew his flag in *Sheffield*. Once the exercises were over *Sheffield*

made two high-profile visits, the first to Bari in Italy and the second to the Yugoslavian port of Split, which is now part of Croatia. On 18 March *Sheffield* was back at Malta and she remained in local waters until late April when she took part, with *Ark Royal, Cavendish, Corunna, Decoy* and *Duchess*, in 'Exercise Shotgun', returning to Grand Harbour at the end of the month. During early May there were more local exercises and a visit to Tripoli. On 17 May the cruiser took part in the NATO exercise 'Medflex Fort', during which she operated with the US Navy's cruiser *Salem*. The exercise took *Sheffield* as far north as Gallipoli, and the highlight of the exercise came on 23 May during a 20-minute jackstay transfer with *Salem*, for which the US cruiser provided the full ceremonial of white uniforms and a brass band. *Sheffield*'s return to Malta was to prepare for her first summer cruise, which was to have included visits to Istanbul and Beirut, but instead in early June, together with *Bermuda*, the destroyers *Cavendish, Decoy* and *Diamond* and the aircraft carrier *Eagle*, she was deployed to the eastern Mediterranean again, using the anchorages at Dhekelia, Akrotiri and Limassol off the coast of Cyprus. Unsettling events in Britain's 'informal' Empire in the Middle East where the wider effects of the Suez Crisis were making themselves felt were the reason for the large concentration of naval power in the area. In February 1958 Egypt and Syria had joined together in a single centralised state, the United Arab Republic, and there were fears that President Chamoun of Lebanon and the British-installed King Hussein of Jordan, whom Britain had pledged to support militarily in the event of aggression, would be toppled from power by the wave of Arab nationalism which was sweeping the region. Along with a US Navy task force, the ships of the Mediterranean Fleet carried out patrols off Cyprus, awaiting events. The crisis came to a head on 14 July 1958 when the British-installed King Faisal of Iraq was assassinated and power in that country was seized by the Army. Fears by the leaders of Lebanon and Jordan that they too faced similar coups prompted both Chamoun and King Hussein to call for military help from the USA and Britain. At 1612 on 15 July, in support of *Eagle* whose aircraft would escort troop-carrying aircraft into Amman, *Sheffield* and the other ships of the Mediterranean Fleet operated just over the horizon off the coast of Lebanon, where US Marines were streaming ashore to occupy Beirut. In Jordan the men of the Parachute Regiment touched down without any opposition during the morning of 17 July, and two days later, with the political tensions having eased and both Lebanon and Jordan remaining quiet, *Sheffield* and most other ships of the fleet returned to Cypriot ports where they remained until 28 July. For most of that period *Sheffield* was anchored off Famagusta, but on 27 July, with still no signs of the expected coups, she moved to Limassol where she embarked 250 men of 40 Commando, Royal Marines, for passage to Malta, where she arrived on 30 July.

For three weeks after her return to Grand Harbour *Sheffield* underwent a maintenance and docking period and on 20 August she left Malta for her summer cruise, the first port of call being Venice. By 27 August, however, her cruise had been cut short and she had returned to Malta for four very hectic days of storing ship before leaving for the Persian Gulf. The unstable political situation in the oil-rich country of Iraq, which had come about after the assassination of the British 'Puppet' King Faisal, was causing a great deal of concern in London. This had come to a head when the new regime ordered the closure of Britain's last remaining military base in the country, RAF Habbaniya, west of Baghdad. As a result it had been decided to station a cruiser in the Persian Gulf, but *Ceylon*, which had been earmarked, had only just completed a refit in Portsmouth and was still working up in the Mediterranean, so *Sheffield* was dispatched to the area for a month to relieve *Newfoundland*, which could then return to the Far East Station. Leaving Malta on 2 September and making her southbound transit of the Suez Canal four days later, *Sheffield* arrived on station and relieved *Newfoundland* on 14 September. The ship's company had been warned to expect a month-long stay in the sweltering heat of

HMS Sheffield *at Whale Island in the 1960's as the Headquarters ship of the Reserve Fleet. There followed various attempts to raise funds to have the ship preserved as a museum but they were not successful.*

(Tim Meredith (top) & T. Ferrers-Walker (below))

the Bahrain area, but to their immense relief the requirement for a cruiser at immediate notice to cover what had become known as 'the war that never was' was reduced to just a week. During this time the ship took part in 'Exercise Longboat', which involved landing men of the 1st Battalion Royal Fusiliers on the sun baked island of Halul, where the ship's Royal Marines Detachment formed the first assault wave in the ship's boats. As one marine commented: '*We spent two hours ashore, but that was quite long enough on Halul.*'

Meanwhile, on 13 September in the Gulf of Oman, two oil tankers, the 10,715-ton, French-registered *Fernand Gilabert* and the 20,551-ton Liberian-registered *Melika* had collided, as a result of which both ships caught fire, killing 22 men. The Liberian vessel had been abandoned by her crew, but was still steaming south, ablaze and deserted, in the busy shipping lanes. She was soon discovered by an aircraft from *Bulwark* which was in the area, and it was not long before boarding parties from both the commando carrier and the frigate *Puma* had climbed aboard, stopped the ship and put out the fires. *Bulwark* had then taken the vessel in tow and brought her into the safety of an anchorage outside Muscat. When *Sheffield* arrived the tanker was at anchor and in the words of one of the cruiser's marines: '*Our job was to correct the list, transfer the cargo of oil to other ships and get her ready for further towing. The cutter was in almost constant use ferrying to and fro, and the size of the hole in* Melika*'s side can be judged by the fact that our cutter had no difficulty in driving in and out.*' The task of transferring the fuel, and for the supply department the extremely unpleasant job of clearing rotten food from different freezers in the ship, took nine days, and in early October *Sheffield* was heading back to Aden where she was duly relieved by *Ceylon*. Six days later *Sheffield* had passed through the Suez Canal and, after her unscheduled five weeks' 'Foreign Service', was back in the Mediterranean. However, she did not return directly to Malta, but carried out exercises in the Eastern Mediterranean, before all three ships visited Istanbul.

During November there were visits to Toulon and Valencia, and after that came the postponed C-in-C's inspection after which one member of the ship's company commented: '*Despite the lack of preparation we came out of it pretty well and sat back for a quiet Christmas.*' No sooner were the festivities over, however, than *Sheffield* left Malta for the last time bound for Naples where she arrived in time for the New Year festivities. But as one marine commented: '*Naples was rather a busted flush, as very few of us had any money and those who did were keeping it for home. However, we were able to witness a Neapolitan new year, when everyone throws the old crockery into the streets, and a few of us more hardy ones climbed Vesuvius the hard way.*' On 5 January 1959 *Sheffield* left Naples and three days later she called at Gibraltar for a 48-hour stopover before continuing her passage to Portsmouth. It was 2359 on 12 January when she anchored at Spithead and at 1035 next day the Royal Marines Band of the C-in-C Portsmouth and numerous press representatives were embarked. They were followed at 1145 by HRH the Duchess of Gloucester who, some 23 years earlier, had launched the cruiser. During the next two hours the ship's company mustered by Divisions to perform a final march past at which the Duchess took the salute before making a farewell address and leaving the ship. Finally, at 1426 *Sheffield* weighed anchor to steam up harbour and to secure alongside Fountain Lake Jetty.

No sooner was she alongside than the job of de-ammunitioning and de-storing began. A few weeks later the ship was shifted to No 14 dry dock where preservation work was carried out, and those few members of the ship's company who remained aboard were accommodated in the Royal Naval Barracks. At noon on 24 June 1959 the ship was finally paid off, with the White Ensign being lowered for the last time, and the reserve fleet personnel still aboard moved to join HMS *Vanguard*, the last of the Royal Navy's battleships, which was acting as an accommodation ship. In June 1960, however, *Vanguard* was decommissioned and reserve

With the former HMS Sheffield *secure alongside at Faslane, the task of scrapping the ship could begin.* *(T. Ferrers-Walker)*

fleet personnel moved back to *Sheffield* which, by all accounts, after the battleship they considered to be very cramped. *Sheffield* was now the Flagship and Headquarters ship of the Reserve Fleet, a role which, at her moorings off Whale Island, she would fulfil for some six years.

With the demise of *Birmingham* in September 1960, of the original ten cruisers of the Town-class only *Sheffield* and *Belfast* remained, and in August 1963 the latter paid off for the last time to become the new Headquarters ship of the Reserve Fleet. During the years that followed there were various attempts to raise funds for *Sheffield*'s preservation as a museum ship, but with at least £500,000 being required they were not successful. In January 1967 she was towed to Rosyth where she was laid up and put on the sales list, but there were no realistic offers. Eight months later *Sheffield* was sold to Shipbreaking Industries Ltd for demolition and shortly afterwards, on 18 September 1967, she began her final passage under tow from Rosyth to the breaker's yard at Faslane.

Chapter Four

HMS BIRMINGHAM

1937-1960

HMS Birmingham *seen nearing completion at Devonport in November 1937. Note the 'flared' bow, rather than the 'knuckle' type as fitted to the remainder of the class.* *(Syd Goodman Collection)*

In mid-December 1934 it was announced that Devonport Dockyard would build the fifth cruiser for what had been originally intended as the Minotaur class, but which, only a few weeks before, had been altered to bear the names of towns and British cities. At the same time it was announced that the new ship would be called *Birmingham*, and that she would enter service in the autumn of 1937, a deadline which was easily met by the Royal Dockyard. The first keel plates were laid on the slipway at Devonport on Thursday 18 July 1935 by the wife of the C-in-C Plymouth, Lady Kathleen Plunkett-Ernle-Erle-Drax[1], at a time when naval affairs were very much in the news, for just a few weeks earlier the British Government had unilaterally agreed what was known as the Anglo-German Naval Accord. This allowed Germany to increase its fleet of three pocket battleships (heavy cruisers), six light cruisers and smaller warships to five battleships, two aircraft carriers, five heavy cruisers, 11 light cruisers and 65 destroyers. The thinking of the British Government was that the Royal Navy would always be able to maintain its superiority. They failed to take into account, however, the country's worldwide commitments at that time. It was also in direct contradiction to the announcement in March that year that in view of a possible German military threat in Europe, defence spending would increase and there would be an increase in the size of the fleet. The increase in naval expenditure meant that work on *Birmingham* proceeded rapidly and by late August 1936 the ship

[1] Her husband, Admiral the Hon. Sir Reginald Aylmer Ranfurnly Plunkett-Ernle-Erle-Drax, we have already met in the story of HMS *Sheffield* when, in 1939, he was appointed to the Allied Commission to the Soviet Union.

was ready for launching.

Given that the new cruiser was to be named after Britain's second biggest city, it was only fitting that the launching ceremony should be carried out by a member of one of Birmingham's most influential families, the Chamberlains, with the honour going to Lady Ivy Chamberlain, wife of the former Chancellor of the Exchequer and Foreign Secretary and, in 1931 for a brief period, First Lord of the Admiralty. The ceremony, which took place during the afternoon of Tuesday 1 September 1936, was attended by other notable dignitaries from the city of Birmingham, including the Lord Mayor, Alderman S. J. Grey, who was one of the original directors of what in those days was known as the Halford Cycle Company, and the Minister of Transport, Leslie Hore-Belisha, a native of Devonport whose name became associated with the uncontrolled pedestrian road crossings, with their familiar Belisha Beacons and zebra stripes in the road. At 1700 Lady Chamberlain sent the cruiser down into the waters of the Hamoaze, where tugs took her in tow and moved her into a tidal basin. No sooner had she entered the water than the slipway was being prepared to receive the first keel plates of another Town-class cruiser, *Gloucester*.

Following her launch work on *Birmingham* proceeded apace, and on 4 August 1937 her first commanding officer was appointed. Captain C. F. Harris RN had served in the battleship *Conqueror* during the Great War and in the early 1930s commanded destroyers in the Mediterranean. A few weeks later, on 13 September, with the ship lying at No 5 wharf and steam having been raised, a steaming crew from RNB Portsmouth arrived on board, and at 1600 *Birmingham* was commissioned for builder's trials. Next afternoon she slipped her moorings to begin ten days of sea trials in the Channel and on the measured mile off Whitesand Bay. During the afternoon of 24 September, with the trials completed, she secured alongside Devonport's No 7 wharf and next day her steaming crew returned by train to Portsmouth and the ship paid off into dockyard hands for final adjustments to her machinery and for completion of fitting out, a process which would take seven and a half weeks. During this period it was announced that after commissioning and undergoing her initial acceptance trials *Birmingham* would be sent east to join the China Station at Hong Kong, and the more northerly port of Wei hai wei, where it was planned she would relieve *Capetown*, which in turn would return to home waters.

At 1630 on Tuesday 16 November, with fitting-out work completed, Captain Harris and 28 of his officers returned to the ship and half an hour later they were joined by an advance party of 378 ratings and a detachment of 30 Royal Marines, all of whom had travelled by train from Portsmouth. Two days later, at 1120 on 18 November, *Birmingham* slipped her moorings to carry out six hours of steaming trials before returning to Plymouth Sound where all the dockyard employees were disembarked. Later that evening she weighed anchor and set course for Spithead where she anchored at 0730 the next morning. During the forenoon she steamed up harbour to secure alongside Portsmouth's Pitch House Jetty and over the next four days her ship's company was brought up to full strength. This included 89 boys who joined from the old training battleship *Iron Duke* which, during the Great War, had been Jellicoe's proud flagship. At 1000 on 23 November *Birmingham* was commissioned for operational service, which brought the number of operational cruisers on the Royal Navy's lists up to 60.

On 29 November *Birmingham* began her first trials and work-up exercises, mostly in the Channel off the south coast of the Isle of Wight. By December 1937 not only were political tensions in Europe rising, but in the Far East Japan's brutal invasion of China was affecting the various European Concessions in that country, bringing both Britain and America into confrontations with Japanese forces in China. By mid-December the fighting had spread along the Yangtze River and Japanese aircraft had 'accidentally' bombed Royal and US Navy river gunboats, notably HMS *Ladybird* at Wahu, when one rating was killed and

A party of about 400 representative citizens of Birmingham visited Portsmouth on 31 January 1938 to make presentations prior to the ship leaving for the China Station on her maiden commission. The party was headed by the Lord Mayor and Lady Mayoress of Birmingham. Among the presents were 32 silver bugles and a ceremonial white ensign made of pure silk. *(Syd Goodman Collection)*

another badly wounded. Although Britain was powerless to take any meaningful military action against Japan, diplomatic tensions ran high and in Portsmouth there were strong rumours that *Hood*, the flagship of the battlecruiser squadron, was standing by at a moment's notice to sail for the Far East and that she would be accompanied by *Birmingham*. In the event the rumours proved unfounded and the cruiser spent Christmas and New Year high and dry in No 15 dry dock. At 2200 on the evening of Sunday 2 January 1938, with the main body of the ship's company on seasonal leave and all quiet on board, smoke was seen billowing from the starboard aircraft hangar and the fire alarms rang out. Fortunately, the duty fire party was soon on the scene and in just over half an hour they had extinguished the blaze, but not before it had destroyed RAF stores and spare parts for the Walrus

aircraft. This was the second and worst fire in the hangar within a matter of days, and soon after this incident one of the Walrus's wings was found to have been deliberately damaged. All the incidents were thought to have been connected, and although there was insufficient evidence to convict any individual a change of ship's flight personnel put a stop to further incidents. Next day there was a change of command when Captain E. J. P. Brind took over from Captain Harris, and shortly afterwards *Birmingham* was moved out of dry dock and secured to a buoy in the harbour. Later that month, on 19 January, the ship began her work-up in earnest, with flying trials of a Walrus aircraft.

On the last day of January 1938, with *Birmingham* lying alongside Portsmouth's South Railway Jetty, a deputation of 400 guests from the city of Birmingham, led by the Lord Mayor, arrived alongside by special train direct from the city. Among the gifts presented to the ship was a silver cup which, in 1914, had been taken from the beached German cruiser *Emden*. After thanking the Lord Mayor, Brind told the assembled guests that he had been instructed by the C-in-C Home Fleet, to turn over the 'Emden Cup' to *Glasgow* in order that a suitable occasion might be chosen for its presentation to a German warship. Unfortunately, by early 1938 time was rapidly running out for such acts of European co-operation, and whether an opportunity arose for the return of the cup is not recorded. With the departure of the Lord Mayor and his guests preparations began to get *Birmingham* ready for sea, and at 1000 the next morning the ship was given a final inspection by the C-in-C Portsmouth.

En route to the China Station Birmingham *passed close to Spanish waters during her transit of the Mediterranean - as Spain was still embroiled in a civil war she displayed neutrality markings on 'B' and 'X' turrets.*
(Steve Bush Collection)

Finally, at 1345 that afternoon, the cruiser left South Railway Jetty and set course for Gibraltar.

As *Birmingham* left the sheltered waters of Spithead she steamed down Channel in severe south-westerly gales and torrential rain, and it was not until she reached the southern edge of the Bay of Biscay that the weather began to ease. Making only a brief stop at Gibraltar and spending just 48 hours at Malta, on 14 February she steamed south through the Suez Canal. After leaving Aden on 21 February and spending four days at Colombo, on 9 March *Birmingham* anchored in Singapore Roads, south of the city, where she officially joined the 5th Cruiser Squadron on the China Station. Other ships of the squadron included *Cumberland, Dorsetshire, Kent* and *Suffolk*. Six days later *Birmingham* put to sea for a series of exercises and manoeuvres with other ships which were based at Singapore, including the destroyer *Tenedos* which had followed *Birmingham* out from Portsmouth. Two days later, with the exercises over, *Birmingham* steamed up the eastern end of the Johore Strait to secure alongside at the newly completed and much-vaunted naval base on the north shore of Singapore Island. During the last days of March, after gunnery and towing exercises in the South China Sea, she returned to the naval base to carry out a short docking and maintenance period.

On 18 April *Birmingham* left Singapore to carry out flying exercises with her two Walrus aircraft, L2187 and L2189, on completion of which she set course for Hong Kong where, on 23 April, she secured to a buoy in the harbour. Three days later her ship's company manned and cheered ship as they bade farewell to *Capetown* which, after a two-year commission on the China Station, was leaving harbour bound for Devonport. The experiences of her ship's company were a clear indication of just how, for the Chinese, the Second World War had already begun. Japanese troops had first invaded Chinese territory in 1931, and the continual fighting was increasingly encroaching upon the European-occupied Treaty Ports, including Shanghai. In October 1937, after Chinese forces blocked the Yangtze River against the advancing Japanese, *Capetown* had been temporarily stuck at Hankow. In the event most of her ship's company were sent back to Hong Kong by train, a precarious journey during which the train was bombed. The ship's company eventually returned safely to Hong Kong, but it was an indication of just how the Sino-Japanese War of the 1930s would increasingly threaten the European Treaty Ports, which neither the Chinese nor the Japanese had any love for, and how it would inevitably involve the ships serving on the China Station.

Birmingham remained at Hong Kong until the afternoon of 3 May, when she sailed north for the naval base at Wei hai wei (now Weihai). Although it is largely forgotten today, between 1898 and 1940 the Royal Navy maintained a naval base at Wei hai wei, which was situated on Liugong Island. Its acquisition by Britain came about as a result of China's defeat in the first Sino-Japanese War of 1894-95, after which Britain and other Western powers, including the USA, Germany and France, took advantage of a weakened and politically divided China to begin what became known as the 'scramble for Concessions'. Among the more blatant examples of this Imperialist predation of Chinese territories were the leased areas and the surrounding hinterland such as Kowloon and Wei hai wei. Known to the Chinese as the 'unequal treaties' these complicated agreements infringed upon Chinese sovereignty, administrative and legal integrity, and economic viability. Extraterritorial rights exempting foreigners from Chinese justice, and putting all administration in the hands of foreigners, which included the country's ability to collect revenue through its Maritime Customs Service, all became part of the elaborate edifice of extraordinary rights and privileges that the outside powers created for themselves. Desperately in need of capital to pay a war indemnity imposed by Japan, in the late 1890s China found itself beset by European demands for territorial concessions. One such British concession was the 99-year lease of Kowloon and what became known as the New

Territories; another lesser known concession was the lease of the 285 square-mile area around the northern town of Wei hai wei, which included the six-mile-wide harbour and naval base. The terms of the lease were ambiguous, but originally it was designed to last for as long as Russia occupied Port Arthur (Dalian). However, in 1905 when Japan occupied Port Arthur, the lease was kept on. In Britain the Wei hai wei lease was always politically controversial, and no effort was made to invest in or to develop the territory. In 1930 the territory was nominally returned to China in a diplomatic deal known as 'rendition', a condition of which was that China should make it a Special Administrative Region, similar to Hong Kong's current status, and that the Royal Navy should continue to use the naval base. In November 1940, with the Japanese Army having occupied most of Wei hai wei, the Royal Navy abandoned the naval base and a year later, with the outbreak of war with Japan, all the European Concessions in China were swept away within the space of a few weeks. In the post-war world only Hong Kong and Portuguese Macau survived for any length of time, but both were totally dependent upon Chinese consent, for had they so wished China could have swiftly swallowed them up at any time. Today, the only surviving relics from the Royal Navy's Wei hai wei base are two very ornate Chinese-made guns which once stood outside the Naval Commissioner's House there, but now grace the entrance to the Senior Rates Mess at HMS *Excellent* on Whale Island.

This then was the situation on 8 May 1938, when *Birmingham* anchored at Wei hai wei to join the aircraft carrier *Eagle* along with *Cumberland, Suffolk, Falmouth* and *Folkestone*. More ominous, however, was the presence of the Japanese light cruiser *Kuma*, whose two seaplanes were regularly bombing Chinese villages in the area, usually in retaliation for the activities of Chinese guerrillas in the area, and often in full view of ships in the anchorage. To provide some relief from the swelteringly hot summer months in Hong Kong, the ships of the China Station would steam north to the cooler climes of Wei hai wei, and *Birmingham* was due to remain at the base until the end of September, when she and the rest of the fleet would return to Hong Kong. During May and June she carried out a series of day-running exercises with *Eagle* and *Cumberland*, and the first break from this routine and the rather dull canteen leave on Liekung tao Island, came in mid-July when *Birmingham* steamed up the Yangtze River to Shanghai to join French, US and Italian warships. By the end of the month she had returned to Wei hai wei, where she remained during the whole of August and the first two weeks of September.In September 1938 came the Munich Crisis and the threat of another European war, which saw the China Fleet concentrated at Hong Kong and Wei hai wei. The Royal Navy's river gunboats were ordered to move closer to Hong Kong, and if they were confronted by hostile Japanese warships to burn all confidential documents and attempt to force their way through. On 17 September *Birmingham* was ordered to curtail a convoy escort exercise with *Suffolk* and escort RFA *Appleleaf*, which had embarked naval wives and families at Wei hai wei and was evacuating them to the relative safety of Hong Kong. Half way through the passage *Birmingham* was ordered to hand the escort over to *Suffolk* and to put into Tsingtao in order that at least one major warship remained in northern waters. During *Birmingham*'s five-day stay packed Japanese transports were arriving at the port and landing thousands of troops. All around them *Birmingham*'s men could see the war between Japan and China gathering pace, but Britain was powerless to influence events and by the last week in September all attention was on the political situation in Europe where the Munich Crisis was nearing its climax, and war seemed imminent. This was the situation during the afternoon of 24 September when *Birmingham* was ordered to sail immediately for Woosung, where she was to embark the 1st Battalion The Seaforth Highlanders for immediate passage to Hong Kong. It was all part of a prearranged plan that, in the event of a European war, the bulk of Britain's armed forces would be sent

home from many colonial and quasi-colonial outposts, such as those in China. At just before midnight on 25 September *Birmingham* anchored at Woosung, and next afternoon a fleet of tugs ferried them from the Customs Jetty to the ship. The official explanation was that the regiment was going to take part in manoeuvres at Hong Kong, but this fooled no one and there was great concern in the British Concession at Shanghai, which was being left defenceless. Within two hours of embarkation *Birmingham* was at sea bound for Hong Kong where, two days later, the Army battalion was landed. By the end of September, with the Munich Crisis over and Prime Minister Neville Chamberlain having promised '*Peace for our time*', the threat of an immediate European war receded, and *Birmingham* remained at Hong Kong until 19 October. She and *Kent* then sailed north, via Amoy (Xiamen) to Shanghai where, to the relief of the British community, she remained until the second week of November.

During the evening of 6 November 1938 there was a graphic example of just how European influence in the Treaty Ports was quickly slipping away when a bomb was thrown into a Shanghai central district bar which was frequented by British servicemen. Seven men were badly injured by the blast, including three of *Birmingham*'s Royal Marines Detachment. Six days later the cruiser once again sailed south to Hong Kong, where she carried out exercises and manoeuvres with *Eagle*, *Kent* and four destroyers, all closely monitored by the Japanese cruiser *Myoko*. *Birmingham* remained in and around Hong Kong for the rest of the year, with seasonal festivities taking place in the Colony, where the China Fleet Club provided a slap-up Christmas dinner and the Peninsular Hotel was the venue for the fleet's New Year Ball. To many people it seemed that with the Munich Crisis over there really would be '*Peace for our time*'.

On 6 January 1939, *Birmingham*, accompanied by the sloops *Folkestone* and *Lowestoft*, left Hong

The cleaner lines of her bows are evident in this early view of Birmingham. *Such bows were used by US Navy cruisers and the Admiralty wished to determine the seakeeping merits of this bow over the traditional RN knuckle design. (National Museum of the Royal Navy)*

Kong to steam south through severe storms to Manila, but after four days the visit was cut short and *Birmingham* was ordered to return to Wei hai wei. Japanese interference with British-registered shipping was becoming more and more frequent, and the SS *St Vincent de Paul*, which had unloaded cargo near Haichow, had been stopped some nine miles out to sea by a Chinese Customs vessel and two Japanese destroyers, and ordered to proceed to Tsingtao, where it was detained. As soon as the British naval authorities at Shanghai learned about the incident *Birmingham* and *Folkestone* were ordered to free the British ship. Arriving at Tsingtao during the forenoon of 29 January, they were met by a hostile force of Japanese heavy cruisers led by *Ashigara*. There then followed a very tense 24-hour period of negotiations between Captain Brind and British consular officials and Japanese naval officers from *Ashigara*. Some 18 months earlier the Japanese cruiser had paid a friendly courtesy visit to Spithead for the Coronation Review, but now it was very different and at one stage the Japanese threatened to open fire on *Birmingham*, *Folkestone* and *St Vincent de Paul*. Seeing that negotiations were getting nowhere Brind stated quite bluntly that at 0800 the next morning he intended sailing with the captured merchantman and with that he returned to *Birmingham*. Next morning the situation was tense as the three British ships prepared to put to sea, but at exactly 0800, with *Folkestone* leading the way, followed by *St Vincent de Paul* and *Birmingham* bringing up the rear, the three ships sailed. As they left harbour *Ashigara*'s 8-inch guns were trained on *Birmingham*, and with the ship's company at their Action Stations the British cruiser trained her main armament on the Japanese cruiser. Although the incident passed off peacefully it was a clear indication of the deteriorating relations between Britain and Japan. After clearing the harbour *Birmingham* led the escort of *St Paul de Vincent* for most of the way to Hong Kong, before handing over to *Folkestone* and returning north to Wei hai wei. Although the incident made world news it was soon overshadowed by another more serious incident when, just four miles outside Hong Kong, Japanese naval ships stopped, boarded and attempted to detain the P&O passenger liner *Ranpura*. However, this incident was dealt with by ships from Hong Kong and when the cruiser returned to the colony on 24 February it was to begin a ten-week docking and maintenance period.

In early May 1939 *Birmingham* was at sea again, and in company with *Cornwall* and *Diamond* she carried out post-refit trials and manoeuvres. On 14 May, flying the flag of the C-in-C China Station, Vice-Admiral Sir Percy Noble, and in company with *Defender* and *Duncan*, she left Hong Kong for Amoy and Foochow (Xiamen and Fuzhou respectively). The C-in-C was travelling to meet with senior US Navy officers in the cruiser USS *Marblehead* at Shanghai, where the British ships were also going to show the flag, for rumours were circulating that the Japanese Army was planning to seize the International Concessions in the city. During the eight days *Birmingham* spent at Shanghai Noble made strong protests to Japanese Vice-Admiral Oikawa about the conduct of his ships in stopping and detaining British vessels, as well as the Japanese military occupation of Kulangsu Island in Fujian Province, not far north of Hong Kong. By all accounts the protests were listened to politely, but ignored. Japan was well aware of the weakness of Britain in all its Far Eastern possessions, from Singapore to Wei hai wei. The direct talks between the two admirals on board *Birmingham* failed to achieve anything and the aggressive Japanese tactics continued. Indeed, on 7 June, while *Birmingham* was returning to Hong Kong from Shanghai she was closely shadowed by two Japanese seaplane carriers. On 12 June 1939, for the last time, the ships on the China Station left Hong Kong to sail north to spend the summer months at Wei hai wei. *Birmingham* escorted the aircraft carrier *Eagle* which, with *Hermes*, had been a regular visitor to the China Station. Once at sea they were joined by *Cornwall, Kent* and four destroyers. The whole fleet remained in the vicinity of Wei hai wei until late July. By the summer of

1939, however, Wei hai wei was completely dominated by the Japanese base, and their troop transports escorted by powerful warships were coming and going continually. During the last week of July *Birmingham* sailed for Amoy, where she remained at anchor for three weeks and once again her ship's company watched as Japanese troop transports landed their human cargoes by the thousand. On 24 August *Birmingham* arrived back in Hong Kong, but her stay in harbour was brief, for next day she was ordered to sail for Singapore to undergo maintenance. She arrived at the naval base three days later and was immediately secured in the floating dry dock. It was on Saturday 2 September when, in company with *Eagle*, she put to sea again to patrol the Strait of Malacca. Next day, when war was declared, she was off the Sumatran port of Pankalanlunang, in what were then Dutch territorial waters. During her patrol *Birmingham* rendezvoused with the submarines *Regent, Rover* and *Grampus*, which were also patrolling the Strait, to provide them with fresh provisions. On 15 September she anchored in the Sunda Strait, within sight of Krakatau, to refuel from RFA *Appleleaf*, and two days later she rendezvoused with the Dutch destroyer *Banckert* off Sumatra's south coast. *Birmingham*'s long patrol ended on 28 September at Singapore Naval Base.

During October 1939 *Birmingham* continued to patrol the waters and sea lanes around Singapore and the Dutch East Indies (Indonesia), regularly supplying the submarines *Odin* and *Olympus* with fresh provisions, and refuelling at sea from RFA *Appleleaf*. She also carried out joint manoeuvres with the Australian cruiser *Hobart* (ex-*Apollo*) and the elderly *Durban*. During the first months of the European War the Navy's presence in South-East Asia was weak, consisting of the 5th Cruiser Squadron which, in addition to *Birmingham* and *Durban*, included *Kent* (flag C-in-C), *Cornwall* and *Dorsetshire*, the 21st Destroyer Flotilla with nine destroyers, five escort vessels and the outdated aircraft carrier *Eagle*. There was also the 17th Submarine Flotilla with 17 submarines, seven based at Hong Kong and ten at Singapore. With the naval base at Wei hai wei having been virtually abandoned, the only two bases were at Singapore and Hong Kong. However, it had long been recognised that Hong Kong could not be defended against any determined and well-equipped army. The seizure by Japan of Amoy and the landings at Bias Bay, some 50 miles north of Hong Kong, by a large Japanese force had completed the isolation of Hong Kong and the adjoining leased territories. The war in Europe had also created serious problems for the defence of the Malay Peninsula and the island of Singapore. It had become very clear that the dispatch of a large battlefleet to the brand new and much-vaunted naval base on Singapore Island would be impossible, and Britain's weakness in the Far East had been known to Japanese Intelligence since at least 1915, when Britain had to call upon Japanese forces to assist in quelling a mutiny in the small Indian garrison on the island. As the Japanese Army steadily increased its hold on large areas of China and its government waited for an opportunity to rid South-East Asia of its European colonists, the best Britain could do was to attempt to maintain a good relationship with an increasingly aggressive Japan.

During the second week of November, with *Cornwall, Dorsetshire* and *Eagle* having been dispatched to Trincomalee, *Birmingham* left Singapore to return to Hong Kong where she remained for the rest of the year. On 25 November, while patrolling in heavy seas off Hong Kong, a rating was lost overboard and despite a long search of the area no trace of him could be found. Christmas Day was spent on patrol with the armed merchant cruiser *Moreton Bay* (ex-Aberdeen & Commonwealth passenger liner), and two days later she returned to Hong Kong to undergo a short, five-day docking prior to leaving the China Station and sailing west.

On Tuesday 2 January 1940, the C-in-C China Station addressed the ship's company and next day *Birmingham* sailed for the Mediterranean. Calling briefly at Singapore, Colombo and Aden, she made her northbound transit of the Suez Canal on 19

January, and two days later she secured alongside Somerset Wharf in Malta's Grand Harbour to begin a 14-day maintenance period. *Birmingham* remained with the Mediterranean Fleet for just four weeks, during which time she briefly hoisted the flag of the C-in-C, Admiral Cunningham, and took part in fleet manoeuvres between Alexandria and Malta. On 19 February she was ordered to sail for home waters and making a fast, non-stop passage she arrived at Spithead during the afternoon of 24 February. Later that day she steamed up harbour to secure alongside Portsmouth's Pitch House Jetty, from where the ship's company began a period of well-earned leave, and for many there were draft chits to other ships.

On 4 March 1940 there was a change of command when Captain A. C. G. Madden RN[2] took over from Captain Brind, and 12 days later *Birmingham* sailed to join the Home Fleet, and her sister *Manchester*, on Northern Patrol blockade duties in the waters between Iceland and the Shetland Islands. Those members of the ship's company who had remained with the ship now experienced the bitterly cold Arctic waters, in sharp contrast to those of the South China and Yellow Seas. On 25 March, six days into her first patrol, *Birmingham* intercepted and stopped her first merchantman, the Norwegian cargo steamer *Norge Athene*, which was dispatched under armed guard to Kirkwall in order that her cargo could be checked. On 31 March *Birmingham* left Scapa Flow for her second patrol in northern waters, most of which was conducted in blinding blizzards and heavy seas. During the patrol she supplied trawlers with fresh provisions, and on 9 April she rendezvoused with the battlefleet, which included *Renown, Rodney, Valiant, Warspite* and the aircraft carrier *Furious*, as it returned to Scapa Flow. At 1545, however, just three hours away from her destination, *Birmingham* was attacked by a lone German aircraft which dropped three bombs, all of which missed the ship, and that evening she anchored safely in Scapa Flow.

During the second week of April the German Army invaded Norway and on 13 April, in company with *Manchester*, *Birmingham* left Scapa Flow to escort a troop convoy to Lillesjona Fjord, where they arrived safely three days later. During the period at anchor in the fjord she was attacked by enemy aircraft, but once again she came through unscathed. During the early hours of 17 April she weighed anchor and left the fjord to rendezvous with the fast Canadian Pacific liner, turned troop transport, *Empress of Australia*, which she escorted back to home waters before returning to Scapa Flow. Four days later, on 23 April, she joined *Manchester* and *York* at Rosyth to embark troop reinforcements for Andalsnes in central Norway. With a screen of three destroyers, the three cruisers left Rosyth at 0700 on 24 April to make a fast passage to Andalsnes. During the afternoon of the next day they came under attack from the air, but fortunately there were no hits or casualties and five hours later, at 2119, *Birmingham* anchored off the Norwegian port. Within minutes of her arrival the destroyer *Acheron* was alongside and the work of disembarking troops, stores and equipment began. By 0209 on 26 April the disembarkation had been completed and *Birmingham* weighed anchor and set course for Scapa Flow. At 0740, some five hours after sailing, a suspicious trawler flying the Dutch flag was sighted; it was quickly identified as the German *Schleswig*, and within ten minutes the cruiser's main armament had sunk the vessel. *Birmingham* arrived back at Scapa on 29 April, but by this time all British forces in central and southern Norway were being evacuated, leaving only a small force at Narvik. On the last day of April *Birmingham* was once again ordered to sail for Andalsnes, this time to assist with the evacuation.

During the passage across the Norwegian Sea *Birmingham* was twice attacked by enemy aircraft, but by skilful manoeuvring she managed to evade all the bombs. At 2300 on 1 May she anchored off Andalsnes where she, *Manchester*, *Calcutta* and *Auckland* embarked a mixed military force of Royal Marines, Green Howards and the King's Own

[2] Later Admiral Sir Alexander Cumming Gordon Madden. Retired 1955 as C-in-C Plymouth.

Yorkshire Light Infantry. At just after midnight on 2 May, *Birmingham* and *Manchester* weighed anchor to make a fast passage back to Scapa Flow, where they arrived without further incident during the morning of 3 May. It was the end of *Birmingham*'s brief involvement in the Norwegian campaign, and on 9 May she was ordered south to Immingham to bolster the North Sea naval defences between there and Rosyth, during which time she spent long periods at anchor in the mouth of the River Humber. On 21 June, while she and *York* were on patrol in the North Sea they were attacked by enemy aircraft, but they emerged unscathed. Five days later *Birmingham* underwent a five-day docking period at Rosyth, after which she steamed south to Sheerness from where she formed part of the Thames Estuary defences for the next six weeks. With most of Western Europe having been overrun by German forces, Britain was on high invasion alert, and *Birmingham* remained in the Thames Estuary until mid-August, rarely straying from her buoy off Sheerness. With steam continually raised and with very limited shore leave for the ship's company, she remained at immediate notice for sea. On 17 August, however, she was ordered north to Scapa Flow from where, with *Manchester*, she patrolled between the Orkney Islands and Immingham. During three weeks of September she remained at anchor in the mouth of the River Humber, then in the last week of that month she sailed north and through the Pentland Firth, down into the Irish Sea to Birkenhead to undergo a major 13-week refit, which would keep her out of commission until the end of the year.

During her refit *Birmingham* was fitted with Type 286M surface warning radar, which was the first ship-borne radar capable of detecting surface vessels and was actually modified RAF equipment. On Christmas Day 1940 *Birmingham* was shifted from dry dock to Liverpool's Albert Dock, and next day she sailed north to Scapa Flow where, on New Year's Eve, she rejoined the 18th Cruiser Squadron for contraband control duties on the Northern Patrol between Iceland and the Orkney Islands. During January 1941, sometimes in company with *Edinburgh*, she patrolled the icy waters of the Norwegian Sea. In early February, however, there was a change of scenery when she sailed south to Greenock to refuel and await the formation of a large convoy, WS6, which was bound for Cape Town and the Indian Ocean. In addition to *Birmingham* other escorts included *Rodney*, *Renown*, *Ark Royal*, *Malaya* and a destroyer flotilla. The whole force, together with the convoy, left Greenock on 9 February to set course into mid-Atlantic before turning south. The first break in the long, slow passage came on 2 March when the convoy reached Freetown, but six days later the passage south was resumed. During the forenoon of 12 March there was time to mark the crossing of the equator and nine days later, having delivered the convoy safely to its next destination, *Birmingham* secured alongside Cape Town's Duncan Dock. For the ship's company there was a weekend to enjoy shore leave in a country which was largely untouched by war, before sailing on Monday 24 March for home waters. Two days out, however, her passage was slowed somewhat when she encountered the merchantman *Christian Huygens*, which had been partially disabled with engine trouble, and she escorted her to Freetown. On leaving Freetown *Birmingham* was ordered to accompany the armed merchant cruiser *Bulolo* and also assist in the escort of a homeward-bound convoy. In the event it was 22 April before *Birmingham* arrived back in Scapa Flow, where she rejoined the cruiser squadron. With Germany having occupied much of Europe the Northern Patrol was not going to be as effective as it had proved in the Great War, but the Home Fleet's priority in the spring of 1941 was indicated by a major tactical exercise which took place between 5 and 7 May, involving *Birmingham*, *Edinburgh*, *Manchester* and a destroyer flotilla. *Manchester* took the role of a German pocket battleship while the destroyer *Nestor* acted as an accompanying heavy cruiser, both of which were attempting to break through the northern blockade to prey on Allied shipping in the Atlantic Ocean. The two

'enemy' ships were spotted and shadowed by *Birmingham*, *Edinburgh* and their escorting destroyers, *Bedouin, Eskimo* and *Walpole*, which bore an uncanny resemblance to the events which would unfold later that month. During the latter part of the exercise *Birmingham* herself was shadowed by a German Focke-Wulf aircraft, which was obviously monitoring naval activity in the area. However, after several bursts of anti-aircraft fire from the naval ships it left the scene. No sooner was the exercise over than *Edinburgh* intercepted the German weather ship *München*. On 18 May *Birmingham* and *Manchester* left Scapa Flow for another patrol between Iceland and the Orkney Islands, but this time the exercise practised earlier in the month was to become a reality, for later that day *Bismarck* and the cruiser *Prinz Eugen* left Danzig (Gdynia) in their bid to break out into the Atlantic. In the event the two German ships took the route north of Iceland, while *Birmingham* and *Manchester* had been ordered to patrol much further south to cover the Iceland-Faeroes gap. As events transpired neither of the two cruisers took any part in the sea battles which saw the destruction of *Hood*, and on the last day of May *Birmingham* returned from the area around the Faeroes to secure at a buoy in Scapa Flow.

On 2 June *Birmingham* left Scapa Flow to steam south to Greenock, where she had been ordered to act as ocean escort to an important troop convoy, WS9A, which was routed via Cape Town to the Indian Ocean. Leaving Greenock on 4 June the convoy steamed well out into the Atlantic before turning south and Freetown was reached on 16 June. On 3 July, having detached the convoy safely to Cape Town, *Birmingham* secured alongside the naval base at Simonstown. This time, however, she did not return home, but continued to escort the convoy towards Durban, handing it over to *Hawkins* when it was some 24 hours from its destination. *Birmingham* then retraced her route to Simonstown from where, on 25 July, she sailed north with another convoy. Arriving in Freetown on 1 August, there was a short weekend break before the cruiser sailed for South America to patrol the waters off the River Plate.

She had been ordered to the South Atlantic Station to join *Newcastle* and the armed merchant cruisers *Carnarvon Castle* and *Alcantara* patrolling the vital South American trade routes. On 14 August *Birmingham* anchored off Cabo San Antonio, on the south side of the River Plate estuary, where Rear-Admiral F. H. Pegram hoisted his flag. Next day, in company with *Newcastle* and *Alcantara*, she began her first patrol of the River Plate area, during which *Newcastle* left for Freetown. The patrol lasted for ten uneventful days, before she again anchored off Cabo San Antonio to embark provisions and to refuel from RFA *Abbeydale*. At the end of August there was a rare treat when *Birmingham* called at Rio de Janeiro, but visits to neutral ports lasted only 48 hours at the most and they were limited to just one every five to six weeks. In September the long days of patrolling the Atlantic Ocean between the River Plate and the Abrolhos Rocks, off the west coast of Australia, were broken by a short stay at Buenos Aires, and at the end of October she paid another visit to Rio de Janeiro. In mid-November, however, there was a change to her routine when, after spending 48 hours at Montevideo, *Birmingham* steamed south to Port Stanley in the Falkland Islands, where she was scheduled to remain for a week to carry out maintenance. At 1500 on 23 November, however, memories of December 1914 were evoked when lookouts spotted smoke from an unidentified ship approaching from the south. All the cruiser's liberty men were immediately recalled and steam was raised, but two hours later as she was about to sail, the unknown vessel was identified as a friendly merchantman. By the end of November *Birmingham* was back in her patrol area off the River Plate. During the first week of December, following the entry of Japan into the war, *Birmingham* was ordered to Simonstown, where she arrived alongside the naval base on 10 December. Rumours on board were flying around thick and fast, the two favourites being that the ship was to join the hard-

pressed East Indies Fleet at Colombo, while the more optimistic speculated that the ship would return home. In the meantime, during the brief stay at Simonstown, there was a change of command when Captain H. B. Crane RN, who had travelled from Australia where he had commanded the shore establishment HMAS *Cerberus*, took over from Captain Madden. In the event neither of the two main rumours about *Birmingham*'s future were correct and after a brief stay at Simonstown the ship returned to patrol the South American trade routes, with Christmas Day spent off the coast of Uruguay and the new year being seen in at Rio de Janeiro. On New Year's Day 1942 the cruiser was ordered south.

With the Japanese Navy temporarily in control of the Pacific Ocean, and in a position to attack at will in almost all of the Indian Ocean, there were concerns as to the safety of the Falkland Islands and so *Birmingham* was dispatched to Port Stanley. During the whole of January the cruiser patrolled that region of the South Atlantic, on one occasion making a brief visit to the Argentine port of Punta Arenas, but by early February she was back in the River Plate area. She remained there until the third week of February, when she sailed via Tristan da Cunha to Simonstown to begin a five-week refit and docking period.

During *Birmingham*'s stay at Simonstown her AA armament was improved by the fitting of 20mm close-range anti-aircraft guns, and the Type 286M radar which had been installed at Liverpool in the autumn of 1940 was replaced with an improved Type 291; fire control Type 284 radar for the 6-inch armament was also fitted. The refit provided a welcome period of relaxation for the ship's company, and after its completion on 6 April the ship remained in or around Simonstown for the rest of the month. *Birmingham* had been allocated to the 4th Cruiser Squadron of the Eastern Fleet, and on the last day of April she steamed north for Kilindini Harbour, Mombasa, where, on 7 May, she joined

HMS Birmingham *in the Indian Ocean in 1942 wearing an Admiralty Light Disruptive type camouflage comprising blue, grey and cream panels.* *(Crown Copyright/MoD 1942)*

Newcastle, Caledon, Emerald and *Enterprise*. During the rest of May *Birmingham* took part in exercises with other ships of the fleet, including the aircraft carrier *Formidable*, and paid a short visit to Tanga. During the last week of May she sailed north to Aden to refuel before steaming on through the Red Sea and the Suez Canal.

HMS *Birmingham* had been temporarily loaned to the Mediterranean Fleet specifically for 'Operation Vigorous', the running of eleven merchant ships from Alexandria to Malta, in conjunction with 'Operation Harpoon', a supply convoy from Gibraltar to Malta. Accompanying *Birmingham* to the Mediterranean was *Newcastle* and on 2 June, when 24 hours away from Suez, the two cruisers passed the old Great War veteran battleship, now a target ship, HMS *Centurion*, which had been mocked up to resemble *Anson*. After a delay outside Port Suez they made their northbound transit of the Suez Canal on 6 June, and next afternoon arrived at Alexandria. *Birmingham*'s first operational duty with the Mediterranean Fleet, which would also be her last with them, began on 13 June when, with *Newcastle*, she took part in what has been described as one of the 'most disturbing' operations in the Mediterranean war at sea. The 11 merchantmen involved in 'Operation Vigorous', together with the escorts, left Alexandria during the afternoon of 13 June, but next day one merchantman was sunk. Soon after this strong winds and heavy seas forced the escorting MTBs to return to Alexandria, and that afternoon the convoy came under air attack and another merchantman was lost. However, there was worse to come when, at 0400 on 15 June, enemy E-boats torpedoed and seriously damaged *Newcastle*. The explosion tore out so much of her starboard shell plating she was unfit for further service and had to return to Alexandria. Eight hours later *Birmingham* and the rest of the convoy were subjected to fierce air attacks by German Ju-87 'Stuka' dive-bombers. One attack saw *Birmingham* straddled by bombs, one of which exploded very close to her starboard side aft, causing extensive splinter damage and disabling her after gun turrets. Soon after this the convoy was ordered to return to Alexandria, but during the night of 15/16 June the cruiser *Hermione* was torpedoed and sunk by *U-205*, with the destroyer *Exmoor* rescuing over 400 survivors. At 2045 on 16 June *Birmingham* arrived back at Alexandria, where she remained for five days for repairs to her splinter damage. She then sailed south through the Suez Canal to Aden where, on 2 July, she rejoined the Eastern Fleet.

Much to everyone's relief *Birmingham*'s stay in Aden lasted for only ten hours before she sailed south to Mombasa, the Eastern Fleet's base since March 1942. She arrived on 8 July to undergo a seven-day maintenance period before joining other ships of the Eastern Fleet, including *Formidable, Illustrious, Resolution* and *Mauritius*, for manoeuvres off the Kenyan coast. In the summer of 1942 the Eastern Fleet was on high alert for an expected Japanese offensive against Ceylon and on 21 July, in company with *Formidable* and *Mauritius*, she left Kilindini Harbour for the island. On arrival eight days later the three ships did not go to the naval base at Trincomalee, which was more vulnerable to air attack, putting in instead to Colombo Harbour. Admiral Somerville, the C-in-C, Eastern Fleet, wished to provide some sort of Indian Ocean naval diversion in order to assist the hard-pressed US Navy in the Pacific Ocean. This was codenamed 'Operation Stab' and involved sailing three dummy convoys from three separate ports, Trincomalee, Madras and Visagapatam (Vishakhapatnam), into the Bay of Bengal, suggesting an invasion and attempt to retake the Andaman Islands, which had been occupied by Japan some four months earlier. It was at 1715 on 30 July that *Birmingham*, the elderly *Warspite* (flag C-in-C), *Illustrious, Formidable, Mauritius* and four destroyers, comprising Force A, sailed from Colombo ostensibly to provide cover for the three convoys, which were under orders to reverse during the night of 2 August and return to their ports. However, the presence of a powerful Japanese naval force in the Strait of Malacca was detached

causing Somerville to cancel the operation. Force A, including *Birmingham*, returned to Colombo from where, after refuelling, it sailed for Kilindini.

During the whole of August *Birmingham* underwent maintenance at Kilindini, but on 6 September, in company with *Dauntless, Gambia, Caradoc, Illustrious*, the monitor *Erebus*, the HQ ship *Albatross*, *Manxman*, 12 destroyers, an assortment of minesweepers and an invasion convoy of transports, she left the port as part of 'Operation Stream', the invasion and capture of Majunga (Mahajanga) on the northern end of Madagascar's west coast. Earlier that year, with US Government approval, a mainly British force had invaded and occupied the Vichy naval base at Diego Suarez, and this latest invasion was a move to consolidate the Allied occupation of Madagascar in order to forestall any Japanese attempt to set up bases on the island. US assurances that Madagascar would be fully restored as a French colonial possession after the war were given in the hope that there would be little or no resistance to the invasion, and these proved to be well founded, for at just after midnight on 10 September the landings began. By 0830 the same day all resistance had ceased and by the evening the town had returned to normal. *Birmingham*'s liberty men were allowed ashore where they found the population to be pro-France rather than pro-Vichy. By 13 September, with her presence off Majunga no longer required she steamed north to Diego Suarez to prepare for the next stage of the operation, the invasion of the eastern port of Tamatave. This got under way during the early hours of 18 September with *Illustrious* and *Warspite* also taking part. After a short naval bombardment all resistance ashore ceased and *Birmingham*'s log entry for 0853 reads: '*Ceasefire, white flag hoisted ashore*'. Next day *Birmingham* returned to Diego Suarez.

Her final involvement in what was known as the 'United Nations' occupation of Madagascar came on 29 September, when at 0713 she anchored off the south-western port of Tuléar where her detachment of Royal Marines led the assault force ashore. This landing was accomplished without any opposition, and next day the cruiser steamed north to Diego Suarez from where, on 5 October, she sailed for Kilindini Harbour en route to Simonstown to undergo a short docking and maintenance period. The refit ended on the last day of October, when *Birmingham* steamed north, via Durban, for Kilindini and from there to Bombay where, on arrival in mid-November, she received a visit from the C-in-C. For the foreseeable future the cruiser would carry out trade protection duties in the Indian Ocean, where at least four Japanese submarines were attacking and sinking Allied shipping. On Friday 20 November, as *Birmingham* lay at anchor in Bombay Harbour preparing for her first patrol, the 10,000-gross ton passenger-cargo steamer *Tilawa*, belonging to the British-India Steam Navigation Company, slid by her and cleared the harbour to set course for East African ports. On board, in addition to some 6,472 tons of cargo and a crew of 220, she was carrying some 715 Indian people, most of whom were deck passengers who lived on the upper decks and slept below in large dormitories. Over 100 of these passengers were women and children. The ship was equipped with ten lifeboats and 25 life rafts, which in an emergency with the ship undamaged would have been barely sufficient for the numbers carried. Three days later during the early hours of 23 November, she was torpedoed by the patrolling Japanese submarine *I-29*. Although *Tilawa* remained afloat the huge explosion caused many of the deck passengers to panic and many of them jumped overboard. Others tried desperately to launch lifeboats. One passenger, Mr Chunilal Novsaria, who was a teenager at the time, remembers the night: '*I was just falling into a deep sleep when I was woken by a loud and violent explosion. Expecting the worst I grabbed my life jacket and headed for the upper decks. There was chaos and panic everywhere as everyone headed for the upper decks. As they climbed the main stairs everyone was scrambling and stamping about and before I knew it I was hurtling back down the way I had come.*' Eventually

Chunilal managed to get into a lifeboat which he remembers thus: '*We drifted for an entire day and night, the sea was choppy, a cold wind was blowing and all I had to keep me warm were the pyjamas I was wearing. During the day it rained hard and our boat was tossed about perilously. On the morning of the 25 November we sighted a small plane which approached and signalled to us. Later we saw a cruiser on the horizon.*'

Before *Tilawa* had been hit by a second torpedo her radio operator managed to send distress signals and at 0405 on 24 November *Birmingham* was ordered to search for survivors. As she steamed towards *Tilawa*'s last known position, 07°36'N 006°08'E, some 500 miles east of Socotra, she began flying off her aircraft in an attempt to locate any lifeboats. That afternoon the search was delayed when one of the cruiser's own ship's company fell overboard, but fortunately he was recovered safely, and at 2046 the first of *Tilawa*'s lifeboats was sighted just over a mile away. At 2131, with these survivors having been embarked, the search was resumed, but it was dawn on 25 November before the next boat was sighted. After that, from 0600 until 1830, *Birmingham* was searching for and rescuing survivors from boats and rafts, and by nightfall she had picked up 661 people. Chunilal Novsaria describes his own rescue: '*We saw the ship on the horizon coming closer and closer. It was* HMS Birmingham *and we were picked up and taken aboard, where we were issued with blankets and given tea and sandwiches. The medical staff on board were very busy and they successfully carried out five major operations, 20 minor operations and treated over 400 cases of burns, abrasions and shock. Accommodation on board was allocated as follows: European men – wardroom, gunroom and warrant officers mess; European women and children – captain's day and sleeping cabins; Indian women and children – admiral's day and dining cabins;* Tilawa *crew – in the cruiser's waist; Male deck passengers – on the hangar deck and in the starboard hangar. Most of us were very inadequately clad in either nightwear or underwear, and everyone was kitted out with clothing of some sort. During the journey to safety two survivors died and were buried at sea.*'

At 1840 on 25 November, having embarked the last of *Tilawa*'s survivors, *Birmingham* set course for Bombay, where she secured alongside Ballard Pier at 1745 on 27 November. Chunilal Novsaria again: '*The quayside was packed with anxious relatives and friends enquiring after the safety of their loved ones. A massive reception awaited us, with tables laid out and piled high with food, refreshments and clean clothing. Even in the hustle and bustle of the huge crowd my mother quickly spotted me and she was so overjoyed and overcome with emotion that she started telling everyone that it was because of her generosity to the destitute and poor that she had been blessed with the survival and safe return of her son. Sadly though, 242 passengers and 28 of* Tilawa*'s crew were lost at sea on that tragic night.*' Three days later *Birmingham* left Bombay for Kilindini Harbour, from where she operated for the rest of that year.

The new year of 1943 for *Birmingham* began with intensive exercises in the western Indian Ocean, often in company with *Warspite, Illustrious* and *Hawkins*. By the end of the month, however, she had returned to trade protection duties and was escorting convoys between Mombasa and Durban; this continued through to the third week of March. On 18 March came the day that the ship's company had been long waiting for when, at 1050, she slipped quietly out of Kilindini Harbour to steam south to Durban and Simonstown, pausing only briefly at each port, before heading north into the Atlantic Ocean and to Freetown, where she arrived on 9 April. Next day she left harbour to set course for a non-stop passage home. Finally, at 0730 on 19 April, two Spitfires, which were to escort her for the final leg of the voyage, circled overhead and two hours later she anchored in Plymouth Sound. The first visitors to arrive on board were from HM Customs, but three hours later she was given clearance to proceed up harbour, and at 1330 she secured alongside Devonport Dockyard's No 5 wharf. It

HMS Birmingham *in 1943 following her repair and refit at Devonport.* *(Syd Goodman Collection)*

was the end of the commission, and as soon as *Birmingham* had been placed in dockyard hands to begin a five-month refit, her complement was reduced to just a small care and maintenance party.

For over two months *Birmingham* lay in Devonport's No 8 dry dock. Work on the ship included the fitting of anti-aircraft fire control, Type 284 air warning radar, and a Type 281 radar installation. On 7 September 1943 Captain H. W. Williams RN relieved Captain Crane and took command of the ship. Six days later *Birmingham* moved out to a buoy in Plymouth Sound, and on 16 September she undertook two days of sea trials before returning to Devonport for final adjustments to her machinery before sailing north to Scapa Flow to carry out a five-week programme of work-up exercises. By the second week in November the work-up period had been completed and she had steamed south to Greenock, prior to sailing for the Mediterranean where she was to be based at Alexandria. With the Italian Fleet having surrendered a few weeks earlier the Mediterranean was a much quieter theatre of war than it had been when she had last sailed from Alexandria, although it was known that some German U-boats were still operating off North Africa. After leaving Greenock during the early hours of 16 November *Birmingham* and the armed merchant cruiser *Ranchi* made a long detour into mid-Atlantic, finally arriving in Gibraltar on 24 November.

After a 36-hour break at Gibraltar *Birmingham*, accompanied by the Greek destroyer *Themistocles* and the Polish *Krakowiak*, sailed for Alexandria. The first two days at sea passed without incident, and as far as possible the RAF provided air cover in the form of Beaufort and Hurricane aircraft. By the forenoon of Sunday 28 November the cruiser was off the coast of Cyrenaica (eastern Libya), north east of Benghazi. At 1112 she altered course to make the starboard leg of her zigzag and six minutes later she was in a position 33°04'N 021°42'E, steering 080° and steaming at 23 knots. Unfortunately, the cruiser had crossed the path of the patrolling German submarine *U-407*, which fired one torpedo. The missile slammed into *Birmingham*'s port side under the keel between stations 22 and 25. The massive explosion caused the ship to whip violently and a huge column of water and debris was thrown high above the bridge. Twenty-three men were killed instantly, all but one of whom were never found, and four more died within two hours. Twelve men were very seriously wounded and 78 others suffered minor injuries. After the spray had subsided speed was reduced to just ten knots, and the ship took on a seven-degree list to port. About 30 seconds after the explosion one of the cruiser's lookouts sighted what he thought was an air bubble swirling on the surface

some 1,000 yards away on the port beam and the cruiser's stern was turned towards the position.

The damage to *Birmingham*'s superstructure on the port side was severe, with the centre of the damage clearly visible from the upper deck where a large jagged opening could be seen. However, the ship's main propulsion machinery and steering gear was undamaged, and at just after midday, at a speed of ten knots, the ship resumed her passage to Alexandria. That afternoon, with the two destroyers forming a tight anti-submarine screen, the five dead were buried at sea. In the event it was at 1000 on the last day of November when *Birmingham* secured alongside at Alexandria, where she was to remain for the next six months as temporary repairs were made to the damaged forward section of the ship. It was virtually the end of her operational wartime career.

HMS *Birmingham* finally left Alexandria during the forenoon of 21 June 1944, then joined a westbound convoy, which included the troopships *Monarch of Bermuda* and *Strathaird*, to make a slow, six-day passage to Gibraltar. On 29 June she left Gibraltar for a ten-day transatlantic voyage to the USA. She secured alongside the US naval base at Norfolk, Virginia, on 9 July and remained there until late November. During this period major repairs were carried out to the whole of the cruiser's bow section which was virtually rebuilt. On 14 November she was hauled out of dry dock and nine days later she began a four-day period of trials in Chesapeake Bay. Finally, on 29 November she left US waters to make her transatlantic passage home, and after refuelling at sea from RFA *Empire Gordon* she arrived at Portsmouth on 8 December, where almost half the ship's company left for new drafts. Next day she was taken in hand for work on her radar system, with a new Type 282 anti-aircraft fire control for close-range weapons being fitted. In addition 'X' turret and the aircraft catapult were both removed.

By mid-January 1945, with her ship's company having been brought back to full strength, *Birmingham* was once again ready for operational service. At just after midnight on 13 January 1945 she left Spithead to steam north to Scapa Flow, where next day she joined the 10th Cruiser Squadron of the Home Fleet and began a four-week work-up period, during which she rarely ventured beyond the confines of Scapa Flow for more than a few hours at a time. On 14 February, with her work-up completed, she hoisted the flag of CS10, Vice-Admiral F. H. G. Dalrymple-Hamilton. On 8 March, in company with *Rodney* and *Devonshire*, she took part in a sweep against enemy shipping off the Norwegian coast, but owing to foul weather conditions the operation was cut short and the force returned to Scapa Flow. *Birmingham*'s next foray into the Norwegian Sea took place shortly before the end of the war in Europe, when she and *Bellona* provided anti-aircraft cover for the escort carriers *Queen, Searcher* and *Trumpeter*, which were flying sorties to seek out and attack enemy shipping off Norway. They left Scapa Flow during the early morning of 6 April, but once again severe weather disrupted flying and the operation was cut short; not, however, before *Birmingham* had steamed into the Arctic Circle. On 12 April, she returned to Scapa Flow. It was her final operational duty of the Second World War.

On 5 May 1945, three days before the end of the war in Europe, *Birmingham* steamed south to Rosyth. Here she embarked additional naval personnel for duties in connection with the German surrender of naval forces in Denmark, where a large proportion of the Kriegsmarine was based. Next day, at 1700, in company with *Dido*, four destroyers and a flotilla of minesweepers, she sailed from Rosyth bound for Copenhagen. Their passage through German minefields in the Skagerrak and the Kattegat was difficult and slow, but finally at 1000 on 9 May they entered Copenhagen Harbour, where they found what were virtually the last remnants of the German surface fleet, including the powerful cruisers *Prinz Eugen* and *Nürnberg*, which only days earlier had been shelling Copenhagen. With them in harbour were three destroyers, two torpedo boats, ten minesweepers

HMS Birmingham *in November 1944 following her second major repair and refit, this time conducted at Norfolk, Virginia in the USA. The markings on the image highlight the revised armament changes. Note also the removal of the aircraft catapults and the blanked off hangars.* *(Courtesy of James Flynn)*

The last remnants of the German Fleet, including the cruisers Prinz Eugen *and* Nürnberg, *came under the guns of the Royal Navy in Copenhagen Harbour at 0900 on 10 May 1945. The British warships under the command of Captain H.W. Williams RN had been steaming for two days forcing a passage through the German minefields in the Skagerrak and Kattegat to reach Copenhagen after the German surrender. This image shows ratings and Royal Marines from* HMS Birmingham *throwing cigarettes to Danish sightseers.* *(Crown Copyright/MoD 1945)*

and an assortment of armed auxiliaries. An eyewitness on board *Birmingham* describes the entry into harbour thus: '*On board* HMS Birmingham *our Royal Marines Band was playing on the quarter-deck and the ship was dressed with three of the largest White Ensigns on board, but we were taking no chances and the rest of the ship's company was at Actions Stations and on the alert for the slightest hostile movement. There was none that mattered. One ship, a merchantman, had its crew fallen in with their backs to us as we steamed by. Another, a torpedo boat, passed close to us with her officers looking the other way, but that was all. As we made our way slowly to the quayside we passed* Prinz Eugen *lying alongside. Although she towered above all else in the harbour she was a defeated ship, with her guns in wild disorder, some pointing up, others down, some trained one way and the rest another.*'

Once alongside, the additional officers from *Birmingham* and *Dido* served on the various surrender committees whose duties included inspections of the German warships. Under pressure from

the Danish Government priority was given to moving the German warships from Danish ports and waters, with boarding parties from *Birmingham* working to prepare a number of German destroyers for sea. On 20 May, however, having been relieved by *Devonshire*, she left Copenhagen to return to Rosyth and prepare for her next duty in connection with the aftermath of the war in Europe. After her arrival in Rosyth on 21 May she began embarking a battalion of troops and their equipment for passage to Norway where they were to carry out PoW camp guard and repatriation duties in respect of the German garrisons still remaining in the country. During the early evening of 24 May *Birmingham* secured alongside a jetty at Bergen, where the troops and their equipment were disembarked. She remained at Bergen for a further seven days to provide support for the troops, before returning to Rosyth via Lerwick. On 11 June she arrived in Portsmouth to begin a four-week maintenance and docking period which ended on 11 July when she left for Scapa Flow, stopping enroute in Plymouth Sound. On arrival at Scapa Flow she once again hoisted the flag of CS10, this time Rear-Admiral Cunninghame-Graham, and seven days later she sailed for a flag-showing visit to the seaside town of Llandudno which, after six years of war, was once again attracting day trippers. With the visit over *Birmingham* remained in the vicinity of Liverpool Bay, carrying out radar trials on day-running trips. In early August she moved north to Greenock where she carried out a series of RAS exercises, before steaming via the Pentland Firth to Rosyth where ships of the Home Fleet were gathering.

Led by *Rodney* (Flag C-in-C Home Fleet) and *King George V*, the fleet had gathered for a post-war inspection by King George VI, and this took place on Friday 28 September. During the afternoon of the inspection the King visited *Birmingham* to inspect Divisions and to walk round the ship. At 1750, some three hours after the King's departure, *Birmingham* weighed anchor and rendezvoused with the destroyers *Orwell* and *Offa* and set course for the Baltic. The three ships were making a series of visits to Swedish ports, the first by Royal Navy warships since the early summer of 1939. At 0335 on 29 September, as they were crossing the North Sea and some 28 miles from Lister Head, a distress message was received from the Danish steamer *Rosnaes* which had hit a drifting mine and was badly damaged aft. In the event, until she was relieved by a Norwegian corvette, *Orwell* stood by the damaged ship. Next day the three ships passed through the Kattegat and into the Baltic, but speed was much reduced, for the danger from floating mines in this area was still very real. Finally, however, during the afternoon of 1 October they anchored in Stockholm Harbour. As this was a high-profile diplomatic visit there was a full programme of receptions, luncheons and dinners, cocktail parties and sporting events. King Gustav took a close interest in the three ships, and on one evening the city of Stockholm laid on a banquet in the Golden Hall of the Stadhus (City Hall), for 20 officers and 350 ratings from the three vessels. On 7 October the squadron sailed for Malmo, where they arrived on the following morning and once again received a warm welcome. The final port was Gothenburg. Fortunately the weather stayed fine and when they were opened to the public, all the three ships attracted thousands of visitors. At Whitehall the series of visits was considered to have been a resounding success. On 19 October the squadron returned to Rosyth where CS10 struck his flag and transferred it to the battleship *Queen Elizabeth*, which had recently returned from the East Indies Station and was being prepared for the reserve fleet and disposal. On 4 November *Birmingham* left Rosyth for Portsmouth where, on 19 November, there was a change of command with Captain G. W. G. Simpson CBE RN relieving Captain Williams.

HMS *Birmingham* remained in and around the Portsmouth area until the second week of February 1946, when she arrived at Portland to join other ships of the Home Fleet, including *Nelson* (flag C-in-C Home Fleet) for three weeks of exercises. During this period *Birmingham* re-hoisted the flag of Rear-Admiral Cunninghame-Graham, and after three weeks off Portland she rendezvoused with *Diadem* and *Bellona* to set course for the Caribbean, for what was to be a short spring cruise. A member of *Birmingham*'s Royal Marines Detachment remembers the first week: '*We arrived at Port of Spain on 22 March, where the combined detachments of* Birmingham, Diadem *and* Bellona *provided a praiseworthy Guard of Honour for the Governor. After a three-day orgy of rum and cokes, and a ship's dance at the Overseas Club, at which our band excelled itself, we started, alone this time, for our next port of call, namely Kingston, Jamaica, arriving there on 28 March. Once again the main beverage seemed to be rum and coke, so much so that someone procured a gramophone record entitled Rum and Coca-Cola, the strains of which can often be heard during the record-playing session from our SRE. We stayed at Kingston for four days, during which time everyone enjoyed themselves, due in large part to the kind hospitality of the people there, who provided entertainment and "grippo" runs to places of interest. The First of April saw us once more at sea and on our way to Nassau, Bahamas. We arrived there on the 3rd and the ship's company were given an "at home" and dance by the RAF at Oakes Field, who did their best to see that our stay was a pleasant one.*' *Birmingham*'s final stop was at Bermuda where, after two days alongside at Hamilton, she moved round to the naval base at Ireland Island where she rejoined *Diadem* and *Bellona*. Finally, on 10 April the three cruisers left Bermuda and nine days later they arrived at Portland.

In June 1946 Victory celebrations were held throughout Britain, and during the extended holiday weekend break of 7 to 11 June *Birmingham* visited Cardiff, after which she joined the flag of the C-in-C Home Fleet in *King George V* to take part in the summer cruise. *Birmingham* then made visits to east coast ports, including Hull, Hartlepool, Berwick and Scarborough, before she steamed south again to take up guard ship duties for Cowes Week. On 10 August *Birmingham* anchored at Portland and four days later, with the commission coming to an end, the C-in-C Home Fleet visited the ship to bid farewell to the ship's company. Next day the cruiser steamed to Portsmouth where CS10 struck his flag and transferred to *Superb*. For *Birmingham* and a much reduced ship's company there was a short maintenance period before the ship was reduced to reserve.

For ten months *Birmingham* lay alongside at Portsmouth, but in the spring of 1947 it was decided that she would be recommissioned, and on 6 June Captain J. R. S. Harris CBE RN joined the ship and took command. By the third week of August her complement had been brought up to full strength and she was ready for sea. On 19 August *Birmingham* steamed out to Spithead where she was inspected by the C-in-C Portsmouth, and three days later she began a series of trials and work-up exercises which continued through to October. Finally, on 12 October *Birmingham* left Spithead to set course for the Mediterranean and the East Indies Station at Trincomalee.

After calling briefly at Gibraltar and Malta, on 23 October *Birmingham* passed through the Suez Canal, and five days later she arrived at Aden, where her presence was eagerly awaited by *Jamaica*'s ship's company, whose place on the East Indies Station she was taking. On 2 November *Birmingham* rendezvoused with *Norfolk* in Ceylonese waters and four days later the two ships put into Trincomalee Harbour. During November and December *Birmingham* spent a great deal of time swinging round a buoy at Trincomalee, but on 27 December she left harbour and set course for the Burmese capital of Rangoon (Yangon). The visit, which was to last for five days, was to represent the Royal Navy at the Burmese Independence ceremonies and celebrations. Not only was the cruiser representing the Royal Navy, but she was also carrying an Intelligence Officer who would supervise the withdrawal of confidential books and signals from the Burmese RNVR. Her final duty would be to evacuate the outgoing British Governor, Major-General Rance, his wife and personal staff.

During the forenoon of 30 December

Birmingham arrived off the entrance to the Rangoon River where she picked up the pilot, and there then followed a long, slow passage upriver before, at 1700, she secured alongside Phayre Jetty, off the Strand Road, and not far from the Sule Pagoda and the City Hall, which was where the ceremonies were to take place. Just five months earlier the leader of Burma's Executive Council, and the country's first Independent Prime Minister-in-waiting, U. Aug San, and six other members of the Council had been assassinated, and so the political situation in the capital was tense. Despite this, however, *Birmingham*'s ship's company received a warm welcome, and on the two afternoons the ship was opened to the public some 10,000 people managed to get on board, with many more having to be turned away. Independence for Burma was officially proclaimed at 0420 on Sunday 4 January, with the signal for the handover of power being a blank salvo from one of the cruiser's 4-inch guns. This was followed by the beating of ceremonial drums and the ringing of temple bells throughout the country. At the City Hall in Rangoon *Birmingham*'s Chief Yeoman hauled down the Union Flag, which was then safely stowed away on board the ship for onward transit to the British Museum in London. With the hoisting of the Burmese Flag the Governor handed over the seals of office to the incoming President Sao Shwe Thaik, who formally declared the country's new Constitution. After a two-minute silence in memory of the murdered Prime Minister the ceremony ended with a march past, which included a company of seamen and the Royal Marines detachment from *Birmingham*. At 0755, with the formal ceremonies over, the Governor and his entourage embarked in the cruiser which, after firing a 21-gun salute to the new State, slipped her moorings to head downriver to set course for Colombo. Although it is largely forgotten now, at the time *Birmingham*'s involvement in Burma's Independence ceremonies was considered to be politically important and Captain Harris's Report of

HMS Birmingham *sailing from Devonport in March 1946, her peacetime colours restored but still mounting her augmented AA armament.* *(Steve Bush Collection)*

Proceedings concluded with this paragraph: '*At 0830, the ship slipped and proceeded downriver, to the strains of "Auld Lang Syne" and the cheers and waving of thousands of people, who lined the riverside. Every available craft in Rangoon seemed to have been commandeered and manned by cheering men, women and children, and the sirens of every ship in the harbour went into action.*' His report continued: '*I consider that the visit to Rangoon was undoubtedly a success. On all hands I was told that the local populace had been much impressed by the bearing and good manners of both officers and men. It is recommended that visits should be paid at regular intervals.*'

After arriving at Colombo on 7 January 1948, and disembarking her VIP passengers, *Birmingham* was shifted into Colombo's graving dock where the underwater hull was completely scraped and painted. It was 22 January before she returned to Trincomalee, and a week later she sailed again, this time to cruise the Bay of Bengal and to pay goodwill visits to cities on India's east coast, including Madras and Calcutta. From there she moved south to the Andaman Islands where she anchored off Port Blair for five days. By 5 March she was back at Trincomalee, where she remained until early May.

During the months of March and April, while *Birmingham* swung round her buoy at Trincomalee, the ships' companies of the fleet trained hard for the annual fleet regattas. There was also a full programme of sports, with *Norfolk*'s ship's company providing fierce competition for *Birmingham*'s teams. The various games and matches were invariably followed by a 'get-together' in the fleet canteen at Trincomalee. On 8 May, however, *Birmingham* left the harbour to set sail for Mauritius and the six-day passage was punctuated by a colourful 'Crossing the Line' ceremony, which broke the monotony of the long days at sea. After four days at Port Louis *Birmingham* steamed to Simonstown for a short maintenance period before cruising along South Africa's east coast, calling at Port Elizabeth, East London and Durban where, on 28 June, Captain T. A. C. Pakenham RN took over command of the ship. On leaving Durban *Birmingham* returned to Simonstown for a longer docking and maintenance period. One ship's company member remembers that period: '*Our two months in South African waters was a welcome break from the sweltering heat of the East Indies, and it was with regret that on 29 July we said farewell and sailed for Ceylon.*'

During the return passage from South Africa *Birmingham* called at Addu Atoll, the famous 'Port T' of the Second World War, but better known today as Gan[3], where there were still many signs of the wartime occupation. Soon after arriving at Trincomalee *Birmingham* hoisted the flag of the C-in-C East Indies Station, Vice-Admiral C. H. Woodehouse, before setting off on a two-month cruise round the Indian Ocean, which took her to the Seychelles, Dar-es-Salaam, Mombasa, Mogadishu, Aden and Berbera, which was then a part of British Somaliland on the African side of the Gulf of Aden. After leaving Berbera on 11 October *Birmingham* returned briefly to Trincomalee, where the C-in-C left the ship. The cruiser then steamed on to the naval base at Singapore to begin a nine-week maintenance and docking period.

For six weeks of *Birmingham*'s refit the ship's company were accommodated ashore in the spacious barrack blocks of HMS *Terror*, with all its facilities, swimming pools and sports fields. All too soon, however, the period of relaxation was over and on 19 December the ship was moved out of dry dock and everyone returned on board. On 29 December, having been inspected by the C-in-C, the cruiser left Singapore to sail via Penang, where the new year was seen in, to Trincomalee. Her return to Ceylon coincided with the island's first anniversary of Independence, and a naval contingent from the ship marched in the parade held on Galle Face Green in Colombo. During the first three months of 1949 *Birmingham* remained largely in

[3] The RAF base and naval refuelling facility, well known to sailors of the 1960s and 1970s, was not opened until 1957.

and around the island of Ceylon. For the second week of April she left on a flag-showing cruise along India's Coromondel coast to Madras, and on to Visangapatam (Vishakhapatnam) and Calcutta, before steaming south to the Andaman Islands then returning to Trincomalee in mid-May.

On 2 June *Birmingham* left Trincomalee for Penang and Singapore, spending four days at the former and two days at anchor in Singapore Roads, just off the city's waterfront. During this time the ship was inspected by the C-in-C and she was opened to the public before, on 13 June, she moved round to the naval base to begin another maintenance and docking period, during which the ship's company were once again accommodated ashore at HMS *Terror*. This time *Birmingham*'s refit lasted for just over three weeks and on 12 July she returned to Trincomalee. Later that month, flying the flag of the C-in-C, she was ordered to East Africa to cruise the various ports which were still British possessions. The C-in-C took advantage of the cruiser's visit to Mombasa to hold talks with the Governors of Kenya, Tanganyika (Tanzania) and Uganda concerning arrangements for forming an 'East African Naval Force', a prospect which, with the rapid growth of African nationalism, would soon become outdated. During the third week of August, after a visit to Dar-es-Salaam, the cruiser anchored off Zanzibar[4] to take part in the birthday celebrations of the pro-British Sultan of Zanzibar, who paid a short visit to the ship. From Zanzibar *Birmingham* visited Tanga, before returning to Mombasa to collect the C-in-C and return to Trincomalee, where she remained until mid-October. Meanwhile, back in East Africa, the first stirrings of African nationalist unrest against European colonial rule were starting to make themselves felt.

In the late 19th century, what we now know as the Republic of Somalia had been divided up between Britain, France and Italy, with the section from the Kenyan border to the Gulf of Aden being Italian Somaliland, and the northern section whose coast ran along the Gulf of Aden being British Somaliland, with its capital at Berbera. The smallest colonial territory was the French enclave at Djibouti, which even today retains strong links with France. In June 1940, when Italy declared war on Britain and France, Mussolini's Army was ill-equipped for any major campaigns, but it was ordered to invade and occupy British Somaliland. If the Italian Army was ill-equipped, the defenders of British Somaliland were even less well equipped or prepared and the Italians quickly overran and occupied the whole colony, with the cruisers *Ceres* and HMAS *Hobart* evacuating 7,000 troops and civilians from Berbera to Aden. Although Britain recaptured the former colony, and itself overran Italian Somaliland, the sight of two European powers fighting over the country was an unedifying spectacle and it led to a nationalist movement which encompassed both territories. Following the British conquest of Italian Somaliland the former Italian colony came under a British administration, but after 1945 the US President insisted on a United Nations Trusteeship. In early 1949 the United Nations began considering the long-term future of the former Italian colony and by the autumn of that year it was clear that it would be returned to some form of Italian rule; this led to serious civil unrest, which the British authorities feared would lead to a popular uprising against any European rule. With the United Nations decision due to be announced during November 1949 the British Administration requested military assistance at what was then known as Mogadiscio (Mogadishu).

Meanwhile, *Birmingham* was at Colombo in Ceylon when, on 3 October 1949, there was a change of command with Captain C. F. J. Lloyd-Davies taking over from Captain Pakenham. Thirteen days later, during the evening of 16 October, *Birmingham* was ordered to leave Colombo the next day for Mogadiscio and all liberty men were recalled to the ship. Next day, at 0900,

[4] The Sultans of Zanzibar had been British 'puppet' rulers of the island since 1896, but within a month of being granted Independence by Britain, in a bloody revolution by the indigenous African population, the dynasty was overthrown.

HMS Birmingham *on the River Medway in 1950 after modernisation. Note the revised bridge, lattice foremast and much reduced close-range weapons fit.* *(Syd Goodman Collection)*

Birmingham and *Loch Glendhu* sailed for East Africa, and five days later they anchored at Mogadiscio. On arrival anti-European feeling was running high and large crowds were gathering in the city. It was decided that if civil unrest ashore became more threatening all the Europeans in the city would be evacuated to the two naval ships and, if necessary, *Birmingham*'s engine room department were to take over guarding and manning the city's power station. For five weeks, with only a short four-day break at Mombasa, *Birmingham* remained off Mogadiscio and fortunately, possibly due to her presence, the expected civil unrest never got beyond levels which the civil authorities could manage. In the event the United Nations decided to make the former Italian colony a Trustee Territory under Italian administration, but only for ten years after which it would become Independent[5]. Meanwhile, on 29 November, with the UN decision having been begrudgingly accepted by the nationalists, the threat of serious civil unrest receded, and *Birmingham* sailed south to Mombasa before returning to Trincomalee for Christmas and the New Year.

By mid-January 1950 *Birmingham*'s commission was drawing to a close and on 12 January, with her paying-off pennant flying, she left Trincomalee for Colombo where she embarked as a passenger the Foreign Secretary, Ernest Bevin, who had been attending a Commonwealth Conference at Colombo. Leaving on 17 January she steamed north-west to Aden and on to Suez, where she anchored ten days later. As soon as the ship was moored the Foreign Secretary disembarked to travel by road to Cairo for talks with Egyptian Government ministers. Meanwhile, *Birmingham* made her northbound transit of the Suez Canal and steamed on to Alexandria where the Foreign Secretary was re-embarked for the three-day passage to Naples where he left the ship for Rome, and talks with Italian Government ministers. No sooner had he disembarked than the cruiser sailed for

[5] In the event the territory gained Independence in 1960, at the same time as British Somaliland, and the two territories were united as the Republic of Somalia.

Portsmouth, pausing only briefly at Gibraltar, and arriving at Spithead during the afternoon of 8 February. Next day she steamed up harbour to secure alongside Portsmouth Dockyard's North Corner Jetty. Despite the cold, wet and foggy day a large crowd of families and friends waited on the jetty and within minutes of the last mooring ropes being secured they were streaming aboard to greet the men who had been away for two years. During that period *Birmingham* had steamed over 6,000 miles. She had carried the last British Governor of Burma from Rangoon to Colombo, she had assisted the military in keeping the peace in Italian Somaliland, and she had carried the Foreign Secretary from Colombo to Egypt and on to Italy. It was the end of the commission and by May 1950 her ship's company had been reduced to a small care and maintenance party. It would be two years before she went to sea again.

Had it not been for events in South-East Asia it is possible that *Birmingham* would never again have sailed under her own power, but on 25 June 1950 North Korean troops invaded the south of the country, and under the auspices of the United Nations Britain followed America into what would be the long and inconclusive Korean War. It was a war in which the Royal Navy would be heavily involved in blockade duties off Korea's west coast, and by the end of 1951 it had become a major commitment. For *Birmingham* this period was spent laid up in reserve, but in the new year of 1952 the cruiser was taken in hand by the dockyard at Portsmouth to undergo a refit in order to prepare her for recommissioning and further operational duties.

At 0800 on Friday 9 May 1952, with the ship lying at Portsmouth's Middle Slip Jetty, *Birmingham* was recommissioned under the command of Captain J. D. Luce DSO OBE RN, and on 5 June she put to sea for the first time in over two years. Over the weeks which followed *Birmingham* underwent an intensive post-refit trials and work-up period. On 9 July, having exercised with *Vanguard* for most of the day, she sailed for Gibraltar and Malta to continue her work-up before sailing for the Far East. On 23 July, six days after her arrival at Grand Harbour, *Birmingham* began a series of exercises and manoeuvres with ships of the Mediterranean Fleet and four days later she was one of a number of vessels ordered to search for survivors from a Dakota aircraft which had crashed into the Mediterranean while en route from Malta to Tripoli with 32 people aboard. In the event other ships arrived on the scene before her, and she was ordered to proceed to Tobruk where she was to stand by in case her presence was required at Alexandria. Four days earlier a military coup in Cairo had seen the British puppet ruler of Egypt, the notoriously corrupt King Farouk, overthrown by Major-General Neguib, a move seen by the British Government as a serious threat to its military occupation of the Suez Canal Zone. In the event, however, the Egyptians did not use the occasion to make difficulties with Britain, and it was soon made clear that Neguib was willing to accept the British presence until the summer of 1956, although the tenure of the bases would become more and more difficult as Egyptian nationalists found ways of disrupting life there. By 1 August, however, it had become evident that *Birmingham*'s precautionary presence at Alexandria was not required, and she returned to Malta to continue her work-up.

On 5 September, with her work-up completed, *Birmingham* left Malta bound for the Far East. Her southbound transit of the Suez Canal took longer than usual with an extended 30-hour stopover at the British military base at El-Fayid on the west bank of the Great Bitter Lake. However, after leaving Suez on 10 September *Birmingham* paused only briefly at Aden before making a non-stop passage to Singapore. On 25 September she arrived in the Johore Strait and at Singapore Naval Base, where she officially joined the Far East Station. Her stay there was brief and six days later she secured alongside Hong Kong Dockyard's North Arm, where the ship's company of *Belfast* were eagerly awaiting her arrival for, next day, having been relieved on station by *Birmingham*, they sailed for home. For *Birmingham*'s ship's company there was a four-day

An aerial view of HMS Birmingham *in 1952. Note the single crane mounted amidships for handling the boats.* *(Syd Goodman Collection)*

break at Hong Kong before she sailed to the Japanese port of Sasebo, in the Nagasaki Prefecture of Kyushu Island which, during the course of the Korean War, was the forward operating base for the Royal Navy.

By the autumn of 1952 the Korean War had been dragging on for two years, with no indication of an early conclusion. The Royal Navy's role was to provide air strikes against enemy targets in support of the Army ashore, to prevent enemy infiltration and troop landings behind Allied lines on the west coast, to provide naval gunfire support to Army units ashore and to protect the Allied garrisons on the many offshore islands situated around the 38th Parallel which, since September 1945, had been the artificial Western-imposed border between the north of Korea which had been occupied by Russian forces, and the American-occupied south.

HMS *Birmingham*'s first duties, which began on 11 October, took her to the area off Inchon where she rendezvoused with *Newcastle* and on 13 October she embarked the First Sea Lord, Admiral Sir Rhoderick McGrigor, who was on a two-week visit to the operational area. A leading proponent of naval air power, McGrigor arrived on board *Birmingham* by Westland Dragonfly helicopter, which hovered some six feet above the cruiser's quarterdeck. During his time on board he visited the aircraft carrier *Ocean* to watch flying operations, and he also visited Canadian, Australian and New Zealand frigates and destroyers engaged on blockade duties. He observed a bombardment of enemy gun positions and on 19 October, after *Birmingham* returned to Sasebo, he left the ship. For the cruiser, however, it was straight back to the operational area to begin her first patrol off the waters around the island of Cho-do, some 40 miles north of the 38th Parallel, which had been occupied by over 1,500 South Korean guerrilla fighters. On 22 October she anchored south of the town of Hauju and carried out a half-hour bombardment of enemy gun positions, command posts, storage concentrations and troop positions. The operation was repeated on 23, 26 and 28 October. During the final stages of the patrol *Birmingham* joined *Ocean* and her planeguard escort *Cossack* before, on the last day of October, she returned to Sasebo.

On 8 November, after an eight-day break, *Birmingham* began her second patrol, during which she flew the flag of FO2, FES, Rear-Admiral E. G. A. Clifford, and once again her time at sea was spent off the islands on both sides of the 38th Parallel. Since her last patrol there had been a build-up of enemy forces in the Changyon-San Peninsula, particularly opposite Cho-do Island, and both 6-inch and 4-inch bombardments were carried out. At 2120 on 12 November, while at anchor off Paengyong-do, *Birmingham* detected two unidentified aircraft which shortly afterwards bombed UN military installations on the island. Although she was not in a position to intervene, next day she carried out a 4-inch bombardment of what were thought to be airfield facilities close to Haeju. On 29 November, while *Birmingham* and *Cossack* were at anchor off Cho-do, a floating mine drifted down from the north coast on an ebb tide. The mine passed some 25 yards clear of *Cossack*'s starboard side, but *Birmingham* had to quickly slip her cable and go full astern to avoid it. It was thought that the mine had broken adrift from a minefield further north, and as the two warships were directly in the tidal stream they shifted their night anchorage to a position further south. During the final days of the patrol the Korean winter rapidly set in, with severe northerly gales, heavy snow and temperatures which dropped sharply from 7°C to -7°C within the space of just a few hours. *Birmingham*'s second patrol ended on 6 December, this time at Kure where, for the ship's company, there would be an 11-day period of rest and relaxation.

The cruiser's third patrol off Korea's west coast began on 17 December, and took in both the Christmas and New Year periods. This time she operated with the aircraft carrier *Glory*, and it had been the intention to anchor the cruiser for the whole of Christmas Day off Cho-do, but a mutiny in a South Korean Army regiment stationed on the small island of Taesuap-to, west of Yonan, meant

she had to steam within range of the rebellious units and fire several salvoes from her 4-inch armament over the island. This quickly brought the mutiny to an end, but *Birmingham* remained in the vicinity. During the latter stages of the patrol the cruiser exercised with the battleship USS *Missouri*, during the course of which the latter's helicopter landed on the cruiser's quarterdeck. It was perhaps to be an early indication of the next advance in naval aviation, which was not far away. At the conclusion of the joint manoeuvres *Birmingham*'s patrol ended and three days later, on 9 January 1953, she secured alongside the North Arm of Hong Kong's naval dockyard.

On 12 January 1953, three days into the ship's maintenance period, there was a change of command when Captain C. W. Greening DSC RN took over from Luce. On 19 January *Birmingham* left Hong Kong to return to Sasebo and five days later she began her next patrol around Cho-do. This time, however, with winter having set in, the ship's movements were badly affected by freezing conditions and on a number of occasions she was brought to a standstill by ice up to four feet thick. Although the patrol was largely quiet *Birmingham* did carry out bombardments of enemy positions in order to break up troop concentrations. The patrol ended at Kure on 6 February and while the ship underwent a three-week maintenance period the ship's company could enjoy a welcome break from the constant defence watches which were kept by the ship when on patrol. By the end of February 1953, with peace talks under way, there were hopes for an agreement which would end the war, although during two further patrols between 28 February and 18 April, *Birmingham* continued to provide naval gunfire support for the Army units ashore. In May and June, however, as the wrangling of the peace talks dragged on, fighting around the 38th Parallel escalated and during those months *Birmingham* carried out some long and fierce 6-inch bombardments of enemy positions. She also undertook escort duties for *Ocean*, which had relieved *Glory*. On 27 July 1953, after three years of war, an Armistice Agreement ended the Korean War, but on both sides of the 38th Parallel much of the country had been reduced to rubble. Two days before the Armistice *Birmingham*, having transported the C-in-C and FO2, FES, from Kure to Sasebo, began another patrol off the west coast. This time, however, conditions on board were much more relaxed and on 7 August, with the patrol at an end, *Birmingham* set course for Hong Kong.

During the afternoon of 12 August, five days after the ship's arrival there, with only a few hours warning, the colony was hit by one of the tropical cyclones which are particularly prevalent during August and September. On this occasion 'Typhoon Susan' proved to be very severe and after an urgent recall of her ship's company *Birmingham* sailed to ride out the storms, which lasted two days. During the third week of August she returned to Korean waters to patrol off the west coast again in the area around the 38th Parallel, but with the Armistice holding fast the patrols were more relaxed and shorter in duration. In late September *Birmingham* left for Hong Kong then Singapore where, on 12 October, she began a 13-week refit and docking period.

It was mid-January 1954 when *Birmingham* returned to Hong Kong, to join her sister *Newcastle*, and the destroyers *Cockade, Constance* and *Cossack*, for joint exercises before returning to the Japanese ports of Kure and Sasebo for joint manoeuvres with the US Navy's 7th Fleet. By mid-April, however, the commission was drawing to a close and on 21 May, after undergoing a five-week maintenance and docking period in Hong Kong, with her paying-off pennant flying, she left Hong Kong to steam home by way of Singapore, Aden, Suez and Gibraltar, arriving in Chatham on 28 June. During her two-year commission she had steamed some 66,000 miles.

On Wednesday 7 July under the command of Captain J. R. Barnes DSO RN, *Birmingham* was recommissioned at Chatham and 16 days later she sailed for Malta to undergo a three-week work-up period. During these exercises from Grand Harbour

she often operated with her sister *Glasgow* and the new aircraft carrier *Centaur*. On 20 August, during the final day of the exercises, she was ordered to break off a 6-inch naval gunfire support exercise to search for two Fleet Air Arm aircraft which had crashed off Malta. Some hours later she recovered pieces of wreckage, but there was no trace of the pilots. Seven days later, having successfully come through the Admiral's inspection, *Birmingham* left Malta for Port Said, Aden and Singapore where, on 15 September, she rejoined the Far East Station. Two days after her arrival she hoisted the flag of FO2, FES, Rear-Admiral G. V. Gladstone. Next day there was more ceremonial when the First Lord of the Admiralty and the First Sea Lord visited the ship for a conference. It was during this high-level visit that it was publicly disclosed that the Government had received an offer from a Japanese company to salvage the battleship *Prince of Wales* and the battlecruiser *Repulse*, which had been sunk by Japanese torpedo-bombers in 1941. It is interesting to read, in the records of that time, that the first consideration in response to the offer had been the price quoted. However, public disquiet concerning these war graves ensured that the matter was not pursued.

At the end of September *Birmingham* steamed to Hong Kong from where she, *Defender, Cockade, Concord* and *Consort* took part in a joint US/UK/Australian naval exercise centred around Manus Island. Also involved was the Australian aircraft carrier *Sydney*, together with the destroyers *Anzac* and *Tobruk*, and for *Birmingham* the exercise ended with a 6-inch bombardment of Manus, after which she steamed north to Hong Kong, on to Sasebo and the Korean port of Chinhae, where she represented the Royal Navy at a parade to mark the ninth anniversary of the Republic of Korea's Navy. After the ceremonies were over *Birmingham* remained in Korean waters until mid-November when she returned via Kure to Hong Kong, to join her sister *Newcastle* for air defence exercises in the South China Sea; this was followed by Christmas and New Year at Hong Kong. On 26 January 1955 *Birmingham* navigated the Saigon River for a six-day visit to Saigon. After the defeat of the French in 1954 a Geneva Peace Agreement saw Vietnam divided into two halves at the 17th Parallel. It had been intended only as a temporary measure, but Cold War ideology saw the north of the country become a client state of China, while the south was a puppet of the USA. It would be another four years before the start of the Vietnam War and *Birmingham*'s visit was intended to reinforce the West's support for the regime in the south of the country.

After leaving Saigon *Birmingham* returned to Singapore to begin a three-month refit, and on 5 February, when the cruiser went into dry dock, the ship's company were accommodated ashore until the third week of April when they moved back on board. On 2 May, still flying the flag of FO2, *Birmingham* left Singapore for the last time to begin a cruise of Indian Ocean ports, which included calls at Mauritius, Durban, Lourenco Marques (Maputo), Diego Suarez, Tulear, East London and finally, on 18 June, the naval base at Simonstown, where FO2 hauled down his flag and the ship prepared to steam north into the Atlantic Ocean as she made her way home. After leaving South African waters on 21 June, ten days later she made a brief 24-hour call at Freetown, and on Monday 11 July she arrived at Sheerness. Next day *Birmingham* steamed up the River Medway and secured alongside the basin in Chatham Dockyard. Her commission was over, and within days her ship's company had dispersed to new drafts leaving only a small care and maintenance party on board.

On Monday 18 July, Captain J. R. B. Longden OBE RN took command of the cruiser, and next forenoon the main body of her ship's company joined from the naval barracks. A few hours later, at 1250, the ship was recommissioned for service with the Mediterranean Fleet. On 4 August *Birmingham* left Sheerness for Gibraltar where she underwent a three-day docking period before steaming east to Malta where, on 14 August, she anchored in Marsaxlokk Bay and officially joined the fleet. For

the next three weeks *Birmingham* and her ship's company were put through their paces as they underwent an intensive work-up period in the waters around Malta. On 8 September, however, the exercises were cut short and *Birmingham* was ordered to return to Grand Harbour. In the early 1950s Greek Cypriot nationalists had begun stirring civil unrest when they demanded that the island be linked to Greece in a political union. That Cyprus was a British Crown Colony at all was due to Lord Beaconsfield (Benjamin Disraeli) who, when he returned from the Congress of Berlin in 1878, had acquired the island from the Ottoman Turks in exchange for vague guarantees that Britain would use the island as a base to help protect the Ottoman Empire from Russian aggression. The island's population was made up of Greek Orthodox Christians and Muslims, the former being in the majority. During the Great War Britain had actually offered to cede the island to Constantine I, the King of the Hellenes, in exchange for a Greek declaration of war on the side of the Allies. Constantine wisely refused the offer, but the idea of a future political union with Greece was firmly planted in the minds of Greek Cypriot nationalists. It was not until 1925 that the island became a British Crown Colony, and during the Second World War 'Enosis', or union with Greece, became a definite objective of Greek Cypriot leaders; naturally this idea was not at all welcomed by the island's Muslim minority. By the autumn of 1955 civil disorder in Cyprus was becoming increasingly widespread and a Greek Cypriot insurgency, with terrorist atrocities aimed at both the British colonial authorities and the minority Muslim community, was becoming more violent. It was time for urgent military reinforcements to be be sent to Cyprus from garrisons in Egypt and Malta.

During the night of 8/9 September some 528 officers and men of 40 Commando Royal Marines, and the Headquarters 3rd Commando Brigade, together with their equipment and vehicles, were ferried out to *Birmingham* and embarked. The frigate *Roebuck* also took on board a number of marines and their equipment after which both ships left Malta to make a very uncomfortable 30-hour passage to Famagusta, where the Royal Marines and their equipment were disembarked. Within hours of their arrival the marines were deployed to the docks at Limassol, where nationalist protesters had taken control of the facilities there. As soon as her disembarkation was complete, *Birmingham* weighed anchor to return to Malta from where, after refuelling and storing, she sailed for a three-day visit to the Italian naval base at Taranto. On 21 September *Birmingham*, together with *Roebuck, Wakeful, Whirlwind* and RFA *Blue Ranger*, took part in 'Exercise Medflex Champion', which also included the Turkish destroyer *Sultanhisar* (ex-HMS *Oribi*). The exercises were controversial in that the Greek Government, which was at loggerheads with Turkey, refused to let their ships take part. At the end of the manoeuvres *Birmingham* anchored off Izmir before returning to Malta.

For most of October *Birmingham* joined the destroyers *Defender* and *Delight* for various Mediterranean exercises and visits to Algiers and Naples, before she returned to Malta to undergo maintenance and docking. It was the second week of December before she was ready for sea again. On 9 December she hoisted the flag of the C-in-C Mediterranean and steamed via Algiers to Gibraltar for joint Home and Mediterranean Fleet exercises in the Western Mediterranean and Atlantic. These exercises had been an annual event in pre-war years, but by the mid-1950s they were but a shadow of the earlier manoeuvres, for the Mediterranean Fleet had been reduced to little more than an aircraft carrier, a cruiser and a few destroyers and frigates. After spending Christmas and New Year at Malta, the first two months of 1956 were spent day running from Malta, then in March she took part once again in joint Home and Mediterranean Fleet exercises.This time the manoeuvres took the form of a convoy escort exercise, where *Maidstone*, the royal yacht *Britannia* and two RFAs made up the convoy, which was 'attacked' by *Ark Royal*'s aircraft. These exercises were immediately followed by 'Exercise Medflex Dragon', a five-nation NATO exercise which saw *Birmingham* acting as host to three journalists and two US Army cameramen, who covered the ship's activities, including AA, surface and bombardment shoots throughout the exercises. It was even said that the two US Army Sergeants were instructed in the art of 'tea wetting' and were given certificates of merit to prove their ability. On 20 April the exercise ended with a spectacular naval and air event just three miles off the entrance to Valletta's Grand Harbour, when more than 50 NATO ships steamed past the dispatch vessel *Surprise* while an array of NATO admirals and generals took the salute. The proceedings were concluded with a fly-past of some 70 aircraft from the participating NATO countries, after which the ships entered Grand Harbour and Sliema Creek. To the careful observer the ships in the harbour represented a major post-war change in the balance of power in the Mediterranean, for the Stars and Stripes of the US Navy's 6th Fleet now dominated the scene. In just six months time when the Suez Crisis broke, the realities of this change would be exposed for the world to see.

After spending the first three weeks of May carrying out self-maintenance at Malta, *Birmingham* and the destroyer *Diamond* were ordered to transport men of the Royal Marines and their stores and equipment to Cyprus, where the nationalist insurgency was gaining strength and the security situation in the major cities and towns was deteriorating. On 25 May *Birmingham* and *Diamond* left Malta, and three days later anchored off Larnaca. After disembarking the marines the two ships remained in the waters off Cyprus for six days, but shore leave for liberty men was restricted to the canteen and recreational facilities at the Royal Marines camp, which was an indication of the tense security situation. During the first week of June *Birmingham* joined the aircraft carrier *Eagle*, the minelayer *Manxman*, the destroyers *Chevron* and *Duchess*, two RFAs and the dispatch vessel *Surprise* (flag C-in-C) for a high-profile visit to Istanbul, after which *Birmingham*, *Eagle*, *Duchess*

A series of images showing HMS Birmingham *in a 'lively' sea.* *(Mr Leary)*

and *Surprise* visited Beirut which, in 1956, gave the superficial appearance of being a politically stable city. During the visit *Birmingham* played host to the Prime Minister of Lebanon, and *Eagle* put to sea to demonstrate her projection of air power. After leaving Beirut *Birmingham* returned briefly to Cyprus before steaming west to Grand Harbour.

On 15 July 1956 the C-in-C struck his flag and next day, with the paying-off pennant flying, *Birmingham* left Malta to begin her passage home to Chatham. Pausing briefly at Gibraltar, she arrived off Sheerness on 25 July and next day steamed up the Medway to Chatham Dockyard where she paid off and began a six-month refit. That same day, as *Birmingham* was being moved into Chatham's No 3 basin, back in the Middle East, in retaliation for America's and Britain's refusal to provide financial assistance for the building of the Aswan Dam, President Nasser of Egypt announced the nationalisation of the Anglo-French owned Suez Canal Company. It was the start of the Suez Crisis which by the end of the year would be played out and would end in humiliation for both Britain and France. It was confirmation of the post-war reality that neither country was a superpower, and that their ability to influence world events was greatly diminished. For *Birmingham*, however, most of the events of the Suez Crisis took place while she lay in Chatham's No 9 dry dock.

On 18 January 1957 Captain T. D. Ross took over the command of *Birmingham* and a week later, during the afternoon of 25 January, with the ship's company having been brought up to full strength, the cruiser was recommissioned. Three days later she began a three-week trials and work-up period, which also included a few more days in dry dock. On 20 February, however, she left Portland for Gibraltar and Malta where, on 4 March, she rejoined the Mediterranean Fleet. *Birmingham*'s new commission was to take the form of the recently introduced General Service Commission, by which ships' companies were changed every 18 months, while the ships served alternately in foreign and home waters. It was designed primarily to shorten the period of separation of men from their homes in an effort to encourage experienced men to remain in the Service, and it was proving popular. Under this system *Birmingham*'s Mediterranean deployment was due to end in late 1957, after which she would return home to undergo a refit before returning to the Mediterranean to take part in a major exercise and then complete her commission in home waters.

Following her arrival in Malta *Birmingham* carried out an intensive eight-week work-up after which she paid a five-day visit to Cannes which coincided with the annual film festival. This was followed by exercises with the destroyers *Comet* and *Contest*, with visits to Izmir and Istanbul, after which she returned, via Tobruk, to Malta. In July *Birmingham* joined *Cumberland* and *Kenya* for manoeuvres off the island, before all three cruisers rendezvoused with a squadron of the US Navy's 6th Fleet led by the aircraft carrier *Randolph* and the heavy cruiser *Newport News.* They were all to take part in a joint exercise code-named 'Combine', during which *Birmingham* and *Newport News* carried out main armament bombardments of Sardinia's Isola Rossa. During August and September *Birmingham* remained close to Malta, with short visits to Venice and Split. During the second week of October, flying the flag of the C-in-C, the cruiser paid a nine-day visit to Barcelona, during which the C-in-C had an audience with General Franco; the thorny subject of Gibraltar was not raised. On 20 October, while on passage between Barcelona and Malta and off the Tunisian coast, she was called to search for survivors from a USAF F-86 Sabre jet aircraft, which had crashed in the vicinity, and after a four-hour search the pilot was located and rescued. After returning to Malta *Birmingham* remained in local waters until the first week of December when she paid a short visit to Naples. On 7 December, however, the C-in-C struck his flag and next day the cruiser sailed for home, arriving alongside in Chatham Dockyard on 18 December.

During the rest of December and during January 1958, as *Birmingham* languished in dry dock, her

HMS Birmingham *in Grand Harbour, Malta, in 1958, with her sister ship* Sheffield *moored astern and the cruiser* Kenya *to starboard.* *(Crown Copyright/Mod 1958)*

ship's company took seasonal leave before, on 4 February, she left Chatham to follow the aircraft carriers *Ark Royal* and *Eagle* out to Malta again. For the rest of the month she carried out training exercises in the area, then on 4 March joined 40 other ships of the Mediterranean Fleet and the US Navy's 6th Fleet for a three-day programme designed to familiarise the two fleets in combined operating. *Ark Royal*, *Eagle*, *Birmingham*, *Kenya* and *Sheffield* led the Royal Navy's contingent of heavy ships, while representing the US Navy were the aircraft carriers *Essex, Randolph* and *Saratoga*, and the cruisers *Des Moines* and *Salem*. On completion of this exercise *Birmingham* steamed west to Gibraltar, from where she took part in the Royal Navy's 'Exercise Dawn Breeze' in the Western Mediterranean and Atlantic. Once again the aircraft carriers *Ark Royal* and *Eagle* led the manoeuvres, and on 25 March, after she was released from the exercise, *Birmingham* set course for home, arriving off Sheerness on 30 March and two days later steaming up harbour to Chatham.

It was on 7 May 1958 when, flying the flag of the newly appointed C-in-C Home Fleet, Admiral Sir William Davis, *Birmingham* left home waters for Gibraltar, before proceeding to Casablanca and

Lisbon where the C-in-C attended NATO conferences. On 20 May, while homeward bound, she made a 48-hour visit to Brest, after which she steamed north to Greenock to join 20 other ships of the Home Fleet which were beginning their summer training programme. At Greenock the C-in-C transferred to the depot ship *Tyne*, and after a weekend of harbour drills the ships sailed for exercises in the Atlantic and North Sea, with breaks at Loch Eriboll, Invergordon and Rosyth. The manoeuvres followed a similar pattern to those which the pre-war fleet had undertaken in those same waters. On 5 June, after two days at Rosyth, *Birmingham* steamed south to Dover where she embarked a battalion of the Cameron Highlanders and their equipment before sailing north to the Southwold area of Suffolk, where the troops were ferried ashore in a simulated unopposed landing. With the Army ashore *Birmingham*'s role in the exercises was complete, and she crossed the North Sea to make a seven-day visit to Amsterdam, after which she steamed down Channel to anchor at Spithead.

HMS *Birmingham*'s next deployment, which began on 17 June, saw her steaming west across the Atlantic to the St Lawrence River and on up to Quebec where, on 26 June, she secured alongside a berth at Wolfe Cove. The cruiser was representing the Royal Navy at the 350th anniversary celebrations of the founding of the city by the distinguished French navigator and cartographer, Samuel de Champlain. Also in the river for the occasion, lying beneath the magnificent Chateau Frontenac which stands sentinel on a high rock above the city, were the French destroyer *Du Chayla*, the US Navy's aircraft carrier *Leyte* and four Canadian warships. The celebrations took place between 1 and 3 July, with banquets, parades and night fireworks on the plains. During the early hours of 3 July *Birmingham* slipped her moorings to steam down the St Lawrence River to make her return transatlantic crossing, arriving in Chatham on 9 July. Six days later, with her ship's company having moved into barracks, she paid off. However, as was quite common in those days, within minutes of having paid off, she was recommissioned with her new complement under her new commanding officer, Captain S. H. Beattie VC RN.

Eight days after recommissioning *Birmingham* left Chatham for Portland from where, over a period of two weeks, she carried out work-up exercises before returning to Chatham to give seasonal leave. On 29 August, Flag Officer Flotillas (H), Rear-Admiral R. H. Wright, hoisted his flag and five days later *Birmingham* left Chatham to steam north for Rosyth to join other ships of the Home Fleet for the autumn training exercises and cruises. Over 20 ships, led by the depot ship *Tyne* (flag C-in-C), had assembled in the Firth of Forth, and during the weeks which followed they were engaged in an intensive programme of weapons training, NATO exercises and visits to various ports in and around the British Isles.

HMS *Birmingham*, in company with the destroyers *Hogue* and *Solebay*, began the manoeuvres with anti-submarine exercises in the North Sea, as they hunted down the submarine *Astute*. In mid-September there was a weekend break at Rosyth when the ship was opened to the public and over 7,600 people were counted over her gangways. Leaving Rosyth on 15 September she moved south to Portland where she joined *Camperdown, Duchess, Murray, Orwell, Paladin* and *Pellow* for 'Exercise Shipshape', which also involved vessels and aircraft from Belgium, Germany, the Netherlands and Portugal. *Birmingham*'s role was to escort a convoy from the Atlantic Ocean through to the Western Approaches, with submarines of 'Orange Force' attacking the surface ships. However, the manoeuvres were cut short when fire broke out in *Camperdown*'s boiler room and most of the ships were required to stand by the destroyer. In the event she was able to make Gibraltar under her own steam, and three days later *Birmingham* secured alongside at Devonport.

During October *Birmingham* joined the destroyers *Decoy* and *Duchess* at Portland for manoeuvres in the Channel and Western Approaches, and on 7 October the cruiser paid a four-day visit to

Glengariff in Bantry Bay on Ireland's south-west coast. Prior to the Great War Bantry Bay had been an anchorage for ships of the Atlantic and Channel Fleets, but after 1921 when Ireland broke its ties with Britain, naval visits had been rare. From Glengariff *Birmingham* visited Bordeaux and on 21 October, after leaving the French port, she once again rendezvoused with *Decoy* and *Duchess* to steam south for Gibraltar, where they arrived three days later. For most of November *Birmingham* and the two Darings exercised in the Western Mediterranean and Atlantic. The final exercise saw the warships escorting a convoy which was represented by RFA *Tidereach* from Gibraltar out into mid-Atlantic, where they turned north for home waters. It was a similar route to that which Second World War convoys had used. For *Birmingham* the exercise ended on 29 November when she put into Brest for a four-day visit, after which she steamed home to Chatham to undergo maintenance and prepare for her final year of operational service.

On 15 January 1959 *Birmingham* was manoeuvred out of Chatham's No 3 basin to secure at a buoy off Folly Point, and four days later she left the Thames Estuary to rendezvous with *Centaur* and *Gambia* in the Channel and set course for Gibraltar. During the passage the three ships carried out anti-submarine exercises off Ushant, with the submarines *Talent* and *Tireless* acting as both attackers and prey. Taking place during a severe storm, the exercise was brought to a premature end when *Tireless* developed engine trouble and the cruiser had to stand by her until the arrival of a French ocean-going tug, which took over and escorted *Tireless* to Portsmouth, which she managed under her own power. In the meantime *Birmingham*, *Centaur* and *Gambia* completed their passage to Gibraltar where they arrived on 24 January. For the cruiser there followed an eight-week maintenance and docking period, and in early April she steamed east to Malta to join the Mediterranean Station. In mid-April she paid a three-day visit to Istanbul, before returning to Malta to join *Battleaxe, Defender, Delight, Solebay, Saintes, Llandaff* and the RFAs *Fort Duquesne* and *Wave Sovereign*, for fleet exercises off the Libyan coast.

On 6 July *Birmingham* left Malta to join *Battleaxe, Blackpool, Camperdown, Defender, Delight* and *Ulysses* in local exercises before sailing north to Istanbul. At 1750 that day *Delight* took station on *Birmingham*'s starboard side to carry out a jackstay transfer, but three minutes later the two ships collided and the evolution was terminated. In fact the collision had been a glancing blow as the sea brought the two together and the damage appeared to be superficial. By 1850 they were under way again. Down below, however, the engine room department had the task of checking the double bottom compartments to ensure that they were still watertight, but at 1940, while checking *Birmingham*'s forepeak, an engineer officer and three ratings were overcome by fumes. Although rescue operations were quickly under way and the four men were soon extricated, that evening two of them, a Petty Officer and an M(E)1 died from the asphyxia they had suffered. Next day, at 1125, everything was halted while their funeral services were held. On 9 July the ships arrived at Istanbul for a visit of five days, after which the squadron carried out more exercises in the Aegean before anchoring in Phaleron Bay for a five-day goodwill visit to Athens. It was the first visit to a Greek port by British warships for almost five years, for all such calls were suspended during the insurgency in Cyprus. On 23 July *Birmingham* returned to Malta, where she remained for the rest of the month.On 4 August *Birmingham* left Malta to join the rest of the fleet for the short passage to Augusta Bay, where over three days the annual fleet sailing and rowing regattas were held. Later in the month, with other ships of the fleet, she took part in 'Exercise Passex' and paid a short visit to Messina before returning to Malta to begin a four-week period of self-maintenance. On 28 August, while she was in Grand Harbour, *Birmingham*'s sister ship *Belfast* arrived in Malta from home waters. The two cruisers were the last survivors from the original ten ships of the pre-1939 years. One member of *Birmingham*'s

The remains of HMS Birmingham *at Thomas H. Ward shipbreakers at Inverkeithing. (T. Ferrers-Walker)*

ship's company who visited *Belfast* at this time remembers: '*I had the opportunity to visit* HMS Belfast *to see the modernisation of the living accommodation and messing. Those of us who went on board found living conditions much improved and really quite comfortable.*'

On 23 September *Birmingham*'s final maintenance period was completed and she sailed from Grand Harbour to join *Belfast*, which was undergoing her work-up before sailing east to Singapore. With three destroyers and a frigate, the two cruisers carried out a 24-hour exercise off Malta, which culminated in *Belfast*'s final inspection after which she left for Suez and *Birmingham* returned to Grand Harbour. Four days later *Birmingham* steamed west to Gibraltar, which for the ships' companies was always a pleasant change from Malta. While at Gibraltar *Birmingham* joined the Spanish cruiser *Canarias* for joint exercises in the Western Mediterranean, during which they were joined by three Daring-class ships. The exercises ended with a six-day visit to Palma, Majorca, but by 23 October she was back in Grand Harbour.

By early November *Birmingham*'s commission and her career were drawing to a close, and the first two weeks of the month were spent in and around Malta, with a five-day visit to Naples. On Monday 23 November came the Admiralty announcement that *Birmingham* was to be withdrawn from active service and laid up to join the rapidly growing list of superannuated cruisers, which included *Sheffield, Jamaica* and *Superb*. Later that forenoon, with her ship's company manning the upper decks and with her paying-off pennant flying, *Birmingham* left Grand Harbour to make a ten-day passage, which included a weekend break in Gibraltar, home to Devonport. At 0430 on 3 December Eddystone Light was raised, and three hours later she entered The Sound, where she anchored pending Customs clearance. That afternoon she weighed anchor to steam up harbour and secure alongside Devonport Dockyard's No 8 wharf. Most of the ship's company were due foreign service leave and by the end of the week her complement was much reduced. De-ammunitioning and de-storing began almost as soon as she arrived alongside, and by 10 December even the ship's cat had been drafted into quarantine before going to a new home ashore. That same day the Mayor of the city of *Birmingham* paid a farewell visit and next day Captain Beattie relinquished his command. Finally, at 1220 on 15 December, the remaining members of the ship's company moved ashore to barracks and *Birmingham* was reduced to reserve.

HMS *Birmingham* lay idle at the Reserve Fleet Trot in the Hamoaze for eight months until, in early September 1960, she was sold to Thomas H. Ward of Sheffield. On 7 September she arrived under tow in the Firth of Forth, from where she was towed to Inverkeithing for breaking up.

Chapter Five

HMS GLASGOW
1937-1958

During the afternoon of Saturday 20 June 1936, HMS Glasgow *was launched down the slipway into the River Clyde at Greenock.* *(World Ship Photo Library)*

In April 1935 Nazi Germany unilaterally repudiated the Treaty of Versailles and introduced conscription into the country's armed forces. Since its inception in June 1919 previous German Governments had been secretly breaking the terms of the Treaty, but 16 years later the circumstances were different. This time it was done openly and defiantly, signalling the first of many breakdowns in European diplomacy which would end with the continent's second catastrophic war within the space of 25 years. The result would be, in the words of the historian A. J. P. Taylor that '*...Europe ceased to be the centre of the world*'. Meanwhile, in 1935, where Britain was emerging from the Great Depression, on the River Clyde there was some good news when, on 16 April, at Scott's Shipbuilding and Engineering Company's Greenock shipyard the first keel plates of HMS *Glasgow* were laid as work began on the fourth of the Royal Navy's Town-class cruisers. The contract was part of the 1934 Naval Estimates, worth some £500,000 to the shipbuilding company, which was a real boost to employment in an area which had been hard hit by the Depression.

Work on the cruiser proceeded rapidly, and by the summer of 1936 the hull was ready for launching. It had already been announced that Mrs Lucy Baldwin, the wife of the Prime Minister, would carry out the ceremony while in the Glasgow area for party political meetings. *Glasgow* was in fact the first cruiser of the 1934 building programme to take to the water and the ceremony took place at 1345 on Saturday 20 June, which coincided with high tide on the Clyde. A contemporary description of the proceedings reads thus: '*The company on the launching platform heard prayers read, and then*

heard Mrs Baldwin break the customary bottle of wine against the stem of the new ship. The vessel started so slowly that the movement was discernable only to those who could see the tall black perpendicular line of the stem widen its gap from the nearest object on land: but in a few seconds additional speed was gathered and soon the Glasgow *was not only moving but, in Mrs Baldwin's words, "a living thing", in her own element, the water. It was a leisurely, but also a beautifully effective launch, and the tugs in attendance had no difficulty in pulling the* Glasgow *to her allotted position afloat.'* In December 1936, with building work proceeding apace, it was announced that Captain C. A. Browne RN was to be *Glasgow*'s first commanding officer, but this was changed at short notice, and in April 1937 Captain F. N. Attwood RN, who had just returned from two years on the China Station, was appointed. On 8 September 1937 a navigating party of 27 officers and 406 ratings, who had travelled from Portsmouth by special train, joined the ship and next day she left Greenock to begin a six-hour series of acceptance trials in the Firth of Clyde, which culminated at 1430 with the ship being formally accepted from the builders. Later that day, with the trials party having been disembarked, she sailed for Portsmouth and two days later arrived alongside in the tidal basin. For three days *Glasgow* embarked stores and ammunition, and on 14 September she completed to her full complement and was commissioned into service with the 2nd Cruiser Squadron of the Home Fleet in place of *Neptune*, which was to be deployed on the African Station.

During the rest of September and into October *Glasgow* remained alongside at Portsmouth as she continued to embark stores and ammunition, and prepared for sea. At 1530 on 8 October however, there was a loud explosion in the auxiliary boiler room, and both the ship's fire parties and the dockyard fire brigade were quickly on the scene. Fortunately, no onc was injured and there was little damage. It was soon ascertained that the blast had been caused by the accumulation and ignition of unburnt fuel in the funnel uptakes. On 18 October the C-in-C Portsmouth inspected the ship, and next day she sailed to Portland to begin her trials. After anchoring overnight in Weymouth Bay *Glasgow*'s trials began at 0900 the next day, but at 1405, after successfully undergoing some six hours of machinery trials and torpedo firing, she was manoeuvring to a buoy in Portland Harbour when her bows embedded in the muddy bottom and she became firmly stuck. Despite putting the engines full speed astern thc ship would not budge, and it eventually took the combined efforts of the destroyer *Winchester* and a tug to pull the cruiser clear and refloat her. She had been stranded for an hour and a half, but, fortunately, the ship's divers found nothing more than scraping to the paintwork. After a short visit to Milford Haven the trials were resumed, and when they were completed in early December *Glasgow* was dry docked at Portsmouth, where she remained until the beginning of January 1938.

On 20 January 1938 there came *Glasgow*'s first change of command, when Captain C. G. B Coltart RN joined the ship and took over from Attwood. Just over two weeks later, on 5 February, *Glasgow* left Portsmouth to join the Home Fleet at Gibraltar for the annual combined Home/Mediterranean Fleet exercises. Also taking part were the battleships *Nelson, Royal Oak, Rodney* and *Revenge*, together with the cruisers *Newcastle, Sheffield* and *Southampton*. Flying his flag in *Cornwall* was the First Sea Lord, Admiral-of-the-Fleet Lord Chatfield, and, in the battleship *Nelson*, the outgoing C-in-C of the Home Fleet, Admiral Sir Roger Backhouse. In November that year, on Chatfield's retirement, his place as First Sea Lord would be taken by Backhouse. The main exercise in mid-March 1938 saw the ships of the Home Fleet searching for an enemy commerce raider which was attacking a convoy, with *Glasgow* taking the role of the enemy raider. At 0115 on 15 March an entry in *Glasgow*'s log read: '*Ship Sunk*'. There is no doubt that this particular exercise serial bore an uncanny resemblance to various encounters which would

take place during the Second World War, the start of which was only 18 months away. On 29 March, as they steamed up-Channel, the ships of the Home Fleet ceremoniously steamed past *Nelson* as a salute to the soon to be departing C-in-C, and later that evening *Glasgow* anchored at Spithead. Next day she steamed up harbour to secure alongside the elderly training battleship *Iron Duke* at Pitch House Jetty.

During the whole of April *Glasgow* remained alongside at Portsmouth, and at one stage she hoisted the flag of the incoming C-in-C Home Fleet, Admiral Sir Charles Forbes. On 10 May she left Portsmouth for Portland where she joined the flag of the C-in-C in *Nelson*, in company with her sisters *Newcastle, Sheffield* and *Southampton*. She remained in the Portland area until the last week of June when she paid a nine-day visit to the Clyde,

Sister ships HMS Glasgow *and* Newcastle, *seen from* Sheffield, *during exercises off Portland in 1938.*
(Ken Kelly Collection)

Two pre-war images of HMS Glasgow *showing her as completed, with four triple 6-inch turrets, triod masts and a square-fronted bridge structure.* *(National Museum of the Royal Navy)*

where she secured in the King George V Dock at Govan. Also present on the Clyde were *Nelson, Rodney, Royal Sovereign, Courageous, Newcastle*, the 6th Destroyer Flotilla and two submarines, whose visit was timed to coincide with the Empire Exhibition which was being held in Glasgow between May and October 1938. On 4 July, after leaving the Clyde, *Glasgow* set course for an eight-day visit to Stavanger before returning to Portsmouth at the end of the month for maintenance and dry docking.

On 12 September *Glasgow* left Portsmouth to join the Home Fleet at Invergordon for what were to be the last autumn manoeuvres before the outbreak of war. Leading the fleet was the battleship *Nelson*, but also taking a prominent part in the exercises in which air defence was a major feature, was the aircraft carrier *Courageous*. On 24 September the fleet anchored in Scapa Flow, and despite the fact that war was only 12 months away, not much had changed there since February 1920, when the Admiral Commanding Orkney and Shetland hauled down his flag and the base was closed down. Most of the defences erected during the Great War had long gone, and Metal Industries Ltd were still working to raise the sunken wrecks of the German High Seas Fleet, which had been scuttled in the summer of 1919. Some of the more observant witnesses on board *Glasgow* may well have spotted two rather contradictory activities being carried out, with boom defence vessels laying anti-submarine nets, while working parties of Royal Marines were dismantling the last of the Great War gun emplacements. For all but a handful of *Glasgow*'s ship's company this was their first glimpse of the legendary base which had once been the home of the mighty Grand Fleet, but for the C-in-C, Admiral Forbes, the lack of any meaningful defences at Scapa Flow was alarming and as a result of the fleet's visit in September 1938 he made urgent recommendations that adequate defences be constructed. Unfortunately, during the next 12 months his pleas were largely ignored. For 12 days, as political events in Munich unfolded, Forbes kept the Home Fleet at Scapa Flow, but on 6 October with Chamberlain having declared, '*Peace for our time*', the ships sailed south for Invergordon to continue the autumn manoeuvres in the North Sea. For *Glasgow* these concluded with catapult and flying trials off the Firth of Forth. On 17 November she returned to Portsmouth where she remained undergoing maintenance until mid-January 1939.

For the ships of the Home Fleet the new year of 1939 began on 17 January, when they left their base ports to steam south to Gibraltar for the annual combined Home and Mediterranean Fleet exercises, which took place in the Western Mediterranean and Atlantic. On 24 January, when *Glasgow* secured alongside Gibraltar's detached mole, all the major warships of the Home Fleet, including *Nelson, Rodney, Royal Sovereign* and the cruisers *Aurora, Newcastle, Sheffield* and *Southampton*, had already arrived. The exercises began at the end of January, and it is interesting to note that *Glasgow* was assigned to screen the aircraft carrier *Glorious* which was employed on anti-submarine duties, hunting down the two submarines *Cachalot* and *Narwhal*. The deployment of fleet aircraft carriers in this role was, during the first weeks of the war, to lead to the catastrophic loss of *Courageous*.

As well as joining the fleet manoeuvres there was also a diplomatic purpose to *Glasgow*'s visit to Gibraltar, and in mid-February she and her sister *Newcastle* were ordered to convey the Governor of Gibraltar, General Sir Edmund Ironside, to Morocco for talks with his French opposite number about the future defence of the area, and in particular the all-important Strait of Gibraltar. While the talks were in progress the two cruisers spent four days at Casablanca before they returned to Gibraltar to resume their roles in the fleet manoeuvres. It was at this time that Adolf Hitler travelled from Berlin to Hamburg to launch the battleship *Bismarck*. At Gibraltar the fleet exercises ended on 10 March when the fleet anchored in Gibraltar Bay. Three days later, with her sisters *Newcastle* and *Southampton*, she steamed north via Portland to Dover where, with other ships of the Home Fleet,

she provided an escort for SS *Côte d'Azur,* which was carrying the French President, Albert F. Lebrun, from Calais to Dover for a four-day State Visit to Britain. On 24 March, having saluted the French President as he returned to Calais, *Glasgow* returned to Portsmouth where, later that day, she secured alongside *Iron Duke* at Middle Slip Jetty.

During the whole of April *Glasgow* remained alongside at Portsmouth undergoing maintenance, and on 6 May sailed to join her sister *Southampton* (flag Vice-Admiral G. F. B. Edward-Collins) and the Canadian Pacific Line's passenger ship *Empress of Australia*, to set course for Quebec. The two cruisers were to act as escorts to the liner which had been chartered by the Government to carry King George VI and Queen Elizabeth to Quebec for a State Visit to Canada and, more importantly, to the USA. The high-profile visit was intended firstly to act as a deterrent to Germany at a time when Hitler was seeking ever more urgently and forcefully to overturn the Treaty of Versailles and, secondly, if possible, to cement an alliance between the USA and Britain. In the event neither of those aims was achieved, but the visit did make for easier diplomatic negotiations in the future.

At 1500 on 6 May *Empress of Australia*, which had arrived in Portsmouth Harbour the previous day, sailed out to Spithead and through the Needles Channel where she rendezvoused with *Southampton* and *Glasgow*. Between the western edge of the Isle of Wight as far as Portland the three ships were led by *Nelson* and *Rodney* and the Home Fleet, but once clear of home waters *Glasgow* took station some four cables ahead of the liner, a position she maintained for most of the ten-day transatlantic passage. When the ships were some seven days out from Portsmouth they ran into thick pack ice and fog, and for over 24 hours speed was reduced to just four knots, during which time they made only five miles. To avoid running into even thicker ice, course was altered southward, and as they ploughed through the belt large chunks of ice bumped and scraped along their sides, carrying away paintwork, but causing no real damage to the hulls. Finally arriving in Quebec on 17 May the royal party began their tour of Canada and the USA by train, and two days later the cruisers steamed south to New York. On 20 May, while they were exercising their aircraft off the US coast, a rating from *Glasgow* was killed in an accident involving a Walrus aircraft. Three days later the two ships arrived in New York, where *Glasgow* anchored in one of the harbour's US Navy berths; the eight days spent in the city, with its reputation for hospitality, were much appreciated. On 27 May *Glasgow* shifted her berth and secured alongside Pier 54, which ran alongside the west side of Manhattan, a berth usually reserved for the prestigious Cunard passenger ships. The visit ended on the last day of May when the two cruisers left New York to steam north to the Canadian port of St John's, New Brunswick, where they secured alongside the quay wall of Navy Island in the inner harbour. After the bright lights of New York the Canadian port was rather a backwater, and on 8 June they left for Halifax, Nova Scotia where, on 15 June, the royal party were embarked in a different Canadian Pacific passenger liner, the newer *Empress of Britain*. During the return passage the squadron was joined by the cruiser *Berwick*, and the first day at sea was spent avoiding floating ice around the Canadian seaboard, which slowed down progress for another 24 hours. However, once clear of the ice a fast passage was achieved and at 1300 on 22 June, having escorted her to Spithead, *Glasgow* and *Southampton* parted company with *Empress of Britain*. That evening the two cruisers anchored in Portland Harbour, and five days later *Glasgow* made the short passage to Portsmouth to begin a four-week maintenance period.

With the outbreak of war only a matter of weeks away the ships of the Home Fleet had been ordered to advance the period for summer leave, and also to take every opportunity to carry out maintenance work on the ships. At this stage it had been planned that in late August *Glasgow* would hoist the broad pennant of Commodore F. H. Pegram, and would sail to join the 8th Cruiser Squadron on the America

& West Indies Station based at Bermuda, where she was to have taken the place of *Exeter* (Commodore H. H. Harwood). *Glasgow*'s place in the Home Fleet was to have been taken by the newly commissioned *Belfast*. Plans for the deployment were well advanced, with Pegram's appointment having been announced in the press. However, as the political situation in Europe deteriorated, the deployment was cancelled and although *Exeter* would return home briefly in August 1939, she was to remain on the America & West Indies Station. Pegram's appointment was cancelled, and when on 10 July there was a change of command he took over *Glasgow* as Captain, for further service with the Home Fleet. On 20 July *Glasgow* was shifted out of dry dock and nine days later she joined other ships of the Home Fleet for the passage north to Invergordon. During the weeks that she operated from the Moray Firth *Glasgow* steamed north into the Norwegian Sea and south as far as the Thames Estuary, with just one break when she spent a weekend at Grimsby. On 25 August, however, the Home Fleet was ordered to its war station and *Glasgow*, together with other ships of the fleet, steamed north to Scapa Flow, where she joined Admiral Forbes' North Sea Force. Next day the elderly battleship *Iron Duke* entered the Flow, not as the C-in-C's flagship, but as a disarmed hulk to carry out duties as an administrative and depot ship. It was, however, a reminder of events some 25 years earlier which were now a distant memory.

On 29 August *Glasgow* left Scapa Flow in company with the destroyers *Bedouin* and *Punjabi* to patrol the North Sea on a line between the Shetland Isles and the River Humber, and at 1100 on 3 September, when war was declared, they were off the east coast. During the remainder of September and into October *Glasgow* continued to patrol between Rosyth and Sheerness.

At 0800 on 9 October 1939, when *Glasgow* and *Southampton* were patrolling off the Norwegian coast, two German aircraft were sighted and within minutes the cruisers were subjected to the first of many high-level bombing attacks, which lasted continually for some seven hours, only ceasing at 1545 when daylight began to fade. Altogether over 112 bombs were dropped, but despite some near misses there were no casualties, nor was there any damage inflicted. However, the hours of fast manoeuvring had depleted the fuel tanks, and next day she put into Scapa Flow to refuel.

On 12 October *Glasgow* left Scapa Flow to rendezvous with *Newcastle* to act as ocean escort to a convoy bound for the Middle East. The route took the ships out into mid-Atlantic before they turned south, and nine days later when the convoy had safely crossed Latitude 50°N, *Glasgow* was detached and ordered to steam up Channel to Spithead from where, on the last day of the month, she sailed to escort a slow northbound coastal convoy into the North Sea to Immingham, where she arrived on 11 November. Four days later *Glasgow* joined *Belfast* and *Southampton* to steam north to Rosyth and on to Scapa Flow, from where she continued to patrol the North Sea, and escort vital coastal convoys, occasionally taking her turn on the Northern Patrol blockade. *Glasgow*'s first Christmas of the Second World War was spent at Rosyth which, with most ships being either at sea or at Scapa Flow, was a rare treat for her ship's company. The new year, however, was spent at sea patrolling the North Sea with *Edinburgh*.

On 9 February 1940 *Glasgow* left Scapa Flow in company with *Southampton* to patrol the area around Iceland, enforcing the trade embargo on Germany. Three days later, at 1010 on Monday 12 February, in a position 69°44'N 016°40'E, some 200 miles north of Iceland and well within the Arctic Circle, *Glasgow* intercepted the German trawler *Herrlichkeit*, which immediately surrendered to the cruiser. Fortunately, there was little wind and the sea was calm and *Glasgow* was able to send over a prize crew to take off members of the trawler's crew. No sooner had this been accomplished than *Southampton* arrived on the scene, and *Herrlichkeit* was handed over to her, thus allowing *Glasgow* to continue her patrol, which lasted for another seven days before she returned to Scapa Flow. Four days

HMS Glasgow *in a disruptive camouflage scheme early in the Second World War - notice the camouflage on the 6-inch gun barrels and the false bow wave.* *(Syd Goodman Collection)*

later, on 23 February, *Glasgow* steamed south to Belfast where she was taken into Harland & Wolff's shipyard to begin a four-week refit and docking period, during which degaussing equipment was fitted.

On 22 March, with her refit over, *Glasgow* steamed north to the Clyde from where she began her first patrol in northern waters. This ended at Rosyth on 2 April, the day that an over-confident Prime Minister announced to Parliament that, '*Hitler has missed the bus*'. Far from missing buses, as early as mid-February 1940, when some 299 British merchant seamen had been released from *Altmark* at Trondheim, Hitler had been convinced that Britain would not respect Norwegian neutrality and he ordered his Army to prepare for a full-scale invasion of Norway. In the meantime, back in Britain, similar plans were afoot, with the British and French Governments planning to lay mines in Norwegian territorial waters in an attempt to prevent German shipping from obtaining iron-ore supplies through the port of Narvik. In the almost certain knowledge that the mining of a neutral port would provoke a German response, a separate operation code-named 'R4', or 'Rupert', after the naive humanised bear in a children's comic strip, was planned as a back-up to the mining operation in case a military presence was required. It was 'Operation Rupert' for which *Glasgow* had been earmarked, and having arrived in Rosyth on 2 April, *Glasgow* joined the cruisers *York, Berwick* and *Devonshire* alongside the dockyard's north wall. During the morning of 7 April the four cruisers began embarking soldiers of the Royal Lincolnshire

Regiment and their military stores. *Glasgow* embarked one whole infantry battalion, an HQ brigade, and all their equipment. However, during the night of 7/8 April, British Intelligence became aware that a full-scale German invasion of Norway was about to be launched, and during the forenoon of 8 April, with 'Operation Rupert' having been cancelled, *Glasgow*'s troops and their equipment were rapidly disembarked and the ship was prepared for sea. At 1305 the same afternoon, in company with the French cruiser *Emile Bertin*, flagship of the French 'Force Z', a squadron which had been sent to support the Allied operations in Norway, *Glasgow* put to sea. Next forenoon they joined the cruisers *Aurora, Manchester, Sheffield* and *Southampton*, which had been detailed to attack German invasion shipping off Bergen. However, before this could be attempted, the operation was cancelled, but at 1421 enemy aircraft were sighted and a few minutes later the ships came under heavy air attack, during which *Glasgow* suffered damage and casualties from two near misses on her port side. Two ratings, a Leading Signalman and a Stoker, were killed outright by flying shrapnel, but, fortunately, damage to the ship was superficial. During the evening of 10 April *Glasgow* put into Scapa Flow to refuel and embark stores and 24 hours later she put to sea with *Sheffield* and six destroyers to carry out a search of Norwegian waters in the vicinity of Alesund, where the presence of German warships had been reported. Although no enemy ships were sighted, the force again came under air attack, but this time there were no casualties or damage. At this point the force was making for the port of Namsos, for at 0545 that morning orders had been received at the Admiralty that in order to forestall a German landing at the port, *Glasgow* and *Sheffield* were to land a Royal Naval and Royal Marines Battalion, which would be equipped and supplied to be self-sufficient for seven days. It was stressed that the force should only make a landing if it was unopposed, and that once ashore it should secure the quay and other strategic points in the area. At this stage the nearest German troops were at Snåsa, some 38 miles from Namsos. It was envisaged that the naval force would, by 20 April at the latest, be relieved by an Army Infantry Brigade.

By 2130 on 14 April, the joint Naval and Royal Marines Battalion of some 300 men, drawn from *Glasgow* and *Sheffield*, had been ferried ashore and for three days, while the battalion secured its objectives, *Glasgow* and *Sheffield* patrolled offshore. On 16 April the first Army units arrived in Namsos, and by the early hours of the next day there were sufficient troops in position to be able to withdraw the naval personnel, and destroyers ferried the men back to their ships. Finally, at 0410 on 17 April, with the last of the Royal Marines and seamen having been embarked from *Matabele*, *Glasgow* sailed for Scapa Flow to refuel and from there south to Rosyth where, on 21 April, she secured alongside the south wall. *Glasgow*'s part in the Norwegian campaign was far from over, however, and it was not long before tons of military stores were being loaded on board. Later the same day base party troops arrived on board and at 0330 on 22 April, 650 men of the King's Own Yorkshire Light Infantry, together with their equipment, were embarked. Two hours later *Glasgow*, in company with *Galatea*, left Scapa Flow bound for Andalsnes to augment a British force which was under severe pressure from enemy troops. Having arrived safely at her destination during the evening of 23 April, *Glasgow* remained at anchor just long enough to disembark the military personnel before weighing anchor and putting to sea again. By this stage of the Norwegian campaign German bombing was both accurate and fierce, and once into open waters where they could manoeuvre freely she joined *Sheffield*. During the early hours of 25 April both ships went to the assistance of *Curacoa*, which had been badly damaged by bombs. Next day, however, *Glasgow* arrived safely back in Scapa Flow.

During the evening of Sunday 28 April, *Glasgow* slipped quietly out of Scapa Flow to make a fast 24-hour passage to the Norwegian port of Molde where, on arrival at 2210 the next day, those on

board found that the town, '*appeared to be on fire in many places*'. This included the jetty alongside which *Glasgow* secured. Twenty-five minutes after her arrival King Haakon of Norway, together with his staff, Norwegian Government ministers, British and French diplomatic staff, and survivors from Allied ships sunk in and around the harbour, were embarked. In total *Glasgow* had on board some 258 passengers as well as several tons of gold bullion. At 0110 on 30 April, as she was leaving Molde Harbour, both the ship and the town were subjected to a fierce air attack.

After leaving Molde *Glasgow* set course north for Malangenfjord, close to Tromso, where at 1915 the next day she rendezvoused with the elderly Norwegian auxiliary warship *Heimdal*, which had once been a royal yacht. Once she had secured alongside the Norwegian ship King Haakon and his entourage were transferred and *Glasgow*, together with the destroyer *Javelin*, set course for Greenock where, after an uneventful passage, she arrived during the afternoon of 4 May and all the remaining passengers were disembarked. Later that evening, heavily guarded by the ship's Royal Marines Detachment, the gold bullion was unloaded and shipped ashore.

HMS *Glasgow*'s arrival in Greenock marked the end of her involvement in the Norwegian campaign, but she still had one duty to carry out which was an indirect result of the German invasion of Denmark and Norway. In order to deny their valuable facilities to Germany, in mid-April Britain occupied the Danish Faroe Islands, and in early May planning began for the military occupation of Iceland, which, as it did not maintain any defence forces, was not considered to be too difficult an operation. This was just as well, because although the actual invasion force was to consist of some 750 Royal Marines, they were ill-equipped and many were still undergoing their basic training. In addition to *Glasgow* the invasion force included *Berwick* and the destroyers *Fearless* and *Fortune*. By the early hours of 8 May the marines and most of their equipment had been embarked, and at just after 0400 the force sailed into heavy seas and gale force winds for Reykjavik. Contemporary accounts indicate that the unrelenting weather conditions continued throughout the 48-hour passage north, and by the early hours of the morning of 10 May when Reykjavik was reached, many of the inexperienced marines were prostrate with seasickness. Fortunately, as expected, although the fiercely independent Icelanders were hostile to the 'invasion', it was not opposed and later that day, having embarked some 70 German detainees, the staff from the German Consulate and the crew of a merchantman which had foundered off Iceland after hitting an iceberg, the three warships sailed south, arriving on 12 May in the River Mersey where the detainees were disembarked. No sooner was *Glasgow* secured alongside Liverpool's Princes Landing Stage than de-ammunitioning began and next day the ship crossed the Mersey to Cammell Laird's shipyard, where she was placed in dockyard hands.

On 6 June 1940, as the ship lay in dry dock, there was a change of command, with Captain H. Hickling DSO RN taking over from Pegram. Four days later boarding parties from *Glasgow* took over the Italian cargo ship *Gambiano*, which had the bad luck to be in Liverpool when Italy entered the war on the side of Germany and was berthed close to the cruiser. By the first week of July *Glasgow*'s refit was almost completed and during the evening of 7 July she left the River Mersey to steam north to Scapa Flow, where she arrived the next day. During the next seven days the ship carried out work-up exercises in and around Scapa Flow, and at 0830 on 16 July, together with *Southampton* (flag CS18), *Shropshire, Sussex* and *Glasgow*, the destroyers *Cossack* (Captain D), *Fortune, Fury* and *Sikh* of the 7th Division, and *Inglefield* (Captain D), *Imogen, Maori* and *Zulu* of the 5th Division, both of the 4th Destroyer Flotilla, she sailed from Scapa Flow to carry out joint manoeuvres in and around the Pentland Firth, before beginning a patrol of the North Sea. The manoeuvres were dogged by thick fog, and by 2210 the force was off the Pentland Skerries, after being forced to turn back towards

Scapa. The cruisers were in single line ahead in close order, with *Southampton* leading and *Glasgow* bringing up the rear. The destroyers were astern and in line ahead and abeam to starboard, maintaining a position a mile astern of the rear cruiser, which was *Glasgow*. Unfortunately, it had not been made clear that for manoeuvring purposes the destroyers should not form part of the fleet, but should follow astern and generally conform to the cruisers' movements. At 2250 thick fog again descended and the cruisers were ordered to turn in succession 180° to port. The destroyers also conformed to this manoeuvre, and at 2300 when the fog lifted they were approximately a mile astern of *Glasgow* in the rear. At 2322 the cruisers were turned 330° in succession, and the destroyers once again followed suit. Some 20 minutes later, with fog ahead, the cruisers were ordered to make a turn of 160° to starboard, but by the time this had been executed the thick fog had once again enveloped the ships.

By now the whole force was off Duncansby Head and steaming towards Scapa Flow, but manoeuvring signals were not being correctly received and Captain Hickling later recounted events thus: '*The cruisers actually turned in fog. A short blast from only two ships ahead was heard as wheels were put over; it was thought from* Sussex *and* Shropshire. *At 2348, when steadied on a course of 130°,* Glasgow *sounded one long blast.*' At this stage Glasgow's speed was 15 knots, and the story is taken up once again by Hickling: '*At 2353 a destroyer was observed broad on the port bow of* Glasgow *steering on an opposite course. This was* Inglefield. *One long blast on the siren was given and the engines put to slow ahead. About 15 to 20 seconds later a second destroyer (*Imogen*) appeared out of the fog right ahead. The wheel was put hard-a-starboard and the engines to full astern.* Glasgow *struck* Imogen *just before the bridge at an angle of about 20° to her fore and aft line. The two ships remained locked together.*'

On impact a huge sheet of flame shot up from *Imogen*'s funnel, the heat of which was felt on *Glasgow*'s bridge. Almost immediately another fire started under *Glasgow*'s bow, which was locked into the destroyer's side, and this was thought to have been caused by the cruiser's stem coming into contact with *Imogen*'s 4.7-inch ready-use ammunition locker, and possibly a petrol store. This fire, which was in the vicinity of the destroyer's forward magazine, was extremely serious, with a risk of one or even both ships blowing up. As many of the cruiser's forward hoses as possible were brought to bear from the forecastle and from lower deck scuttles, and although at first it appeared that it would be extinguished, with *Imogen*'s firemain system smashed beyond repair, the blaze rapidly began to take hold. In view of this grave situation, the severe damage to *Imogen* and the weather conditions, Hickling ordered the destroyer to be abandoned and her ship's company to transfer by way of the lower boom and emergency ladders onto *Glasgow*'s bows.

Despite the efforts of *Glasgow*'s firefighters the blaze on board *Imogen* became even more intense, and there was a very real danger that her forward magazine would explode. In view of this, at just after midnight on 17 July, having embarked ten officers and 135 ratings, and launched her Carley floats and boats for survivors, Hickling decided to break away from *Imogen* as soon as possible and at 0030 *Glasgow*'s engines went astern. With much grinding of jagged metal the cruiser was manoeuvred free of the destroyer's side, and she then circled *Imogen* whose ammunition was exploding. With fire-fighting efforts abandoned the destroyer was left blazing fiercely in a sea of burning oil fuel. She was last seen at 0045, and it is believed she sank soon afterwards. Two of *Glasgow*'s ship's company, a Midshipman and an Able Seaman, were killed, while in *Imogen* 18 men lost their lives and ten were seriously injured. *Glasgow*, with extensive damage to her bow, limped at eight knots back to Scapa Flow, and anchored there during the forenoon. Two days later, with her bulkheads having been shored up, she steamed south to the River Mersey where, during the afternoon of 21 July, she entered the Canada Graving Dock for major repairs.

HMS *Glasgow*'s second visit to the River Mersey in the space of three months lasted until 4 September 1940, when she steamed north once again to Scapa Flow, to complete the programme of work-up manoeuvres which had been cut short by her collision with *Imogen*. These continued until the last week of September when she put into Immingham for further repair and refit work which lasted until 20 October; she then steamed north to Rosyth Dockyard where the work was completed over the next nine days. During her short stay at Rosyth *Glasgow* was fitted with Type 286 surface radar equipment and at the end of October, with her repairs and maintenance completed, she sailed for Greenock and from there, on the last day of the month, to Gibraltar and the Mediterranean.

After leaving Greenock *Glasgow* rendezvoused with *Ark Royal*, which was returning to Force H after a refit on the Mersey, as well as *Berwick* and *Isis*, for a fast passage south. During the forenoon of 6 November they were met by Somerville's flagship *Renown* and escorted into Gibraltar where *Glasgow* secured alongside the main wharf. *Glasgow* and *Berwick* were in port for just over 24 hours, en route to Alexandria where they were to reinforce Cunningham's Mediterranean Fleet. At 1827 on 7 November, when the two ships sailed, they were accompanied by ships of Force H, including *Ark Royal, Sheffield* and eight destroyers. Also in company was the battleship *Barham* and three other destroyers, all of which, like *Glasgow* and *Berwick*, were intended as reinforcements for the Mediterranean Fleet. Between them *Glasgow*, *Berwick* and the three destroyers were also carrying 2,150 troops and their equipment, none of whom were allowed onto upper decks until the ships were some six miles clear of Europa Point. The whole operation was code-named 'Coat' and as well as escorting the reinforcements *Ark Royal* was also to fly off much-needed RAF Hurricanes for Malta. Although they were expecting, and prepared for, fierce enemy air attacks, in the event there was only one high-level bombing raid on the force, and during the afternoon the Mediterranean Fleet reinforcements, including *Glasgow*, arrived safely in Malta's Grand Harbour. Later the same day, having landed their troops and refuelled, *Glasgow* and *Berwick*, which were now accompanied by *Illustrious, Gloucester, York* and *Valiant*, sailed for what was code-named 'Operation Judgement', the Fleet Air Arm's attack on the Italian Fleet based at Taranto. On 14 November, with the highly successful attack on Taranto having far exceeded Cunningham's expectations, *Glasgow* finally arrived at Alexandria.

The cruiser's arrival in the Eastern Mediterranean coincided with the start of the German reinforcement of the poorly equipped Italian forces which had invaded Greece, and the British intervention which would end disastrously for the war effort in the Middle East, proving a real setback for the campaign in North Africa. Just 24 hours after her arrival at Alexandria, during the forenoon of 15 November, *Glasgow* embarked some 426 RAF and RASC personnel. No sooner were they aboard than she put to sea to make a fast 24-hour passage to Piraeus where all the troops were disembarked, and the ship returned to Alexandria. Eight days later, during the early hours of 25 November, in company with *Gloucester, York* and four destroyers, she was deployed as escort to a Crete-bound troop and supply convoy; five days later she arrived safely at Souda Bay on the north-west of the island.

It had been intended that *Glasgow* would remain there as guardship and on 2 December, after a short patrol off Crete, she returned to Souda Bay and opened her gangways to Army units who were based ashore; by 1350 some 100 soldiers had come on board for a special film show in the ship's hangar. Although anti-aircraft guns were manned there was a generally relaxed atmosphere on board, for at this stage of the Greek campaign the enemy air forces had not fully demonstrated their lethal capabilities. At 1538, with the cinema show in full swing, two enemy aircraft were sighted and the anti-aircraft gunners opened fire. Five minutes later, however, a torpedo struck the forward part of the ship, exploding in the cable locker, and a minute

later a second torpedo slammed into the ship's side aft, destroying the spirit room, damaging two propeller shafts and starting a fire. There were a few casualties when a Surgeon Lieutenant and a marine were killed, with seven ratings being injured. While all the visiting Army personnel were quickly ferried ashore the engine room department began to raise steam and carry out temporary repairs. At 2042 the same day, with the ship some two feet down at the stem, and with two propeller shafts disabled and locked, *Glasgow* weighed anchor and set course at reduced speed for Alexandria. Next day, during the first dogwatch, she slowed down for the funerals of Surgeon Lieutenant G. R. E. Maxted and Marine A. Bragg, and some 11 hours later arrived safely at Alexandria. It was the end of *Glasgow*'s part in the campaigns in Greece and Crete.

For ten weeks *Glasgow* remained at Alexandria, either at No 60 Jetty or in the port's floating dry dock, as she underwent major repairs. However, the dockyard facilities at Alexandria were not sufficient to fully repair the damaged propeller shafts, and when *Glasgow* left Alexandria on 12 February 1941 her speed was limited to 24 knots. After sailing she carried out an 18-hour series of trials before anchoring at Port Said. *Glasgow* had been ordered to join the East Indies Fleet at Trincomalee and on 13 February she weighed anchor to make a slow 28-hour passage south through the Suez Canal, three hours of which were spent being slowly warped around the wreck of the merchantman SS *Ranee*, which only eight days earlier had been sunk by a mine and was now partially blocking the canal. By the morning of 15 February, however, she had cleared Port Suez and set course for Aden where, on 18 February, she joined the East Indies Fleet. Later the same day, after refuelling, *Glasgow* sailed south for Durban and three days later, with full ceremony, she crossed the equator. However, just 40 minutes after the end of the ceremonies, at 1920 on 21 February, she received a 'Raider Report' which turned out to be for the German heavy cruiser *Admiral Scheer*. This powerful warship had left Germany in mid-October 1940, and by mid-January 1941 she had sunk the armed merchant cruiser HMS *Jervis Bay* and ten merchant ships. By 20 January she was in the Indian Ocean west of the Seychelles and that day she intercepted four Allied merchantmen, sinking three of them and capturing the 6,994-ton oil tanker *British Advocate*. Next day she intercepted the 7,000-ton British cargo ship SS *Canadian Cruiser*, and although she sank the vessel it was not before the 'Raider Report' had been transmitted. As *Glasgow* altered course from her intended destination of Durban towards the Seychelles it was estimated that she was at least 160 miles from *Admiral Scheer*'s last known position. Next day, at 1300, when *Glasgow* was in a position 07° 45'S 051°10'E, west of the Seychelles, one of her Walrus aircraft reported *Admiral Scheer* some 80 miles ahead. However, on its next mission it failed to locate the cruiser and, in fact, contact was never regained. By 24 February *Glasgow* was running short of fuel, and that afternoon she put into Port Louis, Mauritius, to replenish her tanks.

Leaving Mauritius within 24 hours of her arrival *Glasgow* was released from her search for *Admiral Scheer* and ordered to join *Caledon* and *Dorsetshire* to escort a vital convoy north to Aden and Suez. Fourteen days later *Glasgow* was back at Aden preparing for her next operational commitment, the invasion and reoccupation of an almost forgotten corner of Britain's Middle Eastern Empire, British Somaliland. This neglected and often overlooked territory, which had been a British Protectorate since 1888, was bordered by Ethiopia, Italian Somaliland and French Somaliland (Djibouti) and it had always been administered from Aden. When Italy entered the war one of its early campaigns was the invasion of British Somaliland, and the territory was quickly overrun, with British forces evacuating through the port of Berbera. It was the first British overseas possession to fall to Axis forces during the Second World War and, as one astute journalist noted, '*Britain's greatest loss was in prestige, especially among Arabs*.' During the Italian occupation the port of Berbera was used as a submarine base, which posed a direct threat to Allied shipping in the

Red Sea. It was inevitable that Britain would soon attempt to recapture the territory. In early 1941 the planning started for the reoccupation of British Somaliland, and *Glasgow*'s arrival at Aden on 11 March was directly connected to this operation, which was codenamed 'Appearance'.

The assault on Berbera was to be carried out by two Indian Army battalions together with a detachment of Somali irregulars, and the invasion fleet was to be escorted by *Glasgow*, *Caledon, Kingston* and *Kandahar*. Leaving Aden at 1623 on 15 March, the fleet arrived off Berbera some ten hours later and the landings began at 0420 on 16 March, with the assault force quickly overpowering the Italian garrison which had been severely weakened by an outbreak of malaria. Both *Glasgow* and *Caledon* provided naval gunfire support during the landings, and *Glasgow* remained at anchor off Berbera until 20 March when she sailed for Aden, arriving there the following day.

Three days after her arrival in Aden *Glasgow* began a series of convoy escort duties in the Indian Ocean, starting with convoy SO2, that was heading south to Mombasa and which included the troop transport *Arundel Castle* and the badly damaged aircraft carrier *Illustrious*. During April, May and the first two weeks of June *Glasgow*, often in company with *Cornwall*, continued to escort convoys across the Indian Ocean. On 25 June, however, she left Colombo bound for the naval base at Singapore where, on the last day of the month, she began an 11-week refit, during which the ship's company moved ashore to the spacious new barrack accommodation at the naval base. During the refit the cruiser spent seven weeks in the base's graving dock, during which time repairs were finally carried out on her damaged propeller shafts.

HMS *Glasgow*'s refit ended on 14 September, and two days later she sailed for Trincomalee where she underwent a six-day work-up before steaming south into the Indian Ocean to join HMAS *Sydney* as escort to the vital troop convoy, US12B, which had left Fremantle on 28 September. The convoy consisted of three large troop transports, Cunard's SS *Aquitania*, and the Dutch ships *Johan van Oldenbarnevelt* and *Marnix van St Aldgorde*, which between them were carrying 7,851 troops to the Middle East. Having escorted these troopships as far as Bombay, *Glasgow* then took over escorting convoy BA8, consisting of the French troopship *Felix Roussel* and SS *Westernland*, from Bombay to Aden. On 15 November she then took over the escort of another troop convoy, which this time included the ex-passenger liners *Dominion Monarch* and *Duchess of Richmond*. With war against Japan only a few weeks away frantic efforts were being made to reinforce Britain's scattered and pitifully inadequate defences east of Suez. On 29 November *Glasgow* left the convoy at Madras, and on 1 December she sailed south once again to arrive at Trincomalee three days later. On 8 December 1941, when Japan entered the Second World War (7 December at Pearl Harbor) *Glasgow* was at sea and on patrol off Southern India. She was under orders to search the area around the Laccadive Islands (Lakshadweep), where it was thought a Japanese submarine and possibly its parent ship might be operating. Having completed the search she was then ordered to the coast of Marmagoa, where the presence of another submarine was suspected, and in the port itself three German merchantmen and one Italian vessel were interned, but were thought to be about to attempt to break out. The first island visited was Kalperi where the Headman declared that nothing untoward had been seen, so *Glasgow* then steamed on towards the island of Kavaratti. At 0800 on 8 December the signal to '*commence hostilities against Japan*' was received, which was followed by another signal warning of the presence of Japanese submarines in the area. By 1830 on 8 December she had completed her search of the Laccadive Islands, and set course northwards to carry out a reconnaissance of Marmagoa Harbour. Shortly after this another submarine report was received giving a position some ten miles off Aguada Point, just north of Marmagoa. Confirmation of the report came from the Indian

auxiliary patrol vessel *Dipavati*.

At 2320 on 8 December *Glasgow* was in a position 15°14'N 078°28'E, when her bridge lookouts sighted a white light bearing 336° some ten miles away, and speed was increased to 20 knots. By 2340, with the moon up and visibility good, the 'vessel' appeared to resemble a submarine lying on the surface. When she approached the 'vessel' *Glasgow* called by light, but received no answer. As she moved closer it appeared that there were two or three lights low down, and not being able to make them out the cruiser manoeuvred with a view to getting into the moonlight. Although the possibility of lighters being in the vicinity was considered, as there were no reports of any coastal tows so far out to sea, it was quickly dismissed. At just after 2340 *Glasgow*'s ship's company were called to Action Stations.

By 2355 the 'vessel' could be seen against the moonlight, and at a range of some 7,000 yards the 'unknown vessel' appeared to have the distinct appearance of a large ocean-going submarine. However, as Hickling had a nagging doubt about the type of vessel it was, he manoeuvred *Glasgow* so that the 'submarine' was out of the moon's direct light; Hickling then got the impression that the 'submarine' was actually on the surface and carrying out repairs. At midnight *Glasgow*'s searchlights were switched on and immediately what appeared to be the vessel's deck lights went out. Hickling thought this was a crash dive and he ordered the cruiser to open fire. The first salvo was seen to hit, and after eight salvoes 'cease fire' was ordered as *Glasgow* closed to pick up survivors. However, as she approached what had been thought to be a submarine, it proved to be a large ocean-going tug, HMIS *Prabhavati*, flying the White Ensign, with two lighters in tow. Although the tug was still afloat and on an even keel, large volumes of steam were blowing from her engine room hatches. The operation to rescue survivors continued until 0200 on 9 December, after which the cruiser set course for Bombay, where she arrived at just before midnight.

Following this tragic accident *Glasgow* resumed convoy escort duties in the Indian Ocean, where desperate measures were being taken to reinforce the garrison at Singapore, while at the same time women, children and key military personnel were being hastily evacuated from the island. After spending Christmas at Colombo *Glasgow* steamed into the Indian Ocean to begin escorting the troop convoys to an area off Sumatra, where they were handed over to *Exeter, Encounter* or *Dragon* for the final run via the Sunda Strait to Singapore. On 22 January, off Colombo, she took over as the escort to convoy BM11, which was carrying some 11,665 troops in the transports *Duchess of Bedford*, *Empress of Japan*, *Wakefield* and *West Point*, the last two being US troopships. At 0654 on 27 January she handed the convoy over to *Exeter* and *Encounter*, but in the event the troops arrived in Singapore just in time to surrender to the Japanese. As for *Glasgow*, on the last day of January she arrived back in Colombo.

During February and March 1942, as catastrophe upon catastrophe befell the British forces in South-East Asia, and British overseas territories from Hong Kong, to Singapore, Burma and even over the borders of India, quickly fell to the Japanese, *Glasgow* continued her Indian Ocean escort duties. After the fall of Singapore, Malaya and the Dutch East Indies, however, she was confined to the western half of the Indian Ocean, between Colombo and Durban and along the coast of East Africa. On 2 April, however, *Glasgow* was ordered to sail for New York to undergo a thorough overhaul and full repairs to the torpedo damage sustained in December 1941. Leaving Mombasa she called at Durban, Simonstown, where initial preparations were made for her American refit, and Freetown, before making her ten-day westbound transatlantic crossing to arrive alongside No 13 berth of New York's Navy Yard for the 14-week refit. For those members of the ship's company who remained with the ship there was a welcome move ashore into US Navy barracks, and on 14 July there was a change of command when Captain E. M. Evans-Lombe RN took over the ship. During this refit *Glasgow*'s radar

HMS Glasgow *passing the Statue of Liberty following a repair and refit at New York Navy Yard in 1942. Note the unusual block style camouflage.* *(Courtesy of James Flynn)*

outfit was updated, with her existing Type 285 and 282 being replaced by a new Type 271. Additional 20mm Oerlikon guns were also fitted.

On 5 August 1942 the ship's company moved back on board and nine days later *Glasgow* left the naval yard at New York for an anchorage in Gravesend Bay, from where she steamed to Chesapeake Bay to carry out four days of trials before sailing south to Bermuda and the naval base at Ireland Island. During a 48-hour stay in Bermuda *Glasgow* embarked over 50 military personnel for the seven-day passage home, arriving at Spithead during the afternoon of 3 September. By 1900 that evening she had secured alongside Portsmouth Dockyard's Pitch House Jetty. Five days later most of her ship's company had left the ship on foreign service leave and new drafts, and *Glasgow* was recommissioned with a new draft from the naval barracks.

On 17 October *Glasgow* left Spithead and steamed north to Scapa Flow where, two days later, she joined the 10th Cruiser Squadron of the Home Fleet. During the remainder of the year she carried out work-up with the battlefleet in and around Scapa Flow. On 5 December she arrived in the Clyde at John Brown's Dalmuir Basin, to undergo a 19-day refit, during which time the ship's company were able to take long leave. On Christmas Day, however, with the work completed, *Glasgow* returned to Scapa Flow where she rejoined her squadron, which also included *Belfast*, *Carlisle* and *Penelope*.

On 18 January 1943 *Glasgow* steamed north to the Icelandic base at Seydisfjord, and three days later, in company with *Kent* and *Bermuda*, sailed to carry out escort duties for convoy JW52, consisting of 15 merchant ships. The convoy had left Loch Ewe on 17 January with the battleship *Anson* providing distant cover, and on 26 January arrived safely at the Kola Inlet. Four days later, this time with *Malaya* providing cover, *Glasgow* returned safely to Iceland having escorted the ten merchant ships of the homeward-bound convoy RA52. After her return to Iceland *Glasgow* was based at Akureyri, a sheltered port on the north coast, and from there she undertook blockade and patrol duties north of the island. On 7 March, after exercising with the Home Fleet, *Glasgow* returned south to Scapa Flow where, during the forenoon of 19 March, she was visited by King George VI. Next

day, however, she returned to Icelandic waters to patrol the Denmark Strait, between the north-western tip of Iceland and the coast of Greenland.

Meanwhile, on 7 February 1943, the 8,068-gross ton Norddeutscher Lloyd passenger cargo liner *Regensburg* had left Djakarta in the Dutch East Indies (Indonesia) bound for Germany. She was one of several German merchant ships making their way back home and, in the process, they were hoping to evade the ships of the Royal Navy's Northern Patrol. *Regensburg* had left her home port of Hamburg in late June 1939 bound for the Far East on a voyage which would terminate at Yokohama. On 24 August, just ten days before the start of the war, she had left Hong Kong bound ostensibly for Bremen, but in fact she disappeared into the Pacific Ocean, hiding around former German colonies which had been administered by the Japanese since 1919, to refuel and restock her supplies. During the first three years of the war she made two successful round voyages between Japan and Bordeaux, on one occasion carrying a valuable cargo of rubber. However, on 7 February 1942 she left Djakarta with cargo and passengers to make the long and hazardous journey home to Germany by way of the southern Indian Ocean and north through the Atlantic Ocean. She would keep well clear of shipping lanes, and once into the North Atlantic she was routed to pass through the Denmark Strait, the narrowest part during the hours of darkness, from where she was hoping to steam undetected round Iceland's north coast and into Norwegian waters, where she would be under the protection of German naval and air patrols. By the early hours of Tuesday 30 March she was well into the Denmark Strait, and for her Master, Kapitän Harder and his 121 passengers and crew, there must have been a mood of cautious optimism that they would make it to the relative safety of Norwegian waters.

At 0400 on 30 March, however, in a position 60°40'N 025°31'W, *Regensburg*'s luck finally ran out, when *Glasgow*'s radar operators detected an unknown ship about an hour's steaming away. Speed was immediately increased and course was set to intercept the contact which, an hour later, was sighted and identified as a darkened, single-funnelled merchantman. From intelligence reports received Evans-Lombe was certain that the ship was German, and the cruiser went to Action Stations. Initially it was intended to direct the merchantman into more sheltered waters and *Glasgow* signalled *Regensburg* to stop; to this the merchantman replied, '*I stop*'. However, within minutes there was a series of explosions and the crew began lowering boats and jumping over the side. Although the sea was reasonably calm, the heavy swell soon carried them away from their ship. Although she was settling in the water it was clear to those on board *Glasgow* that she would not sink quickly, and with submarines thought to be in the area the cruiser could not afford to linger too long. When everyone from the vessel appeared to be in lifeboats Evans-Lombe ordered the main and secondary armament to open fire on the derelict ship, taking care not to hit any lifeboats. In the event it took two torpedoes from the cruiser to sink *Regensburg* which, at 0625, finally upended and disappeared beneath the waves. By now heavy snow was sweeping across the area, and before she left *Glasgow* was able to rescue only six men from one lifeboat. *Glasgow*'s patrol ended at Hvalfjord on 2 April when there was a nine-day break, before she resumed her patrolling of the Denmark Strait until the end of April when there was a five-day break at Scapa Flow. Following this she steamed into the Atlantic to take over as escort to the giant Cunarder *Queen Mary* as she left the Clyde bound for New York. In mid-May she was transferred to Plymouth to cover the South-Western Approaches, but it was only a short while before she was recalled to Scapa Flow. She remained there until mid-July, when she returned to Plymouth and began patrolling the Bay of Biscay. On 7 August she again escorted *Queen Mary* out of home waters and eight days later, while patrolling the northern end of the Bay of Biscay, she was attacked by seven Ju-88 bombers, but emerged unscathed. During the afternoon of 22 August she anchored in Plymouth Sound, where de-ammunitioning took place and three days later she steamed up harbour to Devonport Dockyard's No 5 basin to begin a seven-week refit.

During this refit *Glasgow*'s aircraft catapults were removed, additional 20mm anti-aircraft guns were fitted in order to improve her close-range air defences, and with the fitting of Type 283 Fire Control outfit, her radar was modernised. The maintenance and repair work was completed during the third week of October, and over the ten days which followed she ran a series of trials in local waters. On 26 October she left Plymouth Sound to make a fast passage up-Channel to Spithead and Portsmouth Dockyard where, that same afternoon, she secured alongside South Railway Jetty. At 1108 the next day the First Sea Lord, Admiral Sir Andrew Cunningham, together with a funeral party carrying the ashes of the late Admiral of the Fleet Sir Dudley Pound, and those of his late wife, both of whom had died within three months of each other, were embarked. Shortly afterwards *Glasgow* slipped and, escorted by two destroyers, steamed out to Spithead where, in the vicinity of A buoy, she stopped, and after a simple funeral service the two caskets were committed to the deep. Following the ceremony Admiral Cunningham left the ship by barge and *Glasgow*, after spending the night at Portsmouth, returned to Plymouth Sound from where she carried out a short work-up before resuming convoy escort duties. Her first such duty involved escorting a slow southbound convoy by way of the circuitous mid-Atlantic route to Gibraltar. The passage took a week, and after a three-day break she steamed back to home waters with a northbound convoy. During this return passage, at midnight on 18/19 November, some 36 hours out of Plymouth, an unidentified aircraft appeared over the ship. As it did not show any recognition signals, the cruiser's gunners opened fire and damaged the aircraft before it was realised that it was an Allied Liberator reconnaissance aircraft. *Glasgow*'s homeward passage ended during the forenoon of 20 November, when she anchored in Plymouth Sound.

For the ship's company the return to Plymouth was the start of a rare wartime treat, a week's break from operations in a port city. It also signalled a change of command when, on 25 November, Captain C. P. Clarke DSO RN joined the ship and took over from Evans-Lombe. Next day *Glasgow* sailed for Horta in the Azores where she refuelled and patrolled the area searching for the German blockade-runner *Alsterufer*, a small 2,729-ton steamer with refrigerated cargo facilities which was ideal for service as a supply ship for surface raiders. Between September 1939 and the end of 1943 *Alsterufer* had steamed between Bordeaux and Japan without having been detected, but on 27 December 1943, some 500 miles west-north-west of Cape Finisterre, she was spotted by Allied aircraft. They launched an attack on her but failed to damage her and she had sent out a radio request for air and sea protection. In the event the air support was not forthcoming, and another air attack on the ship did, in fact, sink her. Meanwhile, however, a force of 11 German destroyers and torpedo boats from the Bordeaux Flotilla put to sea to locate and provide an escort for *Alsterufer*. The destroyers were armed with five 127mm (roughly 5-inch) guns, while the torpedo boats, which were, in fact, small destroyers, were each armed with four 105mm (roughly 4-inch) guns. As soon as it became known that they were at sea *Glasgow* and *Enterprise* were ordered to intercept them, and by midday on 28 December the two cruisers were some 500 miles north of Corunna. Although they came under attack by German Condor FW-200 aircraft the two cruisers continued their search and at 1332, some six minutes after the third air attack had been repelled, the masts of what appeared to be four destroyers were sighted to port, bearing 238°. Both *Glasgow* and *Enterprise* immediately ceased their zigzag course and increased speed towards what, from aerial reconnaissance, they knew to be the enemy destroyers.

Although the German flotilla had left Bordeaux to locate and escort *Alsterufer*, for some reason four of the enemy ships steamed on a north-westerly

course, while seven others steamed southwards. It was the four isolated ships that *Glasgow* and *Enterprise* had sighted, and the two cruisers were able to place themselves between them and the safety of the French coast. At 1345, with the German ships some eight miles to port and steering south-east, some 350 miles west of Bordeaux, *Glasgow* opened fire with her main armament, followed a minute or two later by *Enterprise*. The four enemy ships immediately laid a smokescreen and fired a number of torpedoes at the two cruisers, and as *Glasgow* manoeuvred to avoid them, one passed astern and two ahead of her. For some three hours the running battle raged, but by 1505 one of the torpedo boats was stopped dead in the water with its funnel shot away and propulsion machinery badly damaged. By 1542 *Glasgow*'s A and B turrets had almost completely expended their ammunition, but by that time a second torpedo boat and the destroyer, *Z27*, were battered hulks. At 1641, *Z27* sank in a position 46°24'N 012°35'W, the torpedo boats *T25* and *T26* having already sunk, with the fourth torpedo boat managing to escape. In addition to a number of near misses, a 150mm shell fired by *Z26* had hit *Glasgow*'s forward boiler room forced draught intakes, causing damage and also leading to erratic changes of speed. Splinters from the shell also killed an Ordnance Artificer and an Able Seaman. At 1530 the funeral service was held on the quarterdeck, and 20 minutes later *Glasgow* was heading back to Plymouth Sound. As she left the area the cruiser passed a boatload of survivors from one of the enemy torpedo boats, but with the very real threat of air and submarine attack there was no question of stopping. In the event 164 German survivors were rescued by the Irish merchantman *Kerlogue*, on passage from Lisbon, and she landed them at Cobh where they were interned. By 1700 that afternoon RAF aircraft were providing air cover for the two cruisers, and just over an hour later Eddystone Light was sighted. At 1950 *Glasgow* anchored in Plymouth Sound.

Following her success in the Bay of Biscay *Glasgow* remained at Devonport undergoing maintenance and repairs to the damaged boiler room intakes. By mid-January 1944 she was ready for sea again and she left Plymouth to patrol the Western Approaches and to join manoeuvres with *King George V* and *Mauritius*. Over the next few weeks she continued these patrols, and also escorted convoys as far as Gibraltar. In early March, after embarking over 90 RAF and Army personnel, she made a fast passage to Horta in the Azores, but on 10 March, while leaving the Atlantic Island, she ran aground and stuck fast by the stern in the muddy harbour. Fortunately, several tugs managed to pull her free, and later in the day she was able to join the escort carrier *Nairana* in escorting a Clyde-bound convoy. By the end of March she was back at Devonport and undergoing a short maintenance period.

In mid-April, having embarked a detachment of US Army gunners, *Glasgow* steamed north to join *Belfast* on the Clyde, and for the remainder of the month the two ships carried out naval gunfire support exercises in preparation for the D-Day landings. On 22 April *Glasgow* left the Clyde to steam south to the Slapton Sands exercise area, where full-scale dress rehearsals for the landings were being staged. Three days later, on 25 April, the cruiser carried out a bombardment of the Slapton Sands assault area before returning to Plymouth Sound where she anchored for eight days. *Glasgow* had been earmarked as part of the naval bombardment force which would cover the US Army's Utah Beach assault force, who had also begun a joint training programme in readiness for the landings. It was during the morning of 27 April, while *Glasgow* was at anchor in Plymouth Sound, that 'Operation Tiger' began. The American troops and their equipment were embarked in landing craft before sailing in convoy across Lyme Bay. Unfortunately, one of the naval escorts had been damaged and there was a gap in the defences which was penetrated by German E-Boats, resulting in the loss of two LSTs and over 600 US naval and army personnel. Although *Glasgow* did take part in the exercise, her role was confined to that of communication com-

mand centre in Plymouth Sound.

Despite the tragic incident in Lyme Bay the landings went ahead and on 4 May, after putting to sea in company with USS *Augusta*, *Glasgow* anchored off Slapton Sands for a naval bombardment exercise which lasted all day, and in the evening returned to Plymouth Sound. During the whole of May the bombardment exercises continued, and the cruiser also took part in squadron manoeuvres in the Irish Sea with US Navy ships, *Arkansas, Augusta* and *Texas*. Finally, on 26 May, with the D-Day rehearsals and training exercises having been completed, *Glasgow* anchored in Northern Ireland's Dundrum Bay, before moving north to Belfast Lough where leave was granted to the ship's company. At 1315 on 1 June, with everyone back on board the ship, Captain Clarke cleared lower deck and briefed the ship's company on their forthcoming role in 'Operation Neptune', the cross-Channel passage of the invasion fleet leading to the invasion itself, 'Operation Overlord'. At this stage the exact timing of the D-Day landings was not known, but *Glasgow* was to escort ships of the invasion fleet down the Irish Sea and across the Channel to the landing beaches, after which she would provide naval gunfire support for the US Army ashore.

For *Glasgow* the operation began at 0753 on Saturday 3 June when, in company with *Hawkins, Enterprise, Black Prince* and the US Navy's *Arkansas, Texas, Tuscaloosa* and *Quincy*, she weighed anchor to leave Belfast Lough and begin a slow passage down the Irish Sea. The powerful naval force was under the command of Rear-Admiral A. G. Kirk USN, escorting the Western Task Force which was to land the US Army's 29th Infantry Division and US Army Rangers along a five-mile stretch of coast from Sainte-Honorine-des-Pertes to Pointe du Hoc on the right bank of the Douvre River estuary. By the early evening of the next day they were off Hartland Point, and on 5 June, the day on which the invasion was to have taken place, with strong winds and choppy seas, the whole operation was postponed for 24 hours. The troop convoys and their escorts remained at sea, or took shelter for the night in bays and inlets. During the daytime on 5 June *Glasgow* remained in company with *Arkansas* and *Texas* and steamed up-Channel as far as the south coast of the Isle of Wight. However, with the assault definitely confirmed for the early hours of the next day, she steamed across the Channel that evening to a constant drone of aircraft overhead as bombers pounded the German defences along the landing areas. By 0430 *Glasgow* was in her allotted position, 49°27'N 000°52'W, just north of St Laurent-ser-Mer from where, at 0554, she began a half-hour bombardment of enemy coastal defences. At 0630, as the first assault troops of the Allied Expeditionary Force began their landings, *Glasgow* and all the other naval ships ceased fire. By 0645, however, the cruiser had recommenced her bombardment, this time on targets further inland and this continued throughout the day until 2000, when the naval bombardments ceased.

Next day, 7 June, *Glasgow* began her bombardment at 0700, firing at military targets around the village of Formigny, famous for another battle which took place there some 494 years earlier, during the Hundred Years' War. Once again *Glasgow*'s main armament was in action on and off throughout that and the next day. The bombardments continued until 10 June. During the forenoon of 11 June, however, *Glasgow* was ordered to weigh anchor, and wending her way through the massive invasion fleet made her way across the Channel to Spithead where she anchored in Stokes Bay. For 24 hours the cruiser replenished her ammunition and stores, and by midday on 12 June she was once again anchored off Omaha Beach; for the next nine days she continued to bombard enemy defences and troop concentrations inland. During the evening of 21 June, in company with *Enterprise* and USS *Quincy*, she left the Normandy beaches to make an overnight crossing to Portland where, during her 72 hours in harbour, the ship's company were granted shore leave, for the first time since 31 May.

HMS *Glasgow* left Portland at 0430 on Saturday 25 June and set course for Cherbourg, where she

had been ordered to bombard military targets to the east and west of the city. By midday she was in position off the Cherbourg Peninsula and had begun her bombardment. However, this time the shore defences were returning fire and despite manoeuvring, two shells in quick succession hit the cruiser, causing damage in the hangar area and to her fire control system. *Glasgow* was immediately ordered to cease fire and return to Portland where she arrived that evening. Three days later she was officially withdrawn from the Western Task Force and ordered to the River Tyne for repairs and a major refit. Sailing by way of Plymouth Sound, Belfast Lough and Stornaway, once alongside the Tyne Commission Quay de-ammunitioning began before she was moved upriver to Palmer's Shipyard at Hebburn on the River Tyne for a major refit which would keep her out of commission for almost 12 months.

During *Glasgow*'s long months at Palmer's Yard, as well as undergoing repairs and a lengthy dry docking, the ship's radar was again modernised, with an Aircraft Homing Beacon and an updated Type 281 long-range early warning radar outfit, which required the use of only one mast, being installed. Her surface warning Type 272 radar was replaced by a new Type 293 and new gunnery radar was fitted. The biggest task was the removal of the after 6-inch 'X' turret and the conversion of its associated magazines and shell rooms for storage purposes and additional accommodation space. With the ship having been earmarked for service east of Suez in the continuing war against Japan, some work was also carried out to improve messdeck ventilation. During the refit the ship's complement was reduced, but for those who remained with the ship, VE-Day was celebrated on 8 May 1945 with an additional tot of rum. On 13 May detachments from the ship's company took part in the Victory Parade through Newcastle's city centre. Five weeks later, on 17 June, with the ship's company numbers back up to strength, the refit came to an end and *Glasgow* was prepared for sea.

At 0939 on 18 June, for the first time in over 10 months, *Glasgow* slipped her moorings and left harbour under her own steam to begin a six-week series of trials and work-up exercises from Rosyth and Scapa Flow. On the last day of July she arrived in Portsmouth where the ship's company took foreign service leave. It was during this period, on 15 August, that Japan surrendered and the Second World War was finally over. However, although the war had ended, the Japanese victories of 1941 and 1942 had led to a rise in national consciousness and civil unrest, and with the European colonial powers having to deal with turmoil in South-East Asia *Glasgow* would still find herself being kept busy during her first post-war commission.

On 22 August 1945 *Glasgow* left Portsmouth to steam via Gibraltar to Malta where she spent three weeks completing her work-up and on 19 September left Grand Harbour in company with *Jamaica* to set course for Suez. Nine days later the two cruisers arrived at Aden to refuel before continuing their passage to Colombo, where they arrived on 5 October and joined the 5th Cruiser Squadron of the East Indies Fleet. *Glasgow* had relieved *Phoebe* and one of her first duties on arrival was to assist in the transfer of naval personnel from Ceylon (Sri Lanka) to Singapore, where the newly liberated naval base was being remanned. Three days after her arrival in Ceylon, she embarked 250 naval ratings and sailed for Singapore, via Port Swettenham, where she also embarked a draft of Royal Marines who had been part of the Malayan liberation force. She arrived in Singapore on 14 October, but with major mine clearance operations under way in the Johore Strait, she anchored in the outer roads off Singapore city where the personnel were disembarked. After leaving Singapore *Glasgow* returned to Ceylon, but this time to the naval base at Trincomalee. She remained in local waters until 1 December. Having embarked 60 Royal Marines Bandsmen who were touring India, she ferried them to Mandapan, the closest town to north-west Ceylon, and after her passengers disembarked remained in the area for a week. In mid-December she made her second trooping trip

and after embarking over 300 naval personnel she sailed for Singapore where, once again, she anchored south of the city. Although Christmas was spent at anchor off Singapore, because the island was still recovering from the worst effects of the Japanese occupation only very limited shore leave was granted. On 27 December, having embarked another 326 naval personnel, she returned to Colombo and Trincomalee.

On 13 January 1946 there was a change of command when Captain A. G. V. Hubbock CBE RN joined the ship and took over from Clarke. Two days later *Glasgow* sailed for a short exercise programme with the escort carrier *Fencer*, before returning to Colombo to embark another 325 naval personnel bound for the naval base at Singapore. On arrival at Singapore during the forenoon of 22 January the passengers were disembarked, and next day in company with *Petard* and *Sussex* she sailed for manoeuvres in local waters. However, after only 24 hours the exercises were interrupted when *Glasgow* was ordered to proceed with all dispatch to the port city of Surabaya on the island of Java, which in those days was still part of the Netherlands East Indies. During the Japanese occupation of Java, as well as removing much of the Dutch governmental structure, the Japanese had also appointed a large number of Indonesian people to senior administrative positions, which had heightened national consciousness. Following the Japanese surrender in August 1945 the nationalist leader Achmed Soekarno had proclaimed the Netherland East Indies to be an Independent nation under the new name of Indonesia, and he had actually formed a government. This, however, was not what the European colonial powers had in mind, but it was October 1945 before the former Dutch Governor and Dutch troops, who were supported by British troops, arrived. Ostensibly the British Army was there to evacuate British civilians, but in reality their duties included assisting the Dutch to regain control of the country. In the event, in November 1945 both British and Dutch troops were involved in fierce fighting with Indonesian nationalists in

A post-war image of HMS Glasgow *entering Portsmouth. Her 6 inch turret at 'X' position had by then been removed. She could be distinguished from her sisters by the YE60 beacon aerial carried on a pole mast aft of the second funnel.* *(National Museum of the Royal Navy)*

and around the port of Surabaya, and although by late January 1946 much of the fighting was over, there were still tensions and *Glasgow*'s presence was intended to reinforce the British Army in and around the city. By the time she anchored at Jammang Reef, off Surabaya, all was quiet and almost deserted, and after four days *Glasgow* was ordered back to Singapore. Here she embarked ten naval officers and returned to Colombo to begin an eight-day maintenance and docking period, after which she steamed round to Trincomalee. Late that same afternoon, however, all libertymen were recalled and the cruiser was order to raise steam and proceed with all dispatch, this time to Bombay.

Following the Japanese surrender most of the European colonies in Asia were gripped by nationalist unrest, and for Britain the biggest headache of all was India where, between November 1945 and June 1946, at Courts Martial in Delhi, a number of Indian Army personnel who had actively collaborated with the Japanese by joining the Japanese Indian National Army to fight against the British, so inflamed public opinion in India that it erupted into widespread civil disorder. As a result the British C-in-C India was forced to commute the sentences of transportation for life which had been imposed. In January 1946 there were widespread mutinies among British RAF personnel stationed in India, which involved over 40,000 servicemen in some 50 RAF stations in both India and Ceylon. Described officially at the time as 'strikes' this widespread breakdown in discipline had a profound effect on men serving in the Indian Air Force and, perhaps more so, on men of the Indian Navy where, generally, morale was already low. On 18 February ratings of the Royal Indian Navy 'went on strike' and within 24 hours this had spread to most ships and shore establishments in Bombay, Calcutta, Madras, Karachi and other ports. The centre of the mutiny was at Bombay, and on 21 February, in a show of force, a squadron of RAF bombers flew low over the harbour. If anything this had the effect of hardening the attitudes of the mutineers, and what was even more worrying for the British authorities was the fact that a brigade of Gurkhas refused to fire on the Indian naval mutineers. Added to this was the fact that the mutiny spread to the Indian Air Force, and at a time when there was also significant unrest among British service personnel in India. As *Glasgow* steamed north the order came for the Royal Navy to quell the unrest by force if necessary, something which would have been difficult and without a doubt would have seriously exacerbated a situation which would almost certainly have led to very serious civil disorder throughout India. In a secret report British Military Intelligence had already concluded that '*... the Indian armed forces could no longer be relied upon to prop up the Raj*'.

At 1925 on 23 February *Glasgow* anchored in Bombay Harbour, just off the Gateway of India, itself a symbolic landmark, but by this time the mutiny was virtually over. The British administration had sensibly called upon India's own political leaders for help, and the mutineers had got no support from them at all, with Mahatma Gandhi condemning them outright. However, during *Glasgow*'s passage north her Royal Marines Detachment had been busy preparing equipment and weapons ready for boarding or landing, but fortunately they were not required. In the event, the cruiser's seven days at Bombay were marked by many 'good runs ashore' and when the ship was opened to visitors the people on board were estimated at one stage to number some 6,000, making movement around the upper decks almost impossible. Eventually the Royal Marines were turned out, but only to control the huge crowds of good-natured visitors to the ship. At a higher political level it was obvious that Indian Independence, which had been promised during the Second World War, could not be delayed much longer. *Glasgow* left Bombay during the evening of 2 March to steam south to Colombo where she paused just long enough to refuel, before sailing via Port Louis, Mauritius, for Simonstown to begin a 15-week refit.

By all accounts the four months spent at the Cape were happy ones for the ship's company, with the hospitality of the people of Cape Town being

described by one Royal Marine as '*overwhelming*'. During the refit it was learned that *Glasgow* was to become the flagship of the C-in-C, East Indies, Vice-Admiral Sir Arthur Palliser, an officer with wide experience of pre-war and wartime service east of Suez. To mark the appointment there was a nostalgic return to a pre-war tradition with the ship's funnels being painted a buff colour, and the hull white – the peacetime colours of the East Indies Fleet. In early July, with the refit coming to an end, the Royal Marines and platoons of seamen put on a full ceremonial parade in Cape Town, with the local newspapers describing both marines and seamen as '*Excelling themselves in appearance and drill*'. On 8 July *Glasgow* put to sea for the first day of post-refit trials, during which there appeared to be excessive vibration on the port outer propeller. During the forenoon the ship anchored in Simons Bay and the ship's divers began operations to examine both the propeller and the A bracket by which the shaft is held. Unfortunately, one of the divers got into difficulties and by the time he was pulled from the water he had died. In the event the propeller was given a clean bill of health and on 15 July, at the end of the trials period, *Glasgow* left South African waters to return via Mauritius to Trincomalee, where upon her arrival she hoisted the flag of the C-in-C.

On *Glasgow*'s return to the fleet it appeared that much of the nationalist agitation and civil unrest in many of the European colonial territories had abated and the countries were settling back into old prewar routines. This would, in the longer term, be an illusion, but for *Glasgow* it allowed for the first full peacetime 'Showing the Flag' cruise of Indian Ocean and East African territories. Having embarked additional Royal Marines, together with the C-in-C's Band, *Glasgow* left Trincomalee to set course for visits to Mauritius, the Seychelles, Dar-es-Salaam, Zanzibar, Tanga, Mombasa, Aden and the Maldives. The two and a half-month cruise was packed with official high-level diplomatic receptions and parades, which kept the Royal Marines and the Bands busy. For the ship's company, however, after wartime conditions and long periods spent at sea in Defence Watches, the cruise was a relaxed affair. It came as a surprise when, on arrival back at Colombo, the island of Ceylon was found to be paralysed by a general strike amid a tense situation on the streets where large crowds were gathered demanding an end to colonial rule. Almost as soon as she was secured to her buoys in Colombo Harbour the Royal Marines Detachment and platoons of seamen were landed to march through the city in a show of force.

During the whole of November *Glasgow* remained at Trincomalee, and on the 28th of the month before she sailed for Singapore, the C-in-C struck his flag. Arriving at the naval base on 3 December, the ship began a ten-day docking period in the floating dry dock, but by 18 December she was back at Trincomalee, where Christmas and the New Year were spent. On 2 January 1947 *Glasgow* left Trincomalee for her second, much shorter, 'Flag Showing' cruise, this time to Rangoon, Calcutta and Madras, which lasted only three weeks. On her return to Trincomalee there was a short break before she made a third cruise, this time to the Persian Gulf, where she visited Bahrain, the Iraqi port of Basra and Kuwait. On the last day of February, to the relief of the ship's company, *Glasgow* left Bahrain to steam back into the cooler and fresher waters of the Indian Ocean, where she joined the aircraft carrier *Glory*, and *Jamaica* for manoeuvres before ending the cruise with visits to Karachi and Bombay. By the third week in March she had returned to Trincomalee and during April she joined *Glory, Jamaica* and *Contest* for regular day-running exercises. The first two weeks of May saw the East Indies Fleet holding its Fleet Sailing and Pulling Regatta, for which a formidable force had assembled at Trincomalee, including *Glory, Theseus, Jamaica, Contest* and *Consort*, with the shore establishments *Highflyer* and *Bambara* also providing boats and crews. In mid-May, with the regattas over, *Glasgow* steamed round to Colombo, where station leave was enjoyed at Diyatalawa Cantonment, an Army camp almost in the centre of

the island, which during the Second World War had housed enemy internees. However, before the second leave period was over, further nationalist unrest in Colombo had led to more widespread strikes and disorder on the streets. *Glasgow*'s personnel were recalled from leave and once again the cruiser's Royal Marines and platoons of seamen were organised into mobile units ready to land at short notice should the civil police be unable to cope or, as was feared at one stage, should they join the protesters. With India about to gain its independence, nationalist feelings in Ceylon were once again running high, but with the announcement that in February 1948 the island would gain its own independence, the tense situation in Colombo was eased.

On 21 June *Glasgow* made her final cruise of the commission, which took her to Singapore, where she anchored off the city, then to Penang, and to Nancowry and Port Blair in the Andaman Islands. On 10 July she returned to Trincomalee where she remained until 6 August when she left harbour to begin her passage home. Sailing via Aden, Port Said and Gibraltar, at 0315 on Wednesday 27 August she raised St Catherine's Light on the Isle of Wight and four hours later she was anchored at Spithead. For the ship's company, who had been away from home for two years, there was a frustrating seven-hour wait until Customs clearance was given, but finally, during the afternoon, she weighed anchor and steamed up harbour to secure alongside Portsmouth's North Corner Jetty. The commission was over and by the end of September she had been reduced to reserve prior to beginning a long refit.

On 1 August 1948, as *Glasgow* lay in Portsmouth Dockyard with her refit coming to an end, her new Commanding Officer, Captain C. L. Firth DSO MVO RN, joined the ship. During the three weeks which followed, the ship's company was brought up to full strength. For the new company there was the herculean task of making the ship habitable after 12 months in dockyard hands. On 23 August *Glasgow* was recommissioned and finally, at 1015 on 30 September, she left Portsmouth Harbour to

HMS Glasgow *steams past Southsea seafront on 30 September 1948 to begin post-refit trials.*
(Maritime Photo Library)

begin her post-refit trials. It had been recently announced that the America and West Indies Station of the Royal Navy, which was based on Bermuda at the Ireland Island Dockyard, was to be strengthened with the arrival of a second cruiser, *Glasgow*; she was to take the place of *Sheffield*, which would return home for refit.

HMS *Glasgow*'s two weeks of trials off Portland were carried out with such illustrious names as *Anson* and *King George V*, but on 14 October, leaving the two battleships at Portland (from where they rarely strayed) she sailed for Bermuda. During her first two months on station *Glasgow* remained in local waters, where she carried out regular training exercises with *Cleopatra, Diadem* and *Snipe*. Christmas and the New Year were spent at Ireland Island, but on 3 January 1949, with *Bigbury Bay* and *Snipe*, she sailed for a three-month cruise to the southern area of the station, which included the Falkland Islands, South Georgia and visits to South American ports. The visits to the British Dependencies in the South Atlantic were a direct response to increasingly loud Argentinean claims to sovereignty. After refuelling at Trinidad the squadron steamed south to Rio de Janeiro for a week's courtesy visit, after which *Glasgow* steamed up the River Plate to Buenos Aires. The point of the cruise was to provide a 'show of strength' in the Falkland Islands, South Georgia and the British Antarctic Territories, but on arrival in the Argentine capital on 28 January there were no signs of diplomatic tensions. Admiral Tennant addressed the country's press in Spanish and the newspapers gave a positive and friendly reception to *Glasgow*'s arrival. On Tennant's personal invitation President Peron and his Minister of Marine, Admiral Garcia, visited the ship, and when on 4 February *Glasgow* left harbour, the visit was considered to have been a diplomatic success. The tensions had eased somewhat, but the Argentine claims lay dormant, and in another 33 years the threats would became a reality.

After leaving the River Plate the squadron steamed south once again and on 7 February they arrived at Port Stanley, the small capital of the Falkland Islands. On her arrival in the South Atlantic *Glasgow* had rendezvoused with the sloop *Sparrow*, also visiting the Falkland Islands Dependencies; at one stage she had been trapped in ice in Admiralty Bay on the south side of King George I Island in the South Shetlands. Having made a four-day visit to Port Stanley the two ships steamed through thick fog, made all the more dangerous by the presence of large icebergs, to Grytviken in South Georgia. In those days Grytviken was inhabited by a large whaling community, and during the 48-hour visit the ships' companies were granted shore leave and the cruiser was opened to visitors. After leaving Grytviken *Glasgow* steamed along the coast to another large whaling station at Husvik in Stromness Bay, where she loaded a large cargo of tallow to take back to Port Stanley. The return passage to the Falkland Islands was once again hampered by fog and icebergs, but on 20 February the cruiser anchored back at Port Stanley. This time the visit lasted for just 48 hours, but long enough for the ship's company to put on a party for local children.

Leaving Port Stanley *Glasgow* steamed north again to call at the Uruguayan port of Montevideo, where she embarked the country's President, Luis Batle Berres, and took him down the coast to Punta del Este, at the mouth of the River Plate estuary. After leaving Montevideo *Glasgow* returned to Bermuda via Trinidad and Antigua, rendezvousing en route with *Jamaica, Bigbury Bay* and *Whitesand Bay* to carry out air defence exercises with USS *Coral Sea*. During the second phase of the exercise, which lasted for two days, they were joined by the Canadian aircraft carrier *Magnificent*, together with *Ontario*, the destroyers *Athabaska, Nootka* and *Haida*, and the submarine *Tudor*. This part of the exercise saw RFA *Gold Ranger* acting as a convoy, with *Magnificent, Jamaica*, three destroyers and three frigates making up the escort. Ahead of the convoy, between Cuba and Bermuda, lurked the submarine *Tudor* and close to her were *Glasgow* and *Ontario*, all acting as enemy raiders, but in the event they were unable to penetrate the defensive

screen of aircraft from *Magnificent*, and the destroyers. During the exercise *Glasgow* paid a visit to the US naval base at Cuba's Guantanamo Bay, until on 2 April she secured alongside Bermuda's Ireland Island naval base to begin a 13-week refit.

It was early July 1949 before *Glasgow* was ready for sea again, and after a short trials period she left Bermuda to begin a three-month cruise to ports on the eastern seaboard of the USA and Canada. The first calls were at Portsmouth, New Hampshire, and Cornerbrook, Newfoundland. During the latter part of July and into August she remained in Canadian waters and on 8 August she arrived in Halifax, Nova Scotia, for the Canadian Navy Week. The end of August saw *Glasgow* at Quebec, and from there she steamed upriver to Montreal. The real highlight of the American cruise came on 16 September when, after exercising with the submarine *Tally Ho*, she entered New York Harbour, to secure alongside Pier No 54. During her ten-day stay in the city *Glasgow* proved an extremely popular visitor, for she was warmly remembered by many Americans as the cruiser which gave covering fire to the 1st American Division at Omaha Beach on D-Day. During the visit the ship was opened to the public, and on one afternoon alone over 3,000 people crowded over her gangways. After leaving New York *Glasgow* called at Annapolis and the US naval base at Norfolk, Virginia, before returning on 14 October to the dockyard at Bermuda to begin her annual refit and docking period.

After spending the Christmas and New Year of 1949/1950 at Bermuda, on 2 January *Glasgow* left the island to carry out trials prior to a five-day passage to the Caribbean island of Antigua at the start of a three-month cruise of the area. On 13 February she arrived at Kingston, Jamaica, on a ten-day visit. Primarily the ship was in Jamaica for the official installation of Princess Alice of Athlone, Queen Victoria's last surviving granddaughter, as the first Chancellor of the University of the West Indies, whose main campus was on the island. However, the occasion coincided with nationalist unrest on the island which had manifested itself in widespread strikes and rioting in the capital, Kingston. At one stage the riots had turned ugly and had threatened to overwhelm the Police contingent guarding the Myrtle Palace Hotel where Princess Alice and her husband were staying. In the event, however, neither *Glasgow*'s Royal Marines nor landing parties were required and the ceremonies at the University passed off peacefully. On 23 February, after Princess Alice and her husband had embarked in *Glasgow*, the ship sailed for a tour of what were then British colonial territories in the Caribbean, including Dominica, St Lucia, St Vincent, Grenada, Barbados and finally, on 12 March, Port of Spain, Trinidad, where the royal visitors disembarked. With her royal tour over, *Glasgow* spent five days at Trinidad before joining the frigates *Snipe* and *Sparrow*, and the Canadian warships *Magnificent* and *Micmac*, to begin a joint exercise code-named 'Caribex'. As well as the British and Canadian warships, also taking part were four US Navy aircraft carriers, *Franklin D Roosevelt, Leyte, Philippine Sea* and *Wright*, together with cruisers, destroyers and submarines. The exercises were led by the US Navy's Vice-Admiral B. Duncan, and consisted chiefly of submarine and air attacks and counter-attacks, which continued through to the last week of March and ended at Guantanamo Bay. On 30 March, after leaving the US base, the British and Canadian ships made for Caribbean ports, with *Glasgow* spending five days at Nassau, before returning to Bermuda to carry out an 11-week maintenance period.

On 26 April there was a change of command for *Glasgow* when Captain W. J. Yendell RN took over the ship. At this time it was also announced that in November 1950 *Superb* would transfer from the Home Fleet's 2nd Cruiser Squadron to the America and West Indies Station and take the place of *Glasgow*, which, on her return to home waters, would be reduced to reserve. Before *Glasgow* sailed, however, she was to make two more short cruises. The first of these began on 28 June when, in company with *Snipe*, she sailed for Panama on the first leg of a cruise to ports on the west coast of

North America. On 2 July, four days into the passage to Cristobal, the two ships were suddenly ordered to refuel at Kingston, Jamaica and then return to Bermuda. In South-East Asia the Korean War had broken out and in the words of the official Admiralty statement: '*It would be inappropriate to pay flag-showing visits to ports which have been placed on an operational footing on account of the Far East situation.*' *Glasgow* and *Snipe* arrived back in Bermuda on 10 July, and over the next week it became clear that neither ship would be immediately required in the Far East. On 18 July, *Glasgow* and HMCS *Swansea* left Bermuda bound for ports on Canada's east coast. During the three-week cruise *Glasgow* visited Halifax, Nova Scotia, and Cornerbrook, the small city located on Newfoundland's Bay of Islands. From Cornerbrook she paid an eight-day visit to Montreal, before returning to the Atlantic to exercise with the Canadian frigates *La Hulloise* and *Swansea*, arriving back at Bermuda on 18 August.

HMS *Glasgow*'s final cruise of the commission began ten days later on 28 August, with her first call being the Dominican Republic, whose capital in those days was named Ciudad Trujillo (now Santo Domingo), after the country's President, General Rafael Leonidas Trujillo (assassinated in 1961). During the ship's five-day stay Trujillo paid a short visit on board, and when *Glasgow* was opened to the public over a thousand people visited her which, for a country under the iron grip of a ruthless dictator, was considered a good number. From the Dominican Republic *Glasgow* steamed on to Kingston, Jamaica, and to Vera Cruz in Mexico, where she spent six days before making a four-day passage to Belize (British Honduras). The final call was at the Puerto Rican capital of San Juan, and on 6 October she returned to Bermuda for the last time.

On 16 October 1950 *Glasgow* left Bermuda to begin her nine-day passage home, and later she anchored at Spithead from where, after a three-hour delay for Customs clearance, she steamed up harbour to secure alongside in the dockyard as families and friends waited to go aboard. It was the end of the commission and four days later Captain Yendell transferred to *Superb*. By 9 November *Glasgow*'s ship's company had been reduced to little more than a steaming crew, and that afternoon she left Spithead to make the short passage to Chatham, where she arrived the next morning to pay off and begin a long refit.

There is little doubt that had it not been for the Korean War *Glasgow*'s operational career would have been over, but as it was she was scheduled to undergo a long refit after which, contrary to the Admiralty press release which had previously been given out, she would recommission. During her refit *Glasgow*'s close-range armament was reduced to 24, 2-pdrs in six quadruple mountings, and eight single 40mm anti-aircraft guns. In early 1951 she spent three months in dry dock and it was not until 18 September that her new commanding officer, Captain J. Holmes RN, was appointed to the ship. Four days later *Glasgow* was recommissioned, and on 14 November she left Chatham Dockyard to secure at a Sheerness buoy. Two days later she began her post-refit trials, which were carried out off Portsmouth and Portland. On 6 December *Glasgow* left Portland to set course for Gibraltar and Malta where, 11 days later, she joined the 1st Cruiser Squadron of the Mediterranean Fleet, which also included *Liverpool, Cleopatra* and *Euryalus*. *Glasgow*'s arrival in Malta coincided with the start of the Christmas and New Year break, and it was New Year's Day 1952 when she sailed to begin a three-week work-up in the local exercise areas around the island. On 28 January, flying the flag of FO2 Mediterranean, she was joined by *Cleopatra, Manxman, Chequers* and *Chivalrous* to become the first British warships to pay an official visit to Libya following the granting of the country's independence. In the 1950s the full extent of that country's oil reserves had not been discovered, and at the time Britain's main interest was in keeping large military bases which had grown up during the Second World War in the area of Tobruk. It was to Tobruk that *Glasgow*'s 12-day Libyan visit took her, where she anchored in the harbour.

After leaving Tobruk *Glasgow* returned to Maltese waters to join manoeuvres with the aircraft carrier *Theseus*, as well as *Liverpool, Cleopatra* and the destroyers *Cheviot, Chevron, St James* and *Vigo*, during the course of which she visited Cagliari and Naples. On 22 March *Glasgow* left Grand Harbour for fleet exercises off the island, which, as well as *Theseus* and the destroyers, also included *Indomitable*. Next day, however, *St James* was ordered to Port Said, and over the course of the next 24 hours most of the fleet, including *Glasgow*, were ordered to the Egyptian port. Ever since the end of the Second World War the presence of large British military bases close to Ismailia, in what was known as the Suez Canal Zone, had become increasingly resented by Egyptian people, with the result that serious nationalist unrest and attacks on British service personnel and their families had put the bases themselves virtually under siege. Although diplomatic negotiations were under way in an effort to improve the situation, the British Government decided to put on a show of naval force, which, in addition to *St James* and *Glasgow*, included *Cleopatra, Liverpool, Armada, Saintes, Aisne, Agincourt, Corunna* and *Jutland*. In the event *Glasgow* arrived in Port Said during the morning of 26 March, and remained there for almost three weeks. The dangerous security situation for British service personnel is highlighted by the fact that libertymen were restricted to a canteen within the naval compound at Port Said, and on board the ships additional sentries were posted round the upper deck, with ships' divers conducting regular searches of underwater hulls. In mid-April, however, with the civil disorder having subsided, *Glasgow* left Port Said and returned to Malta.

Three days after her return to Grand Harbour *Glasgow* hoisted the flag of the C-in-C Mediterranean Fleet, Admiral Sir John Edelstone, and led *Theseus, Euryalus, Manxman, Surprise, Armada, Cheviot, Sluys, St James, Solebay* and *Vigo* to Piraeus. They were visiting Athens to take part in a high-profile ceremony at the unveiling of a memorial to men of the Commonwealth forces who died in Greece during the Second World War. The ceremonies took place over five days between 23 and 28 April, and on 26 April King Paul of the Hellenes paid two visits to *Glasgow*, where he met the elderly British politician Lord Halifax. On 28 May *Glasgow*, accompanied by *Euryalus*, steamed back to Malta where the former began a five-week docking and maintenance period.

When *Glasgow* put to sea again in mid-June she had hoisted the flag of the new C-in-C, Admiral Lord Mountbatten, and was leading the fleet on a programme of exercises code-named 'B2', which were marked by tragedy when an officer and rating on board *Daring* were killed when a round of ammunition exploded while they were attempting to clear a jammed breach. The manoeuvres also included *Gambia, Surprise, Armada, Gravelines, Saintes, Vigo*, five submarines and ships of the 5th Frigate Flotilla. The programme also included a short visit to Taranto, and on 25 June *Glasgow* arrived at what was then the Yugoslav port of Rijeka (formerly Fiume, and now part of Croatia), where the C-in-C held a series of meetings with President Tito. On 26 June *Glasgow* anchored off Brioni Island, which in those days was virtually Tito's own private property, where he frequently entertained foreign guests. On this occasion it was the venue for further meetings with Mountbatten, and that evening Tito came out to the ship where he inspected a Royal Marines Guard of Honour. From Brioni *Glasgow* visited Trieste where she anchored off the harbour entrance. During the early hours of 29 June the duty watch at the gangway saw a car being driven, apparently deliberately, off a nearby jetty and into the sea. Fortunately a member of the cruiser's ship's company who witnessed the incident immediately swam to the sinking vehicle and, at great risk to himself, successfully rescued the occupant. On 1 July, after the C-in-C had concluded talks with the British Military Governor of Trieste (between 1945 and 1954 the northern half of Trieste was administered by joint US/British Military Governors), *Glasgow* sailed south to join the fleet. They had now been joined by HMCS

Magnificent, at anchor in Phaleron Bay off Athens, where the C-in-C met senior Greek military officers. In the last week of July, however, further nationalist unrest in Egypt, mainly directed against the British military bases, saw *Glasgow* and other ships of the fleet return to Port Said, where they remained for some weeks, with *Glasgow* returning to Malta in mid-August. The latter half of 1952 saw *Glasgow* being used for trials of the centralised messing system, but because of the difficulty in providing adequate dining halls in a ship not originally designed with such facilities, they were not considered to have been a success.

During the remainder of the year, apart from short visits to Algiers and a high-profile visit to Naples, where the C-in-C held talks at NATO's southern headquarters, *Glasgow* remained close to Malta. In October *Glasgow*, *Manxman* and *Loch Dunvegan* starred in the filming of 20th Century Fox's movie '*Single Handed*', an adaptation of C. S. Forester's novel '*Brown on Resolution*'. In the event, however, when the film was released the cruiser was seen in just a few distant scenes. These shots of the warships had been mostly taken from the air by cameramen in an RAF bomber operating from Malta. In mid-November *Glasgow* began a 12-week docking and maintenance period, and it was not until 9 February 1953 that she was at sea once more, this time exercising with *Kenya* and *Gravelines*. On 1 March she left Malta to rendezvous with *Eagle, Indomitable, Gambia, Chivalrous, Daring, Euryalus* and *Manxman*, and two days later, east of Gibraltar, with ships of the Home Fleet, among them the battleship *Vanguard, Theseus, Implacable, Indefatigable, Swiftsure* and the Daring-class ships, *Diamond* and *Duchess*, as well as two other destroyer and frigate squadrons.

The meeting of the Home and Mediterranean Fleets evoked memories of the annual pre-war combined manoeuvres, usually held in the Eastern Atlantic and Western Mediterranean. The opening phase of what was code-named 'Exercise Crossbar' began with a four-day convoy exercise which was witnessed by the First Sea Lord in the battleship *Vanguard*. The ships of the Home Fleet represented the 'Red' force, which were attempting to pass a convoy through the Strait of Gibraltar to the Eastern Mediterranean. Opposing them was a 'Blue' force, which included *Eagle*, *Glasgow*, *Gambia* and other ships of the Mediterranean Fleet. The first phase ended on 5 March when the fleets steamed into Gibraltar for a ten-day break, which also included a great deal of ceremonial and harbour evolutions. The second phase of 'Crossbar' took place in the Mediterranean, south of Toulon and in the Aegean, with French warships also taking part. For *Glasgow* the manoeuvres ended on 24 March when she anchored in Phaleron Bay, once again hosting a short visit by King Paul of the Hellenes. By 1 April, however, she had returned to Malta and for the next six weeks remained in local waters.

On 12 May *Glasgow* led *Gambia* and *Manxman* out of Grand Harbour to steam west for Gibraltar and on to Spithead, where they arrived on 21 May. The three ships were representing the Mediterranean Fleet at the Coronation Fleet Review at Spithead, and during the three and a half weeks in home waters both watches of the ship's company were able to take some leave, and the ship herself spent just over two weeks in the dockyard undergoing maintenance. The Review itself took place on Monday 15 June, and next day *Glasgow* left Spithead to return to the Mediterranean, exercising en route with the Indian Navy's destroyer *Ranjit* (ex-HMS *Redoubt*) and New Zealand's cruiser *Black Prince*. Immediately upon her return to Grand Harbour *Glasgow* began a short docking and maintenance period, before leading 19 ships of the Mediterranean Fleet, including *Theseus* and *Black Prince*, on a high-profile visit to Athens and Istanbul. However, no sooner had she returned to Grand Harbour than further unrest erupted in Port Said and the area of the British military bases in the Suez Canal Zone, during which two British soldiers were shot dead and others wounded, whereupon *Glasgow* departed for the Egyptian port. On her arrival on 13 August security on board the ship was high and as before leave was confined to the can-

HMS Glasgow *anchored at Spithead for the Coronation Naval Review of 1953.* *(National Maritime Museum)*

teen in the naval compound. However, unlike previous occasions, the arrival of the Royal Navy did not see an end to the civil unrest and it was 8 September before *Glasgow* was able to leave Egypt and return to Malta. In the meantime diplomatic negotiations between the British and Egyptian Governments dragged on, but there would be no final settlement until November 1956, when the fiasco of the Suez Crisis settled the matter once and for all.

Following her return to Grand Harbour *Glasgow* led the Mediterranean Fleet to Navarin Bay, attended by the First Lord of the Admiralty and the C-in-C, for the fleet regattas, after which the cruiser paid a two-week visit to Piraeus before returning to Malta. On 24 October, accompanied by *Surprise*, she steamed south for Port Said. This time, however, she passed through the Suez Canal to the southern Jordanian port of Aqaba, where King Hussein and his Prime Minister embarked for a two and a half-hour trip to sea to watch a gunnery display. From Aqaba the two warships steamed south again into the Red Sea for a five-day visit to the Eritrean island port of Massawa which, in those days, was ruled by Ethiopia. Here the C-in-C met with the President of the Eritrean Assembly, who was also Emperor Haile Selassie's very unpopular representative in the province. After leaving Massawa on 11 November *Glasgow* and *Surprise* retraced their route through the Suez Canal before returning to Malta.

The new year of 1954 began for *Glasgow* on 4 January, when she left Malta to begin four days of intensive exercises in local waters, before joining *Glory, Gambia, Daring* and other ships of the Mediterranean Fleet for 'Exercise Janex IV', a prelude to the bigger Home and Mediterranean Fleet combined manoeuvres which were to take place in

March. Before that *Glasgow* joined *Daring* for an amphibious landing and bombardment exercise off the north-east corner of Cyprus, during which she landed men of 40 Commando Royal Marines, and bombarded Cape Arnanti, after which she carried out another stint as guardship at Port Said. On 14 March *Glasgow* left Malta to rendezvous with ships of both the Home and Mediterranean Fleets, including *Eagle, Vanguard, Superb, Bermuda, Daring, Duchess* and other destroyers and frigates. The joint manoeuvres included 'Exercise Medflex A', in which both French and Dutch ships participated, giving them a truly international flavour. *Glasgow*'s part in them ended in the second week of April, when she arrived at Naples for a short visit before returning to Grand Harbour.

On 1 May 1954 *Glasgow* led 25 ships of the Mediterranean Fleet to sea to rendezvous with the Royal Yacht *Britannia*, which had left Tobruk the same day carrying the Queen and Prince Philip on the final leg of what had been a six-month tour of Commonwealth countries. After exchanging salutes the warships had formed two columns, swept in on either side of the Royal Yacht, which was described in a contemporary newspaper thus: '*With little slackening of speed both lines wheeled inward, a gallant sight in the Mediterranean sun, and this time passed within half a cable of* Britannia *as officers and ratings lining the sides gave three cheers for the Queen. Lord Mountbatten went on board the Royal Yacht by jackstay, and after the ships had taken their stations around her, aircraft from the carrier* Eagle, *both piston and jet-propelled, flew past at intervals.*' With the rendezvous ceremony over, *Glasgow* took up station ahead of the fleet and during the forenoon of 3 May all the ships arrived in Grand Harbour.

HMS *Glasgow*, which was coming to the end of her commission, had been chosen to continue her escort duties with the Royal Yacht, and on 7 May, in company with *Barfleur, Chequers* and *Saintes*, she left Malta bound for Portsmouth via Gibraltar. After a short 24-hour stop at Gibraltar during the afternoon of 11 May, *Britannia* and her escorts sailed for the final leg of the passage home. As she left Gibraltar *Glasgow* was flying her 600ft paying-off pennant, and as they approached Eddystone Light, led by *Vanguard*, they were met by ships of the Home Fleet. At 1000 that forenoon *Glasgow*, *Barfleur* and *Saintes* completed their escort duties and parted company from the Royal Yacht. Finally, at 1100 on 14 May 1954 *Glasgow* secured alongside Portsmouth Dockyard's Middle Slip Jetty. The commission was over.

On 19 May there was a change of command when Captain P. Dawnay MVO DSC RN took over the ship and next day, with a new ship's company, *Glasgow* was recommissioned. Eight days later, on 28 May, she sailed once again for the Mediterranean, and on 7 June, after arriving in Malta, once again hoisted the flag of the C-in-C Mediterranean Fleet, Admiral Lord Mountbatten, before leaving on a four-week work-up period, during which she was ably assisted by her sister *Birmingham* and the destroyers *Comet* and *St Kitts*. It was on 13 August that she began her operational duties and left Malta with *Gambia* for Port Said. Once again nationalist unrest was sweeping the Suez Canal Zone, but upon their arrival in Egypt the situation had calmed down following diplomatic negotiations. This time *Glasgow*'s visit was confined to just 12 hours, during which she embarked 450 officers and men of 40 Commando Royal Marines who had been sent to reinforce the garrison, and were now being evacuated. A similar number were also embarked in *Gambia* and during the evening of 16 August the two cruisers sailed for Malta, where they arrived three days later.

During September *Glasgow* took part in a major fleet exercise, which included visits to Kotor and Dubrovnik, and in early October at the end of her Adriatic cruise she formed part of the Mediterranean Fleet which escorted *Surprise*, carrying Emperor Haile Sellasie of Ethiopia to Malta, and then accompanied *Gambia* out of Grand Harbour as she took Haile Sellasie from Malta to Britain for a State Visit. Once clear of the harbour, during the forenoon of 8 October, led by the aircraft

HMS Glasgow *at Malta's Grand Harbour with the Royal Yacht* Britannia *passing her in the background.*
(Michael Cassar)

carrier *Centaur*, the ships of the Mediterranean Fleet put on a flying and gunnery display for the Emperor, before *Glasgow* returned to Grand Harbour for a 14-week refit and docking period, which kept her out of action for the rest of the year.

On 13 January 1955, with her refit completed, *Glasgow* put to sea again, and for nine weeks she remained in local waters carrying out air defence exercises with RAF Meteor jets, and anti-submarine exercises with *Diamond, Duchess, Jamaica* and the Dutch aircraft carrier *Karel Doorman*, which was operating Sea Furies. During the second week of March there came the joint Home and Mediterranean Fleet manoeuvres, during which *Glasgow*, *Jamaica* and *Diana* took an amphibious role. The three ships embarked men of 40 and 45 Commando Royal Marines and sailed as part of a convoy, which also included RFAs, through the Mediterranean between Malta and Sardinia. The escorts included Daring-class ships as well as other destroyers and frigates, with aircraft from both *Albion* and *Centaur* providing the attacking force. It was reminiscent of some of the wartime Mediterranean convoys, and after landing the marines in southern Sardinia, the combined Home and Mediterranean Fleets returned to Malta to make a ceremonial entry into Grand Harbour. With some 50 ships at their moorings, including two aircraft carriers and five cruisers at the various buoys, the harbour and its creeks were almost filled to capacity. After a short break here the ships of the Mediterranean Fleet paid a weekend visit to Naples before dispersing for courtesy visits to French and Western Mediterranean ports, with *Glasgow* calling at Villefranche, Tangier and Algiers.

HMS *Glasgow* left Algiers during the forenoon of 17 April at the end of her deployment with the Mediterranean Fleet, sailing for home waters where she would join the Home Fleet. On arrival in Portsmouth the ship's company were granted ten days' leave before she steamed north to Rosyth Dockyard for a short self-maintenance period, before joining the remainder of the fleet at Invergordon for the annual Home Fleet manoeuvres. When the exercises and evolutions, which also included fleet regattas at Scapa Flow, were completed the fleet dispersed for summer cruises, with *Glasgow* visiting Southend and Amsterdam, before she steamed north through the Kiel Canal and into the Baltic to make a four-day goodwill visit to the Polish port of Gdynia. The Polish Government placed great importance upon the visit, for it was the first by a Royal Navy warship since the end of the Second World War. As *Glasgow* approached to within 20 miles of the shore she was met by a Polish destroyer, with other ships of the Polish Navy drawn up to greet *Glasgow* as she approached the harbour entrance. As she neared her berth it became apparent that at least 1,000 people had turned out to welcome the ship, and according to Captain Dawnay, '*It was the unofficial welcome that was most impressive.*'

That afternoon the ship was opened to visitors and during the weekend a delegation of 150 officers and ratings were invited by the C-in-C of the Polish Navy to the Ministry of Defence, where they were entertained to lunch. One member of the ship's company remembered the event thus: '*After large helpings of big eats and vodka, the 'Iron Curtain' was torn down and, fuelled by more vodka, we had a really good get-together.*' After leaving Gdynia *Glasgow* steamed directly to Rosyth where a special press contingent who had accompanied the Polish visit were landed, before the ship went on to visit Sunderland. Following this she steamed south to Portsmouth for Navy Days which took place during the last weekend of July.

On the last day of August *Glasgow* left Portsmouth to steam north to Invergordon where she took part in the annual autumn exercises in the North Sea, which also included the Canadian aircraft carrier *Magnificent*. One important aspect of the exercise, code-named 'Sea Enterprise', was the use of carrier-borne aircraft, namely Seahawks from *Eagle, Albion, Bulwark* and *Centaur*, to attack targets in Norway. It was a recognition by NATO that the support of forces ashore in Norway was one of the organisation's most important commitments. There were also anti-submarine exercises with *Tiptoe* and other NATO submarines providing the opposition, with *Glasgow* 'falling victim' to a torpedo. It was also becoming apparent that even the big guns of cruisers were, like those of the battleships, becoming irrelevant in modern maritime warfare. For *Glasgow* the exercises ended on 28 September when, with other ships of the Home Fleet, she anchored at Trondheim.

In early October, after a short visit to Rosyth, *Glasgow* steamed via the Pentland Firth to the Firth of Clyde to visit her namesake city. It was during the forenoon of Friday 14 October that she secured alongside Springfield Quay for what was a rare and, as it transpired, her final visit to the city. During each of the five days spent alongside the ship was opened to the public, and on each occasion at least 4,000 Glaswegians took the opportunity to go on board. While in the city itself the civic authorities put on a number of official functions. When, during the afternoon of 19 October, *Glasgow* steamed back down the River Clyde, she passed and saluted her birthplace, the still busy shipyard of Scott's Shipbuilding and Engineering works at Greenock; she then headed north to the Pentland Firth again and Rosyth. On 2 November she steamed south to Portsmouth and two days later secured alongside North Corner Jetty. Five days after her arrival, during the forenoon of 9 November, *Glasgow* paid off and shortly after her old ship's company had marched from the dockyard to the naval barracks, her new complement, commanded by Captain C. D. Bonham-Carter RN, joined the ship for her final recommissioning.

HMS *Glasgow*'s final commission was to last for less than 12 months. It began in earnest when she left Portsmouth for a two-week work-up at Portland, which took her through to the second week of December when she returned to Portsmouth to give seasonal leave. On Monday 16 January 1956, *Glasgow* put to sea to join *Diamond, Duchess, Roebuck* and *Whirlwind* for the passage south to Gibraltar, carrying out various manoeuvres and evolutions en route. During the first week of

HMS Glasgow *in 1956, probably preparing for participation in Navy Days at Rosyth.* *(T. Ferrers-Walker)*

February she made a short visit to Tangier, and on 7 February began a seven-week maintenance and docking period at Gibraltar, on completion of which she returned to Portsmouth in time to take part in the spring Navy Days. During May that year, after exercising off Portland and visiting Cherbourg, she sailed north to Invergordon from where, wearing the flag of the C-in-C Home Fleet, she exercised with *Defender, Delight, Roebuck* and *Whirlwind.* This period of manoeuvres ended with five days of bombardment practice at Cape Wrath, after which she underwent C-in-C's Inspection before sailing south to the naval base at Den Helder in the Netherlands. She also called at Rotterdam, before steaming north via the Kiel Canal to the Swedish port of Malmo.

After leaving Malmo on 3 July *Glasgow* rendezvoused with *Apollo, Defender, Reward, Theseus* and *Tyne*, for two days of exercises in the North Sea, before securing alongside in Rosyth Dockyard to take part in that port's Navy Days. She then returned to Portsmouth via Whitby and Brighton,

arriving alongside South Railway Jetty on 23 July. Three days later President Nasser of Egypt announced the nationalisation of the Suez Canal Company, thereby precipitating the ill-fated Suez Crisis.

During August 1956, in what was usually a quiet period in the dockyard when half of all ships' companies would be on seasonal leave, urgent preparations were under way for what was to be an ill-judged invasion of Egypt. In late July most ships in Portsmouth Dockyard, including *Glasgow*, had been placed under sailing orders and leave for all personnel was cancelled. It appeared that once again the now elderly cruiser would have an active part to play in the nation's affairs. However, it was not to be, and in early August, when *Bulwark, Ocean* and *Theseus* sailed for an 'unknown destination', the Admiralty specifically denied that *Glasgow* would be joining them. Indeed, it was 4 September before the cruiser left Portsmouth, but not for the Mediterranean, but Portland where she joined *Apollo, Armada* and *Daring* in assisting ships of what would eventually be the invasion fleet as they worked up to full operational efficiency. In mid-September she steamed north to Invergordon where she continued to exercise with ships that had been earmarked for the invasion fleet, including *Comet, Contest, Daring* and *Delight*. By mid-October, however, with all the 'Operation Musketeer' ships having sailed for the Mediterranean, *Glasgow* left Rosyth to make a five-day goodwill visit to the West German naval base at Kiel, followed by three days at Den Helder. Finally, at 0600 on Monday 29 October 1956, she anchored at Spithead for the last time and seven hours later, with her paying-off pennant flying, she steamed up harbour to secure alongside, where '*Finished with Engines*' was rung for the last time. For the duration of the Suez Crisis *Glasgow* remained at eight-hours' notice for steam, but by mid-November she had been paid off and placed on the disposal list. The end came in late June 1958 when she was sold to the Hughes Bolckow Shipbreaking Company Ltd, a subsidiary of the Metal Industries Group, for demolition at the company's new deep-water quay at Blyth in Northumberland where, on 8 July, she arrived under tow.

Chapter Six

HMS MANCHESTER
1938-1942

Pristine in her East Indies livery HMS Manchester *is seen here departing the shipbuilders.* *(Steve Bush Collection)*

The loss of *Manchester* in the summer of 1942 still remains, 70 years later, very controversial. The question as to whether Captain Harold Drew was right to scuttle his ship is still fiercely argued, but in retrospect it has become clear that whatever decision he made he would have been open to criticism. I hope the story of the ship's final hours will shed light on the almost impossible position that Drew was in as HMS *Manchester* lay drifting and helpless only two miles from a shallow shoreline with sandbanks to one side and a minefield on the other. The story begins, however, some seven years earlier in the autumn of 1935. It was at a time when political tensions in Europe were beginning to heighten, and with the Italian invasion of Abyssinia, the Continent was drifting inexorably towards its second war in the space of 25 years. In Britain, on the domestic front, Malcolm Campbell had set a new world land speed record and, in order to relieve air traffic congestion at Croydon, Gatwick was opened as the new London Airport. Almost buried by other news came the announcement that a new British device had been patented which could, '*detect aeroplanes by reflecting radio waves off them*'. This had enormous implications for warfare at sea and for the Royal Navy since this new device would also be able to detect ships at sea.

The Admiralty's immediate priority, however, was the building of new cruisers and on 22 October 1935 it was announced that, '*Subject to the settlement of certain points of detail,*' they had decided to, '*entrust the construction of two Southampton-class cruisers of the 1935 programme to the following shipbuilders: - Hawthorn, Leslie & Co Ltd, Hebburn-on-Tyne; and Fairfield Shipbuilding & Engineering Co Ltd, Govan.*' Although no names were announced at that stage, the two ships were the fifth and sixth of a proposed class of eight cruisers, sufficient to form two squadrons. Just over three weeks after that announcement came the news that the cruiser which was to be built by Hawthorn, Leslie, would be named *Manchester*. The naval correspondent of *The Times* newspaper wrote: '*Just as a departure was made last year to include the name of Sheffield so another innovation is made this year in order that* Manchester *may have a representative ship in the fleet. Neither city has been commemorated in this way before, although there was apparently an auxiliary ship called Manchester in the Navy about 1814.*' It was on 28 March 1936, some four months after the announcement of the name that *Manchester*'s first keel plates were laid and building began.

During the months which followed the laying of the first keel plates at Hebburn-on-Tyne political tensions in Europe continued to rise, stoked primarily by particularly unpleasant politicians in Germany who stoked up fires of extreme nationalism, the foundations for which had been laid in 1920 by the Treaty of Versailles. Most of Germany's grievances could be traced directly to the 'unfinished business' of the Great War and the spirit of revenge which had arbitrarily reset international borders with scant regard for the populations who were affected, thus leaving unresolved the centuries-old '*struggle for mastery in Europe*'. Britain was encountering problems connected with Empire and in India the growing demands for Home Rule could not be ignored. It was clear that the end of the Raj was drawing ever closer. Further east Japanese Imperialism was challenging British Imperialism. The Japanese were very aware that during the Great War Britain had been unable to properly defend its Far Eastern territories without the direct help of Japan herself. In the spring of 1937, therefore, the new cruiser *Manchester* would take to the water in an atmosphere where the prospect of a second European War was becoming ever more a reality.

In January 1937 the first key naval personnel, under the command of Commander (E) G. C. Ross, travelled to Tyneside to stand by the ship and by early April that year plans were well in hand for *Manchester*'s launch. The ceremony took place on Monday 12 April, and witnessed by over 600 guests the occasion was a major event on Tyneside. Among those present was a detachment of officers and men from the Manchester Regiment, whose regimental fleur-de-lis was linked with the arms of the city of Manchester in the ship's badge. The ship was launched by the Lady Mayoress of Manchester, Mrs J. Toole, and at a reception afterwards in the company's woodworking shop, the Lord Mayor spoke of the pride the citizens of Manchester felt in having the cruiser named after their city. Nine months after the launch ceremony, on 17 January 1938, *Manchester*'s first commanding officer, Captain H. H. Bousfield, the former Captain of the Royal Naval College, Greenwich, was appointed to stand by the ship during the final stages of fitting out. By the early summer of 1938, with the appointment of nine Midshipmen to *Manchester* on 9 August, it was apparent that the ship was nearing completion and that she would be at her base port of Portsmouth by that date.

During the afternoon of 3 August 1938, as *Manchester* lay alongside Hawthorn, Leslie's shipbuilding yard at Hebburn-on-Tyne, the first major draft of 424 ratings joined the ship after travelling up from Portsmouth. At 0927 the next day, in the charge of a Hawthorn, Leslie pilot and steaming crew, *Manchester* slipped her moorings and was towed stern first downriver to Jarrow Slake where she was turned. Then at 1030, under her own steam, she passed the Tyne Piers to begin her acceptance trials in the North Sea. After an hour, however, defects were found in after engine room machinery which took almost four hours to rectify. During the afternoon, with the ship under way again, gunnery trials were carried out and at 2042 *Manchester* anchored off South Shields, less than a mile from South Tyne Pier. At 2115 Captain Bousfield formally received *Manchester* from the shipbuilder, the White Ensign was hoisted and at 2230 the ship weighed anchor and set course for Portsmouth.

HMS Manchester *alongside at Portsmouth. Note the open hangar door to port of the forward funnel.*
(Ken Kelly Collection)

During the early hours of 5 August thick fog was encountered, but by the evening she was passing through the Strait of Dover and during the next forenoon she secured to a buoy in Portsmouth Harbour. Two days later she was moved to Pitch House Jetty alongside Jellicoe's old flagship, *Iron Duke*, which had been reduced to the role of training ship. Here the cruiser's ship's company was brought up to full strength. On the last day of August she began her sea trials, which were initially carried out while day-running from Portsmouth and these included catapult trials with a Walrus aircraft from Lee-on-Solent. During the second week of September *Manchester*'s trials were continued from Portland, and during the afternoon of 9 September she returned to Portsmouth where she secured alongside the battlecruiser *Repulse* at South Railway Jetty.

During the 18 days she lay alongside at Portsmouth *Manchester* was prepared for service on the East Indies Station, based on Trincomalee, where she was to replace *Enterprise*, which had left Portsmouth in February 1936 and which was due to return home in October 1938. On 10 September 1938 *Manchester* was visited by a deputation from the Corporation of Manchester, led by the Lord Mayor, and at a ceremony on the cruiser's quarterdeck a number of gifts were presented to Captain Bousfield on behalf of the city[1]. Seven days later the Colonel of the Manchester Regiment, together with a regimental detachment, visited the ship to present a silver bugle and framed paintings. Finally, on 24 September, *Manchester* slipped her moorings at Fountain Lake Jetty and set course for Gibraltar, Malta and Alexandria, where she paused for four days. Leaving Alexandria during the morning of 7

[1] These gifts were: A silver centrepiece with city arms and crest for the wardroom table; silver sports trophy for annual competition among ship's company; silk Union Flag and White Ensign; Cricket Cup; cigarette boxes; silver centrepiece for CO's cabin; Shield for gunnery efficiency; ashtrays for wardroom; radio gramophone for wardroom; complete Manchester United FC colours for the ship's football team.

October *Manchester* reached Port Said that same evening where her southbound transit of the Suez Canal was delayed by the giant Cunarder, SS *Aquitania*, which had steamed south through the canal and back again during a Mediterranean cruise. By late afternoon on 8 October, however, *Manchester* was steaming south through the Red Sea to Aden where she arrived on 12 October and officially joined the East Indies Station. Next day, in company with *Norfolk* which was flying the flag of the C-in-C, Vice-Admiral James Somerville, she sailed for Bombay and during the passage carried out joint manoeuvres with the flagship. By the end of the month she had arrived at Trincomalee, the Ceylonese base of the East Indies Fleet, and during November, often in company with *Norfolk*, she carried out day-running work-up exercises.

On 1 December 1938 both *Norfolk* and *Manchester* left Trincomalee to carry out a series of flag-showing visits to ports on the Indian sub-continent, and at the same time carry out surveys as to their suitability as temporary naval bases in case of war. Both cruisers made a joint visit to Karachi and Goa, in those days a small Portuguese colony, where they anchored off the port of Marmagoa. Leaving Goa on 19 December, *Manchester* steamed south to the port of Cochin (now Kochi) where, next day she secured to a buoy in the outer harbour, with her Walrus aircraft at head and stern buoys in the inner harbour. As well as a goodwill visit which would encompass both Christmas Day and Boxing Day, this was one of the ports which Captain Bousfield had been asked to survey and report on regarding the defences and security from enemy raiders. In his report Bousfield made the following observations: '*The ship arrived at the end of the channel at 0900 Tuesday 20 December. There was a slight haze over the land, which made it extremely difficult to distinguish anything ashore until the outer buoy was reached. I heard ashore that she ship had been clearly visible from the port about an hour before. This land haze is apparently prevalent in the morning at this time of year, and would make it extremely difficult for a raider to bombard the port without coming very close in.*' As to the goodwill side of the visit, however, the Port Health Officer warned Bousfield that the whole of Cochin State was infected by an outbreak of plague and he strongly advised against landing liberty men. After a long discussion it was agreed that only organised sports parties would be allowed ashore, and there were also severe restrictions placed on visitors to the ship, which was not opened to the public. During the visit one of *Manchester*'s two Walrus seaplanes was employed taking Army officers of the local Nilgini Malabar Volunteer Battalion, who were responsible for the areas defences, on survey flights. At 0900 on Friday 23 December the aircraft took off on a photographic mission over the harbour. A short time later, at about 1020, having taken the photographs, the aircraft was coming in to land once again when, whilst still travelling at speed, it hit telephone wires across the harbour breakwater and crashed upside down in a nearby creek. The pilot was killed instantly and another officer was missing presumed drowned, but the observer managed to get clear with only minor injuries. Operations to search for the missing passenger and to recover the pilot's body and the wreckage of the aircraft took the rest of the day[2]. In his Report of Proceedings Bousfield describes the atmosphere on board: '*Social events for the day were cancelled. These included a cricket match, and a visit to the ship by some of the leading families from Ernakulam. I decided that it was best for everyone that other entertainments should continue, and addressed the ship's company accordingly. Consequently, Christmas Day was celebrated in the usual manner, and I am glad to say that despite the real and deep sorrow of the whole ship's company, I have never seen a Christmas so thoroughly enjoyed on board ship. The day finished off with a*

[2] The three officers were: Sub-Lt J.F.R Collis RN, pilot; Sub-Lt P.N. Boxer RN, passenger; Lt F.M. Griffiths RN, observer. The body of Sub-Lt Boxer was recovered on 27 December and was buried at sea, some five miles west of Cochin Lighthouse.

very successful concert, the first of the commission.' During the morning watch of 27 December *Manchester* weighed anchor and set course for the port of Trivandrum (now Thiruvanarithapuram), situated almost at the southern tip of the Indian subcontinent, where she arrived that afternoon for a three-day visit. By New Year's Eve, however, the ship had arrived in Colombo for a ten-day maintenance period.

Following her short refit and a mini work-up with *Norfolk*, *Manchester* returned to Trincomalee from where she carried out day-running exercises for the rest of January. On 7 February, for a period of eight days, she hoisted the flag of the C-in-C, Vice-Admiral Somerville, but on 15 February he returned to *Norfolk* and three days later the two cruisers exercised together before steaming round to India's east coast to show the flag at Madras (now Chennai) and Calcutta (now Kolkata). From here they steamed across the Bay of Bengal to Rangoon and then south to Singapore, where for two days they were anchored in Singapore Roads, off the city itself. Following this visit they put to sea with four destroyers for joint exercises and then steamed round to the north-east shores of the island to the new and much-vaunted naval base. After putting to sea again on 21 March *Norfolk* and *Manchester* carried out joint manoeuvres with *Eagle, Kent* and *Medway*, in the waters off Malaya's east coast. Two days later *Manchester* returned briefly to Singapore Naval Base to embark new elevating machinery for a faulty X turret, which had been dispatched by air from the UK to Singapore. Next day *Manchester* sailed to complete the exercises and then set course through the Strait of Malacca to the Andaman Sea to visit the Nicobar and Andaman Islands, the little known and seldom visited group of islands which form a chain between northern Sumatra and Burma which, for administrative reasons, had always been part of Britain's Indian Empire.

HMS *Manchester*'s presence in the Andaman Sea was not only to 'show the flag' and remind the citizens of the islands that they were not forgotten, but also to locate Japanese fishing vessels in the area. By 1939 it was apparent to anyone who was familiar with South East-Asia that Japanese Imperialism appeared to be on a collision course with the Western Imperial powers in the region, which was not only Britain, but also France, the Netherlands and, to a lesser extent, Portugal. It had long been suspected that the large Japanese fishing fleet in the waters around Malaya and the Netherlands East Indies was being extensively used to chart and photograph strategic ports, seaways and shipping. During *Manchester*'s cruise around the Andaman Sea the ship's Walrus was kept busy searching for Japanese fishing boats, but only two were identified and one of those was licensed to be in the area.

On 26 March *Manchester* anchored in Nancowry's False Bay, where Captain Bousfield made contact with the island's officials, but owing to lack of facilities ashore no leave was granted to the ship's company. Two days later the cruiser arrived at Port Blair where once again official contacts were made, and this time there was canteen leave for off-duty watches at the small NAAFI facility which had been set up for the small resident detachment of the Northamptonshire Regiment stationed on South Andaman Island. On 2 April *Manchester* sailed for Trincomalee where, three days later, she anchored to de-store and de-ammunition prior to undergoing a refit at Colombo. This also gave the ship's company an opportunity for station leave and an advance party left the ship for a rest camp on the island. However, on Sunday 9 April, political events in Europe, which were continuing to deteriorate, temporarily put paid to any thoughts of leave. Italy had invaded Albania and just a few weeks earlier German troops had marched into what had been left of Czechoslovakia after the previous year's Munich Agreement. The British Government put the Royal Navy on alert worldwide and *Manchester* was ordered to remain at short notice for steam in Trincomalee. The advance leave party was recalled, but in comic opera fashion all the victualling stores ashore were firmly closed for the Easter holiday weekend and despite the alert would not reopen. On board

Manchester, with the ship having been de-stored there was barely enough food on board to cater for what should have been a much reduced ship's company, so food rationing was experienced even before war broke out. Seven days later, however, the fleet was stood down and *Manchester* was ordered to carry on to Colombo for her scheduled refit. On 18 April she secured alongside the port's Guide Pier, where the leave parties finally left the ship and the refit began.

It was the middle of June 1939 before *Manchester*'s maintenance work was completed, and on 3 June she returned to Trincomalee. Three days later she left the East Indies base for what was to be the last time to begin a cruise of the Indian Ocean and East African ports. She was also ordered to remain in radio contact with the Australian Government's long-range Catalina flying boat, *Guba*, which was carrying out a joint British and Australian survey of the Indian Ocean to find the best air routes between Britain, East Africa and Australia. On 10 June both *Manchester* and *Guba* arrived at Diego Garcia in the Chagos Archipelago, where the flying boat was able to refuel and embark stores from the cruiser. *Guba*'s survey crew identified Diego Garcia, which had once been a French colonial possession, but was now British, as being the ideal location for a flying boat station and a civil airfield for commercial flights between Perth and Kilindini Harbour, Kenya, but these plans were soon forgotten as war swept them away. Instead a military airfield was built, the inhabitants of the island were forcibly removed and, under Lend-Lease agreements, the island was virtually handed over to the USA, which continues to cause controversy. On 14 June, having replenished *Guba* and supplied hot food, baths and rest facilities for her crew, *Manchester* sailed for Zanzibar where she remained for eight days. During this time she took on board 50 local East African RNVR ratings for training courses. By the end of July she was at Dar-es-Salaam, the port for Tanganyika (Tanzania) which, being the former German East Africa, had only been British for 20 years, and was mandated by the League of Nations. From Dar-es-Salaam the cruiser moved up the coast of Tanganyika to the port of Tanga and on to Pembo Island, where she anchored for two days in the small harbour of Mkoani. On 14 July she anchored in Kilindini Harbour where she joined her sister *Gloucester* and hoisted the flag of the new C-in-C East Indies, Rear-Admiral Ralph Leatham CB, who had relieved Somerville after the latter had been diagnosed with tuberculosis and placed on the retired list. On 25 July *Manchester*'s cruise came to an end when, in company with *Gloucester*, she sailed north to Aden where the two cruisers joined the sloops *Egret* and *Fleetwood* to carry out a series of convoy escort exercises between Aden and Port Sudan in the Red Sea. On 14 August *Manchester* spent 48 hours alongside at Port Sudan, before returning to Aden to refuel. At 1215 on 18 August she sailed from Aden, as had been originally planned, to return to Trincomalee but the following evening she received orders to return to Aden where she arrived during the forenoon of 20 August.

A week after her return to the barren, inhospitable rocks of Aden, *Manchester* was ordered to rendezvous at sea with the troop transport *Dilwara*, which was bound from Bombay to Alexandria, and escort her into the Red Sea and clear of the potentially hostile Italian-occupied coast of Eritrea as far as the border with Sudan, after which she steamed back to Aden, arriving on the last day of August. Next day, late during the evening of 1 September, *Manchester* was ordered to sail to carry out a patrol of the Gulf of Aden and the southern waters of the Red Sea. This time, however, the ship was darkened and the ship's company were working defence watches. The patrol ended back at Aden on Sunday 3 September, some two and a half hours before war was declared (1300 local time) and no sooner had she completed refuelling than she was ordered to sail for Colombo from where she made one short patrol before beginning convoy escort duties. On 25 September, in company with *Rochester*, she acted as ocean escort to the troop transports *Indora* and *Rohna*, two former British India Line passenger

ships, which had been requisitioned by the Government and were carrying Indian troops from Bombay to Suez. After seeing the convoy safely into the Red Sea *Manchester* returned to Aden for a short break before escorting a combined British/French convoy from Aden to a point just south of the Gulf of Suez. Here she rendezvoused with the fast troop transport, *Empress of Australia*, a 21,000-ton passenger liner which had been launched in 1913 as *Admiral von Tirpitz* for the Hamburg-Amerika Line, but in 1919 had been handed over to Britain as part of the Great War reparations, and then acquired by the Canadian Pacific Line. *Manchester* escorted the former liner via Aden to Colombo, before steaming north to Bombay where, on 29 October, she underwent a 12-day dry docking and maintenance period. On 10 November, when *Manchester* put to sea again, for the ship's company it was in the knowledge that they were homeward bound and less than a week after leaving Bombay she was passing north through the Suez Canal. There was a two-day stopover at Malta, but by 24 November she was off Ushant where a severe storm reduced her speed to six knots. The following afternoon she was approaching Spithead and at 1800 she secured alongside Portsmouth Dockyard's Pitch House Jetty. A great deal had changed in the 14 months since she had left for the East Indies Station for now Portsmouth was a city at war. *Manchester* underwent three weeks of essential maintenance in the dockyard while most of her ship's company left her on draft to other ships, and everyone was granted ten days leave.

On 22 December 1939, *Manchester* left Portsmouth as part of the Home Fleet after carrying out three days of trials, to steam north via the Irish Sea to Scapa Flow where, on Christmas Eve, she joined the C-in-C Home Fleet, Admiral Sir Charles Forbes' North Sea Force, and became flagship of the 18th Cruiser Squadron, flying the flag of Vice-Admiral Geoffrey Layton (CS18). The North Sea Force based at Scapa Flow during the years between 1939 and early 1945 was very different from Jellicoe's Grand Fleet of 1914. The largest survivor of the previous conflict was Jellicoe's old flagship, the battleship *Iron Duke*, but she was a disarmed hulk which had been damaged in an early German air raid on Scapa Flow and then beached. She would, however, survive this second conflict as a very useful depot ship. Gone too were the long lines of super-dreadnoughts. There were battleships, but only a handful of them and lined up in Scapa Flow there were now aircraft carriers of various shapes and sizes, cruisers and destroyers. The cruisers, including *Manchester*, were to endure seemingly endless days and weeks at sea in the cold, inhospitable waters between the Shetland Islands and Iceland, as they enforced the trade blockade on German imports and exports. On Christmas morning, after an introductory talk by Admiral Forbes, *Manchester* was at sea and on patrol north of the Shetland Islands. During her first nine-day patrol there was no shortage of merchantmen to stop and check, but they were all neutral vessels such as the Swedish SS *Virginia*, which was boarded during the afternoon of 28 December but, as her cargo was ostensibly bound for neutral Sweden, she was allowed to proceed.

HMS *Manchester*'s patrols continued through the bitterly cold and often violently stormy months of January and February 1940, and sometimes the ships which were intercepted required further investigation. One such vessel was the Norwegian SS *Cetus*, which was intercepted and overhauled during the evening of 5 February. In the inky darkness and heavy seas it was not safe to dispatch a boarding party, so *Manchester* remained in company with the merchantman overnight. Next morning, with the weather conditions still too rough to attempt a boat transfer, the ship was handed over to an armed trawler which escorted it into Kirkwall.

Over the following days numerous Scandinavian ships were intercepted, but at 1526 on Wednesday 21 February, some 80 miles south-west of Iceland, alert lookouts in *Manchester* and the accompanying destroyer *Kimberley*, spotted a 4,700-ton merchantman sailing east. With strong gale-force winds,

HMS Manchester *with later modifications to her close range armament, including a 40mm Bofor on the roof of B turret and a 20mm on the roof of X turret.* *(T. Ferrers-Walker Collection)*

heavy seas and poor visibility which at times was down to less than a mile, it took some time to identify her, but after some 20 minutes it was apparent that she was the German, Hamburg-registered, MV *Wahehe*. She had left Hamburg before war broke out with a mixed cargo and before attempting to run the blockade on her return trip she had taken refuge in Vigo Bay, on Spain's Atlantic coast, to await the most opportune time to attempt her breakthrough. This came with the severe weather conditions, but as the two warships approached her *Wahehe*'s crew began lowering boats and making preparations to scuttle their ship. A signal was flashed from *Manchester* warning them against such a move but two boats were skilfully launched into the stormy seas. *Manchester*'s log reads: *'1355 Commence circling ship and fired two bursts of pom-pom near boats.*' That this was successful in achieving the desired result is shown by the next entry: *'1600 Ship surrendered boats returned to ship and crew re-embark.*' All that remained was for *Kimberley* to escort her to Kirkwall while *Manchester* resumed her patrol until 25 February, when she returned to Scapa Flow.

During March 1940 *Manchester* carried out two further ten-day patrols, and on 7 April she left Scapa Flow to begin a third. Two days into the patrol, however, she was ordered to make for the Norwegian coast and to establish a patrol between Latitudes 60° and 61°, which covered the area off Bergen. Scandinavia was suddenly becoming of major interest to both the warring Allies and Germany. In early March Germany was concerned that Britain and France were planning to invade both Norway and Sweden in order to control the Swedish iron ore fields, which was in fact the case, and the British and French governments had requested Norwegian and Swedish approval to send Allied troops to Finland through the two Scandinavian countries. Ostensibly it was said the troops would aid Finland in its war against Russia, but the governments in London and Paris were primarily interested in occupying the Swedish iron ore fields. In retrospect it is probably just as well that both Norway and Sweden flatly refused the Allied request, for the difficulties which might have arisen by antagonising the Scandinavian countries and Russia, as well as fighting the war against Germany, do not bear thinking about. On 9 April, however, pre-empting any Allied moves in the area, Germany invaded both Denmark and Norway and completely altered the strategic situation in the area. *Manchester*'s arrival in her patrol area off Bergen brought fierce German air attacks on the ship, and at one point some 50 aircraft made a high-level air raid on her. Fortunately the cruiser was able to take evasive action and dodge what was estimated to be over 100 bombs. Later, at just after midnight, the cruiser sighted and attacked a U-boat off her port bow, but the depth charges she launched failed to explode and the submarine escaped. Soon after this she was ordered back to Scapa Flow, where she arrived some 24 hours later. Next day, while at anchor, there was no respite for the high-angle gunnery crews, for enemy air raids continued at regular intervals throughout the hours of daylight. So frequent were they that all shore leave was cancelled. Next afternoon, on Friday 12 April, there was a change of command when Captain H. G. Packer took over the ship. At 1530, just 15 minutes after Captain Bousfield had left the ship, *Manchester* sailed from Scapa Flow to rendezvous with her sister *Birmingham* to take over the escorting of a troop convoy, which included her old friend from the early days of the war, *Empress of Australia*. Next day the battleship *Valiant*, together with the battlecruiser *Repulse*, joined the convoy and during the morning watch of 16 April they anchored close to the Norwegian port of Namsos, where the troops were disembarked. That afternoon there were fierce German air attacks on the warships and transports at anchor, but fortunately there were no casualties and during the early hours of 17 April *Manchester*, *Birmingham* and a destroyer screen sailed to escort the now empty transports on their return passage to home waters. During the passage, however, *Manchester* was ordered to leave the convoy in the care of *Birmingham* and return to Norwegian waters, where she took over as the main escort to an empty French troop convoy which was also homeward bound. It was 21 April before she returned to Scapa Flow. Events in Norway were by then moving quickly and next day she was ordered to steam south to Rosyth.

HMS *Manchester* and other cruisers of the Home Fleet were urgently required to transport troops and equipment directly to Norway, and once alongside Rosyth Dockyard *Manchester* embarked some 500 soldiers, together with their stores and equipment, a process which took the best part of 24 hours. Finally, at 0600 on 24 April, together with *Birmingham* and *York*, she left the Firth of Forth to make a fast passage to Norway. *Manchester* was bound for Molde where, during the evening of 25 April, she completed the disembarkation of troops and then sailed for home waters again, her destination being Scapa Flow. No sooner had she anchored, however, than she was once again ordered to sail for Norwegian waters and the port of Andalsnes. The Allied intervention in Norway, which was largely one of Churchill's ideas, was rapidly turning into a disaster - for which Churchill managed to deflect the blame onto Chamberlain - and by the end of April a hasty evacuation of all Allied troops, apart from those in Narvik, was under way. This time *Manchester* would come under heavy air attack. As she neared the approaches to Romsdalsfjord the first German reconnaissance aircraft began to shadow her, and shortly afterwards the first enemy bombers appeared overhead. That evening, as she was about to anchor off Andalsnes, a more determined air attack was made on the ship with three bombs coming very close to hitting the cruiser's port bow. In the event it was 2300 before she was able to anchor and the embarkation of troops, as well as eight German PoWs, began immediately. Two and a quarter hours later *Manchester* was making her way back down Romsdalsfjord and by daylight she had received an RAF escort of three Blenheims who saw her safely to Scapa Flow, where she arrived at just before 0100 on 3 May.

HMS *Manchester*'s return to Scapa signalled the end of her participation in the ill-fated Norwegian campaign, but at just after midnight on 10 May Germany invaded Belgium and the Netherlands, in a move which was aimed primarily at France and to be a quick knockout blow in the west. *Manchester* was ordered to raise steam immediately and put to sea, but engine defects, which required urgent attention, meant she was quickly diverted to Rosyth, where for ten days she was in dockyard hands. On 22 May she put to sea for machinery trials and after another five days in Rosyth Dockyard she steamed south to Immingham to join a hastily assembled naval force based around the Humber estuary to guard against any invasion attempts along the east coast. Arriving at Immingham during the afternoon of 27 May, further maintenance work was carried out to the ship's main propulsion machinery and a section of the ship's company was granted seven days' leave. By 10 June she was back at Rosyth where, five days later, Vice-Admiral G. F. Edward-Collins relieved Layton as CS18. *Manchester* remained at Rosyth for the remainder of the month. On 1 July 1940 she received orders to sail south and next day she paused for 48 hours off Sheerness before continuing her passage to Portsmouth where she arrived during the morning of 5 July. Her main propulsion machinery was continuing to give problems and for the next six and a half weeks she was laid up in Portsmouth's No 14 dry dock, during which time her ship's company were given leave and the ship herself was visited by both King George VI and Winston Churchill.

During the evening of 20 August *Manchester* left Portsmouth and steamed via the Irish Sea to Scapa Flow. Before she had left the Channel, however, she came under attack from a lone German aircraft and one of the two bombs it dropped exploded some 800 yards from *Manchester*'s starboard beam. Four days after her arrival in Scapa Flow an air-laid mine exploded very close to *Manchester*'s anchorage, but once again she was fortunate in avoiding any damage. On 29 August she again hoisted the flag of Vice-Admiral Edward-Collins (CS18), and next

HMS Manchester *is straddled by shells from the Italian fleet during the Battle of Spartivento.* *(Syd Goodman Collection)*

day steamed south to Rosyth and on to Immingham for anti-invasion duties on the east coast. During the first week of November she returned to Rosyth where, on 12 November, Vice-Admiral Lancelot Holland took over as CS18 from Edward-Collins. Two days later *Manchester* steamed north to Scapa Flow from where, after refuelling, she sailed to rendezvous with the merchantmen of a vital Mediterranean convoy which, under the code name 'Operation Collar', was to carry urgently needed heavy equipment, including an armoured tank brigade, to Alexandria to reinforce the hard-pressed Western Desert Force in Egypt. The convoy was made up of the reasonably fast steamships *Clan Forbes, Clan Fraser* and *New Zealand Star*. In addition there was the troop transport *Franconia*, an ex-Cunard passenger liner, which was carrying over 1,400 troops who would be transferred to *Manchester* and her sister *Southampton* at Gibraltar. Between them they would carry the soldiers to Alexandria, *Franconia* being too big and vulnerable a target to risk in the Mediterranean.

After leaving Scapa Flow *Manchester* steamed well out into the Atlantic Ocean and west of Ireland before rendezvousing with the convoy during the forenoon of 16 November. Soon afterwards *Southampton* joined the escort and course was set through heavy seas and gale force winds for Gibraltar. During the early evening of 20 November, with the severe weather having abated and while *Manchester* was off the coast of southern Portugal operating her Walrus aircraft L2257, she stopped to hoist it inboard, an evolution that was always tricky even in flat calm seas. On this occasion the aircraft capsized before it could be hoisted, throwing a naval airman into the sea. Although the sea boat was launched within minutes, and *Manchester* herself carried out a thorough search, there was no trace of the lost man, so the cruiser resumed her passage and rejoined the convoy. Next day she arrived alongside Gibraltar's south mole where the embarkation of troops from *Franconia* began. During the 12 hours alongside at Gibraltar *Manchester* and *Southampton* embarked 660 and 760 RAF and military personnel respectively, together with large quantities of stores and equipment. The addition of almost 700 extra men on board *Manchester*, almost twice as many again as the ship's normal complement, meant that her fighting capabilities would be severely hampered. Both CS18, Admiral Holland, and Flag Officer Force H, the reinstated Admiral Somerville, agreed that the two cruisers would not, '*be in a satisfactory state to fight an action*'. However, although it was agreed that the safe passage of the personnel and heavy equipment was to be the priority, a contradictory instruction was received from the Admiralty. This appeared to bear Churchill's hallmark and was that if Italian forces were sighted, action taken by the two cruisers must be the same as if personnel were not embarked.

The force which left Gibraltar during the morning of Monday 25 November was made up as follows:
- Force B: ships of Force H based on Gibraltar and commanded by Vice-Admiral Somerville; *Renown, Ark Royal, Sheffield, Despatch* and nine destroyers;
- Force F: *Manchester* (CS18) and *Southampton*, between them carrying some 1,400 RAF and military personnel, one destroyer and four corvettes;
- Merchant ships of the convoy: *Clan Forbes, Clan Fraser, New Zealand Star*, all carrying tanks and heavy equipment. Maximum speed 16 knots.

The first 48 hours of the passage east passed quietly, and at 1015 on 27 November *Ark Royal*'s reconnaissance aircraft sighted an Italian battlefleet of two battleships, six cruisers and seven destroyers just over 40 miles to the north of the convoy which, at this time, was south-east of Sardinia. Approaching from the east was Force D, made up of ships of the Mediterranean Fleet from Alexandria: *Ramillies, Newcastle, Berwick, Coventry* and four destroyers, which were to take over the escort south of Sardinia at noon that day. Somerville ordered *Ark Royal* to fly off a striking force while *Renown*, the cruisers and destroyers set off at 28 knots in an attempt to intercept the Italian ships. They were soon joined by *Ramillies* and at 1212 the Italian 8-inch cruisers came into sight and opened fire. At 1222 this was returned by *Renown* and the British cruisers at a distance of some 27,000 yards. The Italian cruisers started to withdraw under cover of smoke and at 1250 *Renown* sighted the two Italian Littorio-class battleships, which drew away to the east. Although *Renown*, *Manchester* and *Southampton* gave chase, smoke prevented accurate fire and by 1320 they were within 30 miles of the Sardinian coast and within range of Italian air, submarine and E-boat bases at Cagliari. By then the Italian ships were out of range and Somerville called off the chase. He was right in supposing that the withdrawal of the Italian ships was a deliberate attempt to lure the British force to well within range of bombing forces which, at that point, were hurriedly being prepared to carry out air strikes on both the convoy and escorts. During the chase *Berwick* had received two hits, killing an officer and six ratings, but suffered only slight damage which did not affect her operational capabilities. Somerville's decision to abandon the chase and return to the all-important convoy which had been left dangerously exposed to attack was, in the circumstances, correct; it was not long before both the warships and merchant vessels came under air attack, and this continued all afternoon. *Manchester* and *Southampton* rejoined the convoy at 1740, and at 0930 next day Malta was sighted. An hour later they were on station with the ships of Cunningham's Mediterranean Fleet, and at 0950 on 30 November *Manchester* secured alongside in Alexandria Harbour, to be followed 25 minutes later by *Southampton*. Both ships were then able to disembark their RAF and military passengers.

Having delivered her military reinforcements safely to Alexandria *Manchester*'s return to home waters was made by way of Crete, Malta and Gibraltar. Leaving Alexandria during the afternoon of 4 December she made a fast passage to Suda Bay where she arrived the next forenoon to disembark stores and military personnel. After refuelling she continued her passage, arriving in Grand Harbour at 1235 on 2 December. Once again she remained just long enough to disembark military stores and personnel before, at 1700 the same day, she left harbour to make a fast passage west, arriving in

Gibraltar some 42 hours later. After a two-day halt there, a welcome break for the ship's company, *Manchester* sailed north and on 13 December arrived back in Scapa Flow. Christmas Day was spent at Scapa, where the only relief was the rather basic beer canteen, then on 26 December she sailed on another patrol of the icy-cold waters between the Shetland Islands and Iceland before returning to Scapa for New Year's Day. On 8 January 1941 Vice-Admiral Holland transferred his flag to *Edinburgh*[3]. Three days later, at 0100 on 11 January, *Manchester* left Scapa under cover of darkness to make a fast 15-hour passage south to the River Tyne where she secured alongside the Tyne Commission Quay to begin a 13-week refit.

During *Manchester*'s refit, which was carried out by Palmer's Shipbuilding & Engineering Company, her main propulsion machinery was thoroughly overhauled and Type 297 air warning radar was installed. Most of her ship's company were drafted to other ships, so when she sailed from the River Tyne during the afternoon of 10 April she was virtually beginning another commission. That evening she arrived at Rosyth where she underwent a short docking period and further maintenance work. Finally, during the afternoon of 17 April, she left the Firth of Forth to sail north for Scapa Flow where, next morning at 0621, she rejoined the 18th Cruiser Squadron. During the rest of April *Manchester* carried out work-up exercises in the relative safety of Scapa Flow, and occasionally at sea in the Pentland Firth. During the forenoon of 24 April, while at sea in the waters around the Orkney Islands, she was attacked by a lone German Ju-88, but the aircraft was driven off by the combined efforts of the 4-inch and pom-pom gun crews. By the first week of May the work-up was completed and on Monday 5 May, in company with *Edinburgh* (flag CS18), *Birmingham* and the destroyers *Nestor* and *Somali*, she left Scapa Flow to carry out another patrol of the area between the Shetland Islands and Iceland. They had also been ordered to search for and intercept the German weather ship, the trawler *München*, which was operating in a position approximately 67°12'N 003°36'W, just south-west of Iceland. The trawler was actually located at 1710 on 7 May, and although her crew attempted to scuttle her, a boarding party from the destroyer *Somali* managed to retrieve vital parts of her 'Enigma' coding machine. Three days later the patrol ended back in Scapa Flow.

By the second week of May British Intelligence reports had indicated that the powerful new German battleship *Bismarck* was about to break out into the Atlantic, and it was this possibility which dominated *Manchester*'s next patrol in northern waters. It was at 0600 on Sunday 18 May, the same day that *Bismarck* and the heavy cruiser *Prinz Eugen* sailed from Gdynia bound for the Norwegian Sea and the Denmark Strait, that *Manchester* and *Birmingham* left Scapa Flow to patrol the area between the Faroe Islands and south-east Iceland. The two cruisers flew their Walrus aircraft on continuous reconnaissance patrols and on 22 May, when *Bismarck* and *Prinz Eugen* were refuelling off Bergen, *Manchester* and *Birmingham* had to enter Icelandic waters to refuel from RFAs. The two cruisers put to sea again that same evening and returned to their patrol line. On 23 May they were joined by *Arethusa*, and during the morning of 24 May were still south-east of Iceland and in no position to influence the action between *Bismarck* and *Prinz Eugen*, *Hood* and *Prince of Wales* in the Denmark Strait. During 25 May the three cruisers were ordered to move north in case the two German warships should attempt to return to their own home waters, and that evening *Manchester* and *Birmingham* had to put into Hvalfjord to refuel from RFA *British Governor*. By 0300 on 26 May they were back at sea and patrolling the Iceland-Faroes gap. Apart from encountering Norwegian and Polish fishing trawlers their patrol was

[3] He did not remain in *Edinburgh* long. On 9 May 1941 he was appointed Vice-Admiral Commanding Battlecruiser Squadron, flying his flag in HMS *Hood*. Fifteen days later, on 24 May, he was one of the 1,415 lost when *Hood was sunk*.

uneventful. During the forenoon of 3 June *Manchester* returned once again to Scapa Flow.

Next day there was a change of command, when Captain Harold Drew DSC RN, who had joined the RNR in 1915 and transferred to the Regular Navy the following year, took command. Drew was a gunnery specialist and in 1917 had been awarded the DSC for operations in coastal motor boats off the French coast. During the inter-war years he was commended for his technical work on the design of the Navy's high-angle gunfire control systems. Another man who joined the ship that day was Petty Officer (Writer) Charles Heath. He had originally been drafted to *Laforey*, but before he could join the ship the billet was downgraded from PO to Leading Writer. At the same time the post on board *Manchester* had been downgraded from CPO to PO Writer, so on 19 May he left RNB Portsmouth to travel by rail and ferry to Scapa Flow. There, for a short time until *Manchester* came back in from her patrol, he was billeted in the elderly depot ship *Dunluce Castle*, a former Union Castle liner which had come to the end of her useful life in 1939. It was said that every Royal Navy sailor who passed through Scapa Flow spent at least one night on board *Dunluce Castle* which, as Charles Heath remarked, was one of the most uncomfortable periods in his naval service.

HMS Manchester *in July 1941, listing after being hit by a torpedo which struck a fuel tank. Men in adjacent compartments, overcome by fumes, are being brought on deck.* *(Syd Goodman Collection)*

On 9 June 1941, five days after the change of command, *Manchester* put to sea in company with *Edinburgh, Hermione* and the destroyer *Icarus*, this time to patrol the waters of the Denmark Strait, north and west of Iceland. During the patrol *Manchester* refuelled and stored ship at Hvalfjord where, during the short breaks, canteen leave was granted. This routine continued up to the end of June, then on 3 July she finally returned to Scapa Flow where she remained for six days, storing and ammunitioning ship in preparation for her next deployment.

HMS *Manchester*'s next duties would take her a long way from the northern waters to which her ship's company had become accustomed when on 9 July, in company with *Arethusa*, she left Scapa Flow to make a fast overnight passage south to Greenock. *Manchester* was to take part in another attempt to run a convoy from Gibraltar, through the Mediterranean, once again acting as both escort and troop transport. The convoy was the first organised attempt to bring relief to the beleaguered island of Malta, hence the code name 'Operation Substance'. The convoy itself consisted of five merchant ships: *City of Pretoria, Durham, Melbourne Star, Port Chalmers* and *Sydney Star,* all of which were reasonably fast vessels with a good cargo capacity. However, with Malta lying so close to Italian military bases, major fleet operations were needed to get even a single merchant ship through to the island. To escort this convoy were the ships of Force H: *Renown* (flag), *Nelson, Ark Royal, Hermione* and eight destroyers, augmented by *Edinburgh*, *Manchester* and *Arethusa*, the fast minelayer *Manxman* and eight destroyers from the Home Fleet. Once again *Manchester*, together with *Arethusa* and four of the destroyers, would carry military personnel and during the afternoon of 12 July, while at anchor off Greenock, embarked the first 200 men of the King's Own Royal Lancaster Regiment. The remainder of the troops were embarked in the French transport *Pasteur* for the passage to Gibraltar and at 2125, as soon as the embarkation was completed, *Manchester* sailed for Gibraltar.

Ten hours after leaving Greenock *Manchester* caught up with the convoy which, in order to avoid U-boats, steamed well out into the Atlantic before turning south. The long roundabout route to Gibraltar meant that the passage took eight days, but finally, at 0255 on 20 July, under cover of darkness, *Manchester* secured alongside Gibraltar's south mole. That same forenoon Admiral Somerville addressed the ship's company and at 2200, after darkness had fallen, another 536 men of the King's Own Royal Lancaster Regiment, together with their equipment, stores and baggage, were transferred from *Pasteur*. It was gone midnight before the embarkation was completed and just over an hour later, at 0245 on 21 July, *Manchester* sailed to take station astern of the convoy as course was set for Malta. During the first two days at sea *Manchester* took station either astern of, or between two columns of the convoy. On the second day at sea, however, Italian reconnaissance aircraft located and began shadowing the convoy. The first air attacks came at 0940 on 23 July, when the convoy was some 100 miles north-east of Algiers and well out of sight of land. The first Italian torpedo bombers made a determined attack on the convoy and its escorts and at 0947 a torpedo smashed into *Manchester*'s port side, where it exploded with terrific force in Y4 oil fuel tank. The deck of X flat port side was blown up almost to the deckhead above. The after engine room, the 4-inch magazine, the Wireless Transmission Office, the Midshipmen's Chest Flat, X magazine and the port provisions room were all destroyed, severely damaged or flooded. The flooding extended over the lower deck along the port side and with the ship listing between 12 and 15 degrees to port, the flooding was almost level with the scuttles. Petty Officer (Writer) Charles Heath has left vivid memories of the incident: '*I was in the forward Petty Officers' mess when Action Stations was sounded. My station was in the Wireless Transmission Room where, as code/cipher assistant, I produced the relevant figure and the officer would look up the number in the*

cipher book and come up with the word. I received a small payment for each watch I served in the wireless office, which was a very small compartment behind the main radio transmitter and had just enough room for two people. Should anything happen to the equipment there was not much hope for the duty cipher watch. We had a large number of Army personnel aboard and, being dispersed all round the ship and in passageways, their presence made it difficult to move from forward to aft at speed. I reached the Pay Office (aft) just as Paymaster Midshipman Pooley came out of it. He immediately went through the watertight door and was climbing down into the wireless office when the torpedo hit the ship. He was killed. I had popped into the Pay Office to pick up my gas mask, torch and sailor's knife, and was about to open the watertight door leading to the wireless office hatch when I felt the terrific shock of the explosion as the torpedo hit the ship. Manchester *immediately heeled over and gave no indication she was going to stop. She did, of course, and I then returned forward and made my way to the upper deck. I was met by the Deputy Pusser, Lieutenant A. A. D. Cope RNVR, who couldn't believe his eyes, he had written me off. The Paymaster Commander, Captain's Secretary and the Midshipman (S) were all killed, as were the wireless office staff. I owed my life to the fact that the soldiers who were sitting and lying about the passageways hampered my progress and slowed me down as I made my way to my action station.'*

Although *Manchester* was listing some 12 to 15 degrees to port, this was corrected by counter-flooding and she then took on a list to starboard of one degree. Three of the ship's main engines were out of action, but only one turbo-generator was disabled. Although the ship was initially able to maintain some 12 knots, this gradually reduced as the hours went by. However, being in open sea the lack of manoeuvrability was not a serious problem. Meanwhile, on the upper deck rescue efforts to help the trapped and injured were under way. Charles

HMS Manchester *in May 1942. At the time she was painted overall in a 'Mountbatten Pink' scheme.*
(Syd Goodman Collection)

Heath remembers: '*I made my way to the quarter-deck to help. Those brought out alive were covered in thick oil fuel and those who had swallowed the black oily mass did not stand much chance of surviving. I was busy cleaning up the Gunroom PO Steward*[4] *when he died on me.*' Altogether 26 officers and men of the ship's company had been killed in the explosion, or died later of their wounds. In addition 23 officers and men of the King's Own Regiment who were in the vicinity of the explosion were killed. At 1007 *Manchester* was ordered to return to Gibraltar, and with the engine room personnel able to maintain some 220rpm on the starboard outer propeller shaft, she began the slow and dangerous return passage to Gibraltar, screened by the destroyers *Avon Vale, Eridge* and *Vidette*. At just after 1800 that day, however, the damaged cruiser was again attacked by Italian bombers, but this time by the combined efforts of the ship's gunners and the barrage put up by the destroyer screen they were beaten off with no further damage being done. That evening the first of three burial services was held as the bodies of the 23 soldiers and ten members of the ship's company were committed to the sea. By the forenoon of 24 July *Manchester* was within range of air cover from Gibraltar and from 1100 onwards a patrolling Sunderland flying boat flew reassuringly overhead. At just after midnight on 26 July two tugs from Gibraltar had taken the cruiser in tow, and by 0430 she had been secured alongside Gibraltar's detached mole. Once alongside, while the injured were being transferred to hospital and the troops disembarked, the ship's divers inspected the damaged hull and by 1930 that evening the cruiser had been secured in Gibraltar Dockyard's No 2 dry dock.

During the days which followed there were more funeral services as some of the more badly wounded succumbed to their injuries, and by the second week of September temporary repairs to *Manchester* were almost completed. Finally, on 13 September, with the destroyer *Firedrake* escorting her, *Manchester* left Gibraltar to make a ten-day transatlantic passage to the US Navy yard at Philadelphia where she spent five months in dockyard hands for more permanent repairs to be carried out. For those members of the ship's company who remained with the ship it was a welcome respite from the war in Europe with the privations of rationing and government controls in Britain. For much of the time they were accommodated ashore with generous families who welcomed them into their homes. Charles Heath stayed with the Johnson family, who made sure he was well looked after and even drove him to New York in their large Buick saloon car. It was, as he once told the author, '*like another world*'. Back in the Navy Yard, as well as carrying out repairs, preparations were made to fit more up-to-date radar, with the original equipment being removed. She was also fitted with three single 20mm anti-aircraft guns.

On 12 February 1942, with the work completed, *Manchester* sailed to carry out two days of trials, after which she was dry-docked for six days. Finally, on the last day of the month, *Manchester* left Philadelphia for seven days of post-refit trials, anchoring each evening in Chesapeake Bay. On 8 March she left US waters to make a 24-hour passage to Bermuda from where, after refuelling and embarking stores, she sailed for Portsmouth. During the evening of 17 March the Nab Tower was sighted and an hour later, at 2135, she anchored at Spithead. Next forenoon she weighed anchor and steamed up harbour to secure alongside Pitch House Jetty.

HMS *Manchester* spent the next six weeks at Portsmouth where work was carried out to fit Types 284 and 285 radar equipment for the main and secondary armament, as well as a new Type 273 surface warning radar, the preparatory work having been done in the USA. During this refit, however, conditions were very different from those in Philadelphia for there were regular air raids on both the city of Portsmouth and the dockyard. Fortunately, *Manchester* suffered no further damage and on 2 May 1942, escorted by the destroyer

[4] This was Petty Officer W. Buckett.

At anchor in Scapa Flow and hoisting her Walrus aicraft. This photo was taken in 1942 shortly before she left home waters for the 'Pedestal' convoy. *(C.H.G. Heath BEM MBE)*

Berkeley, she left Portsmouth for the last time and set course for Scapa Flow. Sailing by way of the Irish Sea she anchored in Scapa during the evening of 4 May. She had left in July 1941 for what was to have been no more than a two-week deployment, but had been away for some ten months. During the rest of May *Manchester* carried out a series of work-up exercises in or around Scapa Flow. On 29 May, with the work-up completed, she left the anchorage to rendezvous with *Kenya* and *Newark* for another patrol between Iceland and the Shetland Islands, and to provide cover for mine-laying by ships of the 1st Minelaying Squadron on the northern barrage, code-named 'Operation SN 72'. She returned to Scapa during the afternoon of 4 June and two days later, while at anchor, she was visited by King George VI, who was on an official visit to the Home Fleet and its wartime base.

During the first half of June *Manchester* remained in or around Scapa Flow, sailing for day-running exercises with other ships of the Home Fleet and, on one occasion, with the US Navy's heavy cruiser *Wichita*. On 18 June she escorted the brand new battleship *Anson*, which was not long out of the builder's yard, from Scapa to Rosyth before returning to the anchorage the next morning, where she hoisted the flag of Vice-Admiral. During the next two weeks *Manchester* remained in and around the Scapa Flow area, making only one short passage to Greenock. During the ship's 48-hour stay there she had embarked stores and equipment for a detachment of Norwegian commandos, who were themselves embarked at Scapa Flow. On 27 June she left Scapa to steam to Iceland's Seydisfjord where she refuelled and, on the last day of June, sailed for Spitsbergen.

Just a few weeks earlier, in mid-May, a small Norwegian garrison had been landed at Spitsbergen in order to run a radio and weather station on the island, and *Manchester* was now delivering stores and reinforcements of military personnel. Charles Heath remembers one of the Norwegian sergeants

who was accommodated in the Petty Officers' mess: '*He spent a lot of time honing his commando knife, and as he told me he had been a medical student in civilian life, he would certainly have known where to stick it. During the passage into the freezing Arctic waters the commandos, all stripped to the waist, mustered on the quarterdeck each morning to carry out physical jerks. We were all muffled up in duffel coats.*' *Manchester* was accompanied by the destroyer *Eclipse* and after passing Jan Mayen Island at midnight on 30 June, she anchored off Spitsbergen two days later, where the commandos were landed. Charles Heath remembers: '*We came away from Spitsbergen with a number of huge Russian radio transmitter valves and other bits and pieces. I was given a packet of Russian cigarettes which I carried around for a number of years. They were only half tobacco, the rest being just a cardboard tube.*'

On leaving Spitsbergen *Manchester* joined the battleships HMS *Duke of York* and USS *Washington*, the aircraft carrier *Victorious* and the cruisers *Cumberland* and *Nigeria*, to provide distant cover for the ill-fated convoy PQ17. After arriving back at Scapa *Manchester* remained in home waters and continued to carry out patrols in the waters north of the Shetland Islands. In mid-July Vice-Admiral S. Bonham Carter (CS18) struck his flag and the ship was prepared for her next deployment, the escorting of a third Mediterranean convoy. Twelve months had passed since *Manchester*'s last foray into the Mediterranean and during that period there had been two major operations to run merchant ships east from Gibraltar to resupply and reinforce the island of Malta: 'Operation Halberd' in September 1941 and 'Operation Harpoon' in June 1942. Both had been major fleet operations and they had succeeded in the aim of getting some relief to the besieged island. However, even on greatly reduced rations it was estimated that Malta's population had only enough food to last until the end of August 1942, and if supplies were not forthcoming that was the date which had been set as the longest the island could hold out. Each relief convoy was more difficult than the previous and, given the losses which were being incurred, there were those who considered that Malta should be allowed to fall. Planning for the latest convoy began in early July 1942. Code-named 'Operation Pedestal' this vital convoy was to be the biggest yet and would consist of 14 merchant ships: *Almeira Lykes, Brisbane Star, Clan Ferguson, Deucalion, Dorset, Empire Hope, Glenorchy, Melbourne Star, Port Chalmers, Rochester Castle, Santa Elisa, Waimarama, Wairangi* and the oil tanker *Ohio*. Also within 'Operation Pedestal' were three smaller operations code-named 'Berserk', 'Bellows' and 'Ascendant', which were an aircraft carrier co-operation exercise, a reinforcement of RAF Spitfires to be flown off to Malta and the sailing of a small convoy from Malta to Gibraltar. The escort force for the convoy was made up as follows:

Force Z: *Nelson, Rodney, Victorious, Indomitable, Eagle, Furious* (for 'Operation Bellows'), *Phoebe, Sirius, Charybdis* and 14 destroyers.

Force X: *Nigeria* (Flag CS10), *Kenya, Manchester, Cairo* and 11 destroyers.

There were also various smaller ships such as corvettes, two RFA oil tankers, *Brown Ranger* and *Dingledale*, as well as tugs.

By Thursday 30 July, *Manchester* was at Greenock awaiting orders to sail south for Gibraltar. The main body of the convoy and escorts sailed on 31 July, but *Manchester*'s departure was delayed after the aircraft carrier *Furious* grounded while loading Spitfires in Glasgow's King George V Dock, and then had further difficulties stowing the RAF aircraft which, unlike those of the Fleet Air Arm, were unable to fold their wings. Finally, however, at 2350 on 4 August *Manchester*, *Furious* and the Polish destroyer *Blyskawica* left Greenock and, steaming at high speed, set course to join the convoy and escorts led by *Nelson* (Vice-Admiral E. N. Syfret). After some 62 hours at high speed the three ships met the convoy off the west coast of Portugal, but as *Manchester* was running low on fuel she was

sent ahead to Gibraltar. Although she rejoined the convoy as it approached Cap Trafalgar she was still some 600 tons short of furnace fuel oil, and that evening she was again detached to Gibraltar to complete the operation. She did not rejoin the convoy until 1130 on 10 August, by which time it had passed into the Mediterranean. Next afternoon at 1316, when the convoy was south-east of Formentera Island, the aircraft carrier *Eagle* was torpedoed by *U-73* and sank in just eight minutes with the loss of 163 lives. At the time *Furious* was flying off Spitfires for their long flight to Malta, and as soon as this had been completed was ordered to return to Gibraltar. From that point onwards the convoy and escorts were under constant attack from aircraft and submarines.

As the force approached the area near Galite Island, just north of the Algerian/Tunisian border, there was some success when the destroyer *Ithuriel* depth charged, then rammed and sank the Italian submarine *Cobalto*, but during the day the convoy was subjected to four fierce air attacks as a result of which the merchantman *Deucalion* suffered damage from a near miss and her speed had to be reduced. By 1800 on 12 August the convoy and escorts were preparing to pass through the Skerki Channel, between Cape Bon and Pantelleria Island, and it was not long before another very heavy air raid developed. As a result of this attack *Indomitable* was badly damaged by three large bombs and several near misses, as was the destroyer *Foresight*. At 2030, with darkness falling, Force Z was ordered to withdraw westwards and return to Gibraltar.

Meanwhile, at 1900, Force X and the convoy, which included *Manchester*, had been ordered to keep close in to the Tunisian coast from Cape Bon to Ras-el-Mustafa, before sailing almost due east to Malta. Less than an hour later, however, *Nigeria, Cairo,* the merchantmen *Ohio* and *Brisbane Star* were all hit by torpedoes fired by the Italian submarine *Axum*. Despite serious damage *Nigeria* was able to return to Gibraltar, but *Cairo*'s stern had been blown off and she was scuttled. The two merchantmen eventually got under way again, but at 2038 a fierce dive- and torpedo-bomber attack developed and despite the best efforts of *Ashanti* and *Penn*, which put up a fierce anti-aircraft barrage, the merchant ship *Empire Hope* was lost. At just after 2110 the cruiser *Kenya* was hit by a torpedo fired by a submarine, but she remained operational.

By midnight on 13/14 August the ships of Force X had passed Cape Bon and were steaming close in to the shore. *Manchester* was in the lead, closely followed by *Ashanti, Kenya* and two merchant ships. As *Manchester* was passing Zambra Island a mine exploded under her port bow and, although no damage was caused, it prompted Captain Drew to modify the ship's company's action stations to the extent that the shell room and magazine crews and other exposed personnel, including Petty Officer Charles Heath, moved up one deck to the lobbies. In the previous year's incident when *Manchester* had been torpedoed, a number of men in the shell, magazine and wireless rooms had been killed unnecessarily and by moving men up a deck Drew hoped, without reducing the fighting efficiency of the ship, to avoid more needless loss of life. What was not known at the time was that not far ahead of the force there were a number of Italian E-boats patiently awaiting their arrival in the area. They were hiding behind the wreck of *Havock* which, not long before, while trying to run the gauntlet between Gibraltar and Malta had grounded on one of the many sandbanks off Kilibia on this part of the Tunisian coast.

At 0015 on 14 August, in the inky blackness an Italian E-boat was sighted on *Manchester*'s port beam and within seconds her gunners had turned all the ship's armament onto the tiny target and sunk it in an engagement which lasted for just ten minutes. Just over an hour later, as *Manchester* approached the vicinity of Kilibia, while Drew was looking for *Havock*'s wreck, he spotted what he later described as a '*suspicious object*' partly hidden by the background shoreline on the starboard bow. Rightly suspecting that it might be another Italian E-boat he

An aerial view of HMS Manchester *taken in June 1942. Note the positions of boats and the Walrus aircraft. Additional AA guns and Carley floats take up any available space.* *(Crown Copyright/MoD 1942)*

quickly ordered hard-a-starboard, full ahead port. However, seconds later as *Manchester* began to swing to starboard, Drew and others on the bridge heard the sound of torpedoes being discharged, after which there was the noise of diesel engines being started as two E-boats made off at speed towards the shore. They were, in fact, the Italian *Ms16* and *Ms22*[5] which had been lying patiently in wait before firing their torpedoes from as close as 100 yards. Of the two torpedo tracks spotted by Drew the first passed harmlessly ahead of the ship, but the second smashed into *Manchester*'s starboard side abreast the after engine room, where it exploded with devastating effect, instantly killing the officer and eight ratings who were on watch in the engine room.

Commander (E) William Robb, who was in the forward engine room at the time, described the situation below: '*I felt an explosion with severe shaking or bouncing of the ship, and I knew we had been hit. I heard a loud knocking on the starboard outer shaft. I gave orders to stop the shaft and saw by the repeat revolution indicator that the starboard inner shaft had stopped. The ship immediately assumed a list to starboard, settling eventually at 10½ degrees.*' Leading Stoker Albert Slater was in the after engine room, which had taken the force of the explosion: '*I was standing some 20 feet above the engine room starting platform when this terrific explosion plunged everything into darkness. I was actually blown bodily off the platform on which I was standing and it was only the water rushing into the compartment which saved me from serious injury or death, as I fell into the water of the flooded engine room rather than onto the deck plates. The water carried me quickly upwards towards the deck head and there appeared to be nothing to stop me from drowning. Suddenly, the water ceased rising and I pulled myself onto what I thought was the top of a turbine. I could see a faint glimmer of light,*

[5] *Ms16* and *Ms22* were modern MTBs, built specifically for operations in the Sicilian Narrows. They each carried two 533mm torpedoes.

but I couldn't climb over the superheated steam pipes without being badly burned, so I took a chance and plunged into the water and came back up at a place where the air was a bit fresher. I groped my way along the deck head, cutting my hand on a broken lamp. I went on until I found myself beneath an open hatch and was pulled clear.'

With great difficulty Commander Robb and a rescue team managed to get to the after engine room hatch, where Robb found: '*One man covered in fuel oil astride the cofferdam of the engine room door, exhausted and calling for air. Fumes were thick and more like vapour. I put the man into the fan chamber for air. I shone a torch into the engine room, which was flooded up to the crown. There was one man with his head above the oil fuel and grasping the top rung of the ladder, and another man was calling for help.'*

Both men were pulled to safety by the rescue team and were guided to the upper deck by way of a fan trunking.

Three of *Manchester*'s main engines were wrecked beyond repair, and although the port inner engine was functioning it too was damaged and with the steering gone the ship began to steam round in circles. Eventually, after almost half an hour the engine was stopped and the ship came to a rest with a 12½ degrees list to starboard, just two miles from the shoreline at Point Kilibia. *Manchester*'s predicament was very different from that in which she had found herself in July 1941 after being torpedoed in the open sea, with a destroyer escort and much closer to air cover from Gibraltar. This time she was close to a shallow and hostile shoreline riddled with sandbanks, such as the one on which the *Havock* had foundered. In addition she was on the edge of a minefield, which was close to seaward on her port side. If he could get his ship under way at all Drew decided it would be unwise to try to reach Malta, for that would mean passing very close to Pantelleria during daylight hours and all available aircraft at Malta would be fully occupied providing cover for the merchant ships of the convoy. He decided that to stand any chance at all of reaching safety he must have the ship under way before daylight, and even then the track west at ten knots would take the ship to within 20 miles of Pantelleria and within easy range of Italian E-boat and torpedo-bomber bases. It would also mean committing the ship to navigating the channel only a mile and a half from the coast and inside the minefield until clear of the shore. However, both options depended upon the port inner engine being serviceable for, having been stopped, problems had arisen with the main cooling water circulating pump and it could not immediately be restarted.

As *Manchester* lay helpless and virtually dead in the water and Drew waited for full reports on the extent of damage to the ship, damage control and rescue parties worked to transfer fuel, shore up bulkheads and hatches, and attempted to rig up emergency steering, as well as rescuing those trapped. Charles Heath remembers:'*When the ship was hit I was sitting by the hatch which led down to my action station, the wireless office. As there had been a lull in the proceedings Captain Drew had brought us up one deck when, suddenly, there was a loud thud, and the compartment filled with smoke and debris; at the same time we were plunged into darkness as the lights went out and the ship started to heel over to starboard. After a while I moved up another deck where I found a number of the ship's company milling around in the dark, and as I had a torch I was able to guide them onto the open deck via a gun turret, but when I tried to get out onto the quarterdeck myself I found the heavy watertight door firmly closed and I couldn't get the strongback clips off. Fortunately there was a scuttle alongside the door which I managed to open and I was pulled unceremoniously through it and onto the quarterdeck by one of the Royal Marines. By then the ship had stopped heeling over and it had settled with a permanent list.'*

By 0300, with daylight only two hours away and with Commander (E) still unable to give an estimate of how long it would take to restart the port

inner engine and rig up emergency steering, Drew was faced with a real dilemma. It was by no means certain that the engine could be restarted and, even if it was, it would not be until after daylight. Then, having come to rest so close to the shore, he estimated it would take at least an hour backing and filling on one screw in order to work her round so that she was pointing towards Cape Bon once again. With a maximum speed of only ten knots there was little chance that the ship could clear the coastal waters that day, and if the already seriously damaged ship were subjected to air attacks while close inshore, effective avoiding action would be impossible and there was every chance the ship would end up going aground, as the much smaller *Havock* had done. Once aground it was doubtful whether she would have enough power or manoeuvrability to get free and would almost certainly fall into enemy hands. The continued presence in the area of Italian E-boats and the certainty of enemy torpedo-bombing attacks again raised the possibility of the ship going aground and falling into enemy hands, something Drew was determined at all cost to avoid.

From reports which reached him it was clear that the torpedo had hit the ship on the starboard side between 179 and 198 stations. As a result primary flooding had occurred between stations 155 and 198, which included Y3 oil fuel tank. The compartments known to have been flooded were the after engine room, Y1 oil fuel tank, the 4-inch high-angle magazine, the clothing issue room and its associated stores and the main Wireless Transmitter Office. It was also clear that the watertight compartments and oil fuel tanks on the starboard side of the after engine room were open to the sea. The after engine room had flooded quickly, putting both port and starboard outer shafts out of action, and as time went on superheated steam was escaping into the flood water in this engine room and it started to boil. The starboard inner shaft had also suffered serious damage and was out of action, which meant that no electrical power was available aft of 155 section, thus putting the steering gear out of action. Structurally a large split had appeared on the lower deck of the gunroom flat, which was also flooded with oil and water, and there was serious structural damage to the wardroom flat.

Meanwhile, at about 0154 the destroyer *Pathfinder*, which was passing, came upon *Manchester* stopped and listing heavily to starboard some 095 degrees and 2.2 miles from Kelibia Light. This was the first indication for the rest of Force X of *Manchester*'s plight. The destroyer immediately requested help, but at that stage it was not possible to detach any of the convoy escorts. *Pathfinder* manoeuvred alongside *Manchester*'s starboard quarter and took off ten officers and 163 ratings who were not required. At 0220 the destroyer cast off and an hour later, with still no indication of how long it would be, or whether the port inner engine could be restarted, Drew made the decision that to prevent it from falling into enemy hands preparations must be made to scuttle the ship. The problem was that engineers who were still trying to work out how to restart the only possible serviceable engine were now required to begin the preparations to sink the ship. Drew ordered that the ship's company be mustered on the flight deck where, in total darkness, he explained the situation to them and told them of his decision to sink the ship. He then went on to explain the steps he wanted taken, including the total destruction of all RDF (radar) sets and the launching of rafts. He concluded by telling them to work as quietly as possible as E-boats were still in the area, in the hope that the presence of a crippled cruiser might go undetected for a while longer. However, despite his plea for silence the loyalty of his ship's company was such that: '*They gave me three hearty cheers together with expressions of sympathy and friendship.*'

Having addressed the ship's company Drew then instructed Commander (E) and the Torpedo Officer to make the necessary arrangements for opening the sea cocks and magazine floods, and for placing explosive charges on the condenser doors in the forward engine room. He also ordered the Executive Commander to start getting the ship's company

away in the Carley rafts, preparations which took over two hours to complete. Down below all the nuts holding the doors were slackened off and personnel were stationed on all flooding valves to await the order to open them and start flooding the ship. Eventually when all the ship's company apart from Captain Drew and other key officers were away in the rafts, with the ship's whalers being reserved for the flooding parties, the order was given to sink the ship. Commander (E) Robb left this account: '*I saw the Captain standing on the pom-pom deck. I called up to him, "Commander says he is ready to carry on flooding sir." Captain replied "Carry on" and he came down to the flight deck. I waited for the last raft to go out, then went down to Damage Control HQ and gave orders for the forward and after sections to carry on flooding. After receiving reports from Lt Fletcher (fwd) and Lt Malim (aft), I ordered Mr Budden to open forward floods and abandon both boiler rooms. On receiving his report, I ordered forward engine room to flood and place scuttling charges. Mr George and Mr Casey (Warrant Engineer and Gunner respectively) went down to the forward engine room. I checked that the diesel watch keepers were up, and ordered all officers and men with no further duties to abandon ship. All the Engineer Officers were reluctant to leave the workshop flat and I had to tell each one personally and definitely, to go. Lt Rambaut returned to wait until we had finished in the engine room and I again told him to leave the ship. Mr George's party with CERA Pedder removed the condenser doors, came up and reported. I told them to abandon ship. I ordered Mr Casey to fix his charges. Mr Casey was the last man to leave the forward engine room. I told him to abandon ship, and followed him up the ladder and went to the starboard waist. I found a crowd around the starboard whaler, which was in the water alongside and was full. The Captain was in the whaler. I suggested to the Commander that we should all go aft to the quarter deck until the scuttling charges had gone off. He agreed and we began to make our way aft. Lt Sutton and myself got aft to the quarterdeck, but in the darkness we could not find anything floatable. I missed the Commander and Lt Malim and went forward to look for them. I met the Commander who said: "If you want to catch the whaler, hop in now." I got back to the starboard whaler and found Lt-Cdr Duff and Mr Casey working with some ropes. I climbed down the whaler's falls and Duff and Casey got some kind of wooden raft, which was towed by the whaler with them and two ratings hanging on. The Commander and Lt Malim got a plank and were picked up by the whaler. Lt Sutton was picked up off the quarterdeck by the second whaler. I estimated it was 05.00 when the whaler left the ship.*'

One of those on the flooding parties was Charles Heath, who remembered: '*Eventually it became obvious that it would be impossible to get* Manchester *under way again and we were told that the Captain had decided to scuttle the ship. As my shirt had been torn during my struggle to get through the scuttle onto the quarterdeck, and shorts were hardly appropriate to go ashore in, I went along to the Petty Officers' mess and "borrowed" a serge suit from a mess mate. My kit locker was in the area of the explosion and was destroyed. After I changed I then joined several other senior ratings in opening various hatches around the ship in order to ensure that she did in fact sink, and I was one of the last to leave in the ship's whaler.*'

Dawn was breaking as the whalers and rafts made their way slowly to the shore and, as one occupant of a whaler observed: '*An Italian plane arrived overhead and aimed a torpedo at the ship. It ran close to the whaler, but missed ahead of the ship. On the way ashore planes circled the boats several times. The ship herself listed over to starboard and we heard shell cases on the pom-pom deck rattling as they rolled over the side. I estimate it was at just after 0530 that the stern of the ship went under, her bow then lifted up and she sank.*' Progress of the survivors towards the shore was slow, and one whaler was handicapped by the fact that it was towing the makeshift wooden raft. By 0545 there were at least six Italian torpedo-bombers flying low over

the water examining the rafts, and two of them flew off south towards the merchant ship *Glenorchy*, whose masts and funnel were just visible to the survivors in *Manchester*'s whalers. She was torpedoed and, as she was sinking, blew up in a huge column of smoke and flame.

As *Manchester*'s survivors made their way towards the shore one of several Italian E-boats that were cruising around the area took a Lieutenant and a Midshipman from one of *Manchester*'s rafts and unsuccessfully attempted to find out from them the whereabouts of Captain Drew. The rest of the survivors took almost three hours to reach the shore and some of the Carley rafts were actually assisted by local fishing boats. By 0830, however, the majority of them had landed and about half an hour later they had made their way round to Kilibia village, where they were interned by the Vichy French authorities.

Initially *Manchester*'s ship's company were held in a temporary camp in Tunisia, before being sent by rail to the Algerian town of Langhouat, built around an oasis some 400 kilometres south of the Algerian capital Algiers. Today it is an important centre for the production of natural gas, situated on the trans-Saharan Highway on the northern edge of the Saharan Atlas Mountains. Charles Heath described the PoW camp in which they were interned at Langhouat as: '*looking just like a Foreign Legion fort, straight out of the* Boys' Own *paper.*' Conditions in the camp were harsh with many privations, but fortunately their internment did not last for too long and in November 1942, following the Allied landings in North Africa, they were released and returned home via Gibraltar.

For Captain Drew, four of his officers and a Petty Officer, the ordeal was not over, for on their return home they faced a court martial and were found guilty of various offences of negligence. In Drew's case it was for abandoning and scuttling *Manchester* when: '*Having regard to the conditions prevailing at the time, it was his duty to stand by the ship and do his utmost to bring her into harbour.*' In the author's

Four of HMS Manchester*'s Senior Ratings on their release from the Lahout Internment Camp, Algeria, in November 1942.* *(C.H.G. Heath BEM MBE)*

opinion, having studied all the evidence in detail, the verdict hung on whether *Manchester*'s port inner engine could be restarted, and little heed was taken of Drew's main concern , considering the fate of SS *Glenorchy*, whether the engine was working or not, of what fate *Manchester* would have met had she still been afloat during the forenoon of 14 August. Had she suffered further damage and grounded she would almost certainly have fallen into the hands of the enemy for, despite the fact that Tunisia was administered by a Vichy French regime, the Italians were using the coast as their own. What is abundantly clear is that whatever decision Drew made it is unlikely he would have escaped criticism. To his credit, for the rest of his life he bore the stigma uncomplainingly and with great dignity, supported wholeheartedly by his ship's company who kept a very strong bond with their old commanding officer.

Chapter Seven

HMS LIVERPOOL
1938-1958

HMS Liverpool *alongside the Fairfield Shipbuilding & Engineering Company's fitting-out berth at Govan. The interior of the starboard hangar can be clearly seen.* *(Maritime Photo Library)*

The Royal Navy's 1935 building programme provided for the construction of 28 ships of all sizes, from coastal sloops to cruisers, one of which, it was announced in October 1935, as '*...being of the Southampton-class, the building of which is, subject to the settlement of certain points of detail, to be entrusted to the Fairfield Shipbuilding & Engineering Company Ltd, Govan, Glasgow*'. It was predicted that the ship would take some two and a half years to build at a cost of £1,750,000. The announcement also predicted that eventually there would be eight ships of the class or, '*enough for two squadrons*'. The other two cruisers of that year's programme were, of course, *Gloucester* and *Manchester*. Three weeks after this initial announcement came the news that the Fairfield-built cruiser would be named *Liverpool*, a name which had been given to five earlier ships of the Royal Navy, four of them being frigates of the sailing fleets, and the last a cruiser which served throughout the Great War of 1914-18.

On 17 February 1936 the keel for the new *Liverpool* was laid, and some 13 months later the hull was ready for launching. The ceremony took place on Wednesday 24 March 1937, performed by Mrs Montague Norman, the wife of the Governor of the Bank of England. In May 1938 the ship's first commanding officer, Captain A. N. Read RN, was appointed. In the early 1930s Captain Read had commanded the seaplane carrier *Ark Royal*, and later the sloop *Folkestone* on the China Station. During the Great War he served as Gunnery Officer in the cruisers *Castor, Donegal* and *Yarmouth*, and immediately after the war in the battleship *Warspite*. Originally it had been expected that *Liverpool* would commission in early September

A pre-war image of HMS Liverpool *entering Grand Harbour, Malta, displaying neutrality markings on 'B' and 'X' turrets.* *(T. Ferrers-Walker Collection)*

1938, and that during the second week of October she would take the place of *Emerald* on the East Indies Station. However, as work on fitting out *Liverpool* neared completion, delays began to creep in, and it was 26 October before a steaming crew arrived at Govan from their depot at Chatham, and the ship was commissioned for her builder's trials the following week. Finally, during the forenoon of 1 November a navigating party of 368 ratings from the naval barracks at Chatham, who had travelled up by special train, joined the ship and at 0630 the next day *Liverpool* slipped her moorings and steamed downriver for Greenock and the Firth of Clyde to undergo a full eight hours of machinery trials. At this stage the ship was still in the charge of the builder's pilot, but at 1720 *Liverpool* anchored off Greenock where, just over an hour later, Captain Read accepted the ship and the White Ensign was hoisted. Later that evening, sailing by way of the Irish Sea and the Channel, *Liverpool* set course for Chatham Dockyard where, during the forenoon of 5 November, she secured alongside No 3 basin.

Originally she had been scheduled to sail for the East Indies Station to relieve *Emerald* on 11 October, but the building delays meant that this schedule was no longer possible and most of November was spent alongside at Chatham embarking stores and ammunition. She also hoisted on board the Walrus seaplanes of 714 Flight. By the end of November the cruiser was moored off Sheerness, and on 4 December she began three weeks of trials and work-up exercises in the Channel, between Dover and the Isle of Wight, before returning to Chatham for Christmas and New Year.

On 3 January 1939, *Liverpool* left Sheerness for further trials before setting course for the River Mersey and the city of Liverpool where, three days later, she secured alongside in Gladstone Dock. During her three-day visit the Lord Mayor of the city visited the ship to present a silver plate, then finally during the afternoon of 10 January she put to sea and set course for the Mediterranean and her delayed passage to the East Indies Station. The passage east was broken at Malta where the cruiser remained for 13 weeks. Initially she had been due to

carry out a three-week work-up programme from Grand Harbour, but in the event mechanical problems with her main propulsion machinery kept her in dockyard hands for six weeks, and it was 6 March when she began her work-up programme. Just nine days into the exercises, which were undertaken in company with her sister *Gloucester*, Germany occupied what remained of Czechoslovakia after the Munich 'carve-up', and *Liverpool* was ordered to remain in the Malta area. On 8 April 1939 Italian troops invaded Albania and Prime Minister Neville Chamberlain warned Mussolini of the '*serious consequences*' of his actions. In Malta this diplomatic activity translated itself, at 1900 on 9 April, into a general recall of all liberty men and for some 48 hours the fleet at Malta, including *Liverpool*, remained at immediate notice for sea. By 11 April, however, the immediate crisis had passed and limited leave was granted to ships' companies again. Finally, during the forenoon of 21 April *Liverpool* left Grand Harbour to continue her passage east, with her transit of the Suez Canal being interrupted by a three-day break at Ismailia. After clearing the Suez Canal during the early hours of 28 April, later that day she rendezvoused with *Gloucester*, and the two cruisers steamed south to Aden where, on 2 May, they officially joined the East Indies Fleet as part of the 4th Cruiser Squadron.

After leaving Aden *Liverpool* and *Gloucester* remained together in the Indian Ocean. On 18 May they set out from Colombo on a summer cruise of Indian Ocean islands, which took *Liverpool* to Male Island in the Maldives and Diego Garcia in the Chagos Islands, which in those days was administered from Mauritius and still supported an indigenous native population. From Diego Garcia *Liverpool* made a short stop at Port Mathurin on Rodrigues Island, and then Port Louis, Mauritius. Finally, in mid-June, in company with *Gloucester*, she visited Farquhar Island with its small settlement, before steaming via the Seychelles to Trincomalee. On 4 July *Liverpool* made the short passage to Colombo to begin a six-week docking and maintenance period, during which further repair work was carried out on the ship's main engines. For the ship's company there was some relief in that both watches were granted leave at the Diyatawala Rest Camp in the centre of the island.

It was Saturday 19 August when *Liverpool* put to sea again to carry out a short trials period before returning to Trincomalee where she refuelled and took on board stores and ammunition to put her on a war footing. On 24 August 1939, *Liverpool* had been at Trincomalee for four days when the worsening political situation in Europe made itself felt in Ceylon (Sri Lanka). With German troops massing on the Polish border, and Prime Minister Chamberlain having been granted wide-ranging emergency powers, *Liverpool* was ordered to sail immediately for Bombay, where two days later she took on more stores and equipment, before steaming at 18 knots into a strong south-westerly monsoon across the Arabian Sea to anchor just out of sight of land off the island of Masirah. During the next six days, assisted by the sloop *Rochester*, her ship's company laid buoys and marked out deep water channels in order to provide an emergency wartime anchorage for shipping. The task was completed just hours before war was declared on 3 September, and next day *Liverpool* was ordered to sea, where she joined the Indian ships *Indus* and *Hindustan*. Two days later however she was ordered to Aden and after a rough passage at high speed she arrived in the harbour on 8 September.

For over two weeks *Liverpool* remained in local waters around Aden, carrying out gunnery practice in the area of Perim Island, as well as launching her Walrus aircraft to carry out bombing practice. On 22 September she left Aden with a convoy, which included the troop transport *Reina del Pacifico*, bound for the Far East and three days later, having handed the escort over to the aircraft carrier *Eagle*, she put into Bombay. During October 1939 *Liverpool* continued to patrol the Indian Ocean, and at one stage she was literally island-hopping around the remote atolls of the Seychelles, including St Pierre, Aldabra and Providence Islands. In addition to showing the flag, the main purpose of this patrol was to brief the inhabitants on action to be taken should German commerce raiders seek shelter or supplies. During this period *Liverpool* refuelled and stored ship at the French naval base at Diego Suarez, but during the second week of November she returned to Colombo. Two days later, on 15 November, she left the East Indies Fleet for Singapore, where she joined the China Station and on 21 November, two days after her arrival, underwent a short docking period. After hoisting the flag of the C-in-C China Station, Admiral Sir Percy Noble, the cruiser's first duty was to steam north to Saigon which was then the southern capital of the French colony of Indo-China, in what was the region of Cochin China. There, during a visit lasting for just over 24 hours, Noble met his French counterparts. *Liverpool* then steamed on to Hong Kong, where she arrived on 10 December. Eleven days later she sailed for her first patrol in the waters around southern Japan.

The Royal Navy's contraband patrols in the waters around Japan were primarily intended to intercept German ships which had taken refuge in German ports, and also to intercept ships of other nationalities, including Japanese vessels, which were suspected of carrying German nationals. Given the fact that at that time Japan was the most powerful military nation in South-East Asia and that her foreign policy, linked as it was to the Axis powers, was becoming ever more aggressive towards the Western colonial powers in the region, Noble had been instructed not to antagonise the Japanese Government unnecessarily. On 23 December *Liverpool* arrived off southern Japan and began her patrolling well outside territorial waters. Initially all went smoothly, and there was no necessity to stop any ships entering or leaving Japanese ports. In order to refuel and take on stores *Liverpool* would rendezvous with an RFA, but again well outside territorial waters. On 2 January 1940 *Liverpool* stopped and sent a boarding party to a Japanese passenger ship, *Toya Maru*, and before she returned to Hong Kong on 12 January she had intercepted and boarded two more vessels.

HMS *Liverpool*'s second patrol began on 16 January, and four days later she received information that 21 people on board the 16,975-gross ton Japanese passenger liner, MV *Asama Maru*, which was on passage from Honolulu to Yokohama, were German nationals and survivors from the 32,354-gross ton Norddeutscher Lloyd passenger ship *Columbus* which, in December 1939, had been intercepted by the destroyer *Hyperion* some 400 miles off the coast of the USA. In order to avoid being captured *Columbus* was scuttled by her crew, who were then picked up by the cruiser USS *Tuscaloosa* and taken to New York. The signal received by *Liverpool* indicated the 21 members of *Columbus*' crew had made their way from New York to San Francisco, where they had taken passage on board *Asama Maru*, bound for Japan on what was to be the first stage of their journey back to Germany via Japan and the trans-Siberian Railway. *Liverpool* was ordered to intercept *Asama Maru*, but well outside Japanese territorial waters and also out of sight of the coast. In the event she sighted the Japanese liner at 1255 on Sunday 21 January, some 35 miles off the Nojima Promontory, Chiba Prefecture, close to the volcanic island of Ni Ijima, which is just over 20 miles south of Shimoda on the Izu Peninsula. After the cruiser had signalled and fired a blank 3pdr round *Asama Maru* stopped, and a boarding party was quickly on board the liner. According to surviving records the encounter between the master of the liner and the officer in charge of the boarding party was very formal, but initially the captain refused to hand over the German passengers. However, as he was unable to prevent them from being forcibly seized by the boarding party he eventually submitted to the demand and they were handed over. By 1445 they were prisoners on board *Liverpool* and the Japanese passenger ship was allowed to continue her voyage. As the German seamen, of whom 13 were officers and eight were technical ratings, all fell within the category of military personnel, they were accommodated in a messdeck which had been hurriedly

cleared for them. The diplomatic repercussions, however, were yet to come.

Within 24 hours the incident was making the headlines in newspapers the world over, as the Japanese Government protested in the strongest terms to the British Ambassador in Tokyo. Despite the fact that international law was on the British side, Japan began to retaliate and it was not long before powerful Japanese warships were stopping and detaining British-registered shipping not only in the waters off Japan, but also off the Chinese coast. It was a problem which, after the fall of France in June 1940, and the withdrawal of more Royal Navy ships from South-East Asia, would escalate even further.

For *Liverpool* the patrol ended on 28 January when she returned to Hong Kong and the prisoners were landed. It was the last patrol she made off the Japanese coast for the British Government decided that the benefits were far outweighed by the high diplomatic cost at a time when Britain was desperately trying to avoid antagonising Japan. During February 1940 and through early March *Liverpool* remained in local waters around Hong Kong, carrying out training exercises with the cruiser *Danae* and the destroyer *Thanet*. That Japan was becoming an ever-increasing threat to British interests in the region is indicated by the fact that *Liverpool* was regularly shadowed by Japanese military aircraft. During March *Liverpool* patrolled the waters of China's Chusan (Zhoushan) Archipelago and the approaches to Shanghai. In early April she was operating close to Hong Kong again, and on the 14th of the month she was ordered west to rejoin the East Indies Fleet.

Steaming via the naval base at Singapore, *Liverpool* arrived in Colombo on 21 April, and at Aden nine days later. Operating from here the cruiser began a series of patrols and convoy escort duties between Aden and Suez, and on 19 May she evacuated a number of British families from the colony of French Somaliland (Djibouti) to Aden. With the barren island of Perim as the sheltered anchorage between patrols, there were few breaks for the ship's company, but on 4 June, with Norway having been overrun, the British Expeditionary Force having been evacuated from Dunkirk and Italy expected to declare war against Britain and France, *Liverpool* was ordered to steam north to join the Mediterranean Fleet. After making her transit of the Suez Canal during the night of 6 June, the next day she arrived in Alexandria where she joined the 7th Cruiser Squadron. Three days after her arrival Italy entered the war on Germany's side.

With Italy now a belligerent power the Mediterranean Fleet's bases at Malta and Alexandria were both on Italy's doorstep, the latter being very close to the Italian North African colony of Libya, with its military base at Tobruk less than 100 miles from the Egyptian border. On 11 June *Liverpool* was involved in her first operation aimed at blocking the port facilities at Tobruk. Sailing from Alexandria as part of Admiral Cunningham's battlefleet at 0100, the plan was to intercept and attack an Italian convoy in the region of Crete, while *Liverpool*, *Gloucester* and four destroyers were detached to bombard the port of Tobruk. The attack was carried out in conjunction with an RAF bombing raid by Blenheims of the Western Desert Air Force, supported by elderly Gloster Gladiators of 274 Squadron. The bombardment by the cruisers was primarily intended to divert the defenders' attention from the RAF raid, and the two cruisers arrived off Tobruk at 0500 on 12 June, where they soon engaged four gunboats, one of which, *Giovanni Berta*, was quickly sunk. Within minutes, however, the shore batteries at Tobruk had engaged the cruisers with accurate fire, and after sinking the gunboat they retired under cover of a smokescreen to rejoin the battlefleet at just after midday. The fleet, including *Liverpool*, returned to Alexandria the same evening.

HMS *Liverpool*'s next operational foray began during the forenoon of 27 June when, in company with other cruisers of her squadron, including *Gloucester, Neptune, Orion* and HMAS *Sydney*, she left Alexandria to cover the sailing of Malta convoys. Soon after leaving harbour an RAF recon-

naissance aircraft sighted an Italian supply convoy some 100 miles north of Tobruk and heading towards the port. The convoy actually consisted of three elderly Italian destroyers, *Espero, Ostro* and *Zeffiro*, which were carrying heavy military equipment and troops to reinforce the Tobruk garrison. The cruisers were ordered to intercept the Italian force, and at 1831 on 28 June, *Liverpool* was the first to sight them. Three minutes later she opened fire on the leading ship, which was *Espero*. The destroyer suffered severe damage which reduced her speed, but she still managed to fire torpedoes, which *Liverpool* had to manoeuvre to avoid. *Espero* then put herself in the line of fire in order that the other two destroyers could escape which, with night falling, they managed to do. With the destroyers within range of air cover from shore bases the cruisers abandoned the chase, but *Espero*, which had taken the brunt of the fire, quickly sank. Before leaving the scene *Sydney* rescued some 47 survivors; *Liverpool* had sustained one hit on her armoured belt some three feet above the waterline, but this did not affect her operational capabilities. However, instead of returning to Alexandria, she was ordered to steam south through the Suez Canal, first to Ismailia where she took on stores, ammunition and fuel, and then on to Port Tewfik at the southern entrance to the Suez Canal, where she secured alongside the harbour wall.

With Italy now in the war the two British colonial possessions of Aden and British Somaliland were now vulnerable to enemy attack, particularly the latter which adjoined Italian Somaliland and was virtually undefended. *Liverpool* had been ordered to embark the 2nd Battalion the Black Watch, together with their equipment, and leaving Port Tewfik during the early evening of 1 July, she arrived in Aden two days later where the troops were disembarked[1]. On 4 July *Liverpool* steamed north once again and four days later she returned to Alexandria to find the fleet had sailed. Pausing just long enough to refuel *Liverpool* put to sea again to join Force A, the ships of the 7th Cruiser squadron, including *Gloucester, Neptune, Orion, Sydney* and HMAS *Stuart*, which was part of Cunningham's fleet. They had put to sea the day before to provide cover for convoy MW2 sailing from Alexandria to Malta, and the returning convoy ME4. She quickly joined the main cruiser force which was steaming ahead of the main battlefleet, led by *Warspite* (flag C-in-C), with *Malaya, Royal Sovereign, Eagle* and 16 destroyers. Two days earlier, on 6 July, a convoy of four Italian merchantmen had left Naples bound for Benghazi, and that evening were joined by two torpedo boats and another merchantman from Messina. Altogether the Italian convoy was carrying 2,190 troops, 72 tanks, 232 vehicles, plus thousands of tons of fuel and supplies. The convoy's escort was formed of three groups, the first being eight destroyers and four torpedo boats which provided the close escort. The second group, which was some 35 miles to the east, consisted of six heavy cruisers, *Zara, Fiume, Gorizia, Pola, Bolzana* and *Trento*, together with a destroyer screen. The third group was the main Italian battlefleet made up of the battleships *Giulio Cesare* (flag Admiral Inigo Campioni) and *Conte di Cavour*, together with a screen of eight destroyers.

During 8 July both Cunningham and Campioni became aware of the other's presence at sea and for most of that day, between 1000 and 1830, Cunningham's fleet came under heavy air attack, with some 70 Italian bombers almost constantly overhead. The heaviest attacks were directed at the ships of the 7th Cruiser Squadron, and it was at 1814, during the last of these attacks, that *Gloucester* received a direct hit which wrecked her bridge and caused heavy casualties. *Liverpool* emerged unscathed, as she did from further air raids the next day. During the afternoon of 8 July, with air reconnaissance having located the exact position of the Italian fleet, Cunningham turned his force

[1] The 2nd Battalion the Black Watch were transferred from Aden to British Somaliland in order to reinforce the tiny local garrison. It was however, a case of too little, too late, and on 19 August 1940 the Italian Army occupied this forgotten British colony.

towards Taranto hoping to be able to cut off the Italian ships from their base. As luck would have it this came at a time when Campioni had temporarily lost track of Cunningham, and at 1452 the ships of the 7th Cruiser Squadron, which were steaming ahead of *Warspite*, sighted the Italian cruiser force some 30 to 40 miles east of Calabria. The first sighting was made by *Neptune*, when she reported '*Two enemy vessels in sight bearing 238 degrees*'. The cruisers were rapidly closing the enemy battlefleet which was some 15 miles away, and at 1512 they were ordered to engage. *Liverpool* and *Neptune* both opened fire at a range of 22,100 yards, and by 1520 both sides were firing accurately. Splinters from a near miss damaged *Neptune*'s catapult and aircraft, but shortly before 1525 *Warspite* opened fire with ten salvoes and soon after this the Italian cruisers turned away under cover of a smokescreen.

Although they later engaged enemy destroyers, the 7th Cruiser Squadron's part in the battle was virtually over. At 1552 there was another inconclusive engagement, this time between the two main battlefleets, during which *Warspite* inflicted damage on *Giulio Cesare*, but by 1605 the Italian fleet had moved north hoping to draw Cunningham closer to their air bases, but this ended the surface engagement. At 1640 Italian bombers again began to launch high-level air attacks and Cunningham realised that he would be unable to intercept the Italian ships before they were within close range of their air bases at Messina, nor, at this stage, would he be able to catch the Italian convoy, so he concentrated on ensuring the safe passages of the two Malta convoys. During 11 and 12 July the fleet was subjected to constant high-level bombing attacks, and for *Liverpool* the worst of these came between 1400 and 1500 on 12 July when she suffered slight damage from a near miss in which a 21-year-old Seaman was killed. Next day, however, at 0710, *Liverpool* arrived back in Alexandria.

For nine days *Liverpool* remained in the vicinity of Alexandria, but at just after midnight on Monday 22 July she left harbour in company with *Capetown* and the destroyers *Defender, Diamond, Dainty* and *Stuart*, as the escort for a convoy bound for the Aegean. During the forenoon of 25 July the convoy reached Athens, and after refuelling from an RFA, *Liverpool* and her group took over a convoy of empty merchant ships for the return passage to Alexandria. By the forenoon of Monday 29 July the convoy was well south of Crete, just over 24 hours' steaming from their base and not far from the safety of air cover provided by *Eagle*'s aircraft. At 1030, however, came the first of a number of high-level bombing raids by the Italian Air Force. For almost three hours *Liverpool* avoided the attacks, but at 1320 a bomb struck the forward end of the bridge and although it did not explode, it penetrated into B gun deck recreation space flat, hitting and killing a stoker outright. Damage to the ship, however, was limited and the cruiser managed to avoid the bombs which continued to rain down until well into the afternoon. Although one of *Eagle*'s aircraft managed to shoot down one Italian bomber, one of the carrier's own aircraft was also brought down. During the afternoon of 30 July *Liverpool* arrived back at Alexandria.

After only a five-day break in harbour, on 4 August *Liverpool* again left Alexandria to escort a convoy as far as the Gulf of Athens. This time she was accompanied by the destroyers *Hostile* and *Jervis*. Although enemy aircraft were sighted the force returned safely to Alexandria, and on 20 August, this time in company with *Janus* and *Jervis*, she left harbour to patrol the convoy route between Alexandria and Crete. Within a few hours of leaving harbour the ships came under air attack, but they avoided all the bombs and three days later returned to harbour. It was 30 August before *Liverpool* put to sea again, this time as part of the battlefleet led by *Malaya* and *Eagle*, and also including *Gloucester, Kent, Orion, Sydney* and nine destroyers. Once again the fleet was escorting a convoy which was bound for Malta. During the afternoon of 2 September, south of the island, the fleet came under heavy air attack from waves of both high-level and dive-bombers, but all emerged

unscathed. Two days later, as they turned south with a returning convoy, they again came under heavy air attack, and these raids continued at frequent intervals until 6 September when they arrived back at Alexandria.

Following her return to the Egyptian port there was a six-day break for *Liverpool*'s ship's company before, on 14 September, she joined *Gloucester* and *Kent* to escort a fast supply and munitions convoy to Malta, and to support *Illustrious* as her aircraft bombed and mined the Benghazi harbour area in an attempt to disrupt Italian supplies and reinforcements into the port. The carrier's air attack took place in the early hours of 17 September, before, 48 hours later, the force returned to Alexandria. Nine days after her return to harbour *Liverpool* shifted from her buoy to the quayside where for three hours she embarked troops, together with their stores and equipment, before sailing to join *Gloucester* and *York* for a fast passage to Malta. The main battlefleet provided cover for the three cruisers, but some 14 hours after sailing the force came under attack by torpedo-bombers and only by some skilful manoeuvring did *Liverpool* avoid being hit. At five minutes past midnight on 10 October the cruiser secured alongside Parlatorio Wharf in Malta's Grand Harbour. Two hours later, with the troops having been disembarked, *Liverpool* put to sea again and rejoined the battlefleet for the 42-hour passage to Alexandria.

At midnight on 8/9 October, *Liverpool* put to sea again to join the battlefleet led by *Warspite, Malaya* and *Ramillies*, the aircraft carriers *Eagle* and *Illustrious*, the cruisers *Ajax, Gloucester, Sydney* and *York*, together with a screen of nine destroyers, which had sailed to provide escort cover for the supply convoy MW2 bound for Malta. By Friday 11 October the convoy had been delivered safely and in the early hours of the next morning the fleet was south-east of Malta and escorting an empty convoy on its return passage to Alexandria. Also in the vicinity was the Italian destroyer *Artigliere* and the torpedo boats *Airone* and *Ariel*. Further away were three other enemy destroyers. At 0200 *Airone* fired four torpedoes at *Ajax*, all of which missed, and then opened fire on the cruiser. Three shells hit *Ajax*, which reacted quickly to the surprise attack and within 20 minutes she had destroyed the gunboat. She then turned her attention to *Artigliere*, and despite being hit four times herself she reduced the destroyer to a disabled wreck. By 0305 *Ajax* had sighted more Italian destroyers, which she mistook and reported as cruisers, but having suffered 13 killed and 22 wounded she was ordered to rejoin the main force and *York* was detailed to sink the crippled *Artigliere*. During the chase which followed *Liverpool* opened fire on one enemy destroyer as it retired at high speed, but with the ship well out of range this action was soon abandoned, and as *Liverpool* rejoined the fleet she passed survivors from the two Italian ships in the water.

At 1245 that day came the first of many air attacks on the fleet, when formations of Italian bombers made high-level raids. Although *Liverpool* came through unscathed, she suffered two very near misses and by 1330 all the cruisers were back with the convoy. During the next day the convoy made steady progress towards Alexandria and most of Monday 14 October passed quietly. However, at 1852 lookouts in *Liverpool* sighted a single Italian torpedo-bomber which had overflown the ship before the anti-aircraft gunners had time to open fire. Two minutes later there was a terrific explosion as a torpedo slammed into *Liverpool*'s bow. The force of the blast almost blew off the ship's bow and it also started a fierce fire which, at 1920, ignited petrol storage tanks in the bow causing another huge explosion. Altogether three officers and 27 ratings died as a result of the two very violent explosions, the second of which left the cruiser's bow section as far aft as 30 Station hanging precariously. The forward section was evacuated and as preparations were made for her to be taken in tow aft, the pinnace, motor boats and Carley floats were hoisted out in case it became necessary to abandon the ship. In the forward section, emergency fire and damage control parties struggled to control the raging fires and to assist them in this the

A view forward following the torpedo strike of 14 October. The bows are still attached, but twisted to starboard, and the roof has been torn away from 'A' turret. *(T. Ferrers-Walker Collection)*

On 16 October, HMS Liverpool *arrived, under tow, at Alexandria, minus the complete bow section which had fallen away during the morning of 15 October.* *(Syd Goodman Collection)*

engines were driven slow astern. In the meantime *Orion* and two destroyers stood by until, at 2320, with the fires out and lines secured, *Orion* commenced towing the crippled *Liverpool* by the stern.

After two hours of slowly being towed towards her destination, at just after 1100 on 15 October the tow line parted and *Liverpool* was left wallowing helplessly. By 1430 new towing lines had been prepared and were being passed to *Orion* when, without any warning whatever and with a terrific crash and grinding of metal, *Liverpool*'s bow section, right up to 30 Station, fell away into the sea. Immediately the cruiser's engines were driven astern and thereafter, at between 7½ and 9½ knots, *Liverpool* set course, astern, for Alexandria. Although steering the ship proved to be very difficult she maintained a steady course, and finally at 1415 on Wednesday 16 October she was secured alongside No 81 quay at Alexandria.

It was clear that *Liverpool* would be out of service for many months and on 27 October Captain Read left the ship for *Ramillies*. On 13 January 1941 *Liverpool*'s new commanding officer, Captain A. L. Poland DSO DSC RN, assumed command. The ship herself lay alongside the dock at Alexandria for six months while forward compartments were sealed off and a temporary bow structure was built. It was 29 April before the work was completed and the ship put to sea to run an eight-hour series of trials. At 1030 the next day she again put to sea, this time bound for Suez and Aden. On 5 May she reached Aden, where she was secured to a specially laid buoy, and during her 24-hour visit a full survey of the temporary bow was carried out. The cruiser was bound for San Francisco, by way of Colombo and Singapore where, on 17 May, she secured alongside the naval base and the temporary bow was strengthened. Three days later *Liverpool* continued her passage via Manila and Pearl Harbor, finally arriving during the early hours of Monday 16 June alongside Mare Island Naval Base, San Francisco. Ten days later, having been de-stored and de-ammunitioned, she was shifted into dry dock where the task of rebuilding the bow began.

HMS Liverpool, *on 22 October 1941, following repairs at Mare Island Navy Yard, California.*
(Steve Bush Collection)

These permanent repairs took three months, and it was the second week of September before she was moved from dry dock to secure alongside *Orion*, which was also undergoing major repairs for damage caused by bombs during the battle for Crete. On 21 September *Liverpool*'s new commanding officer, Captain W. R. Slayter DSO RN, arrived onboard, and on 22 October the ship began a series of trials off San Francisco. Finally, on 3 November, she left the city to steam via Panama and Norfolk, Virginia, to the naval base at Ireland Island, Bermuda, where she remained for ten days to carry out a programme of work-up exercises. On 29 November she left Bermuda to make a fast six-day transatlantic crossing to Greenock where she anchored during the evening of 5 December. Five days later she steamed upriver to secure in Glasgow's King George V Dock where, over the next seven weeks, her refit would be completed.

During *Liverpool*'s stay on the Clyde work was carried out to fit and update her radar outfit, with Type 273 and Type 281 surface and aircraft warning sets, together with Type 284 and 285 main armament and anti-aircraft fire control radar being installed. The cruiser remained in Glasgow until 28 January 1942, when she moved downriver to Greenock. Nine days later she sailed north to Scapa Flow where, during the afternoon of 17 February, she rejoined the fleet and became part of the 18th Cruiser Squadron.

For six weeks after her return to Scapa Flow *Liverpool* carried out a busy work-up programme, with an emphasis on anti-aircraft firings against Spitfires from nearby RAF bases, and it was 29 March when the schedule was completed with an inspection by Rear-Admiral Bonham Carter (CS18). *Liverpool*'s first operational duties began on 3 April when she left Scapa Flow to begin her first Arctic convoy escort. The cruiser made a fast passage to the Kola Inlet in order to escort the empty, homeward-bound convoy QP10. Arriving during the early evening of 7 April she spent four days in the bleak Russian waterway, before leaving with the convoy and being closely shadowed by German reconnaissance aircraft. Also forming part of the escort were the cruisers *Kent* and *Nigeria*, together with destroyers and smaller vessels. Providing distant cover were capital ships of the Home Fleet, and for three days the convoy and escorts came under attack by U-boats; on one occasion a torpedo passed just ahead of *Liverpool*'s port bow. The convoy arrived at Reykjavik on 21 April, but four of the 16 merchantmen had been lost to the U-boats. On 18 April, however, *Liverpool* was ordered to detach from the convoy, first to Seydisfjord and then to Scapa Flow.

After returning to Scapa *Liverpool* carried out a further programme of training exercises, but on 6 May she returned north to Seydisfjord. Together with *Nigeria* and a destroyer screen, she was under orders to steam from Iceland to a position close to Bear Island, where they were to rendezvous with the damaged cruiser *Trinidad* and escort her to Iceland and Scapa Flow. In March *Trinidad* had been badly damaged by one of her own torpedoes which it was believed had suffered a faulty gyro mechanism. She had managed to reach Murmansk where she underwent temporary repairs, before leaving the Russian port on 13 May to return home. However, with her speed limited to 20 knots and poor manoeuvrability, she was obviously vulnerable to attack by both aircraft and submarines. On 12 May *Liverpool*, *Nigeria* and the destroyer screen left Seydisfjord intending to make the rendezvous with *Trinidad*, but three days later when in the vicinity of Bear Island the two cruisers came under heavy air attack by 12 Ju-88 bombers. One bomb exploded very close to *Liverpool*'s port side aft, but she came through undamaged. Further east, however, *Trinidad* had also come under heavy air attack and had suffered further severe damage, which led to the decision to scuttle her. All that remained was for *Liverpool* and *Nigeria* to return to Icelandic waters. During the afternoon of 17 May they anchored in Hvalfjord. Six days later, this time in company with *Kent, Nigeria, Norfolk* and a destroyer screen, she left Iceland to escort a large 36-ship convoy, PQ16, bound for Archangel and

Murmansk. On 25 and 26 May the convoy came under heavy air and submarine attack, which took its toll on the merchant ships, with seven being lost. However, *Liverpool* did not complete the passage to the Kola Inlet, as she was detached to escort the empty homeward-bound convoy, QP12, and on 28 May she again anchored in Scapa Flow.

On Wednesday 3 June 1942, *Liverpool* and *Kenya* were ordered south to Greenock, from where they were to form part of the escort for a convoy of six merchant ships[2] which were transporting vital relief supplies to Malta. The convoy was code-named 'WS 192' within the whole massive escort operation known as 'Operation Harpoon'. In addition to *Kenya* (Vice-Admiral T. B. Curteis), *Liverpool*, and ten destroyers of the 17th Flotilla, at Gibraltar they would be joined by *Malaya, Eagle, Argus, Cairo, Charybdis*, seven more destroyers, plus minesweepers and motor launches. The operation was being mounted simultaneously with a similar convoy which would sail to Malta from Alexandria. *Kenya*, *Liverpool* and the ten destroyers left Greenock during the late evening of 4 June, and next day they rendezvoused with the six merchant ships, which had formed up and set course, via mid-Atlantic, to Gibraltar. During the passage to Gibraltar both Portuguese and Spanish merchant ships were encountered, and it was almost certain that the presence of the convoy was reported to German and Italian embassies in those countries. At 2300 on 11 June *Liverpool* was ordered to make a fast passage under cover of darkness through the Strait of Gibraltar in order to refuel, and to rejoin the convoy the next day. At half past midnight on 12 June she anchored in Gibraltar Bay where she refuelled from an RFA and four hours later she was under way, rejoining the convoy at 0800.

During Saturday 13 June, as the convoy slowly steamed east through the Mediterranean, *Liverpool* and *Argus* were on station ahead of the convoy, and although the day passed quietly, enemy reconnaissance aircraft kept the ships under constant observation. The next day, Sunday 14 June, began quietly, but at 0700 enemy reconnaissance aircraft were detected by radar and it became apparent that an air attack was imminent. With *Liverpool* on station ahead of the convoy she was in a vulnerable position, and she would be one of the first targets for the attacking bombers. By 1028 the convoy was some 120 miles south-west of Sardinia, when the first air attack by three formations of high-level bombers began. Although all the bombs missed their targets, several dropped uncomfortably close to *Argus* and another crashed into the sea close to *Liverpool*'s starboard bow. No sooner had that raid cleared than at 1108 torpedo-bombers were sighted low on the horizon and 20 minutes later an attack by 28 of the aircraft developed, with 13 coming in on *Liverpool*'s starboard side and 15 on the port side. On the cruiser's port side the fierce AA barrage ensured that few of the torpedo-bombers got through, but on the starboard side the three groups of aircraft forced their attacks home. At 1125 a torpedo crashed into *Liverpool*'s starboard side where it exploded with terrific force in the after engine room, killing 13 men and wounding many more. Two seamen were also killed by cannon fire from one aircraft as it flew low over the ship. In the same attack MV *Tanimbar* was also hit and later sank.

Once again *Liverpool* had been very seriously damaged by an airborne torpedo, and she was detached immediately from the convoy to return to Gibraltar, with the destroyers *Antelope* and *Westcott* standing by her. This time, however, with her main propulsion machinery badly damaged *Liverpool* could make only two to three knots, and at 1240 she was taken in tow by *Antelope*, while *Westcott* provided anti-submarine protection. Her troubles, however, were still far from over for, at 1626, the tow line parted and ten minutes later the cruiser was attacked by five dive-bombers. Although she emerged unscathed, two bombs exploded very close to her damaged starboard side. At 1422 the cruiser was subjected to an audacious attack by three tor-

[2] The six merchantmen were: SS *Kentucky* (oil tanker), SS *Troilus*, SS *Chant*, SS *Orari*, SS *Bundawan* and MV *Tanimbar*.

pedo boats, with one torpedo passing close to the stern of the ship, and between 1700 and 2300 she was subjected to three more air attacks, but there were no further hits. It was not long, however, before the cruiser was within range of air protection from Gibraltar and two tugs from the Colony took over the tow. The remainder of the passage passed without incident, and at 1740 on 17 June she was secured alongside the detached mole at Gibraltar.

Once alongside the damage to *Liverpool*'s wrecked after engine room could be properly surveyed, and the bodies of the 12 ratings killed in the compartment were recovered by the ship's divers and landed for burial. The ship herself remained in Gibraltar undergoing temporary repairs for seven weeks, but finally, at 2230 on 5 August, she left Gibraltar bound for Rosyth where she arrived safely seven days later. For *Liverpool* it was the end of the war, for she would remain in dockyard hands for three years. By mid-September 1942 her ship's company had been reduced to just a small care and maintenance party, and on 14 October the ship was paid off completely and placed in dockyard hands.

Although the repair work to the action damage sustained by *Liverpool* was completed by the summer of 1943, she remained in dockyard hands for another two years. During this time X turret and the aircraft catapult were removed, and additional AA armament in the form of pom-poms and 20mm Oerlikon cannons was fitted. The ship's radar outfit was again modernised with the installation of Type 281B air warning, and Type 293 surface warning, with its associated height finder Type 277. The main armament fire control radar was replaced by Type 274; barrage control Type 283 radar was also fitted. In July 1945 the ship's complement was increased to three-fifths full strength, and on 30 July she left the main basin at Rosyth for the first time since August 1942 to anchor in midriver. Next day she put to sea to carry out the first of a series of post-refit trials which continued through to 12 August, when she sailed for Portland. She arrived two days later – the same day that Japan agreed to surrender unconditionally.

On the last day of August *Liverpool* was ordered north to Cairnryan, where she secured alongside to act as an accommodation ship for a large delegation of senior British, Russian and American naval officers, all members of the Allied Control Commission employed to oversee the disarming of the German Navy and the disposal of large numbers of U-boats. At that time there were over 80 surrendered German submarines in Loch Ryan and one of them, *U-369*, was secured alongside *Liverpool* for two days and opened to the public[3]. On Monday 10 September, with the Commission having decided which U-boats would be allocated to particular Navies and which should be sunk at sea, they left the ship and *Liverpool* returned, via Greenock and Portsmouth, to Portland. On 1 October she was back in Portsmouth Dockyard.

HMS *Liverpool* had been allocated to the Mediterranean Fleet and on 10 October 1945, after embarking Sir D'Arcy Osborne, the British Ambassador to the Holy See, and his retinue of staff for passage, the cruiser left Portsmouth for Malta. For seven weeks after her arrival in Grand Harbour she carried out an intense programme of work-up exercises, with the first relaxation coming on 7 December with a six-day visit to Naples. After the end of the Second World War certain parts of Europe presented the USA and Britain with particular problems, and one such area was Trieste. Once part of the Austro-Hungarian Empire, at the end of the Great War the city had been occupied by the Italian Army, which in those days was an Allied nation. In May 1945, however, Yugoslavia under Communist President Tito held full control of the city and it was only after difficult negotiations that Tito's Army withdrew, leaving Trieste to a joint US/British Administration. It was, however, an uneasy agreement and the US and Britain were in an awkward position in that they found it distasteful to hand it over to Tito who was a Communist, and impossible

[3] In the winter of 1945/46, as part of 'Operation Deadlight', *U-369* was towed out to sea and sunk some 130 miles north-west of Loch Foyle.

to hand it over to Italy which had until recently been a hostile power. During this difficult period, which lasted until 1947, America and Britain stationed troops in the city and also kept a strong naval presence in the Adriatic. On 18 December *Liverpool* was ordered to sail for Trieste, where she arrived three days later to spend Christmas and the New Year in the port city. On 7 January she left Trieste to return to Malta, passing en route her sister *Newcastle* which was employed carrying troops to Colombo, and once back in Grand Harbour hoisted the flag of the C-in-C Mediterranean Fleet, Admiral Sir John Cunningham.

As the flagship of the Mediterranean Fleet *Liverpool* began the new year of 1946 with official visits to Tangier, where she was the first major warship to secure alongside the quay, Algiers and Casablanca, where the C-in-C attended conferences with French and American counterparts. In early February she joined with French warships in the Western Mediterranean, and after calling at Gibraltar and Naples returned to Malta. On 19 March, after exercising with the destroyers *Marne, Matchless, Milne* and *Musketeer*, the five ships began a tour of French Riviera ports, with *Liverpool* visiting Toulon and Cannes. During her four-day stay in Cannes she was joined by the four destroyers, and on 30 March the C-in-C hosted a luncheon on board the cruiser where, as well as civic officials, the principal guests were the Duke and Duchess of Windsor. By 3 April *Liverpool* was back in Malta, but 48 hours later she left for the troubled Mandate territory of Palestine, where the consequences of A. J. Balfour's infamous 'Declaration' of 1917 were having appalling repercussions which its author had been warned of, but which had been ignored – namely a vicious insurgency, fought by mainly Eastern European Zionist immigrants to Palestine, designed to oust Britain from its UN role as the Mandatory Power. In April 1946 Jewish extremists had detonated a large bomb on the railway line outside Haifa, and at the same time the indigenous Palestinian workforce in Haifa had gone on strike. *Liverpool* was ordered to the port in order to assist generally with the security situation, and to ensure that the harbour facilities were kept open. The cruiser arrived at Haifa on 7 April, and after securing stern to at the main jetty, strict security precautions were put in place including the exploding of small TNT charges in the water alongside, and the ship's divers making regular round-the-clock searches beneath the ship[4]. Shore leave for the ship's company was strictly limited, and working parties from the ship assisted the port authorities. By late April, with the security situation having improved and the strikes having been called off, *Liverpool* sailed for Alexandria and Port Said, but by 10 May she had returned to Malta.

During the remainder of that month, flying the flag of the C-in-C, now Admiral Sir Algernon Willis, and accompanied by the destroyer *Volage*, *Liverpool* paid flag-showing visits to Villefranche and Algiers before returning to Malta. On 10 June, however, she was once again ordered to Trieste where there was concern that unrest in Italy, where people had voted by a large majority to become a Republic, might spill over into the city. In the event, however, the fears were unfounded and after a short visit to Venice, on the last day of June *Liverpool* returned to Malta. On 3 July, as she lay in Grand Harbour, the battleship *Duke of York,* flying the flag of Admiral Sir Bruce Fraser, the outgoing C-in-C of the British Pacific Fleet, passed through on her way home from the Pacific to Devonport. During the first two weeks of July *Liverpool* took part in joint manoeuvres with *Chivalrous, Venus, Virago* and *Volage*, but the latter half of the month was spent in Palestinian waters and the ports of Jaffa and Haifa, and at anchor off Gaza, where the violence orchestrated by the three terrorist organisations, Hagana, Irgun Zvia Leumi and the Stern Group, had reached new heights. In the event *Liverpool*'s role was confined to patrolling the coast, with only brief calls at the strife-torn ports. These patrols continued at intervals through to mid-September when, after visiting ports in the southern Aegean she called at

[4] On 31 April 1946 an attempt was made to detonate a bomb on board the destroyer *Chevron* at Haifa.

Piraeus, from where she left in company with *Childers* to carry out an anti-submarine exercise prior to a meeting of the Mediterranean Fleet. In a throwback to pre-war days the Mediterranean Fleet manoeuvres were to have taken place south of Greece, with weekend breaks at Argostoli where the Fleet Regatta would be held. At the same time as *Liverpool* had been visiting Piraeus, other ships of the fleet, including the cruisers *Leander* and *Mauritius*, together with the destroyers *Saumarez* and *Volage*, had been visiting the island of Corfu. During the afternoon of 22 October the four ships began leaving Corfu harbour to join *Liverpool* (flag C-in-C) and the rest of the fleet south of Greece. Some months earlier, in mid-May, Albanian coastal batteries had shelled the cruisers *Orion* and *Superb* as they passed through the narrow channel between Corfu and the Albanian coast, so during the afternoon of 22 October all eyes on board the four warships were closely watching the Albanian shore. However, as they navigated the North Corfu Channel the danger did not come from gun batteries, but from mines, two of which were detonated by *Saumarez* and *Volage*, causing severe damage and heavy casualties in both ships. The force of the explosion almost blew *Volage*'s bow off, while *Saumarez* suffered severe damage forward, between 'A' and 'B' gun turrets, which started a large fire. Eventually the two destroyers were towed back into Corfu. Meanwhile, as soon as the C-in-C learned of the incident, he immediately ordered *Liverpool* and *Childers* to abandon their anti-submarine exercises and return to Corfu with all dispatch.They arrived off Corfu in the early hours of 23 October, but waited for daylight before proceeding very slowly into the harbour and it was almost 0900 before *Liverpool* finally anchored. As soon as the ship was safely at rest the C-in-C left the cruiser to make an inspection of the two damaged ships, and later that day the heavy repair ship *Ranpura* arrived in harbour; she had facilities and equipment to begin the major repairs necessary to keep them afloat and to get them back to the dockyard facilities in Malta. *Liverpool* remained at Corfu for three days during which time a Court of Inquiry met and opened before adjourning. At 0900 on 26 October, *Liverpool* weighed anchor and, accompanied by *Cardigan Bay* and *Childers*, sailed for Argostoli to join the ships which had assembled. However, there were no joint manoeuvres, evolutions or regattas, with the fleet gathering being a very subdued affair, and on the last day of October *Liverpool* returned to Grand Harbour.

On 11 November *Liverpool* left Malta and anchored later in the day off Augusta, Sicily, from where, seven days later, she sailed to stand by and escort the hulk of *Saumarez* which, with her bow section having been deliberately blown off in Corfu Harbour, was being towed stern first to Malta. Later that day she rendezvoused with *Saumarez* and remained with her for over 24 hours, but as the tow neared Augusta she was detached for Naples, where she made an eight-day visit to the Italian port. By the end of November *Liverpool* was back in Malta, which is where she remained for nine weeks as she underwent docking and maintenance. According to one member of the ship's company: '*The ship was invaded by hordes of dockyard mateys, with their spanners and well-stocked lunch boxes*'. For the ship's company Christmas and the New Year came and went all too quickly and on 3 February 1947 *Liverpool* was once again at sea and undergoing post-refit trials. By 17 February she had once again hoisted the flag of the C-in-C Mediterranean before leading *Cheviot, Childers* and *Verulam* to the Western Mediterranean for training exercises and visits to Tangier, Algiers and Bizerta. During March *Liverpool* visited Naples, after which she was joined by the aircraft carriers *Ocean* and *Triumph*. In early April she carried out amphibious landing exercises during which she carried a detachment of Gordon Highlanders to assault beaches close to their base at Trieste. Much of late April was spent in and around Trieste, with a short visit to Venice, but during May *Liverpool* remained in Grand Harbour undergoing maintenance. She remained close to Malta in June, with only one 'foreign' weekend visit to Palermo.

On Thursday 17 July, flying the flag of the C-in-C, *Liverpool* led the Mediterranean Fleet out of Grand Harbour to begin a summer cruise to ports in Turkey, Russia and the Eastern Mediterranean. In the late 1940s the Royal Navy could still boast a powerful fleet based on Malta, and accompanying her on the joint manoeuvres and cruise were the aircraft carriers *Triumph* (Flag FO (Air) Med) and *Ocean*, the cruisers *Mauritius, Phoebe* and *Leander*, as well as 17 destroyers and frigates. After two days of exercises the first port of call for the whole fleet was Istanbul, where thousands of local people turned out to see the ships arrive. From there the fleet split up to visit ports in Russia, Greece, Cyprus and Palestine, with *Liverpool*, *Chaplet* and *Chequers* steaming through the Bosporus into the Black Sea for Sevastopol where, during the morning of 28 July, they rendezvoused with the Russian destroyer *Zheleznyakov*, which escorted them into harbour. The visit to the Black Sea Fleet had been organised by the C-in-C at the personal request of Ernest Bevin, the Home Secretary, in order to '*make contact with the Russian people wherever and whenever possible and at any level*', which to the C-in-C seemed '*eminently sensible*'. According to contemporary reports: '*The C-in-C and his officers and men were very cordially received by Admiral Oktiaberski, the commander of the Black Sea Fleet, and men of his command. Official lunches and receptions were held, and a number of sporting events and excursions were arranged*'. These included trips to Yalta, the Crimean holiday resort, which was still in the process of being rebuilt following the devastation caused by the severe fighting in 1943 and again in 1944 when the German Army was finally driven out. After the visit the C-in-C reported: '*The officers and men under my command supported me so well with their usual tact, good humour and common sense on what was not an easy visit to a foreign port. Moreover they created an excellent impression on the local inhabitants.*' The visit ended during the forenoon of 31 July when *Liverpool*, *Chaplet* and *Chequers* steamed south and, early next morning, passed through the Bosporus on their way to the Dardanelles where they stopped for two hours to allow for visits to war graves. On 2 August, having joined the rest of the fleet at Nauplia (Novplio), the C-in-C hosted a reception on board *Liverpool* for the King and Queen of the Hellenes. On 11 August, with the fleet having reassembled, a major convoy escort exercise took place around Cyprus, with *Triumph* and *Mauritius* taking the role of the convoy. On 22 August *Liverpool* returned to Malta to begin a four-week docking and maintenance period.

On 19 September, once again flying the flag of the C-in-C, *Liverpool* was joined by the destroyers *Chequers, Childers, Chivalrous* and *Troubridge* for training exercises and manoeuvres in the Western Mediterranean, which culminated in a three-day visit to Toulon. On 10 October she returned to Grand Harbour where the C-in-C struck his flag, but after just nine days' stay she embarked 19 officers and 118 ratings for the passage home. Finally, at 0900 on 20 October, with her decks manned, her band playing and her paying-off pennant flying, she left Grand Harbour to make a fast non-stop homeward passage. Seven days later, during the early morning of 27 October, she passed the South Goodwin Light Vessel, and at just before midday she secured to a buoy off Sheerness. Three days later she steamed up the River Medway to Chatham Dockyard where she paid off.

It was March 1948 before *Liverpool* was once again ready for sea, and on 17 March her new commanding officer, Captain K. Mackintosh RN assumed command. On the last day of the month, with her ship's company having been brought up to full strength, basin trials began, and six days later the cruiser left the dockyard to secure to a buoy off Folly Point. On 9 April *Liverpool* left Sheerness to spend a weekend alongside the submarine depot ship *Adamant* at Portsmouth's Pitch House Jetty before moving on to Portland where she spent three days, before sailing for Gibraltar and Malta. During her outward passage she carried 27 cases of Olympic torches which would be relayed back to London for the start of that year's Games. She

HMS Liverpool *at Spithead on 10 April 1948.* *(National Museum of the Royal Navy)*

arrived in Grand Harbour on 24 April, where she took over from *Mauritius* which left for Portsmouth. The Olympic torches were disembarked for onward transmission to Athens. Soon after her arrival she briefly hoisted the flag of the C-in-C Mediterranean Fleet, Sir Algernon Willis, then on 13 May he was relieved by Admiral Sir Arthur Power, who arrived on board and hoisted his flag that same morning. Four days later *Liverpool* sailed to begin a two-week programme of work-up exercises.

On 4 July, having embarked the C-in-C and his staff, *Liverpool* left Grand Harbour to make her summer cruise to Greek ports and the Eastern Mediterranean. At Piraeus she received a visit from the King and Queen of the Hellenes, after which she steamed on to Salonika and Santorini before joining *Chequers* at anchor off Famagusta. The next port of call was at the British military base close to the Suez port of El-Fayid. As one member of the ship's company remembers: '*Our trip through the Canal was without incident, as was our arrival at El-Fayid. The organisation and reception read like a debutante's diary. Plenty of dancing, swimming, cricket and football, not forgetting that ancient but not forgotten art, "elbow bending". We said good-bye to Fayid with much regret and on to pastures new.*' The 'pastures new' were in fact Port Said and Alexandria, the latter being a port in which *Liverpool* had spent some months when it was the former wartime base for the fleet. This time, however, local feelings about the continued British military presence in the country were running high, and the security situation ashore meant there was no general leave granted, with recreation limited to a few organised and heavily guarded sports parties. From Alexandria *Liverpool* steamed north to Argostoli to join fleet manoeuvres, before detaching for a short visit to Trieste and returning on the last day of July to Malta.

During the whole of August and the first three weeks of September, *Liverpool* remained in Grand Harbour carrying out maintenance, but in the last week of the month she put to sea and resumed her

duties as the fleet's flagship. It was in this capacity that she paid official visits to Naples, Aranci Bay and Toulon, then after a short break at Gibraltar, she continued the cruise with visits to Tangier and the French naval base at Oran. On 25 October she returned to Malta, and for the rest of the year she remained in local waters around the island. On 6 December 1948, with the C-in-C having transferred his flag to *Newcastle*, the newly arrived Flag Officer 1st Cruiser Squadron (CS1), Rear-Admiral Lord Mountbatten, hoisted his flag in *Liverpool* – an appointment which earned her the reputation of being a 'high society' ship.

On 4 January 1949, flying Mountbatten's flag, *Liverpool* was accompanied by *Phoebe* and *Euryalus* for visits to Trieste, Venice and Phaleron Bay, before returning to Malta to join up with the main body of the Mediterranean Fleet. Among the ships present at the time were the battleship *Vanguard*, as well as the light fleet carrier *Triumph*, the cruiser *Newcastle* and the destroyers *Chequers, Cheviot, Chieftain, Childers, Chivalrous, Venus, Verulam* and the recently repaired *Volage*, as well as the submarines *Tabard, Tantivy, Templar* and *Teredo*. At Gibraltar they joined ships of the Home Fleet, which included the battleship *Duke of York*, the aircraft carriers *Implacable* and *Theseus*, the cruisers *Cleopatra, Diadem, Sirius* and *Superb*, together with destroyers *Agincourt, Aisne, Alamein, Barossa, Jutland, St James, Sluys* and *Solebay*, and the submarine *Andrew*. It was the largest gathering of Royal Navy warships at Gibraltar since 'Operation Torch', the North African landings in November 1942. This exercise was 'Operation Twostep', a programme of joint Home and Mediterranean Fleet exercises in the Western Mediterranean and Eastern Atlantic. The main manoeuvres took place between 5 and 9 March, and ended with what was described as, '*... a confused "battle" in the western end of the Strait of Gibraltar between 2230 and 0230 this morning. Vice-Admiral Russell's Blue defending forces felt confident that Rear-Admiral Lord Mountbatten's raiders had all been destroyed, and that Vice-Admiral Douglas-Pennant's supporting force had been staved off until it was too late to help them. Admiral Russell decided yesterday afternoon that his best plan was to lie in wait west of Tarifa. The speed of the supporting force had been reduced because of air attack, which gave good hope that the raiders could be destroyed before assistance could come to them. Surface contact was first made with Lord Mountbatten's main force along the Spanish coast at 2320. By 0210 this force of two cruisers and one destroyer was attacked by four cruisers and destroyed at the cost of one cruiser,* Diadem, *which was out of action for an hour. Admiral Russell had sent his two carriers to anchor under the guns of Gibraltar for the night, so he was able to dispatch five destroyers to intercept three of Lord Mountbatten's which were seen on Monday creeping up the Moroccan coast. This left one destroyer and one cruiser of the raiders to be accounted for. The former was discovered disguised as a merchantman by the destroyer* Jutland *and sunk. The missing cruiser, also disguised, was located by the* Duke of York, *and was engaged and sunk just before radar reports made it known that* Vanguard *(representing two Red battleships) and destroyers were approaching in the rear 11 miles to the east.* Vanguard *had been engaged by the guns of Gibraltar's fixed defences, but not damaged. Admiral Russell's defending forces therefore claimed that before 0300 they had completely destroyed the raiders and were free to turn east to engage the supporting battleships with superior forces. Before returning to Gibraltar today (9 March), the combined fleets engaged in manoeuvres east of Gibraltar in which air striking forces from the three carriers attacked the ships, which were defended by combat air patrols. Rain and mist prevented the full scheme of the manoeuvres from being carried out.*' With the exercises over the ships of the Mediterranean Fleet remained at Gibraltar for six days before returning to Malta, with *Liverpool* calling at Golfe Juan and Villefranche en route, and arriving in Grand Harbour on 1 April.

Five days after her return to Malta, *Liverpool* was

HMS Liverpool *on exercise in the Mediterranean post-war.* *(Ken Kelly Collection)*

at sea again, this time to take part in a short 48-hour amphibious landing exercise with *Newcastle*, during which both cruisers embarked troops for landings on Malta's north coast, after which *Liverpool* returned to Grand Harbour to begin a seven-week maintenance and docking period. This kept her out of routine until 30 May, after which she carried out two days of trials. At 0921 on 14 June *Liverpool* joined *Vanguard* (flag C-in-C), *Ocean* and *Surprise* at sea for a mini fleet review which was staged to bid farewell to the outgoing British Governor of Malta, the politician Sir Francis Douglas. The Governor, who was embarked in *Surprise*, took the salute as first *Vanguard*, followed by the light fleet carrier *Ocean*, then *Liverpool* leading the 1st Cruiser Squadron, and finally destroyers, frigates, minesweepers and submarines, steamed past, after which aircraft from *Ocean* flew overhead dipping their wings in salute. On completion of the fly past the fleet returned to harbour and four days later left for its summer manoeuvres and cruise. Some 20 ships took part in the cruise that year, over a period of four weeks visiting four countries and showing the flag in a dozen different ports. For *Liverpool* the first call was in Libya, which in those days was the home of a number of Second World War British military bases. The visit coincided with an inspection of the Army bases by the Chief of the Imperial General Staff, Field Marshal Sir William Slim, who visited *Liverpool* for a conference with Mountbatten. During the week which followed Slim's visit *Liverpool* embarked Army personnel to carry out an amphibious landing exercise on the Libyan coast at Zwara, close to the border with

Tunisia. After leaving Libyan waters, on 27 June *Liverpool* rendezvoused off Cyprus with other ships of her squadron including *Euryalus*, *Newcastle* and *Phoebe*, to carry out four days of exercises before *Liverpool* detached to visit Rhodes and Navarin, where she again hosted a visit by the King and Queen of the Hellenes. The last two ports of call on her agenda were Argostoli and Corfu before she returned to Malta on 24 July.

After remaining in and around Malta during August and the first week of September, *Liverpool* joined *Newcastle* (flag C-in-C, Admiral Sir Arthur Power), *Chaplet, Childers* and *Chivalrous*, for a cruise which took them to ports in southern France, Italy, Sicily, Sardinia, Corsica, Algeria and Tunisia. *Liverpool* herself visited San Remo, Villefranche, Naples, Capri and Palermo, arriving back in Malta on 12 October. Three days later, at 1012 on 15 October, Captain J. D. Shaw-Hamilton RN joined the ship and took over from Mackintosh. Following the change of command *Liverpool* remained in local waters for the remainder of the year, and in December she was the venue for a number of social occasions arranged by Mountbatten for his nephew the Duke of Edinburgh who, with HRH Princess Elizabeth, was based in Malta.

On 2 January 1950 *Liverpool* left Malta on a short cruise to Piraeus, Beirut and finally Alexandria. This final port of call was the most important, and during the five days the cruiser spent alongside, Mountbatten had a long meeting with King Farouk about the presence of the British military bases at Suez, which were becoming ever more a focus for nationalist unrest and discontent in the country. On 23 January Mountbatten's visit to Cairo was reciprocated when King Farouk paid a visit to *Liverpool* and Mountbatten entertained him to lunch. This was a prelude to a visit by the Foreign Secretary Ernest Bevin the following week, when high on the agenda would be the subject of the British bases in the

In March 1950, HMS Liverpool *took part in a series of Anglo-French exercises in the Mediterranean, for which she was the British Flagship.* *(Ken Kelly Collection)*

Suez Canal Zone. As it turned out the courting of King Farouk by British politicians was all in vain for within two years he was ousted, to be replaced by nationalist military leaders. By 25 January, however, *Liverpool* was back in Malta and remained in local waters until early March.

On Friday 3 March 1950, *Liverpool* arrived at Toulon in advance of a series of joint exercises with ships of a French squadron from the city's naval base. During the manoeuvres the ships came under the command of the French Vice-Admiral Lambert, flying his flag in the aircraft carrier FS *Arromanches* (ex-HMS *Colossus*). They lasted for nine days, and included short visits to French naval bases at Mers-el-Kebir in Algeria. These exercises were closely followed by joint manoeuvres involving ships of both the Home and Mediterranean Fleets, during which the Blue side, consisting mainly of the Mediterranean Fleet, escorted a convoy out of the Mediterranean through a 'hostile' Strait of Gibraltar, while the Red Home Fleet was given the task of intercepting and destroying the convoy. These manoeuvres lasted for three days, and it was not until the last day of March that *Liverpool* returned to Malta.

During April 1950 she remained in local waters around Malta, and on 27 April she embarked HRH Princess Elizabeth for a day at sea to watch anti-submarine exercises and amphibious landing operations in and around Marsaxlokk Bay. Next day the cruiser returned to Grand Harbour, and on 8 May Mountbatten hauled down his flag and handed command of the 1st Cruiser squadron to his successor Rear-Admiral C. T. M. Pizey, who hoisted his flag in *Phoebe*. It was the end of *Liverpool*'s commission and she was taken in hand by Malta Dockyard to undergo a 12-week docking and maintenance period. During the months that *Liverpool* was laid up high and dry in Malta's No 5 dry dock almost the whole of her ship's company was changed, with the troopship *Empress of Australia* bringing out the main body of the new personnel to Malta, and in the last week of July the cruiser recommissioned for the last time. In mid-August *Liverpool* put to sea to carry out a three-week trials and work-up period, during which she was assisted by *Saintes* and the aircraft carrier *Warrior*.

In mid-September, together with *Euryalus*, *Chieftain*, and briefly at the end of September with *Belfast*, which was returning home from the Far East, *Liverpool* operated in the Western Mediterranean, sometimes in company with French warships from Toulon. During October she remained close to Malta, carrying out anti-submarine exercises in company with *Gambia* (flag C-in-C Mediterranean, Admiral Sir John Edelstone). During the remainder of the year *Liverpool* did not leave Maltese waters, and in the new year of 1951 she hoisted the flag of the C-in-C for joint exercises with ships of the Home Fleet and the 6th Fleet. This took her briefly into the Eastern Atlantic, where the manoeuvres included *Vanguard* and *Indomitable*, and ended with a four-day visit to Casablanca. She returned to Malta by way of Algiers, and at the end of March she began a three-week self-maintenance period which kept her out of routine until the third week of April. It was during this period, on 23 April, that the ship's final change of command occurred, when Captain J. D. Luce DSO OBE RN took over from Shaw-Hamilton. Following her maintenance *Liverpool* remained in local waters until the first week of June.

On 4 June she left Malta to join the flag of the C-in-C in *Surprise*, and the destroyers *Armada*, *Chieftain, Chevron, Chivalrous* and the RFA *Fort Duquesne*, acting as the 'convoy' during manoeuvres which took the ships into the Adriatic to Trieste, returning to Malta by way of Taranto, Venice, Milos and the Turkish port of Marmaris. Here firefighting parties were landed to assist the local fire brigades in extinguishing bush fires in the countryside around the port which, owing to abnormally high temperatures and lack of rain, were spontaneously breaking out in the surrounding hills. By mid-July, however, she had returned to Grand Harbour.

During August *Liverpool* and other ships of the fleet operated in Greek waters, and in the area

HMS Liverpool *at Grand Harbour, Malta, in June 1951.* *(Maritime Photo Library)*

around Cyprus. It had been intended that, flying the flag of the C-in-C, she would make a five-day official visit to the Egyptian ports of Alexandria and Port Said, but deteriorating diplomatic relations between Britain and Egypt over the continued presence of British military bases in the Suez Canal Zone led to the visits being cancelled. It was a problem which would dog British/Egyptian relations for at least four more years, until the ill-fated Suez Crisis decided the matter decisively in Egypt's favour. Instead of steaming south *Liverpool* remained in Greek waters and in early September, with other ships of the Mediterranean Fleet, carried out bombardment exercises off the south coast of Cyprus. On completion of these *Liverpool* set course for Split in Yugoslavia (now Croatia) for the first official visit of a British warship since before the start of the Second World War. The British Government naturally was keen that it should be seen as a success, as was President Tito, and the day before the ship's arrival he had transferred to his villa in Split[5]. When *Liverpool* entered harbour at 0805 on Tuesday 11 September it was with full ceremony, including a 21-gun salute. Within hours of the cruiser's arrival the C-in-C had been invited to the President's villa for lunch, and later in the day, an hour earlier than the time scheduled for his visit '*...the Marshal's barge was observed under way with his standard flying*'. With most of the ship's company in working rig and employed clearing up decks there was a flurry of activity on board, described by the C-in-C as '*a creditable evolution*', with the Royal Marines Guard and Band and the ship's company changing quickly into ceremonial uniforms and dashing up to the quarterdeck to fall in for Divisions at exactly the time that Tito's barge drew alongside. The C-in-C's report of proceedings went on to describe the meeting thus: '*The Marshal*

[5] Tito was, in fact, himself Croatian.

inspected the Royal Marines Guard and was then introduced to the officers. He subsequently inspected the whole ship's company at Divisions and then accompanied me to my day cabin. At the end of a short period of conversation in the cabin, the Marshal suddenly said, "Now I would like to look round the ship." He was taken on a tour of the upper deck, armament and bridges and showed great interest in all that he saw. In all, he stayed on board for about one hour and appeared to enjoy the visit very much. He recalled that the last time he was on board one of HM ships was in 1944 when he was transported from Italy to Vis by HMS Blackmore, *a trip that he appeared still to remember with pleasure.*' Three days later, when *Liverpool* left harbour to complete her cruise, with visits to Naples, Thasos and Istanbul, large crowds of local people turned out to bid farewell. By the end of the month she had returned to Malta.

During the first two weeks of October *Liverpool* operated in the Western Mediterranean, but in the latter half of the month serious riots in Egypt's Suez Canal Zone, directed against the British military bases, saw *Liverpool* placed at immediate notice for sea as ships of the Mediterranean Fleet prepared to leave for Port Said. On 24 October, having embarked a brigade of Grenadier Guards, she sailed for Tobruk, where the soldiers disembarked to be held in reserve should it become necessary to reinforce the Suez Canal garrisons. After disembarking her troops, with no let-up in the unrest in Egypt, on 14 November she joined *Manxman* and the landing ship *Striker* at Tobruk to transfer the Guards brigade to the Canal Zone. On 17 November, with the troops having been embarked, the three ships sailed in convoy to Port Said, where they arrived during the forenoon of 19 November. However, once the troops had disembarked, a general strike in Port Said and sabotage to the port facilities meant *Liverpool* had to remain for over four weeks. Each day armed landing parties went ashore to ensure that the port remained open to shipping, and while she was in harbour no leave was granted amid tight security precautions. On 19 December, however,

Since the middle of October 1951 HMS Liverpool *had been lying off Navy House, Port Said, providing officers and men to handle the berthing and unberthing of some 1500 merchant ships in the Suez Canal.* *(Ken Kelly Collection)*

having been relieved by *Gambia*, the ship returned to Malta for the Christmas and New Year festivities.

After spending a week in dry dock, on 8 January 1952 *Liverpool* left Malta to return once again to Port Said, where she joined *Agincourt, Cheviot* and *Chieftain*, and relieved *Gambia*. Once again her ship's company was required to maintain the harbour services necessary to keep the Suez Canal open. A contemporary report describes the situation: '*From the destroyer* Corunna *lying in Lake Timsah off Ismailia, your correspondent was taken in the frigate* Loch Scavaig, *which was leading the morning convoy, northward through the canal to Port Said, and shown a few of the many unfamiliar tasks undertaken by the crew of the cruiser* Liverpool *in their successful efforts to restore the port to conditions as near normal as possible. The cruiser lies off Navy House, dominating the entrance of the canal; her boats range all over the harbour, their crews sometimes armed to the teeth to search for criminals and sometimes stripped to the waist for the slippery job of mooring ships to buoys.*' On 26 January, however, *Liverpool* was ordered to withdraw to Tobruk where she would remain at four hours' notice in case she was required to return to Port Said. In the event her presence was not needed, and on 9 February she was

On 24 April 1952 friends and family greet HMS Liverpool *as she returns to Portsmouth to pay off following a four year commission in the Mediterranean as fleet flagship. Note the balloons supporting her paying-off pennant.*
(Ken Kelly Collection)

ordered to return to Malta, where she arrived three days later.

HMS *Liverpool*'s commission, and operational career, was drawing to a close and on 26 February she left Malta to take part in a large four-power naval training exercise which was designed to increase the ability of allied naval forces and their air arms normally stationed in the Mediterranean to operate together and communicate with one another in the defence of the area. Also taking part were ships of the Home Fleet, the US Navy's 6th Fleet, the French Mediterranean Fleet and 19 ships of the Italian Fleet. The exercises ranged over half the Mediterranean, with ships putting to sea from Gibraltar, Toulon, Genoa, La Spezia, Leghorn (Livorno), Valletta, Algiers and Oran. Salient features of the manoeuvres were a bombardment exercise in the Tyrrhenian Sea, far-ranging anti-submarine exercises, refuelling at sea, an operation in which French warships were fuelled by US tankers, and an air attack on targets off the Italian coast by British, French and US carrier aircraft. The 200 or so ships formed 20 separate task units which were grouped without regard to nationality, although throughout her part *Liverpool* remained in close company, with *Cleopatra* and *Cheviot*, and for a major convoy escort exercise she also operated with *Glasgow*. During the manoeuvres there was a short weekend break at Cagliari and the exercise ended on 6 March at Naples for the wash-up and debriefings. On 15 March *Liverpool* arrived back in Grand Harbour where, seven days later, she embarked the

By July 1958 the former HMS Liverpool *had been moved to P & W MacLellan on the Firth of Forth, for demolition.* *(T. Ferrers-Walker)*

Within months of arriving on the Firth of Forth very little remained of the former cruiser. *(T. Ferrers-Walker)*

First Sea Lord for a 24-hour Mediterranean Fleet exercise off Malta. In addition to *Liverpool* there were two aircraft carriers, three cruisers, 11 destroyers, nine frigates and three submarines. At 1030 on Wednesday 16 April, with her upper decks manned and her paying-off pennant flying, *Liverpool* left Malta to make a fast, seven-day passage to Portsmouth. She arrived at Spithead at just before midnight on 23 April, and next afternoon having cleared Customs, steamed up harbour where she secured alongside North Corner Jetty to be greeted by families and friends. It was the end of *Liverpool*'s operational career. Seventeen days after her arrival Captain Luce had left the ship to take command of *Birmingham* which was lying alongside Middle Slip Jetty.

Within 24 hours of her arrival in Portsmouth Harbour *Liverpool* was being de-stored and de-ammunitioned, and by the end of the month her ship's company had been reduced to a care and maintenance party. By mid-June the ship had been reduced to Reserve and for two years she was used to accommodate the Senior Officer Reserve Fleet and his staff. She was also used as an accommodation ship for ships' companies whose own vessels were being refitted. However, in November 1956 this role was taken over by *Vanguard*. The end for *Liverpool* came in the summer of 1958, when she was sold to P & W MacLellan of Glasgow, for demolition, and on 2 July that year she arrived at the company's Bo'ness yard on the Firth of Forth.

Chapter Eight

HMS GLOUCESTER
1939-1941

HMS Gloucester *is seen here in Plymouth Sound during her work-up period in 1939.* *(Syd Goodman Collection)*

Of the ten Town-class cruisers the one which had the shortest career was *Gloucester* but, almost 70 years after her tragic loss, the ship and those who lost their lives are still remembered in the city after which she was named. She was the third and last cruiser authorized under the 1935 construction programme, only one of which would survive the Second World War. On 2 March 1936 the contract to build the ship was awarded to Devonport Royal Dockyard, with the order for the main propulsion machinery going to Scotts' Shipbuilding & Engineering Company of Greenock. However, with the Devonport slipway still occupied by *Birmingham* it was 23 September 1936, three weeks after *Birmingham*'s launch, that Mrs A. L. Snagge, the wife of the Admiral Superintendent of the dockyard, laid the first keel plate for *Gloucester* at a small ceremony. By the second half of the 1930s the pace of shipbuilding had been speeded up and it was hoped that by the spring or early summer of 1938 the new cruiser would be entering service. In the event, however, it was the autumn of 1937 before the hull was ready for launching. The ceremony took place on the afternoon of Tuesday 19 October. It was an important event in Plymouth and Devonport and a large crowd of over 18,000 spectators turned out to watch the Duchess of Gloucester name the ship and send her down into the waters of the Hamoaze, thus clearing the slipway for the construction of another ill-fated warship, the Colony-class cruiser, *Trinidad*.

In mid-November 1938, under the temporary command of Captain W. N. T. Beckett, who had transferred from the fleet target ship *Centurion* in order to take the new cruiser to sea, *Gloucester* was

commissioned to run a series of builder's trials in the Channel, before returning to the dockyard to be paid off into dockyard hands once again. At the same time that she was undergoing these initial trials it was announced that, on commissioning in January 1939, *Gloucester* was to become the flagship on the East Indies Station, where she would hoist the flag of Vice-Admiral J. F. Somerville and take the place of *Norfolk*. Her sisters *Liverpool* and *Manchester* had also been allocated to the East Indies Station where they were to take the places of *Emerald* and *Enterprise* respectively. On 2 January 1939 *Gloucester*'s first commanding officer, Captain F. R. Garside CBE RN, joined the ship which was secured alongside in Devonport's No 5 basin. Captain Garside had entered the Navy as a 13-year-old in 1910 and in October 1914, as a midshipman, he joined the battleship *Orion* in the Grand Fleet. He served in *Orion* throughout the Great War, being promoted to Lieutenant in 1917. After the war he specialized in gunnery and for some years in the 1920s he went on loan to the Royal Australian Navy, serving in the cruisers *Adelaide* and *Sydney*, before being appointed Gunnery Officer of the battleship *Royal Sovereign*. In the mid-1930s he became the Executive Officer of the cruiser *Devonshire* on the China Station and at the end of 1935 he was promoted to Captain.

Just over three weeks after Captain Garside was appointed to the ship, on Friday 27 January 1939, *Gloucester* was commissioned and the main body of her ship's company marched down from the Royal Naval Barracks to No 5 basin. Three days later the ship was moved round to the coaling jetty to begin ammunitioning, and next day put to sea for seven hours of trials before returning to Devonport Dockyard. During the next three weeks there was a succession of visitors to the ship, including the Mayor of the City of Gloucester, and the Duke and Duchess of Gloucester, who made an hour-long inspection of the ship, taking in an engine room, the bridge, a forward gun turret, a mess deck and the wardroom. At 1320 on 21 February, an hour after her sponsor's departure, *Gloucester* slipped her moorings and sailed for Portland for a four-day work-up before returning to Devonport for dry docking. By the end of February she was back at sea and undergoing catapult trials, and on 7 March, at Spithead, embarked three Walrus aircraft. Finally, on 15 March she left her base port of Devonport bound for the Mediterranean and the Indian Ocean. She was destined never to return to home waters.

After only a brief pause at Gibraltar, which lasted just long enough for mail to be transferred, *Gloucester* continued her passage east and on 22 March arrived in Malta's Grand Harbour, from where she carried out a four-week work-up, followed by a maintenance period. During the work-up she carried out joint manoeuvres with *Liverpool* and *Shropshire*, but on 21 April the former left for Port Said and the Red Sea and three days later *Gloucester* followed her. After making her southbound transit of the Suez Canal on 27 April *Gloucester* again rendezvoused with *Liverpool* in the Red Sea, and the two cruisers remained in company until mid-June.

On 2 May 1939 *Gloucester* arrived in Aden where, later that day, she officially joined the East Indies Station and relieved *Norfolk*, which sailed for Devonport. *Gloucester* had been due to hoist the flag of Vice-Admiral Somerville, but in early April ill health had unexpectedly forced him to relinquish his command and Rear-Admiral Ralph Leatham CB had been appointed in his place. However, as Leatham had only left England on 27 April to travel by train to Marseilles before sailing in the P&O liner SS *Ranpura* some 24 hours later, *Gloucester* had an unexpected extension to her stay in Aden. The liner arrived there on 7 May, and later that day Leatham was able to hoist his flag. Next day, with the new C-in-C aboard, *Gloucester* and *Liverpool* sailed for the island of Ceylon (now Sri Lanka) and the naval base in the picturesque harbour at Trincomalee. Within days of their arrival the two cruisers were back at sea to begin their summer cruise of the Indian Ocean islands and East African ports which all came under the East Indies

Two views of HMS Gloucester *entering Grand Harbour, Malta, in March 1939. During her passage from Devonport she had steamed close to the Spanish coast, and although the civil war in that country was drawing to a close, as a precaution 'B' and 'X' turrets have been painted with red, white and blue neutrality markings.*
(National Museum of the Royal Navy)

Command. Two days after leaving Trincomalee *Gloucester* had to part company with *Liverpool* in order to make an urgent diversion to Aden to land an urgent medical case at the military hospital there, resulting in another unscheduled stay in this most inhospitable of ports. By 9 June, however, she had rejoined *Liverpool* for visits to, among other places, the Seychelles, Farquhar Island and Tanganyika (Tanzania), a relatively new possession in East Africa for Britain since being granted a League of Nations Mandate to run the country. There was also a nine-day visit to the island of Zanzibar, which was dominated by formal ceremonies and a visit to the ship by the Sultan. The final visit of the cruise was to Mombasa, where the ship remained for 19 days and where, on 14 July, she was joined by *Manchester*. On the last day of July the two cruisers arrived in Aden, where they spent three days before putting to sea for a series of convoy escort exercises in the Indian Ocean and the Red Sea. It marked the end of *Gloucester*'s peacetime cruises in the Indian Ocean and, although it was not apparent at the time, the end of a way of life on the East Indies Station, for soon war would sweep it all away and bring about a premature end to the British Raj in India.

On 18 August 1939, just days before war was declared, *Gloucester* arrived in Colombo where formal peacetime rituals and ceremonies were still being rigidly adhered to, and that afternoon Admiral Leatham took official calls from the German, Italian and Japanese Consuls in the city. Seven days later *Gloucester* was dispatched to Aden where she arrived on 29 August to remain until further orders were received. These were not long in coming and , at 1620 on Friday 1 September, *Gloucester* left Aden, with her ship's company at Defence Stations. Although there were still two days before war was declared Allied merchant ships east of Suez were already forming convoys, and *Gloucester* was ordered to escort the first of these, northbound through the Red Sea, until it was clear of the Italian-held coastline. At this time, in company with the minelaying submarine *Seal*, she was patrolling the sea lanes between the Red Sea and the Gulf of Aden. She was in the Red Sea at 1316 (local time) when war was declared. During the days which followed she called at Aden for just long enough to refuel, before resuming her patrols. On 26 September she relieved *Seal* so that the latter could return to home waters[1].

In early October *Gloucester* was back at Aden, from where she steamed to Colombo, a passage which took her via the Gulf of Oman with a refuelling stop at the island of Masirah. During her three days in Colombo Harbour it seemed that Europe's second war in the space of 25 years was having little effect on the social life in Britain's far-flung colonies, for when the Italian cruiser *Bartolomeo Colleoni* secured to a buoy astern of *Gloucester*, her commanding officer and officers were invited to a cocktail party in the British ship. During the rest of October *Gloucester* patrolled and exercised from Colombo, sometimes in company with *Cornwall, Dorsetshire* or the aircraft carrier *Eagle*. She also acted as escort to important troop convoys, which included the transport *Ettrick* and the P&O liner *Viceroy of India*. This pattern of operations continued into November, but in the middle of the month she was ordered into the Bay of Bengal where, as well as patrolling, she was ordered to 'show the flag' in the more remote corners of the Empire. The first of these visits was to Nancowry in the Nicobar Islands, and from there she sailed north to the mouth of the Rangoon River. After a slow three and a half-hour passage she secured to a buoy at Rangoon. The ship's company could look forward to the pleasant prospect of a weekend in the city. At 1330 shore leave was piped to the off-duty watch, but just over an hour later Intelligence reports were received that, having sailed round the Cape of Good Hope, the German heavy cruiser *Admiral Graf Spee* was at large in the Indian Ocean. Immediately all *Gloucester*'s shore leave was cancelled and those already ashore were recalled. At 1920 *Gloucester* slipped her moorings

[1] On 5 May 1940 the submarine *Seal* was lost off the coast of Sweden and captured by the German Navy.

HMS Gloucester *in Grand Harbour prior to her passage east of Suez.* *(Maritime Photo Library)*

to make her way back down the Rangoon River to the Bay of Bengal and a two-day passage to Trincomalee. In fact, although *Admiral Graf Spee* had made a foray into the southern Indian Ocean, sinking a small oil tanker *Africa Shell*[2] and stopping a Dutch merchantman, the trail had then gone cold and it was not until the first week of December that she claimed her next victim in the South Atlantic. Meanwhile, after refuelling at Trincomalee, *Gloucester* steamed south to the French naval base at Diego Suarez, from where she patrolled until the second week of December.

On 12 December 1939 *Gloucester* put into Durban for what, apart from 24 hours at sea with *Eagle* and *Cornwall*, was a pleasant ten-day break for the ship's company. On 22 December the three ships put to sea to patrol the shipping lanes between Durban, Mauritius and the Seychelles. On Boxing Day she anchored off Mauritius, but no shore leave was granted, and New Year's Day saw her in company with *Eagle* heading for Colombo where she arrived on 4 January 1940 to undergo a four-week refit, which included a docking period.

On the last day of January 1940, with the refit completed, *Gloucester*, *Kent* and the French cruiser *Suffren*, sailed to continue the patrols of the Indian Ocean sea lanes. During her passage south she made her seventh crossing of the equator and took short breaks at Mombasa, Zanzibar, Durban, the French island of Rèunion, the Seychelles and the ports of Tulèar (Taliara) and Fort Dauphine (Taolanaro) in southern Madagascar, with recreational leave being granted at the latter two ports. By the first week of March *Gloucester* had returned to Colombo to undergo further maintenance and on the 22nd of the month steamed north to Bombay for a brief docking period before returning to Colombo where, on 29 March, the C-in-C East Indies struck his flag. Later that day she sailed via Mauritius to the naval base at Simonstown from where, for the rest of April, she patrolled the trade routes round the Cape of Good Hope. During the first two weeks of May *Gloucester* was at Simonstown undergoing maintenance, but on 13 May, three days after

[2] Ten and a half miles south by south-west of Cape Zavora in Mozambique.

Germany invaded Belgium, Holland, Luxembourg and France, she was ordered to leave Simonstown and steam north to Aden, calling briefly at Mombasa to refuel. Arriving in Aden on 22 May, *Gloucester* joined *Eagle* and later that day, in company with HMAS *Sydney*, steamed north to Suez. Having been ordered to join the Mediterranean Fleet they passed through the Suez Canal on 26 May and arrived in Alexandria the next day where she joined the 7th Cruiser Squadron of the Mediterranean Fleet; it was the same day that the evacuation of the BEF from Dunkirk and the Belgian coast began.

Eight days after joining the Mediterranean Fleet, *Gloucester* sailed to rendezvous with *Eagle, Neptune, Orion, Sydney* and two destroyer flotillas for joint exercises. Then, on 7 June she sailed to Malta where, two days later, she embarked an additional draft of Royal Marines. On 10 June, when Italy declared war on the side of Germany, *Gloucester* arrived back in Alexandria. The war in the Mediterranean was about to begin in earnest.

The first major naval operations in the Mediterranean war were the laying of extensive mine barrages around the Italian coastline, and off the Italian North African Dependency, Libya, which, of course, bordered the British Protectorate of Egypt. At just after midnight on 11 June, in company with *Warspite* (flag C-in-C, Mediterranean, Vice-Admiral A. B. Cunningham), *Malaya, Eagle, Liverpool, Sydney, Neptune* and a destroyer flotilla, *Gloucester* left Alexandria to join the cruisers *Calypso* and *Caledon*, after which the fleet steamed west towards the Libyan coast to test Italian reactions. In the early hours of 12 June *Gloucester* and *Liverpool* were detached to steam to within sight of the port of Tobruk in order to bombard the Italian defences. At 0510, not only were they within sight of land, but 'suspicious vessels' were sighted off the port bow, which turned out to be enemy minesweepers in the process of laying mines. Both cruisers opened fire on them, and on the elderly cruiser *San Georgio*, which was acting as a floating shore battery just inside the breakwater. One of the minesweepers was sunk, but accurate fire from *San Giorgio*'s 10-inch guns, and from other shore batteries, forced the two cruisers to withdraw under cover of a smokescreen, to rejoin *Warspite* and the fleet later in the day. That same day, however, south of Crete, the cruiser *Calypso*, commanded by Captain H. A. Rowley RN, was sunk by a torpedo from the Italian submarine *Alpino Bagnolini*. Fortunately, her commanding officer was amongst the survivors, and on the following day the fleet returned to Alexandria.

Having been thrust straight into the Mediterranean war there was little time for joint training with either squadron or fleet, and during the forenoon of 27 June *Gloucester*, in company with *Liverpool*, *Sydney* and *Neptune*, left Alexandria to escort as far as Crete two convoys bound from Alexandria to Malta. With France having concluded an Armistice with Germany and Italy, this foray into the Mediterranean was an opportunity for Cunningham to carry out a sweep of the eastern Mediterranean. On 28 June, when the cruisers were some 90 miles south-west of Crete, reconnaissance aircraft spotted an Italian convoy sailing towards Tobruk, carrying large quantities of stores and equipment to resupply their Libyan garrison. The convoy was escorted by the destroyers *Espero, Ostro* and *Zeffiro*, all three of them heavily laden down with equipment which severely hampered their fighting abilities. The cruisers were immediately ordered to give chase to the enemy convoy which was steaming towards the south west, and at 1831 *Liverpool* sighted the destroyers and both she and *Gloucester* opened fire. Although the Italian destroyers laid a very effective smokescreen, by 2020 when darkness had fallen, *Espero* had been badly damaged and *Sydney* was ordered to finish her off, which she did before rescuing 47 survivors. Next day the other two destroyers reached the safety of Benghazi. On the last day of June both *Gloucester* and *Liverpool* steamed south through the Suez Canal to anchor in the Great Bitter Lake, where they refuelled and stored ship.

On 1 July *Gloucester* left the Suez Canal and after

taking the opportunity to exercise with *Ramillies* returned to Alexandria the next day. When she put to sea again, during the late evening of 7 July, together with Cunningham's main battlefleet, including *Warspite* (flag), *Royal Sovereign, Malaya, Orion* and *Sydney*, it was to cover the passage of two convoys of merchant ships carrying military personnel and equipment from Malta to Alexandria. At the same time the Italians were also sailing an important and heavily defended convoy of their own from Naples to reinforce the garrison in Libya. Within hours aerial reconnaissance on both sides had located the respective fleets and convoys. By mid-forenoon on 8 July the battlefleet, including *Gloucester*, was some 90 to 100 miles north of the Gulf of Salum on the Egyptian-Libyan border. At 1020 the first of 13 heavy air attacks was launched on the fleet by Italian SM-81 bombers. The attacks continued all day, keeping the anti-aircraft gunners very busy, but right up to 1800 *Gloucester* had managed to successfully evade each onslaught and there was some optimism that with dusk approaching she would get through unscathed. At 1813, however, the last air attack of the day came suddenly and devastatingly, and a minute later a 500lb bomb hit and almost completely destroyed *Gloucester*'s bridge, instantly killing seven officers, including Captain F. R. Garside and the Executive Officer, Commander J. R. H. D'Aeth, and ten ratings. The First Lieutenant, Lt-Cdr R. P. Tanner, took over command; with the navigating bridge having been so badly damaged *Gloucester* had to be steered from the emergency steering position, but her main propulsion machinery was unscathed so she was able to remain at sea and with the fleet. That evening, after the wreckage of the bridge had been cleared, the funeral service for the 17 dead took place. Next day *Gloucester* was detached from the fleet to join *Eagle* and her destroyer screen, so she took no part in the Battle of Punto Stilo on 9 July. During the afternoon of 10 July an 18th member of the ship's company died of his wounds and was buried at sea. At 0833 on 11 July, south-west of Crete, fast troop convoy MF1 was sighted. Some 24 hours later the convoy and *Gloucester* arrived safely at Alexandria, and three days later, on 16 July, Captain H. A. Rowley DSO RN, who had been kicking his heels in the port since the sinking of his ship *Calypso*, took command of *Gloucester*. His Executive Officer was the newly promoted Commander R. P. Tanner, who had so ably taken command after the deaths of Captain Garside and Commander D'Aeth, for which he was awarded the DSC. As for *Gloucester* herself, much of the repair work to her bridge was carried out at Alexandria, but on 28 July she made an overnight passage to Port Said where she remained for four days while a new Director Control Tower was fitted. By the evening of 2 August the repairs were completed and the ship returned to Alexandria.

On her return to Alexandria *Gloucester* hoisted the flag of Rear-Admiral E. De F. Renouf, Flag Officer 3rd Cruiser Squadron (CS3). On 4 August, together with *Liverpool* and the destroyers *Jervis* and *Hostile*, she sailed from Alexandria to an area north of Crete in a search for enemy shipping. However, apart from a sighting of an enemy reconnaissance aircraft, the four days at sea were largely uneventful and on 8 August the force returned to Alexandria. On 14 August, together with *Liverpool* and a destroyer screen, *Gloucester* took part in a night encounter exercise returning to Alexandria the following afternoon. That night five Italian torpedo-bombers attacked the fleet anchorage at Alexandria and *Gloucester* had a lucky escape when two torpedoes, which had been launched at too high an altitude for the relatively shallow waters of the harbour, embedded themselves harmlessly in mud close to the ship and failed to explode. As a precaution, however, she was taken into the port's floating dry dock for a survey to her hull.

Gloucester's next foray into the Mediterranean began on 24 August when she sailed in company with *Kent* to carry out another offensive sweep into the Aegean, and to escort an incoming convoy from Malta. Two days later they were spotted by Italian reconnaissance aircraft, and at 0750 on 27 August they were attacked by torpedo-bombers, but both cruisers were able to manoeuvre and comb the tracks. Later that day they returned to Alexandria. *Gloucester*'s next major operation began three days later, on 30 August, when with *Liverpool* and the main battlefleet she sailed to provide escort cover for convoy MF2, bound from Malta to Alexandria. Then, with the battlefleet, she took part in 'Operation Hats', the reinforcement of the Mediterranean Fleet with the battleship *Valiant* and the aircraft carrier *Illustrious*, both of which had steamed east from Gibraltar, escorted by the ships of Force H as far as the Skerki Narrows. During the seven days spent at sea the fleet twice came under heavy air attack, the first time by high-level bombers during the afternoon of 2 September south of Malta, and on the second occasion at midday on 5 September when four Italian bombers attacked the fleet. On both occasions the cruiser emerged unscathed and on 6 September she returned to Alexandria.

Seven days later, on 13 September, *Gloucester* left Alexandria once again, this time in company with *Kent*, *Liverpool* and a destroyer screen to provide anti-aircraft defences for convoy AN3, sailing from Alexandria to Malta. The three cruisers rendezvoused with the convoy next day, and on 16 September they met *Illustrious* to provide cover for the aircraft carrier as she launched air strikes on the Italian defences at Benghazi. During the night of 16/17 September the cruisers came under attack by torpedo-bombers, which left *Kent* badly damaged, but still afloat, and she was towed back to Alexandria by the destroyer *Nubian*. Both *Gloucester* and *Liverpool* returned unscathed on 19 September, and for *Gloucester*'s ship's company there was a welcome ten-day break from opera-

An excellent close-up view of HMS Gloucester's *midships section showing her Walrus aircraft, catapult and aircraft handling cranes.* *(Maritime Photo Library)*

tions. On 29 September, however, she sailed once again, this time in company with *York*, *Liverpool* and the battlefleet. Both *Gloucester* and *Liverpool* were carrying troop reinforcements for the garrison at Malta, which meant that their fighting capabilities were severely hampered. Some 15 hours after leaving Alexandria, at just after midnight on 29 September, the fleet came under heavy air attack from torpedo-bombers, but fortunately no damage was done. Sporadic air attacks continued until shortly before midnight on 30 September, when the two cruisers arrived in Grand Harbour, where *Gloucester* secured alongside Hamilton Wharf and disembarked her troops.

HMS *Gloucester*'s visit to Malta lasted for just two and a half hours, during which time, as well as disembarking the military personnel, she refuelled and embarked a number of naval as well as RAF personnel and Maltese civilians for the return passage to Alexandria. Leaving Grand Harbour at 0233 on 1 October, she rendezvoused with *Liverpool* and *Calcutta* for a fast passage to Alexandria, where they arrived without incident the next day. Once again there were only a few days between operations, and during the forenoon of 8 October *Gloucester* sailed to rendezvous with the main battlefleet, including *Warspite, Valiant, Ramillies, Illustrious, Eagle, Ajax, Orion, Sydney* and a destroyer screen, to provide the escort for the passage of convoy MF3 from Alexandria to Malta. Three days after leaving harbour the northbound convoy arrived safely at Malta, and another small convoy was picked up for escort back to Egypt. Soon after beginning the southbound passage, during the early hours of 12 October, *Ajax* reported sighting what were initially thought to be three Italian cruisers, but were in fact the destroyer *Artigliere* with the smaller E-boats *Airone, Alcione* and *Ariel* which were hoping to ambush and attack the battlefleet or convoy on its way back to Alexandria. During the spirited action which followed *Artigliere* was hit and badly damaged, *Airone* was sunk and *Ajax* herself was damaged. However, before she could sink *Artigliere* she was ordered to rejoin the battlefleet so she broke off the action. At 0800, however, *Gloucester*, *Liverpool* and *York* found the crippled Italian destroyer which was under tow and she was destroyed by gunfire from *York*. By 1000 the three cruisers had rejoined the battlefleet, but two hours later the first of a number of air attacks began. Initially no damage was caused to the fleet and at 1330 the cruisers parted company to support the convoy and, as the forenoon of 13 October passed quietly, it was thought that all the ships would reach Alexandria safely. At 1433, however, these hopes were shattered when the first wave of Italian torpedo-bombers attacked the battlefleet. These attacks continued for over four hours, and at 1856 *Liverpool* was hit by a torpedo which caused severe damage to her bow. *Gloucester* immediately circled the crippled cruiser while *Orion* took her in tow. For the rest of the passage, until they were within 15 miles of Alexandria, *Gloucester* provided the escort for the two ships; they all arrived safely on 16 October.

It was Monday 28 October when *Gloucester* put to sea again. Just a few hours after sailing a signal was received to the effect that there was now, '*a state of war between Greece and Italy*', the latter country having invaded Greece from Albania. *Gloucester* was ordered to return to Alexandria and by 0950 she was secured alongside. One strategic effect of the Italian action was to drain off Italian Army strength from North Africa where an advance to the Suez Canal had been a distinct possibility. However, within days and against all military advice, Churchill decided to go to the aid of Greece. Soon British Army and RAF units from North Africa began landing in Athens and on the Greek island of Crete. These operations would cost Britain dearly, and would severely handicap the main campaign in North Africa. At just after midnight on 29 October, the battlefleet, which included *Gloucester*, sailed from Alexandria once more, this time to provide escort cover for troop convoys between Alexandria and Crete. By 2 November they were back at Alexandria, but four days later they again left their Egyptian base to provide protection for

convoys running between Egypt and Greece. As well as providing cover for the convoys *Gloucester* rendezvoused with the battleship *Barham*, together with the cruisers *Berwick* and *Glasgow* and three destroyers which had left Gibraltar three days earlier to reinforce the Mediterranean Fleet. After refuelling at Malta *Berwick* and *Glasgow* rejoined *Gloucester* and *York* off Grand Harbour, and during the forenoon of 14 November arrived safely at Alexandria. Next day *Gloucester* shifted berths to lie alongside the quay in order to embark Army and RAF personnel[3] for passage to Greece. Later that day, in company with *Berwick, Glasgow, Sydney* and *York*, she sailed for Piraeus, making a fast 24-hour passage to arrive in the Greek port the next afternoon. Pausing just long enough to disembark the military personnel and their equipment and to refuel, the five cruisers sailed the same day and next afternoon returned to Alexandria in the middle of an air raid on the harbour where Italian aircraft were seen dropping mines inside the breakwater.

Eight days later, on 25 November, *Gloucester* left Alexandria to join the battlefleet for convoy protection duties and to escort *Illustrious* which was carrying out air strikes on Port Laki on the island of Rhodes. On 28 November, while south of Malta, *Gloucester* was detached from the battlefleet to escort four corvettes, which had been steamed east from Gibraltar to reinforce the fleet, to Crete's Suda Bay where they arrived on the last day of November. During the days spent at anchor off Crete both *Gloucester* and *Glasgow* acted as a kind of recreation facility for the troops ashore who came on board 100 at a time for cinema shows and to use the washrooms. During the afternoon of the third day, however, the fleet was attacked by Italian torpedo-bombers, one of which damaged *Glasgow*, but that evening both cruisers were able to weigh anchor and steam south to Alexandria, where they arrived safely during the forenoon of 7 December. Three days later *Gloucester* was at sea once again, this time as escort to *Illustrious*, which was operating her aircraft in support of the Army in Egypt; after this she returned to Alexandria for a two-day break. Her next duty, together with *Dainty* and *Greyhound*, was to escort a convoy to Suda Bay before steaming on to Piraeus where, during the afternoon on 23 December, she secured alongside. Next day, during the afternoon of Christmas Eve, she sailed once again for Crete, coming under attack by an Italian torpedo-bomber just outside Suda Bay, where she refuelled before returning to Piraeus. Once again she remained alongside for just over 24 hours and at the end of December returned to Alexandria, just in time for the New Year.

The start of 1941 saw the British Army in Egypt back on the Libyan border and about to launch an attack on the Italian strong point at Bardia. During the evening of 2 January, in company with *Illustrious, Barham, Warspite* and *Valiant*, *Gloucester* left Alexandria to steam west along the Egyptian coast to carry out a bombardment of the Italian garrison there. This began at 0730 the next morning and continued throughout the forenoon, but by the evening *Gloucester* had returned to her base. Two days later Bardia fell to the British offensive and the Italian Army retreated to Tobruk. During the forenoon of 6 January *Gloucester* embarked 160 officers and men of the Royal Artillery who were bound for Malta to reinforce the garrison, and at 1252, in company with *Southampton*, slipped her moorings and set course for Grand Harbour. The passage to Malta passed without incident, and at just after 0900 on 8 January she steamed past the breakwater to secure alongside Boat House Wharf where the Army personnel were disembarked. That same afternoon, as soon as refuelling was completed, *Gloucester* and *Southampton* sailed to rendezvous with the battlefleet at a point in the Sicilian Narrows off the island of Pantelleria, where they were to meet an eastbound convoy of four merchant ships which had been escorted that far by the ships of Force H. At 2100 that evening Pantelleria was sighted and shortly afterwards the two cruisers were challenged from the shore, which meant their presence had not gone unnoticed. However, despite the fact that they

[3] Mainly RAF ground crews from 80 Fighter and 211 Bomber Squadrons.

had been seen, the night passed quietly and at 0940 on 9 January the convoy being escorted by *Bonaventure* and three destroyers was sighted. The good fortune did not last for much longer, however, and at 1345 the first enemy air attacks began, with ten bombers dropping sticks of bombs on *Gloucester*. These exploded all around her, but fortunately there were no casualties and two of the aircraft were shot down by anti-aircraft fire. That night the destroyers made a submarine contact, which turned out to be the Italian *Settimo*. It was driven off by depth charges. With nightfall came a lull in the action which lasted until the next morning, 10 January, when at 0740 the torpedo boats *Circe* and *Vega* were sighted off *Gloucester*'s port quarter. Both the cruisers and the destroyers went to intercept them but, despite being heavily outgunned, the Italian ships managed to close the range to 5,000 metres and fire seven torpedoes before *Vega* was sunk; *Circe* escaped. Soon after this the destroyer *Gallant* hit a mine which blew her bow off, and *Gloucester* spent the rest of that day and the night on a zigzag circular course around the crippled ship, which was being towed by *Mohawk,* in an effort to protect her from further damage.

At 0400 on Saturday 11 January *Gloucester*, *Southampton* and the destroyer *Diamond* were ordered to part company with *Gallant* and rejoin the battlefleet, and soon afterwards they received further orders to provide cover for convoy ME6, on passage from Malta to Egypt. By 1520 that day they were some 180 miles south-west of Sicily when they were suddenly attacked by a force of German Ju-87 dive-bombers. The attack was fast and ferocious and one 500lb bomb hit *Gloucester*'s forward director tower and penetrated five of the cruiser's decks without exploding. A second 500lb bomb exploded very close to *Gloucester*'s starboard side, amidships, blowing a hole through the hull and into the Royal Marines' messdeck, killing a sub-lieutenant, a leading seaman and seven marines outright, and critically wounding another who died the next day. Another 13 ship's company members were wounded. At the same time the dive-bombers hit *Southampton* with at least two and possibly up to four 500lb bombs, leaving her very badly damaged, disabled and on fire. The unexploded bomb in *Gloucester* had ended up in the ship's Meteorological Office where, in order to prevent it rolling around with the movement of the ship, a young NAAFI canteen assistant, William Black, sat on it until it could be thrown over the side.

As work went on to tend the injured and clear up the wreckage on board *Gloucester*, the cruiser was able to maintain her speed and manoeuvrability in order to circle the crippled *Southampton* in an effort to shield her from further attack as desperate efforts were made to fight the fires. At 1615 *Gloucester*'s Walrus aircraft, which had been launched an hour before the attack, returned and landed in the sea close to *Diamond*, the crew were recovered from the sea and the aircraft sunk. By 1900, with daylight fading, attempts to save *Southampton* were abandoned and *Diamond* was ordered to go alongside the cruiser's forecastle in order to transfer the wounded, and then the remainder of the ship's company. By 2020 this operation had been completed and *Gloucester* was ordered to sink the burning and crippled hulk. She fired a torpedo at her sister ship which hit and exploded under 'B' turret, but did not sink her. An hour later *Orion* arrived on the scene and she fired two torpedoes at the blazing wreck, one of which caused a massive explosion and finally sent her beneath the waves. Meanwhile *Diamond*, which was heavily overcrowded with personnel, was ordered to go alongside *Gloucester* to transfer a large number of *Southampton*'s survivors, which included 67 badly wounded men. By 2145 the operation had been completed and, escorted by *Orion* and *Perth*, *Gloucester* was able to set course for Alexandria. At 0715 next day, south of Crete, she joined the main battlefleet and took station some eight cables astern of *Warspite*. That day three of *Southampton*'s critically injured men died of their wounds and were buried at sea. With no more enemy attacks on the fleet they arrived safely at Alexandria during the forenoon of 13 January.

Gloucester secured alongside No 43 wharf at Alexandria Docks to disembark her own wounded and *Southampton*'s survivors.

During the rest of January, and for almost three weeks of February 1941, *Gloucester* underwent repairs at Alexandria, making two short passages to Port Said, but staying there only a few hours before returning to her base. Finally, on 18 February, with all the repairs completed, *Gloucester* left harbour for a day of sea trials, before returning to harbour. Next day she was declared fully operational again and embarked 630 officers and men of the Cheshire Regiment, together with equipment and stores, before sailing that evening to make a fast passage to Malta, where she arrived alongside Hamilton Wharf at 0820 on 21 February. There then followed an intense period of activity disembarking her passengers and their equipment, a task made much more difficult by constant enemy air raids on Grand Harbour throughout the day. Finally, at just after 1900, *Gloucester* sailed for Suda Bay where, next day, Army stores were unloaded. She remained at anchor off Crete for almost 30 hours and, leaving at just before midnight on 23 February, she then steamed east as far as Cyprus before turning south, thus avoiding air attacks en route to Alexandria where she arrived on 26 February.

On 4 March 1941, as a result of Churchill's ill-considered plans to open a Balkan front (almost a Second World War version of Gallipoli), 'Operation Lustre', the large-scale insertion of British troops into Greece began. However, this new British theatre of war was opened at the expense of the increasingly successful North African theatre and would result in more unnecessary disasters for both the Army and the Navy. For the remaining months of her career *Gloucester*, like most of the Mediterranean Fleet, would be employed almost solely with the reinforcement, supply and then the evacuations of the Army from both Greece and Crete, back to their original bases in Egypt. On 6 March she embarked officers and men, plus baggage and stores of the 1st Armoured Division, before making a fast passage from Alexandria to Piraeus. She remained there just long enough to disembark the troops before making another fast passage back to Alexandria, where she arrived on 8 March. No sooner had she refuelled and embarked more troops than she sailed once again for Piraeus, but instead of returning to Egypt, in company with *Bonaventure* and *York* she spent nine days escorting convoys between Suda Bay and Piraeus. It was 18 March before *Gloucester* returned to Alexandria where she embarked officers and men of the Australia and New Zealand Brigade (ANZACs) for another fast passage to Piraeus. She then remained at anchor in the harbour for two days before sailing on 21 March to rendezvous with the battlefleet which included *Barham, Valiant, Warspite, Formidable, York* and a screen of 15 destroyers, to cover the passage of convoy MW6 from Alexandria to Malta. All passed quietly until the afternoon of 24 March when, some 80 miles south-west of Crete, the whole force was subjected to fierce bombing attacks. Fortunately, there were no casualties or damage sustained.

In mid-March intelligence reports were being received to the effect that the Italian Navy was planning to steam into the Aegean with the aim of seriously disrupting the Greek reinforcement convoys. Cunningham began planning the disposition of the fleet in order to bring the Italians to action. For *Gloucester* and *York* this meant remaining in the vicinity of Crete. At 1440 on 25 March, having been detached from the main force, the two ships arrived in Suda Bay to refuel and anchor for the night. At 0500 the following morning, however, in a daring and audacious attack on the warships at anchor, six Italian motor launches loaded with explosives, all of which had been transported to the waters off Crete by the torpedo boats *Dardo* and *Strake*, launched themselves at the anchored ships. The oil tanker *Pericles*, from which *Gloucester* had refuelled the previous evening, was seriously damaged and *York* was crippled and had to be written off. The motor launches had each targeted one of the ships in harbour and, when only 100 yards from the target, the crews slid off backwards into the sea

leaving their launch and its explosives to smash into its target. In the event *York* was hit on her starboard side leaving a gaping hole which flooded all her main machinery spaces. She was, in fact, beached, but subsequent events prevented salvage operations and she was eventually abandoned at Suda Bay. Before the Italian crews were located and interrogated it was thought that a submarine had penetrated the defences of Suda Bay and *Gloucester*, which only escaped the attacks because the launch targeting her had suffered mechanical problems, quickly raised steam. By 0730 on 26 March she had cleared Suda Bay, but no sooner had she left harbour than she was subjected to a fierce air attack, although fortunately, she avoided any hits. A few hours later, as she was steaming towards Piraeus, the plummer block on the port inner screw began to seriously overheat and the ship was stopped while the engineers put the brakes on the shaft to stop it from turning. The remainder of the passage was made at 20 knots and that evening *Gloucester* anchored in the sheltered waters of Salamis Bay off Piraeus, where the ship's divers went down to inspect the A bracket on the port inner propeller. They found that there was excessive slackness between the propeller shaft and the A bracket, and that this was the probable cause of the overheating. Although the plummer block was repaired there was nothing that could be done about the cause and it was decided that wherever possible the ship's maximum safe speed had to be regarded as 24 knots. However, in the dramatic 48 hours which followed she would regularly exceed this limit.

At just after 1300 on 27 March, having refuelled from RFA *Olna*, *Gloucester* weighed anchor and sailed to rendezvous with *Orion* (flag Vice-Admiral Light Forces {Med}, H. D. Pridham-Wippell), *Ajax* and *Perth*, as well as the destroyers *Hereward* and *Vendetta*, before the whole squadron set course for a rendezvous point some 30 miles south of Gavdo Island (Gavdhos Island). Reports had been received to the effect that the Italian fleet, including a battleship, were about to attack the troop convoys in the Aegean Sea and so at dusk on 27 March Cunningham, flying his flag in *Warspite*, sailed the battlefleet from Alexandria to the rendezvous point. Designated as Force A it consisted of *Warspite, Barham, Valiant, Formidable*, and a screen of nine destroyers[4]. Pridham-Wippell's light cruiser squadron was designated as Force B, and at 0644 on 28 March it rendezvoused with *Hasty* and *Ilex* from Suda Bay. At roughly the same time an enemy aircraft was seen shadowing Force B, and it was identified as a type which was carried in Italian cruisers. For the first time it was realised that enemy surface forces were likely to be in the vicinity, and an hour later a reconnaissance aircraft from *Formidable* reported a force of Italian cruisers and destroyers just out of sight of Force B, but in a position to cut it off from Force A, which was still over 90 miles away to the south-east.

The Italian naval force was made up of the 8-inch heavy cruisers *Pola, Zara, Fiume, Bolzano, Trento* and *Trieste*, together with three destroyers. Without the presence of Force A the Italian force could outrange and outgun the light cruisers and put them in a very uncomfortable position. Pridham-Wippell decided to attempt to lure the Italian cruisers towards the direction of the main battlefleet, but by 0812 the enemy were within range and they opened fire, concentrating their accurate shooting on *Gloucester*, which was forced to snake the line in order to avoid being hit. Some 15 minutes later *Gloucester* replied with three 6-inch salvoes, but as the enemy had the benefit of greater range these all fell short. For some 25 minutes the Italian cruisers followed Force B as it steamed towards the battlefleet, before they suspected, quite rightly, that they were being lured into a trap and they turned away. As soon as the Italian cruisers altered course Force B began to shadow them, but they too were being lured towards the Italian battleship *Vittorio Veneto* (flag Vice-Admiral Iachino); the entry at 1057 in *Gloucester*'s log reads: '*Unknown battleship*

[4] The 14th Destroyer Flotilla: *Jervis* (Captain D), *Janus*, *Nubian* and *Mohawk*. The 10th Destroyer Flotilla: *Stuart*, *Greyhound*, *Griffin*, *Hotspur* and *Havock*.

opened fire on squadron.' These were the opening 15-inch salvoes from *Vittorio Veneto* which was firing accurately from 32,000 yards, first at *Orion*, which suffered minor damage from a near miss, then, after she put up an effective smokescreen, at *Gloucester*, which was repeatedly straddled. Pridham-Wippell lost no time in turning his force to the south and increasing to full speed as the light cruisers and destroyers escaped from what would have been for them a devastating action. Information on the enemy's movements during this 28-minute action was scant, but at 1148 there was no sign of them.

Meanwhile, as the main battlefleet approached from the south-east, Cunningham ordered *Formidable* to launch an air strike on the Italian ships. At 1127 the entry in *Gloucester*'s log reads: '*Battleship attacked by torpedo-bombers.*' Initially it was thought that one torpedo had found its target, but, in fact, all had passed astern of her. The attack did have the effect of relieving the pressure on Force B, and with his battlefleet closing the distance, Cunningham requested assistance from shore-based aircraft in Crete and Greece. The attack by *Formidable*'s aircraft forced *Vittorio Veneto* and the accompanying cruisers to take evasive action, and contact with Force B was lost until 1224 when lookouts in *Gloucester* sighted *Warspite* and the battlefleet. An hour later *Gloucester* took station on *Valiant*.

Although Iachino was aware that the Mediterranean Fleet was at sea and steaming towards his force, because of faulty air reconnaissance he was under the impression that Cunningham and his battleships were much further to the south-east than they were, affording them a real opportunity to catch the Italian ships. That afternoon a further air attack by three Albacores and two Swordfish from *Formidable*, supported by three Blenheims from Greece, was more successful when a torpedo from an Albacore hit *Vittorio Veneto* on her port side aft, damaging a propeller and causing serious flooding. Soon after this a near miss from a Blenheim caused further flooding and damaged her steering gear. As a result of this damage the battleship's speed was reduced to 19½ knots, and she took up a position in the centre of the Italian fleet. Even at this stage Iachino did not fully appreciate the danger his force was in, but with an aircraft carrier in the vicinity and with insufficient air cover available to his force, he decided to turn for home. Had he been able to muster sufficient air cover there was a possibility he would have been able to reach safety with his force intact, but with the chase now on Cunningham was determined to bring the Italians to action.

During the course of the afternoon aircraft from *Formidable* and other ships made numerous reconnaissance flights, and soon after 1800 *Warspite*'s Walrus presented Cunningham with an accurate picture of the situation. His dilemma, however, was that the Italian warships had concentrated in mass round *Vittorio Veneto*, thus creating a formidable obstacle to an attack by the light cruisers and destroyers. It was also apparent that by daylight on 29 March the Italian ships would be well within the cover of dive-bombing aircraft based in Sicily. He had to decide whether to send in the light cruisers and destroyers and to follow up with the battlefleet, or to wait until the morning in the hope of engaging with his whole fleet – with the certainty of exposing his ships to heavy air attacks. In the event he chose the first option, but the resulting success was assured through the intervention of the Fleet Air Arm.

By 1707 the four light cruisers of Force B had formed into single line ahead and, including *Gloucester*, were steaming at 30 knots towards the Italian force. By dusk they were drawing close to the enemy when, at 1934, six Albacores from *Formidable* attacked the Italian heavy cruisers and one of their torpedoes hit and severely damaged *Pola*. Having suffered damage to her boilers she lost all power and lay completely disabled and dead in the water. On board *Gloucester* this was recorded in the log as: '*Underwater explosions.*' Although *Pola* was in no immediate danger of sinking it was some time before she could be got under way, and

then only at six knots. Meanwhile Iachino ordered *Fiume* and *Zara*, together with the destroyers *Vittorio Alfiere* and *Giosue Carducci*, to assist and if necessary tow *Pola* to safety. With the British battlefleet bearing down on them their fate was sealed.

At 2033 the entry in *Gloucester*'s log reads: '*Dark object smelling of smoke by 235°*,' followed at 2040 by: '*Unknown bg 270°*.' The light cruisers had found the crippled *Pola*, and as soon as he was informed of this Cunningham turned his battlefleet towards the spot. By 2210, on what was a dark, moonless night, *Warspite* was just six miles from *Pola, Fiume* and *Zara*; in the action which began at 2226, with *Warspite, Valiant,* and *Barham* opening a devastating fire with their 15-inch guns, all three cruisers were sunk, together with the destroyers *Vittorio Alfieri* and *Giosue Carducci*. During the battlefleet action contact was lost with the damaged *Vittorio Veneto*, and at 2243 Cunningham broke off the main action and ordered the battlefleet to rendezvous at 0700 in a position 35°54'N 021°38'E in order to sweep the area; it was at this point that Force B joined them. Between 0950 and 1100 on the forenoon of 29 March, many rafts and boats containing Italian survivors were spotted and the destroyers *Hasty, Havock* and *Juno* were ordered to rescue as many men as possible. However, by 1100 enemy reconnaissance aircraft had begun to appear and as there was no further sign of Italian surface ships Cunningham ordered his fleet to set course for Alexandria. Iachino had paid heavily for his decision to assist the crippled *Pola* and an Italian commission of inquiry later confirmed that it had been a major error. At the Battle of Cape Matapan, as it became known, the Italian Navy lost five ships, some 2,300 dead and 1,411 taken prisoner. The return passage was not without incident, for during the afternoon of 29 March the battlefleet came under attack from German Ju-88 bombers and both *Valiant* and *Formidable* were narrowly missed by several bombs. Finally, during the early evening of 30 March, the Mediterranean Fleet arrived back at Alexandria. Any elation at the Matapan victory was, however, to be short-lived, for the full consequences of Churchill's ill-advised Balkan Front and his decision to defend Crete were soon to end in unmitigated disaster for both the Army and Royal Navy.

On 6 April 1941, while *Gloucester* was undergoing repairs to the plummer block and A bracket of her port inner propeller shaft, the German Army invaded Yugoslavia and Greece, and within three days all Greek forces in the Salonika Peninsula had surrendered. By mid-April it was apparent that the Royal Navy would be required to withdraw the Desert Army, and as much of its equipment as was possible, from Greece; they would also have to provide support for the forces who had remained in Egypt and were now desperately trying to fend off a major offensive by the Axis Army in North Africa, which had seized control of Benghazi and was moving quickly east across Cyrenaica towards the Egyptian border. Once *Gloucester*'s repairs were completed she was ordered to sea to act as convoy escort and on 18 April sailed in company with *Warspite, Valiant, Barham, Formidable, Orion, Ajax, Perth* and a destroyer screen to cover vital convoys between Egypt and Malta, on conclusion of which the whole battlefleet put into Suda Bay to refuel. *Gloucester*'s stay was brief and during the early hours of 21 April she was back at sea with the battlefleet off Tripoli where, between 0517 and 0550, the military depots around the city were bombarded. The engagement was not one-sided, for Italian shore batteries returned fire with some accurate shooting. At 0600, as dawn broke, the fleet left the scene to make a fast return passage to Alexandria, with *Gloucester* being detached to steam north to Malta where she was to support the Malta Strike Force, the newly arrived 5th Destroyer Flotilla, which had been given the task of disrupting enemy convoys between Italian ports and Libya.

HMS *Gloucester* arrived in Grand Harbour on 22 April 1941, to an island which had been under siege for almost a year and which was being subjected to almost constant air attacks on Valletta and all the military installations. Despite their recent disaster off Cape Matapan, the Italian Navy had continued

An undated image of HMS Gloucester *at Grand Harbour, Malta, presumably taken in 1941.*
(Syd Goodman Collection)

to run vital troop and supply convoys to Tripoli, which were crucial for the Axis forces in North Africa. *Gloucester*'s new role was to provide support for the destroyer flotilla as its ships attacked these convoys, and given the fact that the routes were well within air cover of aircraft operating from bases in Sicily they were extremely dangerous operations. In the event *Gloucester* did not last long in this role for on 30 April, while waiting behind the destroyer flotilla to enter Grand Harbour, *Jersey* hit a mine off Fort Ricasoli and sank right across the harbour entrance. *Gloucester* was then ordered to steam west to Gibraltar to assist Force H with 'Operation Tiger', a vital convoy carrying tanks for the Desert Army in Egypt, most of which were replacements for those lost in the Greek campaign. During the early hours of the morning, as she passed through the Sicilian Narrows, a mine exploded in the ship's paravanes, causing some damage to the hull but not affecting her manoeuvrability from both high-level and dive-bombing aircraft. One bomb passed right through the stern of the ship without exploding; had it done so she would have been left totally disabled, with further attacks inevitable. As it was she was able to reach Gibraltar where she was quickly dry-docked for emergency repairs to her hull. By the forenoon of 16 May these were completed and when the five merchantmen, *Clan Campbell, Clan Lamont, Clan Chattan, Empire Song* and *New Zealand Star*, passed through the Strait of Gibraltar and assembled in the Western Mediterranean for the perilous passage east, *Gloucester* was able to join the other escorts, which included *Renown*, *Ark Royal, Sheffield*, and six destroyers. Also augmenting the escort was the newly refitted battleship *Queen Elizabeth* together with the cruisers *Fiji* and *Naiad*, which were being sent east to reinforce Cunningham's hard-pressed Mediterranean Fleet. It was during the afternoon of the third day that enemy air attacks began. Although a gunnery accident on board *Renown* left seven dead and 25

injured, there were no hits on the convoy. Also lost were two Fulmars from *Ark Royal*, which had been repelling air attacks by Ju-87s, Ju-88s and Me-110s.

On 9 May, when the convoy was off Malta, the merchantman *Empire Song* hit a mine and sank, taking her valuable cargo with her. Later that afternoon, some 50 miles south of Malta, the rendezvous was made with the Mediterranean Fleet. The entry in *Warspite*'s log reads: '*1639 Identified* Queen Elizabeth, Gloucester, Fiji, Naiad, *destroyers and merchant ships.*' By early evening *Gloucester* was stationed astern of *Valiant* and during the forenoon of 12 May anchored in Alexandria Harbour.

HMS *Gloucester* had been absent from her Egyptian base for just over three weeks, but during that time the strategic situation had deteriorated badly. Churchill's idea of a Balkan Front in Greece had collapsed, and he had become fixated with the apparent vital need to defend and hold the island of Crete[5]. Many of the Army units defending Crete had been withdrawn from Greece and were without their heavy equipment. The Navy's task was to prevent a seaborne invasion which, despite being well within range of enemy air attack, it was eminently capable of doing. However, although a seaborne assault was attempted, the decisive attacks came from the air; over 400 Luftwaffe bombers and 230 fighters launched their attacks on Crete which began in earnest on 14 May and continued unabated for six days. These initial raids succeeded in their objective of destroying most of the island's anti-aircraft defences and heavily cratering main roads, thus making them virtually impassable to all but the lightest traffic. Meanwhile, following her return to Alexandria, *Gloucester* was prepared for her part in the defence of Crete[6], but first she steamed the short distance to Port Said for urgent work to be carried out on her rangefinder. By 15 May she was back at Alexandria where, with *Fiji*, she embarked the officers and men of the 2nd Battalion, Leicester Regiment, together with all their equipment. The two cruisers left Alexandria at just after midnight and, making a fast passage north, arrived off Heraklion during the hours of darkness on 16 May, thus avoiding the heavy air attacks which were taking place on a daily basis. Having completed this task, *Gloucester* and *Fiji* were then designated as Force B and ordered to carry out anti-invasion patrols off the north-western shores of Crete. They were also to act in support of Force D (*Naiad, Phoebe* and two destroyers) which were covering the west coast of Crete. Intelligence reports had indicated that the main invasion would be from the sea, and that it was imminent. But with over 600 Axis bombers in the vicinity all the defending ships were vulnerable to attack from the air. *Gloucester* and *Fiji*, positioned off the north-west of the island, were in the most vulnerable position, particularly as both were running low on anti-aircraft ammunition. By 17 May, having carried out night sweeps off Cape Matapan, *Gloucester* was also running short of fuel and on 18 May she returned to Alexandria in order to refuel. However, during the night of 19/20 May she was ordered to return to the patrol area off north-west Crete.

At 0800 on 20 May the German 'Operation Merkur' had begun, with eight battalions of airborne troops landing in the Maleme, Retimo and

[5] The need to occupy and hold the island of Crete as a vital strategic base was shown to be false when, following the German occupation, it simply became a military backwater. Churchill's decision to defend the island was made in spite of strong military objections from both the Army and Navy C-in-Cs.

[6] The naval forces defending Crete were deployed as follows:-
Force A - *Queen Elizabeth* (Vice-Admiral 1st Battle Squadron) and *Barham* in position west of Crete to cover all other naval forces
Force B - *Gloucester* and *Fiji* to cover the north-west of Crete, or to support Force D.
Force C - *Dido* (Rear-Admiral D), *Kandahar*, *Nubian*, *Kingston*, *Juno* and *Coventry* to defend the approaches to Heraklion and Sitia.
Force D - *Naiad*, *Phoebe* and two destroyers to deal with landings west of Retimo.
Reserve - At Alexandria, *Warspite*, *Valiant*, *Formidable*, *Orion*, *Ajax* and all remaining destroyers.

Heraklion areas on Crete either by parachute or by glider. Fighting was fierce and German losses were heavy, but by dawn on 21 May they had captured the airport at Maleme on the north-west coast. It was at this point that the defenders lost the battle for the island, for once in possession of the airfield the Luftwaffe pushed more and more transport aircraft in. Despite losing over 80 transports, more and more German infantrymen were disgorged onto the island and it was not long before there was no possibility of a counter-attack to recover Maleme.

During 21 May the naval forces off Crete were subjected to heavy air attacks and Force A1 (*Warspite, Valiant, Ajax* and eight destroyers), which had relieved Force A, was attacked once in the forenoon and again for over two hours during the afternoon. *Gloucester* and *Fiji* had joined up with A1 some 60 miles west of the Andikithiri Strait and were steaming to join Force D, which now consisted of *Orion* and *Ajax* with four destroyers. During these air attacks *Ajax* was damaged by near misses, and it was becoming very apparent that if they continued unabated serious losses would be incurred. At 2000 that evening *Gloucester* and *Fiji* parted company with A1 to patrol the area off north-west Crete and that evening, although no major seaborne operation had taken place, groups of small coastal craft carrying over 2,300 German troops, escorted by the torpedo boat *Lupo*, were sighted making their way from the island of Milos, towards Crete. They were heading towards the German stronghold of Maleme when they were intercepted by Force D and over a period of two and a half hours at least ten of the small caiques and the escort *Lupo* were sunk, but not before the latter had fired its torpedoes and damaged the destroyer *Kingston*.

In all some 297 German soldiers were killed, but it made no difference to the outcome of the Battle of Crete which, for the British Army, was already lost. Very soon the Navy's role would change from that of preventing a seaborne invasion to the evacuation of the Army before it was overwhelmed.

During the night of 21/22 May *Gloucester* and *Fiji*, together with the destroyers *Greyhound* and *Griffin*, patrolled off Cape Matapan and in the early hours of 22 May a signal was sent ordering them to proceed to Heraklion. However this signal was not received by them in time for it to be carried out. At daylight on 22 May they were some 25 miles north of Canea (Khania) steaming towards Force A1. From 0630 to 0800 the four warships were almost continuously attacked by dive-bombers, and both *Gloucester* and *Fiji* suffered some minor damage from near misses. Surgeon Lt-Cdr Hugh Singer, who was the Deputy MO on board *Gloucester*, has left an account of this action: '*It was a perfect spring morning. The sky was cloudless and the sea flat calm. It was difficult to appreciate that a major battle was in progress. However, our peace was soon shattered. As I was walking on the quarterdeck soon after dawn the loudspeakers blared out the "Alarm to Arms", and at the same time I saw a few apparently harmless dots appear over the horizon astern of us. The specks rapidly grew larger and soon resolved themselves into a squadron of German aircraft. I went below to my action station in the Stokers' bathroom, port side. I had seen a great deal of it in the Mediterranean, especially since the beginning of the Battle of Crete. Since leaving Alexandria on 20 May we had been subjected to one air attack after another during daylight hours. As I reached the Stokers' bathroom the 4-inch guns opened fire. They were soon joined by the pom-poms and the 0.5s. The ship heeled over as she was put hard-a-starboard. Almost immediately there were some dull thuds and the ship shook a little. Splinters from the exploding bombs spattered against the ship's side.*' After this first attack the two cruisers were left for a short time, and Hugh Singer takes up the story again: '*I went up to the wardroom to arrange for some breakfast in my capacity as mess caterer. Right beside the seat I habitually occupied was a new splinter hole in the bulkhead, and I was duly thankful the attack had not taken us by surprise. While I was lingering over my coffee we were again ordered to action stations. Almost at once the ship could be felt to increase speed and the guns again opened fire. The same routine was*

repeated and from that time until we were sunk in the afternoon we were constantly at action stations, and attack followed attack with little interruption.'

At about 1100 *Gloucester* and *Fiji* joined Force A1 with *Gloucester* taking station on the port side of the battle squadron, inside the destroyer screen. Although the air attacks continued she and *Fiji* were no longer the sole targets. During the forenoon the German pilots changed their strategy from targeting the major warships to concentrating on the destroyer screen and at 1249 they had their first success when *Juno* suffered a number of direct hits and sank within the space of two minutes. Hugh Singer again recalls the events which followed: '*Just after the loss of the destroyer I went foraging for something to eat. We were released from our action stations in small groups for this purpose. I found a bully-beef sandwich in the wardroom and decided to get some fresh air while I still had the chance. As I stepped out on deck I saw that an attack was being made on* Warspite. *She was hit amidships but appeared to be keeping station in spite of the large quantities of black smoke billowing up from her*[7]*. I was not able to watch for long as a few of the dive-bombers directed themselves towards us, and I repaired below without undue delay.*'

By this time *Gloucester*'s anti-aircraft ammunition was running dangerously low, and in some cases had been reduced to 20 rounds per gun. Meanwhile, at 1351, *Greyhound*, which had been detached form Force A1 to sink a caique, which had been sighted between Pori and Andikithiri Islands, was bombed and sunk whilst returning to her position in the screen. The air attacks continued without a break, and as Hugh Singer remembered: '*During the afternoon air attacks our retaliatory fire was more noticeably economical than it had been earlier in the day.*' At just after 1400 *Gloucester* and *Fiji* were ordered to detach from the main battlefleet to give AA support to *Kandahar* and *Kingston* who were picking up survivors from *Greyhound* and were themselves coming under fierce air attack. However, at 1457, when the low state of their high-angle stocks became clear, the two cruisers were ordered to rejoin Force A1.

While all this was going on Hugh Singer remembers conditions down below: '*I had not been on deck since the lunch interval, but we were kept well informed below decks by means of the tannoy, through which the torpedo officer kept up a running commentary for our benefit. Also one comes to be able to form a fairly accurate picture of what is happening from the movements of the ship, the vibrations of the engines and the nature of the HA fire.*' By 1530 both *Gloucester* and *Fiji* were sighted coming up astern of Force A1 at high speed, and at the same time engaging enemy aircraft which were making determined attacks on both ships. At about 1550 *Gloucester* was seen to be hit by several bombs and immobilized. Hugh Singer describes the events: '*We were warned through the loudspeakers of the imminence of another attack. The 4-inch fired. The pom-pom opened fire. The voice of the torpedo officer told us that this looked like being, "a pretty close one". Almost immediately afterwards the ship shook violently, and all the lights in my part of the ship went out. The loudspeakers went dead. Again there was a dull explosion and the ship heaved, throwing us into the air. I switched on my torch and got to my feet. The ship was shaken by more explosions. About 1550 we were hit by at least two bombs in the after part of the ship. One of them entered through X barbette and exploded in the gunroom flat. Either this bomb or another damaged B boiler room and compressor room, and the main WT office. Another was responsible for blowing clean over the side the after DCT, the after HA director and the main topmast.*' A witness on board *Kingston* remembers seeing this attack and he described it thus: '*I saw a Stuka diving and as I followed its progress I saw a bomb leave the aircraft and hit* Gloucester*'s mainmast which seemed to come down with a shudder and then fall over the side of the ship.*' Hugh Singer again takes up the story: '*Another bomb landed on*

[7] One officer and 22 ratings were killed in the attack on *Warspite*.

the 4-inch gun deck between P1 and P2. All the port torpedoes had been fired before the explosion owing, I believe, to the prompt action of the torpedo officer, Lt E. O. Daniel. No doubt many more would have been killed had the warheads exploded. Yet another bomb penetrated the port pom-pom platform, went through the port hangar and exploded in the canteen flat. Up to this time the ship had been able to steam on the forward engine, but in a very short time we lost steam altogether and the ship rapidly lost way.'

Petty Officer Wainwright also remembers the action: '*When we ran out of ammunition we finished up firing the 6-inch guns and starshell, it was a waste of time really. Wave after wave of Stukas were concentrating on us. By the time we came to abandon ship we had gone another half mile from where we were first hit. A bomb hit the ship aft and the after Director Control Tower went up in the air, then toppled over the side, it took half of the main mast away. The aerials came crashing down and I took cover. I went back to the bridge and assisted a Sub-Lieutenant to throw the cipher books over the side. Captain Rowley told me to make a signal to* Fiji *and ask her to come alongside, but before I could do so the Captain took the flags and sent the signal himself. The reply came back, "Sorry, but I will drop Carley floats".'*

As well as the direct hits to *Gloucester* a number of near misses on the port side had ripped open large holes in the ship's side, and it was not long before the cruiser took a severe list to port. In the meantime, down below, Hugh Singer whose distribution station was the gunroom, attempted to make his way to the compartment where necessary arrangements had been made for dealing with casualties. He describes his attempts thus: '*After we had been hit my first concern was to reach the gunroom. I got as far as the armoured door on the port side, but found this had jammed. I managed to get it open a few inches and was at this stage joined by Commander (E) Brown and Lieutenant (E) Setton, but our combined efforts failed to open it any further. Large quantities of smoke began to pour out from the Marines' after messdeck and we were forced to abandon any further attempt to reach the after part of the ship by this route. At this stage all hands were ordered on to the upper deck. Those of us who were in the midships section reached the upper deck through the hatch leading up from the workshop flat.'*

With the ship heeling over to port and uncontrollable fires raging below deck, Hugh Singer goes on to describe events once he had reached the upper deck: '*Abandon ship had already begun. I had not actually heard the order myself, but that is hardly surprising in the circumstances. The starboard whaler had been lowered and I heard later that owing to some confusion while getting it away it had gone straight to the bottom, and many men were leaving by shinning down the falls. We were by this time listing quite heavily to port. The port whaler was also away, but judging from the surrounding damage I imagine it would have proved unseaworthy. As I came on deck* Fiji *was steaming past dropping her Carley floats into the water. She then increased speed and left us*[8]*.'*

Despite the fact that *Gloucester* was sinking and that Abandon Ship had been ordered, Hugh Singer continued to tend the wounded, as he remembers: '*I established an emergency dressing station on the starboard side well deck against the bakery. There we were sheltered from any stray splinters which might have come from the pom-pom shells which were exploding at intervals as a result of a fire raging round the pom-pom magazine. I attended a few casualties here, mostly from the port 4-inch and pom-pom guns' crews. The two most seriously injured were put into the two remaining Neil Robertson stretchers and passed into a Carley float kept alongside for the purpose. Others were dealt with as the circumstances permitted. Dressings were applied as necessary and fractures splinted. Those who were not too gravely wounded were given only ¼ gr of morphine, in order that they might help themselves as much as possible. The*

[8] At 2015 that evening, having been hit by at least four bombs, *Fiji* too was sunk.

An aerial view of HMS Gloucester *under attack, taken from the attacking aircraft. (Syd Goodman Collection)*

dangerously wounded were given at least ½ gr, as their survival under these conditions seemed highly unlikely, and there seemed no point in allowing unnecessary suffering. Owing to the intensity of enemy air activity we could not expect any ship to stop to pick us up during daylight hours. While I was thus engaged the PMO came aft from the sickbay and asked me if I had everything under control. On being assured that I needed no help, he reminded me to take off my shoes before leaving and he abandoned ship by the falls of the starboard whaler. Shortly afterwards SBCPO George Hicks, who had been assisting me, left. I did not see either of them again. Shortly after they left a few Ju-87s and -88s came over the ship and dropped sticks of bombs among the survivors swimming near the starboard side. I cannot say whether this was deliberate or whether they were actually trying to hit the ship. In any case I did not observe the effect as I was fully occupied at the time. When all the wounded who were brought to me had been dealt with and put on the Carley float I went aft along the 4-inch gun deck to see if it were possible to reach the after part of the ship by this route. Unfortunately, the wardroom flat and the wardroom galley flat above it were badly on fire and there was no hope at all. On my return to the waist of the ship I joined for a short time Commander Turner, who was with a small party on the flight deck throwing loose wood over the side for the benefit of the swimmers. After a few minutes, however, another casualty was brought to me from somewhere forward. After his leg had been splinted he was put into a Carley float which was still alongside. By this time it was full to capacity, and those who were in it were up to their chests in water. Some of the badly wounded were already in a critical state. There seemed to be no more wounded who could be reached, so I ordered the float to cast off.'

By this time *Gloucester* had been reduced to a blazing wreck and with the list to port increasing it was clear that the ship was in danger of capsizing completely. Hugh Singer again takes up the story: '*During the time I was running the emergency dressing station I was greatly assisted by LSBA Priestly, who stayed with me until the last of the wounded was aboard the Carley float. He was for most of the time my only assistant apart from the Chaplain, Rev William Bonsey, who made excellent use of the knowledge of first aid he had acquired in the ship. At about 1715, at least that is the time my watch stopped, there being nothing further to do, I abandoned ship with the padre. The port gunwales were by this time awash and it was simply a matter*

A souvenir postcard which was typical of a type published during the Second World War in memory of ships and their companies who had been lost at sea. In this case, as well as the loss of the ship on 28 March 1941, the citation on the card mentions the attack on 8 July 1940. (World Ship Photo Library)

of stepping into the water.'

Shortly after this and within sight of the hilltops of Kithira, *Gloucester* rolled over onto her port side, before rising vertically in the water and sinking by the stern. For the hundreds of men in the water it was the end of one ordeal and the beginning of another.

With the ferocious air attacks continuing it was impossible for any of the destroyers to attempt to rescue *Gloucester*'s survivors, and some of those who had managed to get into the water were killed or wounded by machine-gun fire from the attacking aircraft. After nightfall the air attacks ceased, but the overnight exposure in the sea took its toll and is summed up by Hugh Singer: '*Initially I found the water pleasantly warm, but soon found that water which is pleasant for bathing is not necessarily a suitable medium in which to spend a day and a night.*' As the night wore on Hugh Singer describes how some men just appeared to give up the struggle to stay alive: '*One of the astonishing features of this unfortunate business was the ease with which some men gave up the struggle for existence and allowed themselves to drown without apparently making any effort at all. Admittedly the Mae West proved a most unsatisfactory form of lifejacket, but it did give valuable support and was effective if the swimmer helped himself a little. And yet from the time I abandoned ship until far into the night I saw men, among them several first-class swimmers, just give up. There was no panic. They died very peacefully. Two of them actually smiled to me and said "good bye". I think they must have been affected sooner, and to a greater degree, by a sort of lethargy, which one*

had to fight. I found that even I could contemplate drowning without any qualms, and at times I had an overwhelming urge to let down my Mae West and give up what seemed an unending and pointless struggle.'

Rescue eventually came in the form of locally requisitioned caiques which the German Army was using to search for survivors from one of their own troop convoys that the Royal Navy had devastated. Eventually all the survivors were sent to PoW camps in Germany and it would be four years before they were liberated. Of *Gloucester*'s 805 officers and men only two officers and 83 ratings survived[9]. Captain Rowley was not one of them. Some four weeks later, in late June, his body was washed up on the North African coast, near the Egyptian town of Marsa Matruh. Churchill's ill-judged decision to try to open a Balkan front, and to try to defend the island of Crete led to disaster for both the Army and particularly the Navy which, by the end of the campaign, had lost three cruisers, *Gloucester*, *Fiji* and *Calcutta* (it could also be argued *York* as well) and six destroyers, *Greyhound, Juno, Kelly, Kashmir, Imperial* and *Hereward*, with 1,828 naval personnel killed in total. In addition the battleships *Warspite, Barham* and *Valiant* were damaged, as were six cruisers and seven destroyers. As Cunningham later reported; '*Losses and damage were sustained which would normally only occur during a major fleet action, in which the enemy fleet might be expected to suffer greater losses than our own.*' In the event the Axis forces lost only a handful of aircraft. The lessons of air power as a major factor in the war at sea would be hard-learned by the Royal Navy and later in 1941, in the Far East, there would be another disaster when major warships were left vulnerable to attack from the air.

As for *Gloucester* the C-in-C Mediterranean, Admiral Cunningham, said of her: '*Thus went the gallant Gloucester. She had endured all things and no ship had worked harder or had taken more risky tasks. She had been hit by bombs more times than any other vessel and had always come up smiling.*'

[9] Two ratings died in captivity, so only 81 made it home in 1945.

Chapter Nine

HMS EDINBURGH

1939-1942

HMS Edinburgh *on the River Tyne on 4 April 1939, after completing long duration sea trials in the North Sea (Steve Bush Collection)*

Of the four Town-class cruisers which were lost to enemy action during the Second World War, the one which is best remembered today is HMS *Edinburgh*. Her name will be forever linked with the fascination for gold, and a great deal of it. Like *Belfast* she was part of the 1936 construction programme, with the order going to Swan, Hunter and Wigham Richardson, at Wallsend on the River Tyne. When her first keel plates were laid on 30 December 1936 there were ten cruisers of the class under construction, enough for two squadrons. On 20 October 1937, with the hull of the new cruiser taking shape, the first officer to be appointed for duty with the ship arrived at the Tyneside shipyard, but it was to be another five months before the vessel was launched. In January 1938 progress was delayed by a strike of platers in a dispute over whether platers or shipwrights should make the armour plating. At the end of March that year, however, the ship was ready for launching, being the last of the ten Town-class cruisers to take to the water. The ceremony took place on Thursday 31 March 1938, being performed by Lady Gumley, the wife of Sir Louis Gumley, Lord Provost of the city of Edinburgh. It was almost 12 months later, on 15 February 1939, that *Edinburgh*'s first commanding officer, Captain F. C. Bradley RN, was appointed to the ship which was still fitting out on the Tyne. Captain Bradley had seen service during the Great War of 1914-18,

HMS Edinburgh *in July 1939, leaving Devonport for exercises in the North Sea which, only a few weeks before the outbreak of war, would take her close to the German coast.* *(World Ship Photo Library)*

when he had commanded torpedo boats and the destroyers *Rocket* and *Unity*. During the post-war years he had served with the Royal Australian Navy, during which time he had commanded the cruisers *Australia* and *Canberra*.

On 9 March 1939, just days before German troops occupied Prague and the 21-year-old Republic of Czechoslovakia, *Edinburgh* left the River Tyne for her first full day of contractor's trials at sea. However, that same evening while entering the River Tyne to return to her fitting-out berth, she was in collision with the 6,000-ton petroleum tanker SS *Rosewood*, which was secured to the Howdon Buoys opposite Jarrow Slake. Fortunately the tanker was empty, but the force of the collision cut *Rosewood* adrift and holed her above the waterline. Luckily nobody was injured and a tug soon had her secured once again. *Edinburgh*, which was in charge of Swan Hunters' trials master, had dropped her anchor when a collision appeared inevitable, but she sustained damage to her bows, also above the waterline, and she was able to continue her passage to Swan, Hunters' Wallsend shipyard. The repairs cut short the trials period, and it was the end of March before they were resumed. On 29 March, during the course of the trials, *Edinburgh* anchored at Rosyth and Captain Bradley, who had not yet taken over command, visited Edinburgh's City Chambers, where he called on the Lord Mayor and other civic dignitaries. By the first week of April the cruiser had returned to Wallsend to complete her fitting out.

During the forenoon of 6 July 1939, with all shipyard work on *Edinburgh* having been completed, the cruiser left the River Tyne for a day of machinery trials in the North Sea, when the White Ensign was hoisted for the first time. That evening the ship stopped off Tynemouth to disembark the civilian workmen who had sailed for the acceptance trials, after which the ship set course south. Next day progress was hindered by thick fog, but by the early forenoon of 8 July she was off Start Point. At 1715 that day she secured alongside the battleship *Rodney* at Devonport Dockyard, where she remained for ten days while a steady stream of VIPs came to look her over.

By mid-July 1939 the immediate euphoria which had followed the Munich Agreement just ten

months earlier had evaporated and, as Adolf Hitler's eyes turned towards the city of Danzig, in Britain and France a sense of the inevitability of another catastrophic European war gathered pace. It was clear that in the circumstances *Edinburgh*'s trials and work-up would be short, for she would need to be operational as soon as possible and on 18 July she left Devonport for Spithead where, with a Walrus from RAF Gosport, she carried out catapult launching and aircraft recovery trials. On 30 July, following an inspection by the C-in-C Plymouth, Admiral Dunbar-Nasmith VC, she sailed north to Rosyth.

Arriving in the Firth of Forth on the last day of July *Edinburgh* joined her sisters *Glasgow, Sheffield, Southampton*, the battleship *Ramillies*, the battlecruiser *Hood*, the aircraft carrier *Ark Royal*, the cruisers *Cumberland* and *Dunedin* and numerous destroyers for what was to be the last prewar naval exercise in the North Sea. The exercise, code-named 'KD', began on Friday 11 August and took the Royal Navy's ships close to the German coast. Here, during the afternoon of 15 August, when *Edinburgh* was north-west of Heligoland, she was shadowed by a German seaplane which slowly circled the ship before it left the scene. The exercise ended at Invergordon on 21 August and four days later, with other ships of the Home Fleet, she anchored in Scapa Flow as part of Admiral Sir Charles Forbes' 'North Sea Force', an altogether smaller fleet than Jellicoe's Grand Fleet 25 years earlier. During *Edinburgh*'s three days at the anchorage she carried out daily work-up exercises in the Pentland Firth, and on the afternoon of 26 August there were faint echoes of Jellicoe and the Grand Fleet when she met and escorted his Great War flagship, the elderly and demilitarised battleship *Iron Duke*, into Scapa Flow where she was to take her final role as a depot ship. Two days later *Edinburgh* was dry docked at Glasgow, and it was 1 September before she returned to Scapa Flow, in time for Chamberlain's declaration of war at 1100 on Sunday 3 September 1939.

HMS *Edinburgh*'s war began in earnest on Saturday 9 September when, in company with *Belfast*, she left Scapa Flow for the area east of Iceland and the icy-cold waters of the Denmark Strait to search for any German merchant shipping which might be using the northbound route home in an effort to avoid the contraband patrols operating between the Shetlands and Iceland. The two cruisers steamed round Iceland's north shores some 14 miles off the coast, but the only vessels encountered were Norwegian trawlers. In the Denmark Strait visibility was reduced to less than a mile, ideal conditions for blockade-runners. On Wednesday 13 September *Edinburgh* and *Belfast* took their places in the line of the Northern Patrol, between the Faroe Islands and Iceland, but gale force winds, heavy seas and torrential rain again reduced visibility. During the height of the storm, *Edinburgh*'s boats suffered damage and both she and *Belfast* hove to until weather conditions improved. It was 0600 on 14 September before the two ships were able to rejoin their patrol lines and two hours later, just north of the Faroe Islands, *Edinburgh* intercepted and stopped her first merchant ship, the Norwegian steamer *Idefjord*. However, weather conditions still precluded the dispatch of a boarding party, and on learning that she was from Montreal bound for Stavanger with a cargo of grain, she was allowed to proceed. In the meantime, on board *Edinburgh*, her details were checked so that if necessary she could be overhauled and stopped. That night two more neutral Norwegian vessels were stopped and interrogated, but as they did not give rise to any suspicions, they were allowed to proceed. Finally, at 0715 on 15 September, *Edinburgh* and *Belfast* were ordered to Sullum Voe where they anchored later that day. *Edinburgh* continued her duties on the Northern Patrol, operating between the Shetland Islands and Iceland, enforcing the trade embargo on Germany which had been so successful during the Great War. On the last day of September, however, she was ordered south to Rosyth from where she would operate through to the spring of 1940.

At 0915 on Monday 9 October 1939, *Edinburgh*, together with her sisters *Glasgow* and

Southampton, were on patrol in the North Sea some 100 miles west of the Skagerrak, when they came under a sustained attack by a strong force of Heinkel He-111 bombers. Initially the attacks were made from a high level, but later in the forenoon further waves of aircraft dive-bombed both *Glasgow* and *Southampton*. The attacks continued for most of the day and only ended at 1700, when daylight was fading. Next day *Edinburgh* returned to Rosyth, and during the early hours of 13 October, following a collision between the armed merchant cruiser *Jervis Bay* and the destroyer *Sabre*, *Edinburgh*'s boats assisted with the search for survivors. Three days later, during the afternoon of 16 October, as *Edinburgh* and *Southampton* lay at anchor at Rosyth, they came under heavy air attack from successive waves of Heinkel He-111 bombers. It was the first enemy air attack directed at Rosyth and the Firth of Forth, and at 1530 *Southampton* took a direct hit by a bomb which failed to explode. Splinters from another bomb which exploded close to *Edinburgh* killed a Commissioned Gunner and an Able Seaman aboard the cruiser, and wounded another five men. The very minor damage did not affect *Edinburgh*'s operational capability, and on 23 September she put to sea for a six-day patrol of the North Sea.

During November 1939 *Edinburgh* carried out convoy escort duties in the North Sea, escorting vital merchant ships between the Firth of Forth and Immingham, where the shipping was vulnerable to both U-boat and air attacks. These duties, alternating with North Sea patrols, continued through December and on until March 1940. During this period *Edinburgh* operated closely with *Arethusa* and *Glasgow*. On 11 December 1939, while at Rosyth, Captain C. M. Blackman DSO RN took over command of the ship from Bradley. She made a final patrol in early March, which took her close to the Norwegian coast, ending on the 12 of the month at Scapa Flow. That same evening she left Scapa with a convoy of merchant ships to make a slow, five-day passage to the River Tyne where, during the forenoon of 17 March, she secured alongside a berth at Jarrow Slake to begin a seven-month refit. By 22 April her ship's company had been reduced to a small care and maintenance party.

It was October 1940 before *Edinburgh*, with a new ship's company, recommissioned for operational service. By that time the military and political situation in Europe had changed out of all recognition since the spring of that year, with most of Western Europe under German occupation. After a short work-up at Scapa Flow *Edinburgh* began her new commission by escorting convoys between Greenock and Freetown, returning to Scapa at the end of each round voyage. On 18 December she joined her sister *Manchester* for two days of exercises, before carrying out patrol duties from Scapa Flow, which continued into the first two months of 1941. In late February she began convoy escort duties between Scapa Flow and Greenock, and on 25 March she left Greenock with a southbound convoy which she escorted as far as Gibraltar. From there she escorted a northbound convoy back to the Clyde, and by 15 April she had returned to Scapa Flow. On Saturday 19 April, *Edinburgh* and *Exeter* escorted a force of minelayers from Scapa Flow to the Denmark Strait where mines were laid between Iceland and Greenland in an attempt to block the strait to shipping. Following this operation the force returned to Scapa Flow by way of Reykjavik.

HMS *Edinburgh*'s next patrol from Scapa Flow began during the forenoon of 5 May when, in company with *Birmingham* and *Manchester*, she left for the patrol areas between the Shetland and Faroe Islands. Two days later, just south of the Faroe Islands she intercepted and captured the German weather ship *München*. The crew were embarked in *Edinburgh* and men from the accompanying destroyer *Somali* put a prize crew aboard the weather ship, which was in fact a trawler, to sail her to Sullum Voe. On 10 May the three cruisers returned to Scapa Flow and two days later Vice-Admiral L. E. Holland, who had been flying his flag in *Edinburgh*, was appointed Vice-Admiral Battlecruiser Squadron and he left *Edinburgh* to hoist his flag in *Hood*. His new appointment would

HMS Edinburgh *outboard of a Nelson-class battleship prior to the outbreak of the Second World War. Note the positioning of 'X' and 'Y' turrets, mounted one deck higher than in the previous ships.* *(Steve Bush Collection)*

last barely 14 days, and ended with the catastrophic loss of *Hood*[1].

On Sunday 18 May, having completed two days of exercises with the brand new battleship *Prince of Wales*, which was working up from Scapa Flow, *Edinburgh* sailed on a patrol of the Western Atlantic from Iceland as far south as the coast of Portugal. These were uncertain times, for Intelligence reports indicated that the formidable new battleship *Bismarck*, together with a heavy cruiser, was about to break out into the Atlantic. It was intended that they should join forces with *Scharnhorst* and *Gneisenau* to create havoc among British convoys. Four days into the patrol, during the afternoon of 22 May, when *Edinburgh* was in mid-Atlantic, over 500 miles west of La Corunna, she sighted a suspicious merchant ship which, when challenged, did not reply. As *Edinburgh* closed the merchantman her crew were seen to be abandoning ship and shortly afterwards a huge explosion ripped through the vessel, which rapidly began to sink. All that was left for *Edinburgh* was to lower her boats and pick up the German crewmen. The ship was in fact the German SS *Lech*, which was homeward-bound from Rio de Janeiro. She had been intending to run the British blockade south of Iceland, but her passage had been interrupted two days earlier than her master had expected. Having taken on the survivors, *Edinburgh* continued her patrol and some 38 hours later, at 0600 on 24 May, *Hood* and *Prince of Wales* met *Bismarck* and *Prinz Eugen* in the ill-fated encounter in the Denmark Strait. *Edinburgh* at that time was in mid-Atlantic, west of Ireland, and two days later she joined *Rodney* in the South-Western Approaches, some 150 miles south-west of Bantry. During the course of the day she was involved in the search for the two German warships and at noon on 27 May she received the signal, '*Bismarck sunk*', and was ordered to Lough Foyle in the north of Ireland where, during the afternoon of 28 May, her

[1] The author's uncle, Telegraphist George McCart, was already serving in *Hood*, on the staff of Vice-Admiral Battlecruiser Squadron. He too lost his life when *Hood* was sunk.

HMS Edinburgh *at anchor, prior to 1941, as she has yet to receive her wartime modifications.*
(Steve Bush Collection)

prisoners were disembarked before *Edinburgh* herself sailed north for Scapa Flow.

On 19 June 1941, at Scapa Flow, there was a change of command with Captain H. W. Faulkner RN relieving Blackman. With the threat of *Bismarck* now gone *Edinburgh* spent most of June 1941 operating with her sister *Manchester* on the Northern Patrol, between the Shetland Islands and Iceland, and on 19 June Rear-Admiral E. N. Syfret, (CS18) hoisted his flag. Six days later the cruiser headed south to Greenock from where, on 29 June, she sailed as part of the escort to the southbound convoy WS9B. Once off the Portuguese coast *Edinburgh* was detached and on 10 July she secured alongside Gibraltar's detached mole, where she remained for ten days. With Axis forces now in complete control of Crete and Greece, and dominating the north-east Mediterranean and much of North Africa, the island of Malta was almost completely isolated. Naval operations in the Eastern Mediterranean were extremely hazardous and if the island were not to fall to the Axis powers most of its supplies would have to be shipped in from the west. The first major convoy to bring relief to the beleaguered island was code-named 'Operation Substance' and it consisted of seven large merchantmen carrying military personnel, military equipment and stores. The escort comprised the battleships *Nelson* and *Rodney, Ark Royal*, the cruisers *Edinburgh*, *Manchester, Hermione* and *Arethusa*, eight destroyers and the fast minelayer *Manxman*. However, three of the cruisers, *Edinburgh*, *Manchester* and *Arethusa* would each be carrying over 500 troops, who had been brought to Gibraltar in the French troop transport *Pasteur*, and this would seriously hamper their fighting efficiency. The convoy left Gibraltar during the early hours of 20 July and initially it steamed west towards the Atlantic, until it passed Tarifa Point when it turned about and set course into the Mediterranean. The first two days of the passage west passed without incident, but at 0735 on 23 July, an enemy seaplane

was sighted and it was not long before the first air attack. At 0940 nine Italian S79 torpedo bombers attacked at low level, while at the same time five Cant Z1007 bombers made a high-level attack. They were quickly attacked by Fulmars from *Ark Royal*, but not before *Manchester* was hit by a torpedo and was forced to limp back to Gibraltar[2]. Almost simultaneously the destroyer *Fearless* was also hit by another torpedo, and she was eventually scuttled. A near miss from a bomb disabled the destroyer *Firedrake*'s engines. A second attack later in the forenoon was driven off by fighters from *Ark Royal*. Later that day RAF Beaufighters from Malta were able to provide air cover, but just over an hour later, at 1902, another enemy torpedo and bombing attack developed and during the night Italian torpedo boats hit the freighter *Sydney Star*, while *Edinburgh* herself had to manoeuvre hard in order to avoid torpedoes. By 0600 on 24 July the convoy was once again covered by aircraft from Malta, but at 0700 it was subjected to another fierce aerial attack. Fortunately no further damage was caused to the convoy or to the escorts, and at 1145 *Edinburgh* secured to a buoy in Grand Harbour where her troops were safely disembarked. By 1730 that day she had refuelled and embarked a number of officers and ratings for the return voyage. After leaving Malta, the eastbound passage passed without serious incident, and at 0755 on 25 July she was met by Force H, including *Renown* and *Ark Royal*. Two days later, at 0930 on 27 July, she secured alongside at Gibraltar.

Following her safe return to Gibraltar *Edinburgh* relieved *London* on convoy escort duties in the Atlantic, sailing south to Freetown and Cape Town. In mid-September, however, she returned to Gibraltar where she joined a formidable force of warships which would provide the escort for eight large merchant ships, again bound for Malta. The operation, code-named 'Halberd', was, in the autumn of 1941, the largest attempt to run merchant ships through the Mediterranean and, as they were carrying over 80,000 tons of military equipment and civilian food supplies, it was vital that the ships got through to their destination. As well as *Nelson, Ark Royal, Sheffield, Hermione* and six destroyers of Force H, the Home Fleet provided *Prince of Wales, Rodney, Edinburgh, Euryalus, Kenya* and 13 destroyers. During the night of 24/25 September the convoy passed through the Strait of Gibraltar and once into the Mediterranean *Ark Royal, Nelson, Hermione* and five destroyers steamed ahead as if they were on one of the regular air reinforcement runs hoping, as they steamed towards the Balearic Islands, to avoid Italian reconnaissance aircraft for as long as possible. During the forenoon of 27 September both groups joined up and 18 destroyers fanned out ahead of the convoy, with *Edinburgh* leading the right hand column of four merchant ships[3], and the battleship *Nelson* to starboard. The left column of merchantmen was led by *Kenya*, with *Prince of Wales* and *Rodney* screening them. Astern and between the two columns was *Sheffield*.

The first Italian air attacks came at 1300 that day when torpedo bombers attacked from the port side, with two being shot down by a barrage of fire from *Prince of Wales, Rodney* and *Kenya*. Half an hour later a second air attack, this time from the starboard side of the convoy, resulted in *Nelson* being hit by a torpedo and being badly damaged. She was, however, able to continue as part of the escort. That afternoon reconnaissance aircraft from *Ark Royal* reported an Italian naval force of two battleships, four cruisers and at least 16 destroyers some 80 miles north-east of the convoy, which Somerville in *Nelson* thought were either planning to intercept the convoy in the Skerki Channel, or were attempting to draw the main escort away to the north-east, thus leaving the convoy open to attack from the air. In the event, at 1430 he ordered *Nelson, Prince of Wales, Rodney, Edinburgh, Sheffield* and six destroyers to haul out of line and set course to inter-

[2] See chapter on HMS *Manchester* and the memories of Petty Officer Writer C.H.G. Heath BEM MBE. He also highlights the difficulties the ship's company had fighting the ship with over 500 troops embarked.
[3] These were *Clan Ferguson*, *Dunedin Star*, *Breconshire* and *City of Lincoln*.

HMS Edinburgh *at speed in late 1941 after her refit. She was fitted with Type 279 air search radar and six single 20mm Oerlikon mountings (two on 'B' turret; two on the quarterdeck and one either side of the bridge on 'B' gun deck level.)* *(Maritime Photo Library)*

cept the Italian ships. Soon after the chase began *Nelson*, which had been unable to make more than 15 knots, fell behind and at about the same time the Italian Admiral Iachino, who had orders not to attack unless in '*decisive superiority of forces*', received reports that he was facing at least three battleships and he reversed course. In the event the two naval forces came within 50 miles of each other. At 1900, with the convoy having been handed over to *Edinburgh, Kenya, Sheffield, Euryalus* and *Hermione*, the three battleships and *Ark Royal* turned back for Gibraltar. Just an hour after they parted company the first of two air attacks on the convoy began, and at 2030 SS *Imperial Star* was torpedoed, but she was the only casualty. At 0140 the next morning *Hermione* was detached to bombard Pantelleria, and at 1130 the convoy and escorts, minus *Imperial Star*, arrived at Malta's Grand Harbour. Five hours later, having refuelled and embarked mail and military passengers, *Edinburgh*, *Kenya* and the destroyer *Oribi* sailed from Malta to rendezvous with *Sheffield, Euryalus* and *Hermione*, to escort the Gibraltar-bound convoy 'MG2', which consisted of five merchant ships. Soon after leaving Malta *Edinburgh* and *Oribi* were detailed to search for two Italian destroyers which were reported to be north-west of Gozo. In the event they did not find either of them and by 2035 they had rejoined the escort. During the early evening of 30 September the convoy and escorts arrived safely at Gibraltar. With 'Operation Halberd' having been completed successfully *Edinburgh* returned to Scapa Flow which was her base during the rest of October and November 1941 while she operated in the North-Western Approaches. The first day of December saw her at Scapa Flow preparing for a very different operation.

On Monday 8 December 1941 *Edinburgh* left Scapa Flow to escort an Arctic convoy from Iceland's Seydisfjord to the Kola Inlet (Koskiy Zaliv), the part of the Barents Sea kept free of ice by the warm waters of the Gulf Stream, which also gave access to the port of Murmansk. On 22 June that year Germany and its Axis partners invaded the Soviet Union along a 1,800-mile front from the Arctic to the Black Sea. This would lead to the greatest clash of armies the world has ever known, and would determine the eventual outcome of the

Second World War. Both Britain and the United States pledged their support for the hard-pressed Soviet Red Army which, having been taken by surprise, was in headlong retreat. On the northern front Germany demanded, and got, free passage through Sweden and into Finland for its troops. Finland then declared war on Russia, hoping that with German help it might recover parts of the Karelian Peninsular which it had lost to Russia in the spring of 1940[4]. The new front in Finland and the German occupation of Norway brought the fighting front to within artillery range of the city of Murmansk, which added to the dangers faced by Arctic convoys. Both militarily and politically the supply convoys to Russia during the first months when the Red Army was being hard-pressed by the German Army were vitally important. As well as the hazards of air attack by German aircraft, surface attack by German Naval units and attack by U-boats from their bases in northern Norway, during the winter months the convoys and their escorts had to contend with unimaginable freezing weather conditions, with gale force winds, blinding snowstorms and ice deposits up to three feet thick on ships' upper works, which made even remaining on one's feet difficult. Once at the Kola Inlet, with the area under constant siege from frequent air raids, there was nothing in the way of luxuries and even basic food supplies were in short supply, for both local people and visiting service personnel alike.

At just after midday on 20 December, when *Edinburgh* and her convoy were only a few hours' steaming from the Kola Inlet, they were attacked by two enemy Ju-88 aircraft, which left one merchant ship damaged. Only one of the bombs, a near miss, exploded, blowing one crew member of the merchantman overboard. Luckily he was quickly picked up by *Echo* as survival time in those northern waters is measured in just a few minutes. That afternoon, without further mishap, *Edinburgh* and her convoy anchored in the Kola Inlet, where the cruiser remained for just over two weeks. During this period there was no shore leave for the ship's company, and the ship herself came under air attack by enemy aircraft operating from German-occupied airfields near the Finnish town of Petsamo close to the Russian border. On 5 January 1942 she sailed as part of the escort for convoy QP4, and ten days later all the ships arrived safely at their destination of Seydisfjord.

HMS *Edinburgh* then steamed south to the River Tyne where she underwent a seven-week refit and both watches were able to take two weeks' leave. On 8 March she left the Tyne to rejoin the Home Fleet at Scapa Flow, where she rejoined the Northern Patrol. On 21 March she joined *King George V*, *Duke of York*, *Renown*, the aircraft carrier *Victorious*, the cruiser *Kent*, and a destroyer screen, to make up a powerful force providing distant cover for the Arctic convoys PQ13 and the returning QP9, in the area north of Trondheim. These ships would be able to deal with *Tirpitz*, *Admiral Scheer* or *Hipper* if they showed themselves. On 3 April *Edinburgh* formed part of the 'welcoming squadron' which escorted the US Navy Task Force 69 to Scapa Flow. The battleship USS *Washington*, the aircraft carrier USS *Wasp*, the cruisers *Tuscaloosa* and *Wichita* and a screen of nine US Navy destroyers were reinforcing the Home Fleet at Scapa, while Royal Navy warships were deployed east of Suez for the invasion and occupation of Madagascar. On 9 April *Edinburgh* was again deployed as a convoy escort, this time for PQ14 bound for Murmansk from Seydisfjord. She was also carrying a large quantity of steel plating which was urgently required for repairs to the cruiser *Trinidad*, which had suffered damage while escorting convoy PQ13 and was in dry dock at the Russian port of Rosta, north of Murmansk. *Edinburgh* anchored in the Kola Inlet at just before midnight on 19 April, having lost only one merchant ship, SS *Empire Howard*, which had been tor-

[4] Ironically, Britain and France had come within a whisker of joining Finland in its war against Russia. However, the two Allied countries were also secretly hoping to occupy parts of Sweden, thus controlling that country's iron ore deposits. Military planners, however, knew how utterly unrealistic this was when Britain and France were already at war with Germany.

HMS Edinburgh *seen alongside in late 1941. The two 20mm Oerlikons mounted on 'B' turret are quite prominent in this picture.* *(Steve Bush Collection)*

pedoed three days earlier.

Although it was mid-April, the winter in northern Russia that year was particularly severe, a factor which the German invaders, like others before them, had grossly underestimated, and when *Edinburgh* arrived at her anchorage in Vaenga Bay her upper decks, superstructure, masts and yardarms were encrusted with thick coatings of ice. During her stay the steel plating and stores for *Trinidad* were unloaded into lighters, for with Murmansk virtually under siege by German forces there were barely enough food supplies to feed the city's population, and visiting ships had to remain self-sufficient in everything but fuel oil and fresh water. On 26 April, seven days after her arrival, *Edinburgh* embarked 28 injured personnel from the Murmansk Russian Naval Hospital, 24 of whom were cot cases, four of them suffering fractured limbs. The remainder were victims of frostbite, which ranged from mild to gangrenous. Several of the more severe cases required blood transfusions and limb amputations, and some of these operations were carried out on board. Although the worst of the medical cases were accommodated in the sick-bay, others were slung in stretchers in the Seamen's forecastle recreation space and in the Chief and Petty Officers' recreation area. In addition to the invalids *Edinburgh* also embarked a number of passengers for the voyage home, including one Polish Government Cabinet Minister and his Private Secretary, a Czechoslovakian Army Colonel and three other Czech Army Officers, three Russian Naval Officers, together with eight other officers and 30 other ranks. The overcrowding caused by the invalids and additional passengers made living conditions on board very uncomfortable for the ship's company, and to a certain extent hampered them in their efforts to fight the ship.

In addition to the invalids and other passengers, *Edinburgh* also embarked a secret and extremely valuable cargo which, when it arrived alongside in two tarpaulin-covered lighters, was guarded by a

heavily armed detachment of Red Army soldiers. The lighters were, in fact, carrying over five tons of gold bullion which had been packed into 93 small, rough, wooden crates. Each crate held four 28lb ingots packed in sawdust, and even at 1942 values the consignment was worth millions of pounds. It was destined for the US Treasury Department and as Russian payment for American weapons which had been supplied for the Soviet Union's desperate struggle for survival against the German invasion, the brutality of which far exceeded anything experienced on the Western Fronts. As the cases were hoisted on board and stowed in the aircraft bomb room there was much speculation as to their contents, and when one of the wooden crates slipped from its sling and burst open as it crashed onto the deck, narrowly missing Royal Marine Bill Miles, the secret was out. One Chief Petty Officer remembered that bitterly cold day, with a cutting, icy wind and sleet falling, and that the moisture trickling off the red stencilling on the crates gave the appearance of 'dripping blood', a sight which made him somewhat apprehensive about the homeward passage.

During the afternoon of 28 April, having assembled in Vaenga Bay, convoy QP11 sailed for Iceland. At 1500 they passed Tore's Island (Ostrov Tores) at the entrance to the Barents Sea and six and a half hours later *Edinburgh*, together with nine other escorts[5], weighed anchor and sailed to catch up with the convoy. It was sighted at 0308 on 29 April and joined just over four hours later. During the next 24 hours, during periods of poor visibility, *Edinburgh* stationed herself in the centre of the convoy, and when visibility improved she zigzagged independently at high speed astern and to port of the vessels. Soon after she joined the merchantmen, however, a German Ju-88 reconnaissance aircraft was sighted to the west and it was clear to Vice-Admiral Bonham-Carter that enemy air, submarine or surface attacks could be expected at any time. At this point Bonham-Carter had the additional problem that the German heavy cruiser *Admiral Scheer*, which had attacked Soviet shipping off northern Norway, was reported to have sailed from Trondheim and could easily be in a position to attack the convoy.

During the early evening of 29 April the 6th Minesweeping Flotilla, which had been operating ahead of the convoy, was ordered to return to Kola Inlet. At 2000 an Admiralty signal informed Bonham-Carter that a U-boat had made a sighting report of the convoy's position and course, and soon after this *Bulldog* reported large icebergs ahead so course was altered to avoid them. That evening the convoy ran into very strong head winds, which reduced its speed to four knots and left one merchantman, SS *Ballot*, unable to keep up. However, when the winds dropped she was able to rejoin the others. During the morning and forenoon of 30 April, with enemy submarines known to be in the vicinity, *Edinburgh* stationed herself some 16 to 20 miles ahead of the convoy and zigzagged at the highest speed permitted by the state of the sea, turning every few hours in order to make contact with the merchant ships.

At 1607 during the afternoon of 30 April *Edinburgh* was in a position 73°00'N 033°00'E. She had just steadied on a course 225° at a speed of 19 knots, when *U-456*, commanded by Kapitänleutnant Max Tiechert, which had been shadowing her for over four hours, fired a salvo of three torpedoes aimed at the cruiser's forward funnel. The first of these smashed into *Edinburgh*'s starboard side abaft the bridge, between stations 70 and 87, and within seconds another torpedo struck the ship again on the starboard side but much further aft, level with station 260. A Boy Telegraphist remembered the first explosion as '*...a terrific explosion and a blinding flash, followed by darkness then cries from the injured and dying in the next compartment.*' As far as the ship was concerned, however, it was a second explosion which was more serious, for it totally wrecked the steering gear compartment. A Chief Petty Officer remem-

[5] These were HM destroyers *Beagle*, *Bulldog*, *Amazon*, *Beverley*, *Forester* and *Foresight*, together with the corvettes *Campanula*, *Saxifrage* and the aptly named *Snowflake*. There were also a number of Russian destroyers.

Looking aft over the wrecked stern of HMS Edinburgh *following the initial torpedo attack.*
(Syd Goodman Collection)

bers both explosions: '*The whole ship bucked like a bronco, throwing me up in the air. No sooner had I come down with a violent bump than there was a second explosion and once again I was thrown into the air and landed on the deck with another violent bump.*'

Although *Edinburgh* was able to continue steaming she took on a seven degree list to starboard. All communications between Damage Control Headquarters, the bridge and the machinery compartments were cut off, but Captain Faulkner was able to establish that steam pressure was being maintained and that three of the cruiser's shafts were still functional, the starboard inner propeller having been destroyed by the second explosion. However, not long afterwards, at 1830, the stern section of the ship abaft Y turret broke off, carrying with it the rudder and the port inner A-bracket and propeller. The ship was now without a rudder and steaming on the two outer engines.

The first torpedo had hit the ship and exploded below the after end of the sickbay, which had to be evacuated to allow for the shoring up of bulkheads in adjacent compartments. The damage caused also rendered the Chief Stokers' and Seamen's bathrooms completely useless as first-aid stations, which in turn severely hampered efforts to treat the injured. The second torpedo had wrecked the steering gear which meant that the ship's course could only be controlled by varying the revolutions on the two outer propeller shafts that were relatively undamaged. At best the stricken cruiser could only maintain a maximum speed of ten knots, and course was set to return to Kola Inlet, over 240 miles away. With the breaking off of the stern section, however, and with the loss of both inner propeller shafts, *Edinburgh*'s speed was reduced still further; nevertheless both Bonham-Carter and Faulkner were optimistic that the ship could make it.

When the first torpedo hit the ship, down below in the machinery spaces sea water, mixed with fuel oil from damaged tanks, flooded into A boiler room, contaminating the oil supply. Steam pressure dropped rapidly and both engine rooms had to be

quickly cross-connected to B boiler room. Fortunately the contamination was cleared and the two boiler rooms could be steamed as separate units again. With Damage Control HQ flooded and out of action, orders were passed from the after engine room, and by counter-flooding the port watertight compartments abreast the machinery rooms the starboard list was checked, so that eventually the ship could be brought upright. Meanwhile, however, in the after unit, with the starboard inner propeller having been carried away, steam was shut off to the engine and two hours later, when the port inner propeller was also lost, steam was isolated from that engine as well. From that point the after engine room was used solely to supply the auxiliary machinery, with the main circulating pumps being kept in use in order to pump out the bilges. The after turbo-generator and evaporators remained in use, the latter for supplying boiler feed water and drinking water. The main steam system was kept open right up to the after throttles so that if necessary it could be cross-connected to the forward engine room.

At 1905 Bonham-Carter ordered *Forester* to take *Edinburgh* in tow, but the cruiser had no stern and being seven feet down by the head came rapidly up into the wind and no headway was made at all. In view of the fact that the attempt to tow *Edinburgh* was unsuccessful, and the fact that the destroyer was now just another 'sitting target' for submarines, Bonham-Carter decided to cast off *Forester* and await the arrival of a Russian tug which had been sent out from Murmansk. It was decided that as *Edinburgh*'s two outer propeller shafts could maintain 120rpm without risk of further damage, she would actually take *Foresight* in tow, with the towed ship controlling the cruiser's steering. This proved to be reasonably efficient, and between 2330 on 30 April and 0600 on 1 May a speed of advance of three knots was maintained. At this stage, with Kola Inlet still some 240 miles away, it was estimated that it would take at least four days to get back, but Bonham-Carter was mildly optimistic.

That day reports were received of enemy submarines ahead and of enemy destroyers at sea so the ship's company was kept at Action Stations, adding to the stresses already being experienced. With only very limited power supplies, the duties of the ship's company, particularly for those in exposed upper deck positions, were particularly arduous. Conditions were made especially difficult for those whose messdecks had been destroyed, for they were deprived of their warm clothing. During the forenoon of 1 May Bonham-Carter considered transferring the wounded and the invalid passengers to a destroyer, but when the vessel came alongside he decided it was too dangerous and the attempt was abandoned. At 2330 that evening the good news was received in an Admiralty signal that *Admiral Scheer* had returned to Trondheim and 15 minutes later saw the arrival of the Russian tug, accompanied by the minesweepers, *Gossamer*, *Harrier, Hussar* and *Niger*, which had been recalled. This lifted the spirits of all on board the cruiser, but soon afterwards came reports that in addition to enemy destroyers being at sea, U-boats were taking up positions between *Edinburgh* and the Kola Inlet.

By 0600 on 1 May the Russian destroyers which had been assisting with the escorting and screening duties were running dangerously short of fuel and they had to return to port. Before they left, Bonham-Carter took the opportunity to muster as many members of *Edinburgh*'s ship's company as could be spared on the flight deck where he informed them frankly of the situation they faced, but told them he had high hopes of getting the ship back to harbour. In his report to the Admiralty he stated: '*...the way they responded to these remarks convinced me that my hopes were shared by them all, that morale was high and that there was no indication of our danger in the behaviour, conversation or other actions of any officer or man with whom I came into contact.*'

By this time, with some amenities restored, including the galley, life on board seemed to be returning almost to normal.

Following the arrival of the Russian tug, *Edinburgh* was taken in tow, but the sea had risen and the vessel was not powerful enough to prevent the cruiser from coming up into the wind. The possibility of steaming the ship stern first was considered, but quickly discounted when it became apparent that the damage to the after bulkheads was such that the '*grave risks could not be entertained*'. At 0530 on 2 May the tug was again taken on ahead with *Gossamer* astern to act as a drogue, and *Edinburgh* was then hauled round until her head was pointing in the desired direction before she went slowly ahead on both engines. For about half an hour she proceeded at a speed of three knots with the tug fine on the starboard bow and *Gossamer* broad on the port quarter. It seemed everything was going well. At 0600, however, gunfire from *Harrier* on the starboard quarter indicated the arrival of enemy surface warships. This was a very unwelcome turn of events, but Bonham-Carter had already foreseen such an attack and had made the following signal to *Foresight* and *Forester*: '*In the event of an attack by German destroyers,* Foresight *and* Forester *are to act independently taking every opportunity to defeat the enemy without taking any undue risks to themselves in defending* Edinburgh. Edinburgh *is to proceed wherever the wind permits, probably straight into the wind.*'

The three German destroyers were in fact *Z7 (Hermann Schoemann) Z24* and *Z25*, which were operating from northern Norway, and a few hours earlier they had harried the convoy, damaging the destroyer *Amazon* with a torpedo and sinking a merchantman, so the attack on *Edinburgh* was not unexpected. The three enemy vessels were more powerfully armed than *Forester* and *Foresight*, both of which quickly moved to engage them. With very limited visibility only one enemy ship was visible at any one time, the others being hidden by heavy snowstorms and smoke, and for both sides it was difficult to distinguish between friend and foe. *Edinburgh*'s gunners were operating under local control, with the Gunnery Officer in charge of 'X' turret, and the forward turrets being controlled by a gunnery lieutenant in 'B' turret. The latter turret was directed onto its targets by the bridge, with Captain Faulkner leaning over and shouting instructions to the lieutenant, who was looking out through the top of the turret. Nearly all *Edinburgh*'s salvoes were from B turret and, despite the fact that the ship was listing, the firing was accurate and rapid. On three occasions the enemy destroyers made determined attempts to close *Edinburgh*, but each time *Foresight, Forester* and *Edinburgh* herself drove them off. One salvo from the cruiser's 'B' turret smashed into *Hermann Schoemann*, wrecking her engine room and leaving her disabled and sinking. The other two destroyers disappeared into the blizzard, but they had not broken off the attack. At 0652 four torpedo tracks were seen at about 5,000 yards on *Edinburgh*'s starboard beam, and at first it seemed they would pass well astern. However, *Edinburgh* was not under control with her head swinging rapidly to port, and while two torpedoes passed harmlessly astern and a third passed close ahead, a fourth torpedo was running deeper than the others and no action could be taken to avoid it. This one smashed into the cruiser's port side, between frames 87 and 108, and she immediately took on a severe list to port. Captain Faulkner received reports that A boiler room was flooding and that steam was failing so he ordered the main engines to be stopped, and boiler and engine room personnel up on deck. Within minutes of the third torpedo hit Bonham-Carter ordered *Gossamer* and *Harrier* to come alongside the cruiser's starboard and port sides respectively, in order to take off the sick, wounded and passengers, of whom there were about 100. The ship continued to list and as the enemy destroyers had disappeared by now, Bonham-Carter told Faulkner to get all personnel not required to fight the ship up on deck. Shortly after this the list reached 20° and he ordered the captain to abandon ship. As *Edinburgh*'s list increased it became more and more difficult to lower men down the starboard side to *Gossamer*, a task not made any easier by the fact that the upper decks were covered in ice and just staying on one's

The extensive damage to the stern of the stricken HMS Edinburgh *is evident in this view. The sloop* HMS Gossamer *is seen alongside* *(Syd Goodman Collection)*

feet became an achievement in itself. In the event *Gossamer* took on board about 450 and *Harrier* 350, including the sick, wounded and civilian passengers, as well as the Polish Government Minister's Secretary who had been killed when the first two torpedoes hit the ship. Fortunately, with the strong wind and heavy seas having abated somewhat the task was not now hampered by the elements. As for the destroyers, *Foresight* had been hit, but was still in action, *Forester* was not in sight and *Hussar* had laid a smokescreen to cover *Edinburgh*.

As soon as Faulkner was satisfied that all men were up from below and embarked in one of the minesweepers, and that all upper deck hatches which could be reached had been opened, he and Bonham-Carter embarked in *Harrier*, which then lay off *Edinburgh* to wait for the ship to sink, an event which everyone involved thought would happen within minutes. However, with the wind and sea having calmed, *Edinburgh* lay listing heavily, crippled and helpless, but showing no signs of sinking. As the enemy destroyers were still in the vicinity Bonham-Carter ordered *Harrier*'s captain to hasten the end by firing 4-inch shells into her, and by dropping depth charges with shallow settings close to the ship. However, although the crippled cruiser settled further in the water she still showed

The sloop HMS Gossamer *is seen alongside preparing to take off survivors shortly before the cruiser sank on 2 May 1942.* *(Syd Goodman Collection)*

no immediate sign of sinking. As *Foresight* had just one remaining torpedo left Bonham-Carter ordered her to fire it into the hulk, and in his own words: 'Edinburgh*, though sinking slowly, was sunk by the remaining torpedo of* Foresight*. A hateful signal to make to* Foresight*, but though sinking slowly I considered it necessary to hasten her sinking in case the enemy destroyers returned. At this time none were in sight. On being hit by* Foresight*'s torpedo* Edinburgh *had had all she could take. She rolled over to port, her back broke and the last seen of her was her bows rising vertically and then disappearing. The after part just rolled over and within three minutes was completely submerged. It was a sad sight, but she could not be left to sink slowly.*' In fact, as will be seen later, Bonham-Carter's impression that *Edinburgh*'s back was broken does not appear to be correct.

As soon as *Edinburgh* had disappeared beneath the waves *Gossamer* and *Harrier*, both of which were overloaded with survivors, set course at their best available speed for the Kola Inlet where they berthed alongside at Polyarnyy, at the mouth of the inlet. It was the first opportunity to muster everyone together in order to establish the total number of casualties, which amounted to 58. After a pep-talk by Captain Faulkner the ship's company was split into groups as required by the local accommodation which was available, with half remaining at Polyarnyy, and the rest being re-embarked in *Gossamer* and taken to Vaenga, with the sick and wounded being sent to Murmansk.

At this point it is worth quoting Faulkner's well-deserved words of praise for his officers and men: '*The ship's company's behaviour during these three trying days left nothing to be desired and although*

they had to work continually in severe cold with only makeshift meals and almost continually at action stations when not repairing or handling tows, all orders were carried out cheerfully and enthusiastically. All emergencies were met with such confidence and calmness that they ceased to be emergencies. Throughout the whole three days the work of all men below decks and in particular the Engine Room department was beyond praise and their behaviour and bearing were in the highest traditions of the Service.'

In September 1945, when the Second World War ended, *Edinburgh* would, but for one factor, have become just another largely forgotten wartime statistic. That factor was the cargo of gold bullion. Interest among would-be salvors first surfaced in 1954, but the wreck of *Edinburgh* lay over 700 feet down in the icy-cold waters of the Barents Sea and in the mid-1950s the technology to locate and dive on the wreck just did not exist. In 1957 the wreck was declared a War Grave, but interest in the recovery of the gold bullion continued unabated. As the years went by the discovery of oil in the North Sea led to rapid advances in deep sea diving techniques, among them the breathing of a mixture of oxygen and helium, making it possible for divers to work for long periods at great depths. Finally, in May 1981 Keith Jessop, a very determined British entrepreneur who was also an experienced diver and marine salvage contractor, won the contract to locate and recover *Edinburgh*'s lost gold. On 16 May 1981, some 39 years after she had slid beneath the waves, the wreck of *Edinburgh* was located and the first video film pictures were obtained. These showed that Bonham-Carter had been mistaken when he thought the cruiser had broken her back, for she was still in one piece and lying on her port side. The hole blasted in the ship's side by the first

A memorial card commemorating the service of HMS Edinburgh *and her Ship's Company.*
(Syd Goodman Collection)

torpedo was reported to be at least 30 feet wide. It was mid-September before the first gold bars were recovered and by 7 October, when weather conditions brought diving operations to an end, some 431 gold ingots had been recovered. The wreck of *Edinburgh*, which still contained human remains, was once again allowed to rest in peace, some 200 miles north of Murmansk and deep down in the Barents Sea.

Chapter Ten

HMS BELFAST
1939-1964

A magnificent view, taken from one of Harland & Wolff's large cranes, of HMS Belfast *as she nears the end of the slipway and takes to the water for the first time.* *(Ulster Folk & Transport Museum)*

With the guns of her main armament at their maximum 45° elevation and aimed in the direction of north-west London, for over 40 years *Belfast* has lain at her permanent mooring in the Pool of London. Below decks in place of the hum of machinery there is an uncanny silence, broken only by the chattering of visitors to the ship. On deck, where once her aircraft hangar was situated, there is now a café complete with its own open-air terrace. On occasion she plays host to contemporary warships from other nations as she now forms part of the Imperial War Museum. Her survival is assured, at least for the foreseeable future. But this was not always so and at one stage, less than six months after commissioning, it appeared that her career might already be over.

HMS *Belfast* was the last of the Town-class cruisers to enter service and, like her sister *Edinburgh*, was authorised by the 1936 Naval Estimates. On 17 August that year it was announced that the contracts for the last two ships of the class would go to Swan Hunter on the River Tyne, and to Harland & Wolff at Belfast. The cost of each cruiser would be £2,000,000 and, according to Samuel Hoare, the First Lord of the Admiralty, the contracts were allocated to those particular areas of the country in

HMS Belfast *alongside her fitting-out berth in 1938. Since little has been added to her superstructure, this photograph must have been taken shortly after her launch.* *(Maritime Photo Library)*

order to help reduce higher than average unemployment figures. Two months later, at a Trafalgar Day dinner, he announced that the new cruisers would be named *Belfast* and *Edinburgh* and six weeks after that, at Harland & Wolff's Belfast shipyard, the first keel plates for *Belfast* were laid.

In the winter of 1936/37 Europe was a deeply divided continent. In Spain a civil war was raging, and repressive fascist regimes dominated both Italy and Germany, with the latter aggressively determined to unravel the Treaty of Versailles. With the continent still recovering from the economic depression which followed the Wall Street Crash in 1929, although there was no widespread talk of a second European war, political tensions were increasing and during the two years and eight months that *Belfast* was under construction the very war, which had been just a distant possibility, became a reality.

Both *Belfast* and *Edinburgh*, coming some two years after the first ships of the class had been laid down, and after the first five had actually been launched, were bound to incorporate many improvements upon the earlier cruisers. First of all they displaced some 10,550 tons, and were over 20 feet longer. There was also increased anti-aircraft armament and a more sophisticated ammunition supply system. In August 1937 the first naval personnel, led by Commissioned Gunner T. Porter, arrived in Belfast to stand by the ship as she was built. In late September and late October respectively the two men who would oversee the fitting of all the main propulsion and auxiliary machinery, Commander (E) K. A. B. Hutson RN, and Lieutenant (E) F. S. Ferguson RN, arrived in the city to add to the growing naval party which was standing by the ship. In December 1937, as the hull took shape on Harland & Wolff's slipway, it was announced that 3 March 1938 had been provisionally set as the launch date. Three weeks later came a further announcement that the wife of the Prime Minister, Mrs Anne Chamberlain, would travel to Belfast to launch the new cruiser, but the launch date itself had been put back by two weeks to 17

March, St Patrick's Day. The ceremony at Queen's Island, Belfast, took place during the forenoon of a blustery, showery and chilly day. Despite the inclement weather large crowds turned out for the event, and *Belfast* was sent safely down the slipway into the Victoria Channel from where she was towed to the fitting-out berth at Thompson Wharf, where she would remain for some 13 months.

In September 1938 came the Munich Crisis and, despite Chamberlain's promises of '*Peace for our time*', rearmament in Britain was speeded up. By the spring of 1939 work on *Belfast* was approaching completion and on 31 March it was announced that Captain G. A. Scott DSC RN was to be the ship's first commanding officer. He had served with distinction during the Great War, having been awarded the DSC for service in the monitor *Severn* off the Belgian coast, and for operations against the German cruiser *Königsberg* in East Africa. He had also commanded five destroyers and, in the early 1930s, the cruiser *Ceres*. It was in early April that drafts of men began to arrive in Belfast, and by the third week in May her complement had been increased sufficiently to provide a full steaming crew. It was at 0915 on 22 May 1939, the day after Hitler and Mussolini signed what became known as the 'Pact of Steel' that *Belfast* cast off her mooring ropes and put to sea for the first time. At this stage she was still in the hands of the builders and so flying the Red Ensign. After carrying out anchor trials she steamed across the North Channel of the Irish Sea to the Firth of Clyde to begin the builder's machinery and speed trials. These included a number of runs on the Skelmorlie measured mile, but the operations were disrupted by auxiliary machinery failures. *Belfast* continued her steaming trials for two days, before returning to Harland & Wolff's shipyard. At the end of May, still flying the Red Ensign, she was at sea again and during the afternoon of Thursday 1 June she was in the Firth of Clyde when the submarine *Thetis* was reported as overdue surfacing while engaged on her builder's trials. Initially, as well as destroyers and minesweepers, *Belfast* steamed towards the point,

On Sunday 5 August 1939, having been accepted into service from the builders, HMS Belfast *enters Portsmouth for the first time.* *(National Museum of the Royal Navy)*

close to the Great Orme where the stricken submarine, its forward compartments flooded, lay helplessly on the bottom. But in the event, as *Belfast* was not equipped or prepared for rescue operations, she was ordered to continue her trials. By the end of July 1939, two months of trials and the final stages of fitting out had been completed. During the forenoon of Thursday 3 August 1939, exactly 31 days before the outbreak of war in Europe, *Belfast* completed final machinery adjustments at Harland & Wolff's Liverpool Yard and subsequently steamed from the River Mersey across the Irish Sea to anchor in Belfast Lough where, at 1815, Captain Scott accepted the ship from the builders and the White Ensign was hoisted. One hour later *Belfast* weighed anchor and set course for Portsmouth where, at 0815 on Saturday 5 August, she secured alongside Pitch House Jetty. Five hours later lower deck was cleared for the Commissioning Ceremony, after which Captain Scott addressed the ship's company.

HMS *Belfast* was now part of the 2nd Cruiser Squadron, which also included *Glasgow* and *Southampton*, under the command of the C-in-C Home Fleet, Admiral Sir Charles Forbes, whose North Sea Force, based at Scapa Flow, was responsible for the sea defences between Rosyth and the Thames Estuary. For eight days after her arrival in Portsmouth stores and ammunition were embarked, and the ship's company numbers were brought up to full strength. Finally, during the forenoon of 14 August *Belfast* left Portsmouth Harbour, and after a brief pause at Spithead for official photographs, steamed via the Strait of Dover into the North Sea to take part in a major fleet exercise, code-named 'XKD'. This was designed to test the Home Fleet in its ability to detect German commerce raiders which were attempting to break out into the Atlantic. *Belfast*'s role was to represent the German cruiser *Admiral Hipper*. Passing through the Strait of Dover during the early evening, by midnight she was clear of the Goodwins and steaming north to rendezvous with *Dunedin* and *Janus* for joint manoeuvres. At this stage, however, with the North Sea basking in warm sunny weather, there was still time for relaxation and recreation, and during the forenoon of 15 August, while off the Lincolnshire resort of Skegness, 'Hands to Bathe' was piped. The exercise began during the early hours of 17 August when, from a position close to the Horns Reef and the Jutland Peninsula, *Belfast* parted company with *Dunedin* and *Janus* and began her fast passage across the North Sea towards the Pentland Firth, where she would attempt to navigate the narrow waterway undetected by air patrols and other ships of the Home Fleet. In the event *Belfast*'s task was made easier by thick fog which was blanketing much of the North Sea, and at 0400 on 18 August she arrived off Cape Wrath, the western edge of the exercise area, from where she retraced her course and steamed south to the River Humber to rejoin *Dunedin* at anchor off Spurn Head. Her role in her first major exercise had been a complete success.

HMS *Belfast* remained in the area of the River Humber for only three days before, having been ordered north, she weighed anchor and in company with *Dunedin* and *Janus*, steamed to Invergordon and on to Scapa Flow, where she arrived during the forenoon of 25 August. It was the same day that Britain and France signed, with Poland, a five-year agreement which as far as the British and French governments were concerned was an unambiguous declaration of an intention to fight should Germany invade Poland. No mention, however, was made of Russia and even at that late stage British politicians were willing, indeed hoping, that there might be a political agreement which would allow Germany to regain control of East Prussia, which in 1919 had been handed over to newly independent Poland as part of the Treaty of Versailles. Unfortunately, rather belatedly, British politicians realised that the hastily entered into treaty left them at the mercy of intransigent Polish politicians. For *Belfast* the arrival at Scapa Flow meant seven days of gunnery exercises, mainly within the confines of Scapa Flow itself, and an inspection by the C-in-C Home Fleet. During the early hours of 31 August she sailed from Scapa Flow to begin her first patrol in the waters

between the north of Scotland and Iceland, with her patrol line being off the Orkney Islands, north of Mull Head and North Ronaldsay. At 1100 on 3 September, when war against Germany was declared, *Belfast* was some three miles off Dennis Head, and four hours later she encountered her first merchantman, which turned out to be the Swedish SS *Tisnanon*. Towards the end of the patrol she rendezvoused with *Renown* and *Edinburgh* for joint manoeuvres and next day, 6 September, she anchored in Scapa Flow, where her Walrus aircraft was embarked.

In the early months of the war the ships of the Northern Patrol spent little time in harbour, and as there were not many facilities for liberty men at Scapa Flow few men objected. On 8 September she put to sea for her second patrol, during which she and *Edinburgh* were ordered to search from the eastward around Iceland's north coast for shipping which might be using this route in order to avoid the Navy's contraband control patrols. *Edinburgh*'s Captain Bradley describes the patrol: '*Passing through the rendezvous at 2345 and with* Belfast *joining, course 030° was steered so as to reach by daylight the track between the north coast of Iceland and the coast of Norway. At 0600 on 10 September course was altered to 300° and* Belfast *was spread to visibility distance on my starboard beam. The only vessels sighted were trawlers and their attendant carriers, mostly Norwegian. Visibility throughout the day was extreme and it was possible to check that no vessels were hugging the coast.*' During the patrol *Belfast* sent one merchantman into harbour for a full search, but most of the time was spent checking fishing vessels. On 20 September she returned to Scapa Flow.

For almost two weeks *Belfast* remained within the confines of Scapa Flow, mainly exercising her newly acquired Walrus aircraft and the catapult equipment, the fitting of which had finally been completed by the contractors. On 2 October *Belfast* left Scapa Flow to carry out a full-calibre firing in the Pentland Firth, on completion of which she relieved *Norfolk* on the Northern Patrol. Throughout the patrol strong southerly winds kept *Belfast*'s speed down to a maximum of 14 knots. On the third day, despite strong winds and heavy seas, she intercepted the 12,000-ton Norwegian whaling parent ship *Suderoy*, accompanied by six whalers, which were all boarded and checked. Three days later, in a position 63°27'N 007°26'W, just 50 miles north-west of the Faroe Islands, *Belfast* sighted the Norwegian merchantman SS *Tai Yin*, which was bound for Oslo from Baltimore. The Admiralty had already signalled to blockading ships that if they spotted *Tai Yin* she should be stopped and sent to Kirkwall for examination. By 1035 a boarding party was away and 25 minutes later *Tai Yin* had set course for the Orkney Islands. At 1104, just as *Belfast* had hoisted her cutter, another merchantman was seen on the horizon, bearing 320°, and *Belfast* closed to investigate. The ship, which was on a course of about 070°, was a passenger-cargo liner of some 13,615 gross tons with a single funnel and substantial white upperworks. Because no vessels of this size had been reported in the vicinity suspicions were immediately aroused. The vessel was flying a Swedish flag, and as the cruiser approached her the name *Ancona* could be discerned on her bow. As there was no Swedish ship of that name it was almost certain that the ship was a German blockade-runner. As *Belfast* got closer this was confirmed for it could be seen that an attempt had been made to paint over another name on the bow, that of *Cap Norte*.

Built for the Hamburg Süd Amerika Line in 1922, *Cap Norte* carried passengers and cargo between Germany and Pernambuco (Recife), usually calling at the Canary Islands and Madeira en route. She had left Pernambuco on 22 September, some 17 days earlier, manned partly by German reservists. On board were some 171 people, seven of them women with children, but *Cap Norte* had been unable to take on sufficient fuel to make a more northerly course round Iceland, which was why she was taking a chance just north of the Faroe Islands. When *Belfast* gave the order to stop *Cap Norte* did so at once, and it was clear that her crew were making no

On 5 October 1939 HMS Belfast *intercepted and captured the 13,615-ton German passenger liner* Cap Norte *which, flying the Swedish flag and with the name* Anacona *painted on her bow, was attempting to break through the Allied blockade.* Cap Norte *was the largest merchant ship captured on the Northern Patrol.*
(Author's Collection)

immediate efforts to scuttle their ship and take to the boats. *Belfast*'s second boarding party of the day, consisting of 20 ratings commanded by Lt-Cdr A. G. L. Seale, was quickly assembled and the cutter was launched. The boarding party was a mix of seamen, Royal Marines and engine room personnel, and despite deteriorating weather conditions by 1210 they were safely alongside *Cap Norte* where a rope ladder had been hung for the 30-foot climb up the ship's side. On reaching the liner's upper deck Seale and a party of Royal Marines were confronted by an empty expanse of deck, and they had to make their way to the bridge to find the ship's master. Although there was no resistance from anyone on board, there was no co-operation either and as the single boarding party would be hard pressed to ensure there were no acts of sabotage during the passage to Kirkwall, a second boarding party was dispatched. At 1350, with *Belfast* astern, *Cap Norte* set course for Kirkwall. At 0730 the next day, in what were now stormy seas, the elderly cruiser *Delhi* took over the escort and *Belfast* returned to her patrol line. *Cap Norte* was the largest merchant ship captured on the Northern Patrol; she was carrying some six tons of quartz crystals which were seized and eventually sold to the GPO and the Standard Telephone Company. *Cap Norte* herself was renamed *Empire Trooper* and saw UK service as a troop transport until 1955, when she was scrapped.

Once back on her patrol *Belfast* intercepted only one more merchant ship when, during the afternoon of 12 October, the Swedish SS *Uddeholm*, bound from Stockholm to Havana, was boarded and ordered into Kirkwall for examination. Next day, however, *Belfast* returned to Scapa Flow where the three prize crews from *Cap Norte* and *Tai Yin* returned to the ship. That night, as *Belfast* lay at anchor, the German submarine *U-47* managed to navigate its way into Scapa Flow. As it happened Admiral Forbes had received intelligence reports of an impending air attack on the Home Fleet and most of the major units had been dispersed, leaving some 51 warships and auxiliaries at Scapa, of which the most important were *Royal Oak, Belfast, Aurora, Cardiff, Caledon, Colombo* and *Delhi*, together with a number of destroyers and minesweepers. Also in the Flow that night was the disarmed battleship *Iron Duke*, which was serving as a depot ship. At one stage during its attack on the

ships at anchor in Scapa Flow, *U-47* headed for *Belfast*'s position, but in the event it was the elderly *Royal Oak* that was hit by the first of four torpedoes fired by the submarine, at 0104 on 14 October. Within 15 minutes the old battleship had rolled over and sunk with the loss of 833 lives, including over 100 boys. At 0741 that same morning, as rescue efforts for *Royal Oak* survivors were still going on in Scapa Flow, *Belfast* and *Aurora* were ordered to weigh anchor and steam south to join the Home Fleet in the relative safety of Loch Ewe.

Twenty-four hours after arriving at Loch Ewe *Belfast* put to sea again, this time as part of the main battlefleet which was providing cover for the vulnerable armed merchant cruisers on the Northern Patrol. *Belfast*'s patrol lasted seven days, during which time she intercepted two Scandinavian merchantmen and again dispatched them under armed guard to Kirkwall. On 22 October she returned to Loch Ewe, and next day she steamed south for the River Clyde to begin a 14-day refit in Glasgow's Princes Dock. It was 7 November when the refit ended and *Belfast* steamed down the Clyde to anchor off Greenock and two days later, having been allocated to the 2nd Cruiser Squadron, she sailed for Immingham where she arrived during the evening of 11 November. After four days at anchor in the River Humber *Belfast* was sent north to Rosyth to undergo a short training and work-up period with her sisters *Glasgow* and *Southampton*, also *Aurora*, *Enterprise* and ten destroyers, before they formed a North Sea strike force based on Rosyth. At 0753 on Monday 20 November she weighed anchor and put to sea for gunnery and torpedo-firing practice. At 1753, after a successful day, she returned to her anchorage at Rosyth and at 0917 the next day she once again weighed anchor and this time followed *Southampton* and two destroyers to sea, where it was intended that a programme of sub-calibre gunnery firings would be carried out. At 0947 *Belfast* passed through the anti-submarine boom and at 1030, the three cruisers were about to begin their practice shoot. The events which followed are described in Captain Scott's report: '*At 1037 course was altered together to 295°, at 1042 to 115°, and at 1049 to 060°. The rudder had just been put amidships at the conclusion of the last alteration of course - the ship's head at that time being about 065° - when, at 1052, a violent explosion occurred, apparently under the foremast. At this time* Southampton *bore 030°, approximately four-and-a-half cables. The order, "Stop Both" was given and subsequently "Half Ahead Both - Hard-a-Starboard." The ship answered the rudder until she lost steerage way and was put on course for Inchkeith, but from the moment of the explosion the main engines were out of action.*' On what was a calm and clear day, in a position 56°06'N 002°54'-36"W, *Belfast* had in fact detonated one of a number of magnetic mines which had been dropped by German aircraft in British coastal waters. At that early stage of the war very little was known about these weapons, and coming so soon after the *Royal Oak* disaster it was at first thought the ship had been torpedoed by a U-boat. Indeed, that same day, having heard the initial reports the First Lord of the Admiralty issued a memo calling for better anti-submarine measures at Rosyth.

On *Belfast*'s starboard side abreast the mainmast, the massive explosion sent a huge column of water and smoke soaring up into the air. The centre of the explosive force struck the ship under the forward engine room, some 320 feet from the bow. The concussion was severe and caused the ship to vibrate and whip violently, throwing people off their feet and against bulkheads. Remarkably, given the force of the explosion, casualties were light with 19 men being seriously injured, three critically, and 22 suffering minor injuries, the most common being broken and fractured limbs; the majority of these were incurred in the forward part of the ship. Witnesses in *Southampton* reported seeing *Belfast*'s stern rise some ten feet out of the water, and in the cruiser's forepeak a heavy oil drum was hurled eight feet into the air before crashing into the deckhead. The damage to the ship was extensive and she was completely immobilised.

Direct damage caused by the explosion was centred around 151 station and some 20 feet to starboard of the ship's centre line. In this vicinity the outer bottom plating was indented near the turn of the bilge, mostly in the strakes above and below the bilge keel and extending for a length of about ten feet forward and aft of 151 station. Despite the fact that between 143 and 180 stations the bilge keel had been blown upwards and its edge joints broken, the damage caused no major flooding into the ship and no gratings were disturbed. In the forward engine room itself the main transverse girder which formed the forward support to the main turbines was very badly distorted, and the supporting pillars had also been pushed upwards, with all deck plates being thrown up and displaced.

Directly above the centre of the explosion, having been thrown upwards off their roller paths, the starboard 21-inch triple torpedo tubes were badly damaged, but fortunately, although all the tubes were loaded, with pistols and primers in position, none of the weapons exploded. All the ship's boats in the vicinity of the explosion had been badly damaged by their chocks being forced upwards. It was, however, the indirect damage to *Belfast* which was far more serious, and which threatened to sink the ship. The line of the vessel's keel, which was badly distorted, had lifted between 40 and 180 stations. Briefly, this damage to the keel was described at the time as, '*having broken the ship's back in the vicinity of the foremast and as a result the stem has dropped about two feet from its original line.*' So serious was this damage that preparations were made to abandon ship, with Carley Floats slung out and other floating objects being ranged in various places round the ship. But what gave Captain Scott the greatest cause for concern was the structural damage immediately under the foremast. He felt there was a distinct possibility that the forepart of the ship, which included all the forward messdecks, was sagging dangerously and might come adrift altogether so he ordered that part of the ship to be abandoned.

The outer bottom of the ship had been subjected to compressive forces which had caused a very severe buckling which was almost symmetrical on both sides of the ship, and in addition to this the flat keel was completely fractured at the apex of its buckle. Above the waterline the most obvious sign of damage, centred between 104 and 106 stations, was a severe downward crumpling right across the upper deck, with a maximum depression of about 14 inches. Directly under this depression all but one of the upper deck girders were fractured and the sheer strakes on both port and starboard sides, just forward of the aircraft catapult, were badly distorted. On the upper deck the plating right across the ship was fractured, while on the starboard side at 90 station the fracture extended into the sheer strake and through a scuttle, stopping some 18 inches short of the plate's lower edge. Just forward of this the sheer strake was badly damaged and the armour plating on both sides of the ship had been displaced. Directly overhead was a 12-inch depression in the forecastle deck, and the bulkheads between the two decks were severely buckled, as were the lower deck passageways abreast A boiler room. Some flooding in magazines occurred and a provisions room had been flooded with fuel oil.

In the forward engine room the cast iron stools of all four turbines and the main gear case of the port set were fractured, while in the after engine room a large crack had been made across the after end of the starboard LP turbine. In addition the spring supports of both forward condensers had collapsed, and although both inner shafts could turn freely, the port outer shaft was almost seized, and the starboard outer shaft could not be turned at all. However, what had totally immobilised *Belfast* was the shattering or fracturing of the cast iron discharge branches of all oil fuel pumps, including stand-by pumps in the boiler rooms resulting in a rapid loss of steam pressure. With hot oil fuel spraying from all the broken pipes and onto even hotter pipes it was fortunate that in the first ten minutes, while the ship was without any power, this oil did not ignite. As far as the ship's armament was concerned, all the 6-inch turrets 'jumped' from their paths, and although the rollers were undamaged the turrets

themselves were jammed. In the magazines and bomb rooms large numbers of projectiles were thrown about and badly damaged, but once again it was very fortunate that there were no shell or bomb explosions. To add to all these problems *Belfast* was lying helpless in the water, outside the inner anti-submarine defences.

When *Belfast* detonated the magnetic mine, she and *Edinburgh* were within seconds of carrying out a main armament, sub-calibre shoot at a target towed by the tug *Kroonan*. By 1130 she had managed to slip the target and was preparing to take *Belfast* in tow. In the meantime additional tugs were dispatched from Rosyth and as the rescue operation slowly progressed, with her main galley completely wrecked, the ship's company were served an emergency meal of sandwiches and abandon ship provisions, prepared in the undamaged bakery. To the relief of many the rum ration was unaffected by the crisis, and the wardroom galley produced gallons of tea. At 1520 *Belfast* was towed past the anti-submarine boom of Rosyth's inner defences, and just over an hour later, as she prepared to enter the lock, two of her tugs were slipped. By 1700 she had been secured alongside the lock, and 15 of her most serious casualties were transferred to ambulances which took them to Dunfermline Hospital, with the remainder of the ship's company moving ashore to makeshift temporary accommodation in the dockyard canteen. At 2230 that evening *Belfast* was secured in No 2 dry dock and the next day shoring began. As the water level was lowered, however, it became apparent that although the forward and after ends of the ship were bearing down on the blocks, the midships section was still some three to four inches above them. As a result the ship was quickly refloated and urgent assistance from the DNC's department was requested. Divers who inspected the hull reported that: '*...the keel appears to be buckled upwards from 244 station abreast B turret, to 182 station abaft the after funnel. Maximum clearance between the keel is about three inches and occurs at 80 station, except there is a complete fracture of the keel plate at about 75 station. Keel plate sticking down some four inches and is piercing into blocks.*' As a result of their report another dry dock was quickly prepared in which the blocks were, as far as was possible, moulded to fit *Belfast*'s damaged keel. Finally, all her ammunition and oil fuel was removed and the cruiser was towed back into the main basin where all her main armament gun turrets were removed. On 4 January 1940 the ship was paid off and most of her ship's company were dispersed, leaving behind only a small care and maintenance party who were accommodated ashore at a schoolhouse in Rosyth's King's Road. *Belfast*'s new dry dock was prepared with specially formed softwood capped blocks and gantries to support the damaged bottom and to preserve the hull alignment.

Once her hull and machinery spaces had been surveyed it was apparent that although there were no large holes in her hull, the shell plating adjacent to the fractured keel was considerably buckled, and the damage was far more serious than had originally been anticipated. It was also clear that reconstruction of the ship in addition to rebuilding large sections of her hull, would also involve the removal of all her main and auxiliary machinery for rebuilding, repair or realignment. It was also decided that all the ship's gun mountings and torpedo tubes would be reconditioned and gun supports re-machined. At one stage questions were raised as to whether the ship was actually beyond repairing, but with modern cruisers urgently required for the war at sea it was both cheaper and quicker to make the repairs than it would be to build a new cruiser. However, the major rebuilding could not be carried out at Rosyth, so work to make *Belfast* seaworthy again began immediately.

During the four months that *Belfast* spent in dry dock at Rosyth the repairs to her hull entailed the building of temporary steel structures over the buckled and distorted sections, and also temporary repairs to her main propulsion machinery. Finally, on 28 June 1940, *Belfast* left Rosyth to steam down what was now a very hostile North Sea, to make the dangerous transit of the Strait of Dover, where she

would be within range of artillery on the enemy-occupied coast of France, under cover of darkness. She arrived in Plymouth Sound on the last day of June and four days later she was paid off into dockyard hands. It would be over two years before she became operational once again.

HMS *Belfast*'s major reconstruction and refit at Devonport was disrupted by enemy bombing raids on the city of Plymouth, and on the dockyard itself. The first bombs fell on the city in July 1940, but it was in early 1941 that enemy air raids reduced much of Plymouth to rubble and killed over a thousand people. The disruption of the raids, and the subsequent evacuation of residents, which almost halved the city's population, affected the dockyard badly, but fortunately *Belfast* came through unscathed. Before the cruiser could be dry docked specially prepared blocks were fitted into the dock bottom and all her main propulsion machinery, including her boilers, was removed, together with all the remaining stores; it took two weeks to get the ship properly bedded down. During the reconstruction process all the ship's superstructure between 66 and 93 stations was removed and completely rebuilt, which was the only way the deformed hull could be straightened. The thickness of her side armour was increased and her hull was strengthened by the construction of transverse bulkheads at 104 station. After the addition of many tons of top weight, to provide stability side bulges, which added three feet to the ship's beam, were built into her hull. The most important addition at this stage was radar and *Belfast* was equipped with the most advanced available, including Type 284 and Type 283 for main armament gunnery fire control and barrage gunnery fire control respectively. She was also equipped with Types 251 and 252, which were modified RAF transponders coded to give the ship's identity (Identification Friend or Foe – IFF). This comprehensive radar outfit made *Belfast* one of the most formidable cruisers of her day.

The ship's secondary armament was also modernised, with her MkII, 2-pdr pom-poms being replaced with more modern MkVIII remote power control weapons. The MkII directors were replaced by two MkIV pom-pom directors which were positioned close to the guns themselves. The directors were fitted with Type 282, beam-switching, gunnery control radar sets. Also added were ten 20mm Oerlikon guns in five twin mountings which were installed at various positions around the ship, together with eight single Oerlikons, which replaced ·5-inch machine-guns. Another important addition, particularly in view of the fact that *Belfast* had almost been lost to a magnetic mine, was the fitting of degaussing coils. Her hangar and aircraft turntable were strengthened to enable her to operate the heavier Supermarine Sea Otter, the replacement for the Walrus, although she continued to operate the latter until mid-1943, when her catapult was removed.

On 29 September 1942, as *Belfast*'s reconstruction was nearing completion, her new commanding officer, Captain F. R. Parham RN, was appointed, and at around the same time key personnel were drafted to the ship. It was at 0900 on Tuesday 3 November 1942, while she lay alongside the south wall of No 5 basin, that *Belfast* was recommissioned. Shortly after this the main body of her ship's company marched from the barracks to the ship, and almost immediately storing and ammunitioning began. During the forenoon of 18 November, having successfully completed her basin trials, *Belfast* was shifted through the North Lock to the sea wall at No 5 wharf where, the following day, the Admiral Superintendent of the Dockyard carried out his final inspection. Six days later, at 1350 on 25 November 1942, for the first time since the summer of 1940, *Belfast* slipped her moorings and steamed down harbour to Plymouth Sound, where she secured to a buoy for the night. Next day she began a series of day-running trials which took her through into December. During this period she returned briefly to the dockyard for adjustments to her machinery, but finally at 0900 on 10 December *Belfast* left Plymouth Sound to steam north through the Irish Sea to Scapa Flow where she anchored during the early evening of the next

Two views of HMS Belfast *in Plymouth Sound in 1942, immediately after her reconstruction. In the course of repairs bulges were added to improve stability, adding 4ft to her beam, and radar/gunnery control modifications were carried out.* *(Syd Goodman Collection)*

day.

During the rest of the month and into January 1943 *Belfast* underwent an intensive series of work-up exercises, often in company with *Howe, Carlisle* and various destroyers. On 17 December she had officially joined the 10th Cruiser Squadron, under the command of Vice-Admiral R. L. Burnett CB CBE, who hoisted his flag in *Belfast* on 12 January 1943. Throughout January *Belfast* continued her work-up and on the 15th of that month there was a day of ceremony. First came C-in-C's Divisions, followed by an inspection by A. V. Alexander, First Lord of the Admiralty, and finally a high-level conference of Flag Officers and Commanding Officers. During the remainder of January the work-up continued, and on the last day of the month the cruiser was opened to residents of Kirkwall and surrounding villages. *Belfast*'s final exercises began on 4 February when, in company with *King George V, Newfoundland* and *Uganda*, she steamed south to Plymouth Sound. After a short overnight stay the four ships returned via the Atlantic to Scapa Flow. Five days later *Belfast*'s operational career began when, screened by five destroyers, she sailed for Seydisfjord on Iceland's east coast which was the base for US and Royal Navy ships which were deployed as escorts for convoys to Russia. The weather during the passage was atrocious, with severe gales, heavy snow and mountainous seas. So severe were the weather conditions that speed was reduced, and on arrival off the coast of Iceland *Belfast*, *Cumberland, Scylla, Intrepid* and two destroyers were unable to enter harbour. This was to be *Belfast*'s introduction to Arctic convoys and the weather conditions which would dominate the ship's operational life for the next 11 months, until the new year of 1944.

HMS *Belfast*'s first passage to the Kola Inlet began during the afternoon of 21 February when, with *Cumberland* and *Norfolk*, she left Seydisfjord to make a fast passage to the north Russian port which, owing to warming by the Gulf Stream, is the only ice-free area of northern Russia. During the winter months not only did the ships of the Arctic convoys have enemy aircraft, submarines and the ever-present threat of German capital ships to contend with, but also the icy waters of the Norwegian and Barents Seas, which were frequently lashed by gales and mountainous seas. Survival times for those unfortunate to find themselves immersed could be counted in seconds rather than minutes. Less than 24 hours after leaving Icelandic waters German reconnaissance aircraft were sighted, as well as loose drifting mines, but it was not long before the severe weather in the form of blinding blizzards seriously reduced visibility for both the Allied ships and the enemy planes. As the ships neared the Kola Inlet speed was again reduced as thick sludge ice was encountered, but in the early hours of 26 February they anchored safely in Russian waters.

During the four days *Belfast* spent at anchor in Vaenga Bay preparations were made for the homeward-bound convoy, RA 53, to form up. During this period there were numerous conferences involving the Masters of the merchant ships and the commanding officers of the escort ships which, in addition to *Belfast*, also included *Cumberland* and *Norfolk*. Leave was granted to the ship's company, but apart from a very poorly supplied canteen there was little in the way of recreation. With the German base at the nearby Finnish town of Petsamo, and the even closer base at Kirkenes in German-occupied Norway, the local Russian population was itself under siege and existing at below what were considered to be minimum subsistence levels. *Belfast* and the rest of the escorts left the Kola Inlet during the forenoon of 2 March, but after suffering a lubricating oil failure in her after engine room the cruiser was forced to detach from the convoy. Once she had rejoined, however, the passage passed without any serious incidents, although when just 24 hours away from Iceland German reconnaissance aircraft were seen to be shadowing the convoy. At one stage *Belfast*'s gunners opened fire, but the shadowers remained elusively just out of range of their guns. During the morning of 7 March *Belfast* anchored in Seydisfjord. In fact she had completed the last

Russian convoy of the season, and with the next one not due to leave Liverpool until mid-November, she was ordered to return to Scapa Flow. Next afternoon, after leaving Icelandic waters, she once again steamed into severe gales and heavy seas which, at one stage, poured down the air intakes and flooded A boiler room. Fortunately, the next day she arrived back at Scapa Flow where there was a nine-day break from operations.

One of the main reasons for the suspension of the Arctic convoys to Russia was the presence in northern Norway of powerful German naval forces, including *Tirpitz, Scharnhorst, Lützow*, and a number of destroyers, and with the long daylight hours the convoys were considered to be too easy a target for aircraft, submarines and the surface forces. Although during the summer period *Tirpitz* and *Scharnhorst* made only one offensive mission into Arctic waters, when in September 1943 they bombarded Allied facilities on the island of Spitsbergen, they remained a 'fleet in being', and as such an additional and continual threat to Allied shipping.

On 20 March *Belfast* left Scapa Flow to participate in a fleet exercise, during which she took on the role of the German battlecruiser *Scharnhorst*, with *Glasgow* representing an accompanying heavy cruiser. Between them the two ships were ordered to try to make Iceland without being detected, which for the purpose of the exercise simulated a break-out into the Atlantic by German ships. In the event it was air reconnaissance by RAF Catalina and Hudson aircraft which quickly detected and tracked *Belfast* and *Glasgow* for most of the exercise. The weather on *Belfast*'s return to Iceland was in stark contrast to that experienced just two weeks earlier, and this time having anchored at Reykjavik in warm sunny weather, her boats' crews were able to take part in a fleet sailing and pulling regatta. At the end of March *Belfast* began her new duties in the unpredictable northern waters around Iceland where, with *Glasgow* and *Intrepid*, she patrolled the waters of the Denmark Strait, searching for both blockade-runners and the ever-present threat of an attempt by German capital ships to break out into the Atlantic. These patrols continued throughout April and into May, with only short breaks at either Hvalfjord or Scapa Flow. On 25 May she left Scapa Flow as part of the escort for a small convoy of minelayers bound for Norwegian waters to lay their mines off Narvik. During June *Belfast* spent more time at Scapa Flow and in the middle of the month, after exercising with heavy units of the Home Fleet, including *Nelson, Rodney, Valiant* and *Warspite*, she again escorted a minelaying convoy to the Norwegian coast. On 18 June, however, she arrived at Rosyth to undergo an 11-day docking and maintenance period, and it was 1 July before she rejoined the fleet at Scapa Flow.

Once again *Belfast* returned to the unpredictable waters around Iceland and the Norwegian Sea, and while patrolling the latter she was invariably shadowed by enemy reconnaissance aircraft which, very wisely, remained just out of range of her anti-aircraft guns. On 7 July *Belfast* formed part of a diversionary force, which also included *Kent, London* and the US Navy's battleship *South Dakota*, in an operational area off the Norwegian coast. It was the first of several such operations intended to prevent enemy aircraft from being diverted from Norway south to Italy at a time when Allied landings were taking place in Sicily. As always the ships were shadowed by reconnaissance aircraft, which was the intention this time, but there was no enemy attempt to interfere with the force. Later in the month, on 27 July, again forming part of a diversionary force, *Belfast* sailed for the Norwegian coast. This time, however, the recently repaired and refitted aircraft carrier *Illustrious* accompanied the force and, with the help of *Belfast*'s radar, her Martlets were able to shoot down one enemy reconnaissance aircraft, while RAF Beaufighters accounted for another two. During the first two weeks of August *Belfast* continued to patrol in northern waters and was at Scapa Flow on 14 and 15 August when King George VI visited the Home Fleet. During the afternoon of 15 August, *Belfast* left harbour to steam north to Iceland and the inlet of Skaalefjord on the north coast from where, with

Norfolk, she continued to patrol the waters to the north of Iceland. On 2 October, *Belfast*, in company with other ships of her squadron, the battleships *Duke of York* and *Anson*, the aircraft carrier USS *Ranger*, and the heavy cruiser USS *Tuscaloosa*, left Scapa to attack shipping off the northern Norwegian coast. Following this she returned to Scapa to carry out a six-day period of self-maintenance, after which she steamed south to Greenock to embark stores and ammunition. It was during this period of self-maintenance that one watch of the ship's company were granted leave, but on 15 October she steamed north again to Scapa Flow, and on to Iceland to continue her patrols around the island. By now, however, daylight north of the Arctic Circle was limited to just a few hours around midday, and after a break of nine months Arctic convoys to northern Russia were to be resumed.

The first of the winter's Russian convoys, JW52, left Liverpool on 17 November and nine days later it arrived safely in the Kola Inlet. Initially *Belfast* was not directly involved in convoy escort duties and she continued to patrol the waters around Iceland. On 11 December, however, she was ordered from Loch Ewe to Scapa Flow from where, on 15 December, she put to sea with *Norfolk* and *Sheffield* as part of the escort for convoy JW55A, which had left Liverpool three days earlier. Although there were reports of U-boats in its path, on 20 December the convoy and its escorts arrived safely in the Kola Inlet.

By December 1943 the German naval position in Norway had changed, for in late September *Tirpitz* had been seriously damaged in an attack by midget submarines. In addition the heavy cruiser *Lützow* had been forced to return to Kiel for repairs to her main engines, and these would keep her out of service until the new year of 1944. This left *Scharnhorst* and a force of at least five destroyers as a much depleted naval force in northern Norway. During 1943 there had also been significant changes in command, both in the Royal Navy's Home Fleet where Admiral Sir Bruce Fraser had relieved Tovey, and in the German Kriegsmarine, where Grand-Admiral Karl Dönitz had taken over from Raeder. Both men had very definite ideas about the naval war in Arctic waters. Although the resumed Arctic convoys had, since mid-November, all arrived safely at their destinations, Fraser, assisted by intercepted German radio signals, was convinced that, led by *Scharnhorst*, the German surface fleet in Norway would attempt to attack one of the Russian convoys. On his part Dönitz was under the mistaken assumption that by not having suffered any attacks on the Russian convoys following their resumption in mid-November the British would be lulled into a false sense of security and would not be expecting a major surface attack. Dönitz had also to take into account that since the German Army's catastrophic defeat at Stalingrad, one of the bloodiest battles in the history of warfare, it was obvious to the High Command that the war was going to be won or lost on the Eastern Front, and from Germany's point of view it was increasingly important that supplies of all kinds being carried by the Arctic convoys should be stopped or at least severely disrupted. On 19 December the newly appointed Dönitz met with Hitler and told him of his intention to use the battlecruiser *Scharnhorst* to attack the next Arctic convoy, which he believed would present itself sometime over the Christmas period.

Anticipating such an attack Fraser had formed two forces. Force 1 was commanded by Vice-Admiral R. L. Burnett, flying his flag in *Belfast*, and also included *Norfolk* and *Sheffield*. These ships were actually part of the convoy escort which, on 20 December, had arrived in the Kola Inlet. Force 2, commanded by Fraser himself flying his flag in the battleship *Duke of York*, also included the cruiser *Jamaica* and the destroyers *Saumarez, Savage, Scorpion* and *Stord*. Fraser was convinced that *Scharnhorst* would attempt to attack the east-bound convoy, JW55B, which had left Liverpool on 20 December and was due to arrive at the Kola Inlet at the end of the month; he therefore made preparations to intercept and destroy the German battle-cruiser. Writing afterwards he recorded: '*Should* Scharnhorst *be encountered I had decided: - a) To*

Apart from the enemy, another of the major hazards faced by seamen on the Russian convoy routes was the thick ice which quickly formed on the guns and superstructure; it had to be continually be removed by steam jets. *(Imperial War Museum/Ref A20687)*

close the enemy, opening fire with starshell at a range of 12,000 yards. b) To form the four destroyers of my screen into sub-divisions and release them in time to take up positions for torpedo attack. c) To keep Jamaica *in close support of* Duke of York*, but with freedom to take drastic avoiding action and open the distance if required.*' At 2300 on 23 December, Force 2 left the Icelandic port of Akureyri, and after carrying out a practice attack using *Jamaica* as the target, set course for the area of Bear Island. Fraser once again takes up the story: '*The endurance of the destroyers did not permit continuous cover to be given for the whole passage of the convoy and my intention was to reach the covering position at a speed of advance of 15 knots when the convoy was just east of Bear Island. This would allow me to spend some 30 hours in the area.*'

During the evening of 22 December the now empty ships of convoy RA55A left the Kola Inlet for their return passage to home waters. Some hours later, at 0315 on 23 December, *Belfast*, *Norfolk* and *Sheffield* weighed anchor and steamed out of the inlet to provide escort cover for the convoy. Meanwhile, during the forenoon of 22 December, a German meteorological aircraft sighted the outward bound JW55B as it steamed almost parallel to the Norwegian coast, just south of Narvik. Initially the merchant ships were mistaken for troop transports whose intention was to spearhead an invasion of northern Norway in the Narvik region, and U-boats were diverted from their patrol areas around Bear Island to a position off the Norwegian coast. At the same time in Altenfjord, *Scharnhorst* and her battle group of five destroyers were ordered to three hours' notice for steam. Later that day it became clear to the German reconnaissance aircraft, who were now closely shadowing the convoy, that it was not an invasion force, but another supply convoy bound for Russia. By Christmas Eve the convoy

was some 450 miles from the point midway between Altenfjord and Bear Island, where it was at its most vulnerable. Although German surface forces had not previously ventured that far west Fraser was concerned that the convoy, which by midday was in a position 70°40'N 003°10'E, well out of range of Force 1, was unsupported. At 1400 therefore, he broke radio silence and reversed the course of the convoy for three hours. At the same time he increased the speed of Force 2 to 19 knots, so that if enemy surface forces searched to the west they would be unlikely to locate it before darkness closed in.

Since leaving the Kola Inlet convoy RA55A and the escorting Force 1 had steamed steadily westward undetected by enemy reconnaissance. By the forenoon of Christmas Day the ships were in a position 74°07'N 028°45'E, less than 100 miles east of Bear Island. Weather conditions were atrocious with what was described at the time as a '*very unpleasant sea and strong head winds*' and it was said that few people in either the convoy or the naval escorts got much sleep. The foul weather, however, prevented any comprehensive German air reconnaissance, and the enemy remained unaware that a battleship was moving in to support the two convoys. Had this fact become known to them then there is little doubt *Scharnhorst* would not have put to sea. At the same time that Fraser ordered JW55B to alter course, he also detached four destroyers, *Matchless, Musketeer, Opportune* and *Virago*, from their position with RA55A to rendezvous with JW55B. By the afternoon of Christmas Day the weather conditions had virtually precluded any German air reconnaissance, and at just after midday *Scharnhorst* was ordered to one hour's notice for sea, an order which was said to have convinced her ship's company that it was an exercise deliberately designed to ruin their Christmas. In fact this was no exercise and Dönitz had made the decision that the battlecruiser, supported by the five destroyers, *Z29, Z30, Z33, Z34* and *Z38*, would sail to find and attack convoy JW55B.

Code-named 'Operation Eastern Front' the foray that Dönitz was keen to launch against the Arctic convoys was not popular with other senior naval officers. Both Admiral Schniewind, in command at Kiel, and the newly promoted Admiral Erich Bey who, flying his flag in *Scharnhorst*, would command the German force, wanted to postpone the operation; they proposed an alternative plan whereby the five destroyers would lead the attack on the convoy, while *Scharnhorst* was held back in support. There were also concerns regarding the five destroyers, which in heavy weather were not good seaboats. Dönitz overruled all their objections, believing it is said that a hit-and-run operation against the convoy would cause serious damage to the fully laden ships bound for Murmansk, and so he ordered *Scharnhorst* and the destroyers to weigh anchor and leave Altenfjord at 1900 on Christmas Day. By 2300 that evening the German force had reached the open waters and already the heavy seas were affecting the fighting capability of the destroyers.

Dönitz's plan was for three of the destroyers to shadow the convoy, and then during the morning of 26 December the whole force would descend upon the merchant ships sinking and damaging as many as possible before returning at high speed to the safety of Altenfjord. During the night, despite gale force winds and heavy seas, the German force made good progress, but they were dogged by communications problems, a factor which would seriously hamper their operations throughout the forthcoming action. At midnight *Scharnhorst* reported that she was in the operational area, but because of the continuing rough weather conditions she was forced to reduce her speed. During the night Bey received a signal authorising him to steam on ahead if weather conditions were seriously hampering the destroyers' capabilities, and if necessary to make a lone attack on the JW55B. Bey ignored this discretionary offer, and by 0700, as his force headed towards the convoy, the five destroyers were steaming in line abreast some ten miles ahead of the battlecruiser, thus placing them beyond visual signal range. Although the weather conditions had pre-

cluded air reconnaissance, U-boats had still been able to shadow JW55B, and it was their reports which had enabled his force to close to within 50 miles of the convoy by 0800. However, in the atrocious weather conditions Bey lost contact with his destroyers, and they were unaware of a change of course by *Scharnhorst*. They would never regain contact with the battlecruiser.

Meanwhile, *Belfast*, Force 1 and convoy RA55A were steaming west undetected. Then at 0840, when she was in a position 73°35'N 023°21'E, *Belfast*'s radar picked up *Scharnhorst* on a bearing of 295° and at some 35,000 yards distant. At 0855 *Belfast* was ordered to Action Stations, and five minutes later a second radar echo was obtained on a bearing of 299° at 24,500 yards, but it was never clear whether this second echo was a ship of the convoy, or one of the German destroyers which had become detached from the force. Whichever it was Burnett ignored it, for he rightly deduced that the first and larger radar contact was *Scharnhorst*. By this time the German battlecruiser had become separated from her destroyers and at 0921 it was *Sheffield* which made the first sighting of *Scharnhorst* bearing 222° at a range of 13,000 yards. Three minutes later *Belfast* opened fire with starshell. Although *Belfast*'s starshell had failed to illuminate *Scharnhorst*, it took the battlecruiser completely by surprise, but she reacted quickly and immediately altered course 30° to port. Then, at 0930, *Norfolk* opened fire with her 8-inch armament with some excellent gunnery and quickly scored two hits. One shell landed on *Scharnhorst*'s high-angle director close to the bridge, which not only destroyed the director, but also the ship's radar aerial sited on the foretop. Another shell hit the battlecruiser between a gun turret and her torpedo tubes and penetrated into a messdeck, but failed to explode. *Scharnhorst* rapidly increased speed to 30 knots which, given her superior speed, meant the range quickly opened up. As she turned away the battlecruiser returned fire with her after 280mm guns. Initially Burnett decided to follow *Scharnhorst*, but given the fact that the battlecruiser was quickly opening the range and the weather conditions limited the cruisers to 24 knots, and feeling that the enemy ship would try to work her way north of the convoy and attack it from that direction, he decided to place the cruisers in a position where they would be able to intercept such an attack.

At 1024, as Force 1 closed the convoy, they were joined by four destroyers of the 36th Division, *Matchless, Musketeer, Opportune* and *Virago*. At 1045 Force 1 passed through position 73° 49'N 021°58'E, and five minutes later radar contact was made with the convoy. The three cruisers then commenced zigzagging some ten miles ahead of the convoy with the four destroyers disposed ahead of them as a screen. By this time Fraser appreciated that Force 2 would have little chance of finding *Scharnhorst* unless contact was made again, and he informed Burnett of this fact. The latter, however, was reluctant to split his force and he was still confident that *Scharnhorst* would return to attack the convoy from either the north or the north-east.

At noon that day Fraser, with Force 2, found himself in what could have been a very difficult position. *Duke of York* was still some hours steaming from the position of the convoy and his accompanying destroyers were running low on fuel. He had to make a decision as to whether he should continue on towards the Kola Inlet, or turn back and return to Iceland. If *Scharnhorst* had turned for home there was no possibility of Force 2 intercepting her, and there was always the possibility that she might steam west and, while the Home Fleet was concentrating on the Arctic convoys, break out into the Atlantic. However, his dilemma did not last for long, for at 1205, when the convoy was in a position 74°11'N 022°18'E and some nine miles on the port quarter of Force 1, *Belfast* made radar contact with *Scharnhorst* at a range of some 30,500 yards, bearing 075°. It was at that moment Fraser knew that he had every chance of catching the German battlecruiser.

As soon as *Belfast* regained contact with the enemy Burnett concentrated the destroyers of the

36th Division on his starboard bow and altered course towards *Scharnhorst*. At 1221 *Sheffield* reported '*enemy in sight*' and at a range of 11,000 yards Force 1 was ordered to open fire. At the same time the 36th Division was ordered to carry out a torpedo attack, but given the severe weather conditions and the fact that *Scharnhorst* was now retiring at high speed, there was little chance of it succeeding, although at a range of 7,000 yards *Musketeer* opened fire on the battlecruiser and continued to fire at her for some 14 minutes. The second action by Force 1 lasted for some 20 minutes, at ranges from between four and a half and eight miles. Once again *Scharnhorst* was driven off the convoy by Force 1's determined attack and this time the battlecruiser withdrew towards the south-east, increasing her speed to 28 knots. Force 1's shellfire had been opened by *Belfast* with starshell, and quickly followed with her main armament. Once again it appeared that Bey had been taken by surprise, but *Scharnhorst* quickly returned fire, straddling *Sheffield* with a 280mm salvo and, at 1233, hitting *Norfolk* with a shell from her main armament, which smashed and wrecked X turret's barbette. A second shell landed amidships, and most of the ship's radar was rendered unserviceable. In addition to the damage one officer and six ratings were killed, five more men were seriously wounded and others suffered minor wounds. In fact *Sheffield* had a lucky escape for the salvo which straddled her had sent pieces of shrapnel flying, described as '*up to football size*', many of which hit the ship.

By 1241, given *Scharnhorst*'s superior speed, the range had opened to 12,400 yards, and Burnett decided to cease fire, then deploy his whole force to shadow the battlecruiser until such time as Force 2 could intercept her from the south-west. At the same time the destroyers of the 36th Division, which were to the west of the cruisers, continued to pursue *Scharnhorst* at a steady distance of some 20,000 yards. By this time Bey had given up all ideas of attacking the convoy and he was retiring at high speed to the south-east and southward for the Norwegian coast and the safety of Altenfjord. However, despite aerial reconnaissance which had clearly spotted and reported Force 2 and the battleship *Duke of York*, Bey had not received the reports which would have given him an earlier opportunity to take avoiding action. In the event he continued to steam southward, probably confident that by midnight he would have reached safety. In fact the battlecruiser's fate was already sealed.

For four hours, at a range of some seven and a half miles and slightly to the eastward of her, Force 1 shadowed *Scharnhorst* and as the battlecruiser was retiring on such an advantageous course for interception by Force 2, the cruisers remained in close company and did not attempt to engage. With darkness having descended they remained just outside visibility range and relied on their radar for keeping in contact. The 36th Division to the westward of *Scharnhorst* closed the range slightly and although heavy seas prevented a torpedo attack, they were able to guard against the possibility that the battlecruiser might turn in that direction and attempt once again to attack the convoy or to reach Altenfjord. Had that happened, it is unlikely that either Force 1 or Force 2 could, against a head sea, have kept up with her. During the afternoon *Norfolk* had to reduce speed in order to fight a fire onboard, and *Sheffield*'s speed was also reduced when she encountered propeller problems. The delay caused by the latter problem prevented *Sheffield* from taking any further part in the action which was about to ensue.

From 1000 to 1400 on 26 November, from a position about eight and a half miles on her starboard quarter, three enemy reconnaissance aircraft had almost continually shadowed *Duke of York*. For almost three hours one aircraft was heard to be making 'enemy reports', but for some reason the reports of a 'heavy unit' heading on a course to intercept *Scharnhorst* was not relayed to Bey in the battlecruiser. Likewise, during the first two brief engagements involving the cruisers, the exact composition of the German force was not known to either Fraser or Burnett, who were only aware that *Scharnhorst* might be accompanied by destroyers.

Burnett had signalled to Fraser that only one enemy heavy unit was present, and as a result the former decided to engage the battlecruiser at about 13,000 yards with *Jamaica* in support, at the same time detaching the destroyers of his screen to make a torpedo attack. By 1400 Fraser had concluded that if *Scharnhorst* maintained her course and speed, at roughly 1715 Force 2 would be in a position to engage her. In the event, however, after making an alteration of course she was picked up by *Duke of York*'s fire control radar, bearing 020°, at 45,500 yards, at 1617. Ten minutes later Fraser ordered the destroyers to take up the most advantageous position for a torpedo attack.

After this the range closed rapidly and very soon *Belfast*, which was astern of *Scharnhorst*, was picked up by *Duke of York*'s fire control radar. At this point *Scharnhorst* appeared to be zigzagging on a mean course of 160°, and at 1642 altered course slightly to port. Two minutes later Force 2 altered to 080° to open A Arcs, which would allow all guns of the main armament to simultaneously fire at the enemy. At 1647, without any warning to anyone on board *Scharnhorst*, the inky-black Arctic afternoon was suddenly and dramatically flooded with the bright lights of starshell fired by *Belfast*, and three minutes later starshell from *Duke of York* further illuminated the sky. By this time the range was down to 13 miles and it was apparent that Fraser's trap had taken the enemy battlecruiser completely by surprise, for when first sighted the guns of her main armament were trained fore and aft. At 1651 *Duke of York* fired her first extremely accurate ten-gun 14-inch broadside, one shell of which hit the battlecruiser abreast of A turret, putting it out of action. *Jamaica* had also opened fire and with her third salvo she too hit the battlecruiser. A shell from *Duke of York* landed close to *Scharnhorst*'s C turret, destroying the battlecruiser's hangar and causing many casualties among her anti-aircraft guns crews. At 1656 *Scharnhorst* began to return fire, but her opening salvoes were erratic and fell short. However, her gunnery quickly improved in both speed and accuracy and *Duke of York* was soon being straddled, with many near misses. The gun duel between *Duke of York* and *Scharnhorst* continued until 1820 when the range had opened up to 20,000 yards. Just over 20 minutes later, with the range having opened up still further to 21,400 yards, *Duke of York* checked fire.

At this stage, with all the British ships out of range, there was a distinct possibility that *Scharnhorst* would escape, and Fraser was about to abandon the chase and support the convoy for the remainder of its passage to the Kola Inlet. It was at this very moment, just before the German ship fell out of range, that one of the shells fired by *Duke of York* hit *Scharnhorst*'s starboard side and penetrated into the battlecruiser's forward boiler room, where it severed a main steam pipe. Immediately *Scharnhorst*'s speed was reduced to just nine knots, but after some heroic efforts by her engineering department to quickly cross-connect steam supplies from undamaged pipes and units, this was increased to about 22 knots. This, however, was not sufficient to shake off her pursuers, and the four S-class destroyers Fraser had ordered to make a torpedo attack, which up until then had not been making any headway, slowly began to overhaul *Scharnhorst*. Although it was not immediately apparent to Fraser that *Scharnhorst* had been seriously damaged, he gradually became aware of the fact and, as he stated in his report of the battle: '*As the effect of this (*Scharnhorst*'s reduction in speed) was not apparent for some time I had already decided to turn towards the Norwegian coast, hoping the enemy would also lead round and so give my destroyers a chance to attack. When, however, I saw the speed reduction I turned in straight at the* Scharnhorst.'

By 1840 the destroyers *Savage* and *Saumarez* were astern of *Scharnhorst* and gaining on her, while *Scorpion* and *Stord* on her starboard side had closed to about 10,000 yards. *Scharnhorst*, by this time, had opened up a heavy but ineffective fire with her secondary armament which the destroyers were able to return once the range closed to 7,000 yards. Owing to the muddled handling of *Scharnhorst*'s gunnery the full weight of fire was

not directed at all four destroyers. It seemed that when *Duke of York* had first opened fire most of the battlecruiser's secondary armament gun crews had been ordered to take cover, an order which was never countermanded, and only skeleton crews remained at their stations. There had also been disagreements between gunnery officers, which had resulted in a series of contradictory orders and more confusion. Thus, while *Savage* and *Saumarez* drew *Scharnhorst*'s fire *Scorpion* and *Stord* closed in unseen from the south-eastward. By 1849 it was obvious to all that *Scharnhorst*'s speed had been permanently reduced, and she was again illuminated by starshell fired by the first two destroyers. At the same time the other two, at a range of just over 2,000 yards, fired 16 torpedoes between them with at least one hitting the battlecruiser's starboard side. As *Scharnhorst* altered course to starboard in an effort to comb the torpedo tracks, she presented herself as an ideal target for *Savage* and *Saumarez*, both of which had to hastily train their torpedo tubes onto the enemy's starboard side and to get within firing range. At 1855, despite being under heavy fire from the battlecruiser's armament, both destroyers turned in to attack. *Savage* came through the ordeal unscathed, but *Saumarez* took the brunt of the withering fire when 280mm shells passed through her director and under her range-finder. Although they didn't explode she suffered considerable splinter damage which reduced her speed to ten knots on one engine only. During this attack she suffered 11 killed and 11 wounded and, as a result of both the casualties and the damage, one set of torpedo tubes was put out of action. Despite this intense bombardment both destroyers pressed home their attack and when the range was down to 3,500 yards *Savage* fired eight torpedoes and *Saumarez* four. Both destroyers scored repeated hits on *Scharnhorst* with their main 4·7-inch guns, but it was the torpedoes which finally settled matters. Of the 12 torpedoes fired by the two destroyers, at least three found their target, one hitting *Scharnhorst*'s bow, one a boiler room and another hit her after end. Once again the battlecruiser's speed was drastically reduced to little more than ten knots, and although she did manage to increase this to 20 knots Force 2 was once again closing in from the west to re-engage. Fraser described the attack by the destroyers thus: '*This gallant attack was practically unsupported and carried out, particularly in the case of the first sub-division (*Savage *and* Saumarez*), in the face of heavy fire from the enemy.*'

Meanwhile, on board *Belfast* a number of heavy underwater explosions were heard as the torpedoes slammed into *Scharnhorst*'s hull, and by 1901 Force 2 was once again within range of the enemy battlecruiser. At a range of 10,400 yards *Duke of York*, *Jamaica* and *Norfolk* all opened fire on the enemy as she continued to steer southward. However, owing to the difficulty of finding their target, after two salvoes *Norfolk* ceased fire. Within minutes of this engagement being opened *Scharnhorst* was suffering repeated hits, and the flashes from exploding ammunition flared up and illuminated the target still further. The battlecruiser, meanwhile, was firing at the destroyers which by now were retreating northwards, then at a range of some 8,000 yards she shifted her fire to *Duke of York*.

By 1915 *Scharnhorst*'s speed had been reduced to five knots, and at a range of 17,000 yards *Belfast* opened fire. Some 13 minutes later, however, *Duke of York* checked fire in order to allow *Belfast* and *Jamaica* to deliver torpedo attacks. By this time *Scharnhorst* was almost stationary and firing only intermittently from B and C turrets. The torpedo attack by the two cruisers was described by Fraser thus: '*At 1919 I ordered* Jamaica *and at 1920* Belfast *to close the enemy, who by this time appeared to be almost stationary, and sink her with torpedoes. Both ships at once closed.* Jamaica *fired three torpedoes (one of which misfired) to port at 1925 at a range of 3,500 yards but no hits were claimed, probably due to an under-estimation of the enemy's speed.* Belfast *fired three torpedoes to starboard at 1927 and claimed one hit which was unobserved and considered unlikely. Both cruisers*

hauled round to fire their remaining tubes, Jamaica *engaging the enemy with main and secondary armament while doing so and scoring several hits.* Scharnhorst *replied with erratic fire from secondary armament and light weapons causing no damage. Enemy fire ceased before* Jamaica *fired three torpedoes at 1937 at a range of 3,750 yards with the enemy broadside on and almost stopped. Two hits were claimed but were not observed as the target was completely hidden by smoke; they are considered probable as underwater explosions were felt after the correct interval. When* Belfast *turned to fire her torpedoes at 1935 she found such a melee of ships and fire round the target that she altered round to southward to await a more favourable opportunity. She came in again for her final attack at 19.48, but on firing starshell to illuminate the target it was clear from the surrounding wreckage that* Scharnhorst *had by that time sunk.*'

The '*melee of ships*' was, in fact, made up of the destroyers of the 36th Division, which included *Matchless* and *Musketeer*. At a range of 1,000 yards the former had fired four torpedoes, three of which hit *Scharnhorst* between the funnel and mainmast. She was about to follow up with another torpedo attack, but a heavy sea disrupted communications and so she hauled round and came in to attack again on the enemy's port bow. By this time however *Scharnhorst* had sunk, and *Matchless* joined *Scorpion* in picking up survivors. At the same time that *Matchless* and *Musketeer* were attacking, on the battlecruiser's starboard side *Opportune* and *Virago* fired 15 torpedoes between them, at least two of which found their target. At 1938 the last ships to sight *Scharnhorst* were *Jamaica*, *Matchless* and *Virago*. Ten minutes later when *Belfast* closed to deliver a second torpedo, in an approximate position 72°16'N 028°41'E, the German battlecruiser had disappeared from sight beneath the waves.

As soon as it had been confirmed that *Scharnhorst* had, in fact, sunk *Jamaica* joined *Duke of York* and set course for the Kola Inlet, leaving *Belfast*, *Norfolk* and most of the destroyers to search the area for survivors. Decreasing her speed to 16 knots *Belfast* switched on her searchlights to aid the search, and the 36 survivors who were picked up by the destroyers were later transferred to *Duke of York*. Shortly after 2100 Fraser ordered all his forces in the area to proceed independently to the Kola Inlet, and next day during the first dog-watch *Belfast* anchored in the approaches to Murmansk Harbour, where she remained for just over 48 hours.

Without doubt it had been the superiority of British radar, communications and intelligence that had been the deciding factors in the Battle of the North Cape. But once the enemy ship had been detected it was the tenacity and dogged persistence of the cruisers and destroyers, all of which had been outgunned, that had overwhelmed *Scharnhorst*. The British force did not remain long in the Kola Inlet, with *Duke of York* sailing during the afternoon of 28 December, and 31 hours later, after loading some 20 tons of gold bullion, *Belfast* followed her. She arrived in Scapa Flow at just before midnight on New Year's Day 1944. On 6 January there was some relaxation for the ship's company when a special 'Christmas Day' routine was piped, and that evening she weighed anchor to steam south to Rosyth to undergo an 18-day maintenance period and to give ten days long leave to two watches. It was 25 January when she returned to Scapa Flow, and early February before she began operating with the fleet again, as she joined *Anson*, *Furious* and the French battleship *Richelieu*, following up with squadron exercises with *Bermuda, Dragon, Nigeria* and *Sheffield*. On 3 March, Burnett, who had been promoted to Vice-Admiral, struck his flag and his place as CS10 was taken by Rear-Admiral F. H. G. Dalrymple-Hamilton. During the rest of that month *Belfast* continued to undergo training exercises from Scapa Flow, with *Victorious* joining the manoeuvres. The purpose of the training was to practise for a forthcoming operation scheduled for early April code-named 'Tungsten'.

During February 1944 the powerful German battleship *Tirpitz* had arrived in Altenfjord and, once again, the safety of the Arctic convoys was threat-

ened. 'Operation Tungsten' was planned as an air strike by the Fleet Air Arm, with the aircraft carriers *Victorious, Emperor, Furious, Pursuer* and *Fencer*, supported by *Anson* (flag C-in-C), *Belfast* (CS10), *Jamaica, Sheffield* and 16 destroyers. This force was to steam to a point between 100 and 120 miles off Altenfjord, where Barracudas would be flown off the carriers to attack the enemy battleship. The ships left Scapa Flow during the forenoon of 30 March, and after ensuring the safe passage of Arctic convoy JW58, the strike force arrived off Altenfjord during the early hours of Monday 3 April. At 0415 the first Barracudas were flown off *Victorious*, with a second wave following an hour later. By midday, having hit *Tirpitz* with 14 bombs and causing serious damage to the battleship, all but one of the Barracudas had returned; three days later the force returned safely to Scapa Flow. Nine days later *Belfast* steamed south to Greenock from where, in preparation for the D-Day landings, she began practising naval gunfire support exercises off Arran's Catacol Bay. On 22 April, however, she was ordered to Rosyth to undergo a docking and maintenance period, and to give leave to half of the ship's company. It was 9 May when she put to sea again to make the short passage north to Scapa Flow.

Three days after her arrival at the fleet anchorage *Belfast* was present for the visit of King George VI to the Home Fleet, hoisting the Royal Standard for two hours when she carried the King from Scapa Flow to Scrabster. During the remainder of May *Belfast* continued her bombardment exercises off Cape Wrath, and on the last day of the month steamed south to Greenock to join shipping which was gathering in the Firth of Clyde in preparation for the D-Day landings, which originally had been set for 5 June 1944. At Greenock *Belfast* joined *Arethusa, Danae, Dragon, Frobisher, Ramillies* and *Warspite* for 'Operation Neptune,' the landings on the French coast in Normandy, which in both planning and execution were primarily a naval affair. The Allied Expeditionary Force was divided into two naval task forces, the Western commanded by Rear-Admiral A. G. Kirk, and the Eastern, for which *Belfast* was designated as the headquarters ship of the group's bombardment force, which also included *Arethusa, Danae, Diadem, Dragon, Frobisher* and *Mauritius*. The elderly battleships *Ramillies* and *Warspite*, together with the monitor *Roberts*, were also allocated to this force and used to suppress enemy shore batteries east of the Orne River.

It was known that only a few days in June, when there would be both a full moon and spring tides to provide illumination and deep water, would be suitable for launching this massive invasion of mainland Europe. The Supreme Allied Commander, US General Dwight D. Eisenhower, had originally chosen 5 June for the landings, but strong winds and a very choppy sea meant that it would have been virtually impossible to launch landing craft from their parent ships. With a slight, but significant, improvement forecast for 6 June, Eisenhower made the decision to postpone the invasion for 24 hours. Meanwhile, however, at Greenock, during the forenoon of Saturday 3 June, the invasion forces set sail, with *Belfast* slipping her buoy at 1055 and taking station astern of *Emerald* on a southerly course into the Irish Sea. In the event, with the invasion force at sea for some 24 hours longer than had at first been anticipated, *Belfast* spent most of Sunday 4 June cruising in the mouth of the Bristol Channel, between Milford Haven and Lundy Island. During the forenoon of 5 June, however, she passed Land's End and by that same evening she was off Portland.

The D-Day landings began at first light on Tuesday 6 June, and at 0320, along with the other ships of the bombardment group, *Belfast* arrived off the French coast roughly opposite the small seaside town of Ver-sur-Mer. Already the USAF and RAF had begun bombing the German defences and fires could be seen burning on the shore. At 0400 *Belfast*'s company were ordered to Action Stations and an hour later the ship stopped in preparation for the first of many broadsides, aimed at the German gun battery at Mont Fleury; these began at 0527. This set the scene for the next four days, as *Belfast*

fired at enemy positions and infantry concentrations. Throughout this period she also embarked Army casualties for treatment in the ship's sickbay, but despite the efforts of her medical staff, during the first two days of the landings two young soldiers died of their wounds on board. During the bombardment *Belfast* and other ships of the force stood in as close as was possible and engaged all manner of defensive installations. But despite their efforts the enemy fire was still accurate and damage was caused to both ships and vehicles, much of it by accurately directed batteries of artillery.

On 10 June, having completed a bombardment of buildings enclosing enemy artillery batteries, *Belfast* weighed anchor to make a four-hour Channel crossing to Spithead and an anchorage in Stokes Bay. Her stay in the Solent was limited to just 14 hours, during which time she was able to refuel and embark ammunition and stores before returning to the beachheads in the area of Ver-sur-Mer, from where she again bombarded German troop concentrations and defences around the ancient city of Bayeux. Three days after her return to the French coast, however, she was ordered back to Spithead again, but this time for a four-day break, during which leave was granted to the ship's company. On 19 June she returned to the French coast, this time to the area off Baie de la Seine to continue the bombardment. On 24 June *Belfast* came under two separate air attacks, but on both occasions the bombs fell wide on her starboard side. On 5 July she shifted her area of operations to a point north of Colleville-sur-Orne, west of Le Havre where, during the early hours of 8 July, the elderly cruiser *Dragon* was torpedoed by a German Neger human torpedo, manned by Midshipman Potthast. She was eventually towed to Courseulles where she was scuttled to form part of an artificial breakwater. By this stage, with the Allied Armies moving further inland, the requirement for naval gunfire support was diminishing and later that day *Belfast* weighed anchor and made a six-hour passage back to Stokes Bay. Next day she was ordered north to Greenock, and from there to Scapa Flow, where she arrived on 12 July. *Belfast*'s role in the European theatre of war was over.

Although nine months would pass before the war in Europe came to an end, Britain was at last able to turn her attention to the war in South-East Asia and the Pacific, which for many in Britain was a 'forgotten war'. It was an indication of how 'Empire' was becoming an irrelevance for large numbers of Britons. It had been decided that *Belfast* would undergo a nine-month refit on the River Tyne, to prepare her for service east of Suez, and on 27 July she left Scapa Flow for a fast passage south to Newcastle where, at noon the next day, she secured alongside the Tyne Commissioners Quay. That same afternoon Captain R. M. Dick CBE DSC RN joined the ship and next forenoon he took over the command.

During the nine months spent in the hands of the South Shields-based Middle Docks and Engineering Company, numerous alterations were made to the ship's armament and radar outfit. Perhaps the most noticeable of these was the removal of her catapult and aircraft handling facilities, and the conversion of the hangar into a recreation space. In order to cover the vast distances required of what was to become the British Pacific Fleet, *Belfast* was fitted with Refuelling at Sea (RAS) facilities, which were vital for ships that operated with the US Navy. To help the ship's company to cope better with tropical weather conditions, ventilation to messdecks was improved and new laundry facilities were installed. With air attack being one of the main hazards for ships operating in the Far East and Pacific, *Belfast*'s anti-aircraft armament was augmented by 12 twin, 20mm Oerlikon anti-aircraft guns; these were sited on the lower bridge wings, the after corners of the lower bridge, one each abreast the after funnel, and one on the quarterdeck. Two of the ship's HA 4-inch guns were removed, and the remaining ones were modified to operate with Remote Power Control. *Belfast* was also fitted with two eight-barrelled MkVIII pom-poms, one mounting on each side of the mainmast, controlled by two pom-pom directors.

HMS Belfast *as she appeared in 1945. During the immediate post-war period the ship was able to provide relief for the civilians who had been freed from Japanese Internment Camps.* *(Syd Goodman Collection)*

Finally, she was equipped with four, 4-barrelled MkVIII anti-aircraft guns.

It was the spring of 1945 before *Belfast*'s refit ended, with the Admiral's inspection taking place on the 14th April, and three days later she left dry dock to be secured once again alongside the Tyne Commissioners Quay. On 1 May she put to sea to carry out eight hours of machinery and gunnery trials before returning to the River Tyne where, two days later, she underwent her final post-refit inspection. On 6 May she steamed north to Rosyth to complete her refit and was there two days later when Germany surrendered. On 21 May she hoisted the flag of CS10, Rear-Admiral A. E. M. B. Cunninghame-Graham, but not for long, because after carrying out a short post-refit trials period and work-up at Scapa Flow, on Sunday 17 June she sailed for the Mediterranean and the British Pacific Fleet based at Sydney, where she was to be the flagship of the 2nd Cruiser Squadron. After a brief pause at Gibraltar *Belfast* arrived in Malta's Grand Harbour, where she stayed to complete a four-week work-up, with an emphasis on anti-aircraft exercises.

On 24 July 1945, with her work-up completed, *Belfast* left Malta to steam via Alexandria, where her landing parties were exercised, to Port Said where, on 27 and 28 July, she made her southbound transit of the Suez Canal, arriving in Aden on the last day of the month. After a 24-hour break there *Belfast* left for Colombo and Fremantle, crossing the equator for the first time on 8 August and arriving at her destination six days later. Next day, at 0700, while she was anchored in Fremantle's Outer Roads, the ship's company heard Prime Minster Clement Attlee announce the end of the war against Japan. The Second World War was finally over.

Leaving Fremantle on 16 August *Belfast* made the five-day passage to Sydney where, on 21 August, she officially joined the British Pacific Fleet. Nine days later she sailed north for the fleet's forward operating base at Manus where she paused just long enough to refuel before steaming on to Leyte. Once again she stayed only long enough to refuel before steaming north once again, this time to the Formosan port of Kiirun (now Keelung, Taiwan). A member of *Belfast*'s Royal Marines Detachment takes up the story: '*We oiled ship and continued on towards Kiirun in Formosa where many of our lads had been held prisoners of war for some considerable period. Many of them were in a terrible state, caused mainly by malnutrition. The Rising Sun flag was still flying over some of the buildings when we slowly entered this terribly wreck-strewn and horribly demolished harbour. Most of the British prisoners who were able to walk had been taken aboard destroyers, and the remainder were taken aboard a hospital ship which had arrived shortly before us.*'

On her arrival at Kiirun *Belfast* secured alongside *Bermuda* (flag CS2) which, accompanied by *Argonaut* and three destroyers, had arrived before her, leaving the aircraft carrier *Colossus* at sea in order to provide air cover. Between them these ships had managed to evacuate most of the British ex-PoWs, and shortly after she secured alongside *Bermuda*, Rear-Admiral R. M. Servaes (CS2) transferred his flag to *Belfast*. Next day, during the afternoon of 11 September, *Belfast* led the Task Group (designated 111.3) to sea where they joined *Colossus*. After rendezvousing with US Navy warships and leaving *Colossus* at sea again to provide air cover, the rest of the force entered the Yangtze and Whampoa Rivers to make a slow 24-hour passage to Shanghai.

It was the afternoon of 19 September when the four American and five British warships (*Belfast*, *Bermuda* and three destroyers) arrived in the city of Shanghai to secure at buoys opposite the Bund. *Belfast*'s Royal Marine again describes the scene: '*We were given a tremendous welcome by thousands of people of all nationalities who lined the banks of the river, and with the sound of hooters and whistles ringing in our ears, we steamed slowly into Shanghai with the White Ensign floating majestically in the breeze.*' Unlike many cities in China which had been ravaged by eight years of war, Shanghai gave the appearance of having come through the ordeal relatively unscathed, although ashore there were signs of confusion and lawlessness, and there were concerns for the safety of European civilians who had been liberated from Japanese detention camps. In the event seamen and Marines from the British and US warships guarded key buildings in what had been the city's International Settlement, while the ships' companies ferried ashore stores for the freed detainees. During the afternoon of 24 September *Belfast* opened her gangways to British ex-detainees, who were invited on board for a slap-up tea. The children, many of whom had known no other life than that in detention camps, were entertained to cinema shows, swings and see-saws. Each person was given a voucher to obtain from *Belfast*'s canteen such luxuries as chocolate, sweets, fruit and some canned goods. It came as a surprise to the ship's company to find that many of the children had never seen sweets or chocolate before.

HMS *Belfast* remained at Shanghai until 19 December 1945, when she slipped her moorings and steamed back downriver to set course for Hong Kong, where she arrived two days later for a seven-day Christmas break. During her stay a large draft of ratings was exchanged with the battleship *Anson*, and *Belfast* received a visit from the C-in-C, BPF, Admiral Sir Bruce Fraser. On 28 December she left Hong Kong and sailed north to Shanghai again, where she relieved HMS *Black Prince* as the British guardship. In early 1946 the situation in Shanghai had largely stabilised, but for the European population there was to be no return to the pre-war privileges of the International Settlements in the city. *Belfast*'s second tour of duty as the Shanghai guardship lasted for 18 days before she was ordered south to Sydney for a three-week refit and maintenance period. Here further work was carried out to update her anti-aircraft armament, and she also underwent a five-day docking period. All the ship's torpedo armament and depth charges were landed, and on 25 February with all the work completed, *Belfast* left Sydney to begin a three-month cruise round New Zealand, Fiji and Japan.

HMS *Belfast*'s first port of call was Port Chalmers, the main port for the city of Dunedin on New Zealand's south island, where she was the first Royal Navy warship to visit since before the start of the Second World War in 1939. Each afternoon during her six days in the port *Belfast* was opened to the public and each day hundreds of people queued to go aboard. On 6 March she left Port Chalmers to head north for Wellington and then Napier where, over the space of just four days, some 10,000 people visited the ship. On 12 March the cruiser left New Zealand's shores for Fiji, an island which during the Pacific War had felt itself to be very much in the front line. On 20 March, after leaving Suva, *Belfast* steamed north for 12 days then during the forenoon of 1 April, some 62 miles south-west of Tokyo, she sighted Mount Fuji. Five hours later she anchored in Tokyo Bay as part of the Allied Occupation Force.

For ten days *Belfast* remained in Tokyo Bay, and her ship's company were allowed some limited shore leave. On 10 April, in company with HMAS *Warramunga*, she left Tokyo Bay for Kobe and Yokohama where, during the evening of 24 April, she secured to a buoy close to the battleship *Anson*. Six days later Admiral Servaes transferred his flag to the battleship and on 2 May *Belfast* left harbour to steam via Hong Kong to Singapore. Two weeks after leaving Japanese waters *Belfast* anchored in the roads off the city of Singapore. For the newly reinstated British authorities there was an urgent need to restore national prestige, which in February 1942 had been devastated by the ignominious surrender of the island. On 20 May, however, *Belfast* steamed round to the north of Singapore Island to secure alongside the naval base where de-ammunitioning got under way prior to a nine-week refit.

During her stay at the naval base much of the unskilled work carried out on board, such as chipping, scraping and renewing paintwork, was carried out by a 70-strong gang of Japanese PoWs, who were being employed to carry out various tasks in clearing up the island's badly damaged and neglected infrastructure, as well as assisting with work in the naval dockyard. Some members of the ship's

HMS Belfast *in 1946.* *(Maritime Photo Library)*

company enjoyed a seven-day period of station leave at the up-country coastal resort of Port Dickson at this time. In mid-1946 the main base for the British Pacific Fleet was moved to Hong Kong, but this was only a temporary measure and it would not be long before the BPF was disbanded and a new Far East Fleet formed, based at Singapore. In June 1946 Admiral Sir Denis W. Boyd took over from Fraser as C-in-C, BFP, and on the 10th of the month, whilst passing through Singapore he paid a visit to *Belfast*, which was soon to be his flagship. Four weeks later, with the ship now alongside No 12 berth, there was a change of command when Captain H. B. Ellison DSO RN arrived on board and took over from Captain Dick, who left the ship to await a passage home.

On 24 July, with her refit completed, *Belfast* left Singapore for Hong Kong where she arrived five days later to undergo C-in-C's inspection followed by a two-week period of post-refit trials and work-up. On 15 August Admiral Boyd hoisted his flag, and that same afternoon sailed for the Japanese port of Yokohama, at the start of a cruise to Japanese and Chinese ports. After visiting Yokohama, Otaru, Kure and Kobe, *Belfast* sailed for the Chinese port of Woosung, which is virtually a suburb of Shanghai, where the C-in-C held talks with Nationalist Chinese military officers. By September 1946 the Chinese Civil War, which had been raging on and off since the late 1920s, had resumed following a wartime truce. America and Britain were backing the Nationalist leader Chiang Kai-shek, whose Army it appeared had the upper hand over Mao Zedong's Communist forces. With the Nationalists having captured an important Communist base at Kalgan in northern China, both America and Britain were keen to provide Chiang Kai-shek with military aid. Britain provided the Flower-class frigate *Petunia* and various river gunboats including *Gannet*, *Falcon* and *Sandpiper*, all of which were redundant following the relinquishing of the Treaty Ports by the Western nations. In

addition, in May 1948 the Hunt-class frigate *Mendip* was transferred to China, but a year later following the collapse of the Nationalists it was handed back to the Royal Navy.

On 19 September *Belfast* navigated the lower Yangtze River to anchor off the Nationalist-held city of Nanking (Nanjing), where the C-in-C and his staff once again went ashore for talks with the Nationalist Navy's C-in-C. Following her visit to Nanking *Belfast* made a series of calls at former Treaty Ports all of which, in 1943, had been formally relinquished by the relevant Western powers; these included Tsingtao (Qingdao) and Chinwangtao (Qinhuangdao), then, in mid-October returned to Hong Kong where she remained for three weeks. During the last weeks of November *Belfast* visited Penang and Singapore, and during the first week of December returned to Hong Kong where the aircraft carrier *Victorious*, which was being employed as a troop transport, had arrived with naval personnel to replace *Belfast*'s Hostilities Only men who were due home for demobilisation. Shortly after her arrival in Hong Kong *Belfast* shifted from her buoy in the harbour to the north arm of the naval dockyard to begin a six-week maintenance period, which included a five-day docking period in the commercial Taikoo Dry Dock, a facility which the Navy used right into the 1950s.

On 21 January 1947, with *Belfast*'s refit completed, the C-in-C transferred his flag from *Amethyst* back to the cruiser, and that evening from her buoy in the harbour *Belfast* put on a spectacular fireworks display to celebrate the Chinese New Year. Three days later, she and the frigate *Alert* left Hong Kong to begin a two-week flag-showing cruise to the island of Borneo and the ports of Jesselton (Kota Kinabalu) and Sandakan in what was then British North Borneo (now Sabah), before steaming on to Manila and returning to Hong Kong. In late February, this time in company with the destroyer *Comet*, she began a cruise to Japanese and Chinese waters, which took her to Kure, where she underwent Admiral's Inspection, before reaching Shanghai on 5 March.

By the spring of 1947 the civil war in China had been raging for some ten months, and despite substantial US aid to the Nationalist cause, Mao Zedong's Communist PLA had gained the upper hand. In Shanghai, however, the Nationalist forces still controlled the city and it would be two years before it fell to Mao's Communist Army. Although many of the International communities had returned to the city and some of the former concessions were excluded from Chinese municipal control, it was clear that conditions would not return to the pre-war quasi-colonial state of affairs and that the European presence was now very much more on Chinese terms. During *Belfast*'s stay there were more high-level discussions with senior Chinese naval officers regarding aid to the Nationalist Government, and also about the Chinese Navy's access to the newly refurbished and reopened naval dockyard at Hong Kong. After ten days at Shanghai *Belfast*, *Comet*, *Cossack* and *Alert* left the city to steam down to the mouth of the Yangtze River and then north to Tsingtao which, until June 1949 when it was occupied by Mao's Red Army, served as a base for the US Navy's Pacific Fleet. Once again there were more high-level meetings with Nationalist Chinese officers, but on 24 March *Belfast* returned to Hong Kong.

Upon her return the C-in-C transferred his flag ashore, and while the ship herself prepared for a six-week docking and maintenance period at the Singapore Naval Base, where she was scheduled to undergo a three-week dry docking when her rudders would be removed for maintenance. The refit came in the last few months of *Belfast*'s commission in the Far East for in mid-October she was scheduled to return to the UK. On 2 June the work was finally completed and next day the cruiser steamed north into the Strait of Malacca to the small town of Port Dickson where, in the shallow coastal waters, she anchored over a mile out. The cruiser was to spend the rest of the month in Malayan waters, as part of a concerted effort by the British Government to stamp its authority on the new post-1945 Malayan Union, a political settle-

In October 1948 HMS Belfast *paid a belated visit to the city where she was built, for the official presentation of her silver bell.* *(Maritime Photo Library)*

ment which had superseded the pre-war hotchpotch of Federated and Unfederated States. The British reoccupation of Malaya was being undermined by a Communist insurgency which would drag on for over ten years, and would not end until after the country had been granted Independence. *Belfast*'s presence was a flag-showing exercise designed to shore up support for the colonial administration which was struggling to assert its authority. While *Belfast* was anchored off Port Dickson she was visited by the Governor of the Malayan Union, Sir Edward Gent[1]. After six days at Port Dickson *Belfast* steamed north to the island of Penang, where once again the civic authorities were entertained on board. After three days at anchor off Georgetown *Belfast* steamed south to Malacca where once again, owing to the shallow coastal waters, sheanchored over a mile offshore. The series of flag-showing visits ended on 18 June when *Belfast* returned to Singapore to anchor off the city, where she was joined by other ships of the Far East Fleet, including *Glasgow* and *Sussex*. Finally, on 3 July, after exercising in the South China Sea with *Concord, Comet, Hart, Amphion, Constance* and *Quickmatch*, she returned to Hong Kong, remaining in and around the colony for the rest of the month.

On 19 August 1947 the C-in-C struck his flag and transferred it ashore to HMS *Tamar*. Next day, after embarking some 75 passengers, *Belfast* left Hong Kong to begin what was to be a slow passage home. The cruiser's first stop was Singapore Naval Base where she underwent a short 48-hour docking period for bottom scraping and painting, followed by a two-week maintenance period. On 11 September she left Singapore bound for Aden, Port Said, Malta and Gibraltar, and arrived off Spithead during the morning of 15 October. That same afternoon she weighed anchor to steam up harbour and secure alongside North Corner Jetty, where over 1,000 relatives and friends were waiting to greet the ship.

[1] British Governor of the Malayan Union, and later the Federation of Malaya, until June 1948 when he was killed in a plane crash at Northolt when returning home to discuss the deteriorating situation in Malaya.

HMS *Belfast*'s return to the UK saw her being reduced to reserve and at the same time undergoing a major refit. Of her complement of 750, some 150 men were due for immediate demobilisation and roughly the same numbers were due for release within 12 months. In the years which immediately followed the Second World War, Britain, like most of Europe, was virtually bankrupt and there was an urgent need to rebuild manufacturing industry and re-establish the export trade. At the same time, however, Britain still had worldwide Imperial commitments and there were conflicting demands on the country's manpower, so it was inevitable that recruitment to the armed forces would suffer and naval recruitment was particularly difficult. On board *Belfast* the ship's company was soon reduced to little more than a care and maintenance party, while the dockyard gave all the ship's main and auxiliary machinery a thorough overhaul. It was the autumn of 1948 before the refit was completed, and on 22 September, under the command of the newly appointed Captain E. K. Le Mesurier MVO RN, *Belfast* was recommissioned with a new ship's company. Once again the ship was earmarked for service with the Far East Fleet, but before she left home waters there was a much postponed ceremonial presentation to arrange. The question of *Belfast* paying an official visit to the city where she had been built had been first raised at the Admiralty before the outbreak of the Second World War, but the hostilities had precluded this. In Belfast the civic authorities had been pressing for 'their' ship to visit the city for a formal presentation of a magnificent silver ship's bell which had been purchased by public subscriptions and cast before the outbreak of war. It was in late September that the C-in-C Portsmouth worked out a schedule which would allow the cruiser to make a 74-hour visit to Belfast the following month. In the event she left Portsmouth on 5 October to carry out two days of machinery trials in the Channel, before returning to Portsmouth where final adjustments were made to her main propulsion machinery. On 12 October C-in-C Portsmouth inspected the ship, and three days later *Belfast* sailed for Portland to carry out DG ranging. It was during these trials that stormy weather with severe gales battered the south coast, and *Belfast* was at anchor in Portland Harbour during the night of 17/18 October when a pinnace belonging to *Illustrious* sank in the harbour with the loss of 29 men. Unfortunately, on board *Belfast* the ship's boats were out of action, but her Medical Officer was able to get to *Illustrious* to assist with casualties. On 20 October the cruiser arrived alongside Belfast's Dufferin Dock, and next day the ship's ceremonial guard and band of seamen and Royal Marines marched through the city. That afternoon the ship was opened to the public, and many of those who had worked on her construction were able to visit her for the first time in almost ten years. During the forenoon of 22 October the Lord Mayor of Belfast arrived on board for the presentation of the bell, weighing 156lbs and measuring 22 inches in diameter at the bottom. It was in place to mark the passing of noon and at 1300 the next day *Belfast* slipped her moorings, setting course for Gibraltar.

Originally it had been intended that *Belfast*'s stopover at Gibraltar would last only as long as it took to refuel, but in view of the fact that the colony's dockyard facilities were not being fully utilised it was decided that she would undergo a two-week dry docking period. Arriving in Gibraltar on 27 October, she remained until Thursday 11 November when she continued her passage east, via Malta, Port Said, Aden and Trincomalee. On 18 November, the day after leaving Malta, *Belfast* answered an emergency call from a US merchantman, SS *Eastport*, which urgently required a doctor. After four hours steaming at full power *Belfast* sighted the American ship, and it was not long before *Eastport*'s bosun had been transferred to the cruiser's sickbay. So ill was the man that *Belfast*'s surgeon performed an immediate two-hour appendectomy, and next day on arrival at Port Said the patient was transferred to a hospital ashore. *Belfast* arrived alongside Singapore Naval Base on 8 December, and despite the fact that five months earlier the British Pacific Fleet had ceased to exist,

with the Far East Fleet based at Singapore having taken its place, no sooner had the C-in-C hoisted his flag in *Belfast*, than she sailed for Hong Kong where she arrived on 23 December to relieve *Sussex*.

HMS *Belfast* had been away from Hong Kong for some 16 months, and during her absence the civil war in China had continued unabated. However, not only had Mao Zedong's Communist Army gained the upper hand, but it was also rapidly routing the Nationalist forces. After a campaign lasting over seven weeks, by the end of 1948 Mao's Army had won its battle to dominate northern China and Manchuria and was advancing towards the Yangtze River delta and the major cities of Nanking and Shanghai. These advances brought clashes between the Communist forces and Western military warships, which were still operating in China, mainly on the Yangtze River, despite the fact that in 1943 the USA and Britain had declared an end to the Treaty Port system. As Mao had publicly stated that any Chinese Government led by him would no longer tolerate foreign military operations in China, the likelihood of clashes between US or Royal Navy ships and Mao's forces was almost inevitable. However, although Mao had always carefully avoided any mention of Hong Kong, the authorities in the colony were taking no chances and set up a range of security measures in the New Territories frontier districts, although it was recognised by the British Government that against a concerted Communist attack the area would be indefensible. This then, was the military and political situation when *Belfast* returned to the colony.

Before leaving Singapore on 9 December *Belfast* had once again hoisted the flag of the C-in-C, FES, and officially joined the Fleet's 5th Cruiser Squadron. On 3 January 1949, to the cheers of *Belfast*'s ship's company, *Sussex*, whose place *Belfast* had taken, left Hong Kong at the start of her passage home to Portsmouth. Four days later, with the C-in-C having struck his flag, *Belfast* took over as flagship of the 5th Cruiser Squadron and hoisted the flag of Rear-Admiral A. R. G. Madden. During the rest of January she remained in and around the waters of Hong Kong, anchoring in Mirs Bay (Tai Pang Wan) on most evenings. On 11 January she carried out air defence exercises with RAF aircraft, including a de Havilland Vampire jet fighter, flying from Kai Tak. During the exercises one of these jets made a forced landing on the western coastline of Mirs Bay which was firmly in Chinese territory, although the area was still held by the friendly Nationalist Army. It was decided that every effort should be made to recover the aircraft. In the event *Belfast* anchored in the bay, well within Hong Kong waters, for over 36 hours while a landing party went ashore and manhandled the wrecked aircraft onto a lighter which was towed back to the ship before being returned to the RAF. On the last day of January *Belfast* left Hong Kong for Shanghai, where she joined *Black Swan* and *Cossack*. Also in harbour was the US Navy's destroyer USS *Rogers*. During *Belfast*'s nine days at Shanghai it was noticeable that foreign residents in the city, including Britons, were becoming increasingly concerned about the advancing Communist Army, and there were increasing demands for passages out of the city to Hong Kong. Before she sailed for Hong Kong, *Belfast* embarked the British Vice-Consul in Shanghai who was attempting to organise an evacuation of British residents, and during her passage down the Yangtze River passed a Chinese warship evacuating Nationalist troops from the north bank. It was becoming increasingly clear that Chiang Kai-shek's Nationalist Army was facing total defeat.

HMS *Belfast* remained at Hong Kong for the remainder of February and for most of March, but on the 26th of the month she made the two-day passage to Shanghai. Once again her stay in the city was confined to nine days and on 7 April she arrived back in Hong Kong, which is where she was on 19 April when the sloop *Amethyst* left Shanghai for Nanking to relieve *Consort* as the Royal Navy's guardship in the city. Late that afternoon, before darkness fell, *Amethyst* anchored off Kiang Yin Island, and at 0800 the next day she weighed anchor and got under way, entering the fighting zone. The

port (south) bank of the Yangtze River was occupied by Nationalist troops while the starboard (northern) bank was held by troops of Mao's Chinese People's Liberation Army. They had already given notice that Western Navies would no longer be able to operate independently in Chinese territorial waters. At shortly after 0900 *Amethyst* came under fire from gun batteries on the starboard river bank, and after being hit several times went aground in the mud; thus began a 14-week stand-off. As well as suffering damage, 22 of *Amethyst*'s company, including her commanding officer, were killed and 31 were wounded.

The incident came at a time when the C-in-C, FES was in London for conferences, with Vice-Admiral Madden in command during his absence. On 26 April Madden took the cruiser *London* and the sloop *Black Swan* upriver from Shanghai in an attempt to rescue *Amethyst*, which had managed to free herself from the river mud. In the event, both *London* and *Black Swan* came under heavy artillery fire, and after sustaining casualties and damage they were forced to return to Shanghai. Madden then ordered *Belfast* and the destroyer *Crescent* to Woosung, some 14 miles downriver from Shanghai, where they arrived during the morning of 28 April. That afternoon FO2 transferred his flag to *Belfast* and next day *London* and *Black Swan* steamed downriver to the mouth of the Yangtze. *Belfast*, meanwhile, remained at Woosung until 19 May, when with the return of the C-in-C from the UK she returned to Hong Kong. This marked the end of *Belfast*'s role in what became known as the 'Yangtze Incident' and she remained in and around Hong Kong until the second week of August. During the forenoon of Wednesday 3 August the battered *Amethyst*, having made a daring and successful dash downriver, rejoined the fleet at Hong Kong. On 16 August, with the 'Yangtze Incident' over, and with *Jamaica* having arrived from the Caribbean to strengthen the colony's defences, *Belfast* sailed for Singapore and Penang to exercise with the aircraft carrier *Triumph* and the destroyer *Charity*. On 3 September, all three ships returned to Hong Kong. By this time the Nationalist Army in mainland China had collapsed and it was desperately attempting to evacuate as many loyal troops as possible to the island of Formosa (Taiwan) and its outlying islands. As far as mainland China was concerned the civil war was over, and in October 1949, without any preconditions, the British Government formally recognised Mao's People's Republic of China.

Soon after her return to Hong Kong *Belfast* was at sea again and bound for the Japanese port of Kure, which was the home of a US naval base. The cruiser's visit lasted for ten days, before she began an 11-day patrol of the Formosa Strait, where hundreds of ships and boats of all sizes were fleeing from mainland China to Formosa. At one point, on 23 September, *Belfast* went to the assistance of a Chinese merchantman which was towing a disabled Nationalist Chinese gunboat. In the event all that was required was help in reconnecting the tow and on the last day of September returned to Hong Kong. She remained in the area during most of October and on the 28th a large draft of men, who were due for release, were discharged to the P&O liner *Carthage*, their places being taken by others who arrived from the UK in the same ship. Two days later, during the afternoon of Sunday 30 October, *Belfast* was instructed by the C-in-C to sail that evening for Pratas Island, a small coral atoll some 210 miles south-west of Hong Kong, where a Nationalist Chinese tank landing ship with over 700 people on board had run aground. Apart from a small weather station manned by a handful of men, the island was uninhabited and did not have the resources to support such large numbers of people, most of whom were Chinese Nationalist soldiers. After leaving Hong Kong at 1800 on 30 October *Belfast*'s passage to Pratas, as she steamed through a strong monsoon swell, was wet and uncomfortable, but she arrived off the atoll at 0650 the next morning and anchored in 28 fathoms, about a mile south-west of the island where there was a good lee. From the anchorage the wrecked vessel, *Cheung Hsai*, was clearly visible lying on the northern arm

of the reef; anchored close to it was an elderly gunboat, *Kiang Kun*, an ex-Italian river gunboat which dated back to 1918, but they did not appear to be making any effort to rescue those still on board the stricken vessel. As it was clear that nothing would be done about evacuating survivors unless *Belfast* organised it, a pinnace was launched, but for some reason neither those still on board nor those on shore were willing to make a move until the next morning. In view of this *Belfast* withdrew for the night, and at 0645 next day the rescue operation got under way.

As the only approach to the ship was across a lagoon, a tortuous and shallow passage of six miles, it was clear that the whole operation would take some time, but during the day a sampan and a junk arrived and began evacuating the stricken ship. *Belfast* herself took on board 195 military personnel, 12 women, 15 children and four other civilians from the island. The cruiser then made the 24-hour return passage to Hong Kong where, in Junk Bay, the refugees were transferred to a Chinese merchantman, SS *Ming Chung*.

During the remainder of November and the first three weeks of December *Belfast* remained in local waters off Hong Kong, exercising periodically with the aircraft carrier *Triumph* and the destroyers *Charity, Concorde, Constance* and *Consort*. On 9 December she left Hong Kong to pay a visit to the city of Saigon which, in those days, was still the capital of the Cochin China region of French Indo-China. With a guerrilla war against Vietnamese Nationalists led by the French-educated dissident Ho Chi-minh some two years old, the French colonial authorities were struggling to reassert their authority. At the same time Britain had its own post-war colonial unrest in Malaya, and care had to be taken to avoid any indication that *Belfast*'s visit was material support for the French. After steaming up the Saigon River during the forenoon of 12 December *Belfast* secured alongside a berth in the city. On the day of her arrival there were the usual exchanges of visits by civic dignitaries, and one of the visitors to *Belfast* was the former Emperor of Indo-China, Bao Dai, who, in March 1945 had renamed the French colony Vietnam. Although he had abdicated soon afterwards, the French government had recently re-instated him as a puppet head of state. However, with the war in Indo-China making itself felt in Saigon the ship's company had to observe a strict evening curfew, with all liberty men required to be back on board by 2200. The visit lasted for five days, and on 17 December *Belfast* made her way back down the Saigon River, arriving in Hong Kong three days later, where she remained for the Christmas and New Year festivities.

On Monday 16 January 1950, Rear-Admiral W. G. Andrewes took over as FO2, FES, and hoisted his flag in *Belfast*. Two days later the cruiser left Hong Kong to make a five-day passage to Singapore where, on 23 January, she began an 11-week refit at the naval base. For the ship's company, with the accommodation spaces on board being refurbished, there was the luxury of a seven-week stay in shore accommodation at HMS *Terror*. Work on board included the replacement of baths with showers and the sickbay being fitted with air conditioning units. All the ship's boilers were cleaned and repairs were made to her starboard outer propeller which had been damaged. On Saturday 8 April there was a change of command when Le-Mesurier was relieved by Captain Aubrey St Claire Ford DSO RN and three days later, on 11 April, the ship put to sea for eight hours of trials. On 14 April she left Singapore to return to Hong Kong where she began a ten-day post-refit work-up in local waters. On 12 May, with her trials and work-up completed, *Belfast* and *Consort* set course for Kure and a summer cruise to Japanese ports. *Belfast* visited the US naval base at Yokosuka, and from there returned to Kure, where she and *Consort* joined *Triumph, Cossack* and *Contest* for exercises in the Pacific. During the first weeks of June *Belfast* remained in northern Japanese waters, operating with *Triumph* and destroyers out of Ominato Bay.

HMS *Belfast*'s presence in Japanese waters came at a time of international tension in the area, with the focus of disagreement being Korea. Since 1904

Korea had, effectively, been occupied and ruled by Japan, and until the Russo-Japanese War of 1903/04 both China and Tsarist Russia had always exerted a strong influence over the country. In July 1945, at the Potsdam Conference, the USA and Soviet Union had taken the decision to partition Korea at the 38th Parallel, with the northern part being under Soviet influence and the south coming under the US. Both countries stated that the partition would only be temporary, but neither power made any serious moves to address the problem and the 'temporary' border became a fixed frontier between political ideologies. In May 1948 both the Soviet-backed North and the American-backed South claimed jurisdiction over the whole country. Later that year, on 9 September, North Korea proclaimed its independence under its leader Kim Il Sung, who loudly stated that his Communist State was the rightful ruler of the whole Korean Peninsula and that '*whether by force of arms or negotiation*' he would reunite the country. At the same time the American-occupied southern half of the peninsula became the Republic of Korea, and its first leader, Syngman Rhee, also claimed to be the rightful ruler of the divided country. Both States were in fact puppets of the Soviet Union and America, and the stage was set for Korea to become a pawn in the post-war clash of political ideologies.

The Royal Marines Detachment parades on HMS Belfast's *quarterdeck for a visit by the President of the Republic of Korea, Syngman Rhee, at Pusan.* *(Author's Collection)*

During the morning of 24 June *Belfast* weighed anchor and left Ominato Bay to exercise with *Triumph* and *Contest*, and at the end of manoeuvres that evening the ships anchored off the port of Hakodate at the southern end of Hokkaido Prefecture. In the early hours of the next morning and with no prior warning, Communist North Korean troops and tanks stormed over the frontier at the 38th Parallel and began a rapid advance south towards the capital Seoul.

Having initially been taken by surprise, President Truman then reacted quickly and ordered American forces in South Korea to assist in repelling the invasion. On 28 June the British Prime Minister, Clement Attlee, ordered that Royal Navy warships in the Far East be placed under the overall command of US General Douglas MacArthur to aid the UN resistance. It was the first time since the formation of the NATO Alliance in March 1949 that the US and British Fleets had joined forces operationally.

Meanwhile, back at Hakodate, at just before midnight on Sunday 25 June, hands were called and ordered to prepare *Belfast* for sea. As Typhoon Elsie was sweeping the area and torrential rain had reduced visibility to just a few hundred yards, few thought that the early sailing was anything other than a move away from the storms. Rumours soon

began to abound that the ship was bound for Kobe, where she was due to spend a week, and at just after midnight on 26 June *Belfast* weighed anchor and set course for a destination which was still unknown to most on board. Soon, however, the word quickly spread round the ship that North Korean forces had invaded the South and it wasn't long before many theories concerning the ship's future movements were being put forward. At noon on Tuesday 27 June, with most of the ship's company still in the dark as to where the ship was bound, *Belfast* arrived at the US naval base of Yokosuka, only 40 miles from Tokyo, and hopes were raised of some good runs ashore. With the stay lasting for only a few hours these hopes were soon dashed, and at 1800, with Admiral Andrewes having returned from a conference with senior US Navy officers, *Belfast* sailed again. This time, however, the ship's company were closed up at Defence Stations and in two watches. On 29 June she joined forces with *Jamaica, Triumph* and the destroyers *Consort, Contest* and *Cossack*, before steaming on towards the island of Okinawa. Arriving off the island at just after first light on Saturday 1 July, *Belfast* anchored well offshore. Once again, however, the stay was short and as soon as Andrewes had returned from conferences ashore *Belfast* set sail once more. As one member of the ship's company noted: '*We were beginning to consider that the whole atmosphere was becoming uncomfortably warlike.*'

On 2 July, *Belfast*, *Triumph* and the destroyers made a rendezvous with a US Navy strike force led by the aircraft carrier *Valley Forge*, together with a cruiser and destroyer escort, to form a formidable task group of two aircraft carriers, with approximately 130 aircraft, two cruisers and ten destroyers. All that day and the next night the force steamed north, and at 0520 on Monday 3 July the ships' companies went to Action Stations. At dawn the two aircraft carriers began flying off their aircraft. A member of *Belfast*'s ship's company remembers the events: '*They came off very fast, and within a few minutes the air seemed to be full of aeroplanes orbiting the task group – Panther jets, Seafires, Skyraiders, Corsairs and finally the Fireflies which, with everything but the kitchen sink under their wings, seemed to struggle to get off* Triumph*'s flight deck. After a while they all streamed off east to strike at North Korean airfields and we were left to await their return. A couple of aerial incidents broke the monotony of the day; first when a helicopter running a mail trip delivered some signals to our quarterdeck, and later when one of the CAP Corsairs ditched and went into the sea right alongside an American destroyer, which quickly rescued the crew.*' For two days the aircraft carriers flew off a constant stream of air strikes against enemy positions and troop concentrations, until at 1800 on 4 July the operations ceased and the task group set course for Sasebo, where they arrived late the next afternoon.

Sasebo, situated as it is on the western side of the island of Kyushu, and facing the Korea Strait, was an ideal base for the Allied naval operations off the Korean coast. But as a member of *Belfast*'s company remembers, in July 1949 it was: '*...rather a small town with a few shops, a pearl farm and a couple of rather dubious cabarets for the benefit of the US occupation troops. There were American officers' and other-ranks' clubs, but owing to the dollar exchange rate we ratings could usually only afford rather inferior Japanese beer. The American Club boasted a large canteen with many amenities, including Japanese taxi dancers.*' In the event *Belfast*'s first stopover at Sasebo lasted for just four days before she sailed to begin her first patrol off Korea's west coast. According to a ship's company member this was: '*The most unpopular task in the fleet. A five- or six-day patrol was spent steaming up and down at various distances off the coastline searching for blockade-runners, of which there seemed to be remarkably few. It was well summed up by one officer who, when we returned to base, reported that we had seen, "Nothing but two fogs and one junk."*' In fact *Belfast*'s first patrol was uneventful, but during her second patrol, which began on 17 July, she was rather busier.

As well as patrolling the coast *Belfast* also had to

HMS Belfast *bombarding enemy positions on the Korean Coast.* *(Author's Collection)*

carry out shore bombardment duties, and just 24 hours after starting her second patrol was called upon to do just this. While she was sailing close inshore, at midnight on the 18th, lights were seen moving along the main coastal road. As she was well north of the 38th Parallel she opened fire with her main armament, but the results of this first bombardment could not be seen. At dawn *Belfast* arrived off the town of Yangyang, where there was known to be a large concentration of enemy troops. Once again *Belfast* opened fire with her main armament and this time the results were observed. As a member of the ship's company remembers: '*We in our 4-inch directors had a grandstand view of the whole proceedings, including some very surprised North Koreans sprinting for the hills in what looked like their nightshirts, and a beautiful bit of target practice on a tall chimney. After this we steamed slowly back down the coast, firing occasionally at the coast road and railway, and once at an imposing-looking mansion which was thought to be the local naval headquarters.*' Early the same afternoon *Belfast* arrived off Yongduk where she rendezvoused with the US Navy's 5-inch anti-aircraft cruiser USS *Juneau*, which was carrying out a bombardment in support of the 1st US Cavalry Division. Here *Belfast*'s spotting was carried out by an American aircraft, and therefore very little could be seen by those on board the cruiser. However, there was one very spectacular explosion when a broadside from *Belfast* hit an ammunition dump. Soon after *Belfast*'s arrival *Juneau* asked if she would like to take over the bombardment, and after 18 broadsides the spotting aircraft told her to cease fire as there appeared to be nothing left of the target. Next day *Belfast* carried out another bombardment, and on 22 July the patrol ended when she returned to Sasebo. After that there followed two more west coast patrols before she returned to Sasebo at 0630 on 3 August to spend three days before she was scheduled to sail for Hong Kong en route to Chatham. However, next day she was ordered to sail, not for the UK, but to Korea's west coast once again where, on Saturday 5 August, she carried out a 4-inch bombardment of Inchon, the port at the mouth of the Han River which served Seoul. Early that morning she rendezvoused with *Kenya* and the two ships entered the Han River estuary to open fire on Inchon. Once again spotting was carried out by US aircraft, so for those on board, apart from some dense clouds of black smoke, there was little to be seen. Afterwards, however, *Belfast* learned that her bombardment of barracks, factories and a power station had been successful. As they returned through the narrow channel on their way out from the estuary the two cruisers were ordered to open fire on enemy pillboxes, and although their targets were almost immediately

The scene on HMS Belfast's *open bridge during bombardment duties.* *(Author's Collection)*

obscured by clouds of dust and smoke, *Belfast* managed to get away ten 4-inch broadsides before she was ordered to cease fire. Next day *Belfast* returned to Sasebo, and on 9 August sailed for Hong Kong. For the time being it was the end of her involvement in the Korean War.

From Hong Kong *Belfast* steamed to the naval base at Singapore where, on 14 August, she began a four-week refit and docking period, during which the ship's company again moved into shore accommodation. On 11 September *Belfast* left Singapore to make her passage home by way of Aden, Port Said, Malta and Gibraltar. On Thursday 5 October she passed the Isle of Wight and later that evening she anchored off the Great Nore Light Vessel. Next day she moved upriver to Sheerness and on 9 October secured alongside No 3 basin in Chatham Dockyard. The commission which had begun in September 1948 was over.

HMS *Belfast* was scheduled to stay in home waters for just over thirteen weeks, so during her stay in Chatham Dockyard the ship was a busy hive of activity. On 19 October, having been paid off, she recommissioned with a full wartime complement of over 900 men, for further service on the Far East Station. To make up numbers in a Navy which

was still suffering severe manpower shortages, both reservists and time-expired men who would have been due for discharge were enlisted and in order to accommodate the additional personnel the recreation space on board was hastily converted into a messdeck. Finally, on Friday 27 October 1950, *Belfast* slipped her mooring buoy at Sheerness and set course for the Far East, sailing by way of Gibraltar, Malta, where she carried out a ten-day mini work-up, Suez, Aden and Singapore. On 4 December, some 16 weeks after her departure in August, *Belfast* returned to Hong Kong. During December and into the first weeks of January 1951, the cruiser carried out an intensive work-up programme from Hong Kong but it was not until the last day of January that she arrived in Sasebo to begin operations off Korea's west coast once again.

HMS *Belfast*'s first operational patrol of the commission began at first light on Friday 2 February when, at 0700, she left Sasebo for the west coast. At the end of January 1951 the UN forces had only just managed to halt a joint North Korean and Chinese offensive which had been launched on a broad front close to the 38th Parallel. The offensive had achieved considerable success and within four days the Communist Army had captured Seoul. When *Belfast* arrived off Inchon that same afternoon, large fires and thick black smoke could be seen ashore as battles raged around the city. That evening *Belfast* engaged shore targets with her

HMS Belfast *bombarding enemy positions in Korea.* *(Author's Collection)*

main armament, and it was not long before more columns of black smoke were seen rising from the targets. For three days *Belfast* remained in the area off Inchon, laying down a slow but harassing bombardment of enemy positions. On 5 February, however, she resumed her patrol, this time searching for enemy minelaying junks, and although she intercepted and boarded a number of vessels each day, none of them was hostile. During the patrol she also rescued a USAF pilot who had been forced to ditch in the sea, but unfortunately he later died from his injuries. The patrol finally ended at Sasebo on 15 February, where the ship's company could enjoy a three-day respite.

HMS *Belfast*'s second patrol began on Sunday 18 February, and this time she was ordered to assist with the naval blockade of the strategically important port of Worsan, which had begun three days earlier and which would last for some 861 days. The naval bombardment of the port had begun on 17 February, and next day *Belfast* carried out an intensive attack, with her 4-inch armament engaging enemy troop concentrations and shore batteries on an island off Worsan, during which a direct hit on a machine-gun position was observed, while the 6-inch armament targeted the port area of the city. By the early evening of 20 February *Belfast* had returned to Sasebo, where there was a 48-hour break before the ship was at sea again. This time *Belfast* was once again off Inchon and bombarding offshore islands which had been occupied by North Korean troops. It was during this patrol that the cruiser encountered sub-zero temperatures and a sea covered with large slabs of floating pack ice. On 6 March she returned to the base at Sasebo.

Between 12 and 21 March, wearing the flag of the C-in-C, FES, *Belfast* made another patrol in the area around Inchon, during which her 6-inch armament engaged enemy troop concentrations in the Chinnampo area. However, while she was at anchor off Inchon, monitoring shipping in and out of the Han River, there was some enemy interest in the cruiser in the form of a few MiG aircraft which circled the ship, while keeping well out of range of her guns. On 20 March *Belfast* was relieved by *Kenya*, and next day returned to Sasebo. Four days later she arrived at the Yokosuka naval base, which provided a welcome change of scenery for the ship's company. The town offered plenty of scope for sightseeing, as well as the US Navy's Enlisted Men's Club, which offered all the amenities of a good canteen. In the harbour there were ever-present reminders of the Second World War, with the remains of a former Japanese cruiser which had been run aground to save it from sinking. For *Belfast* the break from operations was short, and on 29 March she was back on patrol off Korea. She carried out two further patrols before returning to Hong Kong on 7 April. Since leaving the colony on 28 January she had steamed some 12,526 miles, most of which had been in the operational area, and on average she had spent seven out of every nine days at sea. Once again, however, the ship's break from operations was only short, for although she had been due to sail for Singapore to undergo maintenance in the dockyard, an unexpected military offensive by the North Korean Army saw her being recalled to Sasebo, and by mid-April she was once again patrolling off Inchon. This patrol lasted for two weeks, and during the course of it she embarked three North Korean PoWs for interrogation. At the end of April she anchored off Inchon waiting to begin a bombardment of enemy positions, but the order did not come and on 30 April she returned to Sasebo. On 2 May she began another patrol, but within 48 hours of sailing she had been recalled to Sasebo. On 6 May she sailed via Hong Kong to the naval base at Singapore to begin her postponed 14-week maintenance and docking period; the ship's company could now enjoy the long-awaited change from living in the cramped conditions on board to the spacious barracks of HMS *Terror*.

On 18 August 1951, after a short period of machinery trials, *Belfast* left Singapore for Hong Kong, where she carried out a further week of trials and manoeuvres. It was 28 August when she arrived in Sasebo, and on the last day of the month she sailed for her next west coast patrol. At 1330 that

afternoon Action Stations was exercised, and the ship assumed war routine once again. As before *Belfast* carried out blockading and bombardment duties, and the first bombardment came on the second day at sea when she opened fire on concentrations of enemy mortar platoons close to the beaches. Further along the coast the 4-inch guns opened fire on gun positions, and on one occasion during the patrol X turret, manned by the Royal Marines Detachment, opened fire in support of a RM Commando raid on enemy positions ashore. This latter event came at the end of September when, during a five-day operation by 41 Commando, Royal Marines, a Russian-built MiG-15 jet fighter, which had crashed on a coastal shoal, was recovered for Allied experts to examine.

On 10 and 11 October *Belfast* led an international force of warships, including HMAS *Sydney*, HMAS *Tobruk*, the Dutch destroyer *Van Galen* (ex-HMS *Noble*) and HMS *Constance*, which joined US Navy ships *Concord*, *Colohan* and *Shields* off Korea's east coast, some 60 miles north of the 38th Parallel, where they successfully bombarded enemy troop positions in and around the port of Kŏje. Next day *Belfast* returned to harbour, but after two days in Sasebo she was hurriedly ordered to sea to avoid a particularly severe typhoon. In the event she steamed right through the storm and in the enormous seas and howling winds the ammunition in X shell room came adrift. There were some dangerous moments as the Royal Marines, whose turret it was, attempted to control and retrieve the shells which were rolling and crashing about in the compartment. Fortunately, no one was hurt in the mêlée, and after carrying out one further patrol, on 24 October *Belfast* arrived at Kure for a nine-day maintenance period. At the same time some members of the ship's company took weekend leave to Matsuyama, a port town which had been relatively untouched by the presence of the post-war US Occupation Force.

On 2 November, after leaving Kure, *Belfast* returned to Sasebo to embark FO2 and his staff for a patrol off Korea's west coast. During this patrol she joined *Sydney, Constance, Tobruk, Van Galen*, HMCS *Sioux* and USS *Hyman* to take part in 'Operation Athenaeum', a co-ordinated series of air and surface attacks against shore batteries in the coastal areas around Hungnam. These enemy batteries had been particularly effective when firing at UN minesweepers and destroyer patrols. The bombardments and air strikes which were executed on 20 and 21 November were deemed a success. After leaving the operational area *Belfast* set course for Yokosuka, and upon her arrival at just before midday on 23 November, on the jetty waiting to take over command was Captain A. C. A. C. Duckworth DSO DSC RN. Five days later the cruiser returned to Sasebo for a brief stay before sailing on to Hong Kong where the ship's company enjoyed 12 days of rest and recuperation. However, by 22 December she was once again on patrol off Korea's west coast.

For *Belfast* the month of January 1952 was extremely busy, with long periods at sea, and the inevitable bombardments designed to keep large numbers of enemy troops manning coastal defences away from the main fighting front. At the end of January, with spotting duties being carried out by US aircraft, *Belfast* undertook an intensive and prolonged bombardment in support of an Allied landing behind the enemy front line, north of Inchon. The final day of this onslaught came during the afternoon of 1 February, and 24 hours later she left the operational area to return briefly to Sasebo. Next day she arrived in Kure to begin a 19-day maintenance and docking period. It was Saturday 23 February when she put to sea again, sailing first to Sasebo and then to Pusan where FO2 disembarked. Two days later the ship began patrolling the west coast, this time in sub-freezing conditions with floating pack ice often surrounding the ship. Twice during the forenoon of 3 March a helicopter from *Glory* landed on *Belfast*'s quarterdeck to deliver official correspondence, a portent for the future of naval aviation. On 7 March *Belfast* operated in support of marines from the Republic of Korea who were carrying out landings on west coast islands just south of the 38th Parallel. The marines were

embarked in *Belfast* then ferried ashore to their destination by landing craft and helicopters. It was during these operations that two members of *Belfast*'s Royal Marines Detachment, Sergeant J. H. James and Corporal T. R. Hamill, lost their lives. During the remainder of the month *Belfast* continued her bombardment duties, and by the third week of March the front line was more or less back to the 38th Parallel. With the city of Inchon back in Allied hands *Belfast* was able to anchor off the port and limited shore leave was granted.

HMS *Belfast* would continue her patrol and bombardment duties throughout April and May, but in early April she was able to take a temporary break and pay courtesy calls to the ports of Pusan and Chinhae. At the former the Royal Marines Detachment paraded a Guard of Honour for the President of the Republic, Syngman Rhee. However, it was soon back to patrolling the country's west coast until, on 25 April, she was relieved by *Ceylon* and was able to sail for Hong Kong for a 12-day break. It was 10 May before *Belfast* returned to her regular patrol line and after three weeks she was ordered to Kure to undergo an eight-day docking period. On 15 July, after carrying out a bombardment in support of the troops ashore, she embarked six PoWs and four casualties for the passage to Sasebo.

During the forenoon of Monday 28 July, *Belfast* left Sasebo to carry out another routine patrol. Six days later, on Sunday 3 August, she was in the area of the Wolsa-ri Peninsula, north of the 38th Parallel and well within enemy waters. The day had passed quietly with several hours spent at anchor, but at 1448 she weighed anchor to patrol close to the coast. Suddenly, without any warning, at 1740 the ship was engaged with very accurate fire from enemy shore batteries, to which A turret quickly returned fire. However, one enemy 75mm shell hit the ship forward and exploded in the Locally Enlisted Chinese Stewards' messdeck, severely wounding four ratings. In the meantime *Belfast* steamed quickly out of range of the guns and at 1807 anchored in order to assess and repair the damage. At 1205 on Monday 4 August, some six and a half hours after the attack, one of the injured men, Leading Steward Lau So, died of his wounds. At midday, with the shipwrights having temporarily patched up the damaged hull, and after transferring the body of the rating to shore, *Belfast* resumed her patrol. This ended at Sasebo on 10 August and later that day the ship sailed for Hong Kong where more permanent repairs could be made to her hull.

By the end of August 1952 the Korean War had been dragging on for over two years, and although it would be another 11 months before it was finally ended, *Belfast*'s role in the conflict was drawing to a close. When she left Hong Kong on 25 August she had just one more patrol to complete, and already on the messdecks the talk was of home. The final patrol began on 5 September and eight days later, during the afternoon of 13 September, she carried out her final bombardment of enemy positions in Korea. On 27 September *Newcastle* arrived on station to relieve her, and after exchanging salutes *Belfast* set course for Hong Kong.

On 2 October, after two years in eastern waters, *Belfast* left Hong Kong to make her passage home. Sailing by way of Singapore, Aden, Port Said, Malta and Gibraltar, she arrived alongside No 3 basin at Chatham Dockyard during the afternoon of 4 November. On arrival at Chatham a maintenance party of some 150 ratings, which included around 50 per cent of the Engine Room Department, was immediately sent on a week's leave and on their return the main body of the ship's company left on 62 days' foreign service leave. On 26 November Captain Duckworth relinquished his command, the ship's complement was reduced to peacetime numbers and five days later *Belfast* was towed out to Sheerness and secured to a buoy. Work began to reduce the ship to reserve, which initially at Sheerness was confined to the cleaning of watertight compartments, and the inspection and preservation of machinery not required for steaming the ship; A boiler room was also cleaned. On 3 March 1953, steaming on just one main propulsion unit, *Belfast* left Sheerness for Devonport where she

HMS Belfast *steaming through still waters in February 1953.* *(Crown Copyright/MoD 1953)*

would finally be reduced to Class 3 Reserve.

This would involve a thorough overhaul of all her main and auxiliary machinery, and armament, before it was put into a state of preservation. The work was not completed until the end of November 1953, and following this the cruiser languished at a buoy at Devonport, in the shadow of Brunel's Saltash Bridge. At this stage there is no doubt that prospects for *Belfast*'s operational future looked bleak. In the post-war world Britain's role as an Imperial power was virtually at an end, and although the Korean War had meant a reprieve from the scrapyards for many warships, with the end of that conflict and cuts to the Defence Budgets, there was no reason to suppose that *Belfast* would be spared. In March 1955, however, some two years after she had last put to sea, a decision was taken at the Admiralty that *Belfast* would undergo a major modernisation refit then recommission for further operational service. The work would cost some £5,553,000 and would last for over three years, but when completed, events would have overtaken the ship and she would be virtually redundant.

It was not until the spring of 1956 that work commenced on *Belfast*'s modernisation and in the archives there is a document which sheds light on the decision to carry out such an expensive programme of work on a ship which was 17 years old: '*The alterations to the gun armament bring* Belfast *up to a standard similar to that known as the* Birmingham *standard. This is defined as, able to defend themselves against present-day air attack in all conditions, and other ships, to a limited extent in blind fire. The main limitation is that of range in using MRS8 with radar Type 262R for 4-inch guns. Torpedo armament is removed to allow top weight and, particularly, space for other alterations. The electrical system can be described as no more than adequate, but the naval staff agreed that this must be accepted. Main machinery will last the ship about ten years after completion of the extended refit, but there may be some reduction in endurance. Alterations to the accommodation affect the largest improvement to the ship. Provision of centralised*

messing and a reasonable area in Messes and Messdecks have been achieved by reduction in complement and by building in a large portion of the upper deck, which later became possible because of the removal of torpedo tubes.'

Work on *Belfast*'s extended refit began in early 1956 and it would drag on for three years. However, after the Suez Crisis at the end of that year and the swingeing cuts to the Navy's post-war fleet, particularly where pre-1939 warships were concerned, it was already becoming clear that *Belfast*'s future might be limited. The most noticeable alterations were the replacement of the two tripod masts with lattice structures, and the plating-in of the bridge, which ended up as a five-sided arrangement, with a similarly designed Admiral's bridge directly below it. Also included in this arrangement was an Operations Room, which incorporated Air Direction, Gunnery Direction and Radar Direction facilities. In the interior of the ship an airtight citadel was incorporated which, as far as possible, would safeguard most of the ship's company from radioactive contamination. To clear such contamination from the ship's hull and upperworks, prewetting piping and equipment was installed, and cleansing compartments were added. The messdeck accommodation for both senior and junior ratings was modernised by the fitting of three-tier standee bunks, as well as more substantial bunks, which by day could be converted into settees, all fitted with bedside lamps. In addition a full system of centralised messing was provided for all ratings, and in the galley oil-fired cooking equipment was replaced with more modern electrical appliances. *Belfast*'s main 6-inch armament was retained intact, with the DCTs being replaced by more up-to-date directors. The ship's 4-inch mountings were replaced by more modern versions, while the close-range armament gave way to six Twin Bofors MkV mountings controlled by four MRS8 directors sited between each pair of mountings. A helicopter landing pad was built on the quarterdeck, although when in use Y turret had to be trained abeam. In addition to all the other alterations and improvements *Belfast*'s main and auxiliary machinery was thoroughly overhauled, with improvements being made to the steering motors, the refrigeration system and the fresh water evaporators.

On 2 April 1959 *Belfast*'s new commanding officer, Captain J. V. Wilkinson DSC GM RN, arrived on board and took command of the ship which, at that stage, was still lying alongside the dockyard basin, manned only by an advance party. Just over two weeks later, on Monday 11 May, the ship underwent Admiral's Inspection and that evening she was shifted from the basin to the sea wall. At 1015 the next day the ship's company marched down from HMS *Drake* and the Commissioning Ceremony was held. The next weekend saw Navy Days being held at Plymouth, with *Belfast* as one of the star attractions, and over the three days some 10,500 people visited the ship. It was Wednesday 3 June when, for the first time since March 1953, *Belfast* put to sea to begin a 12-week period of trials, staged in the Channel and round into the Bristol Channel. In late July, while carrying out gunnery firings off Land's End, one or two stray shells narrowly missed the trawler *Lyonesse*, which was fishing in the area. In a signal reminiscent of those sent during the Second World War, the trawler reported that she was '*being shelled by an unknown ship*'. Fortunately no damage was caused and the trawler was able to continue fishing. Next day *Belfast* returned to Plymouth Sound to pick up families for a day at sea, after which she secured alongside at Devonport to give leave, and on 20 August, the day after she completed her trials period, left Plymouth Sound bound for the Far East. However, no sooner was she at sea than she was diverted to assist in the search for survivors from an RAF Handley Page Victor II bomber which had crashed somewhere off the Scilly Isles. The aircraft, with its four-man crew and Handley Page's Chief Test Observer, had been on a test flight from Boscombe Down and was last seen by a merchantman some 22 miles from Bishop Rock. Soon afterwards another vessel west of Bishop Rock reported a large explosion which sent up a 50-foot column of water. *Belfast* was the first

With her bridge now enclosed and lattice masts replacing the tripod structures this photorgraph shows HMS Belfast *entering Grand Harbour, Malta, in 1959 following her 3-year-long modernisation refit at Devonport.*
(Syd Goodman Collection)

ship on the scene, and was soon joined by *Grafton, Keppel* and *Trafalgar*, but in the event all that was found was wreckage. This was recovered by *Belfast* and taken to Plymouth Sound where it was unloaded onto a tender. On 23 August *Belfast*, in company with *Crossbow*, set out for the Far East once again.

After arriving in Grand Harbour at the end of August *Belfast* remained in the area for four weeks in order to complete her work-up in company with ships of the Mediterranean Fleet, which included *Gambia, Daring, Dainty, Defender* and *Delight*. At one stage it was thought she might visit Naples, but there was not enough time and on 29 September she left Malta for Port Said and Aden. On 20 October, after an absence of some seven years, she arrived in the Singapore Naval Base. Soon afterwards, in company with *Llandaff*, she sailed for Hong Kong. Less than 24 hours into their passage, as the two ships were carrying out a jackstay transfer, *Belfast* was ordered to disengage and make a rendezvous with the Blue Funnel passenger-cargo liner SS *Memnon*, which had reported an acute case of peritonitis on board. That evening *Belfast* rendezvoused with the merchantman and the patient was quickly and efficiently transferred by sea boat to the cruiser. The patient was so ill that *Belfast*'s PMO operated immediately, and although it was touch-and-go, the operation was a success and the man was delivered safely to hospital in Hong Kong.

HMS *Belfast*'s visit to Hong Kong was short, and by 17 November she had returned to Singapore to undergo a four-week maintenance and docking period, which for the ship's company again meant a move to shore accommodation. Although life ashore in Singapore was more comfortable than on board, for most members of the ship's company the ideal was to return to Hong Kong for Christmas. In mid-December, having hoisted the flag of Rear-Admiral V. C. Begg, FO2 FES, *Belfast* joined the

Australian ships *Quickmatch* and *Vendetta* for a rough passage back. Having kept a respectable distance from Typhoon Gilda, which was an unseasonal visitor, the three ships spent a pleasant week over Christmas and the New Year, although one member of the ship's company remembered that the Colony appeared to have been, '*practically taken over by American Marines on leave from Guadalcanal*'.

On 2 January 1960, with the festivities over, *Belfast* left Hong Kong and made her way across the South China Sea, to the small port of Sandakan in North Borneo, before steaming to the Indian city of Madras, and the naval base of Vizagapatam, some 60 miles north. By the end of the month, however, she was back at Singapore and preparing for major fleet exercises. The first of these came in the form of 'shop window' manoeuvres for the benefit of foreign consuls, political figures and businessmen from Singapore. Code-named 'Exercise Oriel', the cruiser joined *Centaur, Solebay, Finisterre* and *Llandaff*, for a series of anti-submarine, anti-aircraft and minesweeping operations designed to show the Fleet's strength and fighting efficiency. *Belfast*'s role was to fight off a mass attack by *Centaur*'s aircraft, and to fire ten main armament broadsides. On the second day of the exercises, however, the cruiser's second broadside almost hit the target-towing tug and the rest of the day's shoot was cancelled. On 14 February, after a two-day break following the 'Oriel' exercises, *Belfast* left the naval base at Singapore to join *Centaur, Gambia, Quickmatch, Vendetta, Solebay* and *Cavendish*, before setting course for Trincomalee. They were on their way to join 'Exercise Jet 60', an annual Commonwealth maritime exercise which, that year, was taking place in the Bay of Bengal and the approaches to Cochin, Karachi and Trincomalee. Participating were some 50 warships representing seven Commonwealth countries, as well as aircraft from four countries, which included those from *Centaur*. Two days out from Singapore the group was joined by INS *Delhi* and *Mysore*, the former being remembered by many in *Belfast* as the RN cruisers *Achilles* and *Nigeria*. They arrived at Trincomalee on 20 February, in time for a weekend break before the main phase of the manoeuvres began on the following Monday. Six days later *Belfast* led *Centaur, Gambia, Mysore* and *Delhi* into Trincomalee Harbour.

On Monday 29 February *Belfast* and *Gambia* had been scheduled to sail for a tour of Australian ports, but on the previous day the latter had been ordered to leave for Mauritius to assist with clear-up operations following a destructive cyclone which had hit the island. This left *Belfast* to carry out the tour alone and after a rough crossing of the Indian Ocean, on 10 March she arrived in Fremantle, where a large crowd had turned out to welcome her. Within two hours of her arrival coaches had been laid on for sightseeing and brewery tours. That the visit was a resounding success was evidenced by the fact that just 48 hours after her arrival when she put to sea again, even larger crowds turned out to wave her off. The five-day passage to Hobart was uncomfortable with gale force headwinds, but during the six-day stay a large proportion of the ship's company was able to take four days' station leave. From Hobart *Belfast* joined *Cavalier* for a five-day visit to Sydney and from there, wending their way slowly along the length of the Great Barrier Reef, the two ships made their way north to Darwin. On 1 April, as they approached the Torres Strait, *Belfast* responded to a call for medical assistance from RFA *Wave Master*, who had an injured crewman with broken limbs. That evening the two ships rendezvoused and transferred the casualty by jackstay to *Belfast*. Two days later, off the Darwin River, *Belfast* and *Cavalier* joined HMAS *Melbourne* and *Voyager* for forty-eight hours of joint manoeuvres in the Timor Sea. On 6 April the cruiser put into Darwin for a short overnight stop, when the injured man was taken ashore to hospital. From Darwin all four ships, now joined by HMAS *Queenborough*, sailed via the Java Sea to Singapore, where *Belfast* began a ten-day maintenance period.

When *Belfast* left Singapore on 23 April, she was in company with *Albion, Melbourne, Caprice, Cavalier, Vendetta* and *Tenby*, bound for the waters

of the South China Sea, close to the US naval base at Subic Bay. This was in preparation for the SEATO exercise code-named 'Sealion', led by USS *Yorktown*. During the first phase of the exercises *Belfast* carried out a 6-inch full-calibre shoot at targets on the island of Corregidor, and during the second phase the Commonwealth contingent was joined by *Albion*. On conclusion of the manoeuvres *Belfast* accompanied *Albion* back to Singapore and then to Hong Kong prior to undertaking a cruise to Japanese and Korean ports. This got under way on 26 May and took in Inchon, Kobe, Tokyo and Sasebo. The six-day stopover in Kobe was disrupted by the weather, as a member of the ship's company remembers: '*We entered Kobe determined to have a good time on this, for the majority of us, first trip to Japan. Very few people were disappointed. There were bus trips to various places in luxurious coaches, and many people visited the Takarazuka Opera, which was formed entirely of girls. English shows will have to improve by 500 per cent to come anywhere near them for talent, entertainment and real showmanship. The bus trip to the top of Rokko San was breathtaking, and the countryside was among the most picturesque in the world. The highways are feats of workmanship, and the bus appeared to do everything but loop-the-loop. On Saturday the ship should have been open to visitors, but we had to put to sea in a hurry when a typhoon warning was received. However, at the last minute the typhoon veered away and we spent a peaceful night at anchor, before going alongside again on the Sunday morning. That afternoon we had 3,000 visitors in just two hours.*'

The next call was to Tokyo where, during the ship's four-day visit, the rain poured down constantly each day. The final port was Sasebo, before both *Albion* and *Belfast* rendezvoused for the passage back to Hong Kong, via Okinawa. By mid-July *Belfast* was back in Singapore and on 2 August joined *Albion, Cavalier, Cardigan Bay, Tenby, Quiberon* and *Vampire* at sea for the annual FOTEX exercises which, in 1960, took place in the Strait of Malacca and the South China Sea. *Belfast*'s part in the exercises ended on 16 August at Hong Kong and by the end of the month she was back in Singapore undergoing a 15-week refit and docking period. For the ship's company it was effectively the end of the commission, and they moved from the ship to the shore accommodation in HMS *Terror*.

During the refit ship's company numbers were reduced as some personnel were flown home, but the bulk remained in Singapore and on 5 December they moved back on board. Seven days later *Belfast* sailed to begin a series of post-refit trials in local waters, which lasted until 23 December. After a five-day break for Christmas the trials resumed and finally ended on 11 January 1961. Meanwhile, at the Admiralty in London, a large-scale exchange of personnel had been planned for the ship which, had it taken place only a year or two earlier, would have meant virtually a whole ship's company travelling by sea to Singapore and the same number of men returning home, again by sea. The whole operation would have taken the best part of two months, but this time, beginning on 16 January, in the space of three weeks, using seven flights of specially chartered Britannia aircraft of British United Airways and BOAC, some 52 officers and 580 men were flown out to Singapore, with the returning men being flown home in the same aircraft. On 19 January the first contingent of the main body of the new ship's company, which had been assembling in HMS *Terror*, arrived on board. Four days later, on 23 January, *Belfast*'s new commanding officer, Captain Morgan C. Morgan-Giles DSO OBE GM RN, arrived on board and assumed command. Finally, on 31 January 1961, with both the refit and the changeover of personnel complete, *Belfast* was recommissioned at Singapore Naval Base.

After having undergone three weeks of training exercises in the South China Sea, in company with *Carysfort, Cavendish, Quickmatch* and HMNZS *Royalist*, the group was joined by *Melbourne* and *Voyager* for the passage to Trincomalee and 'Exercise Jet 61', with other Commonwealth navies. Once again the manoeuvres ended at

Trincomalee, where there was a five-day break before the force returned to Singapore. During April *Belfast* and *Royalist* joined *Victorious* and the commando carrier *Bulwark* for exercises off Malaya's east coast and the coast of North Borneo. The Royal Navy's role in this US-led exercise code-named 'Pony Express' was, under wartime conditions, to land a company of Australian infantry and 42 Commando, Royal Marines onto the shores of North Borneo close to Pulau Silad on the northern coast. The exercise was the first major test of the effectiveness of the relatively new commando carrier *Bulwark* in the large-scale landing of troops and equipment by helicopter. For *Belfast* the exercise ended at Hong Kong where she, *Queenborough* and *Yarmouth* prepared for a cruise to Japanese ports. On 23 May the three ships left Hong Kong, with *Belfast* paying visits to Nagasaki, Kure and Tokyo, before returning to Singapore to carry out a six-week maintenance and docking period. This was completed on 5 August when she began a cruise to Australian ports. During the passage south she steamed through the Great Barrier Reef to join ships of the RAN and RNZN in a large-scale Commonwealth naval exercise code-named 'Tucker Box', which was undertaken mainly in the Coral Sea. At the conclusion of the exercise *Belfast* spent a night at anchor off the port town of Hervey Bay, and on her arrival in Melbourne on 28 August she was welcomed at Princes Pier by friends and some relatives. When she opened her gangways to the public, over just two afternoons some 5,000 people visited the ship. *Belfast*'s second port of call on 4 September was Sydney, with the ten-day stopover being much appreciated by all on board. Although Sydney's famous beaches were not warm enough for bathing, many members of the ship's company went on organised tours into the surrounding countryside, including the famous Blue Mountains. During the visit Captain Morgan-Giles and his wife arranged a large dance at the Trocadero Ballroom for the whole ship's company, which was a resounding success. On leaving Sydney, to ensure that all the cobwebs were blown away, a full-calibre main armament gunnery shoot was carried out. By the end of September the cruiser was back in Singapore Naval Base.

On 5 October *Belfast* joined the rest of the Far East Fleet for the annual FOTEX exercises in the South China Sea; other ships taking part included *Caesar, Cavalier, Cossack, Cassandra, Vampire* and the submarine *Taciturn*, with the highlight for the seamen being a fleet banyan and barbeque at Pulau Tioman. On 20 October, on completion of the exercises, *Belfast* had been scheduled to visit Saigon, but with severe flooding in the area the visit was cancelled. She remained at Singapore until the end of that month when, wearing the flag of the C-in-C, and in company with *Caesar, Cassandra* and *Vampire*, she sailed for Hong Kong, which coincided with a visit to the Colony by Princess Alexandra. During the visit there was a mini Review of the Fleet in Hong Kong Harbour, but for most of the ship's company the occasion was an opportunity to do some last-minute Christmas shopping, with over 800 sacks of parcels of all shapes and sizes being dispatched through the ship's mail office.

After leaving Hong Kong *Belfast* returned briefly to Singapore before, on 22 November, she sailed for East Africa, having embarked the combined bands of the Third Commando Brigade RM and the C-in-C, FES. She had been ordered to attend the Independence Celebrations of Tanganyika (Tanzania) at Dar-es-Salaam, and to return to Singapore in time for Christmas, a round trip of over 10,000 miles. First, however, a ship's company Honour Guard of Seamen and Royal Marines had to undergo a crash training course in preparation for the ceremonial duties involved. Six days after leaving Singapore *Belfast* called at the Addu Atoll island of Gan where, while the ship refuelled from RFA *Wave Victor*, the bands and the Honour Guard were able to go ashore to rehearse their roles. With the refuelling stop at Gan lasting just over four hours, *Belfast* left harbour and set course for Pemba Island, a small islet situated some 50 miles east of Tanga. There, over a 24-hour period, the ship's sides were painted, and on 5 December it was a

truly spotless and gleaming *Belfast* which arrived in Kilindini Harbour, Mombasa. Here the Flag Officer, Middle East, Rear-Admiral A. A. F. Talbot, joined the ship for the passage to Dar-es-Salaam. Next day, accompanied by HM Ships *Rhyl* and *Loch Alvie*, *Belfast* sailed for the Tanganyikan capital where, during the morning of 7 November, they arrived to find a very congested harbour, crowded with merchant shipping. During *Belfast*'s four-day stay at Dar-es-Salaam there was a full programme of official engagements and functions, with the highlight of the visit being the performance of the Honour Guard and the Combined Bands of the Royal Marines at the flag-raising ceremony at midnight on Friday 8 and Saturday 9 December in front of a large audience of international dignitaries. During the evening of 10 December *Belfast* hosted a major diplomatic event when the President of the new country, Julius Nyerere, joined the Duke of Edinburgh and the Governor-General at a reception on board.

HMS *Belfast* left Dar-es-Salaam during the early evening of 11 December to rendezvous with *Rhyl* and *Centaur*, to return briefly to Mombasa, before making the return passage with *Rhyl* via Gan, to Singapore. As the two ships set course from Addu Atoll *Rhyl* was ordered to divert to the coast of Goa, where India had used force to recover the last European colonial possession on the Indian mainland, in case she was required to evacuate British nationals. *Belfast* accompanied the frigate for a short distance to the south of Ceylon (Sri Lanka) in order to refuel her and although this added a day to her journey, the cruiser arrived in Singapore Naval Base in plenty of time for the Christmas festivities.

For *Belfast* the new year of 1962 began on 4 January when she left Singapore for gunnery practice in the South China Sea, after which she, *Lincoln, Quickmatch* and *Vampire* steamed to the Subic Bay exercise areas for joint manoeuvres with the US Navy. These were led by the cruiser USS *Los Angeles* and were followed by a weekend at the US naval base. On 3 February, after a maintenance period at Singapore, *Belfast* left for a goodwill cruise to Penang and the Indian port of Vishakhapatnam in the Bay of Bengal, finishing at Trincomalee. *Belfast* remained there until the end of February when she joined *Centaur, Carysfort, Plymouth, Rhyl* and the submarine *Andrew*, together with the Indian Navy ships *Mys*ore and *Vikrant* (ex-HM Ships *Nigeria* and *Hercules* respectively), as well as warships from Australia, New Zealand and Canada for the annual SEATO exercise, 'Jet 62', in the Indian Ocean. On 16 March *Belfast* and *Andrew* returned to Singapore Naval Base.

For *Belfast* the return to Singapore marked the end of her service east of Suez, and on 26 March she sailed for Hong Kong where she embarked Army personnel for the passage home, which began on 2 April. The initial part of the voyage to Guam took the cruiser through the centre of a tropical storm, which made for a very uncomfortable five days, but after a weekend at the US naval base in Guam, the weather eased. On Saturday 14 April, as well as crossing the equator with the traditional ceremony, *Belfast* also crossed the International Date Line, which meant that for the ship's company there were two Saturdays 14 April. Five days after the second of these dates the cruiser arrived at the enormous US naval base at Hawaii's Pearl Harbor where, after steaming past 'battleship row' and the memorials to USS *Utah* and *Arizona*, she secured alongside Baker Docks, close to the Kamshamcha Highway. After four days of being made to feel very welcome, with full ceremony the cruiser left Pearl Harbor on the six-day passage to San Francisco where, during the forenoon of Saturday 28 April, she secured alongside Pier 18 on the central waterfront. As a member of her ship's company remembered: '*It was difficult to imagine a more elegant, charming and beautifully located city than San Francisco. From the moment we passed under the Golden Gate Bridge, through a host of white-clad sailing boats and saw the city laid out in the hills and the valleys, we suspected that this was a city we would never forget. And how right we were. Invitations poured in from all sides. Those in the ship's company who were ashore in uniform were*

surrounded by friendly strangers, all anxious to talk about Britain. On open days visitors flooded onto the ship in thousands (over 12,000 in two days), the queue at times extending the length of the ship, along the jetty and out into the street.'

On 5 May *Belfast* left San Francisco to make the two-day passage north to Seattle where, during the early morning of 7 May, she steamed into the picturesque Sound, with its pine-forested slopes and, in the distance, snow-capped mountains. The cruiser's visit to Seattle coincided with the official opening of the World's Fair, and during the four-day stay in the city ten members of the ship's company, all volunteers, were chosen to stand guard at the British Pavilion. So popular was their presence that when the ship sailed for home they agreed to stay behind for the duration of the Fair. After leaving Seattle *Belfast* visited Vancouver and the Canadian naval base at Esquimalt, Victoria, before steaming south. On 3 June she made her seven-hour transit of the Panama Canal, and three days later, after refuelling at Trinidad, set course across the Atlantic. During the afternoon of 17 June she passed Land's End, and that evening anchored in Plymouth Sound. Next day she sailed for Portsmouth and anchored at Spithead during the forenoon of 19 June, moving up

After recommissioning in July 1962 HMS Belfast *left Portsmouth Harbour for northern waters. However, only days later it was noticed that the ship was sluggish in answering the helm and she was ordered to Devonport for a docking period and a rudder change.* *(Syd Goodman Collection)*

harbour later in the day to secure alongside South Railway Jetty. *Belfast*'s commission and her long service east of Suez was finally over.

At 0900 on Monday 2 July, as *Belfast* lay alongside *Bermuda* at Portsmouth's Pitch House Jetty, at a ceremony attended by families and friends of the ship's company, the cruiser was commissioned under Captain M. G. R. Lumby DSO DSC RN, as the flagship of Flag Officer Flotillas, Home Fleet, Vice Admiral J. G. Hamilton, taking over the role from *Bermuda*. Next day Admiral Hamilton hoisted his flag and on 9 July *Belfast* sailed to begin a shakedown cruise which took her to Invergordon. However, soon after leaving Portsmouth it was noticed that the ship was sluggish in answering the helm, and after arriving at Invergordon on 14 July she was ordered to Devonport for a 28-day docking and a rudder change. On 16 August, towards the end of her period in dry dock, Lumby was relieved by Captain W. R. D. Gerard-Pearse MVO RN. Five days later the ship was able to put to sea for Portsmouth where, over the next two weeks, her maintenance was completed. In the event it was 6 September before *Belfast* was able to resume her work-up, during which she operated from Portland. It ended with a six-day visit to Southampton.

The first week of October 1962 was, for *Belfast*, one of the busiest periods of her post-war career when, on the 2nd of the month, she left Devonport to take part in the NATO air and sea exercise 'Sharp Squall', which also included *Chichester, Crossbow, Falmouth, Yarmouth* the Canadian aircraft carrier *Bonaventure*, together with the 1st Canadian Escort Squadron. The exercise took place in the South-Western Approaches, but during the first phase *Belfast* was detached to steam at full speed to the aid of a French trawler, one of whose crew members was badly injured. After steaming at 30 knots for several hours she was able to go alongside the French vessel to take the man onboard before putting him ashore in Falmouth Bay, from where he was flown by helicopter to hospital. On 6 October there was a weekend break when *Belfast* returned to Plymouth Sound, but Phase Two of the exercise saw her once again in the South Western Approaches for anti-submarine exercises in company with *Bonaventure* and *Falmouth*. These manoeuvres were conducted in heavy seas, and for *Belfast* they ended at Portsmouth where she embarked the C-in-C Home Fleet for an overnight passage to Devonport.

Although *Belfast*'s operational schedule appeared full, at the Admiralty moves were already afoot to decommission the ship. A signal dated 24 October 1962, from the ship to the Admiralty, was making provisions for paying off: it read: '*Before paying off it is desired to place* HMS Belfast*'s silver bell in the custody of the city of Belfast for safe keeping until such time as the ship recommissions. Ship's visit to Belfast from 15 to 22 November would provide most suitable opportunity and unofficial inquiries indicate that this would be much appreciated by the civic authorities. Bell is a Category A trophy. Request very early approval so that appropriate ceremony can be arranged.*' The request was quickly approved, and after a short visit to Amsterdam in early November, during the forenoon of 15 November *Belfast* arrived alongside Stormont Wharf in her namesake city. During the afternoon of 21 November, at a ceremony attended by FOF(H) and the Governor of Northern Ireland, the ship's silver bell was returned to the city authorities. Next day *Belfast* made the short passage to Moville on the eastern shore of Lough Foyle, and during this passage, at 1345 on 22 November, she fired her last full 6-inch broadside with her four triple turrets. It was the last time in the Royal Navy when such a broadside would be fired. Next day, 23 November, she sailed in company with *Berwick, Scarborough, Troubridge, Yarmouth* and the submarine *Olympus*, for anti-submarine exercises in the Atlantic and Clyde areas, which for *Belfast* ended at Greenock on 28 November. Two days later the ship sailed south to Portsmouth where, on 3 December, she secured alongside Pitch House Jetty. Later that month *The Times* newspaper ran a small news item under the headline: '*Navy to Scrap Cruiser - £5½m Refit Three Years Ago*' which read: '*The cruiser*

Belfast, *on which £5,553,000 was spent in reconstruction and modernisation three years ago, is to be scrapped. She is likely to join the three other cruisers which the Navy has for disposal,* HMS Bermuda, Gambia *and* Mauritius, *early in spring.*' The withdrawal of *Belfast* was no surprise for she was the last of the wartime cruisers in commission, with only the post-war cruisers *Tiger, Lion* and *Blake* remaining as the last big-gun ships of the Royal Navy. The future for *Belfast* looked bleak.

The new year of 1963 saw *Belfast* lying alongside Portsmouth's South Railway Jetty, and in what was an extremely cold winter her much reduced ship's company were employed in cleaning deep snowdrifts from both the jetty and the ship's upperworks. However, during the afternoon of 30 January, *Belfast* left Portsmouth to make an 18-hour passage to Devonport, where she arrived alongside during the forenoon of the next day to secure alongside No 8 wharf. Five days later the ship's company moved ashore to RNB and on 8 February Captain Gerard-Pearse relinquished his command. Later that month, with the ship having been shifted into No 9 dry dock, *Belfast* paid off into reserve. It seemed her seagoing career was over.

For four months *Belfast* lay in dry dock at Devonport, until 1 July, when she was once again moved to the sea wall, this time at No 5 wharf. As the most recent addition to the Reserve Fleet, and still being maintained at 47-hours' notice for steam, when it came to choosing a ship for a seven-week seagoing training period for men of the RNR, *Belfast* was the obvious choice. Her final operational duties began on Monday 8 July 1963 when, under the command of Captain M. E. Shand DSC RN, *Belfast* was commissioned with a ship's company composed mainly of reservists. On 15 July she steamed down harbour to anchor in Plymouth

An undated image of HMS Belfast *toward the end of her operational career.* *(Syd Goodman Collection)*

HMS Belfast *laid up at Portsmouth in 1968. She was the headquarters ship for the Reserve Fleet moored at Whale Island.* *(Tim Meredith)*

Sound. Her temporary reprieve had come about in order to enable naval reservists, together with some 300 Sea Cadets, to take part in 'Exercise Rock Haul', a joint RNR, CCF and SCC training cruise to Gibraltar. One of the objects of the exercise was aimed at recruiting and showing the youngsters what life was like on board a naval warship. During the cruise the cadets were to take an active part in helping to run the ship, including firing the secondary armament, assisting the Supply Department and the Engine Room Department. In addition they were to attend lectures and films on naval topics, as well as taking part in recreational activities. Between 16 July and 7 August, with a long weekend break for Plymouth Navy Days, *Belfast* ran a series of trials combined with a mini work-up, before steaming to Portsmouth where, on 9 August, she secured alongside South railway Jetty. Next day the main body of Sea Cadets joined the ship and that afternoon, in company with the 7th Minesweeping Squadron, she sailed for Gibraltar. During the forenoon of Monday 12 August, *Belfast*'s guns were fired for the last time when she carried out a 4-inch full-calibre shoot. Two days later she arrived at Gibraltar where six days of organised recreational activities had been arranged for the cadets. The training cruise finally ended during the forenoon of 23 August when *Belfast* returned to Devonport. Within 24 hours of her arrival the Admiral Commanding Reserves had struck his flag and the temporary ship's company had left, closely followed by Captain Shand. De-ammunitioning and de-storing began immediately and by the end of August *Belfast* had paid off into dockyard hands with only a small care and maintenance party remaining with the ship.

Although preservation work had started, *Belfast* still had a role to play at Devonport, and for sever-

al weeks between February and May 1964 she acted as an accommodation ship for *Tiger*'s ship's company while their own ship was under refit. There were also efforts to maintain *Belfast* in an immediate condition for sea, in order that the highly successful 'Rock Haul' recruiting cruise might be repeated, first in the summer of 1964 and thereafter on an annual basis. This idea was seriously considered, but eventually the cost involved, as well as, '*complex manning problem equivalent to commissioning a ship*', meant that in June that year the idea was turned down and the plan was dropped. In May 1966 *Belfast* was moved from Devonport to Portsmouth, where she became the headquarters ship of the Reserve Fleet, under the generic term of HMS *Bellerophon*. As well as looking after ships which were on the disposal list her company was responsible for other jobs, such as Sea Cadet training and teaching seamanship to Royal Marines recruits. Not long after arriving in Portsmouth, however, *Belfast* received a visit from the Government Minister responsible for the Navy, who criticised the living conditions on board, but given the age of the ships which made up the Reserve Fleet there was little that could be done to improve them.

It was in the spring of 1967 that the idea of preservation was first considered. In April that year staff from the Imperial War Museum in London had been inspecting HMS *Gambia*, which was on the disposal list, with a view to obtaining a 6-inch gun turret for the Museum's collection. It was following this visit that the possibility of preserving a whole ship as a floating museum was raised. Initially the Treasury appeared to be positive about the idea, but in 1971 shortly before *Belfast* paid off for the last

HMS Belfast *in 1991 at her permanent mooring in the Pool of London where she is preserved as a museum ship. Moored alongside her is the visiting Type 22 frigate* HMS Brave, *giving a good size comparision between the Second World War era light cruiser and a modern day frigate.* *(Steve Bush)*

In 1999 HMS Belfast *made a rare return to Portsmouth for dry docking. She is seen here leaving under tow of the tug* MT Formidable *on 10 June to return to her London moorings. She has been repainted in an Admiralty Disruptive camouflage scheme as worn during much of her Second World War career (but objected to by some as it was never worn during her post-modernisation service!)* *(Walter Sartori)*

time, the Government refused to contribute to either the £600,000 capital cost, which included the scrap value, of saving the ship or the recurring charges for maintenance, which in the early 1970s were estimated at about £200,000 a year. In January 1971 *Belfast* was shifted from her mooring at Fareham Creek to the dockyard for the removal of heavy equipment and stores, and later that month she was towed back to Fareham Creek. It appeared that, like her contemporaries, she was heading for the scrapyard.

With the Government having refused to help, a private trust was formed, headed by one of *Belfast*'s former commanding officers, Rear-Admiral Morgan-Giles, who was now a Member of Parliament, and after a great deal of effort, in August 1971 the Government agreed to hand the ship over to the trust. During the forenoon of Thursday 2 September *Belfast* was towed from Portsmouth Harbour to Tilbury Docks where she spent a month being fitted out as a museum ship, and undergoing a short docking period. Finally, on 14 October *Belfast* was towed up the River Thames, under Tower Bridge, to a permanent berth on the south bank of the river at Symon's Wharf, Southwark, between Tower Bridge and London Bridge, which had been specially dredged. Once she had been manoeuvred into position she was secured to two large steel dolphins, which would guide her up and down on the 20-foot rise and fall of the tide, while a long, flexible, hinged bridge-gangway connected the ship to the shore. Soon after her arrival in London *Belfast* was opened to the public, and for over 40 years now, apart from periods when she undergoes docking and maintenance, she has remained open. She also plays host to both Royal Navy and foreign warships, from minesweepers and submarines to destroyers. In 1978 she was taken over by the Imperial War Museum to become one of their London venues. Today as *Belfast* lies in the heart of London she continues to play host to many thousands of visitors each year.

Town Class Cruisers

Technical Data

HMS *Southampton*

Programme:	Authorised under the 1933 Construction Programme. Order placed with John Brown & Co Ltd, Clydebank, on 1 May 1934.
Keel Laid:	21 November 1934.
Displacement:	9,083 tons (Standard); 11,540 tons (Full).
Length BP:	589ft
Length OA:	623ft 6in
Beam:	63ft 4in
Draught (Max):	18ft 3in
Propelling Machinery:	Quadruple screw. Four sets Parsons geared steam turbines. Steam provided by four oil-fired, Admiralty three-drum superheated boilers. 75,000SHP, Max Speed 32 knots.
Armament:	12 x 6-inch MkXXIII guns in four triple turrets. 12 x 4-inch HA MkXVI Quick-Firing guns in twin mountings. 2 x four-barrelled pom-poms. 8 x 0.5-inch machine-guns. 2 x triple 21-inch torpedo tubes. Up to three Supermarine Walrus amphibious aircraft.
Major Alterations:	No major alterations.

Commanding Officers:

Captain A. M Peters DSO RN	2 November 1936
Captain G. F. B. Edward-Collins CB CVO RN	18 June 1938
Captain F. W. H. Jeans RN	2 January 1939
Captain B. C. B. Brooke RN	18 June 1940

HMS *Newcastle*

Programme:	Authorised under the 1933 Construction Programme. Order placed with Vickers Armstrong Ltd, Walker-on-Tyne, on 1 May 1934.
Keel Laid:	4 October 1934.
Technical Data:	As *Southampton*
Major Alterations:	October – December 1942: Type 281, Type 284 and Type 285 radar equipment installed. Additional 20mm Oerlikon guns fitted. September/October 1945: X gun turret removed.

Commanding Officers

Captain J. G. P. Vivian RN	15 October 1936
Captain F. Figgins RN	26 July 1939
Captain E. A. Aylmer DSC RN	15 August 1940
Captain P. B. R. W. William-Powlett DSO RN	15 February 1942
Captain J. G. Roper OBE RN	11 June 1944
Captain S. H. Paton CBE RN	7 November 1947
Captain A. F. Campbell RN	23 May 1949
Captain W. F. H. C. Rutherford RN	3 March 1952
Captain Sir John R. J. Tyrwhitt Bt DSO DSC RN	19 August 1953
Captain R. B. Honeywill RN	15 June 1954
Captain A. R. Kennedy OBE RN	15 November 1955
Captain A. H. C. Gordon-Lennox RN	23 May 1957

HMS *Sheffield*

Programme:	Authorised under the 1934 Construction Programme. Order placed with Vickers Armstrong Ltd on 17 December 1934.
Keel Laid:	31 January 1935.
Technical Data:	As *Southampton*.
Major Alterations:	April/May/June 1942: Type 273, Type 284 and Type 285 radar equipment fitted.
	March/April/May 1943: Aircraft catapult removed. Additional 20mm Oerlikon guns fitted.
	July 1944 – May 1945: X turret removed. Additional AA armament, four quadruple 40mm Bofors guns and 27 Oerlikon guns fitted.

Commanding Officers

Captain W. P. Mark-Wardlaw DSO ADC RN	24 July 1936
Captain E. De F. Renouf CVO RN	9 August 1938
Captain C. A. A. Larcom RN	14 December 1939
Captain A. W. Clarke RN	2 August 1941
Captain C. T. Addis RN	11 February 1943
Captain J. W. M. Easton RN	14 February 1945
Captain K. L. Harkness DSC RN	14 November 1945
Captain G. B. H. Fawkes CBE RN	27 November 1946
Captain C. P. Yorke RN	6 May 1948
Captain M. Everard RN	15 December 1950
Captain J. G. T. Inglis OBE RN	17 June 1952
Captain K. McNeill Campbell-Walter RN	17 September 1953
Captain T. E. Podger RN	22 December 1954
Captain L. D. Bourke CBE DSO RN	25 February 1957

HMS *Birmingham*

Programme:	Authorised under the 1934 Construction Programme. Order placed with Devonport Dockyard on 1 March 1935.
Keel Laid:	18 July 1935.
Technical Data:	As *Southampton*.
Major Alterations:	February/March 1942: additional 20mm Oerlikon guns fitted. Type 284 radar equipment installed.
	April – September 1943: Type 273, Type 281 and Type 285 radar equipment fitted.
	December 1944: Type 282 AA fire control radar fitted. X turret and aircraft catapult removed.
	1950 – 1952: Modernisation refit. Bridge enclosed. Lattice masts fitted as well as limited air-conditioning. Two MkVI high-angle directors fitted.

Commanding Officers

Captain C. F. Harris RN	4 August 1937
Captain E. J. P. Brind RN	3 January 1938
Captain A. C. G. Madden RN	4 March 1940
Captain H. B. Crane RN	15 December 1941
Captain H. W. Williams RN	7 September 1943
Captain G. W. G. Simpson CBE RN	19 November 1945
Captain K. L. Harkness DSO DSC RN	15 October 1946
Captain J. R. S. Harris CBE ADC RN	6 June 1947
Captain T. A. C. Packenham RN	28 June 1948
Captain C. F. J. Lloyd-Davies RN	3 October 1949
Captain J. D. Luce DSO OBE RN	9 May 1952
Captain C. W. Greening DSC RN	12 January 1953
Captain J. R. Barnes DSO RN	7 July 1954
Captain J. R. B. Longden OBE RN	18 July 1955
Captain T. D. Ross RN	4 January 1957
Captain S. H. Beattie VC RN	15 July 1958

HMS *Glasgow*

Programme:	Authorised under the 1934 Construction Programme. Order placed with Scott's Shipbuilding & Engineering Co Ltd, Greenock, on 17 December 1934.
Keel Laid:	16 April 1935
Technical Data:	As *Southampton*
Major Alterations:	May/June 1940: Type 286 radar installed.
	May – August 1942: Types 271, 281, 282, 284 and 285 radar outfits installed.
	August/September 1943: Type 283 radar fitted. Additional 20mm Oerlikon guns fitted. Aircraft catapult removed.
	August – December 1944: X turret removed. Radar modernised.

Commanding Officers

Captain F. W. Attwood RN	1 April 1937
Captain C. G. B. Coltart RN	20 January 1938
Captain F. H. Pegram RN	10 April 1939
Captain H. Hickling DSO RN	6 June 1940
Captain E. M. Evans-Lombe RN	14 July 1942
Captain C. P. Clarke DSO RN	25 November 1943
Captain A. G. V. Hubbock CBE RN	13 January 1945
Captain C. L. Firth DSO MVO RN	1 August 1948
Captain W. J. Yendall RN	26 April 1950
Captain J. Holmes RN	18 September 1951
Captain B. Bryant DSO DSC RN	1 April 1953
Captain P. Dawnay MVO DSC RN	19 May 1954
Captain C. D. Bonham-Carter RN	10 November 1955

HMS *Manchester*

Programme:	Authorised under the 1934 Construction Programme. Order placed with R & W Hawthorne Leslie & Co Ltd, Hebburn-on-Tyne, on 23 October 1935.
Keel Laid:	28 March 1936
Technical Data:	As *Southampton*
Major Alterations:	No major alterations.

Commanding Officers

Captain H. H. Bousfield RN	17 January 1938
Captain H. A. Packer RN	13 April 1940
Captain H. Drew DSC RN	4 June 1941

HMS *Liverpool*

Programme:	Authorised under the 1934 Construction Programme. Order placed with Fairfield Shipbuilding & Engineering Co Ltd, Govan, Glasgow, on 23 October 1935.
Keel Laid:	17 February 1936
Technical Data:	As *Southampton*
Major Alterations:	December 1941 – January 1942: Type 273, Type 284 and Type 285 radar outfits installed.
	September 1943 – July 1944: X turret removed. Types 274, 283 281B and 293 radar outfits fitted.

Commanding Officers

Captain A. N. Read RN	5 May 1938
Captain A. L. Poland DSO DSC RN	27 October 1940
Captain W. R. Slayter DSO RN	9 September 1941
Captain P. Dawnay MVO DSC RN	1 April 1945
Captain A. C. Chapman CBE RN	30 November 1946
Captain K. Mackintosh RN	17 March 1948
Captain J. D. Shaw-Hamilton RN	15 October 1949
Captain J. D. Luce DSO OBE RN	23 April 1951

HMS *Gloucester*

Programme:	Authorised under the 1935 Construction Programme. Order placed with Devonport Dockyard on 2 March 1936.
Keel Laid:	23 September 1936.
Technical Data:	As *Southampton*.
Major Alterations:	No major alterations.

Commanding Officers

Captain F. R. Garside CBE RN	2 January 1939
Captain H. A. Rowley DSO RN	16 July 1940

HMS *Edinburgh*

Programme:	Authorised under the 1936 Construction Programme. Order placed with Swan, Hunter & Wigham Richardson, Wallsend, on 17 August 1936.
Keel Laid:	30 December 1936
Displacement:	10,550 tons (Standard); 13,175 tons (Full)
Length BP:	579ft
Length OA:	613ft 6in
Beam:	64ft 9in
Draught:	22ft 6in
Propelling Machinery:	Quadruple screw. Four sets Parsons geared steam turbines. Steam provided by four Admiralty three-drum superheated boilers. 80,000 SHP. 32.5knots.
Armament:	12 x 6-inch guns in four turrets. 12 x 4-inch quick-firing high angle guns. 16 x 2pdr pom-poms. Two triple 21-inch torpedo tubes. Up to three Supermarine Walrus amphibious aircraft.
Major Alterations:	No major alterations.

Commanding Officers

Captain F. C. Bradley RN	15 February 1939
Captain C. M. Blackman DSO RN	11 December 1939
Captain H. W. Faulkner RN	19 June 1941

HMS *Belfast*

Programme:	Authorised under the 1936 Construction Programme. Order placed with Harland & Wolff, Shipbuilders and Engineers, Belfast, on 17 August 1936.
Keel Laid:	30 December 1936.
Technical Data:	As *Edinburgh*.
Major Alterations:	1941/1942: While undergoing major repairs: Types 273, 281, 283, 284 and 285 radar installed. Secondary armament modernised. Catapult modified to operate Supermarine Sea Otter. September – December 1944: Aircraft catapult removed. AA armament augmented by 12 x 20mm Oerlikon guns. Two 4-inch HA guns removed. 1956 – 1959: Torpedo tubes removed. Bridge enclosed. Operations Room installed. Centralised messing system introduced. Hammocks replaced by bunks. Galley equipment modernised.

Commanding Officers

Captain G. A. Scott DSO RN	24 April 1939
Captain F. R. Parham RN	29 September 1942
Captain R. M. Dick CBE DSC RN	24 July 1944
Captain H. B. Ellison DSO RN	9 July 1946
Captain E. K. Le Mesurier MVO RN	22 September 1948
Captain Sir Aubrey St Claire Ford Bt DSO RN	8 April 1950
Captain A. C. A. C. Duckworth DSO DSC RN	23 November 1951
Captain J. V. Wilkinson DSC GM RN	2 April 1959
Captain M. C. Morgan-Giles DSO OBE GM RN	23 January 1961
Captain W. R. D. Gerard-Pearse MVO RN	16 August 1962
Captain H. C. J. Shand DSC RN	1 July 1963